80386

Macro Assembler and Toolkit

80386

Macro Assembler and Toolkit

Penn Brumm and Don Brumm

TAB Professional and Reference Books

Division of TAB BOOKS Inc.
Blue Ridge Summit, PA

FIRST EDITION
FIRST PRINTING

Copyright © 1989 by TAB BOOKS Inc.
Printed in the United States of America

Library of Congress Cataloging in Publication Data

Brumm, Penn.
    80386 Macro assembler and toolkit / by Penn Brumm and Don Brumm.
       p.   cm.
    Includes index.
    ISBN 0-8306-3247-6   ISBN 0-8306-0247-X (hard)
    1. Intel 80386 (Microprocessor)—Programming. I. Brumm, Don.
  II. Title
  QA76.8.I2684B79   1989
  005.265—dc19   88-37559
                                                        CIP

TAB BOOKS Inc. offers software for
sale. For information and a catalog,
please contact TAB Software Department,
Blue Ridge Summit, PA 17294-0850.

Questions regarding the content of this book
should be addressed to:

Reader Inquiry Branch
TAB BOOKS Inc.
Blue Ridge Summit, PA 17294-0214

Edited by B.J. Peterson

Contents

Introduction

Before the mid-1950s, programming was done mainly in machine language—a slow, painful process. To solve a problem, programmers had to code long instruction sequences into numbers in binary or octal. Little by little, mnemonic help was provided through the use of *opcode mnemonics* (operation code mnemonics), which are letter codes for operations. Then additional assistance came from the use of symbolic names instead of numerical addresses to refer to values. Assemblers were written to transform these programs into machine language, which gave rise to the term *assembly language*.

Assembly language is the fastest and most powerful language for programming, giving you the same kind of control a stick-shift transmission does in an automobile. Even for experienced programmers, however, assembly language can be time-consuming, when you have to write routines to perform specific tasks that you do over and over. You keep thinking you will build a library of routines, but you are busy and that task stays on a back burner.

A *macro* (macro instruction) is a predefined set of assembler instructions that can be used in different parts of a program with some optional modifications each time it is used. One of the most powerful features of a macro assembler is its advanced macro capability. Once you master macros—how they are best designed and coded—you will use them like opcode mnemonics, only the macros will be ones that you write to fill needs you have. In their simplest forms, macros are often-used sequences of instructions.

The aim of this book is to make it easy for you to incorporate fast, efficient 80386 macro routines into your programs and to not have to worry about building a macro library. To do so, we review the process you went through to learn your native language. We go from that to artificial languages and then to computer languages, the most common artificial languages in the world today. Then we narrow computer languages to assembly language and its translator, an assembler. We finally focus on Microsoft's Macro Assembler, MASM. All along the way, we remind you that MASM has its own language and that you can ''speak'' to MASM by using that language.

INTENDED AUDIENCE

This book is to help you get to where you want to be, when you are trying to write code to solve a problem. We included some topics that are background, in case you are experienced in one area and not another. We do not expect you to be expert in everything. Also, in case you do not have time to key in all the routines, you can obtain a disk that contains them from TAB BOOKS, Inc.

The information in the book assumes that you have done some assembly language programming, using MS-DOS (a recent version or a look-alike). It also assumes that you generally understand how assembly language works. If you code some clever routines or macros, we would like to hear from you. Write to us in care of TAB BOOKS. Also write to us if you find an error, because they can creep into the best of code.

There are many operating systems for the IBM Personal Computer (and clones). This book concentrates on Microsoft's MS-DOS, at level 3.1 and higher. The code was written on an 80386-based computer (a specially-built-for-us clone), with MS-DOS 3.1 using the Microsoft Macro Assembler, level 5.1. MASM 5.1 has a faster assembly than earlier versions because it makes better use of far memory to hold as much of your source code as possible. Also, MASM 5.1 has OS/2 support, although we do not specifically address OS/2 in this book. There are new directives and predefined equates that let you write more sophisticated macros for powerful and portable code.

Don and I have a combined 45 years in the technical side of data processing: Don from the early 1960s and I (Penn) from the late 1960s. We both got started with IBM mainframe systems, only discovering the fascinating world of owning our own microcomputers in the mid-1970s. We have been part of a team that programmed an IBM mainframe operating system from scratch, written compilers, done network programming, and been systems engineers. Don stayed in systems software programming, and I finally opted for management (product support, quality assurance, and software development). We now own (and use extensively) five microcomputers, two of which were used for this book: an 80286-based computer was used for word processing while an 80386-based computer was used for coding. We have four printers, from a dot-matrix, to a daisy wheel, to a brand-new laser printer (that works at a speedy eight pages of camera-ready output per minute). Don has a college degree in mathematics, and Penn has an MBA. For us, data processing is the only industry in which to work.

BOOK CONTENTS

In this book, we took what we think is a unique approach to macros and the Macro Assembler. We looked at them as a language that a user/programmer defines. We explored, with some excellent help from Carl Ross (see chapter 5, which Carl wrote), how Microsoft designed its macro assembler, in terms of its functioning as a language.

The first portion of this book contains the description of what language is, what components it needs for a human to interact with a machine/computer. We look at Microsoft's MASM in terms of its syntax and grammar. The middle portion of the book describes the options and usage of the Microsoft Macro Assembler. The final portion of the book contains a group of macros that implement some of the *BIOS* (basic input/output system) and MS-DOS interrupts. You can use these macros to begin (or add to) your own macro library. Finally, there are a series of appendices that detail error messages, instruction sets, and support material.

Chapter 1 of this book gives you a background on what the basic parts of a native language are, how you learned it, and what your average vocabulary was at two years old. Chapter 1 ends with a short overview of some interesting artificial languages: those languages that were planned and designed, rather than ones that grew naturally from human use. Chapter 2 covers the most common artificial languages in the world, those used by computers, the binary idiots that we have learned to love.

Chapter 3 introduces you to a specific computer language (assembly language) and its translation into machine language by assemblers. The expanded assemblers that allow you to define your own language pieces—macro assemblers—are also covered. Chapter 4 reviews programming principles and macro writing.

Chapter 5 defines the grammar for Microsoft's Macro Assembler, MASM. Carl Ross wrote this chapter. Carl is cofounder of Fundamental Software, a company that creates language processors and tools for language processor construction. Carl is also the manager of software performance evaluation at Amdahl Corporation. Chapter 6 introduces the MASM character set, type, and data declarations. MASM has a powerful set of assembly language directives that maximizes control of the processors.

Chapter 7 covers MASM operands, operators, and expressions. An *operand* is an argument that defines values to be acted on by instructions or directives. An *operator* is a symbol that represents an operation to be performed on one or more operands. Chapter 8 discusses MASM program structure and file-control directives. MASM program structure directives allow the specification of segment registers, the alignment of data or instruction bytes, the association of a group name with one or more segments, and the setting of the location counter.

Chapter 9 reviews MASM global, conditional, and macro directives. Global-declaration directives allow the definition of labels, variables, and absolute symbols that can be accessed globally, that is, from all modules in a program. Chapter 10 introduces interfacing assembly language with high-level languages. Chapter 11 shows you how to run MASM, and chapter 12 lists the macros.

Appendix A lists the MASM error messages. You will run into these when you have miscoded an instruction or used some of the directives in ways Microsoft did not program for. Appendix B gives you an overview of the full 80386 instruction set. If you need additional help and examples, see the book the *80386: A Programming and Design Handbook* (TAB Book No. 3237), which, among other things, has examples of how the flags are changed as the instruction executes.

Appendix C gives you an introduction to the 80387 numerics coprocessor instruction set. Appendix D is an overview of BIOS interrupts and calls. You will have a lot of use for these interrupts and for the MS-DOS Interrupts overviewed in appendix E when you begin programming with the 80386 processor. These interrupts give you some excellent bypasses for some common problems. The more common BIOS interrupts have been built into macros that are listed in chapter 12. Appendix E discusses MS-DOS interrupts, mainly interrupt 21h and its subfunctions. These interrupts also are written into macros listed in chapter 12.

Appendix F introduces Microsoft's object linker, LINK, and the library handler, LIB. Return codes, messages, and error messages are listed. Appendix G is a lengthy program listing that shows most of the directives examined in this book. Also, the program listing shows how not to code many of the more complex directives. Errors are shown because we feel that viewing errors is an extremely solid way of learning how to program (and how not to program).

Appendix H gives an architectural overview of the 80386 microprocessor. This appendix covers the various registers and the bits and flags that they carry. Knowledge of many of these bits, flags, and fields are critical when you try to use some of the instructions.

Keeping abreast of all sides and aspects of the fast-moving micro technology is a monumental task. That means that when a book comes out that promises to tell readers what is the latest and best, the authors open themselves to the very real possibility of being out of date or wrong. We want to give special thanks to three people who reviewed the manuscript and gave us technical assistance, comments, helpful hints, and updates. Those people are Richard Hudson, Linda Hart, and Kate Payne.

1
Looking at Languages

BEFORE YOU READ ABOUT LANGUAGES AND HOW YOU LEARN THEM, LOOK AT THE PHRASE "like a bull in a china shop." You might have learned that this phrase means clumsy. I didn't, not for a long time. I grew up on a holstein dairy farm, and that meant we had a herd of large black-and-white cows and one bull. That bull was a high-bred, massive creature with a thick chest of rippling muscles. Crowned with wicked horns, his wide forehead was made of heavy bone and tapered to a blunt nose with flaring nostrils.

When he paced slowly from one side of his pen to another, he moved like a heavyweight fighter, conserving his energy until he met his enemy. And his enemies were human. When he saw one, he attacked in a rush that was surgically accurate. To confine that power, the bull pen was built of railroad ties and 4-×-8 inch planks. The boards shuddered and bent alarmingly when the full force of his weight hit them.

That bull was not clumsy. He was a massive, brutally deadly force who was kept because he fathered perfect calves. So, I had to learn that when someone who had not grown up on a farm said "like a bull in a china shop," those words translated to *clumsy*, not *fierce power unleashed* or *deadly force that could destroy an unwary person*.

As you grew up, you learned to translate words in the same way. Those words might have had different meanings to you in the beginning, but you translated and edited until you got what you wanted. You learned to use words like *cat* and *milk* and *cookie*—especially, *cookie*, one of the first multisyllable words that my own kids learned.

This chapter explores languages to find out what makes them tick—if they do tick and not tock or talk. Playing with words and learning about languages will help when you explore the depths of the Microsoft Macro Assembler (MASM) and figure out how it works as a language. Then you can learn to use MASM in the same casual way you use your native language.

WHAT IS LANGUAGE?

Spoken language is based on a series of vocal symbols worked out over the centuries by trial and error. Humans learned to speak some 100,000 years ago, but had to depend on oral history until some genius decided to draw marks and call it written language. This discovery only happened in the comparatively recent time of 10,000 years ago.

The earliest forms of language are no more primitive than modern forms. In fact, many of today's aboriginal tribes have very complex methods of description. For instance, one tribe in Samoa can describe your aunt's sister's son's daughter in one word; an oceanic tribe can describe, in a single word, the high tide with the bad oysters that will poison a person. Another world group can describe the potion from tree bark that yields a pain medicine that helps the ache in your forehead that you get from too much brewed corn or malted grain, in a single word: *aspirin*.

There are about 4,000 *speech communities* (groups speaking the same language) in the world. In descending order, the largest are North Chinese Mandarin, English, Hindustani, Spanish, Russian, and German. The smallest groups have only a few members. Differences within speech communities are called *dialects*. In the United States, the dialect used in a Georgia city differs considerably from that used on a Vermont farm or in a software development shop in Silicon Valley.

Languages change constantly, but various factors (especially literacy) lead to the development of a community's standard verbal language, which is usually one dialect. For instance, in Silicon Valley computer-speak, people now talk about *interfacing* with each other. Literary and colloquial standards might differ, and a group's jargon might be unintelligible to outsiders. (Try and speak assembler language to a banking executive or a football coach.) You do not LOAD a touchdown into the DI register, nor do you order eleven men to MOV EAX,EBX. The differences tend to be primarily in vocabulary, syntax, and content—three concepts that are described further in this chapter and are expanded in chapter 2.

Language Families

Groups of related languages are called *families*. Instead of talking about how Italian and Spanish are part of the Romance language family, consider a computer language. If you use PL/I, you can find a basic (no pun intended, although basic-BASIC is another example of how you can play with words) similarity between one manufacturer's PL/I and another manufacturer's product that they might call XPL, or PL-1. With only a short learning curve, you can move from one dialect to another within the PL/I family. The learning curve is longer if you move from one family to another, for example, from PL/I to C or further afield to assembler.

Basic Linguistics

Linguistics is the study of language, and the historical meaning of the word *language* is "that which pertains to the human tongue." Without stretching the meaning of linguistics, you can view a broader interpretation of language as "that which carries a meaning," or "anything that transmits a meaning from one human mind to another." This expanded meaning nicely includes artificial languages and computer languages. Present-day linguistics, so far, has had two main subdivisions: descriptive and historical. As the name implies, *descriptive linguistics* investigates language patterns and displays; for instance, the sounds or structure of a given language at a given historical stage. *Historical linguistics* traces the development and change of language in the course of time; for instance, the evolution of Latin into the Romance languages, or of Anglo-Saxon into modern English.

Whether descriptive or historical, the study of language has been traditionally subdivided into four areas whose boundaries are perhaps not as well defined as we should like them to be. That is the nature of an elusive beast: to slide away when you try to throw a lasso around it. The boundaries of these four compartments are ill defined in spots (1) because the sounds spoken are often influenced by language forms and vice versa (2) because both sound and form often find themselves dependent on meaning, and (3) because there is frequent interplay of syntax and the way word order changes. Those four areas of language study are:

- *Phonology* is the study of language sounds, which includes both phonetics and phonemes.
- *Morphology* is the study of language forms and particularly those changes in the form of an individual word that modify the meaning of that word (for example, the addition of -*s* to *cat* which turns the word into the plural: *cats*).
- *Syntax* is the arrangement of words within the sentence or word group (such as "John hit George," which informs the reader by the way the words are arranged that John did the hitting and George received the blow). Syntax is a key issue in computer languages. It raises its head in the discussions of the rules of structure.
- *Vocabulary* is the study of individual words: their origin, historical evolution, present meaning, and usage. Here is another creature that makes itself at home in computer languages. Vocabulary comprises *etymology* (the history of words) and *semantics* (the study of meanings). *Lexicography* is the art of dictionary making. It combines etymology and semantics, and adds a statement of how words are pronounced, accented, spelled, and used in present-day language.

Written Language

People write to save what they have thought. The written form of a language is the transmission of meanings across time and space. From the standpoint of linguistics, written language is both a help and a hindrance. It is a help because it provides practical access to speech that has disappeared from the world, such as the mysterious cuneiform triangles cut deep into clay tablets found in archaeological digs. It is a hindrance because it does not always faithfully portray such speech forms and often proves misleading. No better example of this confused state of affairs exists than present-day English spelling.

It gives only a partial and often deceptive clue to present-day English pronunciation. For example, take the splendidly awful spelling of the *ough* words: *though*, *thought*, and *through*.

Writing has two main varieties. The first variety is *pictographic-ideographic* (like the Chinese), where there is no link between the written form and the spoken sounds; the written symbol is directly tied to the thought-concept. The second variety of writing is *syllabic-alphabetic*, where the written form tends to represent the sounds of the spoken language, thereby setting itself up as a symbol of a symbol (the spoken language itself is a series of arbitrary symbols of thought-concepts).

A facet of language that directly affects computer languages is the existence of a written form of a language, particularly when it is in widespread use. The written form acts as a powerful brake upon the tendency of the language to change. Left to itself, a language is subject to rapid changes across time and widespread dialectization across space. For example, remember Valley-speak ("gag me with a spoon" and "for sure")? That flashed into wide usage, became part of a popular song, and then died a rapid and deserved death. Both change and dialectization work against the practical purpose of language: communication. By setting up standards of correctness (or correct operation, when referring to a computer language that must work with a particular processor), the written form retards the twin processes of change and dialectical breakup. Written language thereby leads to improved communications among the members of that language community.

Language Structure and Content

There are two classes of words in English. The first class is *content words*, such as *ball*, *run*, *nice*, and *quickly*, which are otherwise known as nouns, verbs, adjectives, and adverbs. The second class is *structural words*, such as *the*, *and*, *or*, and *on*, which bear less clear meanings (for example, whoever saw a *the*?). Structural words enable you to understand an utterance because they signal that a content word is coming up.

Content words have the qualities of inclusion, abstraction, ambiguity, restriction, and figurativeness. These words sound formidable as they shoulder their way into the chapter, but they describe qualities in our everyday use of language that enrich our speech. Consider them one at a time.

Inclusion means to contain. It is that quality of word meaning that lets you understand that *color* includes *red* and *blue*. Because some words include the meanings of other words, you are able to categorize, a very important conceptual feat. If you could not categorize, conversation and writing would be a jumble of specific detail. For instance, you could not say that you enjoy the colors of autumn. You would have to say that you like oranges, reds, purples, dark greens, and so on. You would have no verbal shorthand.

Abstraction is a quality apart from an object. It allows you to speak very specifically about an antique wooden rocking chair with a quilted seat that was always to be found on Betty Smith's porch, or talk about rocking chairs as a class, furniture in general, or household goods. You can move from a very denotative, descriptive, specific statement about an object to a more open-to-interpretation connotative, highly abstract statement that includes that earlier object.

It is *ambiguity* that produces double meaning within the context of sentences. Thus, "She fed her cat food" could mean that she fed cat food to her cat or that she fed cat food to a female guest. Computer languages are designed to eliminate as much of this ambiguity as possible, and that is why you generally find only one instruction that loads a memory value into a register.

Restriction is the quality that disallows certain combinations of semantic features. For instance, the semantic features of *cat* include *four-legged, furry, clawed, whiskered,* and *tailed.* Thus, "the feathered cat is here" is not semantically sound, although it draws an intriguing mental picture. Likewise, *bachelor* has the semantic features of an unmarried person. This makes the sentence "the bachelor's spouse looked in the mirror" an "illegal" combination of words.

Finally, content words have the conceptual quality of *figurativeness.* This means they can be metaphoric and vision-producing. Consider the example of *disk*, a neutral enough word. In data processing, it is generally agreed that *disk* means: an external storage medium. Yet, when the word is spoken, unless a specific disk is presented, the vision varies from listener to listener. A microprocessor programmer sees a floppy diskette; a mainframe systems programmer sees disk packs or big boxes that look like refrigerators and that contain fixed disks.

LEARNING LANGUAGES

From the time you are born until you are old and sophisticated, you both learn and become confused about your own native language. What is important is not that you become confused, but that your learning is developmental; that is, you learn the nature of language bit by bit (pun intended) as you move from being signal makers (a cry means you are hungry) to metaphor makers (describing fresh strawberries to a friend). You start differentiating between signals and symbols when you are about 18 months old.

You begin using your native language by babbling and cooing. Partly by nature and partly by nurture, you learn that sounds like *a* are different from sounds like *p.* You learn that language is a system of vowels and consonants, and you learn how to move your tongues to make the sounds that represent them. The first sounds you learn are those that are easiest to produce: the sounds produced in the front of the mouth (*b, p, d, t, m, n*), which require the least tongue and air control.

Eventually, you learn that certain combinations of vowels and consonants produce sounds that, in turn, produce action and behavior on the part of another. For instance, you learn that if you utter "up" someone might lift you, and that "book" might produce the result of being read to. As a child, you learned to signal your needs and desires to someone else whom you wished would act on your behalf. The application of this old learning process to programming is clear: if you learn how to instruct a computer to perform a task, you get your needs fulfilled.

Learning Structure and Content Words

When you were two years old, you had a vocabulary of about one hundred words. To put the Intel 80386 microprocessor's instruction set into perspective with this early childhood vocabulary, the 80386 has a language of 95 basic instructions, although some of the instructions have several forms.

As a child, once you established a working vocabulary, you branched out to use it in new ways. No longer content to merely utter single words that were wide open to interpretation by the adults around you, you started putting two words together, making primitive sentences. You learned two rules simultaneously: (1) that language has a structure, and (2) that it has content words. You did not get formal instruction during this learning process. You found the rules for yourself when you combined *up* with *book* which got you both picked up and read to.

Your use of vocabulary was very direct. You used it to name an object (a book), to show possession (my book), to locate (where book?), to describe (red book), and so on. Insofar as you were dependent on word order for meaning, you were still bound to the order in which you placed content words. Today, when you program, you combine verbs and objects to get an action, for example, MOV EAX,EBX moves a value from one register to another.

As you developed, you did not immediately acquire the adult-level sense of word and language meaning as quickly as you learned the order of word formation and word order. Until you were five or six years old, you did not consciously understand conceptual content words. You were more interested in the order of words. Children who learn this lesson early become good programmers because of the continuation of an early sense of order and logic.

Learning Concepts and Relationships

You use metaphorical language anytime you try to express your sense of a thing, an emotion, or an experience in terms of another thing, emotion, or experience that you assume your listeners share. When you describe a new dress to a friend as sky blue, you are comparing the known quality of blue skies to the as yet unseen color of the new dress. When you were a child and attempted to understand and interpret your universe, you related what was new to you to what you already knew.

You used your sense of mechanics to make sense of your world, and you made up words to do so. That made-up world tended to stop when you started school. This was where you learned to read, learned to look up hard words, made spelling lists, and regularly were drilled on word relationships. That is, school was where you learned the formalized basic constructs of your native language.

A popular method of teaching reading is one that taught some children to *decode*, that is, to learn to recognize and pronounce a word or a word element. For instance, you were introduced to the word *ill*. Then you were asked to decode words related to the formation of *ill* such as *Jill* and *hill*.

Notice that it is the formations of those three words that are similar, not their semantic content. The notion of being sick has nothing to do with a woman's name or with a mountain. Although you could decode these kinds of word formations, you were not learning anything about the words' semantic connection to one another. You could read all the right words, but you were not involved in what you were reading about. Those who were taught this way probably have a more difficult time grasping language than children who were taught to memorize and to associate words and their contents.

After memorizing a working vocabulary, your first stage of learning a language is learning the basic rules, the sense of the syntax of that language. Next comes the grasp of the complex nature of content words and the variety of interpretation such words make possible. Then, when you encounter experiences that you do not quite understand, you try to integrate the new experience into what you do understand from your past experiences, which is a process of synthesis. Only after that connection comes the ability to create your own narrations. How do you transfer this to learning computer languages?

In this chapter, you are first introduced to what languages are; this introduction gives you essentials on which to base your learning process. Chapter 2 introduces the fundamental pieces of general computer languages. From there, chapter 3 focuses on a specific language translator: a macro assembler. Chapters 4 through 9 narrow the focus to Microsoft's Macro Assembler (MASM), level 5.1, to dissect its grammar and language. That is were you capitalize on your learning.

Labeling and Naming in a Language

The objects and events of the world do not present themselves readily classified. The categories into which they are divided are the categories into which each person divides them. Languages are not neutral; they are not merely vehicles that carry ideas. Language is itself a shaper of ideas, the program for mental activity. Thus, today the only problems that can be solved on computers are those that can be defined by the computer language used. For example, you cannot load the color red into a register.

To speak metaphorically, brains are quite blind and deaf. They have no direct contact with light and sound, but instead must acquire all their information about the state of the outside world in the form of pulses of bioelectrical activity pumped along bundles of nerve fibers from external surfaces of the body. Nerve fibers are the interface between the brain and the environment. Brains also must interpret. They can only deal in symbols and never know the real thing. The program for encoding and decoding those symbols, for translating and calculating, is set up by the languages that each person possesses. What you "see" in the world around you depends, in a large part, on the principles you have encoded into your language.

In order to live in your world, you name that world. Names are essential for the construction of reality because without a name, it is difficult to accept the existence of an object, an event, or a feeling. *Naming* is the means whereby you attempt to order and structure the chaos of existence that would otherwise have as little order as children in a schoolyard. By assigning names, you impose a pattern and a meaning that allow you to manipulate the world. Naming, however, is not a random or neutral process. It is an application of principles already in use, an extension of existing rules and of the act of naming.

Names that do not draw on past meanings are meaningless. You might know that a register is an object that holds a value for a short term, because you have seen cash registers that hold your money temporarily after you pay a merchant for a product and before the merchant moves the money to a bank. (Where do you think the term *cache register* comes from?)

New names, then, have their origins in the perspective of those doing the naming rather than in the objects or events that are being named. That perspective is the product of the prefigured patterns of language and thought. New names systematically subscribe to old beliefs. The names are locked into principles that already exist, and there seems to be no way out even if those principles are inadequate or false. This book does not address the problem of false principles; it is the subject of another book. Here, you need to understand that when you approach assembly language and a macro assembler, you are going to be working with familiar things.

In researching language principles for this chapter, we ran across a dictionary of language and linguistics (see the bibliography) that dealt with a topic far from the mathematically- based data processing surroundings in which we live and work. Thumbing through the dictionary, we found some words and phrases that are highly similar to what we know as basics in data processing. A small sample follows. See how you can easily convert the linguistics terms to concepts familiar to you.

- *Bracketing* is one of several ways of indicating the hierarchical structure of a sentence.
- *Branching* is the representation of elements of syntactic structure by means of tree diagrams.
- *Cluster* is a group of dialects or languages which share common features as a result of their mutual geographical proximity.
- *Code* is a prearranged set of rules for converting messages from one sign system into another.
- *Command* is an utterance which demands or forbids an action to be carried out.
- *Decoding* is the deciphering of a message from the signals of a code.
- *Grammar*, in its widest sense, is generalized statements of the regularities and irregularities found in a language.
- *String* is a concatenation of elements in linear sequence.
- *Structure* is the organization of the language as a whole and of individual elements into meaningful patterns.
- *Testing* is the setting of exercises and tasks to measure either an aptitude for a particular subject or of an achievement in a particular subject.

WRITING IN A LANGUAGE

While it might not be axiomatic that being a good reader makes you a good writer, it seems to follow that if you read a lot, you will be a better writer. This relationship occurs because humans are superb mimics. Writing cannot be learned in a vacuum (especially the writing of good programs) for two reasons. First, a potential writer, who is also a reader, is exposed to a wider choice of material. Second, a potential writer must have something about which to write. You do not write writing; you tell a story or define an action. As a beginning writer, your material depends on people you have known, places you have visited, or events you have experienced. Potential writers cannot even begin without rudiments of the writer's craft, such as spelling, word choice, diction, a sense of connotation and denotation, and vocabulary.

Along with all the programmers we have asked about this subject, we learned a lot about programming by reading other people's code. Code reading has always been useful because, first, you can learn what the software project is all about by reading what has been done by the programmers already on the project and how they accomplished what was needed. Second, you can find other people who independently have discovered how to code particular knotty functions successfully. If you had to invent a way to fetch a byte into memory each time you wanted to do it, you would always be programming at a primitive level. However, you can copy methodology and modify it each time the environment changes.

ARTIFICIAL LANGUAGES

Artificial languages are those languages that have been deliberately invented, unlike human languages that have developed naturally and without conscious planning. The difference is the planning. Any planning that has gone into natural languages (especially into standard forms taught in schools) has merely involved controlling or modifying natural languages already in use. Artificial languages introduce novel systems of symbols. They are used in such diverse fields as mathematics, formal logic, and computer science.

The idea of artificially composing a more logical language goes back to such thinkers as the seventeenth century philosopher René Descartes. Since his time, hundreds of forms have been suggested. An example is the language *Solresol* developed by Jean Francois Sudre in 1817. All its words were formed of combinations of the syllables designating the notes of the musical scale. Two more recent attempts are James Cooke Brown's *Loglan*, invented for use in exploring the relationship between language and thought, and Hans Freudenthal's *Lincos*, which he intended as a program for establishing communication with extraterrestrial intelligent beings, should they ever be located.

In 1880, Johann Martin Schleyer initiated the first major movement for an international artificial language, called *Volapuk*. He based the Volapuk vocabulary on English, but the words are so distorted in form that Volapuk neither looks nor sounds like English. He did this deliberately to give the artificial language a more neutral appearance. Volapuk rapidly lost favor in competition with *Esperanto*, which Ludwik Lazar Amenhof first presented in 1887. Esperanto has a highly regular system of word information, with roots drawn from French, English, German, and other Indo-European languages. A few general expressions in Esperanto are shown in Fig. 1-1.

In 1932, C.K. Ogden proposed *Basic English* in an attempt to reduce the English vocabulary to a core of 850 words in order to get wider acceptance of English as a world

ENGLISH	ESPERANTO	PRONUNCIATION
Yes	Jes	Yes
No	Ne	Neh
Excuse me	Pardonu min	pahr–DOH–noo meen
Please	Mi petas	mee PEH–tahs
It doesn't matter	Ne gravas	Neh GRAH–vahs
Thanks (very much)	(Multan) dankon	(MOOL–tahn) DAHN–kohn

Fig. 1-1. Some General Expressions in Esperanto.

language. For instance, he replaced *enter* by *go into* and *precede* by *go in front of*. The result of his reduction remains distinctly English.

Of the various rival systems proposed for international adoption in this century, the most successful has been Alexander Gode's *Interlingua*. Interlingua is the culmination of a collaborative effort inspired in part by the Latin-based Interlingua originally proposed in 1903 by the Italian mathematician Guiseppe Peano. Interlingua is based on an international vocabulary of science and technology and can be read with little difficulty by those familiar with English or a Romance language. It has been widely employed at medical conferences and in scientific journals.

Now, read on to look at the basics of computer languages, which are of the most logically pure (a very biased opinion to be sure) of the languages known.

2

The Basics of
Computer Languages

THE FIRST COMPUTER LANGUAGE I LEARNED WAS AUTOCODER FOR THE IBM 1401. IT MADE
so little impression on me that (these many years later) I only remember two items.
First, I had to set word marks to show where one instruction ended and another began.
Second, a systems engineer came to one class and ran a card deck through the system.
The deck contained nonsense instructions that sent signals to the various characters
on the line printer. (The mechanical functioning of the printer caused one character—
say an *A*—to make a different sound than another character—say an *X*). The printer
played the "Battle Hymn of the Republic." Wow! What I learned from the systems
engineer was that data processing was fun. I wanted to be a systems engineer if those
people's minds worked that way. It took me two more years before I reached that goal.

INTRODUCING COMPUTER LANGUAGES

Several terms must be defined before computer languages can be defined.

- *Assembler* is a program that translates symbolically represented instructions
into their binary equivalents.

- *Compiler* is a program that assembles a program from instructions written
by programmers. Compilers allow programs to be written in a high-level
language.

- *Constant* is a value that remains unchanged during a calculation. There are
a variety of types of constants, such as numerical, character, logical, and location.

- *High-level language* is a language in which each instruction or statement
corresponds to several machine language instructions. A high-level language
allows you to write in a notation with which you are familiar rather than in a
language oriented to the machine code of a computer.

- *Machine language* is the final language all computers use, it is binary. All other programming languages must be changed into binary codes (machine language) before entering the processor.

- *Object* is a source program (see below) that has been translated into machine language.

- *Opcode* is operation code, which is the operation to be performed. In the example: 3 + 4 = 7, the + quantity is the opcode or operation to be performed.

- *Source program* is a program that can be translated automatically into machine language by some type of translator. A computer program is written in a language that is designed for ease of expression of a class of problems or procedures.

- *Translator* is a generic term for assemblers and compilers. A translator is a program that allows you to express a program in a language closer to your native language for later translation into a language acceptable by a computer.

- *Variable* is any factor or condition that can be measured, altered, or controlled.

Like human languages, computer languages have three elements: alphabet, grammar, and semantics. The *alphabet* is a limited set of tokens that are used by the language and is set at the time the source language is defined. Every program you will ever write consists of some sequence of tokens that you extract from the alphabet of the source language.

To be useful, a language must contain a number of structure rules. Grammar is that set of rules that define what is legal when you combine language tokens into sentences; for instance, the label on a line of code must appear to the left of the opcode. Semantics is a set of rules that delineate how a program performs when translated and executed on some machine.

The principal difference between English and a programming language is that the grammatical and spelling rules for English are complicated and have many exceptions and ambiguities. The corresponding rules for a programming language are concise, highly structured, and have few (if any) special cases, and (hopefully) no ambiguities.

In the 1950s, computer languages were aimed at helping scientific programmers, and generally each language was restricted to a particular machine. Designers wrote languages that produced efficient machine code, even if efficiency was gained at the expense of clarity. In the late 1950s and early 1960s, objectives changed. A committee of representatives from several organizations was set up to design a machine-independent programming language suitable for use by the business community. The result was COBOL (common business oriented language).

The COBOL design committee decided that computer languages should make maximum use of the native English language so that people with no programming experience could understand programs written in COBOL. Whether or not the committee was correct in its decision, the important thing that came from the committee deliberations was the concept that serious efforts should be made to design languages to ease communications between people and computers. At the same time, the committee decided that effort should be expended to make languages independent of specific hardware.

PROGRAMMER'S VIEW OF COMPUTER LANGUAGES

A *programming language* is a formal notation that describes algorithms to be executed by a computer. The rules of syntax govern only the construction of programs from the symbols and have no concern with what happens when the programs are executed. The semantic rules of the language define a subset of legal statements that have a meaning. A language must assist you in designing, documenting, and validating your programs. As such, there are three design criteria that are most important: writeability, readability, and reliability.

Writeability

A language should not be difficult to master. First, all of its features should be easy to learn and remember. For instance, to add values, the opcode ADD is very logical and easily remembered. Note that it also builds on something familiar from another discipline: mathematics. Second, the effects of any combinations of a language should be predictable and easily understood. In the 80386 instruction set, for instance, a return from an interrupt is coded IRET (interrupt return). If you are programming using the 80386 extended register set (32-bit registers), you will use the return with doubleword (IRETD); see appendices B and C for the 80386 and 80387 instruction sets, respectively.

Third, writeability is adversely affected if the language provides several ways to specify the same concept. In the 80386 assembly instruction set, for example, there is only one way to move values to registers, with the MOV instruction. Providing more than one way to do a task favors the development of dialects (dialects are discussed in chapter 1) that use subsets of the multiple ways. If you become fluent in one dialect, you can have difficulties when you switch to another dialect.

Readability

How well you read a program defines how quickly you can modify and maintain it. Also, if you cannot read it easily, it will take you longer to *fix* (correct) it, which increases the cost of the fix. Because everyone assigns a value to hours of work, the increase is the additional time studying the program. Readability is related to writeability: language features that favor program writeability usually favor readability.

Readability is also related to coding style. Simplicity greatly increases program readability. Simplicity requires adherence to many of the structured programming concepts that keep programs a reasonable size and structure: using modules, keeping program pieces (such as procedures) to fewer than 100 lines of code, limiting each piece so that there is only one entry point and one exit point. If, for instance, all your disk input/output (*I/O*) is in one module, you can check that module first if you get a report of an error in reading data from a disk.

Reliability

Reliability is related to readability: a program that is easy to read is easier to test for correct code and logic. Another point about reliability is that languages should not support features that are either impossible or too difficult to check. An example of the former is provided by the parameter-passing conventions of Ada, which can give different results in the presence of aliasing. An example of the latter is given by Pascal variant records.

Reliability can be enhanced by using a language that allows you to develop and certify one module at a time. You can keep the thoroughly tested modules in a separate library and combine them at any time to build new programs.

LANGUAGE LIMITATIONS

Look at languages (including assembly language) from the point of view of a computer—not a specific machine but computers in general. Because it is what it is, a computer is a limited machine, only able to execute a finite number of actions. That is the bottom line, to borrow a term from the financial world. Those computer actions are defined by the computer instruction set, and each instruction set opts to solve various problems, depending on which way the designers decide. For instance, one instruction set might optimize input/output while another might optimize text handling.

There must be a translator that accepts the alphabet, grammar, and structure of a language and that turns them into the object code that drives the machine. No matter how complex the language, it must be turned into the object code that the machine recognizes. The translators that convert source code into object code are called compilers, assemblers, or interpreters, depending on the functions they perform. Using a translator makes the execution of a program written in a language a two-stage process, as shown in Fig. 2-1. Machine independence of a language means that, in principle, a program written in that language is portable from one machine to another. The reality is that portability requires a suitable translator to generate code for the target machine.

Now, you come to the outer layer of communication between you and the machine: the programming language.

COMPUTER LANGUAGE SIMILARITIES

There are a number of computer language classifications based on the program application or modes of use. The following classifications are general, and many languages fall into more than one category.

- *Command languages* are interfaces between the computer user and the operating system. Among other things, each statement defines the programs to be executed, the conditions under which execution is to take place, and the data files to be manipulated. Today, there are few machine-independent or standard forms for languages of this class.

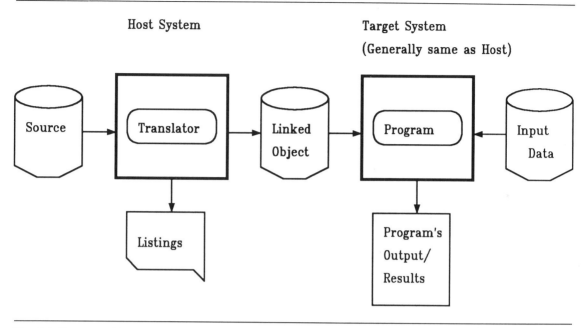

Fig. 2-1. Language Translation.

• *Systems-programming languages* are intended primarily for writing operating systems. These languages tend to be less machine-specific than assembly languages (although assembly languages are also systems programming languages), but they are richer in hardware-associated statements than usual high-level programming languages. The C language is an example.

• *Nonprocedural languages* are ones in which you do not specify the sequence of operations that obtain the problem solution. Instead, only the problem is defined. You specify the forms of the input and the output without a description of the detailed steps required to transform input into output.

• *Scientific languages* are used mainly for the manipulation of numerical data and calculations. FORTRAN is the best known of these languages.

• *Interactive languages* allow you to make changes and corrections from a terminal during execution. Although it is known mainly in the development of artificial intelligence systems, Lisp is designed to be used interactively.

• *Commercial languages* are concerned with the manipulation of files of alphanumeric data and with producing reports. COBOL is the best-known commercial language.

• *Real-Time languages* allow you to program procedures that execute concurrently and can be activated in response to external signals. Ada is a real-time language.

- *Object-oriented languages* are those with which data elements are active; active data elements respond to messages that cause them to act on themselves. Smalltalk is one example of an object-oriented language.

- *Data-Flow languages* permit the flow of data between the statements of a program to be examined so that inherent parallelism is exposed. This program executes on special machines that take advantage of the parallelism for higher speed. Val is a data-flow language.

- *Applicative languages* are languages in which the programs consist of the evaluation of a function that uses the input data as arguments and whose value is the result of the computation.

ELEMENTS OF COMPUTER LANGUAGES

If this were a book on chemistry, the periodic table of elements would be introduced here so you could see that all physical matter is made up of some combination of those elements. Computer languages have not been around as long as, for example, copper, and have not had as many people trying to define their basic factors. However, drawing on our combined experience of more than 45 years, we dissected some languages to see what we could find. We located 10 topics that were common to all languages. The individual languages might treat each topic differently (for example, data attributes) but they must all give at least a nod at that topic. The topics are: symbols, names, data types, attributes references and declarations, procedures and parameters, control structures, input and output, nesting and scope, exception handling, and parallel processing.

Symbols

A *symbol* is something that stands for or suggests something else by reason of relationship or association. For example, the symbol * generally stands for multiplication. Symbols appear in most source languages because they are a shorthand. There are symbols such as + , *, and ( ) that carry at most one or two specific, fixed meanings in a computer language.

Names

Computer languages lets you invent *names* for the entities you wish to have the computer manipulate when your program executes. You can assign properties to these names through the language forms called *declarations*. These properties can then be used to define a particular class of operations for the named entities. For example, the + can be used for a variety of different kinds of addition (real, vector, or fixed) by assigning a type to its operands through declarations. In this way, you can use a few operands for a large number of related mathematical operations to increase the power and clarity of the language.

Names appear in source code more or less at random, at the requirements of the programmer. The association of a name with a set of attributes requires some means of locating a particular name efficiently. Several languages provide a way to limit usage of names, through blocks such as procedures or macros; that name is useful only within its block.

Objects such as numbers, names, and strings have two major attributes. They have a location and a value that might change during the course of program execution. The term *location* is used because *address* is a hardware concept, and this discussion is limited to software at this time.

The object is identified by a name that indicates its location; other times, the name means the value stored at the location. When using a constant, programmers use an identifier that becomes a name for the value. For instance with many computer languages, if you set: STORE = 10, then the constant STORE represents the constant value of 10.

Variables can be modified, and different kinds of values can be associated with the identifier, depending on the type specification. If you declare an identifier as having a constant value, (such as A__NUM = 10) you are saying that the identifier, A__NUM, is identically equal to an integer value, 10. At any point in your program that you wish to use the constant of 10, you can also use the identifier, A__NUM.

A programming language performs the mapping between the abstract concept of a location and the actual storage address. At any point in the program, the language ensures that only one value can be associated with the address that corresponds to a specific location. At another time in the program, the pointer to the location might no longer exist, and some other variable can be mapped into the same address.

The effect of a language declaration of a constant or variable is to find a location that is currently unused, and then to associate that location with the identifier being declared.

An identifier can be associated with any number of entities in a programming language. These entities can be:

- As a reference to some data area.
- As a component of a composite name. The composite name can refer to a data area, but the components refer only to some subset of the data area.
- As a reference to a statement location in a program, that is, a statement label.
- As a procedure name.
- As a macro name.
- As a procedure or macro parameter.
- As a file or a program or as a device connected to an input-output port of the computer.

Every identifier possesses a region of validity within the source program, which is called its scope of definition. That name or identifier is available within its scope and is unavailable outside its scope; in fact, it might not even exist outside its scope. A reference to some datum through its identifier is valid only if the reference lies within the scope of the identifier. You will see how to declare a name as a global identifier.

Data Types

A primitive data object is an object that is normally treated as unit and cannot usually be subdivided by any operation. Every microprocessor has a set of definitions of the primitive data objects with which its instruction set is designed to operate (for example, numbers that are limited to $< = 65535$ and have no decimal points—byte integers).

The data object comes into existence when you execute the program code that contains it. The data is stored in a memory field for the duration of its life and is operated upon by various program instructions. A given object might contain a variety of different values during execution and might reside in physically different sections of memory at different times. Its key property is continuity; its value is preserved between accesses and is only changed through some assignment statement in the program. Its life might or might not end when the program control passes out of the scope of the identifier. Some data objects are created initially and survive for the life of the program, and others survive only while the program control remains in the scope of its identifier, such as within a subprocedure.

Data objects have both an external and internal structure. Externally, its structure is defined by its language declaration (for example, REAL or BYTE). Internally, it is some field of binary information in memory. Remember that the internal form of every data object is some sequence of binary digits that provide no clue to its purpose. It is your task to associate meaning with every data object.

Programs manipulate abstract objects that represent real-world objects. Early languages only allowed numbers as data objects, and everything had to be represented by numbers. As the languages developed, other objects could be used. A consequence of a particular choice of representation of a real-world object is the set of operations that can be performed on the object. For instance, examine calendar dates. If dates are represented by integers, that means that all the operations that are available for integers can be performed on dates. Practically, what does this mean? Two dates can be added or subtracted to find the intervals between them or the sum of their various intervals. However, there is no analog to a multiplication or division of dates in the real world. This leads to a definition of *object types*: a type is the collection of objects and a set of operations that can be validly performed on the objects.

Boolean Types. The simplest of all object types is the Boolean type, which contains one of only two values: true or false. Operations on Boolean values vary from language to language, but typical operators include:

- *And* is a binary operator for computing the logical *and* of two Boolean values, in which both values must be true to make the result true.

- *Not* is a unary operator for negating a Boolean value, which makes the value opposite of what it was.

- *Or* is a binary operator for computing the logical *or* of two Boolean values, in which one or the other or both are true to make the result true.

Character and String Types. Because people generally communicate via characters (for example, the monthly statement you receive from your bank), having a language that manipulates characters is fundamental. However, the requirement is generally not for single characters but multiples of characters, called strings.

There are two types of operations on strings. First, you can divide a string into smaller pieces called substrings. Second, you can treat strings as wholes: comparing them, assigning values to them, and building longer strings (concatenation). In many languages, a string is treated as a series (an array) of single characters and can be a fixed or variable length.

Numeric Types. The numbers that computers use are often not exact and only approximate their real-world equivalents. For instance, there is no way to show a completely accurate value of π (pi) in a computer. Numeric types fall into one of three classes:

- *Integer* is a complete entity, a whole number, that is used for exact arithmetic on whole numbers within a fixed range.

- *Fixed point* is a method of calculation in which operations take place in an invariant manner, and in which the computer does not consider the location of the radix point. Fixed point is used for noninteger values with a fixed number of digits before and after the radix point.

- *Floating point* is a specific number representation system in which each number equals one of those numerals times a power of an implicit fixed positive integer base where the power is equal to the implicit base raised to the exponent represented by the other numeral. It is used for noninteger values with a fixed number of significant digits and a widely varying magnitude.

Integers are the most common of the numeric types and can be represented exactly on all digital computers. Fixed-point values are uniformly spaced over a range and have two quantities: (1) precision that is the total number of digits used for representing the value and (2) scale, the number of digits in the fractional part of the value. For example, the number 154.88 has a precision of five and a scale of two.

A floating-point number has two parts, a fraction (sometimes called a mantissa) and an exponent. Floating-point numbers are written differently than fixed or integer numbers because there is a need for an exponent. Generally, the beginning of the exponent part of the number is marked with the letter E. For example, the number 1000 could be written 10E2.

To aid in human readability, many languages allow a break character to divide lengthy sequences of digits. For example, FORTRAN allows a blank (1 000 000), and Ada allows and underscore (1__000__000).

Attributes References and Declarations

The set of meanings associated with an identifier (for example, a data object) is called its attributes. Some examples of attributes are:

- Whether the identifier represents data, a procedure, a statement label, a file, or a macro.
- If it represents a datum, which of several possible kinds of values it can take on, its location, and its links to related data.
- If it represents a procedure, the location of the procedure, the number and kinds of its parameters, whether it is user- or system-defined, whether it can be called by a user or not, and so on.
- If it represents a file, the characteristics of the file—record size, whether fixed or variable length, whether sequential, random access, and so on.

Clearly, attributes require some kind of classification scheme, as each of the different kinds of identifiers in the language require a different form of attribute specification. The number of attributes also might depend on more than one declaration.

Procedures and Parameters

The use of subprograms is familiar to programmers and has been around for a long time. In 1840, Charles Babbage's analytic engine had a group of punched cards that performed a frequently used part of a larger calculation. Subprograms allow you to package computations and parameterize their behavior. In general, there are two types of subprograms: procedures and functions.

A *procedure* is a sequence of actions that is invoked as though it were a single statement. A *function*, on the other hand, is a sequence of computations that results in a single value and is invoked from within an expression. You might use a procedure to convert an EBCDIC character to ASCII, such as CALL CONVERT, where CONVERT does the actual conversion, and use a function to calculate $A = COT(x)$, where x is some variable and the function COT calculates the contangent of its value. Both forms of subprograms represent operational abstractions that simplify the programs that contain them. In most languages, invoking subprograms is only a matter of coding the name of the subprogram and adding its argument list. Thus, subprograms amount to a language extension that provide a new statement. This is especially true of macros, as you will see in this book.

Subprograms do not exist in isolation. They have some form of data communication with the program code from which they are called. This data communication entity of some kind is called a *parameter*. A parameter is an arbitrary constant that has a particular value under specified circumstances. When you pass a parameter to a subroutine or macro, that parameter usually has one set of attributes throughout any one use, but it might be given different attributes when the subroutine is used in different main routines or in different parts of one main routine. Parameters are important, for it is through them that you generalize the action of a procedure or function.

Control Structures

Computer power comes in large part through your ability to specify in which order the program statements are executed. That ability comes through such techniques as GOTO, loop, and IF statements, which are called control structures.

There are five ways you can specify which statement comes next, as shown in Fig. 2-2. The first is sequential. Here, you can allow the statements to be executed in the order in which they were written. The second is conditional, as shown in the second part of Fig. 2-2.

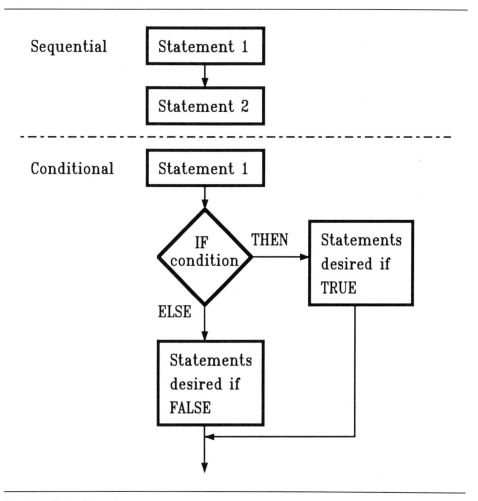

Fig. 2-2. Code Control.

In a conditional control, you code an IF statement which begins with an evaluation of a condition. If its value is true, then the sequence of statements between the THEN and ELSE is executed. If the condition is false, the code between the ELSE and END is executed. In both cases, after the execution of the appropriate code, execution continues with the next consecutive line after the END.

The third type of control is the loop. A loop specifies that a sequence of statements is to be executed repeatedly. There are two types of loops:

- *The WHILE loop*, in which the loop body is prefixed by a condition. Each time control arrives at the top of the loop, the condition is evaluated. If the condition is false, no action is taken, and execution continues after the end of the loop. If the condition is true, the processor executes the body of the loop. Then control goes to the top once again for evaluation.

- *A simple loop*, in which the loop body is executed repeatedly until an explicit exit is found. An explicit exit can be some form of a GOTO, EXIT, or RETURN.

The fourth type of control is the loop exit, as explained in the simple loop above. The last type is an unconditional transfer, such as a JUMP or GOTO. Statements in a sequence execute in the order in which they appear unless some form of program control is encountered, such as a loop, IF, GOTO, JUMP or EXIT.

A special type of control structure found in many languages is the CASE, which is a form of conditional statement where the actions to be carried out depend on the value of an expression given at the head of the case statement. The expression following the CASE is evaluated and its value is compared in turn with each of the values that follow the WHEN symbols. If a match is found, the corresponding sequence of statements is executed. If not, the statements are ignored.

Input and Output

A language must interface with the hardware that handles input and output. The best world is one in which there is an I/O standard that allows the language to simply *present* (output) or *request* (input) the data. That data can be written to a storage device, a screen, or to a printer, or it can be read from storage or a keyboard. By using a standard interface, one manufacturer might implement a language in a way different from another manufacturer, but the exterior interface of both languages to the world would appear the same.

The problem is that there is little agreement on an I/O standard between languages or computer system families (often even within the same family). So, for the time being, you will have to learn the I/O for each hardware family and software family.

In general, the layout of characters for input or output is specified through some kind of format declaration. Given that the device is positioned at some point (on a line for a printer or at an address for storage medium), you specify the text to follow on a character-by-character (or variable-by-variable) basis. Actual I/O is initiated with the input or output statement referencing a particular format declaration.

An input statement generally specifies a list of objects (variables, characters, or character strings) to be input. The external form of the objects can be defined in a named format declaration. In a similar manner, an output statement usually contains a list of objects whose values are to be output. The output forms can also be defined in some named format declaration.

Nesting and Scope

Nesting generally concerns subroutines that are enclosed within each other. Those in the inner ring are not necessarily part of the outer ring or loop. An object holds a value only within a specified program piece or block. For example, a variable might only hold a value within a procedure, in which case the variable is *local* to that procedure. Outside the procedure, the variable either has some other value or is meaningless, because it might not be declared outside that procedure. The part of the program over which an object refers to a value defined in a declaration is the *scope* of the declaration. The process whereby an assembler (or compiler/translator/interpreter) matches an object to its defining declaration is called the *resolution* of the reference.

A variable declaration introduces one or more variables. All program variables must be declared, although some languages allow some variables to be inferred in a way that the first use of the variable is an implicit declaration of its type and usage. Within any one block of a program, a particular variable can be declared only once.

The use of global variables in a block increases the complexity of the block. To use a global variable correctly, you need to understand the computation performed by each block in the entire program that uses the variable. Changes made to global variables outside a nested block affect the use of that variable within the block. Likewise, using a global variable within a block has effects outside the block.

Exception Handling

An exception condition has three aspects. First, an exception is any condition that prevents the completion of the operation that detects it. Second, it cannot be resolved within the local context of the operation. Third, it must be brought to the attention of the invoker of the operation. Bringing the exception to the attention of the invoker is called *raising* the exception. The action taken by the invoker is called *handling* the exception. As a general rule, once an exception condition is raised, it must be dealt with.

There are a number of situations that cause exceptions. The following list is not all inclusive, but it will give you the idea of exceptions that software should handle.

- File-handling conditions:
End of input—The execution of an input statement when there are no more data to be read.
Nonexistent file—You have either misnamed a file, or the file does not exist.

- Program check-out conditions:
Subscript error—The use of an array subscript outside the range 1 through n, where n is the limit of the defined array.

String range—You have attempted to reference a string outside its bounds.
Data error—The characters read during the execution of an input statement do not fit with the type of variable to which they are assigned.
Undefined value—An attempt is made to obtain the value of a variable to which no value has been assigned.

• Computational conditions:
Overflow—The absolute value of a variable exceeds the maximum allowable.
Underflow—The absolute value of a variable is less than can be shown by a defined size.

• System-action conditions:
Error—General error condition.
End—End/termination of program.
Storage—Insufficient storage for requested allocation.

An exception handler diagnoses conditions and initiates some type of action. Often, you design a handler to take control when some specific exception condition is raised that you know the mainline program is not designed to handle. If you know you will have some exceptions you cannot define before they occur, you can write a default handler that will correctly wrap up your program and close the files before you allow the program to terminate.

Parallel Processing

The desire for increased speed has led to overlapping input and output with computation, arithmetic units that work in parallel, and multiprogrammed and multiprocessor operating systems. In the past, this parallelism was hidden from computer users and programmers. This no longer is true. For instance, you will use buffers to allow output to be printed while your program continues to do calculations and prepare for the next line of print.

FINAL THOUGHTS

In chapter 1, you learned the basics of spoken and written language. This chapter overviews general computer language concepts. Now read on to learn about a specific language (assembly language) and language translators (an assembler and a macro assembler).

3

The Basics of a Specific
Language Translator
A Macro Assembler

THE DIFFERENCE BETWEEN PROGRAMMING IN AN ASSEMBLY LANGUAGE AND IN A HIGH-level language is similar to the difference between driving a car with a stick shift and one with an automatic transmission. You are still driving a car. With the manual transmission, you simply exert more direct control over your mechanical helper, the car.

An assembler is simply a program that translates symbolically represented instructions into their binary equivalents. In this chapter, you can take a quick look at assembly language as a basis for examining Microsoft's Macro Assembler, MASM. The discussion moves from general assemblers to macro assemblers and then ends with macros themselves. In chapter 4, the programming process and programming of macros are covered. Beginning with chapter 5, the focus is on MASM itself.

ASSEMBLY LANGUAGE

A machine instruction is a string of binary digits (0s and 1s), represented in the same base in which the machine operates. When interpreted by the hardware, the string causes a unique and well-defined change in the state of the computer. The name *binary digits* has been abbreviated to *bits*. It is important to remember that each processor possesses its own unique instruction set. The same string of bits might mean completely different things on two different computers, even if the number of bits needed for expressing an instruction is the same on both machines. Thus, if you use a bit string that might cause addition of the contents of two registers on an IBM system, the same bit string might decrement the contents of memory on a Radio Shack system.

In the early days of computers, programmers communicated to digital computers with a series of 0s and 1s, the bit strings mentioned above. Whatever it was that you wanted to do, you had to stop and convert into bits. However, the same basic operations performed today were done then. The only time that you now might have to actually work in hexadecimal or binary is when you want or need to modify (*patch*) a system.

Patching becomes expedient when you do not have time to do a reassembly and link of a software system. That is, you only change object code at a specific position where you find a bug. Wanting to avoid a complete assembly, you decide to play the role of the assembly program for the few instructions that need to be added to correct the bug. Remember, however, that you had better go back immediately and change the source code to include the patch. If you do not change the source code immediately, you might forget, and you will end up with a nightmare situation where your source code does not match your operating program.

Today, there is a language in which all operators and almost all operands are represented by names chosen for their explanatory and mnemonic power. ADD is for adding, SUB is for subtracting, and so on. In most assembly languages, assembler designers chose the operand names while leaving it up to you to choose many of the operands as you need them. For instance, if you move a memory value that you have declared into a register (MOVE EAX,VALUE), the MOV and the EAX register are already chosen, but you declared VALUE with all of its attributes.

Probably the most important advantage of programming in symbols rather than bit patterns is the control it gives you over what has come to be called *binding*, the assignment of directly machine-computable values to the symbolic expressions that you coded into your source program. Because the computer cannot execute a program until it is in machine language, a narrow concept of efficiency would seem to dictate that the program be reduced to machine language as quickly as possible. Why do you think that designers include the link as a separate step?

The forced deferral of final translation turns out to have advantages. For instance, you can build a library of object programs, pick and choose which ones you will need in your final program, and then simply link them together. You do not have to write the original programs again and again.

Another advantage of programming in a symbolic language instead of in bits is that the symbols allow you to see the generality of a program. Because you do think of its more widely implementable aspects, you might spend more time writing and documenting it. The reward is that you do not have to rewrite it for each tiny change that comes along; you have already coded in the flexibility. For instance, if you code a variable as TAX_RATE, you can include a tax of 7.5 percent, 12.75 percent, or other value. If you hard coded 7.5, then you would have to change the program each time the tax rate changed or each time you sold the program to a location that had a different rate.

Symbolic programming puts a distance between what you are trying to do and the final task that a user needs. You include adaptability that will save you or a colleague from having to write essentially the same thing over (and over) again.

Although both are symbolic languages, there are at least four areas in which assembly language allows you more control of the computer than does a compiler language:

- Fine Tuning—Only the assembly language programmer directly and consciously determines the machine-language instructions that are to be executed and the detailed representation of the data upon which they are to operate. For these reasons, you alone can guarantee that a program will fit within a given area of storage or execute within a given period of time.

• Early Responsiveness—There is a gap between the time a compiler user finds a need and the time that the compiler writers can respond to it. That gap can be several years. With assembly language, you can turn your need into code right away.

• Pioneering—Assembly language is almost always the choice when a wholly new computer application is being pioneered, even though the necessity for its use might not be clear at the outset. When it is uncertain what the demands of the new species of program are going to be, the safest course is to use the language that imposes the fewest constraints. After a number of programs have been written in the new application area, it might turn out that one of the existing compiler languages (almost always with some modifications) is adequate. Or it might be found that the new application is different and economically important enough to warrant the development of a language tailored to its needs.

In the meantime, assembly language is that language used to keep programmers productively working. Furthermore, a knowledge of assembly language often helps you use compiler languages more efficiently, clarifying the relation between what is written and what the compiler produces, in addition to warning about the hidden points in compiler-language usage where the price of execution might suddenly rise tenfold because the code compiled has exceeded some buffer size or other critical system constraint.

ASSEMBLERS

An *assembler* is a program that allows you to write code in mnemonic instead of having to use long strings of 0s and 1s. *Mnemonics* is the art of improving the efficiency of human memory. *Mnemonic operation code* is an operation code in which the names of the operations are abbreviated and expressed mnemonically to facilitate remembering the operations they represent. The classic assembler takes a routine (or subprogram) and converts it into binary symbolic form for later processing by a linkage editor. As with Microsoft's MASM, the conversion is done by two passes; that is, the source program is scanned twice. This two-pass strategy is very simple. The first pass through the source program collects all the symbol definitions into a symbol table. The second pass converts the program to binary symbolic form, using the definitions collected in the first pass.

The earliest assemblers were little more than routines for translating some of the more convenient representations of machine language instructions, with none of the additional features now expected as a matter of course. It is interesting to note how much extra programming productivity is achieved with even a primitive assembler. It is estimated that there is an improvement of three times the productivity with just that early assembler. You get even more with today's complex macro assemblers, which are discussed in this book.

Assemblers allow use of mnemonic operation codes, allow symbolic names to be assigned to memory location, provide facilities for address calculations in terms of such symbolic names, and usually enable the introduction of numerical and character constants in various forms. Assemblers are used for assembly language programming when it is required to access all the facilities of the machine and the access cannot be accomplished with a high-level language. Returning to the automatic transmission versus manual transmission analogy, you get better gas mileage when you have additional control as to when your car shifts gears. In the same way, you can program a computer to run faster and more efficiently when you do the work yourself instead of allowing some compiler to generate code that someone else decided was the way it should be done.

A typical instruction consists of an operation code, an address, and one or more register fields. The address might refer to a data area or to another instruction. An assembler provides a fixed set of mnemonic operation codes and an open-ended set of programmer-defined symbols for use in address parts. Such address symbols might be defined explicitly or implicitly by attaching them as labels to particular instructions or data words.

Although a symbol stands for an address, an assembler cannot convert label symbols directly into addresses because the address in storage into which a particular instruction will be loaded is not known at assembly time. The difficulty is resolved in two steps. The assembler first records the displacement from the beginning of the code of the instruction in question as the value of the label symbol. Second, it marks the symbol in the assembler output as a relative or relocatable value. This value is adjusted later by the linker or loader.

An assembler usually provides a variety of information about the program that it has assembled. In addition to details of errors such as incorrect syntax or multiple definition of symbols, the following might be provided:

- Listing of symbolic instructions.
- Table of symbols defined/used in the routine.
- Cross-reference table: for each symbol defined, its name, value, and a list of all the instructions that reference it.

Assembler Directives

Assembler directives serve two purposes. Directives provide information to control the assembly process. Also, they provide a way of defining data words in a program. Assembler directives are often called *pseudo-operations* (or pseudo-ops) since they are commonly designated by special codes in the operation field.

The form of the listing is generally controlled by one or more pseudo-ops, for example, LIST FULL. Other common pseudo-ops are EJECT, which causes a page feed on the printer at the point in the listing where it occurs, and SPACE n, where n is the number of blank lines to insert into a listing.

MACRO ASSEMBLERS

In its simplest form, a macro instruction (generally called a macro) is a single computer instruction that stands for a given sequence of instructions. Macros are most often used to represent relatively short sequences of instruction or sequences that involve a relatively large number of insertions of arguments. Often a set of macros is combined into a library; a very common example of this is a library of macros to aid communication with an operating system.

If you program a lot, you will find that a certain pattern of instructions occurs in several places in a program, with only minor variations. This is particularly the case if there is a common operation that requires several instructions for its execution. In this case, it is convenient for you to be able to write one call and have the system generate the sequence of instructions. There are several advantages in this. You write fewer lines of code, which means fewer possible errors. Second, the program can be more readable, mainly because of the fewer code lines. Using macro names that describe their purpose also helps readability. Finally, if at a future stage you need to modify the function the macro performs, you only have to change one place (the macro) instead of multiple places in multiple programs.

To implement macros, you need a piece of software called a macro processor, which is often itself part of an assembly language software system. The job of a macro processor is simple. The programmer supplies some macro definitions, which define the macros and what is to replace them, and the macro processor then replaces any occurrence of the macro accordingly. A macro processor is often combined with an assembler to make it appear to the programmer as if the two are a single unit, called a *macro assembler*.

An important attribute of an assembler is its ability to define and use macros. Figure 3-1 shows an overview of a macro assembler organized as a linear pipeline.

One routine collects input characters into tokens. Another records macro definitions and deletes them from the input stream. A third expands macro calls, and so on. This is just one example of how macro code can be expanded.

Macros are a form of text replacement that provide an automatic code-generation capability under user control. Simply stated, a macro is a predefined set of assembler instructions that can be used in different parts of a program with optional modifications each time it is used. A macro assembler simplifies coding when similar sections of codes are used repeatedly but variations preclude the use of conventional subroutine techniques.

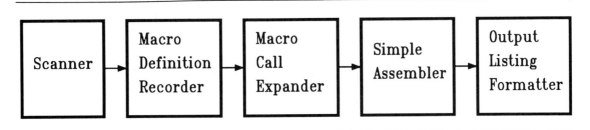

Fig. 3-1. Macro Assembler Organized as a Linear Pipeline.

With a macro assembler, a single instruction turns into the necessary expansion without undue programmer complexity. A macro assembler converts sequences of logical operations directly into machine code.

MACRO LANGUAGES

One approach to designing a macro language is to adapt some existing language to do macro processing as well. Macro facilities are made available through built-in subroutines, such as "define a macro" and "gear a file for macro calls." For each macro, you designate a subroutine, written in the host language, which the language processor calls every time it recognizes the macro name.

A unique property of a macro instruction is its trapping ability. This property enables you to define any standard assembly operator as a macro and thereby trap it for special treatment. This valuable capability rests on two seemingly trivial points: first, the fact that macro calls are (or can be) identical in format to ordinary assembly language operators; second, the fact that macro processing precedes (or can be made to precede) ordinary assembly. Thus, any symbol defined both as an ordinary operator and macro name is effectively a macro name only, and will cause the generation into the object program of whatever instruction you specify. This capability allows you to trap every transfer instruction in a program (or a selected portion of it) and generate instead (or in addition) instructions that compute at execution time the actual addresses to which control is being ordered transferred. It also allows you to compare those transfers with limits that you set, and allow the transfer to be executed only if within those limits.

A macro is a way of packaging routines for future use. As you will see later with MASM, a new macro can be created (or defined) at any point in your program. Because the macro processor, whether embedded in an assembler or not, is put in a special macro-defining mode when it encounters a macro definition, the creation of a macro does not generate any instructions in the program. Only an explicit call generates instructions.

MACROS

There are several advantages to using macros instead of entering individual lines of code. First, you avoid excess typing. (Each time you strike a key, you face a possible error.) Once the macro is entered and tested, you only invoke the macro; you do not have to reenter the keystrokes to get the same task accomplished. Second, you do not need to look up interrupt numbers or service codes each time you need them if you write what you need in a macro. Several of the interrupts are similar (such as those that read a keystroke from the keyboard). Some of the interrupts display the entered key on the screen; others do not. Once you figure out what you want to display, you write it into your macro and name it something descriptive.

One of the disadvantages is that the macro is opaque. For instance, you might code a register to hold an index value inside a macro. You may forget what you have done and use that register for something else entirely outside the macro. That makes debugging difficult, at least until you get the expanded code so that you can debug a line at a time.

This problem is compounded if you use the .SALL (Suppress All macro expansion listings—see chapter 7). You shorten a lengthy listing, but you cannot find cross uses of registers as easily.

A macro is a way of extending a language. Once a macro is defined, you can treat it as an extra assembly language instruction. It is common practice to build an extensive group of macros, and it often happens that a program is built entirely of macros and devoid of true assembly language instructions. In this case, the macros can be thought of as forming a language in their own right.

Macro Components

Macros, like members of a cloistered religious order, are supposed to remain ignorant of the world they live in for the sake of higher things. The macro is intended to limit the area of concern for any one task and to minimize the impact of later changes. It does this by isolating and formalizing the channels of communication, or interfaces between itself and other program components. A common application is the funneling of all a program input/output requests through one module. That module alone makes all the I/O requests to the operating system or the hardware. If the I/O facilities of the system later change in ways that affect a program that you have modularized in this way, only its I/O module needs to be revised. The module, then, accomplishes its objective only if its relations with the rest of the system are sharply restricted.

All MASM macros have a name, a beginning, a body, and an end. They often specify a list of one or more dummy names that can be parameters passed to the macro. Figure 3-2 shows the outline of a basic macro. The *name* is a standard assembler symbol. It can contain 1 to 31 alphanumeric characters including special characters: @ $ __ ?. You use the name to invoke the macro.

```
;
;
; A sample macro skeleton showing the main parts of a macro.
;
; The macro definition statement -  (the beginning)
; name      MACRO directive  dummy parameters

samp01    MACRO           dummy00,dummy01
;; A comment which is internal to a macro - ie it does not print when
;; macro expansion occurs.
;; The body of the macro includes everything between the MACRO line
;; and the ENDM line
          mov     AX,dummy00        ; A prototype statement

          EXITM                     ; A pseudo-op (directive)
ENDM                                ; End of the macro (the end)
```

Fig. 3-2. Basic Macro Outline.

The *dummy* names are a list of parameters, separated by commas, which will be used within the macro. The parameters are temporary variables whose values might be changed with each new macro invocation. You specify the values of these variables when you invoke the macro. These parameters can be numerical or text (including register names), other macro names, opcode mnemonics, and program labels. Labels are concerned with, or correspond to, numerical values or memory locations. The specific absolute address is not necessary, in most cases, because the intent of the label is a general destination. Labels are a requisite for jump and branch instructions.

The macro body consists of opcodes, pseudo-ops, labels, and comments; that is, the macro *body* is lines of assembly language code along with their internal documentation. When you invoke the macro, it is expanded so that the parameters referenced in the body are replaced with the values you've passed it. The *end* is an ENDM, which signals the macro assembler that the macro code has finished.

Self-Modifying Macros

Macros can contain any number of program lines using any of the opcodes, pseudo-ops, labels or macros that the assembler knows. Thus, you can define macros that include procedure, segment, and data definition. You can even write a macro that defines a new macro or redefines itself.

A macro that redefines itself can be used to place subroutine source code into a program. If you write a macro that invokes itself or redefines itself, be sure that a mechanism is provided to exit from the loop.

Macros Versus Subroutines

The difference between a macro and a subroutine is clear cut. A macro is actually replaced by its expanded form in the program after being run through the macro assembler. So, if your program contains n copies of the macro, then n copies of the instructions it stands for are inserted into the program. A subroutine, on the other hand, involves a break in the flow of a program. If a sequence of instructions occurs frequently in a program, then these can be written as a subroutine, and each occurrence in the program is replaced by an instruction to jump to this subroutine, execute it, and then return. There is then only one copy of the sequence of instructions.

PROGRAMMING MACROS

Macros should contain the very best, the most optimal code that you can write. The merits of structured programming have been argued at some length in many books, so they will not be repeated here except for a couple of points. The basis of structure is KISS: keep it simple, stupid.

- Let your code flow from a single entry point and exit only at one other point.
- Let each variable and flag stand for only one thing.
- Document within the program. Each program piece should have a prologue that explains what the piece does, what major decisions are made, and what parameters are passed into and out of the piece.

- Keep each program piece fewer than 100 lines of code. Long programs are complex and difficult to debug. Divide programs into procedures, subroutines, and macros.
- Use few (or no) GOTOs. They break the logic flow, which makes code more difficult to read and maintain.

Programs should be easy to read and understand. You have an obligation to yourself and to other programmers who might have to maintain your code. That obligation is to help them (and yourself) understand what you have coded.

A macro is called by what is, in appearance and placement: just another assembly language operator but one invented by you. The values passed into the defining instructions (when they are inserted into the program text in answer to the particular call) usually follow the macro name on the same line. Also, they are in a format that closely parallels that of the operands supplied with a standard assembly language operator.

FINAL THOUGHTS

It has long been expected, and from time to time announced, that compiler languages would supplant assembly language as it, in turn, has supplanted machine language. This change has not occurred. Assembly language survives and even flourishes. The fundamental reason is clear: assembly language is a language that allows you a great deal of control over your computer environment. Assembly language also allows you to do with the computer anything it can do at all, while compiler languages trade this versatility for applicability to a limited range of problems.

4

The Programming
Process and
Macro Programming

BACK IN THE LATE 1960s, A TOP PROGRAMMER MADE $40,000 A YEAR, AND A COMPUTER WITH 32k (32 kilobytes) of memory sold for $100,000. Today, that same level of programming skill commands salaries in excess of $70,000, and you can buy a desktop computer with four megabytes of memory for less than $5,000. The cost of producing individual units of hardware is decreasing while the production of software is becoming more expensive by the day. An interesting facet of human expense is that often a line of code written by a $25,000 a year programmer is more expensive than a line written by a $75,000 programmer. Why is this?

Expertise in programming is much like expertise in painting. Mistakes are covered by changing them; the new overlays the old. A new programmer has to do a lot of rewriting, but an old pro often gets it right the first time. Also, beginners have problems isolating where errors lie while the pros have been there before so that their time from error discovery to error fix is much less than it is for the beginner.

Too often, the programming process gets fouled because beginning programmers forget that there are actually four distinct steps to the process called programming. First, get a general knowledge about the chosen hardware system, to know if the problem can be solved on this type of hardware. Second, stop and evaluate the problem. Third, design the solution. And only then, fourth, sit down to code. After programming, test the solution and then integrate the solution into production.

Review each of those steps one at a time and then you will see how you can write and use macros to build yourself a language. Then move to chapter 5, which examines MASM's grammatical structure. After that, go to chapter 6 to begin examining Microsoft's MASM.

KNOW THE HARDWARE SYSTEM

Almost all modern computers are based on the stored-program computer concept, generally credited to mathematician John von Neumann. Figure 4-1 shows an overview of a von Neumann machine. The CPU consists of an instruction interpreter, a location counter, an instruction register, and various working registers and general registers.

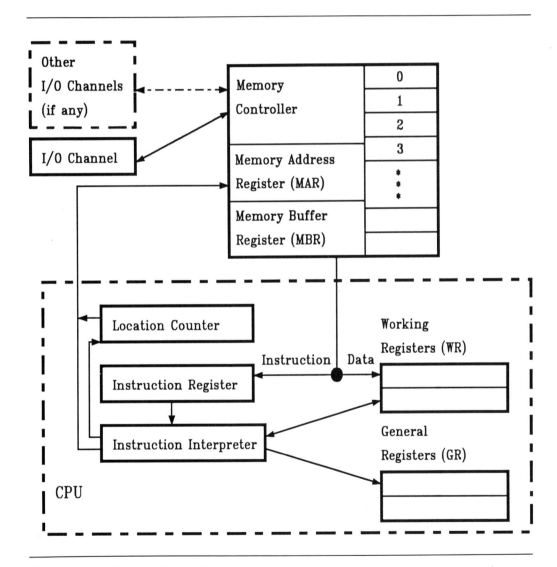

Fig. 4-1. A von Neumann Stored-Program Computer.

The instruction interpreter is a group of electrical circuits (hardware) that performs the instructions that are fetched from memory. The location counter is a hardware memory device that points to the location of the current instruction being executed. A copy of the current instruction is stored in the instruction register. The working registers are memory devices that serve as temporary storage for the instruction interpreter, and the general registers are used by programmers as storage locations and for special functions.

In the von Neumann computer model, the primary interface between memory and the CPU is via the memory address register and the memory buffer register. The memory address register (MAR) contains the address of the memory location that is to be read from or stored into. The memory buffer register (MBR) contains a copy of the designated memory location specified by the MAR after a read, or it contains the new contents of the memory location prior to a write. The memory controller is hardware that transfers data between the MBR and the memory location, the address of which is in the MAR. The I/O channels can be thought of as separate computers that interpret special instructions for inputting and outputting information from memory.

Compare this general computer structure to the 80386.

80386 Microprocessor

In this section is a brief overview of the 80386. For a more complete look, see appendix H. First, a few definitions:

- *Multitasking* is a procedure in which several separate but interrelated tasks operate under a single program identity.

- *Multitasking* is a procedure in which several separate but interrelated tasks operate under a single program identity.

- *On-Chip Memory Management*—Designers of many of the microprocessors chose to manage computer memory in microunits that are auxiliary to the main processor. Intel chose to implement the management on the 80386.

- *Virtual Memory*—Two important concepts of virtual memory systems are those of address space and memory space. Address space is the set of all locations used by a program, both instruction and data. Memory space is the set of actual hardware locations available on the machine. Programs that run under virtual memory generally have their address space much larger than the actual physical memory space. A mapping or some other function from the address space to the memory space is needed. In other words, the address used by a program might not correspond to the actual hardware address of the item being referenced. The virtual memory process, hardware, intercepts all program addresses and sends them to be translated into actual addresses.

- *Paging* is a procedure for transmitting pages (certain amounts of data) of information between main storage and auxiliary storage, especially done for the purpose of assisting the allocation of a limited amount of main storage among a number of executing programs.

• *Pipelining* is the overlapping of fetch and execute cycles within a processor. After the fetch unit has passed a decoded instruction on to the execution unit (see descriptions below), it places the next instruction in the instruction queue.

• *Stack* is a reserved area of memory where the CPU saves the contents of various registers. The stack is referenced in a last-in/first-out (LIFO) basis. It is coordinated with a stack pointer that keeps track of storage and retrieval of each entry in the stack.

The 80386 features multitasking, on-chip memory management, virtual memory with paging, software protection, and large address space. Compatibility with earlier Intel chips (8086 through 80286) is preserved through the instruction set, register handling, and bus sizing.

The 80386 is designed for applications needing high performance and is optimized for multitasking. The 32-bit registers support 32-bit addresses and data types. Instruction pipelining and on-chip address translation ensure execution at sustained rates of between three and four million instructions per second (MIPS).

The 80386 consists of six elements: an execution unit, a segment unit, a paging unit, an instruction decode unit, a code prefetch unit, and a bus interface unit (BIU). See Fig. 4-2 for a graphic view of the six units of the 80386. The BIU provides the interface

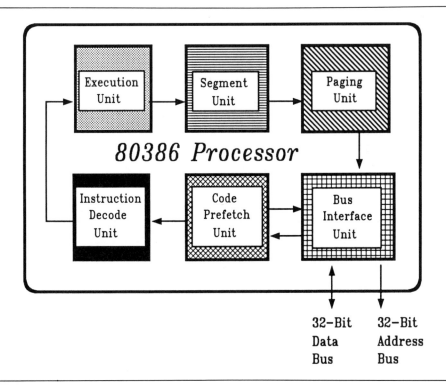

Fig. 4-2. Six Basic Units of the 80386.

between the 80386 and its environment, accepting internal requests for code fetches (from the code prefetch unit) and data transfers (from the execution unit). The code prefetch unit implements the program look-ahead function of the 80386. When the BIU is not performing bus cycles to execute instructions, the code prefetch unit uses the BIU to fetch sequentially along the instruction byte stream. These prefetched instructions are stored in the 16-byte code queue to await processing by the instruction decode unit.

The instruction decode unit takes instruction bytes from the prefetch queue and translates them into microcode. The decoded instructions are then stored in a three-deep instruction queue on a first-in/first-out (FIFO) basis to await processing by the execution unit. Immediate data and opcode offsets are taken from the prefetch queue.

There are valid reasons for knowing the hardware, whichever language you program in. Some languages (notably C) provide constructs (that is, register types) that instruct the compiler to use particular hardware features. The advantage of assembly language lies in the ability to control totally the instructions, registers, and flow of the program. This ability can optimize execution time and/or the size of the resulting object code. It is knowledge of the hardware, not clever tricks, that aids in making a good assembly language program. Knowledge of which instructions set various flags allows the elimination of useless tests, for example:

```
MOV EAX,DATA1
SUB EAX,EBX
MOV DATA2,EAX
OR   EAX,EAX      ;Useless test
JZ   DONE
```

There is no need to OR the EAX register because the subtract already has set the zero flag (Z) if the result is zero. The MOV does not change the Z flag. The 80386 registers and flags are overviewed in appendix H.

PROBLEM EVALUATION

English is a difficult language to use for defining problems formally because it is vague and leads to ambiguous definitions. However, it is the only common language that most people have so it is necessary to develop a formalized way of talking about problems. Allied with that method must be a graphic representation of the problem; that representation is called a flowchart. Both description and charting are used to show how to define a problem.

The first level of problem analysis is the overall problem or, as it is now called, the top view. From there, break the total problem into pieces and work your way down to individual tasks (that is why this method of evaluation is called *top down*). Consider a simple, often-used problem: balancing a checkbook. The top-level problem is to know how much cash there is to spend.

The next level of the problem, level two, is to determine how much cash flows in and out. Call the *in* an A and the *out* a B. A divides down into salary and other; B divides into account management, electronic transfers, and checks. (There are other items, keep the problem simple to show the points of analysis.) Figure 4-3 shows the breakdown.

When you get to this level, the various elements that will need programming begin to appear. At this stage, you are not deciding what kinds of outputs a user needs; that is a later step. Right now, you are trying to decide what has to be done to understand the problem fully.

After flowcharting the problem, you would normally get together with another knowledgeable person and review what you know. That second person checks your analysis and might, with questioning, bring up aspects that you either did not know or had forgotten. For instance, should there be a choice as to whether periodic cash inputs and outputs should be automated? What about the period of retention of records? Should all check numbers be kept for a month, a quarter (three months), or a year? Will you want to subdivide the checks to gather information for tax purposes (for instance, perhaps you have a home-based business, and some of the money is spent for tax-deductible items)?

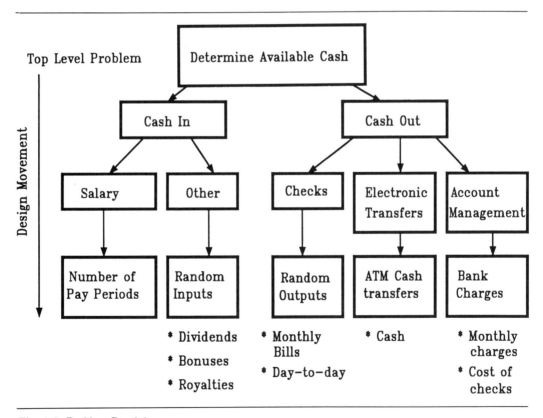

Fig. 4-3. Problem Breakdown.

Continue to define and divide the problem until you feel you have the majority of the problem understood. Realize that you will never know the full problem, because end users will come to you with requests after they have used the software. That is why maintenance and enhancement is such an important part of software development.

DESIGN THE SOLUTION

Now that you have a firm grasp on the problem, it is time to decide how to design the solution. There are problem solution methods that have come to prove themselves. Structured design and analysis is the method that has stood the test of time best.

Structured Programming Concepts

Structured design means that the design of both the components of a system and the interrelationship among those components allows the program to function in the best possible way. Structured design has a significant effect on programming and program maintainability: elements of structured program and their interdependences can be graphed on a structure chart and quickly understood. The quicker the grasp, the shorter the start-up time will be for new programmers.

Well-structured programs have five traits. First, the total program easily divides into modules arranged in a structure that defines the logical relationships. That is, A links to B, which links to C, and so on. Second, execution flows from module to module in easy-to-understand schemes, where control always enters the module at one unique point and always exits at another unique point. After each subroutine call, control always returns to the calling module or program.

The third property of a structured program is that each program variable serves only one purpose, and the scope and limit of that variable is controlled and clear. For example, a variable called *INDEX* might be used as a step value in a loop. It should not also be used in the same program as a condition flag. Fourth, error processing follows normal program control (except in the case of unrecoverable errors). And, finally, each module is documented to explain how it functions, what its data requirements are, how it is invoked, and what it invokes.

Look at each aspect of structured design in detail. When designing program(s), divide each program into independent pieces, called modules. A module is a self-contained unit whose code is physically and logically separate from the code of any other module in the program. So that those programs will be easy to work on, limit independent program pieces to fewer than 100 instructions. This number is not set in concrete but is used to help you concentrate on keeping modules small enough to handle.

Relate the modules to one another in a hierarchical manner. That is, each lower level in the structure should represent a more detailed function. Begin each module with a common block that explains its function, the values passed to it, the values returned, what modules call this one, and what modules this one calls. See the programs included in this book for examples of this point.

Avoid unnecessary labels. MASM allocates space for each of the labels, so if you do not use a label, you are creating extra and unneeded overhead. Unused labels also make the program less readable and less understandable. When a label is encountered, the reader tends to try and locate uses of the label. Unused labels dilute the visual structure of the code. Also, do not use labels as comments because doing so would mix their purposes. If code needs a comment (almost all code should be commented), then use the comment space for the documentation.

Make all variable and module names meaningful. Each name should suggest the function it performs and its purpose in the program. Begin variable names that belong to the same table or to the same module with the same prefix. Limit the scope of a branch statement to the module in which it occurs. Finally, avoid obscure or tricky code because it makes for difficult maintenance, both for yourself and for some unfortunate person who has to work on your code. One aside: it is not obscure to make full use of the instruction set and knowledge of the CPU. The reason that each instruction is present is that it is the optimum one for a particular situation.

Structured techniques also provide some basic project management assistance. Project status information can be attached to the graphic descriptions (the basic blocks in the graphic chart). Managers can then see the status for use in progress reporting. If you are managing your own job, you can easily see at any point in the development cycle just how far into the job you are.

Program Efficiency

Once the basic structuring concepts are in mind, then tackle simple efficiency techniques. Efficiency is the extent to which a program performs its intended function without wasting machine resources such as memory, storage, channel capacity, and execution time.

Efficiency is important, but not when taken to extremes. Some programmers spend so much time being certain that they use the fewest possible lines of code that they lose sight of the fact that the program should be easy to use and maintain. The other side of this argument is that good programmers tend to write code that is efficient almost automatically. After gaining experience, it does not require added effort to be efficient. Even efficient code can often be refined further, but it takes a second pass and significant time. This time should only be spent on high-use program segments and then only after the algorithms have been examined for optimum efficiency. Some things to keep in mind are:

- Modularize the program into logical pieces, for example, keep I/O in one section, error handling in another, and so on.

- Use only a small subset of the program pages at any point during execution to increase efficient use of memory.

- Eliminate all unused labels and expressions to take full advantage of compiler and assembler optimizations. If a label or expression is not used, do not put it in.

• Isolate exception routines and error-handling routines in separate modules. Because errors are out of the mainstream of processing, do not clutter the main line of code with their presence.

• Process all code outside a loop which does not need to be processed within the loop.

• Use integer arithmetic whenever possible, instead of floating-point arithmetic.

• Avoid mixed data types in arithmetic or logical operations whenever possible to eliminate unnecessary data conversions.

• Align program variables in storage.

• Avoid nonstandard subroutine and/or function calls.

• In a complex logical condition, try to break code down so that the "early outs" can be taken; that is, test the most likely TRUE condition first.

• Use the most efficient data type for subscripts.

Program Usability

Usability tends to be defined from the viewpoint of the current participant. End users see usability in ways that depend on their experience, how frequently they use a system, what their ideas of human factoring are, how critical the system is to getting a task done, and exactly how the software interacts with them. Programmers define usability as the ease of maintenance/enhancement/bug fixing. Program managers often see it as how many lines of correct code can be written within a time limit.

Generally, a usable program minimizes confusion, is easy to operate/run, and is tolerant of use errors and changing needs. Usability is simply the extent to which a program is convenient, practical, and easy to use. The following is a usability checklist to measure programs. The points begin with users' viewpoints and moves to programmers' viewpoints.

• Is there a HELP feature for every function and is it available on request?

• Is a correct, complete explanation of each command and/or operating mode available on request?

• Can the user learn the program without human assistance?

• Does the program allow the user to cancel it, at any point, without harmful side effects?

• Does the program have detailed, understandable prompting for input and processes such as starting a printer?

• Are the error messages understandable? Are there suggestions as how to correct the errors?

• Can the program accept reduced input when actions are to be repeated?

• Can commands be abbreviated?

- Does the program edit/validate input data?
- Does the program allow the user to extend the commands?
- Does the program allow an experienced user to work with a faster version, such as abbreviated commands, default values, and so on?
- Are there audit trails so that users and programmers can figure out what went wrong?
- Are all input formats, requirements, and restrictions clearly explained?
- Can the program handle typing errors?
- Does the program allow interruption of a task, and is it able to restart or resume at logical points?
- Does the program do the housekeeping such as deleting temporary files?

If a program is used over a long period of time, it is best to make it easy to use. Human memory is tricky; people forget that one tiny detail that makes a program work correctly instead of incorrectly.

Program Documentation

Well-documented programs are easier to work with than undocumented programs. The key is that a program should be its own documentation. This section describes documentation needed by programmers. User documentation, external manuals, and operations documentation are not addressed. Program documentation describes the program components and data, what the program does, and why and how the program works as it does. There are two types of documentation: internal and external.

External documentation is the written assumptions made before you write code, the hard-copy program listings, and the typed description of inputs, outputs, and processes of the program(s). This external documentation is separate from source code. If the program is well structured, often the programmer allows external documentation to lapse behind the internal.

Internal documentation is defined as those remarks that appear in the actual program source code, the well-defined variables, and the module headers. This is the documentation that does not get lost when it is needed the most. It is also the most accurate documentation of the program. Take a look at the internal documentation on each of the toolkit programs included in this book. No matter if you type in the code or copy it from the available disk, the comments ensure that you will know what the code does and how it does it.

Control Transfer

As part of the process of defining the structure of the program, consider its use of operating system services. If your programming environment is like MS-DOS, the services are invoked by interrupts. Interrupts are simply a means of linking to operating system routines by way of an indirect pointer supported by the hardware. OS/2 replaces the interrupt form of request by using 80286/80386 features that allow operating system services to be called directly (task gates, etc., which resolve to FAR calls in application code).

These interrupts or calls are synchronous with program execution and can be considered the same as CALL instructions, that is a function/procedure described elsewhere that is executed and returns control in line. These calls are best isolated with a macro. Changes between operating systems can then be accomplished by replacing the macro and reassembling the modules that use it. Asynchronous interrupts are handled by the operating system without affecting program execution.

When activated, most modules begin execution at the first executable statement. There are two general ways to transfer control to new code: call and jump. A *call* is made out of the current executing sequence with the assumption that control eventually returns to the execution sequence from which the call was made. The *return* from the call transfers to the location of an instruction in the sequence associated with the most recently conditioned transfer for which a return has not yet been made. In this way, the pattern of call-type transfers and returns always defines a fully nested set of activations. Figure 4-4 shows how the logic appears in a block diagram of transfers and returns. This system is hierarchical because the conditioned transfer sets up its origin as a sequence having control over the target sequence.

Program Initialization
First Program Lines
Call Subroutine 1
    Subroutine 1 Entry
        ⋮
    Subroutine 1 Exit
Next Program Lines
Call Subroutine 2   Fig. 4-4. A Nested Set of CALLs/Activities.
    Subroutine 2 Entry
    Subroutine 2 Lines
    Call Subroutine 3
        Subroutine 3 Entry
          ⋮
        Subroutine 3 Exit
    Subroutine 2 Exit
Final Program Lines
Program Termination

A *jump*, on the other hand, can be either conditional or unconditional. A conditional transfer occurs if a particular predefined condition occurs, such as a carry flag (CF) being set. An unconditional jump forces a mandatory change to the execution sequence. No jump carries any tacit condition of return. These transfers set up a new control stream, activating another portion of the module as an alternate process.

A *subroutine* is a module or procedure activated at execution time by a CALL instruction. Subroutines, as a general rule, can accept arguments and cannot be executed by themselves as stand-alone code. A *macro* is a series of instructions that are copied in line during translation (for example, compilation or assembly) as the result of being invoked by name. The process of copying in line is called *expansion*. A macro is expanded as a result of being invoked. Translation of the macro into the target object code might happen before, during, or after expansion; MASM performs translation after expansion. Macro writing techniques are explored in this chapter.

Termination Processing

You have seen how interrupts and calls transfer control to a second set of code or a subroutine. Once the program has finished its required work, it is time to terminate. When terminating, the software should "clean up" before exiting. It should do this whether it exits in a normal way or as an unexpected exit. At a minimum, the unexpected exit should cause a notification and identification of the error sufficient for debugging or preventing reoccurrence of the error. In the extreme, a serious error should cause a dump. Normally, this cleanup includes closing of files, elimination of temporary files, and doing final input/output (I/O) to clear all buffers.

CODING

One of the most interesting aspects of coding is the great variation in programmer productivity, perhaps as great as a ratio of 10 to 1 from the best to the merely good. For any programmer or coder, there are some traits that are required if a programmer's full potential is to be realized. There is the need for creativity, of course, but it needs to be tempered with great patience and intense discipline if clever but unmanageable programs are to be avoided. Too many programs are written that might be a tribute to a programmer's ability to master complex logical structures but that have no place in a professional environment. The discipline of good programming practices is a severe one.

Just as a great woman once said that she had no time to write a short letter so she wrote a long one. It is easy to ramble and difficult to be concise. Coding in long, rambling macros is a sign of sloppy thinking and sloppy work. Unnecessary tests are probably the most common example of useless instructions; there is also *dead code*, which is code that cannot or is not reached by any branch or line of logic.

Writing two macros (or two subroutines) that are nearly the same is another sign of sloppy practice; usually it indicates a failure in the design process. The two subroutines should probably be three routines: two routines that both call the third for the common function. The macros might be combined into a single, more powerful macro by use of conditional assembly techniques, or they might be split into three macros, one of which is internal to the other two. Clean, simple code cuts down on maintenance because, if the work that the macro or subroutine does has to be changed, you only change one place rather than two. For instance, a macro that handles months might be expanded simply to handle days and years. The total concept would be a macro that handles dates, not pieces of dates.

Once the program is written, it is time to debug it. Finding errors before they get to acceptance testing (whether formal or informal) significantly reduces software cost because fewer hours have been spent working on the program. Another important point that supports early detection of errors is the loss of confidence the end user has when bugs are found in released software.

Debugging means finding errors. These errors come from several common causes. First, the programmer might misunderstand the original design. Second and more often, bugs come from human error in using incorrect code statements or in remembering flags, semaphores, or logic flow. How well programmers find errors depends on the individuals. Often, programmers have difficulty because they make invalid assumptions, and their conjectures become prematurely fixed, which blinds then to other possibilities.

Some of the steps programmers take when coding are:

- Set up file-control directives—INCLUDEs and listing structure (for example, page width and whether to include macro expansion).
- Make GLOBAL declarations.
- Write documentation header.
- Establish program structure directives (for example, register assumptions, segment alignment, and segment origin).
- Set up single entry and exit points.
- Define variables and constants.

MACRO LANGUAGE

It is often necessary to repeat some blocks of code many times in the course of a program. The block might consist of code to save or exchange sets of registers, or code to set up linkages. In these situations, a macro instruction facility becomes very useful.

Macros enable you to assign a symbolic name to a block of source statements and then to use that name in a source file to represent the statements. You can also define parameters to represent arguments passed to the macro. Macro expansion is a text-processing function that occurs at assembly time. Each time MASM encounters the text associated with a macro name, it replaces that text with the text of the statements in the macro definition. Similarly, the text of parameter names is replaced with the text of the corresponding actual arguments. You can define macros within a source file as long as the definition precedes the first source line that calls the macro. Most often, define macros in separate files and make those files available via INCLUDE directives (See chapter 8 for an explanation of INCLUDE).

Defining the appropriate macro instructions tailors a higher-level facility in a convenient manner, at no cost in control over the structure of programs. You can achieve the conciseness and ease in coding of high-level languages without losing the basic advantage of assembly language programming. Integral macro operations simplify debugging and program modification.

In its simplest form, a macro is an abbreviation for a sequence of operations. Consider the program shown in Fig. 4-5.

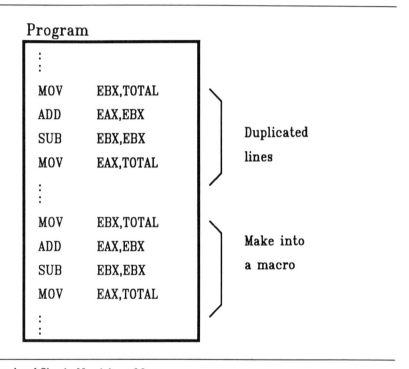

Fig. 4-5. Example of Simple Need for a Macro.

Macro languages and their associated processors represent a distinct form of programming language. When used in conjunction with an assembler (as with MASM), the macro processor provides many useful tools and essentially allows you to define your own personal high-level language.

Because most macros only need to be expanded once, processing them during a single pass of MASM increases efficiency. Do this by enclosing the macros (or an INCLUDE statement that calls them) in a conditional block using the IF1 directive.

...nd Exiting Macros

A macro call directs MASM to copy the statements of the macro to the point of the invocation and to replace any parameters in the macro statements with the corresponding actual arguments. To invoke a macro, use this syntax:

name [argument[,argument],,,]

The *name* must be the name of a macro defined earlier in some source file. The *argument* can be any text; for example—constants, symbols, and registers. You can give any number of arguments, but they must all fit one line, although multiple arguments must be separated by commas, spaces, or tabs. MASM replaces the first parameter with the first argument, the second parameter with the second argument, and so on. If the invocation has more arguments than the macro has parameters, the extra arguments are ignored. If the invocation has too few arguments, any remaining macro parameters are replaced with a null (empty) string.

Generally, MASM processes all the statements in a macro definition and then continues with the next statement after the macro. However, use the EXITM directive to tell MASM to terminate macro expansion before all the statements in the macro have been processed (see chapter 9 for a full description of EXITM). When MASM finds an EXITM, it exits the macro or repeat block immediately. Any remaining statements in the macro or repeat block are not processed. If EXITM is found in a nested macro or repeat block, MASM returns to expanding the outer block. You typically use EXITM with conditional directives to skip the last statements in a macro under specified conditions. Often macros using the EXITM directive contain repeat blocks or are called recursively.

EXAMPLE OF EXTENDING A LANGUAGE

Assume you have been given the job of writing a graphics package. First, specify which basic functions the system needs and then name them with easily rememberable names. For instance, in chapter 11, there is a series of macros that use the major BIOS and MS-DOS interrupts. To tie the macros with explanations in appendices D and E, the characters BIOS and DOS are used appended with the interrupt and functions. For instance, BIOS interrupt 10 function 0A is BIOS100A.MAC.

The general steps of a design process are shown below.

1. Decide that, as a start, you will need to:

   1. Draw a—
      Box
      Circle
      Horizontal line
      Vertical line
   2. Locate the cursor at a particular x,y location on the screen.

3. Fill in a space.
4. Add text.
5. Scroll—
    The entire screen.
    A smaller window.
2. The names will be—
    1. DRAW__BOX
    DRAW__CIR
    LINE__HOR
    LINE__VER
    2. FIND__XY
    3. FILL__REC
    4. ADD__TEXT
    5. SCROLL
3 Sample macros that will accomplish the functions.

A program with four supporting macros and one external procedure can be used. Figure 4-6 shows a listing of the source program. Notice that it was assembled, linked, and tested on an 80286, so the instruction set directive .286 was used. Also, notice that at least half the program is the internal documentation that tells you the purpose and the inputs and outputs. The code lines are also commented so that you know why a line was written. This program shows several things: (1) how to INCLUDE macros, (2) how to nest macros, (3) how to pass parameters to macros, and (4) how easy to read a main program can become when you design the macros to become an extension to assembly language.

```
            PAGE    55,132
            .286
            EXTRN   PAUSE:PROC
STACK       SEGMENT 'STACK' STACK
            DW      100 DUP(?)
STACK       ENDS
CODE        SEGMENT para 'CODE' PUBLIC
            ASSUME  CS:CODE, DS:CODE, SS:STACK
;
; Name:       EXAMPLE
;
; Purpose:    This program does some simple graphics as a
;             demonstration of how to handle macros, to call them
;             and to set variables and then assign values to them
;             and then variable replacement in macros.
;
; Inputs:     ASCII strings are input with DB statements.
;
; Process:    The screen is cleared, lines are drawn vertically
;             and horizontally.
;
; Outputs:    Screen images.
;
; The next are the included macros
;
```

Fig. 4-6. Listing of Program That Invokes Macros.

```
                INCLUDE FIND_XY.ASM
                INCLUDE LINE_VER.ASM
                INCLUDE LINE_HOR.ASM
                INCLUDE END_STD.ASM
;
VERT_LINE       DB      '|$'
HORIZ_LINE      DB      '-$'
CROSS           DB      '+$'
;
EXAMPLE:
                MOV     AX,CS           ; Prepare to set DS
                MOV     DS,AX           ;   and set it.
;
; This first routine clears the screen
;
                MOV     AH,15           ; Read the video mode
                INT     10h
                MOV     AH,0            ; Set the mode
                INT     10h             ; Clear the screen
                MOV     DH,1            ; 1 second wait for PAUSE
                MOV     DL,0            ; No hundredths
                PUSH    DX              ; Save DX on the stack
;
;
;
; Draw the horizontal line
;
                LINE_HOR 80,11,0        ; Width, Row, Column
;
; Draw a vertical line
;
                LINE_VER 24,0,39        ; Height, Row, Column
;
; Now place a cross where the lines cross after first positioning
;   the cursor at the crossing point
;
                FIND_XY 11,39           ; Row, Column to Position Cursor
                LEA     DX,CROSS
                MOV     AH,9            ; Print the "+"
                INT     21h
                POP     DX              ; Retrieve time for PAUSE
                CALL    PAUSE           ; Wait before ending
;
                END_STD                 ; Standard ending macro
CODE            ENDS
                END     EXAMPLE
```

Fig. 4-6. Continued.

The first macro, FIND__XY, which is shown in Fig. 4-7, uses BIOS interrupt INT 10h, with the DX register holding the row and column to position the cursor on the screen. See appendices D and E for the BIOS and MS-DOS interrupts and calls. This macro is nested inside the LINE__HOR macro (see below).

The second macro, LINE__VER, which is shown in Fig. 4-8, draws a vertical line on the screen. It accepts three parameters, the height of the line, the row on which to start, and the column on which to start. Note that it also uses a LOCAL label that appears only within the macro. No matter how many times the macro is called, MASM assigns a new label variable to this label. Because the cursor positioning interrupt (INT 10h), uses DX and the print interrupt (INT 21h) also uses DX, the row and column in DX can be saved, and DX and SI can be swapped. This swapping shows an example of the XCHG instruction.

```
FIND_XY         MACRO   ROW,COLUMN
;
; Position Cursor on the screen.  This macro uses the BIOS
;               INT 10h.
;
;               DX - Row/column to move cursor
;                    where ROW is the row and COLUMN is the column
;
;
                MOV     DH,ROW          ; Row
                MOV     DL,COLUMN       ; Column
                MOV     AH,2
                INT     10h
                ENDM
;
```

Fig. 4-7. FIND__XY Macro Using BIOS INT 10h.

```
LINE_VER        MACRO   HEIGHT,ROW,COLUMN
                LOCAL   LINE            ; Local label
;
; Draw a Vertical Line
;
;               SI - Address of vertical line character
;               DI - Height of the line
;               DX - Row/column to move cursor
;               LT_ROW is the left/top position for row
;               L_COLUMN is the left/top position for column
;
                LEA     SI,VERT_LINE    ; Save address of char string
                MOV     DL,HEIGHT
                MOV     DH,0
                MOV     DI,DX           ; Save height
                MOV     DH,ROW          ; Beginning row
                MOV     DL,COLUMN       ;           column
;
LINE:
                MOV     AH,2
                INT     10h             ; Position the cursor
                XCHG    DX,SI           ; Swap row/col with char addr
                MOV     AH,9            ; Get ready to print '|'
                INT     21h
                XCHG    DX,SI           ; Swap them back
                INC     DH              ; Increment row number
                DEC     DI              ; Printed it enough times?
                JNZ     LINE            ; Is the Z flag set?
;
                ENDM
;
```

Fig. 4-8. LINE__VER Macro Using INT 10 and 21.

The third macro, LINE__HOR, which is shown in Fig. 4-9, draws a horizontal line on the screen, the width of which is passed as the first parameter to the macro. The beginning row and column are the second and third parameters, respectively. This macro also uses a LOCAL label variable; you can see that the external view of the label is the same as in LINE__VER. However, MASM reassigns ascending numerical values so that there is no duplication. This way, you can set an internal coding standard of using a particular variable as the loop variable. LINE__HOR calls FIND__XY to locate the cursor, passing the ROW and COLUMN parameters.

```
LINE_HOR        MACRO   WIDE,ROW,COLUMN
                LOCAL   LINE            ; Local label
;
; Draw a horizontal line
;
;               DX - Row/column to move cursor
;                    Also for address of horizontal line character
;               DI - Width of the horizontal line
;               LT_ROW is the left/top position row
;               L_COLUMN is the left/top column
;
                MOV     DH,0
                MOV     DL,WIDE         ; Move memory reference to reg
                MOV     DI,DX           ; Save width in DI
;
;       Imbedding/nesting a macro to locate cursor
;
                FIND_XY ROW,COLUMN
;
;       Load address of character and ready to print
;
                LEA     DX,HORIZ_LINE
                MOV     AH,9            ; Get ready to print
LINE:
                INT     21h
                DEC     DI              ; Print it enough times?
                JNZ     LINE            ; Is Zero flag set?
;
                ENDM
;
```

Fig. 4-9. LINE__HOR Macro Using INT 21 and Nested Macro.

The fourth and final macro, END__STD, which is shown in Fig. 4-10, provides the standard MS-DOS ending, INT 21 exit 4C. This interrupt returns control to the calling or parent process, which in this case is MS-DOS. All memory that the program has used is also returned with this interrupt. There are various ways to end programs, each of which is discussed in appendix E.

```
END_STD         MACRO                   ; This is the standard ending
;
;               This macro provides code for the standard ending
;               to terminate the current process with a return code
;               and returns control to the calling (parent) process
;               On using this INT 21h call, all memory is freed also.
;
                MOV     Ah,4Ch
                INT     21h
;
                ENDM
;
```

Fig. 4-10. END__STD Macro Using INT 21 and Exit 4C.

To see how to use an external procedure, PAUSE, refer to Fig. 4-11. In the main program, EXTRN PAUSE:PROC is coded, and a CALL is used to call the procedure within the program EXAMPLE. Notice that PAUSE uses the directive PUBLIC to make the name usable by another program. A procedure ends with an ENDP. Again, note the use of internal documentation for easy maintenance and later use or enhancement.

```
            PAGE       55,132
            .286
code        SEGMENT    para 'CODE' PUBLIC
            ASSUME     CS:code, DS:code, SS:code
;
; Name:      PAUSE
;
; Purpose:   The following procedure provides a means of pausing
;            for a time span of from .02 seconds to 59.99 seconds.
;            The clock does not increment smoothly so the granularity
;            is not to the hundredth.
;
;
; Inputs:    DH should contain the number of seconds to delay.
;            DL should contain the number of hundredths to delay.
;
; Process:   The seconds and hundredths are edited for conformance
;            with their value range. (DH 0-59, DL 0-99 and DX >1)
;            If invalid, carry is set and the procedure returns.
;            The procedure then delays for the desired amount of time
;            and returns with carry reset.  The time
;
; Output:    The output is simply the delay in time.  Carry is set
;            if the input values were bad and reset otherwise.
;
;
;
            PUBLIC  Pause               ; Make the name usable
Pause       PROC
            push    DX                  ; Save entry registers
            push    CX
            push    BX
            push    AX
            push    SI
            cmp     DX,2                ; Check for minimum wait
            jb      badwait             ; If < 2 it is bad
            cmp     DL,100              ; Is hundredths 0-99
            jnb     badwait             ; If not - bad
            cmp     DH,60               ; Is seconds 0-59
            jnb     badwait             ; If not - bad
            mov     BX,DX               ; Save for computation
;
; Pause procedure, first compute the time to stop the loop.
;
            mov     AH,2ch              ; Get the Time of Day
            int     21h
            add     BL,DL               ; Add the current time (.01s)
            cmp     BL,100              ; Flow over the max hundredths?
            jb      notover             ; No overflow
            sub     BL,100              ; Get back to less than a sec
            inc     BH                  ; Step the seconds figure
notover:
            add     BH,DH               ; add current seconds
            cmp     BH,60               ; Flow over a minute?
            jb      notovers            ; No
            sub     BH,60               ; If so, bring down to range.
            inc     CL                  : add to minutes

            cmp     CL,60               ; Overflow into hours?
            jb      notovers            ; No - don't change
            sub     CL,60               ; Back to minutes
            inc     CH                  ; Roll to the hour
            cmp     CH,24
            jb      notovers            ; Not across midnight
            sub     CH,CH               ; We are at hour zero
notovers:
            mov     SI,BX               ; Save low order times
            mov     BX,CX               ; Get target time hh:mm
gethour:
```

Fig. 4-11. PAUSE Procedure.

```
                    int     21h                 ; get next time
                    cmp     BH,CH               ; check the hour
                    je      getmin              ; we are there.
                    jb      chkmid              ; If hour is high loop
            ;
            ; New hour is < target - if 0:23 we rolled over midnight
            ;
                    cmp     BH,23               ; Is target 2300
                    jne     gethour             ; If not - not there yet
                    or      CH,CH               ; Is new 0000 (2200)
                    jne     gethour             ; No - let hour roll over
                    jmp     passed              ; Yes - we went across
            ;
            ; Target hour is < new hour - if 0:23 wait for midnight
            ;
            chkmid:
                    or      BH,BH               ; Across midnight
                    jnz     passed              ; if not - time is expired.
                    cmp     CH,23               ; Waiting for midnight?
                    je      gethour             ; Yes - delay some more.
                    jmp     passed              ; No ( 0:1) time expired
            ;
            ; The hour is equal
            ;
            getmin:
                    cmp     BL,CL               ; Check for minute
                    jb      passed              ; If target is low - done
                    ja      gethour             ; If not there - loop
                    mov     CX,SI               ; Get low order times
                    cmp     CH,DH               ; At a second yet?
                    ja      gethour             ; No - get another time
                    jb      passed              ; beyond - we get out.
                    cmp     CL,DL               ; Check hundredths
                    ja      gethour             ; If low, branch
            passed:
                    clc                         ; reset carry
            exit:
                    pop     SI
                    pop     AX                  ; Restore the entry registers
                    pop     BX
                    pop     CX
                    pop     DX
                    ret                         ; and return
            badwait:
                    stc                         ; set carry
                    jmp     exit                ; and return
            Pause   ENDP
            code    ENDS
                    END
```

Fig. 4-11. Continued.

With this many comments, you only have to look at the inputs section to see which registers you have to use to call this procedure. If there are any registers changed or fields modified, comments would have been included in the output section. As you can see in the output section, CF (the carry flag) is set if there is a problem. This allows your calling program to test CF on return from the CALL. The CF test is not used for this simple example program.

Figure 4-12 shows the assembly and linking steps. For this example, the four macros are not built into a MACLIB but are kept as separate pieces of code in an ASM library (which is where all assembly language source code can be put; this library can be an in-house standard). In both the assembly and link steps, commas (,) and a semicolon (;) are entered on the command line to suppress the MASM prompts. From the figure, you can see that MASM 5.1 and LINK 3.64 are used.

```
C:\ASM>MASM EXAMPLE,,,;
Microsoft (R) Macro Assembler Version 5.10
Copyright (C) Microsoft Corp 1981, 1988.  All rights reserved.

    47158 + 404263 Bytes symbol space free

       0 Warning Errors
       0 Severe  Errors

C:\ASM>LINK EXAMPLE+PAUSE,,,;

Microsoft (R) Overlay Linker  Version 3.64
Copyright (C) Microsoft Corp 1983-1988.  All rights reserved.


C:\ASM>
```

Fig. 4-12. Example of Assembly and LINK Steps.

The next figure (Fig. 4-13) shows the assembled and expanded program EXAMPLE. Each of the macros is expanded right after the INCLUDE line that references them; a *C* is listed on the line to the right of the line number to show that it is the line of code which comes from an included macro. In lines 145 through 153 of the listing (and in subsequent lines), you can see a series of lines that have a *1* and *2* to the left of the mnemonics. Those numbers are the levels of nesting of assembled and expanded macro lines.

```
1                                 PAGE    55,132
2                                 .286
3                                 EXTRN   PAUSE:PROC
4 0000                    STACK   SEGMENT 'STACK' STACK
5 0000      0064[                 DW      100 DUP(?)
6             ????
7
8
9 00C8                    STACK   ENDS
10 0000                   CODE    SEGMENT para 'CODE' PUBLIC
11                                ASSUME  CS:CODE, DS:CODE, SS:STACK
12                        ;
13                        ; Name:       EXAMPLE
14                        ;
15                        ; Purpose:    This program does some simple graphics as a
16                        ;             demonstration of how to handle macros, to call them
17                        ;             and to set variables and then assign values to them
18                        ;             and then variable replacement in macros.
19                        ;
20                        ; Inputs:     ASCII strings are input with DB statements.
21                        ;
22                        ; Process:    The screen is cleared, lines are drawn vertically
23                        ;             and horizontally.
24                        ;
25                        ; Outputs:    Screen images.
26                        ;
27                        ; The next are the included macros
28                        ;
29                                INCLUDE FIND_XY.ASM
30     C  FIND_XY          MACRO   ROW,COLUMN
31     C  ;
```

Fig. 4-13. EXAMPLE Assembled and Expanded with the Macros.

```
32    C  ; Position Cursor on the screen.  This macro uses the BIOS
33    C  ;                 INT 10h.
34    C  ;
35    C  ;                 DX - Row/column to move cursor
36    C  ;                      where ROW is the row and COLUMN is the column
37    C  ;
38    C  ;
39    C                    MOV     DH,ROW           ; Row
40    C                    MOV     DL,COLUMN        ; Column
41    C                    MOV     AH,2
42    C                    INT     10h
43    C                    ENDM
44    C  ;
45    C                    INCLUDE LINE_VER.ASM
46    C  LINE_VER          MACRO   HEIGHT,ROW,COLUMN
47    C                    LOCAL   LINE             ; Local label
48    C  ;
49    C  ; Draw a Vertical Line
50    C  ;
51    C  ;                 SI - Address of vertical line character
52    C  ;                 DI - Height of the line
53    C  ;                 DX - Row/column to move cursor
54    C  ;                 LT_ROW is the left/top position for row
55    C  ;                 L_COLUMN is the left/top position for column
56    C  ;
57    C                    LEA     SI,VERT_LINE     ; Save address of char string
58    C                    MOV     DL,HEIGHT
59    C                    MOV     DH,0
60    C                    MOV     DI,DX            ; Save height
61    C                    MOV     DH,ROW           ; Beginning row
62    C                    MOV     DL,COLUMN        ;           column
63    C  ;
64    C  LINE:
65    C                    MOV     AH,2
66    C                    INT     10h              ; Position the cursor
67    C                    XCHG    DX,SI            ; Swap row/col with char addr
68    C                    MOV     AH,9             ; Get ready to print '|'
69    C                    INT     21h
70    C                    XCHG    DX,SI            ; Swap them back
71    C                    INC     DH               ; Increment row number
72    C                    DEC     DI               ; Printed it enough times?
73    C                    JNZ     LINE             ; Is the Z flag set?
74    C  ;
75    C                    ENDM
76    C  ;
77    C                    INCLUDE LINE_HOR.ASM
78    C  LINE_HOR          MACRO   WIDE,ROW,COLUMN
79    C                    LOCAL   LINE             ; Local label
80    C  ;
81    C  ; Draw a horizontal line
82    C  ;
83    C  ;                 DX - Row/column to move cursor
84    C  ;                      Also for address of horizontal line character
85    C  ;                 DI - Width of the horizontal line
86    C  ;                 LT_ROW is the left/top position row
87    C  ;                 L_COLUMN is the left/top column
88    C  ;
89    C                    MOV     DH,0
90    C                    MOV     DL,WIDE          ; Move memory reference to reg
91    C                    MOV     DI,DX            ; Save width in DI
92    C  ;
93    C  ;         Imbedding/nesting a macro to locate cursor
94    C  ;
95    C                    FIND_XY ROW,COLUMN
96    C  ;
97    C  ;         Load address of character and ready to print
98    C  ;
99    C                    LEA     DX,HORIZ_LINE
100   C                    MOV     AH,9             ; Get ready to print
101   C  LINE:
```

Fig. 4-13. Continued.

```
102                        C              INT     21h
103                        C              DEC     DI              ; Print it enough times?
104                        C              JNZ     LINE            ; Is Zero flag set?
105                        C  ;
106                        C              ENDM
107                        C  ;
108                                       INCLUDE END_STD.ASM
109                        C  END_STD     MACRO                   ; This is the standard ending
110                        C  ;
111                        C  ;           This macro provides code for the standard ending
112                        C  ;           to terminate the current process with a return code
113                        C  ;           and returns control to the calling (parent) process
114                        C  ;           On using this INT 21h call, all memory is freed also.
115                        C  ;
116                        C              MOV     Ah,4Ch
117                        C              INT     21h
118                        C  ;
119                        C              ENDM
120                        C  ;
121                           ;
122 0000  B3 24               VERT_LINE   DB      '|$'
123 0002  C4 24               HORIZ_LINE  DB      '—$'
124 0004  C5 24               CROSS       DB      '+$'
125                           ;
126 0006                      EXAMPLE:
127 0006  8C C8                           MOV     AX,CS           ; Prepare to set DS
128 0008  8E D8                           MOV     DS,AX           ;   and set it.
129                           ;
130                           ; This first routine clears the screen
131                           ;
132 000A  B4 0F                           MOV     AH,15           ; Read the video mode
133 000C  CD 10                           INT     10h
134 000E  B4 00                           MOV     AH,0            ; Set the mode
135 0010  CD 10                           INT     10h             ; Clear the screen
136 0012  B6 01                           MOV     DH,1            ; 1 second wait for PAUSE
137 0014  B2 00                           MOV     DL,0            ; No hundredths
138 0016  52                              PUSH    DX              ; Save DX on the stack
139                           ;
140                           ;
141                           ;
142                           ; Draw the horizontal line
143                           ;
144                                        LINE_HOR 80,11,0        ; Width, Row, Column
145 0017  B6 00           1               MOV     DH,0
146 0019  B2 50           1               MOV     DL,80           ; Move memory reference to reg
147 001B  8B FA           1               MOV     DI,DX           ; Save width in DI
148 001D  B6 0B           2               MOV     DH,11           ; Row
149 001F  B2 00           2               MOV     DL,0    ; Column
150 0021  B4 02           2               MOV     AH,2
151 0023  CD 10           2               INT     10h
152 0025  8D 16 0002 R    1               LEA     DX,HORIZ_LINE
153 0029  B4 09           1               MOV     AH,9            ; Get ready to print
154 002B               1   ??0000:
155 002B  CD 21           1               INT     21h
156 002D  4F              1               DEC     DI              ; Print it enough times?
157 002E  75 FB           1               JNZ     ??0000          ; Is Zero flag set?
158                           ;
159                           ; Draw a vertical line
160                           ;
161                                        LINE_VER 24,0,39        ; Height, Row, Column
162 0030  8D 36 0000 R    1               LEA     SI,VERT_LINE    ; Save address of char string
163 0034  B2 18           1               MOV     DL,24
164 0036  B6 00           1               MOV     DH,0
165 0038  8B FA           1               MOV     DI,DX           ; Save height
166 003A  B6 00           1               MOV     DH,0            ; Beginning row
167 003C  B2 27           1               MOV     DL,39   ;          column
168 003E               1   ??0001:
169 003E  B4 02           1               MOV     AH,2
170 0040  CD 10           1               INT     10h             ; Position the cursor
171 0042  87 D6           1               XCHG    DX,SI           ; Swap row/col with char addr
172 0044  B4 09           1               MOV     AH,9            ; Get ready to print '|'
```

Fig. 4-13. Continued.

```
173 0046  CD 21        1              INT     21h
174 0048  87 D6        1              XCHG    DX,SI                ; Swap them back
175 004A  FE C6        1              INC     DH                   ; Increment row number
176 004C  4F           1              DEC     DI                   ; Printed it enough times?
177 004D  75 EF        1              JNZ     ??0001               ; Is the Z flag set?
178                         ;
179                         ; Now place a cross where the lines cross after first positioning
180                         ;    the cursor at the crossing point
181                         ;
182                                    FIND_XY 11,39                ; Row, Column to Position Cursor
183 004F  B6 0B        1              MOV     DH,11                ; Row
184 0051  B2 27        1              MOV     DL,39    ; Column
185 0053  B4 02        1              MOV     AH,2
186 0055  CD 10        1              INT     10h
187 0057  8D 16 0004 R               LEA     DX,CROSS
188 005B  B4 09        1              MOV     AH,9                 ; Print the "+"
189 005D  CD 21        1              INT     21h
190 005F  5A                          POP     DX                   ; Retrieve time for PAUSE
191 0060  E8 0000 E                   CALL    PAUSE                ; Wait before ending
192                         ;
193                                    END_STD                     ; Standard ending macro
194 0063  B4 4C        1              MOV     Ah,4Ch
195 0065  CD 21        1              INT     21h
196 0067                  CODE        ENDS
197                                    END     EXAMPLE
```

Symbols-1

Macros:

```
                 N a m e              Lines

END_STD . . . . . . . . . . .           9
FIND_XY . . . . . . . . . . .          12
LINE_HOR . . . . . . . . . . .         26
LINE_VER . . . . . . . . . . .         27
```

Segments and Groups:

```
                 N a m e              Length  Align  Combine Class

CODE . . . . . . . . . . . . . .       0067    PARA    PUBLIC  'CODE'
STACK . . . . . . . . . . . . .        00C8    PARA    STACK   'STACK'
```

Symbols:

```
                 N a m e              Type     Value   Attr

CROSS . . . . . . . . . . . .         L BYTE   0004    CODE

EXAMPLE . . . . . . . . . . .         L NEAR   0006    CODE

HORIZ_LINE . . . . . . . . . .        L BYTE   0002    CODE

PAUSE . . . . . . . . . . . .         L NEAR   0000            External

VERT_LINE . . . . . . . . . .         L BYTE   0000    CODE

??0000 . . . . . . . . . . . .        L NEAR   002B    CODE
??0001 . . . . . . . . . . . .        L NEAR   003E    CODE
@CPU . . . . . . . . . . . . .        TEXT     1287
@FILENAME . . . . . . . . . .         TEXT     EXAMPLE
@VERSION . . . . . . . . . . .        TEXT     510

     159 Source  Lines
     245 Total   Lines
      18 Symbols

   47158 + 404263 Bytes symbol space free

      0 Warning Errors
      0 Severe  Errors
```

Fig. 4-13. Continued.

On the last page, the Symbols page, notice where MASM shows you that there were four macros used (and lists their names), that PAUSE is an External and renamed the LOCAL labels (??0000 and ??0001) which show as *LINE* in the source listings.

Finally, Fig. 4-14 shows the successful run of this simple graphics program.

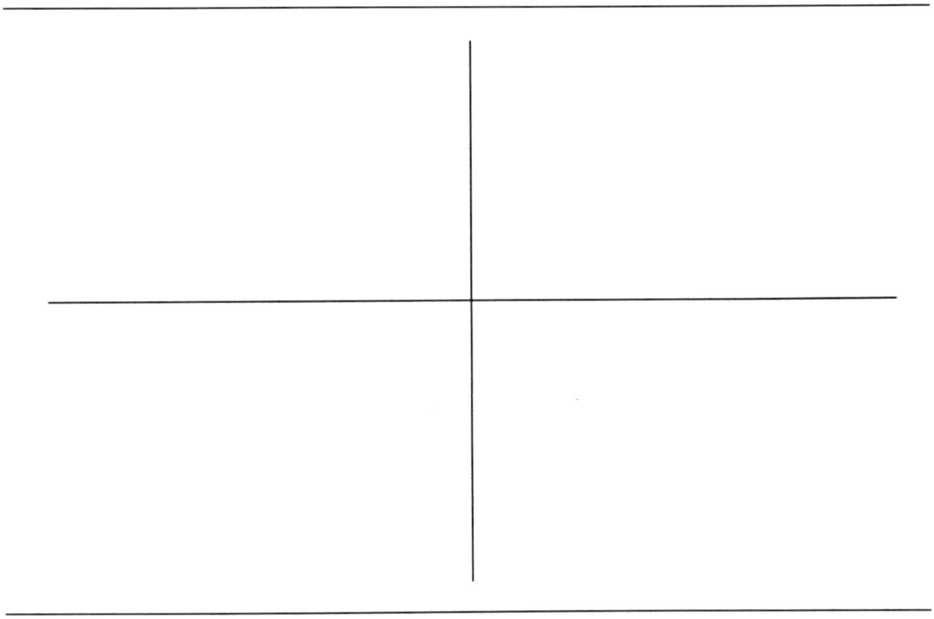

Fig. 4-14. Successful Run of Program EXAMPLE.

5

Languages to Describe Languages

WHEN YOU WRITE WITH A COMPUTER LANGUAGE SUCH AS ASSEMBLY LANGUAGE, IT IS often helpful to have a concise definition of that language. The definition allows you a quick reference to the language rules with a minimum amount of reading. For example, you might need to implement a new function that uses a little-used assembly language instruction. Knowing the rules that govern that instruction allows you to code it correctly.

In order to describe a language, you need to identify its elements. A language can be broken down into three basic parts: characters (or letters), words, and sentences. Characters are the pieces from which all higher elements of a language are constructed. For any language, there are rules that govern the construction of words from characters and sentences from words. In natural languages such as English or German, these rules are very complex and take years of study to master. Computer languages, however, are governed by simpler rules that can be implemented for processing by a computer.

A group of rules that describes a language is called a *grammar*. Often, these grammars are written in high-level languages that are specially designed to describe other languages. These high-level languages are called *meta-languages*. Through the use of grammars, you get a clear description of the language in a concise, almost mathematical form.

A grammar is made up of different types of rules. Each type is used to describe a particular aspect of a language. For example, the rules that govern the grouping of characters into words are called *lexical rules*. Those which govern the grouping of words into sentences are called *phrase-structure rules*. Note that the definition of what a word or sentence is in a particular language is defined by the lexical and phrase-structure rules of the language.

The phrase structure, or syntax, of a language shows the order in which words may appear in a sentence. It does not, however, ensure that a particular sentence is meaningful. For example, the English sentence "The big, tiny cat ate the ocean" is syntactically correct but is meaningless because a cat cannot be both big and tiny, nor can it eat an ocean (maybe drink it, but . . .). The meaning of sentences is governed by a class of rules called *semantic rules.*

There are two general types of semantic rules. *Static semantic rules* describe the tests a compiler performs during compilation to ensure that the statements in a program are potentially meaningful. An example of a static semantic rule is how Pascal ensures that, first, each variable used in a program is defined and, second, that these variables are used in a way appropriate for their definitions. Specifically, it would not be meaningful for a Boolean variable to be assigned a value from a real variable because internal representation of the two types of values are incompatible. The compiler would detect this static semantic error during compilation preventing unpredictable results during execution. Note that when a language is said to be strongly typed, rigid static semantic rules govern the meaning of sentences written in the language.

The second group of semantic rules, called *dynamic semantic* rules, describe the output generated by a compiler for a particular sentence. For example, the Pascal statement "X := Y + Z" becomes the following code on an 80386:

```
MOV     AX,Y
ADD     AX,Z
MOV     X,AX
```

To reduce the size of the grammars so that the description does not hide the information being conveyed, grammars are written in a terse form. Just as with other concise notations, grammars can be read very quickly once you have practice in reading them.

HOW TO READ A GRAMMAR

Grammars consist of a set of interrelated rules. Each rule can be thought of as a subroutine that can be invoked to describe a portion of a language. A rule consists of a name, a body, and an optional action, and is terminated by a semicolon (;).

The name is separated from the *body* with a -> symbol, which can be read as "*is defined as*". For example, the rule:

C -> x y z;

is read:

C is defined as x followed by y followed by z

In this example, C is the name and the x y z is the body of the rule. This rule specifies no action. If a rule has more than one -> symbol, then the rule is satisfied by one of the multiple rule bodies following the -> symbols. As implied in the example, rules are read from left to right.

For example, the rules:

```
hexdigit -> digit | 'A' .. 'F' | 'a' .. 'f';
digit -> '0' .. '9';
```

define a hexadecimal digit as a single character selected from a set of characters that includes all of the numerical characters from '0' to '9' and the alphabetical characters from 'A' to 'F' of both cases.

The rule body is separated from the optional action with a => symbol. The => can be read as "when finished, do this". When the body has been completely processed, the action is performed. In lexical grammars, the action specifies the type of token defined by a particular rule. Tokens are a more general form of words and might include spaces, numbers, and operators as well as what is generally called a *word* in natural languages. In token-processing grammars, the rule action specifies processing that must be performed for a particular token.

Grammatical Expressions

Each rule body contains a one complete grammatical expression. The expressions that appear in a grammar are not the same sort you might find in a Pascal program. The purpose of these expressions is not to perform arithmetic computations but to provide a shorthand mechanism for describing repeated or optional sections of a rule. As in arithmetic expressions, parentheses can be used to group operands and operators within an expression.

There are three types of components that appear in expressions. The first type is identifiers, which is used to reference other rules in the grammar. The second type is strings, which describes expression constants. The third type is the operators that controls the meaning of the expression.

Identifiers. Identifiers reference rules defined in the grammar and predefined rules which identify control character sequences. Essentially, referencing an identifier is analogous to invoking a subroutine.

Strings. There are two types of strings that can appear in grammars. The first type is enclosed in single quotes ('). Enclosing a string in single quotes shows that a specific word must appear at a particular point in a sentence.

The second type of string is enclosed in back quotes ('). The back-quoted string shows that specific type of word that must appear at a particular point in a sentence. These back quote strings can only appear in the phrase-structure grammar. They do not appear in lexical grammar because it is the job of the lexical grammar to define the word types.

Operators. The operators which appear in grammars are: .., *, +, ?, and |.

- The .. operator indicates a consecutive set of characters (for example, A .. F is the same as A or B or C or D or E or F). The set includes the beginning and ending characters.

- The ∗ operator indicates that zero or more of the items immediately to its left may appear in the sentence being described.

- The + operator is similar to the ∗ operator except that it specifies that one or more items may appear.

- The ? operator indicates optional sections (zero or one occurrence) in a sentence.

- The OR (|) operator allows one of many mutually exclusive items to appear in a sentence.

The ∗, +, and ? operators are *postfix* operators, which means that they operate on items immediately to their left. The .. and | operators are *infix* operators, which means that they appear between two operands.

Predefined Rules

In lexical grammars, there are predefined rules that are used to identify control-character sequences. You can think of control characters as those that are generated by simultaneously pressing the CONTROL key on a keyboard and other character(s). The reason they are coded for a grammar is so that you can specify a system-independent symbol for the control character without using the hardware control character itself. Control-character grammar rules start with a $ character. Examples of predefined rules include $EOL and $EOF, which are synonyms for end-of-line and end-of-file character sequences, respectively.

Comments in Grammars

Comments are allowed in grammars as they are in other computer languages. They start with a # character and extend to the end of the line; you will see this character in the grammars shown in this chapter. Comments terminate with a carriage return. The numbers of characters permitted per line is limited by the grammar processor.

OTHER USES FOR GRAMMARS

Because grammars describe languages in a disciplined form, they can also be used to implement portions of language processors (often called compilers or assemblers). This is done using special-purpose compilers that take a grammar as input and generate an implementation of that grammar as output. In lexical grammars, these special-purpose compilers will produce a lexical analyzer. In the case of a phrase-structure grammar, a parser is created. For semantic grammars, programs are generated that implement the rules in the grammars.

Grammars can be used to generate parts of compilers, so it is often said that a grammar recognizes a particular sequence of symbols. What is meant is that the analyzer generated from the grammar recognizes the symbol sequences. There is a one-to-one relationship between grammars and the analyzers that implement them. The grammars that appear in this chapter are written in a language that can be processed by a special-purpose compiler. The analyzers generated from the grammars implement an assembler very similar to MASM (but not quite—the subject is covered in greater detail elsewhere in this book).

MASM AS A LANGUAGE

Describing MASM with grammars presents an interesting challenge. Although it can be done, MASM has some idiosyncrasies that make the grammars difficult to follow. For example, there is the special treatment of %OUT, which is described in this chapter. Languages that were not initially designed using grammars often have features that do not lend themselves to a strict grammatical description. The MASM grammars presented in this book represent a balance between description and implementation. Because the purpose of the grammars is to describe MASM sentences, some MASM implementation details are deliberately excluded from this book. As a result, these grammars will not quite implement a assembler that would take the same input language as MASM. They do give a basic understanding of most MASM sentences. When reading the grammars, you will find that rules that do not fully describe MASM structure are marked with a "frowny" :-(which is the inverse of a "smiley,"   :-)   turn the book sideways to see the frowny and smiley.

Where MASM becomes complicated is in its lexical and phrase-structure rules. For example, the handling of comments in MASM is made difficult by the presence of block comments. The COMMENT string must be identified during lexical analysis. (See the section on comments in the grammars in this chapter.) It is these irregularities that the MASM user should be aware of in order to avoid user-produced errors.

MASM Lexical Grammar

MASM lexical grammar defines rules which govern the clustering of letters into tokens. The MASM lexical structure is complicated because there are situations in MASM where the lexical analyzer must treat characters differently depending on context. As a result, the MASM lexical grammar contains many special cases.

One MASM context-sensitive situation is the END statement. Here, the lines following the END statement are essentially treated as a comment by the assembler. That is, the lexical analyzer must recognize that it is processing an END statement and treat the lines following the END statement by ignoring them. This process is easily done using programming techniques but is difficult to describe in a grammar.

Other MASM context-sensitive constructs include the block comment (COMMENT), subtitle (SUBTTL) and assembler output (%OUT) constructs. In all of these cases, the lexical analyzer must know that a special set of rules are required to process subsequent characters. The difficulty is that the lexical analyzer must recognize complete reserved words; this means that rules must exist that spell out the words letter by letter in upper and lower case.

Having to recognize the reserved words COMMENT, SUBTTL, %OUT, and END in the lexical analyzer means the words can never be used for macro names. This violates the rule that MASM allows any word (reserved or unreserved) to be the name associated with a macro. These context-sensitive constructs are part of the reason the grammars presented in this chapter do not completely implement an assembler for MASM.

MASM Phrase-Structure Grammar

There are three main complications in MASM phrase-structure rules. First, MASM processing of the < and > characters varies because of context. In some cases, < ... > brackets a literal string in which no substitution is performed. In other case, < ... > brackets a group of expressions in which substitution must be performed. One grammatical technique for handling these two cases is to always assume that a literal string is between the < and > characters. In this way, when the parser discovers that a group of expressions is required rather than a literal string, it can invoke a lexical analyzer to decompose the literal string into separate expressions. Although this does not sound difficult, the description of this process in a phrase-structure grammar is not easily followed and is therefore not included in the phrase-structure grammar for MASM presented here.

The second complication is that the MASM macro syntax contains differences from the rest of the MASM syntax. In order to define and process macros properly, other grammars are necessary. Associated with the macros are the repeat blocks constructs (IRP and IRPC—described in chapter 9). These constructs use the macro parameter syntax for their parameters. This syntax is not described in the phrase structure grammar for MASM.

The third complication is that the textual substitution that occurs in MASM requires special processing of each token prior to presenting that token to the parser. In order to process the textual substitution that is used to expand macros in MASM, a special extension to the phrase structure grammar is required. This grammar is called a *token-processing* grammar. A token-processing grammar shows the basic process of macro substitution and identifies different classes of words, which makes the specification of the phrase structure rules easier. This grammar is much simpler, but it is in a different form than the other MASM grammars. The grammars in this chapter show the rules for each type of token. Associated with these rules is a block of pseudo-code that describes the actions to be taken for each token.

The MASM phrase-structure grammar groups tokens into clauses, and clauses into sentences. Thanks to the token-processing grammar, the phrase-structure grammar does not have to define the proper usage of some of the tokens that might be present in an input file. For example, the token processing grammar discards comments, space tokens, and data following the END statement. This means that the parser that implements the definition presented in the phrase structure grammar need not process comment or space tokens. Therefore, the phrase structure rules are simplified.

MASM GRAMMARS

In the following sections are the lexical and phrase-structured grammars for MASM. The # in the left column is the character that distinguishes a comment from a rule.

MASM Lexical Grammar

```
#
# This grammar defines the grouping of letters into words (or tokens) for MASM. The
# lexical analyzer uses a pattern-matching algorithm of one character at a time to form
# these tokens from the data in the input file.
#
# At the highest level, the lexical structure of MASM is a sequence of lines followed
# by an end statement.
masm        ->   masmline * masmend
              ;

#
# Each line in the MASM input file consists of one or more of the following elements
# followed by an EOL character.
#
# Note that $eol is a special built-in function that causes the lexical analyzer to look
# for the end of line character (or characters).
#
masmline ->   (ids | operators | punctuators | numbers |
               ·comments | spaces | strings)* $eol
              ;

#
# The end of a MASM program consists of an END string followed by an optional string
# of tokens which defines the start address for the assembler module being processed.
# Lines following the END line are ignored by the assembler. These lines are skipped
# until an end of file condition occurs.
#
# Note that $eof is a special built-in function that causes the lexical analyzer to look
# for the end of file character.
#
masmend  ->   end masmline masmany $eof
              ;

#
# Allow any printable characters to follow the ,END, line of the MASM input file.
#

masmany   ->   (letters | numbers | allspec | $eol)*
              = > 'follows__end'
              ;
```

```
#
#  It is difficult to have to search for a particular string in a lexical grammar. Unfortunately,
#  MASM requires that you match the 'END' string exactly. The 'END' string is not
#  case sensitive so you must allow both upper- and lower-case letters in it.
#
end               ->    ('E' | 'e') ('N' | 'n') ('D' | 'd')                    => 'end'
                  ;

#
#I D E N T I F I E R S
#
#  An identifier in MASM is a group of characters that conforms to the following rules.
#  Certain characters must be at the beginning of an identifier. Other characters cannot
#  be at the beginning of an identifier. By defining identifiers with the following productions,
#  these constraints are implemented.
#
ids               ->    mustlead anyid+                                        => 'identifier'
                  ->    canlead anyid*                                         => 'identifier'
                  ;

#
#  The characters that must be at the head of an identifier, if they are used at all in an
#  identifier, are defined here.
#
mustlead          ->    '.' | '%'
                  ;

#
#  The characters that can appear as the head of an identifier are defined as all but those
#  that must not appear at the head of an identifier.
#
canlead           ->    letters | uqda | sub
                  ;

#
#  The characters that may appear within the body of an identifier are defined as follows:
#
anyid             ->    letters | uqda | digits | sub
                  ;

#
# O P E R A T O R S
#
#  MASM has only a few simple operators in the input language. Most of the 'operators'
#  are treated as identifiers by the lexical analyzer. Note that the distinction between
#  operators and punctuators is somewhat vague. Generally, punctuators aid in the
#  expression of a sentence but do not directly contribute significantly to the meaning
#  of the sentence.
```

operators   ->   '%'| '+' | '--' | '*' | '/' | '.' | ':'   => 'operator'
                  ;

\#
\# P U N C T U A T O R S
\#
\# The punctuators supported by MASM are as follows:
\#
punctuators   -> '(' | ')' | '[' | ']'   => 'punctuator'
:
\#
\# C O M M E N T S
\#
\# There are three types of comments supported by MASM. The first type of comment
\# is prefaced with a ';'. All of the data on the line following the ';' is considered a
\# comment. The comment ends at the end of the line.
\#
\# The second type of comment is used within macros and starts with a ';;'. This comment
\# has the same conventions as the ';' comment. The difference is that ';;' comments
\# are completely discarded by the assembler during macro processing and do not appear
\# in listing files.
\#
\# The third type of comment is the block comment. It starts with the word 'COMMENT'
\# followed by a delimiter. All of the characters that are between the first instance of
\# the delimiter and the next instance of the delimiter are considered part of the comment.
\#
comments   ->   ';' comany comall*   => 'comment'
            ->   ';' ';' comall*   => 'macro_comment'
            ->   commst delim   => 'comment'
                  ;

commall   ->   allspec | letters | digits;

comany   ->   letters | digits
            ->   ' ' | '!' | '"' | '#' | '$' |'%'| '&' | ''''
            ->   '(' | ')' | '+' | ',' | '-' | '.' | '/' | '@'
            ->   ':' | '<' | '=' | '>' | '?' | '[' | '\'
            ->   ']' | '^' | '_' | ''' | '{' | '|' | '}' | '~
                  ;

\#

```
# A block comment is started by the COMMENT string, which may be followed by
# one or more blanks. Like the END string, the COMMENT string can consist of any
# combination of upper- and lower-case letters.
#
# Unlike other reserved words, the comment reserved word must be defined here in
# the lexical grammar for MASM. This is necessary because different lexical rules are
# used within a comment than outside of a comment.
#
commst          ->      ('C' | 'c') ('O' | 'o') ('M' | 'm') ('M' | 'm')
                        ('E' | 'e') ('N' | 'n') ('T' | 't') ' ' +

                    ;

#
# The first character in the body of the comment is the delimiter. This character will
# also be the last character in the body of the comment. A special function is invoked
# to perform this scanning because looking for the delimiter would be difficult to describe
# in a grammar.
#
delim           ->      (letter | number | anyspec)
                        = > $invoke(delimscan)
                    ;

#
# S P A C E S
#
# MASM treats the blank and the horizontal tab character as spaces. Note that $ht is
# a built-in function which will match a horizontal tab character.
#
spaces          ->      (' ' | $ht) +                                   = > 'space'
                    ;

#
# N U M B E R S
#
# There are two basic types of numerical constants supported by MASM. Integer
# constants can be in base two through base 16 and can be suffixed with a radix specifier.
# Real number constants are specified in decimal and can have an exponent-specifying
# suffix.
numbers         ->      digits hexdigit* radix?                         = > 'integer'
                ->      digits+ '.' digit+ exp?                         = > 'real'

                    ;

#
# Define the exponent structure for real numbers.
#
exp             ->      ('E' | 'e') (' +' | ' −')? digits+
                    ;

#
```

```
#  Hexadecimal digits include the numericals and upper and lower case letters A–F and
#  a–f. Digits are defined later in the grammar.
#
hexdigit          ->      digits | 'A' .. 'F' | 'a' .. 'f'
                       ;

#
#  The radix for an integer can be upper or lower case.
#
radix        ->     'B' | 'b'                          # binary radix
             ->     'Q' | 'q' | 'O' | 'o'              # octal radix
             ->     'D' | 'd'                          # decimal radix
             ->     'H' | 'h'                          # hexadecimal radix
                  ;
```

```
#
# S T R I N G S
#
#  MASM has three different types of strings. The first two types of strings (bracketed
#  by a single or double quote) allow the bracket character to be escaped by repetition
#  of the bracket character. The third type of string (bracketed by < >) allows the
#  bracket characters to be escaped by the '!' character.
#
strings        ->     ('''' notquote* '''')+              = > 'qstring'
               ->     ('"' notdquote* '"')+               = > 'dstring'
               ->     '<' notendlit+ '>'                  = > 'lstring'
#
#  There is a special case when the liberal string consists only of a single '!'. In this
#  case, the '!' does not escape the following '>' character.
#
               ->     '<' '!' '>'                         = > 'lstring'
                    ;
```

```
#
#  Define the characters that may be present in a single quoted string. All characters
#  are allowed except single quotes.
#
notquote          ->     letters | digits | strspec | '"'
                       ;

#
#  Define the characters that might be present in a double quoted string. All characters
#  are allowed except double quotes.
#
notdquote          ->     letters | digits | strspec | squote
                       ;
```

```
#
# Define all of the characters which may appear in a literal string (bracketed by < >).
# All characters are allowed, but the '!' requires special processing. The '!' is defined
# as the literal character operator. Any character following the '!' is placed in the string
# even if it is a '>'.
#
notendlit            ->    letters | digits | strspec | stresc
                     ;

#
# The special characters that are allowed in all types of strings are:
#
strspec              ->    ' ' | '#' | '$' | '%' | sub | '(' | ')'
                     ->    '+' | ',' | '-' | '.' | '/' | '@' | ':'
                     ->    ';' | '<' | '=' | '?' | '[' | '\' | ']' | '\'
                     ->    '^' | '_' | '`' | '{' | '|' | '}' | '~'
                     ;

#
# The ! character, when found in a literal string, escapes any character following the
# '!' into the literal string. The '!' character is discarded because it is not semantically
# part of the string.
#
stresc               ->    escesc (letters | digits | allspec)
                     ;

#
escesc               ->    '!'                                    => $discard
                     ;

#
# M I S C E L L A N E O U S
#
# Define groups of characters that make the definitions of other groups of characters
# easier to write.
#
letters              ->    'A' .. 'Z' | 'a' .. 'z'
                     ;

#
uqda                 ->    '_' | '?' | '$' | '@'
                     ;

#
digits               ->    '0' .. '9'
                     ;

#
# Define all of the special characters that are allowed in a MASM input file.
```

```
#
allspec              ->    ' ' | '!' | '"' | '#' | '$' | '%' | '&' | ''''
                     ->    '(' | ')' | '+' | ',' | '−' | '.' | '/' | '@'
                     ->    ':' | ';' | '<' | '=' | '>' | '?' | '[' | '\'
                     ->    ']' | '^' | '_' | ''' | '{' | '|' | '}' | '~'
                     ;
```

```
#
# Macro substitution processing requires special handling of the '&' character in a string
# (when it is not escaped with an '!') or in a name. In order to remember that substitution
# is required for the string, change the '&' to a special character.
#
sub              ->  '&'                                  = > $replace(sub__char)
                 ;
```

```
#
#
# T O K E N   P R O C E S S I N G   G R A M M A R
#
# This grammar defines the processing which occurs on the token generated by the
# MASM lexical grammar. This token processing grammar defines the reserved words
# for MASM, discards tokens that are not required by the parser, and defines the
# processing associated with MASM macros (to some degree).
#
# The parser is never interested in what follows the END statement of the MASM input
# file, in the contents of a comment, or in spaces. Discard these tokens when they are
# encountered.
#
`follows__end`   = > discard ;
`comment`        = > discard ;
`space`          = > discard ;
```

```
#
# When you encounter the 'macro' identifier, insert a token following it so that the
# statement parser can avoid analyzing the parameters of the macro. Normally, this
# processing would be performed by a special macro parser, which is not presented here.
#

'macro'        = >  upshift
{ generate__following__token(`macro__parms`) } ;
'MACRO'        = >  { generate__following__token(`macro__parms`) } ;
```

```
#
# Each identifier must be processed to ensure that substitution is performed as required.
```

```
# Each identifier must then be processed to ensure that it is not a macro. If it is a macro,
# then that macro must be substituted into the input stream.
#
# After all other processing on the identifier has been performed, the identifier is checked
# against the list of reserved identifiers. If the identifier is in that list, it is marked as
# reserved.
#
# The variable '$current_token' is a reserved, structured variable that contains all of
# the information associated with the current token. The two fields of interest here
# are the token_value and the token_type fields. The token_value field contains the
# string associated with the token. The token_type field contains the type of the to-
# ken (which in this case starts out as 'identifier').
#
'identifier'  = > {   var t: $string
#
```

If the user has not asked for case sensitivity, upshift the identifier.

```
#
        if !case_sensitive_run then
            { $current_token.token_value : =
                upshift($current_token.token_value) }
```

```
#
```

> Try to perform substitution on the current token. If it is successful, then
> the current value token replaced by the substituted value.

```
#
        try_sub($current_token)
```

```
#
```

> Now see if the identifier is a macro name or a reserved word.

```
#
        t := dcl_str_lookup($current_token.token_value)
        if t != $nullstring then
            { if t = = 'def_macro' then
                { expand_macro (t,
                        $input_stream_context,
                        $output_stream)
                }

            else if t = = 'def_resv' then
                    { $current_token.token_type : =
                'reserved_id'
                    }
                else if t = = 'def_oper' then
```

```
                    { $current_token.token_type : =
                          'opcode'
                    }

              else { ERROR('Illegal String Usage') }
                    }
```

\# If this is a case sensitive run, then you must upshift the identifier to see
\# if it matches a reserved identifier.

```
              else if case_sensitive_run then
                 { t := dcl_str_lookup(
                          upshift($current_token.token_value))

                 if t != $nullstring then
                   { if t == 'def_resv' then
                       { $current_token.token_type : =
                             'reserved_id'
                       }

                   else if t == 'def_oper' then
                       { $current_token.token_type : =
                             'opcode'
                       }

                   else if t != 'dev_macro' then
                   else { ERROR('Illegal String Usage') }
                       }
                 }
```

\# If the identifier was not declared anywhere, then it must be a user-defined identifier
\# so no further processing is required.

```
        }
    ;
    #
function initialize_masm_reserved_words
```

\# This function places all the MASM reserved words into the parse-time declaration
\# table.
\#

```
    {    var type:          $string
         var name:          $string
       # con resv:          array of $string init
```

\# Each pair of strings in the following table defines a MASM reserved word. The first
\# string in the table is the type of the reserved word. The second string is the reserved
\# word itself. The 'opcode' reserved word type is an opcode in 80386 assembler. The
\# 'resv' reserved words include all non-opcode reserved words (such as directives).
\# Note that some of the opcode reserved words are also used in assembly time
\# expressions.
\#

```
{'resv', '%out', 'resv', '.186', 'resv', '.286',
 'resv', '.286p', 'resv', '.287', 'resv', '.386',
 'resv', '.386', 'resv', '.387', 'resv', '.8086',
 'resv', '.8087', 'resv', '.alpha', 'resv', '.code',
 'resv', '.const', 'resv', '.cref' 'resv', '.data',
 'resv', '.data?', 'resv', '.err', 'resv', '.err1',
 'resv', '.err2', 'resv', '.errb', 'resv', '.errdef',
 'resv', '.errdif', 'resv', '.erre', 'resv', '.erridn',
 'resv', '.errnb', 'resv', '.errndef', 'resv', '.errnz',
 'resv', '.fardata', 'resv', '.fardata?', 'resv', '.lall',
 'resv', '.lfcond', 'resv', '.list', 'resv', '.model',
 'resv', '.msfloat', 'resv', '.radix', 'resv', '.sall',
 'resv', '.seq', 'resv', '.sfcond', 'resv', '.stack',
 'resv', '.tfcond', 'resv', '.type', 'resv', '.xall',
 'resv', '.xcref', 'resv', '.xlist', 'resv', '@code',
 'resv', '@codesize', 'resv', '@curseg', 'resv', '@data',
 'resv', '@datasize', 'resv', '@fardata',
 'rcsv', '@fardata?', 'rcsv', '@filename', 'opcode', 'aaa',
 'opcode', 'add', 'opcode', 'aam', 'opcode', 'aas',
 'opcode', 'adc', 'opcode', 'add', 'resv', 'align',
 'opcode', 'and', 'opcode', 'arpl', 'resv', 'assume',
 'resv', 'at', 'opcode', 'bound', 'opcode', 'bsf',
 'opcode', 'bsr', 'opcode', 'bt', 'opcode', 'btc',
 'opcode', 'btr', 'opcode', 'bts', 'resv', 'byte',
 'opcode', 'call', 'opcode', 'cbw', 'opcode', 'cdq',
 'opcode', 'clc', 'opcode', 'cld', 'opcode', 'cli',
 'opcode', 'clts', 'opcode', 'cmp', 'opcode', 'cmps',
 'opcode', 'cmpsd', 'comm', 'resv', 'comment',
 'resv', 'common', 'opcode', 'cwd', 'opcode', 'cwde',
 'opcode', 'daa', 'opcode', 'das', 'resv', 'db',
 'resv', 'dd', 'opcode', 'dec', 'resv', 'df',
 'opcode', 'div', 'resv', 'dosseg', 'resv', 'dq',
 'resv', 'ds', 'resv', 'dt', 'resv', 'dup', 'resv', 'dw',
 'resv', 'dword', 'resv', 'else', 'resv', 'end',
 'resv', 'endif', 'resv', 'endm', 'resv', 'endp',
 'resv', 'ends', 'opcode', 'enter', 'resv', 'eq',
 'resv', 'equ', 'opcode', 'esc', 'resv', 'even',
```

'resv', 'exitm', 'resv', 'extrn', 'opcode', 'f2xml',
'opcode', 'fabs', 'opcode', 'fadd', 'opcode', 'faddp',
'resv', 'far', 'opcode', 'fbld', 'opcode', 'fbstp',
'opcode', 'fchs', 'opcode', 'fcom', 'opcode', 'fcomp',
'opcode', 'fcompp', 'opcode', 'fcos', 'opcode', 'fdiv',
'opcode', 'fdivp', 'opcode', 'fdivr', 'opcode', 'fdivrp',
'opcode', 'fiadd', 'opcode', 'ficom', 'opcode', 'ficomp',
'opcode', 'fidiv', 'opcode', 'fidivr', 'opcode', 'fild',
'opcode', 'fimul', 'opcode', 'finit', 'opcode', 'fist',
'opcode', 'fistp', 'opcode', 'fisub', 'opcode', 'fisubr',
'opcode', 'fld', 'opcode', 'fld1', 'opcode', 'fldcw',
'opcode', 'fld12e', 'opcode', 'fldl2t', 'opcode', 'fldlg2',
'opcode', 'fldln2', 'opcode', 'fldpi', 'opcode', 'fldz',
'opcode', 'fmul', 'opcode', 'fmulp', 'opcode', 'fpatan',
'opcode', 'fprem', 'opcode', 'fptan', 'opcode', 'frndint',
'opcode', 'fscale', 'opcode', 'fsin', 'opcode', 'fsincos',
'opcode', 'fsqrt', 'opcode', 'fst', 'opcode', 'fstcw',
'opcode', 'fstp', 'opcode', 'fstsw', 'opcode', 'fsub',
'opcode', 'fsubp', 'opcode', 'fsubr', 'opcode', 'fsubrp',
'opcode', 'ftst', 'opcode', 'fucom', 'opcode', 'fucomp',
'opcode', 'fucompp', 'opcode', 'fwait', 'resv', 'fword',
'opcode', 'fxam', 'opcode', 'fxch', 'opcode', 'fxtract',
'opcode', 'fyl2x', 'opcode', 'fyl2xp1', 'resv', 'ge',
'resv', 'group', 'resv', 'gt', 'resv', 'high',
'opcode', 'hlt', 'opcode', 'idiv', 'resv', 'if',
'resv', 'if1', 'resv', 'if2', 'resv', 'ifb',
'resv', 'ifdef', 'resv', 'ifdif', 'resv', 'ife',
'resv', 'ifidn', 'resv', 'ifnb', 'resv', 'ifndef',
'opcode', 'imul', 'opcode', 'in', 'opcode', 'inc',
'resv', 'include', 'resv', 'includelib', 'opcode', 'ins',
'opcode', 'insb', 'opcode', 'insd', 'opcode', 'insw',
'opcode', 'int', 'opcode', 'into', 'opcode', 'iret',
'opcode', 'iretd', 'resv', 'irp', 'resv', 'irpc',
'opcode', 'ja', 'opcode', 'jae', 'opcode', 'jb',
'opcode', 'jbe', 'opcode', 'jc', 'opcode', 'jcxz',
'opcode', 'je', 'opcode', 'jexcz', 'opcode', 'jg',
'opcode', 'jge', 'opcode', 'jl', 'opcode', 'jle',
'opcode', 'jmp', 'opcode', 'jna', 'opcode', 'jnae',
'opcode', 'jnb', 'opcode', 'jnbe', 'opcode', 'jnc',
'opcode', 'jne', 'opcode', 'jng', 'opcode', 'jnge',
'opcode', 'jnl', 'opcode', 'jnle', 'opcode', 'jno',
'opcode', 'jnp', 'opcode', 'jns', 'opcode', 'jnz',
'opcode', 'jo', 'opcode', 'jp', 'opcode', 'jpe',

'opcode', 'jpo', 'opcode', 'js', 'opcode', 'jz',
'resv', 'label', 'opcode', 'lahf', 'opcode', 'lar',
'opcode', 'lds', 'resv', 'le', 'opcode', 'lea',
'opcode', 'leav', 'resv', 'length', 'opcode', 'les',
'opcode', 'lfs', 'opcode', 'lgdt', 'opcode', 'lgs',
'opcode', 'lidt', 'resv', 'link', 'opcode', 'lldt',
'opcode', 'lmsw', 'resv', 'local', 'opcode', 'lock',
'opcode', 'lods', 'opcode', 'lodsd', 'opcode', 'loop',
'opcode', 'loope', 'opcode', 'loopne', 'opcode', 'loopnz',
'opcode', 'loopz', 'resv', 'low', 'opcode', 'lsl',
'opcode', 'lss', 'resv', 'lt', 'opcode', 'ltr',
'resv', 'macro', 'resv', 'mask', 'resv', 'memory',
'resv', 'mod', 'opcode', 'mov', 'opcode', 'movs',
'opcode', 'movsd', 'opcode', 'movsx', 'opcode', 'movzx',
'opcode', 'mul', 'resv', 'name', 'resv', 'ne',
'resv', 'near', 'opcode', 'neg', 'opcode', 'nop',
'opcode', 'not', 'resv', 'nothing', 'resv', 'offset',
'resv', 'or', 'resv', 'org', 'opcode', 'out',
'opcode', 'outs', 'opcode', 'outsb', 'opcode', 'outsd',
'opcode', 'outsw', 'resv', 'page', 'resv', 'para',
'opcode', 'pop', 'opcode', 'popa', 'opcode', 'popad',
'opcode', 'popd', 'opcode', 'popf', 'opcode', 'popfd',
'resv', 'proc', 'resv', 'ptr', 'resv', 'public',
'resv', 'purge', 'opcode', 'push', 'opcode', 'pusha',
'opcode', 'pushad', 'opcode', 'pushd', 'opcode', 'pushf',
'opcode', 'pushfd', 'resv', 'qword', 'opcode', 'rcl',
'opcode', 'rcr', 'resv', 'record', 'opcode', 'rep',
'opcode', 'repe', 'opcode', 'repnew', 'opcode', 'repnz',
'resv', 'rept', 'opcode', 'repz', 'opcode', 'ret'
'opcode', 'retf', 'opcode', 'retn', 'opcode', 'rol',
'opcode', 'ror', 'opcode', 'sahf', 'opcode', 'sal',
'opcode', 'sar', 'opcode', 'sbb', 'opcode', 'scas',
'opcode','scasd', 'resv', 'seg', 'resv', 'segment',
'opcode', 'seta', 'opcode', 'setae', 'opcode', 'setb',
'opcode', 'setbe', 'opcode', 'setc', 'opcode', 'sete',
'opcode', 'setg', 'opcode', 'setge', 'opcode', 'setl',
'opcode', 'setle', 'opcode', 'setna', 'opcode', 'setnae',
'opcode', 'setnb', 'opcode', 'setnbe', 'opcode', 'setnc',
'opcode', 'setne', 'opcode', 'setng', 'opcode', 'setnge',
'opcode', 'setnl', 'opcode', 'setnle', 'opcode', 'setno',
'opcode', 'setnp', 'opcode', 'setns', 'opcode', 'setnz,'
'opcode', 'seto', 'opcode', 'setp', 'opcode', 'setpe',
'opcode', 'setpo', 'opcode', 'sets', 'opcode', 'setz',
'opcode', 'sgdt', 'opcode', 'shl', 'opcode', 'shld',

```
'resv', 'short', 'resv', 'shr', 'opcode', 'shrd',
'opcode', 'sidt', 'resv', 'size', 'opcode', 'sldt',
'opcode', 'smsw', 'resv', 'st', 'resv', 'stack',
'opcode', 'std', 'opcode', 'sti', 'opcode', 'stos',
'opcode', 'stosd', 'opcode', 'str', 'resv', 'struc',
'opcode', 'sub', 'resv', 'subttl', 'resv', 'tbyte',
'opcode', 'test', 'resv', 'this', 'resv', 'title',
'resv', 'type', 'resv', 'use16', 'resv', 'use32',
'opcode', 'verr', 'opcode', 'verw', 'opcode', 'wait',
'resv', 'width', 'resv', 'word', 'opcode', 'xchg',
'opcode', 'xlat', 'opcode', 'xlatb', 'opcode', 'xor' }
    #
    # For each reserved string, enter the string into the parse-time declaration table
    # along  with its associated type.

    #
#
    for type,name in dopairs(1, element_count(resv)/2, resv )
        { dcl_str_enter(name,type)
            }
    }
#
# P H R A S E    S T R U C T U R E    O F    M A S M
#
# This grammar defines the legal sentences for MASM. The input to this grammar is
# the tokens generated by the lexical grammar and the token processing grammar. There
# are portions of MASM that are not implemented by this grammar. These portions are
# marked with a frowny  :-(  symbol. See above for further information on these
# portions of MASM.
#
# An assembler program is made up of zero or more statements followed by an 'END'
# statement.
#
masm      ->   statement* end
                 ;

#
# The end statement has an optional parameter that specifies the module starting point.
#
end        ->   'end' exp?
                 ;

#
# The following rule defines a MASM statement. Note that comments were stripped out
# during the screening process so the comments are processed here.
```

```
#
statement        ->   stmtbody? `new_line`

                      ;
#
stmtbody         ->   label? `opcode` (exp (',' exp)* )?
                 ->   label 'PROC' procsizes statements*
                          label 'ENDP'
                 ->   label 'LABEL' labsizes
                 ->   label 'SEGMENT' segmenthd
                          statement* label 'ENDS'
                 ->   label 'GROUP' label (',' label)*
                 ->   'ASSUME' assumebody
                 ->   label 'STRUC' fielddef label 'ENDS'
                 ->   label 'RECORD' recfields
                 ->   datadef
```

\#
\# Only some of the macro phrase structure is defined here. The rest is defined in the
\# macro language phrase structure grammar.
\#

```
                 ->   'INCLUDE' name
                 ->   'INCLUDELIB' label ('.' label)?
                 ->   'PURGE' name (',' name)*
                 ->   label '=' exp
                 ->   label 'EQU' exp
                 ->   'REPT' exp `new_line`
                          mstatement* 'ENDM'
```

\#
\# IRP and IRPC do not lend themselves well to description in this grammar. They are
\# processed elsewhere.
\#

```
                 ->   'IRP' irp_parms`       # ( :-( )
                 ->   'IRPC' `irpc_parms`     # ( :-( )
```

\#
\# When a macro expansion is in progress, the screener builds a special token to mark
\# the beginning of the macro expansion. This allows the scoping of local variables to
\# be implemented.
\#

```
                 ->   `mac_exp_start` mstatement*
                          `mac_exp_end`
```

```
#
#  Process a macro definition. As soon as it is possible to determine that a macro definition
#  is being processed, a special processor is invoked to save the macro definition for
#  future expansion.
#
                -> label 'MACRO' 'macro_parms' = > savemac ( )
#
#  The following directives are associated with external variable linkage.
#
                    ->    'PUBLIC' label (',' label)*
                    ->    'EXTRN' extrndef (',' extrndef)*
                    ->    'COMM' commdef (',' commdef)*
#
#  The following directives control the construction of segments.
#
                    ->    'DOSSEG'
                    ->    '.MODEL' memmodel
                    ->    '.STACK' exp?
                    ->    '.CODE' id?
                    ->    '.DATA'
                    ->    '.DATA?'
                    ->    '.FARDATA'
                    ->    '.FARDATA?'
                    ->    '.CONST'
#
#  Define the conditional assembly constructs.
#
                    ->    ifpart elifpart* elpart? 'ENDIF'
                    ->    erchoice exp
#
#  The following directives control the output format of the assembler.
#
                    ->    % 'OUT'   outstr                      # ( :-( )
                    ->    'SUBTTL' `outstr `                     # ( : ( )
                    ->    'PAGE' (exp (',' exp)? ) | '+'
                    ->    '.LIST'
                    ->    '.XLIST'
                    ->    '.LFCOND'
                    ->    '.SFCOND'
                    ->    '.TFCOND'
                    ->    '.LALL'
```

```
                         ->   '.SALL'
                         ->   '.XALL'
                         ->   '.CREF'
                         ->   '.XCREF' (name (',' name)* )?
                              ;
```
#
\# There are two statements that can appear in a macro but cannot appear in any other
\# portion of the assembler input file. These are the LOCAL and EXITM statements.
#
```
mstatement          ->   (mstate1 | stmtbody) 'new_line'
                         ;
```
#
```
mstate1             ->   'LOCAL' label (',' label)*
                    ->   'EXITM'
                         ;
```
#
\# The first portion of a conditional assembly statement is the 'IF' part, If the expression
\# evaluated in the 'IF' part is true, then the associated statement list is assembled.
\# Otherwise, the statement list is skipped.
#
```
ifpart              ->   ifchoice exp 'new_line' statement+
                         ;
```
#
\# The 'ELSEIF' section of the conditional assembly statement also has an expression
\# and a statement list associated with it. As with the 'IF' part, if the expression is true,
\# then the statements are assembled.
#
```
elifpart            ->   elchoice exp   new_line   statement+
                         ;
```
#
\# If all of the expressions in a conditional assembly statement evaluate to false, and
\# if an 'ELSE' part is defined, then the statements in the 'ELSE' part are assembled.
#
```
elsepart            ->   'ELSE' statement+
                         ;
```
#
\# There are many kinds of conditional assembly (IF) statements in MASM. The following
\# productions define the IFs and ELSEIFs which are allowed to start a conditional
\# assembly subblock.
    #

```
ifchoice            ->   'IF' | 'IF1' | 'IF2' | 'IFB' | 'IFNB' | 'IFDEF'
                    ->   'IFNDEF' | 'IFE' | 'IFDIF' | 'IFDIFI' | 'IFIDN'
```

```
                        ->    'IFIDNI'

                              ;
#
elchoice            ->    'ELSEIF' | 'ELSEIF1' |'ELSEIF2' |'ELSEIFB'
                    ->    'ELSEIFNB' | 'ELSEIFDEF' | 'ELSEIFNDEF'
                    ->    'ELSEIFE' | 'ELSEIFDIF' | 'ELSEIFDIFI'
                    ->    'ELSEIFIDN' | 'ELSEIFIDNI'
                              ;
#
# The following production defines the error directives. They have essentially the same
# options as the IF and ELSEIF.
#
elchoice            ->    'ELSEIF' | 'ELSEIF1' | 'ELSEIF2' | 'ELSEIFB|
                    ->    'ELSEIFNB' | 'ELSEIFDEF' | 'ELSEIFNDEF'
                    ->    'ELSEIFE' | 'ELSEIFDIF' | 'ELSEIFDIFI'
                    ->    'ELSEIFIDN' | 'ELSEIFIDNI'
#
# Communal variable definitions are of the following form.
#
commdef             ->    procsizes? label ':' commsize (':' exp)?
                              ;
#
# The following sizes are allowed on COMMUNAL data definitions.
#
commsize            ->    'BYTE' | 'WORD' | 'DWORD' | 'FWORD' | 'QWORD'
                    ->    'TBYTE'
                              ;
#
# Names that are declared with the EXTRN directive have a type associated with them.
# Only one of the type modifiers may be specified in association with an EXTRN name.
#
extrndef            ->    label ':' (labsizes | 'ABS')
                              ;
#
# Record fields definitions associate a number of bits with each field name. Each field
# can be optionally initialized with an expression.
#
recfields           ->    recfield (',' recfield) *
                              ;
#
recfield            ->    label ':' exp ('=' exp)?
                              ;
```

```
#
# The assume statement has three possible forms. Define each of those forms.
#
assumebdy        ->    assumepr (',' assumepr)*
                 ->    segreg ':' 'NOTHING'
                 ->    'NOTHING'
                       ;
#
assumepr         ->    segreg ':' name
                       ;
#
segreg           ->    'CS' | 'DS' | 'ES' | 'FS' | 'GS' | 'SS'
                       ;
#
# The structure of a segment definition statement is defined in the following rules. The
# valid alignments, 'combine' directives and 'use' values, are also defined.
#
segmenthd        ->    alignment? use? combine?
                       'string'? 'new_line'
                       ;
#
alignment        ->    'BYTE' | 'WORD' | 'DWORD' | 'PARA' | 'PAGE'
                       ;
#
use              ->    'USE16' | 'USE32'
                       ;
#
combine          ->    'PUBLIC' | 'STACK' | 'COMMON' | 'MEMORY'
                 ->    'AT' exp
                       ;
#
# Declarations of data areas appear in a structure block or statement block. The label
# for the data area is optional as is the initialization expressions.
#
datadef          ->    label? vardefine varinit
#
# The initialization phrase for a variable definition can consist of multiple expressions
# or a DUP phrase. A DUP phrase requires an initialization phrase (enclosed in
# parentheses) to specify the value(s) to be duplicated. The fields of a structure or rec-
# ord are bracketed by '<' and '>'.
#
varinit          ->    initexp (',' initexp)*
                 ->    '<' varinit '>'                              # ( :-( )
```

```
                  ->    exp 'DUP' '(' varinit ')'
                     ;
#
initexp           ->    '?'
                  ->    exp
                     ;
#
# The following rule defines the legal variable definition directives.
#
vardefine         ->    'DB' | 'DW' | 'DD' | 'DF' | 'DQ' | 'DT'
                     ;
#
# The following sizes are allowed on data definition statements.
#
labsizes          ->    'BYTE' | 'WORD' | 'DWORD' | 'FWORD' | 'QWORD'
                  ->    'TBYTE' | 'PROC'
                  ->    procsizes
                     ;
#
# The following sizes are allowed on PROC statements.
#
procsizes         ->    'FAR'
                  ->    'NEAR'
                     ;
#
# The following memory models are allowed in MASM.
#
memmodel          ->    'SMALL' | 'MEDIUM' | 'COMPACT' | 'LARGE'
                  ->    'HUGE'
                     ;
#
```

EXPRESSIONS

The following rules define an expression syntax and operator precedence hierarchy
that approximates MASM. MASM seems to ignore some portions of some expressions
(without any error messages), so it is difficult to tell if this section of the grammar
is correct. It seems that MASM is defined by its implementation when it comes to
expressions and operands.
#
Note that although this grammar allows some expressions to be parsed in places where
they are semantically incorrect, the semantics rules catch the error rather than the
parser. This makes the phrase-structure grammar easier to follow.

All MASM binary operators are left associative.

```
#
exp   ->   exp0

          ;
#
# The following expressions cannot be part of a more complex expression. The PTR
# operator establishes the type of the expression. MASM does not support complex
# expressions which contain (type) real constants.
#
exp0 ->    labsizes 'PTR' exp
      ->    `real'

          ;
#
# Sentences such as SHORT SHORT LABEL do not seem to be allowed in MASM. They
# are disallowed by these rules.
#
exp1 ->    'SHORT' exp2
      ->    '.TYPE' exp2
      ->    exp2

          ;
#
# The logical, relational, and arithmetic operators are left associative. This means that
# the left-most operator at a particular precedence level is evaluated first.
#
exp2 ->    exp2 'OR' exp3
      ->    exp2 'XOR' exp3
      ->    exp3

          ;
#
exp3 ->    exp3 'AND' exp4
      ->    exp4

          ;
#
exp4 ->    'NOT' exp5
      ->    exp5

          ;
#
exp5 ->    exp5 'EQ' exp6
      ->    exp5 'NE' exp6
      ->    exp5 'LT' exp6
      ->    exp5 'LE' exp6
```

```
                  ->     exp5 'GT' exp6
                  ->     exp5 'GE' exp6
                  ->     exp6
                       ;
#
exp6              ->     exp6 '+' exp7
                  ->     exp6 '-' exp7
                  ->     exp7
                       ;
#
exp7              ->     exp7 '*' exp8
                  ->     exp7 '/' exp8
                  ->     exp7 'MOD' exp8
                  ->     exp7 'SHR' exp8
                  ->     exp7 'SHL' exp8
                  ->     exp8
                       ;
#
exp8              ->     '+' exp9
                  ->     '-' exp9
                  ->     exp9
                       ;
#
exp9              ->     'HIGH' exp10
                  ->     'LOW' exp10
                  ->     exp10
                       ;
#
# The OFFSET and SEG operators must have a variable or label name as their param-
# eter. The THIS operator must have a type specifier as its parameter.
#
exp10             ->     'OFFSET' name
                  ->     'THIS' labsizes
                  ->     'TYPE' exp11
                  ->     'SEG' name
                  ->     exp11
                       ;
#
exp11             ->     segreg ':' exp12
                  ->     exp12
                       ;
#
exp12             ->     name '.' exp13
```

```
                    ->    exp13
                          ;
#
exp13               ->    'LENGTH' exp14
                    ->    'SIZE' exp14
                    ->    'WIDTH' name
                    ->    'MASK' name
                    ->    exp14
                          ;
#
exp14               ->    `qstring`
                    ->    `dstring`
                    ->    `lstring`
                    ->    'identifier'
                    ->    '(' exp1 ')'
                    ->    '[' exp1 ']'
                    ->    '$'
                    ->    `register`'
                          ;
#
# Define some shorthand rules for the rest of the grammar.
#
name                >     `identifier`
                          ;
#
label               ->    `identifier`
                          ;
```

6

MASM Character Set, Type, and Data Declarations

MICROSOFT'S MACRO ASSEMBLER, MASM, IS A SOFTWARE PACKAGE THAT CONVERTS assembly language source files to object code (machine language). MASM runs on the family of Intel 8086 through 80386 microprocessors and the 8087 through 80387 numerics coprocessors. The macro assembler has a powerful set of assembly language directives that maximize control of the processors. In addition, MASM has a set of macro directives that allow you to create and use macros.

MASM checks the syntax of source statements and operand types. It detects questionable usage that could lead to unwanted results, and it prints error and warning messages. As the last step, MASM produces object modules, which are also compatible with object modules created by Microsoft high-level language compilers. This allows the combination of modules created by FORTRAN, Pascal, C, and other Microsoft compilers. See chapter 11 on how to use MASM and the various MASM options.

Every assembly language program contains one or more source files made up of statements that define the program data and instructions. MASM reads these files and assembles the statements to create object modules. LINK (Microsoft's Object Linker) then prepares these object modules for execution. Source files must be in standard *ASCII* (American Standard Code for Information Interchange) format, and they cannot contain control codes. Lines are separated with a carriage-return/line-feed.

A MASM statement is made up of a combination of an optional *name*, a mandatory instruction or directive *mnemonic*, possibly optional *operands*, and an optional comment, in the form:

[*name*] mnemonic [*operands*] [*;comment*]

Examples:

```
                 MOV    EAX,EBX   ;Price Calculation
@DATECALC        ADD    EAX,1
PRINTIT          PROC   NEAR      ;Start the Printing
                 ENDP
```

See appendix A for the full 80386 instruction set and appendix B for the 80387 coprocessor instruction set. Each statement represents an action you want the assembler to take, such as generating a byte of data or generating the machine-code instruction to move a value into a register. Form statements according to the following rules:

- Each statement, except the last one in the file, must be terminated by a carriage-return/line-feed combination. That is, multiple statements cannot be coded on a line.

- A statement may begin in any column.

- Each statement is limited to 128 characters. It cannot contain an embedded carriage-return/line-feed.
Warning: If you were running on MASM 5.0 and ordered the 5.1 update, your documentation will tell you that you can use a backslash (\ ) as a line continuation. This disappears in the full MASM 5.1 release. (We sent for the upgrade for one system and ordered the full 5.1 for a second system. At this point, we suggest you do not use the line continuation until this confusion is resolved.)

- MASM comments must be preceded with a semicolon (;) and terminated with a carriage-return/line-feed. MASM ignores comments, so it's possible to use reserved names within comments.

CHARACTER SET AND NUMERIC CONSTANTS

A given set of symbols constitutes the building blocks of any written language. Each computer language has its own character set, which limits the symbols that may be used in writing programs for that particular language. Implementation of a language in a particular computer might not allow certain characters or might allow characters in addition to the officially defined ones. MASM recognizes the character set as shown in Fig. 6-1.

A *sign* is a binary indicator of the position of the size (magnitude) of a number relative to zero. The sign is represented by a high-order bit added to the front of the number, 0 if positive and 1 if negative. The remaining bits give the absolute value of the number.

Exponents use *biased numbers* for expressing values of floating-point exponents. Biases are 127, 1023, and 16383 for short, long, and temporary real formats. Biased numbers ease numeric comparisons (for example, greater than or less than) and are computed by taking the initial positive or negative number and adding a bias value to it. This bias ensures that the most positive exponent allowable becomes the largest value of the representation and the most negative exponent becomes zero. Note: the IEEE floating-point representation reserves the biased-zero exponent.

	2x	3x	4x	5x	6x	7x	x
	sp	0	@	P	`	p	0
	!	1	A	Q	a	q	1
	"	2	B	R	b	r	2
	#	3	C	S	c	s	3
	$	4	D	T	d	t	4
	%	5	E	U	e	u	5
	&	6	F	V	f	v	6
	'	7	G	W	g	w	7
	(	8	H	X	h	x	8
	)	9	I	Y	i	y	9
	*	:	J	Z	j	z	A
	+	;	K	[	k	{	B
	,	<	L	\	l	|	C
	-	=	M	]	m	}	D
	.	>	N	_	n	~	E
	/	?	O	^	o		F

Note: sp and the horizontal tab character (09h) may be
used interchangeably as 'white space' between
language elements.

del (7Fh) is not a MASM recognized character.

Fig. 6-1. MASM Character Set.

Integers

Syntax: digits
            digitsB
            digitsQ
            digitsO
            digitsD
            digitsH
            digitsR

Examples: 12
           0101b

221q
61o
150d
9Fh
4f3r

MASM recognizes integers which are whole numbers from one of the numerical bases of binary, octal, decimal, or hexadecimal, plus an optional radix. The radix can be: B (binary), Q (octal), O (octal), D (decimal), H (hexadecimal) or R (real). The digits usable with each radix are shown in Fig. 6-2. If a radix is not specified, MASM uses the current default radix, which is decimal unless changed with the .RADIX directive (see chapter 8 for a description of .RADIX). You can use either upper- or lower-case letters to specify the radix, although most people use lower-case letters because they save a keystroke (holding down the SHIFT key).

Name	Digits	Radix Specifier	Example	Base
Binary	01	B or b	10100001b	2
Octal	01234567	O Q o or q	241q	8
Decimal	01234567 89	D or d	161d	10
Hexadecimal	01234567 89ABCDEF	H or h	0A1h *	16

* Hexidecimal numbers which begin with A-F must be prefixed with a zero (0) for the parser to distinguish them from identifiers.

Q is used as an alternate for O to avoid the possible visual confusion with 0.

Fig. 6-2. Type, Radix, and Digits MASM Recognizes.

To distinguish between hexadecimal numbers that start with characters and symbols such as labels, start hexadecimal numbers with a decimal digit 0 through 9. If a number begins with a character, A through F, place a leading 0 to the left of the number. That is, if the hexadecimal number is F6, use 0F6h. The zero is not counted when determining the number of possible digits. For instance, if a 16-bit word needs to show 65535, you can still add the zero as the high-order character. Enter the FFFF as 0FFFFh.

Real Numbers

Syntax: [+|−]*digits.digits*[E[+|−]*digits*]

Examples: − 852.33
            5.43E1
            4952.0E − 2
            91.26

A real number consists of an integer, a fraction, and an exponent in the form shown in the syntax. In the form, the digits can be any combination of decimal digits. The digits in front of the decimal point (.) represent the integer, and those following represent the fraction. The optional exponent is made up of digits following the exponent mark (E). Real numbers can be used only with the DD, DQ, or DT directives (these directives are defined in this chapter). The real number radix, R, can only be used with hexadecimal numbers consisting of 8, 16, or 20 significant digits. A high-order 0 can still be added and not counted as part of the significant digits. The maximum number of digits in an integer depends on the instruction or directive in which the integer is used.

Encoded Real Numbers

Syntax: digitsR

Examples: DD   40F80000R
              DQ   7FD3000000000000R

An encoded real number is an 8-, 16-, or 20-digit hexadecimal number that represents a real number in encoded format. The encoded number has a sign, a biased exponent, and a mantissa with the fields encoded as bit fields within the number. The exact size and meaning of each bit field depends on the number of bits in the number. The digits must be hexadecimal, and the number must begin with a decimal digit (0–9) and must be followed by the real number designator (R). As with any real numbers, encoded real numbers can be used only with the DD, DQ, and DT directives (these directives are defined in this chapter) and must be 8, 16, or 20 digits, respectively.

Binary-coded decimal (BCD) is a system of number representation where each decimal digit is represented by a combination of four binary digits. The largest single digit in BCD is 9 decimal, or 1001 binary. BCD arithmetic is accurate because there is no limit to the size of the operands, and the decimal point can be repositioned easily. The BCD system is based on the fact that each of the decimal digits 0 through 9 can be held conveniently in a single 4-bit *nibble* (half byte). One format, called *packed BCD*, uses the two nibbles of a byte to represent two decimal digits. *Unpacked BCD* ignores the upper half of a byte and uses the lower nibble to hold the decimal digit.

Packed Decimal

Syntax: [+ | −]digits

Examples:	Encoded as:
DT 1234567890	00000000001234567890h
DT −1234567890	80000000001234567890h

A packed decimal number represents a decimal integer to be stored in a packed decimal format, in the form shown in the syntax. Packed decimals cannot have more than 18 digits and can have the same format as other decimal integers, except that they can take an optional plus (+) or minus (−).

Characters

Syntax: 'character' or ''character''

Examples: 'a'
           "a"
           'A message for you.'
           'Can''t find program file.'
           "Can't find program file."
           "The ""file"" wasn't found."
           'The ''file'' wasn''t found.'

A character consists of a single ASCII character stored in a single byte. Characters must be enclosed in single quotation marks or double quotation marks and are case sensitive. A string constant consists of two or more ASCII characters. If using single quotation marks within the string, use two single quotation marks, one for the enclosing quote mark; the same with double quotation marks. For example, the word *can't* is coded *'can''t'*.

Names

Syntax: characters

Examples: SUBRTN
           Subrtn
           __Main__Proc
           $DOLLARS

Names are combinations of letters, digits, and special characters used as a label, variable, or symbol within a line of assembly language code. There are four general rules for names.

- Names can have any number of characters. However, only the first 31 characters are used, and all others are ignored.

• Names must begin with a letter, an underscore (__), a dollar sign ($), a question mark (?), or an at sign (@). Names cannot begin with digits. The period (.) is an operator and cannot be used within a name; it can be used as the first character.

• A name cannot be the same as any reserved name. Note that two special characters, the question mark (?) and the dollar sign ($), are reserved names and therefore cannot stand alone as symbol names.

• Names can have any combination of upper- or lower-case letters because all lower-case letters are converted to upper case by MASM, unless you use the /ML option during assembly, or unless you declare the name with a PUBLIC or EXTRN directive and use the /MX option during assembly. See chapter 11 for the /ML and /MX options.

Reserved names are names with special, predefined meanings to MASM and are shown in Fig. 6-3. Only use the reserved names as defined; all upper- and lower-case combinations of these names are treated by MASM as the same. For instance, the names public, Public, and PUBLIC are the same.

$	%OUT	*	+	-
.	.186	.286	.286P	.287
.386	.386P	.387	.8086	.8087
.ALPHA	.CODE	.CONST	.CREF	.DATA
.DATA?	.ERR	.ERR1	.ERR2	.ERRB
.ERRDEF	.ERRDIF	.ERRDIFI	.ERRE	.ERRIDN
.ERRIDNI	.ERRNB	.ERRNDEF	.ERRNZ	.FARDATA
.FARDATA?	.LALL	.LFCOND	.LIST	.MODEL
.MSFLOAT	.RADIX	.SALL	.SEQ	.SFCOND
.STACK	.TFCOND	.TYPE	.XALL	.XCREF
.XLIST	/	=	?	@CODE
@CODESIZE	@CPU	@CURSEG	@DATA	@DATASIZE
@FARDATA	@FARDATA?	@FILENAME	@VERSION	@WORDSIZE
ALIGN	ASSUME	BYTE	CATSTR	COMM
COMMENT	COMMON	DB	DD	DF
DOSSEG	DQ	DS	DT	DUP
DW	DWORD	ELSE	ELSEIF	ELSEIF1
ELSEIF2	ELSEIFB	ELSEIFDEF	ELSEIFDIF	ELSEIFDIFI
ELSEIFE	ELSEIFIDN	ELSEIFIDNI	ELSEIFNB	ELSEIFNDEF
END	ENDIF	ENDM	ENDP	ENDS
EQ	EQU	EVEN	EXITM	EXTRN
FAR	FWORD	GE	GROUP	GT
HIGH	IF	IF1	IF2	IFB
IFDEF	IFDIF	IFDIFI	IFE	IFIDN
IFIDNI	IFNB	IFNDEF	INCLUDE	INCLUDELIB
INSTR	IRP	IRPC	LABEL	LE
LENGTH	LOCAL	LOW	LT	MACRO
MASK	MEMORY	MOD	NAME	NE
NEAR	NOT	NOTHING	OFFSET	OR
ORG	PAGE	PARA	PROC	PTR
PUBLIC	PURGE	QWORD	RECORD	REPT
SEG	SEGMENT	SHL	SHORT	SHR
SIZE	SIZESTR	STACK	STRUC	SUBSTR
SUBTTL	TBYTE	THIS	TITLE	TYPE
USE16	USE32	WIDTH	WORD	XOR
[	]			

Fig. 6-3. MASM Reserved Names.

In addition to the names in Fig. 6-3, instruction mnemonics and register names are reserved names. These vary depending on the processor directives given in the source file. For example, the name EAX is a reserved word with the .386 directive because the EAX is one of the 32-bit registers. However, a program with the .286 directive can use EAX as a name because the register name is AX. See chapter 8 for the instruction set directives.

Comments

Syntax: ;text

Examples: ; This is a comment.
             ; ENDP means stop
             ;A blank is not required after the semicolon.

Comments are descriptions of code. They are documentation only, and MASM ignores them. Any text following a semicolon is considered a comment. Multiline comments can either be specified with multiple comment statements or with the COMMENT directive (see below).

You can put comments anywhere within the program, although there are two common ways to use them. The first is to place the preceding semicolon in or near column 1 and use the entire line to explain the next section of code. In this way, you can take as many lines as necessary to explain code. The second way comments are commonly used is to place a comment on the same line as the code. If a comment appears this way, it must be to the right of all names, mnemonics and operands. Figure 6-4 shows the four ways to use comments.

Syntax: COMMENT *delimiter* [*text*]
             text
             delimiter

Examples: COMMENT ! This is an example
             of a block of comments
             !

In this type of comment, all *text* between the first *delimiter* and the line containing a second *delimiter* is ignored by the assembler. The *delimiter* character is the first nonblank character after the COMMENT directive. The *text* includes the comments up to and including the line that contains the next occurrence of the delimiter.

DECLARATIONS AND DEFINITIONS

It is possible to generate data, labels, variables, and other symbols for programs. Each of these items are defined; then you can see how they are declared.

```
; name      MACRO directive  dummy parameters

samp01      MACRO             dummy00,dummy01
;; A comment which is internal to a macro - ie it does not print when

              .
              .
              .

            mov     AX,dummy00        ; A prototype statement
              .
              .
              .

COMMENT + This starts a multi-line comment which can contain any
character except the specified delimiter (in this case +
```

Fig. 6-4. Examples of Comments.

First, data is a general term used to denote any or all facts, numbers, letters, symbols, and so on, that can be processed by a computer. A *label* is an identifier prefixed to a mnemonic statement, which enables the statement to be referenced by other statements. Labels are formed as strings of alphanumeric characters. Labels are useful because they are the identifiers of the storage locations in which the assembled statement is located. Where the statement is an instruction, the label allows references to the assembled code for the purpose—among others—of using it as the destination of a branch instruction. Where the label is attached to a declaration of a data element or data area, instructions in the program may use the symbolic label as the name of the element.

A *variable* is a quantity that can assume any of a given set of values. Finally, a *symbol* is letter (or group of alphanumeric characters) that represent particular quantities. A variable symbol refers to assembler programming where a symbol does not have to be declared because MASM assigns it read-only values. The value of a symbol defined as a label is the value of the location counter (see appendix H for an overview of the 80386) at the time the label was encountered. The value of a symbol defined by equality is the value of the expression appearing to the right of the equal sign.

Label Declarations

Some time ago, a genius came up with a clever way to keep from having to hard code specific addresses. Today, you code label declarations to create labels that represent the address of an instruction. This way, it is not a requirement to remember where to transfer program control; let the assembler do the hard work. Labels can be used in jumps, calls, and loop instructions to direct program execution to the instruction at the address of the label.

Near-Label Declarations

Syntax: *name:*

Examples: Strthere:
                   THIS__POINT:

A near-label declaration creates an instruction label that has a NEAR type. You can use the label in instructions in the same segment (see appendix H for an overview of the 80386) to pass execution control to that corresponding instruction. The *name* must be unique (not previously defined), and it must be followed by a colon (:). Also, the segment containing the declaration must be associated with the CS (code segment) register. During program execution when it processes the line of code, MASM sets the name to the current value of the location counter.

The near-label declaration can appear on a line by itself or on a line with an instruction. Labels must be declared with the PUBLIC or EXTRN directive if the labels are located in one module but are called from another module (see chapter 9 for PUBLIC or EXTRN directives).

Procedure Labels

Syntax: *label* PROC [NEAR|FAR]
                   statements
                   RET [*constant*]
                   label ENDP

Examples: THISTIME PROC NEAR
                   [some statements]
                   RET
                   THISTIME ENDP

When using the PROC directive, create a label *name* and optionally assign the PROC a distance which can be NEAR or FAR. Any RET instruction within the procedure automatically has the same distance as the procedure. The *label* represents the address of the first instruction of the procedure. That *label* can be used in a call, jump, or loop instruction to direct execution control to the first instruction of the procedure. If you do not specify the type for a procedure, MASM assumes a default of NEAR. Labels must be declared with the PUBLIC or EXTRN directive if the labels are located in one module but called from another module (see chapter 9 for PUBLIC and EXTRN directives).

When MASM encounters the PROC label definition during execution, it sets the label value to the current value of the location counter and sets the label type to NEAR (default) or FAR. If you code the label as a FAR type, MASM also sets its segment value to that of the enclosing segment. Use NEAR labels with jump, call or loop instructions to transfer program control to any address in the current segment. FAR labels, on the other hand, transfer program control to an address in any segment outside the current segment.

An incorrect label distance is not detected. If you code the wrong distance, the return will be incorrect—a FAR call saves CD:IP (the code segment instruction pointer), and a NEAR return loads what should be just IP. That is, a FAR call to a NEAR return leaves CS on the stack, and the parameters passed are two bytes deeper than expected. An incorrect distance returns into never-never land—LINK does not detect the problem.

LABEL Directive for Code

Syntax: *name* LABEL [NEAR|FAR]

Examples: HERE   PROC   FAR   ; Main entry point
                                  :

                  HERE1   LABEL   FAR   ; Secondary entry point
                                  :

                                  RET
                  HERE   ENDP   ; End of procedure

The LABEL directive provides an alternative method of defining code labels. The *name* is the symbol name assigned to the label. The distance can be a type specifier, such as NEAR, FAR, or PROC. PROC means NEAR or FAR, depending on the default memory model. It is possible to use the LABEL directive to define a second entry point into a procedure. FAR code labels also can be the destination of FAR jumps or of FAR calls that use the RETF instruction. See also the LABEL directive description under symbol declarations in this chapter.

Pointer Variables

Pointer variables (or pointers) are variables that contain the address of a data or code object rather than the object itself. The address in the variable points to another address.

Pointers can be either NEAR addresses or FAR addresses. Near pointers consist of the offset portion of the address. They can be initialized in word variables by using the DW directive. You can use values in near address variables in situations where the segment portion of the address is known to be the current segment. Far pointers consist of both the segment and offset portions of the address. They can be initialized in doubleword variables by using the DD directive. Values in far address variables must be used when the segment portion of the address may be outside the current segment.

In the 80386, pointers are different if the USE32 use type has been specified. In this case, the offset portion of an address consists of 32 bits, and the segment portion consists of 16 bits. A near pointer is 32 bits (a doubleword), and a far pointer is 48 bits.

Data Declarations

The data-definition directives enable you to allocate memory for data. At the same time, you can specify the initial values for the allocated data. Variables consist of one or more named data objects of a specified size.

Syntax: [*name*] *directive initializer* [,*initializer*],,,

The name is the symbol name assigned to the variable. If no *name* is assigned, the data is allocated, but the starting address of the variable has no symbolic name. The size of the variable is determined by the *directive*.

Directives for defining integer variables are listed below with the sizes of the integer they define.

- *DB* (bytes) is a directive that allocates unsigned numbers from 0 to 255 or signed numbers from −128 to 127.
- *DW* (words) is a directive that allocates unsigned numbers from 0 to 65535 or signed numbers from −32768 to 32767. Word values can be used directly in 8086-family instructions. They can also be loaded, used in calculations, and stored with 8087-family instructions.
- *DD* (doublewords) is a directive that allocates unsigned numbers from 0 to 4,294,967,295 or signed numbers from −2,147,483,648 to 2,147,483,647, also for 16-bit FAR pointers.
- *DF* (farwords) is a directive that allocates 6-byte integers (also 32-bit FAR pointers).
- *DQ* (quadwords) is a directive that allocates 64-bit integers. Some calculations can be done on these numbers directly with the 80386 processor, but others require an indirect method of doing calculations on each doubleword separately.
- *DT* (tenbyte) is a directive that allocates 10-byte (80-bit) integers if the D radix specifier is used.

Data definition (declaration) is how you specify a particular layout or format storage. Data formats are the rules that describe the way data is held in a file or record, whether in character form, as binary numbers, as bytes, as words, and so on. Data-formatting statements are the various statements that instruct MASM to set up constants and reserve memory areas to indicate field boundaries.

DB (Define Byte) Directive

Syntax: [*name*] DB *initialvalue*,,,

Examples: INTEGER DB 8
CR__LF   DB 0Ah,0Dh
String   DB 'a'
Nothing DB ?

The DB directive allocates a byte (8 bits) of memory and initializes that storage of each *initialvalue*. The *initialvalue* can be an integer, a character string constant, a DUP (see below) operator, a constant expression or a question mark (?). A string constant can have any number of characters as long as it fits on a single line—that is, no embedded carriage return (C/R). When a string is encoded, the characters are stored in the order given, with the first character in the constant at the lowest address and the last at the highest. Use the question mark to represent an undefined initial value. If coding two or more initial values, you must separate them with commas (,).

The optional *name* creates a variable of type BYTE whose offset value is the current location-counter value.

DD (Define Doubleword) Directive

Syntax: [*name*] DD *initialvalue,,,*

Examples: CHAR__STR   DD   'PB'
             Many   DD   1,2,3,'$'
             pointer   DD   char__str

A doubleword is 4 bytes (32 bits) of storage. DD allocates and initializes a doubleword of storage for each initialvalue. This *initialvalue* can be an integer, a one to four character string constant, a real number, an encoded real number, a DUP (see below) operator, a constant expression, an address expression, or a question mark (?). String constants must not consist of more than four characters because each character uses one byte. The last (or only) character in the string is placed in the low-order byte, and either a 0 or the first character is placed in the high-order byte. (If you are not clear on how the 80386 stores bytes in registers and memory, there is an overview of the 80386 in appendix H.)

To represent an undefined value, use the question mark. If coding two or more expressions, separate them with commas (,). And, if you use the optional *name*, DD creates a variable of the type DWORD whose offset value is the current location-counter value.

DF (Define Farword) Directive

Syntax: *name* DF *initialvalue,,,*

Example: THISONE DF

Farwords are normally used only as pointer variables on the 80386. The *name* is a symbol name assigned to the *initialvalue*.

DQ (Define Quadword) Directive

Syntax: [*name*] DQ *initialvalue,,,*

Examples: REAL   DQ   4.9
             ENC__REAL   DQ   7F000000000000000r

A quadword is 8 bytes (64 bits) of storage. The DQ directive allocates and initializes a quadword for each *initialvalue*. This *initialvalue* can be an integer, a real number, a one- through four-character string constant, an encoded real number, a DUP operator (see below), a constant expression, or a question mark (?). String constants must not consist of more than four characters. The last (or only) character is placed in the low-order byte. If two characters are entered, the first character is placed in the second byte and zeros are placed in all remaining bytes.

To represent an undefined value, use the question mark. If entering two or more *initialvalue*s, separate them by commas (,).

DT (Define Ten Bytes) Directive

Syntax: [*name*] DT *initialvalue*],,,

Example: Hi__Byte   DT- 4164261836005710427110000d

DT allocates and initializes 10 bytes of storage for each *initialvalue* entered. The *initialvalue* can be an integer expression, a packed decimal, a one- through four-character string constant, an encoded real number, a DUP operator (see below), or a question mark (?). As with the other data definition directives, if you use string constants, they must not consist of more than four characters. The last (or only) character in the string is placed in the low-order byte. If you enter a second character, it is placed in the next byte, and so on, with zeros being stored in all remaining bytes.

Notice that DT assumes that constants with decimal digits are packed decimals, not integers. If specifying a 10-byte integer, follow the number with the letter that specifies the number system used. For example, use H or h for hexadecimal.

The optional *name* creates a variable of the type TBYTE, whose offset value is the current location-counter value.

DW (Define Word) Directive

Syntax: [*name*] DW *initialvalue*,,,

Examples: Double   DW   10 DUP(?)
             FORMULA   DW   10*2
             ARRAYPTR   DW   OFFSET AGROUP:ARRAY

A word is 2 bytes (16 bits) of storage. DW allocates and initializes a word of storage for each *initialvalue*. This *initialvalue* can be an integer, a one- or two-character string constant, a DUP (see below) operator, a constant expression, an address expression, or a question mark (?). String constants must not consist of more than two characters, because each character uses one byte. The last (or only) character in the string is placed in the low-order byte, and either a 0 or the first character is placed in the high-order byte.

To represent an undefined value, use the question mark. If coding two or more expressions, separate them with commas (,). And if you use the optional *name*, DW creates a variable of the type WORD whose offset value is the current location-counter value.

DUP Operator

Syntax: *count*   DUP(*initialvalue,,,*)

Examples: DB   2   DUP(5)
            DW 10 DUP(2,4,2,1)
            DD 14 DUP(?)

DUP defines arrays, buffers, and other data structures consisting of multiple data objects of the same size. DUP specifies multiple occurrences of one or more initial values, that always must be placed within parentheses. The *count* sets the number of times to define the *initialvalue*. This *initialvalue* can be any expression that evaluates to an integer value, a character constant, or another DUP operator. It can also be the undefined symbol (?) if there is no initial value. When entering more than one initial value, separate them with commas (,). If multiple values are specified within the parentheses, the sequence of values is allocated *count* times.

If you want to initialize 50 bytes with an initial value of, for instance, 1, code it as follows:

DB 50 DUP(1).

As another example, to generate 80 words of data and initialize each four word groups with the values of 1, 2, 3, and 4, do the following:

DW 20 DUP(1,2,3,4)

DUP nests up to 17 levels. To initialize 125 bytes of data, with each byte having the initial value of 1, you can do the following:

DB 5 DUP(5 DUP(5 DUP(1)))

Finally, do the following for 20 doublewords of uninitialized data:

DD 20 DUP(?)

MASM sometimes generates different object codes when the DUP operator is used rather than when multiple values are given. For example, the statement

THISHERE DB ?,?,?,?,? ; Indeterminate

is indeterminate. It causes MASM to write five zero-value bytes to the object file. The statement:

HERETOO DB 5 DUP (?) ; Undefined

is undefined. It causes MASM to increase the offset of the next record in the object file by five bytes. Therefore, an object file created with the first statement will be larger than one created with the second statement. In most cases, the distinction between indeterminate and undefined definitions is trivial. LINK adjusts the offsets so that the same executable file is generated in either case. If you use the undefined definition, the explicit value is always used in the executable file regardless of link order.

Symbol Declarations

Symbols make programs easier to read and maintain by using descriptive names to represent a number, text, an instruction, or an address. MASM allows the use of symbols anywhere their corresponding values are allowed. Both equates and macros are processed at assembly time. They can simplify writing source code by allowing you to substitute mnemonic names for constants and repetitive code. By changing a macro or an equate, you change the effect of statements throughout the source code.

In exchange for the macro and equate conveniences, you lose some assembly-time efficiency. Assembly might be slightly slower for a program that uses macros and equates extensively than for the same program written without them. However, programs without macros and equates generally take longer to write and are more difficult to maintain.

Equals-Sign Directive (=)

Syntax: *name = expression*

Examples: Number   =   41642
           Initials   =   'PB'
           Formula   =   2 * 8 / 4

Use redefinable numerical equates to assign a numerical constant to a symbol. The symbol value can be redefined at any point during assembly time. Although the value of a redefinable equate might be different at different points in the source code, a constant value is assigned for each use, and that value does not change at run time. Redefinable equates are often used for assembly-time calculations in macros and repeat blocks.

The equals-sign (=) directive allows the creation of a constant symbol by assigning the numerical value of the *expression* to the *name*. In this case, a constant symbol is a name that represents up to a 32-bit value. These constant symbols can be redefined at any time. No storage is allocated; instead, MASM replaces each subsequent occurrence of *name* with the value of *expression*. The value is variable during the assembly process, but is a constant at run time.

Expression can be an integer, a constant expression, an address expression or a one- through four-character string constant. The value of *expression* must not exceed 65535. The *name* must be either a unique name or a name previously defined using the equals sign (=).

EQU Directive

Syntax: *name*   EQU   *expression*

Examples: PI   EQU   3.141592
           CLEAR__REG   EQU   XOR EAX,EAX
           Prompt   EQU   'Enter Number:'
           BYTE__PTR   EQU   BYTE PTR

Nonredefinable numerical equates are often used for assigning mnemonic names to constant values. This can make the code more readable and easier to maintain. If a constant value used in numerous places in the source needs to be changed, then the equate can be changed in one place rather than in many lines of code throughout the program.

There are three types of symbols EQU works on: absolute, alias, and text. An *absolute symbol* is a name that represents a 16-bit value. An *alias* is a name that represents another symbol. Finally, a *text symbol* is a name that represents a character string or other combination of characters. EQU creates constant symbols, aliases, or text symbols by assigning the *expression* to the *name*. MASM replaces each subsequent occurrence of the name with either the text or the value of the expression, depending on the type of expression given. Symbols defined using EQU cannot be redefined, and any attempt to do so generates an error.

Use EQU to create simple macros. MASM replaces a name with the text or value before attempting to assemble the statement containing the name. No storage is allocated for the symbol. You can use symbols defined with numerical values in subsequent statements as immediate operands having the assigned value.

The *name* must be unique, one that has not been previously defined. The *expression* can be an integer, a real number, an encoded real number, a string constant, an instruction mnemonic, an address expression, or a constant expression. These *expressions* that evaluate to values in the range of 00 to 0FFFFFFFF create constant symbols and cause MASM to replace the name with a value (note: they wrap to zero "silently," keeping the low order four bytes). All other expressions cause the assembler to replace the name with text.

See also chapter 9, which describes text macros which also use an EQU.

LABEL Directive for Data

Syntax: *name* LABEL *type*

Example: HERE LABEL BYTE

LABEL creates a new variable or label by assigning the current location-counter value and the given *type* to *name*. This *name* must be unique and not previously defined. The *type* can be the name of a valid structure type or can be any one of the following:

BYTE   (a byte)
WORD   (a word)
DWORD   (a doubleword)
QWORD   (a quadword)
TBYTE   (ten bytes)

See the LABEL directive under Label Declarations, above, for how LABEL uses NEAR and FAR.

Structure Types

In this section, the concern is structure data types. Chapter 8 gets into program structure directives.

STRUC and ENDS Directive

Syntax: *name* STRUC
           fielddefinition
           name ENDS

Examples: TABLE   STRUC
           Count   DB   10
           Value   DW   10 DUP(?)
           TBLNAME   DB   'FONT__3'

           TABLE ENDS

STRUC and ENDS mark the beginning and end of a type definition for a structure. A type definition for a structure defines the name of a structure and the number, type, and default values of the fields contained in the structure.

A structure definition creates a template (a pattern) for data. This template is used by MASM during assembly, but it does not, in itself, create any data. You must declare a structure to create the data. See structure declaration below.

The optional *name* defines the name of the structure type and must be unique. *Fielddefinition* defines the structure's field, where any number of field definitions can be given. The definitions must have one of the following forms:

[*name*]   DB   *defaultvalue,,,*
[*name*]   DW   *defaultvalue,,,*
[*name*]   DD   *defaultvalue,,,*
[*name*]   DQ   *defaultvalue,,,*
[*name*]   DT   *defaultvalue,,,*

In the above definition examples, the optional *name* (which must be unique) specifies the field name and represents the offset from the beginning of the structure to the corresponding field. The DB, DW, DD, DQ, and DT define the size of the field.

The *defaultvalue* defines the value to be given to the field if no initial value is given in the declaration of the structure variable. The *defaultvalue* defines a number, a symbol, a character, or string constant. Also, it might contain the DUP operator to define multiple values for the field. If the *defaultvalue* is a string constant, the field has the same number of bytes as characters in the string. If using multiple default values, separate them with commas (,).

Structures cannot be nested and cannot contain any other statements. A definition of a structure type can contain field definitions and comments only.

RECORD Directive

Syntax: *recordname* RECORD *fieldname:width[= expression],,,*

Example: Code__it RECORD HI:4, MID:3, LO:3

A record variable is a byte or word variable in which specific bit fields can be accessed symbolically. Records can also be doubleword variables with the 80386 processor. Bit fields within the record have different sizes. There are two steps in declaring record variables:

• Declare a record type. RECORD creates a template for data. MASM uses this template during assembly, but the template does not, in itself, create any data. You create the data when declaring a record. See record declaration below.

• Define one or more variables having the record type. For each variable defined, memory is allocated to the object file in the format declared by the type.

The record variable can then be used as an operand in assembler statements. The record variable can be accessed as a whole by using the record name, or individual fields can be specified by using the record name and a field name combined with the field-name operator. A record type can also be used as a constant (immediate data).

RECORD defines a record type for an 8- to 32-bit record that contains one or more fields. The *recordname* is the name of the record type to be used when creating the record. *Fieldname* is the name of a field in the record. *Width* is the number of bits in the field. *Expression* is the initial or default value for the field. See Fig. 6-5 for an example of using RECORD.

The example in Fig. 6-5 creates a record type ENCODE having three fields: HI, MID, and LO. Each record declared using this type occupies 16 bits of memory. HI will be in bits 6 to 9 (bit 9 is bit 1 in the high byte). The MID field is in bits 3 to 5, and the LO field is in bits 0 to 2. The remaining high-order bits are unused.

It is possible to code any number of *fieldname:width = expression* combinations for a record, as long as they're separated with a comma (,). The sum of the widths for all

```
91                          ;
92                          ; Example of record definitions which show the sizes which result,
93                          ; results of initialization (when used below), and masking.
94                          ;
95                          ; Because this is a USE16 segment, record size is limited to 16 bits.
96                          ; (This apears to be a bug in MASM R5.1 - probably associated with the
97                          ;   change in data segment USE defaulting.)  Note that 32 bit records
98                          ; are generated if USE32 is specified for the data segment.
99                          ;
108                         ;
109         encode         record hi:4,mid:3,lo:3

122                          ;
123                          ; Example generation for records
124                          ;
125 0063   03C7                      encode <15,0,7>            ; Initialize hi and lo
126

130                          ;
131                          ; Mask generation examples
132                          ;
133 006B   03C0                      dw        MASK hi          ; A mask to isolate hi
134 006D   0038                      dw        MASK mid         ; A mask to isolate mid
135 006F   0007                      dw        MASK lo          ; A mask to isolate lo
136                          ;
137 0071   FFFF                      dw        NOT MASK mid     ; A mask to clear mid
examples.ASM(124): error A2050: Value out of range
138 0073   FFFFFFC7                  dd        NOT MASK mid     ; A mask to clear mid
139 0077   25 FFC7                   and       AX,NOT MASK mid  ; A mask to clear mid
```

Fig. 6-5. RECORD Example.

fields must not exceed 32 bits. The *width* must be a constant in the range of 1 to 32. If the total width of all declared fields is larger than 8 bits, MASM uses 2 bytes (larger than 16, MASM uses 4 bytes); otherwise, MASM uses 1 byte. The =*expression* defines the initial value for the field. If the field is at least 7 bits wide, it is possible to use an ASCII character for *expression*. This *expression* must not contain a forward reference to any symbol.

Using Structure and Record Types

You can generate blocks of data bytes with many elements or fields by using structure and record declarations. A structure or record declaration consists of the name of a previously defined structure or record and a set of initial values.

Structure Declarations

Syntax: [*name*] *structurename* < [*initialvalue*,,,] >

Examples: STRUCTURE1   TABLE   < >
           STRUCTURE2   TABLE   <1,,>
           STRUCTURE3   TABLE 4 DUP(<7,,>)

A structure variable is a variable with one or more fields; if multiple, the fields can be different sizes. Optionally, it is possible to initialize all the fields in the structure. If you do not, MASM automatically uses the default initial value of the field which was originally determined by the structure. If not established with a default value, the field is uninitialized.

The optional *name* is the name of the variable. If it does not find a *name*, MASM allocates space for the structure, but does not create a name you can use to access the structure. *Structurename* is the name of a structure type created using the STRUC directive. *Initialvalue* is one or more values that define the initial value of the structure. Only one initial value can be given for each field in the structure. The *initialvalue* can be a string constant, an integer, or an expression that evaluates to a value having the same type as the corresponding field.

The angle brackets (< >) must be used even if you do not give an initial value. If coding more than one initial value, separate them with commas (,). If using the DUP operator, enclose the values within the parentheses in the angle brackets. You cannot initialize any structure field that has multiple values if this field has a default initial value from the structure definition.

Like other variables, structure variables can be accessed by name. Fields within structure variables can also be accessed by using the syntax shown below:

Syntax: *variable.field*

Examples:
```
date        STRUC
month       DB      ?
day         DB      ?
year        DB      ?
date        ENDS
            .DATA
yesterday   date    <4,16,42>   ; Declare structure
tomorrow    date    <6,18,36>   ; variables
today       date    <7,22,66>
            .CODE
            :
            :
            MOV     AL,yesterday.day
            MOV     AH,tomorrow.month
            MOV     tomorrow.year,DX
            MOV     BX,OFFSET yesterday
            MOV     AX,[BX].month
```

The *variable* must be the name of a structure (or an operand that resolves to the address of a structure). The *field* must be the name of a field within that structure. The *variable* is separated from *field* by a period (.). The address of a structure operand is the sum of the offsets of *variable* and *field*. The address is relative to the segment or group in which the variable is declared.

Record Variables

Syntax: [*name*] *recordname* < [*initialvalue,,,*] >

Examples: REC   ENCODE   < >
             Table   Item   4 DUP(<'Z',2>)
             PASS   ENCODE   <,,2>

A record variable is an 8- or 16-bit value (or 32-bit if the segment is a USE32 segment) whose bits are divided into one or more fields. The optional *name* is the name of the variable. If it does not find a name, MASM allocates space for the record, but does not create a variable that allows access of the record. *Recordname* is the name of a record type that has been created using the RECORD directive. The *initialvalue* is one or more values that defines the initial value of the record; only one *initialvalue* is allowed for each field in the record.

The optional *initialvalue* can be a string constant, an integer, or any expression that resolves to a value no larger than can be represented in the field width specified in the record definition. Use the angle brackets (< >) even if you do not code an initial value. If coding more than one initial value, separate the values with commas (,). If using the DUP operator, enclose only the values within the parentheses in the angle brackets. Optionally, it is possible to initialize all the fields in a record. If you do not, MASM automatically uses the default initial value of the field, which is defined by the record type. If a default value is not defined, the field is uninitialized.

For example, to create a variable named REC0, whose type is given by the record type ENCODE, do the following:

                    REC0   ENCODE   < >

The initial values of the fields in the record are set to the default values for the record type, if any.

Record operators MASK and WIDTH are discussed in chapter 7.

7

MASM
Operands, Operators,
and Expressions

SYNTAX REFERS TO THE RELATIONSHIP AMONG CHARACTERS OR GROUPS OF CHARACTERS, independent of their meanings and the manner of their interpretation. That is, syntax is the structure of expressions in a language and the rules governing that structure. This chapter describes the syntax and meanings used in MASM operands, operators, and expressions.

Operands are the arguments that define values to be acted on by instructions or directives. Operands can be constants, expressions, keywords, or expressions, depending on the instruction or directive and the context of the statement. A common type of operand is an expression. An *expression* consists of several operands that are combined to describe a value or memory location. Operators indicate the operations to be performed when combining the operands of an expression. By using expressions, you instruct MASM to calculate values that would be difficult or inconvenient to calculate when you write the source code. MASM evaluates expressions during assembly.

OPERANDS

An operand is the fundamental quantity on which a mathematical operation is performed. Usually, an assembly language statement consists of an operator and an operand. The operator indicates an instruction such as ADD and the operand indicates what is to be added. When you work with MASM, you work with operands that are constants, labels, variables, or other symbols that are used in an instruction or directive to represent a value, register, or memory location to be acted upon.

There is a listing in appendix G that shows some additional examples of the various operands described in this chapter. The listing is not a working program. It was written to show directives that work and, almost as important, directives that do not work. If you need a refresher on the 80386 architectural concepts, see appendix H.

Each directive requires a specific type of operand. Most directives take string or numeric constants, or symbols, or expressions that evaluate to such constants. The type of operand varies for each directive, but the operand must always evaluate to a value that is known at assembly time. This differs from instructions, whose operands might not be known at assembly time and might vary at run time.

Some directives, such as those used in data declarations, accept labels or variables as operands. When a symbol that refers to a memory location is used as an operand to a directive, the symbol represents the address of the symbol rather than its contents.

Based Operands

Syntax:
    displacement [BP]
    displacement [BX]
    displacement [Exx]
    where xx is any general register

Alternate Forms:
    [*displacement*][BP]
    [BP + *displacement*]
    [BP].*displacement*
    [BP] + *displacement*

Examples:
    MOV AX,[BX]
    mov cx,[bp] + 16
    MOV BX,32[ECX]

In the 80286 mode, there are two base registers around which the based operands work: BP and BX. In the 80386 mode, it is possible to use any 32-bit general register as a base. If programming in a USE16 mode, ensure that address computation does not exceed 16 bits. A based operand represents a memory address relative to one of these base registers. The *displacement* can be any immediate or direct-memory operand that must evaluate to an absolute number or memory address (see appendix B for the 80386 instruction set). If MASM does not find a *displacement*, it assumes zero. The effective address of a based operand is the sum of the displacement value and the contents of the given register. For BP, the operand address is relative to the segment pointed to by the SS (stack segment) register. For BX, the relative address is based on the DS register.

Based-Indexed Operands

Syntax:
    displacement [BP][SI]
    displacement [BP][DI]
    displacement [BX][SI]
    displacement [BX][DI]

Alternate Form: *[displacement]*[BP][DI]
                 [BP + DI + *displacement]*
                 [BP + DI] + *displacement*
                 [BP] + *displacement* + [DI]
                 [BP + DI].*displacement*

Examples: MOV   EAX,[BP][SI]

A based-indexed operand represents a memory address relative to a combination of base and index registers. The *displacement* can be any immediate or direct-memory operand and must evaluate to an absolute number or memory address. Zero is assumed if MASM does not find a *displacement*. The effective address of a based-indexed operand is the sum of the displacement value and the contents of the base and index registers. If BP is used, the address is relative to the segment pointed to by SS; otherwise, the address is relative to the segment pointed to by DS.

Note that either base register can be combined with either index register; an error occurs if two base or two index registers are combined.

Constant Operands

Syntax: *number|string|expression*

Examples: MOV   EAX,100h
             add   al,40
             MOV   AH,'p'

A constant is a value which remains unchanged during a calculation. It is convenient to refer to constants by their values, since these are what is meaningful in an algorithm. All computer languages are structured to allow the inclusion of actual values, specified directly in the program rather than being read by the program as data. The most common constant is a numerical constant. In MASM, constant operands, unlike other operands, represent values to be acted on, rather than memory addresses. There are a variety of different types of constants: numerical, character, logical, and location.

Numeric constants can be represented in several ways. The first, and most common, is the integer. A second, similar to scientific notation, is particularly useful for expressing very large or very small values. Instead of writing long strings of zeros to establish an order of magnitude for a number, the same value can be designated more concisely by showing only the significant digits in a convenient form. For instance, the constant 0.00000543 can be expressed as 5.43E-06 or 0.543E-5.

A *character constant* is an arbitrary combination of letters, digits, and other symbols; it is treated in the same manner as a numerical constant. That is, it remains the same throughout its use within a program.

There are countless occasions that require explicit references to specific statements. This is done by allowing a distinctive label (location constant) to be attached to a statement, which establishes an identity that is fixed within the context of the program. This identity remains, no matter where the statement resides in storage. In this sense, such labels are constants and references to them are direct.

Direct-Memory Operands

Syntax: *segment:offset*

Examples: MOV   EBX,DATA:0
                    mov   eax,agroup:block1

A direct-memory operand is a pair of segment and offset values that represent an absolute memory register, which can be one or more bytes of memory. When using direct-memory operands, the *segment* can be a segment register (CS, DS, SS, ES, FS, or GS), a segment name, or a group name. The *offset* must be an absolute symbol, an integer, or an expression that resolves to a value within the range of 00 to 0FFFF for a USE16 segment, or 00 to 0FFFFFFFF for a USE32 segment.

Indexed Operands

Syntax: *displacement*[DI]
                               displacement[SI]

Alternate Forms: [*displacement*][DI]
                               [DI] + *displacement*
                               [DI + *displacement*]
                               [DI].*displacement*

Examples: MOV   EAX,[SI]
                              mov   ecx,[di]
                              MOV   EAX,[DI] + 8

An index is a number that represents the relative position of an entity in a record, a file, or memory. Indexed addressing refers to a procedure where data for an instruction is pointed to by the contents of an index register, plus an offset value within a segment.

In the 80386, using MASM, an indexed operand represents a memory address relative to one of the index registers: DI or SI. The *displacement* can be any immediate or direct-memory operand and must evaluate to an absolute number or memory address. Zero is assumed if MASM does not find a *displacement*. The effective address of an indexed operand is the sum of the displacement value and the contents of the given register. The address is relative to the segment pointed to by DS.

Location-Counter Operand

Syntax: $

Example: COUNT EQU $

Used during assembly, the location counter is a special operand that represents the current location within the current segment. This location counter has the same attributes as a NEAR label. Its offset is equal to the number of bytes generated for that segment to that point of the program. Also, it represents an instruction address, relative to the current segment. After each statement in the segment has been assembled, MASM increments the location counter by the number of bytes generated.

Record Operands

Syntax: *recordname*   < [*value*],,, >

Examples: ENCODE   HI:4, MID:3, LO:3
             REC01   ENCODE <3,2,1>
                         MOV   AX,REC01

A record operand refers to the value of a record type and the operands can be in the expressions. The *recordname* must be the name of a record type defined in the source file. The optional *value* is the value of one of the fields in the record. If entering more than one *value*, separate each value with a comma (,). *Value* can include expressions or symbols that evaluate to constants. The enclosing angle brackets (< >) are required, even if no value appears. If MASM does not find a value in the brackets, the default for that value is used. Defaults are defined in the record definitions on a field by field basis by following the field definition with + default.

Record-Field Operands

Syntax: *record-fieldname*: width[= *value*]

Examples: field1: 18 = 03FFFFX

A record-field operand represents the location of a field in its corresponding record, after the record is first specified. The operand evaluates to the bit position of the low-order bit in the field and can be used as a constant operand. The *record-fieldname* must be the name of a previously defined record field.

Register Operands

Syntax: *registername*

Examples: SUB   EAX,EBX
            add   ebx,10h

A *register operand* is any of the CPU registers. These operands direct instructions to carry out actions on the contents of the given registers. Figure 7-1 shows the registers that can be used, and any combination of upper- and lower-case letters is allowed.

The EAX, EBX, ECX, and EDX registers are 32-bit, general-purpose registers. AX, BX, CX, and DX, respectively, are 16-bit, general-purpose registers that are in the low-order 16 bits of the 32-bit registers. Use any of these registers (and the byte registers that make them up, such as AH and AL) for any data or numerical manipulation.

CS, DS, SS, and ES are segment registers that have been with the Intel microprocessors from the 8086 on. Two segment registers, FS and GS, are new with the 80386. CS contains the current code segment address, DS the current data segment, SS the current stack segment, and ES the extra segment. Consider FS and GS as additional extra segment registers. All instructions and data addresses are relative to the segment address selected by the descriptor value in one of these registers.

The 80386 has four 16-bit registers that can be used as base and index registers: BX, BP, DI and SI. You can use them for pointers to program data. Address expressions using BP have offsets in the SS segment by default. Expressions using BX, DI, or SI have offsets in the DS segment by default. DI always has an offset in the ES segment when used with string instructions. Check appendices B and C (80386 and 80387 instruction sets) to determine which registers are used with the various instructions.

Finally, there is the EFLAGS register (see Fig. 7-2), which contains bit flags that are used to control the system with instructions such as LAHF, SAHF, PUSHF, and POPF. (Note that certain of the bits are indicated as reserved by Intel. Do not use these bits because their meaning can change with new releases from the manufacturer.) The 32-bit general registers use DS by default.

Relocatable Operands

Syntax: *symbol*

Examples: MOV   ECX,THIS__ONE
            call   bcdadd

The EAX, EBX, ECX, and EDX registers are 32-bit, general-purpose registers.

A *relocatable operand* is any symbol that represents the memory address (segment and offset) of an instruction, or of data to be acted upon. Unlike direct-memory operands, relocatable operands are relative to the start of the segment or group in which the symbol is defined. They have no explicit value until the program is linked.

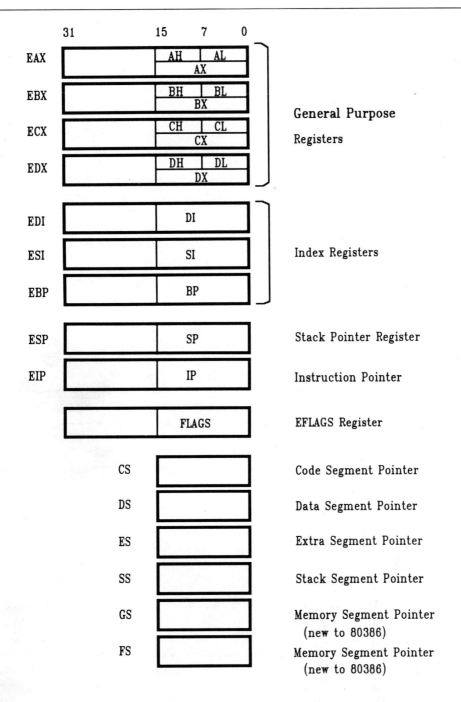

Fig. 7-1. CPU Registers for Register Operands.

```
0000                          data      SEGMENT para
0000  00000000                data32    dd      0              ; a 32 bit data area
0004  0000                    data16    dw      0              ; a 16 bit data area
0006  00                      data8     db      0              ; an 8 bit data area
                              ;
                                           .
                                           .
                                           .

                              ; Registers as operands
                              ;
001B  B1 20                             mov     CL,32          ; 8 bit register as destination
001D  67| 88 0D 00000006 R             mov     data8,CL       ; and as source operand.
0024  8A E1                            mov     AH,CL          ; 8 bit registers as both

0026  67| 8B 35 00000004 R            mov     SI,data16      ; 16 bit register destination
002D  67| 89 25 00000004 R            mov     data16,SP      ; and source operands.
0034  8B F8                           mov     DI,AX          ; 16 bit registers as both.
                              ;
0036  67| 66| 8B 2D 0000             mov     EBP,data32     ; 32 bit register destination
      0000 R
003E  67| 66| 89 15 0000             mov     data32,EDX     ; and source operands.
      0000 R
0046  66| 8B F1                      mov     ESI,ECX        ; 32 bit registers as both.
```

Fig. 7-1. (continued).

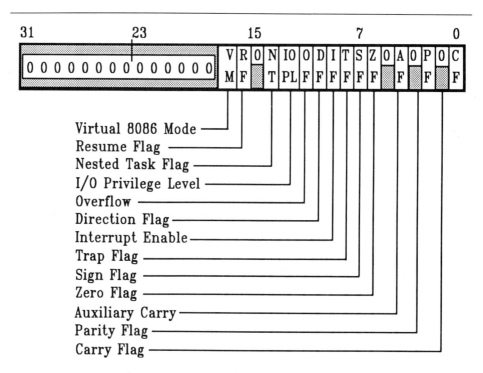

Note: Zero bits (shown by the shaded ares) are Intel reserved.
Do not define in your programs.

Fig. 7-2. EFLAGS Register.

Structure Operands

Syntax: *variable.field*

Example:

```
DATE      STRUC
MONTH     DW ?
DAY       DW ?
YEAR      DW ?
DATE      ENDS
This_date date          <'Ja', '01','89'>
MOV                 EAX,DWORD PTR  This_date.day
```

A structure operand represents the memory address of one member of a structure. A *variable* must be either the name of a structure or a memory operand that resolves to the address of a structure. The *field* must be the name of a field within that structure. Note that the *variable* is separated from the *field* by a structure field-name operator of a period (.). The effective address of a structure operand is the sum of the offsets of *variable* and *field*. This address is relative to the segment or group in which the variable is defined.

OPERATORS AND EXPRESSIONS

An *operator* is a symbol that represents an operation to be performed on one or more operands. It is the character or characters that designate mathematical or logical operations, such as +, −, and so on. An expression is a combination of operands and operators that evaluates to a single value. The result of an expression can be a value or a memory location, depending on what type of operand and operators are used.

It is important to understand the difference between operators and instructions. Operators handle calculations of constant values that are known at assembly time. Instructions handle calculations of values that might not be known until run time. For example, the addition operator (+) handles assembly-time addition, while ADD and ADC instructions handle run-time addition.

MASM provides the following operators: arithmetic, shift, relational, and bit operators. They combine, compare, change, analyze, and manipulate the values of operands. Some operators work with integer constants, some with memory values, and some with both. Operators cannot be used with floating-point constants because MASM does not recognize real numbers in expressions. A special kind of operator, attribute operators, manipulate the attributes of operands, such as their size, address, and type.

Expressions are evaluated according to the rules of operator precedence and order. Operations of highest precedence are performed first, second precedence second, and so on. This default order can be overridden by using enclosing parentheses because operations in parentheses are always performed before any adjacent operations. Figure 7-3 shows the order of precedence. Otherwise, operations of equal precedence are performed left to right.

Operators	Order of Precedence	
LENGTH, SIZE, WIDTH	1	HIGHEST
MASK, (), [],<>		
. (Structure Field–name Operator)	2	
:	3	
PTR, OFFSET, SEG, TYPE, THIS	4	
HIGH, LOW	5	
+, − (unary)	6	
*, /, MOD, SHL, SHR	7	
+, − (binary)	8	
EQ, GE, GT, LE, LT, NE	9	
NOT	10	
AND	11	
OR, XOR	12	
SHORT, .TYPE	13	LOWEST

Fig. 7-3. Order of Precedence.

A forward reference is any use of a name before it has been declared; for instance, a jump to a label before it has been declared. MASM allows forward references to labels, variable names, segment names, and other symbols. Such references can lead to assembly errors if not used correctly. Whenever MASM finds an undefined name in pass 1, it assumes that the name is a forward reference. If it finds only a name, MASM makes assumptions about that name type and segment register and uses these assumptions to generate code or data for the statements. For instance, on a JMP without any other specification, MASM generates three bytes of instruction code for the instruction.

MASM bases its forward reference assumptions on the statement that contains the reference. Errors occur when these assumptions are incorrect. If the JMP discussed above is actually a FAR label, it causes a phase error. That is, MASM needs to generate five bytes of instruction code for the JMP instruction in pass 2 but only allocated three bytes in pass 1. To avoid forward reference errors, use the segment override (:), PTR, and SHORT operators (described below) to override MASMs assumption. Use the following guidelines:

- If the forward reference is a segment name with a segment-override operator (:), use the GROUP statement to associate the segment name with a group name. Then use the ASSUME statement to associate the group name with a segment register. See chapter 8 for GROUP and ASSUME.

- If the forward reference is a variable that is relative to the CS, ES, or SS registers, use the segment-override to specify the variable segment, register, or group. If it does not find a segment-override operator, MASM assumes that the variable is relative to DS.

- If a forward reference is an instruction label in a CALL or JMP instruction, use the PTR operator to specify the label type. MASM assumes that the label has a NEAR type, so PTR need not be used for NEAR labels. If the label is a FAR type, and you do not use FAR PTR, a phase error results.

- If the forward reference is an instruction label in a JMP instruction, use the SHORT operator if the instruction is less than 128 bytes from the point of reference. If it does not find SHORT, MASM assumes that the instruction is further than 128 bytes away. This does not cause an error, but it does cause MASM to generate an extra, and unnecessary, NOP instruction.

MASM carries out strict syntax checks for all instruction statements, including strong typing for operands that refer to memory locations. That means that if you use relocatable operands in an instruction that operates on an implied data type, they must either have that type or have an explicit type override (the PTR operator—see below). As a warning, many assembly-language programs found in magazines are written for assemblers with weak operand typing. These programs may produce error messages such as ''Illegal size for item'' or ''Operand types must match'' when assembled with MASM. Correct these lines by using the PTR operator and assign the correct size to variables.

Arithmetic Operators

Syntax: *operator1 *operator2*
            operator1/operator2
            operator1MODoperator2
            operator1 + operator2
            operator1 – operator2
            + expression
            – expression

Examples: 16 * 4
16 / 4
16 MOD 4
16 + 4
16 − 4
figure1 + figure2

Arithmetic operators provide the common mathematical operations. The operators are + (positive, unary), − (negative, unary), * (multiplication), / (integer division), MOD (remainder after division, modulus), MOD (remainder, modulus), + (addition), and − (subtraction). The unary plus and minus that are used to designate positive or negative numbers are not the same as the binary plus and minus used to designate addition or subtraction. The unary plus and minus have a higher level of precedence. In these operators, for all arithmetic operators except + and −, *expression1* and *expression2* must be integers. It is possible to use the + operator to add an integer number to a relocatable memory operand; in the same manner, you can use the − operator to subtract an integer number from a memory operand. Also, the − operator can be used to subtract one memory operand from another, but only if the operands refer to locations within the same segment; the result is an absolute value.

Bitwise Operators

Syntax: *expression1* AND *expression2*
expression1 OR *expression2*
expression1 XOR *expression2*
NOT *expression*

Examples: 01010101b AND 11110011b
NOT 00001111b
11110000b OR 11110011b
11110000b XOR 11110011b

Logical operators perform logical operations on each bit of the expressions. The operation is performed on each bit in an expression rather than on the expression as a whole. These expressions must resolve to absolute values. Note that, although calculations on expressions using AND, OR, and XOR operators are done using 17-bit numbers (32-bit with the 80386), the results are truncated to 16 bits (32 with the 80386).

It is easy to confuse the AND, NOT, OR, and XOR operators with the 80386 instructions having the same name. However, the operators work on integer constants only at assembly time, and the processor instructions work on register or memory values at run time. MASM can tell the difference between operands and instructions from context.

HIGH and LOW Operators

Syntax: HIGH   *expression*
             LOW   *expression*

Examples: MOV   CH,HIGH THIS__WORD
            mov   al,LOW 0FFCDh

HIGH returns the high-order 8 bits of *expression*. LOW returns the low-order 8 bits. *Expression* can be any value. You cannot use the HIGH and LOW operators on the contents of a memory operand since the contents may change at run time. The HIGH and LOW operators work reliably only with constants and with offsets to external symbols. HIGH and LOW operations are not supported for offsets to local symbols.

Index Operator

Syntax: [*expression1*] '['*expression2*']'

Examples: MOV AL,STRING[2]
            mov   bh,array[5]
            mov   string[first],ah

The index operator ([ ]) adds the value of *expression2* to *expression1*. The single quotes outside the brackets of *expression2* show that, if coding *expression2*, you must use brackets (see the syntax above). The index operator is identical to the + operator, except that *expression1* is optional. If using *expression1*, code the expression on the left of the operator. *Expression1* can be any integer value, absolute symbol, or relocatable operand. If MASM does not find *expression1*, it assumes the integer value 0. If *expression1* is a relocatable operand, *expression2* must be an integer value or absolute symbol. Otherwise, *expression2* can be any integer value, absolute symbol, or relocatable operand. The index operator is typically used to index elements of an array, such as individual characters in a character string.

LENGTH Operator

Syntax: LENGTH *variable*

Examples: In the following examples, assume:
table DW 100 DUP (1,10 DUP(?))
ARRAY1 DW 100 DUP(1)

```
MOV CX,LENGTH array1 ; returns 100
mov  cx,LENGTH table   ; returns 100
```

LENGTH returns the number of BYTE, WORD, DWORD, QWORD, or TBYTE elements in the *variable*. The size of each element depends on how the variable is defined. Only variables defined using DUP return values that are greater than 1. In nested DUP operators, the returned value is always the number preceding the first DUP operator.

MASK Operator

Syntax: MASK {*recordfieldname|record*}

Examples: In the examples below, assume the record definition and record declaration—

```
rtype   RECORD   field1:3,field2:6,field3:7
rec1    rtype        < >

m1    = MASK field1   ; Equals E000h
m2    = MASK field2   ; Equals 1F80h
m3    = MASK field3   ; Equals 007Fh
mrec  = MASK rtype    ; Equals 0FFFFh
```

The *recordfieldname* can be the name of any field in a previously defined record. The *record* can be the name of any previously defined record. The NOT operator is sometimes used with the MASK operator to reverse the bits of a mask.

MASK returns a bit mask for the bit positions of a record occupied by the given record field. A bit in the mask contains a 1 if that bit corresponds to a field bit. All other bits contain 0. (See also Fig. 7-5.) Both MASK and WIDTH (explained in this chapter) are used exclusively with records to return constant values that represent different aspects of previously declared records.

OFFSET Operator

Syntax: OFFSET *expression*

Examples: MOV EBX,OFFSET Count_Date
mov ecx,OFFSET agroup:array

OFFSET returns the offset address of an *expression*. The *expression* can be any variable, label, segment name, or other direct memory operand. The returned value is the number of bytes between the item and the beginning of the segment in which it is defined. For a segment name, the returned value is the offset from the start of the segment to the most recent byte generated for that segment.

It is possible to use the segment-override operator (:) to force OFFSET to return the number of bytes between the item in *expression* and the beginning of a named segment or group. This is the method used to generate valid offsets for items in a group.

If simplified segment directives are given, the returned value varies. If the item is declared in a near data segment, the returned value is the number of bytes between the item and the beginning of its group (normally DGROUP). If the item is declared in a far segment, the returned value is the number of bytes between the item and the beginning of the segment. If full segment definitions are given, the returned value is a memory operand equal to the number of bytes between the item and the beginning of the segment in which it is defined.

PTR Operator

Syntax: *type* PTR *expression*

Examples: CALL FAR PTR SUBROUT__X
             ADD AH,BYTE PTR [BYTE__VALUE]
             mov BYTE PTR [array],1

With the PTR operator, any operand can be the *expression*. The operator forces *expression* to be treated as having *type*. The *type* can be BYTE, WORD, DWORD, FWORD, QWORD, or TBYTE for memory operands. It can be NEAR, FAR, or PROC for labels. Figure 7-4 shows the various *types* and their values which can be used. The PTR operator is typically used with forward references to explicitly define what size or distance a reference has. If MASM does not find a PTR, it assumes a default size or distance for the reference. PTR is also used to enable instruction to access variables in ways that would otherwise generate errors. For instance, use PTR to access the high-order byte of a WORD size variable.

The PTR operator can be used to specify the size of a register indirect operand for a CALL or JMP instruction. However, the size cannot be specified with NEAR or FAR; use WORD or DWORD instead. In 80386 32-bit segments, use DWORD or FWORD. For example:
With 8086, 80286, or 80386 16-bit mode—

```
        JMP     WORD PTR [BX]      ; Legal NEAR jump
        CALL    NEAR PTR [BX]      ; Illegal NEAR call
        CALL    DWORD PTR [BX]     ; Legal FAR call
        JMP     FAR PTR [BX]       ; Illegal FAR jump
```

With 80386 32-bit mode only—

```
        JMP     DWORD PTR [BX]     ; Legal NEAR jump
        CALL    NEAR PTR [BX]      ; Illegal NEAR jump
        CALL    FWORD PTR [BX]     ; Legal FAR call
        JMP     FAR PTR [BX]       ; Illegal FAR jump
```

This limitation only applies to register-indirect operands. NEAR or FAR can be applied to operands associated with labels. For example:

```
        JMP     NEAR PTR pointer[BX]
        CALL    FAR PTR location
```

PTR Type	Value
BYTE	1
WORD	2
DWORD	4
QWORD	8
TBYTE	10
NEAR	OFFFFh
FAR	OFFFEh

```
70                          ; Examples of the use of label to allow access to an area using
71                          ; different types for the same area.
72
73                          ;
74 0007    bytelabel  LABEL   BYTE    ; Refer as byte type,
75 0007    wordtype   LABEL   WORD    ; word type,
76 0007    dwordtype  LABEL   DWORD   ; and as double word type.
77                          ;

526                         ; Use of labels defined as examples of use of the LABEL directive.
527                         ;
528                         ;
529 001B  8A 26 0007 R           mov    AH,bytelabel   ; As a byte,
530 001F  A1 0007 R              mov    AX,wordtype    ; a word, and
531 0022  66| A1 0007 R          mov    EAX,dwordtype  ; a double word.
```

Fig. 7-4. Types and Values of PTR Operators.

Relational Operators

Syntax: *expression1* EQ *expression2*
            expression1 GE *expression2*
            expression1 GT *expression2*
            expression1 LE *expression2*
            expression1 LT *expression2*
            expression1 NE *expression2*

Examples: 1 EQ 0   ; False
            1 GE 0   ; True
            1 GT 0   ; True
            1 LE 0   ; False
            1 LT 0   ; False
            1 NE 0   ; True

Relational operators compare *expression1* and *expression2* and return TRUE (0FFFFh) if the condition specified by the operator is satisfied or FALSE (0000h) if it is·not. The expressions must resolve to constant values and are shown in Fig. 7-5.

Relational Operator	Returned Value
EQ	True (0FFFh) – if expressions are equal
GE	True (0FFFh) – if left expression is greater or equal to the right expression
GT	True (0FFFh) – If left expression is greater than right
LE	True (0FFFh) – if left expression is less than or equal to the right expression
LT	True (0FFFh) – if left expression is less than the right expression
NE	True (0FFFh) – if expressions are not equal

Fig. 7-5. Relational Operators and Values.

Relational operators typically are used with conditional directives and conditional instructions to direct program control. The EQ and NE operators treat their arguments as 16-bit numbers. Numbers specified with the 16th bit on are considered negative

(0FFFFh is −1). Therefore, the expression 01 EQ 0FFFFh is true while the expression 01 NE 0FFFFh is false. GE, GT, LE, and LT operators treat their arguments as 17-bit numbers, where the 17th bit specifies the sign. In this case, 0FFFFh is the largest positive unsigned number (65535); it is not −1. The expression 1 GT −1 is true (0FFFFh), while the expression 1 GT 0FFFFh is false (0).

SEG Operator

Syntax: SEG *operator*

Examples: MOV CX,SEG THIS__VARIABLE
               mov cx,SEG label__name

SEG returns the segment descriptor value of *expression*. This *expression* can be any variable, label, group name, segment name, or other memory operand. The returned value can be used as a memory operand. SEG cannot be used with constant expressions.

Segment-Override Operator

Syntax: *segmentregister:expression*
             segmentname:expression
             groupname:expression

Examples: MOV   AX,ES:[BX][SI]
               mov   al,cs:0001h
               MOV   THIS__TEXT:FAR__LABEL,AX

The segment-override operator (:) forces the address of a given variable or label to be computed using the beginning of the given *segmentregister*, *segmentname*, or *groupname*. If using either *segmentname* or *groupname*, you must have assigned the name to a segment register with a previous ASSUME directive and defined it using a SEGMENT or GROUP directive. (See chapter 8 for SEGMENT and GROUP.)

The *expression* can be an absolute symbol or relocatable operand. The *segmentregister* must be CS, DS, ES, SS, FS, or GS, depending on the instruction and operand type. Also, all labels are assumed to be NEAR. It is possible to override these default types using the segment-override operator.

When you give a segment override with an indexed operand, the segment must be specified outside the index operators. For example, es:[di] is correct, but [es:di] generates an error.

SHORT Operator

Syntax: SHORT *label*

Examples: JMP   SHORT THIS__LABEL
             jmp   SHORT another__place

SHORT sets the type of a given *label* to SHORT. SHORT labels are appropriate in jump (JMP) instructions whenever the distance from the label to the instruction is less than 128 bytes (127 or fewer). Instructions that use SHORT labels are one byte smaller than identical instructions using the default NEAR label.

SHR and SHL Operators

Syntax: *expression* SHR *count*
              expression SHL *count*

Examples: MOV EAX,01110111b SHL 3
             SHR AH,01110111b SHR 2

SHR and SHL operators shift expression right and left by the *count* number of bits. Bits are shifted off the end of the expression and are lost. If the count is greater than or equal to 32, the result is 0. The bits will be shifted by 8 or 16 bits, depending on whether the value being shifted is a byte or a word. These operators are not to be confused with the 80386 instruction set SHR and SHL, which have the same names. Although the effect is the same, these SHL/SHR operators take effect on data at assembly time. The 80386 SHL and SHR instructions take effect on data at run time.

SIZE Operator

Syntax: SIZE *variable*

Example: MOV BX,SIZE ARRAY1

SIZE returns the total number of bytes allocated for an array or variable defined with the DUP operator. The returned value is equal to the value of LENGTH times the value of TYPE. If the variable was declared with nested DUP operators, only the value given for the outside DUP operator is considered. If the variable was not declared with DUP, the value returned is always TYPE *variable*. Assuming that:

      ARRAY1 DW 100 DUP(1)

in the above example,

      MOV BX,SIZE ARRAY1

SIZE returns 200.

Structure Field-Name Operator

Syntax: *variable.field*

Examples: INC   MONTH.DAY
            mov   [bx].destination
            mov   time.min,0

Use the structure field-name operator (.) to designate a field within a structure. The *variable* is an operand, often a previously declared structure variable. The *field* is the name of a field within that structure. This operator is equivalent to the addition operator (+) in based or indexed operands.

THIS Operator

Syntax: THIS *type*

Examples: Tag EQU THIS BYTE
            check = THIS NEAR

The THIS operator creates an operand whose offset and segment values are equal to the current location-counter value and whose type is specified by the operator. The *type* can be BYTE, WORD, DWORD, FWORD, QWORD, or TBYTE for memory operands. It can be NEAR, FAR or PROC for labels. THIS is typically used with EQU or equal sign (=) directive to create labels or variables. This use is similar to using the LABEL directive to create labels and variables.

The example:

      Tag EQU THIS BYTE

is equivalent to the statement

      Tag LABEL BYTE

The example:

      check = THIS NEAR

is equivalent to

      check LABEL NEAR

TYPE Operator

Syntax: TYPE *expression*

Examples: MOV   EAX,TYPE array
            JMP   (TYPE get_this) PTR destiny

TYPE returns a number that represents the type of an *expression*. If *expression* evaluates to a variable, TYPE returns the size of the operand in bytes. Each byte in a string is considered a separate data object, so TYPE returns a 1 for strings. If *expression* is a label, TYPE returns 0FFFFh if the label is NEAR and 0FFFEh if the label is FAR. If *expression* evaluates to a structure or structure variable, TYPE returns the number of bytes in the structure. Note that the returned value can be used to specify the type for a PTR operator.

.TYPE Operator

Syntax: .TYPE *expression*

Examples: x   DB   12
            y   EQU .TYPE x

.TYPE returns a byte that defines the mode and scope of *expression*. If *expression* is not valid, .TYPE returns a 0; otherwise .TYPE returns a byte having bits 0, 1, 5, and 7 affected. If both the scope bit and defined bits are zero, *expression* is not valid. Figure 7-6 shows the .TYPE operator and variable attributes.

Bit Position	If Bit = 0	If Bit = 1
0	Not program related	Program related
1	Not data related	Data related
5	Not defined	Defined
7	Local or Public scope	External scope

Fig. 7-6. .TYPE Operator and Variable Attributes.

.TYPE is typically used with conditional directives, where an argument may need to be tested in order to make a decision regarding program flow.

Warning: If you originally had MASM 5.0 and ordered the update to 5.1, your reference manual indicates that bits 2, 3, and 4 were now assigned. However, if you

simply ordered 5.1 straight (as we did for our second system) and did not pay for th
update step (which we did for our first system), these bits show the same assignments
as in 5.0. As best we can determine, these bits are assigned, but the official 5.1 release
does not document them. So, do not use the bits until this is resolved.

WIDTH Operator

Syntax: WIDTH {*recordfieldname*|*record*}

Examples: In the examples below, assume the following record definition and
             record declaration—
             rtype RECORD field1:3,field2:6,field3:7

```
wid1    =  WIDTH field1   ; Equals 3
wid2    =  WIDTH field2   ; Equals 6
wid3    =  WIDTH field3   ; Equals 7
widrec  =  WIDTH rtype    ; Equals 16
```

WIDTH returns the width (in bits) of the given record field or record. The
recordfieldname must be the name of a field defined in a record. *Record* must be the
name of a record. Both WIDTH and MASK (explained earlier in this chapter) are used
exclusively with records to return constant values that represent different aspects of
previously declared records. Note that the width of a field is the number of bits assigned
for that field. The value of the field is the starting position (from the right) of the field.

8

MASM Program Structure and File-Control Directives

EACH PROGRAM HAS A STRUCTURE THAT DEFINES THE PROGRAM ORGANIZATION. THAT organization specifies where the program begins and ends, what registers and segments it uses, and how subpieces are included. Those subpieces are modules that can be defined as logically self-contained and discrete parts of a larger program.

The purpose of modular programming is to break a complex task into smaller and simpler subtasks, which facilitates writing and testing. To reduce the complexity of a program, restrict the interactions between parts of a program to the interactions between modules. Good program design starts with the most general definition of the function of the program and proceeds through a sequence of increasingly detailed specifications. This technique, top-down design, is an aspect of structured programming and is greatly enhanced by modular programming. See chapter 5, which describes top-down design.

PROGRAM-STRUCTURE DIRECTIVES

Among other things, MASM program-structure directives allow the specification of segment registers, the alignment of data or instruction bytes, the association of a group name with one or more segments, and the setting of the location counter. Also, they let you set the boundaries of your code by specifying a procedure beginning and ending, along with telling MASM where your code ends. For ease of finding them, the program-structure directives are listed in alphabetical order. See the listing in appendix G for additional examples of the structure directives.

This chapter discusses program-structure directives. If you want to look at how to specify simplified or full segment definitions in general, there is a section in chapter 11 that discusses that subject.

ALIGN—Aligning Data

Syntax: ALIGN *number*

Example: ALIGN 4

Some operations are more efficient when the variable used in the operation is lined up on a boundary of a particular size. Use the ALIGN and EVEN (described below) to pad the object file so that the next variable is aligned on a specific boundary.

ALIGN aligns on the next byte that is a multiple of *number*. The *number* must be a power of two. For example, use ALIGN 4 to align on doubleword boundaries and ALIGN 2 (or EVEN) to align on word boundaries. If the location counter value is not on the specified boundary when ALIGN is encountered, the location counter is incremented to a value on the boundary. MASM generates NOP (no operations) instructions to pad the object file. The directive has no effect if the location counter is already on the boundary.

ALIGN and EVEN give no efficiency improvements on the 8088 or 80188 (or any processor with an 8-bit data bus). These processors always fetch data one byte at a time, regardless of the alignment. Using EVEN can speed certain operations on on processors that have a 16-bit data bus, such as the 8086, 80186, and 80286; these processors can fetch a word if the data is word aligned but must do two memory fetches if the data is not word aligned. EVEN should not be used in segments with BYTE align type. Similarly, the number specified with ALIGN should at least be equal to the size of the align type of the segment where the directive is given.

Padding for EVEN and ALIGN is now optimized. Data segments are padded with zeros. Code segments are padded with special two-byte NOP instructions where possible. The two-byte NOP consists of the instruction XCHG BX,BX, which is executed faster than two one-byte NOP instructions.

ASSUME—Segment Registers

Syntax: ASSUME *segmentregister:segmentname,,,*
                 ASSUME *segmentregister*: NOTHING
                 ASSUME NOTHING

Examples: ASSUME CS:CODE
                 ASSUME cs:cgroup,ds:dgroup,ss:nothing
                 ASSUME NOTHING

The ASSUME directive specifies the default segment register *segmentregister* for all labels and variables that are defined in the segment or group given by the *segmentname*. Any subsequent references to the label or variable automatically assumes the selected register when the effective address is computed. ASSUME can define up to six selections, one for each of the six segment registers. *Segmentregister* can be any one of the segment register names: CS, DS, ES, SS, FS and GS. *Segmentname* must be one of the following:

• The keyword NOTHING. This keyword cancels the current segment selection and cancels all register selections made by a previous ASSUME statement.

• A string equate that evaluates to a segment or group name, but not a string equate that evaluates to a SEG expression.

• The name of a segment that was previously defined with the SEGMENT directive.

• The name of a group that was previously defined with the GROUP directive. See below for GROUP.

• A SEG expression.

It is possible to use the segment-override operator (:) to override the current segment register selected by the ASSUME directive.

END—Source File End

Syntax: END [*startaddress*]

Example: END

All source files have zero or more program pieces followed by an END. For instance, a source file that contains only macros might have zero pieces. The END signals the end of the source file and provides a way to define the program entry point or starting address. MASM ignores any statements following the END.

The expression defines the program entry point, that is, the address at which program execution is to start. If the program has more than one module, only one of these modules can define an entry point and that module is called the main module. If an entry point is not specified, none is assumed and the program may not be able to initialize correctly. That program could assemble and link without error messages, but it would probably come to an abnormal ending (abend) when you attempted to run it.

The CS segment is initialized to the value of *startaddress*. The IP register is normally initialized to 0. It is possible to change the initial value of the IP register by using the ORG directive (see below) just before the *startaddress* label. If a program consists of a single source module, then *startaddress* is required for that module. If a program has several modules, all modules must terminate with an END but only one of them can define a *startaddress*.

ENDP—Procedure End

Syntax: ENDP
                    label   ENDP

Examples: ENDP
                    THISPROC   ENDP

This directive marks the end of a procedure and works in conjunction with the PROC directive; every PROC must have an ending ENDP. There can be any number of procedures in a program. Procedures can be assembled separately and brought together during LINK. The *label* is the name used in the PROC statement.

ENDS—Segment End

Syntax: ENDS
           label   ENDS

Examples: ENDS
          CODE1 ENDS

The ENDS directive marks the end of a program segment. It works in conjunction with the SEGMENT directive. The *label* is the same name as started the segment.

EVEN—Segment Alignment

Syntax: EVEN

Example: EVEN

EVEN aligns the next data or instruction byte on a word boundary. If the current value of the location counter is odd, the directive increments the location counter to an even value and generates one NOP (no operation) instruction. If the counter is already even, the directive does nothing.

ALIGN and EVEN give no efficiency improvements on the 8088 or 80188 (or any processor with an 8-bit data bus). These processors always fetch data one byte at a time, regardless of the alignment. Using EVEN can speed certain operations on processors that have a 16-bit data bus, such as the 8086, 80186, and 80286; these processors can fetch a word if the data is word aligned but must do two memory fetches if the data is not word aligned. EVEN should not be used in segments with BYTE align type. Similarly, the *number* specified with ALIGN should be at least equal to the size of the align type of the segment where the directive is given.

Padding for EVEN and ALIGN is now optimized. Data segments are padded with zeros. Code segments are padded with special two-byte NOP instructions where possible. The two-byte NOP consists of the instruction XCHG BX,BX, which is executed faster than two one-byte NOP instructions.

GROUP—Segment Groups

Syntax: *name* GROUP *segmentname,,,*

Examples: dgroup GROUP aseg,bseg,cseg
           ASSUME edx:dgroup

GROUP associates a unique group *name* with one or more segments. It causes all labels and variables defined in the given segments to have addresses relative to the beginning of the group rather than to the beginning of the segments in which they are defined. A group name cannot be used in more than one GROUP directive in any source file. If several segments within the source file belong to the same group, all segment names must be given in the same GROUP directive.

The *segmentname* must be the name of a segment defined using the SEGMENT directive, or a SEG expression. You can use group names with the ASSUME directive and as an operand prefix with the segment override operator (:).

Segments in a group need not to be coded in a contiguous stream. Segments that do not belong to the group can be loaded between segments that do belong. The only limit to remember has to do with the total number of bytes defined in all segments of the group. That is, the segments of a group are combined at LINK time into a single segment; the group can occupy at most 64K of memory.

GROUP does not affect the order in which segments that make up the group are placed in the load module by LINK. That loading order depends on each segment class or on the order in which object modules are given to the linker.

Note that when using the MODEL directive, the offset of a group-relative segment refers to the ending address of the segment, not the beginning. For example, the expression OFFSET STACK evaluates to the end of the stack segment.

INCLUDELIB Directive

Syntax: INCLUDELIB *libraryname*

Examples: INCLUDELIB graphics
                     INCLUDELIB ARITH.MAC

The *libraryname* is written to the comment record of the object file. Intel's title for this record is COMENT. Microsoft's LINK reads this record and links with the specified library file. The *libraryname* must be a file name, rather than a complete file specification. If you do not specify an extension, .LIB is assumed. LINK searches for the library file in the following order:

1. In the current directory.
2. In any directories given in the library field of the LINK command line.
3. In any directories listed in the LIB environment variable.

Instruction-Set Directives

Syntax: .(instruction set)

Examples: .8086
                     .8087

```
.186
.286c
.286p
.287
.386
.386p
.387
```

Instruction-set directives must be placed at the beginning of the program source file to tell MASM which microprocessor instruction set will be used. When a particular set is used, MASM recognizes and assembles any subsequent instructions for that processor. MASM uses .8086 and .8087 default directives, so these are not required if you are programming for these processors. Note that the .8086 and .8088 directives disable assembly of the instructions unique to the 80186, 80286, and 80386 processors.

If MASM finds no instruction set directive, it uses the following defaults:

- 8086/8087 processor instruction set.
- 8087 coprocessor instruction set.
- IEEE format for floating-point variables.

The processor and coprocessor directives are normally used at the start of the source file to define the instruction sets for the entire assembly. If you wish, however, it is possible to use different processor directives at different points in the source file to change assumptions for a section of code. There are two limitations for changing the processor or coprocessor: (1) The directives must be given outside segments. End the current segment, give the processor directive, and then open another segment. (2) You can specify a lower-level coprocessor with a higher-level processor, but an error message is generated if you try to specify a lower-level processor with a higher-level coprocessor.

If using the .8087, .287 or .387 directive, you can also code the /R or /E option in the MASM command line to define how MASM is to assemble floating-point instructions. Note that /R is obsolete, since it generates IEEE, which is the MASM 5.x default. The /E says that an emulator for xx87 instructions will be added at LINK time.

The .286c allows use of 8086 instructions and nonprotected 80286 instructions (which are identical to the 80186 instructions). Use the .286c when writing programs that will be executed only by an 80286 microprocessor, but remember not to use any of the 80286 protected instructions. The .286p uses the protected instructions of the 80286. This does not mean that you have to use the .286p if you are running in protected mode; it is required only if you are using the protected instructions themselves. Use the .286p when writing programs that will be executed only by an 80286 processor and that use both protected and nonprotected instructions.

The .386 directive enables assembly of the 8086 and the nonprivileged instructions of the 80286 and 80386 processors. It also enables 80387 coprocessor instructions. Note that if privileged instructions were previously enabled, this directive disables them. The .386p is equivalent to the .286p, except that it also enables the privileged instructions of the 80386 processor.

Note that the macros in this book all assume the .386 directive, because you should use as much of the full power of the 80386 as you can.

ORG—Segment Origin

Syntax: ORG *expression*

Examples: ORG   150h
            ORG $+10

The location counter is the value MASM maintains to keep track of the current location in the source file. MASM increments the location counter automatically as each source statement is processed. However, you can set the location specifically by using the ORG directive.

ORG sets the location counter to *expression*. Any subsequent instruction and data address begin at the new value. This *expression* must resolve to a constant number. That is, all symbols used in the expression must be known on the first pass of the assembler. It is possible to use the location-counter symbol ($).

If the code reads:

```
ORG 150h
MOV AX,DX
```

The MOV statement begins at byte 150h in the current segment. If the code reads:

```
        ORG $+10
CR__LF  DB 0Ah,0Dh
```

The variable CR__LF is declared to start at the address 10 bytes beyond the current address.

PROC—Procedure Definition

Syntax: *name* PROC [NEAR|FAR]
                :
             name ENDP

Examples: THISONE PROC   NEAR
                       :
            THISONE ENDP

PROC marks the beginning of a procedure, which is a block of instructions that forms a program subroutine. Every procedure has a *name* with which it can be called. This name must be unique, not previously defined in the program. The *name* has the same attributes as a label and can be used as an operand in a jump, call, or loop instruction. Any number of statements can appear between the PROC and its associated ENDP statement. You must code at least one RET directive to return control to the point of call.

The optional distance can be either NEAR or FAR. MASM assumes NEAR if given no distance.

SEGMENT—Segment Definition

Syntax:	*name*	SEGMENT [*align*] [*combine*] [*use*] ['*class*']
		:
	name	ENDS

Examples:	DATAI	SEGMENT USE16 'DATA'
		:
	DATAI	ENDS
	THISTEXT	SEGMENT 'CODE'
		:
	THISTEXT	ENDS
	CODE	SEGMENT PARA PUBLIC 'CODE'
		:
	CODE	ENDS
	CONSTNT	SEGMENT PARA PUBLIC 'CONST'
		:
	CONSTNT	ENDS
	STACK1	SEGMENT PARA STACK 'STACK'
		:
	STACK1	ENDS

A program segment is a collection of instructions and/or data whose addresses are relative to the same segment register, such as the 80386 CS register for the code segment. The SEGMENT directive marks the beginning of a program segment. It works in conjunction with the ENDS (segment ends) directive. The *name* defines the name of the segment; it can be either unique to a program or the same as another segment. If it is the same, MASM treats the two segments as a single segment in two pieces.

Segments can be nested. When MASM encounters a nested segment, it temporarily suspends assembly of the enclosing segment and begins assembly of the nested segment. When the nested segment has been assembled, MASM continues assembly of the enclosing segment. Overlapping segments are not permitted.

The optional align, combine, use and class types give the LINK instructions on how to set up segments. You do not have to use all the types shown, but you should specify them in the order they appear in the syntax example.

The use type specifies the segment word size on the 80386 processor. Segment word size is the default operand and address size of a segment. The use can be USE16 or USE32. These types are only relevant if you have enabled 80386 instructions and addressing modes with the .386 directive. MASM generates an error if you specify use *type* when the 80386 processor is not enabled.

When assembling code for .386 mode, MASM now supports direct-addressing modes between segments with different USE sizes. Segments can have the USE16 or USE32 attribute. These attributes refer to the default size of offsets. Direct-addressing references to labels in other segments are correctly resolved. In the following example, MASM correctly uses a 32-bit offset to access the data at label a32:

```
                .386
SEG32   SEGMENT   USE32
a32     DD        ?
SEG32   ENDS
;
SEG16   SEGMENT   USE16
        ASSUME    DS:SEG32
        MOV       EAX,a32
SEG16   ENDS
```

You can also execute a CALL or JMP to a label in a segment with a different USE size. However, the label must be declared FAR, and the CALL or JMP must not be a forward reference. The following shows a correct method for executing such a CALL or JMP:

```
                .386
COD16   SEGMENT   USE16 'CODE'
PROC16  PROC  FAR
        RET
PROC16  ENDP
;
LAB16   LABEL FAR
COD16   ENDS
```

```
;
COD32     SEGMENT    USE32 'CODE'
          CALL  PROC16
          JMP   LAB16
CODE32            ENDS
```

With the 80286 and other 16-bit processors, the segment word size is always 16 bits. A 16-bit segment can contain up to 65536 (64K) bytes. However, the 80386 is capable of using either 16-bit or 32-bit segments. A 32-bit segment can contain up to 4,294,967,296 (four gigabytes). Although MASM allows you to define four gigabyte segments in 32-bit segments, current versions of MS-DOS limit segment size to 64K. If you do not specify a *use* type, the segment word size is 32 bits by default when the .386 directive is used.

Align—Segment Alignment. *Align* defines the alignment of a given segment and defines the range of memory addresses from which a starting address for the segment is selected. *Align* can be any one of the following:

- BYTE   Use any byte address.
- WORD   Use any word address, with two bytes per word (this is an even location).
- DWORD   Use any doubleword address. This is a location divisible by 4 (bytes/doubleword). DWORD is normally used in 32-bit segments with the 80386.
- PARA   Use any paragraph address, with 16 bytes per paragraph.
- PAGE   Use page addresses with 256 bytes per page.

If it does not find any *align* type, MASM defaults to PARA. The actual start address is not computed until the program is loaded and LINK ensures that the address will be on the given boundary, however it is specified.

The align types BYTE, WORD, and DWORD should not be confused with the BYTE, WORD, and DWORD reserved words that specify data type with operators such as THIS and PTR. Also, PAGE has nothing to do with the PAGE directive. Because the align types are only used on the same line as the SEGMENT directive, the distinctions should be clear in the context in which they are used.

Combine—Segment Combination. The optional *combine* type defines how MASM combines segments. If you do not code any *combine* type, the segments are not combined. Each receives, instead, its own physical segment when loaded into memory. Remember that if you use the same name with more than one segment, each segment definition using that name must have either exactly the same attributes or attributes that do not conflict. *Combine* can be any one of the following:

AT *address*

This causes all label and variable addresses defined in the segment to be relative to the given *address*. This address can be any valid expression; however, it cannot contain a forward reference, a reference to a symbol defined later in the source file. Generally, an AT segment represents an address template that can be placed over code or data already in memory, such as a screen buffer, and contains no code or initialized data. The labels and variables in the AT segments are used to access the fixed instructions and data.

COMMON

All addresses in the segments are relative to the same base address. COMMON creates overlapping segments by placing the start of all segments having the same name at the same address.

The length of the resulting area is the length of the longest segment. If data is declared in more than one segment having the same name and COMMON type, the most recently declared data replaces any previously declared data.

MEMORY

This type is provided for compatibility with other linkers that might support a combine type conforming to the Intel definition of MEMORY type. MEMORY is treated by Microsoft's LINK exactly as a PUBLIC segment. It is possible to define segments with MEMORY type even though LINK does not support a separate MEMORY type.

PUBLIC

This type concatenates all segments having the same name and forms a single, contiguous segment. All the instruction and data addresses in the "new" segment are relative to a single segment register. Also, all offsets are adjusted to represent the distance from the beginning of the "new" segment.

STACK

Like PUBLIC, this type concatenates all segments having the same name to form a single, contiguous segment. However, all addresses in the new segment are relative to the SS (stack segment) register. Also, the stack pointer (SP) register is initialized to the ending address of the segment. Normally, use the STACK type since this automatically initializes the SS register. If using a stack segment and not using the STACK type, specifically code instructions to load the segment address into the SS register. It is recommended that you provide at least one stack segment in each program. Otherwise, LINK gives a warning message, which can be ignored if you have a valid reason for not declaring the stack segment.

The total size of the stack is the total size of all stack definitions. LINK puts initialized data for each defined stack segment at the end of the stack. Data initialized in the last segment linked override data initialized in previous segments. This behavior is usually not relevant, because most programs only define one stack of uninitialized data. Stack data cannot be initialized with simplified segment directives.

USE

USE16 or USE32 tells the assembler which segment size is being defined for an 80386. MS-DOS and OS/2 only support USE16 types—MS-DOS because it is a real-mode operating system without 32-bit capability and OS/2 because of design decisions.

Class Type—Segment Class. All segments belong to a class. Segments without a class name are explicitly stated as having the null-class name. The null-class segments will be loaded as contiguous blocks with other segments having the null-class name. LINK imposes no restriction on the number or size of segments in a class.

The optional *class* type defines which segments are to be loaded into contiguous memory. Enclose the *class* name within single quotation marks ('). The names are not case sensitive unless you are using the /ML or /MX options during assembly, or the /NIGNORECASE option when using LINK.

All segments of a given class name are loaded before segments of any other class and are loaded into memory one immediately after the other. Remember not to use the names assigned for segment class types as other symbol definitions. For instance, if the segment class is coded as 'THISTYPE', do not give the name THISTYPE to any variable or label in the source file. If you do, you will get the error "Symbol already different kind."

If you do not specify class types, LINK copies segments to the executable file in the same order they appear in the object files. The only exception occurs if LINK finds two segments with the same name, in which case it copies them as a contiguous block in the executable file.

There is a limitation to keep in mind when trying to order segments. LINK processes modules in the order it receives them on the command line. Because of this, it is not always easy to specify the order in which segments are loaded. Assume there are two source files that have four segments (STACK, DATA, CONST, CODE) that you want loaded in that order, but DATA is only specified in the second program. LINK will load them STACK, CONST, CODE, and only then DATA, because it found them in that order.

There are two ways to avoid the LINK automatic ordering of segments. The first way is to create and assemble a dummy program that contains empty segment definitions in the order you want the real segments. Be sure to code definitions for all the classes in the program; otherwise LINK chooses a default loading order. Use that dummy as the first object file in an invocation of LINK. LINK then automatically loads the segments in the order given in the dummy.

A second way to control the segment order is with the MASM /A option. The /A option directs the assembler to write segments to the object file in alphabetical order. Give the segments names with an alphabetical order that matches the order you want them loaded and use the /A option. For multiple-module programs, define all segments in the first module specified in the LINK command line.

Note: this bypass is useful only for assembly language programs. Do not use a dummy program with Microsoft FORTRAN, BASIC, C, or Pascal because they must follow the MS-DOS segment-ordering convention specified in the Microsoft *Macro Assembler User's Guide*. Do not modify that order.

Predefined Equates

When defining segments, you have several equates that are predefined for you. Use the equate names at any point in your code to represent the equate values; do not assign equates having these names. Although predefined equates are part of the simplified segment system (see chapter 11), the @curseg and @filename equates are also available when you use full segment definitions.

- @curseg   This name has the segment name of the current segment. This value may be convenient for ASSUME statements, segment overrides, or other cases in which you need to access the current segment. It can also be used to end a segment, as shown in the following example:

```
@curseg     ENDS    ; end current segment
            .286     ; must be outside a segment
            .CODE    ; restart a segment
```

- @filename   This value represents the base name of the current source file. For example, if the current source file is task.asm, the value in @filename is task.

- @codesize   If the .MODEL directive has been used (see chapter 11), the @codesize value is 0 for small

• @datasize	and compact models, or 1 for medium, large, and huge models.
	If the .MODEL directive has been used (see chapter 11), the @datasize value is 0 for small and medium models, 1 for compact and large models, and 2 for huge models.
• segment equates	For each of the primary segment directives (see chapter 11), there is a corresponding equate with the same name, except that the equate starts with an at sign @, and the directive starts with a period. For example, the @code equate represents the segment name defined by the .CODE directive. Similarly, @fardata represents the .FARDATA segment name and @fardata? represents the .FARDATA? segment name. These equates can be used in ASSUME statements and at any other time a segment must be referred to by name. For example:

```
ASSUME    ES:@FARDATA        ; Assume ES to far data
                             ; (.MODEL handles DS)
MOV       AX,@DATA           ; Initialize NEAR to DS
MOV       DS,AX
MOV       AX,@FARDATA        ; Initialize to ES
MOV       ES,AX
```

FILE-CONTROL DIRECTIVES

The term *file* was used before the advent of computers and was one of the first to be incorporated into data processing terminology. In general, a file is a collection of data representing a set of entities with certain aspects in common and organized for some specific purpose. In this definition, an entity is any data object. The word file is used in many ways in data processing. Examples are input file, output file, master file, and program file. The program file contains programs stored in source or object form. It is this latter, program files, that are to be manipulated with the file-control directives described below.

%OUT—Display a Message on the Console

Syntax: %OUT *text*

Examples: IF1

        % OUT End of Test

    ENDIF

%OUT instructs MASM to display *text* when it reaches the line containing the specified *text* during assembly. Normally, the display goes to the screen, but you can reroute it to a file or a printer by using normal rerouting commands. %OUT is useful in debugging; it can show where certain code is in the assembly process of long programs. %OUT generates output for both assembly passes unless you imbed it in the IF1 and/or IF2 directives, used to control when the directive is processed (see chapter 9 for descriptions of IF1 and IF2).

An interesting note: parameter substitution occurs if *text* contains a dummy parameter and the %OUT is in a macro.

INCLUDE—Include a Source File

Syntax: INCLUDE *filename*

Examples: INCLUDE file1   ; file name
              INCLUDE a: \ pgmdir \ file2   ; path name
              INCLUDE /pgmdir1/file2   ; path name
              INCLUDE pgmdir \ file3   ; partial path name

INCLUDE inserts source code from the source file given by *filename* into the current source file during assembly. When MASM finds an INCLUDE, it opens the specified source file and immediately begins to assemble its statements. When all of the statements have been read from the INCLUDE *filename*, assembly continues with the statements immediately following the INCLUDE directive. Nested INCLUDES are allowed; that is, a file named by an INCLUDE can contain INCLUDE directives. MASM marks included statements with the letter *C* in the listings.

Filename must be an existing file, although you can use a full or partial path name if the file is in another directory. MASM first looks for the INCLUDE *filename* in any paths specified with the MASM /I option, then it checks the current directory. Specify a file name but no path name with the INCLUDE directive if you plan to set a search path with the MASM /I option.

If MASM cannot find the file, it displays an error message and terminates assembly. Directories can be specified in INCLUDE pathnames with either the backslash (\ ) or the forward slash (/); this is for XENIX compatibility.

NAME—Copy Name to Object File

Syntax: NAME *modulename*

Examples: NAME THISPGM
              NAME Convert

NAME sets the name of the current module to *modulename*. A module name is used by a linker (such as Microsoft's LINK) when displaying error messages.

Modulename can be any combination of letters and digits, although only the first six characters are used. *Modulename* must be unique and not a reserved word.

If it does not find the NAME directive, MASM creates a default name using the first six characters of the text specified in the TITLE directive. If no TITLE is specified, the default name A is used. Note that each of the macros in this book has a NAME.

PAGE—Set Program-Listing Page Size and Line Width

Syntax: PAGE   [[*length*],*width*
             PAGE   +
             PAGE

Examples: PAGE   25,132
             PAGE   +
             PAGE
             PAGE   ,132

PAGE can be used for three purposes: (1) to designate the page length and line width for the program listing; (2) to increment the section and adjust the section number; or (3) to generate a page break in the listing. If you specify *length* and *width*, PAGE sets the maximum number of lines per page to *length* and the maximum number of characters per line to *width*. *Length* must be in the range of 10 to 255 and *width* must be in the range 60 to 132. The default *width* is 80 characters and the default *length* is 50 lines. If specifying a *width* without stating the *length*, precede the *width* with a comma (,).

If you code a plus sign (+), the section number is incremented, and the page number is reset to 1. Program listing page numbers will then have the form *section-page*, where *section* is the section number within the module, and *page* is the page number within the section. The default section and page numbers begin with 1-1.

If it finds no argument with PAGE, MASM starts a new output page in the program listing. MASM copies a form-feed character to the file and generates a title and subtitle line. See TITLE and SUBTTL below.

Program Listing Controls

The way program listings need to be printed depends on whether you are in preliminary design, debugging, testing, or final listing. You can control what prints, which may shorten or lengthen the time you wait for a listing. For instance, if the macros are already debugged, you might want to suppress the macro expansion while debugging the mainline source program.

.LIST—List statements in Program Listing.

Syntax: .LIST

Example: .list

.LIST specifies that source-program lines are to be copied to the program listing. This directive is typically used with .XLIST (see below), which prevents a section of a source file from being copied to the program listing.

.XLIST—Suppress Listing of Statements.

Syntax: .XLIST

Example: .xlist

.XLIST suppresses the copying of source code onto a program listing. This directive is typically used with .LIST (see above), which copies a section of a source file to the program listing.

.SFCOND—Suppress False-Conditional Listing.

Syntax: .SFCOND

Example: .SFCOND

.SFCOND suppresses the listing of any subsequent conditional blocks whose IF condition is false. See .LFCOND, which restores the listing.

.LFCOND—List False-Conditional in Program Listing.

Syntax: .LFCOND

Example: .lfcond

.LFCOND restores the listing of conditional blocks whose IF condition is false. See .SFCOND, above, which suppresses the listing.

.TFCOND—Toggle False-Conditional Listing.

Syntax: .TFCOND

Example: .TFCOND

.TFCOND toggles the current status of the default mode for listing of conditional blocks. It can work in conjunction with MASM's /X option. By default, conditional blocks are not listed on start-up. If /X is given, .TFCOND causes false-conditional blocks to be listed; that is, /X reverses the meaning of the first .TFCOND in the source file. Each time a new .TFCOND appears in the source code, listing of false-conditionals is turned off if it was on, or on if it was off.

.LALL—Include Macro Expansions in Program Listing.

Syntax: .LALL

Example: .lall

.LALL causes MASM to list all the source statements in a macro, including comments preceded by a single semicolon (;) but not those preceded by a double semicolon (;;).

.SALL—Suppress Listing of Macro Expansions.

Syntax: .SALL

Example: .sall

.SALL suppresses listing of all macro expansions. MASM still copies the macro call to the source listing, but does not copy the source lines generated by the call.

.XALL—Exclude Comments from Macro Listing.

Syntax: .XALL

Example: .xall

.XALL lists only those source statements that generate code or data; comments, equates, and segment definitions are ignored. .XALL is in effect when MASM first begins execution.

.CREF—List Symbols in Cross-Reference File.

Syntax: .CREF

Example: .CREF

.CREF generates cross-references for a MASM cross-reference file.

.XCREF—Suppress Symbol Listing.

Syntax: .XCREF [*name,,,*]

Example: .XCREF

.XCREF suppresses the generation of label, variable, and symbol cross-references. If *name* is specified, only that label, variable, or symbol will be suppressed and omitted from the symbol table of the program listing. All other names will be cross-referenced. If using two or more *names*, separate the *names* with commas (,).

.RADIX—Change Default Input Radix

Syntax: .RADIX *expression*

Examples: .RADIX   10   ; decimal
              .RADIX   2   ; binary
              .RADIX   16   ; hexadecimal

A radix is the total number of distinct marks or symbols used in a numbering system. For example, since the decimal numbering system uses ten symbols (0, 1, 2, 3, 4, 5, 6, 7, 8, and 9), the radix is 10. In the binary system, the radix is 2.

.RADIX sets the input radix for numbers in the source file. The *expression* is a number in the range 2 to 16. .RADIX defines whether the numbers are binary, octal, decimal, hexadecimal, or numbers of some other base. The most common bases are: 2 (binary), 8 (octal), 10 (decimal), and 16 (hexadecimal). Expression is always considered a decimal number, regardless of the current input radix. Also, the default radix is decimal.

.RADIX does not affect DD, DQ, or DT directives. If real numbers are entered in the expression of these directives, they are always evaluated as decimal unless a radix specifier is appended to the value. .RADIX also does not affect the optional radix specifiers used with integer numbers: B or D. When B or D appears at the end of any integer, it is always considered to be a radix specifier even if the current input radix is 16.

SUBTTL—Set Program-Listing Subtitle

Syntax: *text* SUBTTL

Examples: SUBTTL Graphics Routines
              SUBTTL CONVERT SUBROUTINES

SUBTTL specifies the listing subtitle. SUBTTL directs MASM to copy the *text* to the line immediately following the title on each page in the program listing; that is, the *text* appears on the third line of each page. (See TITLE, below, which lists on a separate line of each page.) The *text* can be any combination of characters, although only the first 60 characters are used. If no *text* is given, the subtitle line is left blank. It is possible to use any number of SUBTTL directives in a program. Each new one encountered replaces the current subtitle with new *text*.

TITLE—Set Program-Listing Title

Syntax: TITLE   *text*

Examples: TITLE   THISPROGRAM - This is first program
              TITLE   Graphics

TITLE specifies the program-listing title. TITLE directs MASM to copy the text to the first line of each page in the program listing. The text can be any combination of characters up to 60 characters in length. However, no more than one TITLE directive per module is allowed. The first six nonblank characters of the title are used as the module name if the module does not contain a NAME directive. See NAME, above.

9

MASM Global,
Conditional, and
Macro Directives

GLOBAL CONCEPTS BECAME A PART OF PROGRAMMING EARLY. AS SOON AS PROGRAMMERS were able to divide programs into pieces, they found that certain variables, labels, and calls had to have influence in various of the modules, macros, procedures, and so on. Figure 9-1 gives an overview of global versus local.

Additional examples of the declarations explained in this chapter are shown in a program listing in appendix G. The listing contains both correct and incorrect examples. It is important for you to know what does not work as much as what does work.

GLOBAL DECLARATIONS

MASM global-declaration directives (EXTRN and PUBLIC) allow the definition of labels, variables, and absolute symbols that can be accessed globally, that is, from all modules in a program. These two global declarations make the labels, variables, and symbols available to all of the modules that make up a program. The difference in these two declarations is that PUBLIC makes the label, variable, or symbol global from the source file in which it resides. EXTRN is placed in the source file (not the one in which the label, variable, or symbol resides) from which the label, variable, or symbol will be referenced.

PUBLIC Directive

Syntax: PUBLIC *name,,,*

Examples: PUBLIC THIS__NUMBER,GO__HERE
                    PUBLIC Byte__Change,First__Jump

Variables:	Available:	
CR–LF	Main Program and Macro	GLOBAL
FIGURE	Main Program and Macro	GLOBAL
Number1	Macro only	LOCAL
THISONE	Macro only	LOCAL

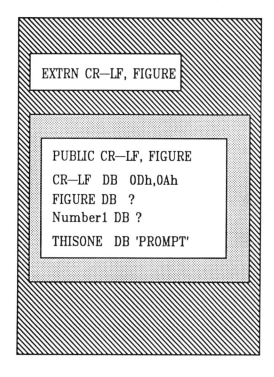

```
EXTRN CR–LF, FIGURE

PUBLIC CR–LF, FIGURE
CR–LF DB  0Dh,0Ah
FIGURE DB  ?
Number1 DB ?
THISONE  DB 'PROMPT'
```

Main Program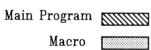

Macro

Fig. 9-1. Global Versus Local.

PUBLIC directives are used in declarations to transform locally defined symbols, variables, and labels into global symbols. This makes any symbols, variables or labels specified by *name* available to other modules in the program. The *name* must be the name of a variable, label, or absolute symbol defined within the current source file.

Absolute symbols, if given, can only represent one- or two-byte integer or string values. These symbols must be declared PUBLIC before they can be used for symbolic debugging with Microsoft's SYMDEB or CodeView.

Case is not important in a *name* since MASM converts all lower-case letters to upper-case before copying the *name* to object files. The /ML and /MX options can be used in the MASM command line to direct the assembler to preserve lower-case letters when copying public and external symbols to object. See chapter 11 for descriptions of /ML and /MX.

Although absolute symbols can be declared PUBLIC, aliases for public symbols might cause errors. The following code is illegal:

```
PUBLIC    lines                     ; Declare symbol public
          lines    EQU    rows       ; Declare alias for 'lines'
          rows     EQU    25         ; Illegal
```

EXTRN Directive

Syntax: EXTRN *name:type,,,*

Examples: EXTRN JUMP__HERE:NEAR
             EXTRN numbr1:byte,chars:dword

The EXTRN directive defines an external label, variable, or symbol of a specified *name* and *type*. This EXTRN item is one that has been declared PUBLIC in another module of the program. The *type* must match the type in the declaration in the other module and can be one of the following:

BYTE   (A byte, 8 bits)
WORD   (Two bytes)
DWORD   (Four bytes)
QWORD   (Eight bytes)
TBYTE   (Ten bytes)
NEAR   (Distance for a label)
FAR   (Distance for a label)
ABS   (For symbols that represent constant numbers such as equates declared with the EQU directive.)

Where you locate EXTRN declaration can be important. The actual address is not determined until the object code is LINKed, so MASM might assume a default segment for the external item that is based on where EXTRN is placed. If coded within a segment, the item is assumed to be relative to that segment, and the PUBLIC declaration of the item in some other module must be in a segment having the same name and attributes. If the EXTRN is outside all segments, no assumption is made about what segment the item is relative to, and the PUBLIC declaration of the item can be in any segment in any module. In either case, it is possible to use the segment-override operator (:) to override the default segment of an external variable or label.

This directive tells MASM not to generate an error, even though the symbol is not in the current module. MASM assumes that the symbol occurs in another module. However, the symbol must actually exist and must be declared PUBLIC in some module; otherwise LINK generates an error.

Program Example

Figures 9-2 and 9-3 illustrate two programs that use PUBLIC and EXTRN declaration. Figure 9-4 is a sample run of the programs.

```
 1                              PAGE    55,132
 2                              .386
 3
 4
 5 0000              stack      SEGMENT para 'STACK' USE16 STACK
 6 0000  0064[                  dw      100 DUP (?)
 7        ????
 8                     ]
 9
10 00C8              stack      ENDS
11
12
13 0000              code       SEGMENT  para 'CODE' USE16 PUBLIC
14                              ASSUME   CS:code, DS:code, SS:stack
15                   ;
16                   ; Name;   CH09P1
17                   ;
18                   ; Purpose: The following procedure provides half of the example use
19                   ;          of PUBLIC and EXTRN usage.
20                   ;
21                   ; Inputs:  No input is needed.
22                   ;
23                   ; Process: When invoked, the program name is displayed along with a
24                   ;          request for input, which when satisfied causes a call to
25                   ;          the companion external procedure.
26                   ;
27                   ; Output:  The display is the only output.
28                   ;
29                   ; Note:    This program is expected to be linked as the second object
30                   ;          file in the command 'LINK ch09p1+ch09p2,,,;'.  The
31                   ;          resulting EXE file (CH09P1.EXE) can then be invoked to
32                   ;          demonstrate the use of PUBLIC and EXTRN.
33                   ;
34                              PUBLIC  CH09P1              ; Make the name usable
35                              EXTRN   CH09P2:FAR          ; and its companion usable.
36                   ;
37                   ; When loaded, DOS transfers control to Start - the label on the END
38                   ; statement.  This allows us to control where the program begins.
39                   ;
40
41 0000              Start:
42 0000  9A 0000 ---- E          call   ch09p2              ; Call the external procedure
43 0005  EB F9                   jmp    start               ; Loop until break out is done.
44
45
46 0007              CH09P1      PROC    FAR
47 0007  EB 2A 90                jmp     begin               ; Skip data definitions
48                   ;
49                   ; The output message
```

Fig. 9-2. Program Listing. (continued)

```
50                              ;
51 000A  0A 0D 69 6E 20 43  opmessg    db      10,13,'in CH09P1 - press any key to continue.$'
52        48 30 39 50 31 20
53        2D 20 70 72 65 73
54        73 20 61 6E 79 20
55        6B 65 79 20 74 6F
56        20 63 6F 6E 74 69
57        6E 75 65 2E 24
58                              ;
59 0033                      begin:
60 0033  52                     push    DX              ; Save entry registers
61 0034  50                     push    AX              ; used by this procedure.
62 0035  1E                     push    DS              ; save DS
63 0036  8C C8                  mov     AX,CS
64 0038  8E D8                  mov     DS,AX           ; Set CS as DS value
65 003A  B4 09                  mov     AH,09h          ; Set the DOS function
66 003C  8D 16 000A R           lea     DX,opmessg      ; the string offset and
67 0040  CD 21                  int     21h             ; display the string.
68 0042  B4 0C                  mov     AH,0ch          ; Request the kbd buffer be
69                              ;                       ; cleared before
70 0044  B0 08                  mov     AL,08h          ; requesting a key-stroke.
71 0046  CD 21                  int     21h             ; from DOS.
72 0048  1F                     pop     DS              ; Restore DS,
73 0049  58                     pop     AX              ; the registers used,
74 004A  5A                     pop     DX
75 004B  CB                     ret                     ; and return.
76 004C                CH09P1   ENDP
77 004C                code     ENDS
78                              END     Start
```

Segments and Groups:

N a m e	Size	Length	Align	Combine	Class
CODE	16 Bit	004C	PARA	PUBLIC	'CODE'
STACK	16 Bit	00C8	PARA	STACK	'STACK'

Symbols:

N a m e	Type	Value	Attr		
BEGIN	L NEAR	0033	CODE		
CH09P1	F PROC	0007	CODE	Global	Length = 0045
CH09P2	L FAR	0000	CODE	External	
OPMESSG	L BYTE	000A	CODE		
START	L NEAR	0000	CODE		
@CPU	TEXT	3343			
@FILENAME	TEXT	ch09p1			
@VERSION	TEXT	510			

```
     69 Source  Lines
     69 Total   Lines
     12 Symbols

  47384 + 120788 Bytes symbol space free

        0 Warning Errors
        0 Severe  Errors
```

Fig. 9-2. (continued)

```
 1                                   PAGE     55,132
 2                                   .386
 3 0000                      code    SEGMENT  para 'CODE' USE16 PUBLIC
 4                                   ASSUME   CS:code, DS:code, SS:code
 5                              ;
 6                              ; Name;   CH09P2
 7                              ;
 8                              ; Purpose: The following procedure provides half of the example use
 9                              ;          of PUBLIC and EXTRN usage.
10                              ;
11                              ; Inputs:  No input is needed.
12                              ;
13                              ; Process: When invoked, the program name is displayed along with a
14                              ;          request for input, which when satisfied causes a call to
15                              ;          the companion external procedure.
16                              ;
17                              ; Output:  The display is the only output.
18                              ;
19                              ; Note:    This program is expected to be linked as the second object
20                              ;          file in the command 'LINK ch09p1+ch09p2,,,;'.  The
21                              ;          resulting EXE file (CH09P1.EXE) can then be invoked to
22                              ;          demonstrate the use of PUBLIC and EXTRN.
23                              ;
24                                   PUBLIC   CH09P2           ; Make the name usable
25                                   EXTRN    CH09P1:FAR       ; and its companion usable.
26
27 0000                      CH09P2  PROC     FAR
28 0000  EB 2A 90                    jmp      begin            ; Skip data definitions
29                              ;
30                              ; The output message
31                              ;
32 0003  0A 0D 69 6E 20 43 opmessg  db       10,13,'in CH09P2 - press any key to continue.$'
33         48 30 39 50 32 20
34         2D 20 70 72 65 73
35         73 20 61 6E 79 20
36         6B 65 79 20 74 6F
37         20 63 6F 6E 74 69
38         6E 75 65 2E 24
39                              ;
40 002C                      begin:
41 002C  52                          push     DX               ; Save entry registers
42 002D  50                          push     AX               ; used by this procedure.
43 002E  1E                          push     DS               ; save DS
44 002F  8C C8                       mov      AX,CS
45 0031  8E D8                       mov      DS,AX            ; Set CS as DS value
46 0033  B4 09                       mov      AH,09h           ; Set the DOS function
47 0035  8D 16 0003 R                lea      DX,opmessg       ; the string offset and
48 0039  CD 21                       int      21h              ; display the string.
49 003B  B4 0C                       mov      AH,0Ch           ; Request the kbd buffer be
50                              ;                               cleared before
51 003D  B0 08                       mov      AL,08h           ; requesting a key-stroke.
52 003F  CD 21                       int      21h              ; from DOS.
53                              ;
54                              ; Use the extrn defined above.
55                              ;
56 0041  9A 0000 ---- E               call     ch09p1           ; Invoke our companion.
57
58 0046  1F                          pop      DS               ; Restore DS,
59 0047  58                          pop      AX               ; the registers used,
60 0048  5A                          pop      DX
61 0049  CB                          ret                       ; and return.
62 004A                      CH09P2  ENDP
63 004A                      code    ENDS
64                                   END
```

Fig. 9-3. Program Listing. (continued)

```
Segments and Groups:

                N a m e               Size    Length   Align  Combine Class

CODE . . . . . . . . . . . . .        16 Bit  004A     PARA    PUBLIC  'CODE'

Symbols:

                N a m e               Type    Value    Attr

BEGIN  . . . . . . . . . . . .        L NEAR  002C     CODE

CH09P1 . . . . . . . . . . . .        L FAR   0000     CODE    External
CH09P2 . . . . . . . . . . . .        F PROC  0000     CODE    Global   Length = 004A

OPMESSG  . . . . . . . . . . .        L BYTE  0003     CODE

@CPU . . . . . . . . . . . . .        TEXT    3343
@FILENAME  . . . . . . . . . .        TEXT    ch09p2
@VERSION . . . . . . . . . . .        TEXT    510


    58 Source  Lines
    58 Total   Lines
    10 Symbols

 47424 + 120748 Bytes symbol space free

     0 Warning Errors
     0 Severe  Errors
```

Fig. 9-3. (continued)

```
(A sample run of CH09P1.EXE)

in CH09P2 - press any key to continue.
in CH09P1 - press any key to continue.
in CH09P2 - press any key to continue.
in CH09P1 - press any key to continue.
in CH09P2 - press any key to continue.
in CH09P1 - press any key to continue.
in CH09P2 - press any key to continue.^C
```

Fig. 9-4. Sample Run.

Communal Symbols

Syntax: COMM *definition*,,,
            where each *definition* has the following syntax:
                [NEAR|FAR] *label:size[count]*

Examples: .DATA   ; Must be inside data segment
             COMM NEAR this bufr:WORD:40

Communal variables are uninitialized variables that are both public and external. They are often declared in INCLUDE files. If a variable must be used by several assembly routines, declare the variable communal in an include file. Then include the file in each of the assembly routines. Although the variable is declared in each source module, it exists at only one address.

A communal variable can be NEAR or FAR. If you specify neither, the type will be that of the default memory model. If you use a simplified segment directive, the default type is NEAR for small and medium models; it is FAR for compact, large, and huge models. If using full segment definitions, the default type is NEAR.

The *label* is the name of the variable. *Size* can be BYTE, WORD, DWORD, QWORD, or TBYTE. The *count* is the number of elements; if MASM finds no *count*, it assumes one element. Multiple variables can be defined with one COMM statements; separate each variable with a comma (,).

Using a communal variable in an include file (and including it in several source modules) is an alternative to defining the variable and declaring it public in one source module and then declaring it external in other modules. If the variable is declared communal in one module and public in another, the public declaration takes precedence; the communal declaration has the same effect as an external declaration.

LINK allocates communal variables, because MASM cannot tell if a communal variable has been used in another module. As a result, communal variables have the following limitations:

- Communal variables are not guaranteed to be allocated in the sequence in which they are declared. Do not use any assembly language techniques that depend on sequence and position of data defined as communal.

- Placement of communal variables follows the same rules as external declarations. That is, they must be declared inside a data segment.

- You cannot initialize communal variables, and initial values are not guaranteed to be 0 or any value. These variables can be used for data that are not given a value until run time, such as file buffers.

- You cannot override the default segment to place communal variables in other segments. Communal variables are allocated in segments that are part of the Microsoft segment conventions.

    > NEAR communal variables are placed in a segment called c__common, which is part of DGROUP. The segment is created and initialized automatically if you use simplified-segment directives. If you use full-segment directives, create a group called DGROUP, and use ASSUME to associate it with the DS register.

    > FAR communal variables are placed in a segment called FAR__BSS. This segment has the combine type private and the class type 'FAR__BSS'. This means that multiple segments with the same name can be created. Such segments cannot be accessed by name. They must be initialized indirectly using the SEG operator.

CONDITIONAL DIRECTIVES

Conditional occurrences are based on the testing of the state of an entity. If the state is found to be true, a program branches one way; if the state is false, the program branches another way. MASM provides two types of conditional directives. Use the first during assembly to test a condition and assemble a block of statements only if the condition is true. Use the second to generate an error condition after testing for a specified condition. Both kinds of conditional directives only test assembly-time conditions and cannot test run-time conditions because these conditions are not known until an executable program is run. You can only compare or test expressions that evaluate to constants during assembly.

Conditional-Assembly Directives

Conditional-assembly directives control which lines of code will be assembled into object form. Conditional-assembly directives include the following, which are explained in detail in this section. The basic lines of code are the IF, ELSE, and END, and they are listed in the left-most column. IF has eight forms that can test some special conditions; those eight are listed in an indented column.

IF

IF1	(Tests during MASM pass 1)
IF2	(Tests during MASM pass 2)
IFB	(Tests if an argument is blank)
IFDEF	(Tests if a name is defined)
IFDIF	(Tests if two arguments are different)
IFE	(Tests value of an expression)
IFIDN	(Tests if two arguments are identical)
IFNB	(Tests if an argument is not blank)
IFNDEF	(Tests if a name is defined)

ELSE
ENDIF

The IF, ELSE, and END directives enclose the statements to be considered for conditional assembly. The conditional block is used as in this example:

IF *test condition*
     statements1
[ELSE
     statements2]
ENDIF

The *statements1* that follow IF can be any valid statements, including other conditional blocks. The ELSE directive and its *statements2* are optional. ENDIF ends the block. The two sets of *statements1* and *statements2* are assembled only if the *test condition* specified in the IF directive is satisfied. If you include an ELSE and its statements (*statements2* in the example), only the IF conditional block statements are assembled;

the *statements2* are assembled only if the IF condition is not met. Include the ENDIF statement to close the conditional block. Each IF can only pair with one ELSE condition within the IF-ENDIF block.

IF directives can nest up to 255 levels. In nested IF-ENDIF blocks, the ELSE directive always belongs to the nearest preceding IF directive that does not have its own ELSE. An ENDIF directive must mark the end of any conditional-assembly block. No more than one ELSE directive is allowed for each IF statement.

IF and IFE Directives.

Syntax: IF *expression*
            IFE *expression*

Examples: IF debug
                EXTRN dump:FAR
                EXTRN trace:FAR
            ENDIF

IF and IFE test the value of the *expression*. IF allows assembly if the value of *expression* is true, or nonzero. IFE allows assembly if the value of *expression* is false, or zero. The *expression* must resolve to a constant value and must not contain forward references.

IF1 and IF2 Directives.

Syntax: IF1
            IF2

Examples: IF1
                    %OUT This is Phase 1
            ELSE
                    %OUT This is Phase 2
            ENDIF

Remember here that MASM is a two-pass assembler. IF1 tests the current assembly pass to determine if it is the first pass, and IF2 tests whether it is the second pass. IF1 allows assembly on the statements only during pass one, and IF2 allows assembly on pass two. There are no arguments with these two directives.

IFDEF and IFNDEF Directives.

Syntax: IFDEF *name*
            IFNDEF *name*

Examples: See the listing in appendix G—listing page numbers 1-5 and 1-6.

IFDEF and IFNDEF both test whether or not the given *name* has been defined.

IFDEF allows assembly only if *name* is a label, variable, or symbol. IFNDEF allows assembly only if *name* has not yet been defined. The *name* can be any valid name. Remember that MASM is a two-pass assembler and, if *name* is a forward reference, it is considered undefined on the first pass and defined on the second pass.

IFB and IFNB Directives.

Syntax: IFB <*argument*>
            IFNB <*argument*>

Examples: See the listing in appendix G—listing page numbers 1-9, 1-10, and 1-11.

IFB and IFNB are intended for use in macro definitions. They control conditional assembly of statements in the macro, based on the parameters passed in the macro call. (In such cases, *argument* should be one of the dummy parameters listed by the MACRO directive.) The angle brackets (<>) are required.

Both IFB and IFNB test the *argument*. IFB allows assembly if the *argument* is blank, and IFNB allows assembly only if *argument* is not blank. *Argument* can be any name, number, or expression.

IFIDN and IFDIF Directives.

Syntax: IFIDN[I] <*argument1*>,<*argument2*>
            IFDIF[I] <*argument1*>,<*argument2*>

Examples: See the listing in appendix G—listing page number 1-11.

IFIDN and IFDIF are both intended for use in macro definitions. They can control conditional assembly of macro statements, based on the parameters passed in the macro call. In these cases, *argument1* and *argument2* should be dummy parameters listed by the MACRO directive.

IFIDN and IFDIF both compare *argument1* and *argument2*. IFIDN allows assembly if *argument1* is identical to *argument2*; case is significant. IFDIF allows assembly if the arguments are different; case is also significant here. The arguments can be any names, numbers, or expressions. The angle brackets (<>) are required and the arguments must be separated by a comma (,).

The optional [I] at the end of the directive name specifies that the directive is case insensitive. If used, the I means that arguments that are spelled the same will be evaluated the same, regardless of case. If the I is not given, the directive is case sensitive.

ELSEIF Directives

MASM Version 5.1 includes an ELSEIF conditional assembly directive that corresponds to each of the IF directives. These ELSEIF directives provide a more compact way of writing some sequences of ELSE and IF directives. The following twelve directives are available.

ELSEIF
ELSEIF1
ELSEIF2
ELSEIFB
ELSEIFDEF
ELSEIFDIF
ELSEIFDIFI
ELSEIFE
ELSEIFIDN
ELSEIFIDNI
ELSEIFNB
ELSEIFNDEF

Conditional Error Directives

An error is any incorrect step, process, or result in a data processing system. The term also refers to machine malfunctions, called *machine errors*, and to human mistakes, called *human errors*. Really, an error is any discrepancy between a computed, observed, recorded, or measured quantity and the true, specified, or theoretically correct value or condition.

Error-detecting code refers to a system of coding so that any single error produces a preplanned event. An automatic detection of an error is usually designed to detect the error and to take a predetermined series of steps. MASM conditional error directives allow the detection and selective processing. The conditional-error directives can be used to debug programs and check for assembly-time errors. Inserting a conditional error directive at a key point in your code allows the testing of assembly-time conditions at that point. Also, the conditional error directives can test for boundary conditions in macros.

Like other severe assembler errors, those generated by conditional error directives cause the assembler to return exit code 7. If MASM encounters a severe error during assembly, it deletes the object code. All conditional error directives except ERR1 (see below) generate fatal errors. Figure 9-5 shows a sample of the error directives and the errors they produce. Note that the assembly parameter /D was necessary to get the pass 1 errors out.

```
                          PAGE     55,132
                          .386
0000              code    SEGMENT  para 'CODE' USE16 PUBLIC
                          ASSUME   CS:code, DS:code, SS:code
                  ;
                  ; Name;    FIG9_ERR
                  ;
                  ; Purpose: The following procedure provides a vehicle for
                  ;          demonstrating the error directives.
                  ;
                  ; Inputs:  None.
                  ;
                  ; Process: None.
```

Fig. 9-5. Conditional Error Directives and Their Error. (continued)

```
                             ;
                             ; Output:  This listing.
                             ;
      0000                   Fig9_err   PROC

    = 0005                   num1       EQU    5
    = 0006                   num2       EQU    6
    = 0005                   num3       EQU    5

                             IF1
                                 %OUT      Pass 1 messages:
                                 .ERR1                             ; Unconditional error pass 1
fig9_err.ASM(25): error A2087: Forced error - pass1
                                 .ERR2                             ; Unconditional error pass 2
                             ENDIF
                                 .ERR                              ; Unconditional error
fig9_err.ASM(33): error A2089: Forced error
                                 .ERRE     num1 EQ num2            ; Force error if 5=6
fig9_err.ASM(34): error A2090: Forced error - expression equals 0
                                 .ERRE     num1 EQ num3            ; Force error if 5=5
                                 .ERRNZ    num1 NE num2            ; Force error if 5=6
fig9_err.ASM(36): error A2091: Forced error - expression not equal 0
                                 .ERRNZ    num1 NE num3            ; Force error if 5=5

                                 .ERRNDEF  Fig9_err               ; No error - fig9_err is def.
                                 .ERRNDEF  FIG9_xxx               ; Error - fig9_xxx is not.
fig9_err.ASM(40): error A2092: Forced error - symbol not defined
                                 .ERRDEF   Fig9_err               ; Error - fig9_err is defined
fig9_err.ASM(41): error A2093: Forced error - symbol defined
                                 .ERRDEF   FIG9_xxx               ; No error - fig9_xxx is not.
                             ;
                             ; The remaining two error directives are valid only within macros.
                             ; Thus we make a macro to demo them.
                             ;
                             demo1     MACRO    param1
                                 IFB   <param1>                    ; ensure param1 is omitted
                                     %OUT     Parameter param1 is omitted
                                     .ERRB    <param1>             ; This generates an error
                                     .ERRNB   <param1>             ; This doesn't
                                 ELSE
                                     %OUT     Parameter param1 is present
                                     .ERRB    <param1>             ; This doesn't generate but
                                     .ERRNB   <param1>             ; this does.
                                 ENDIF
                                     ENDM
                             demo1     present                     ; non-blank error message
                                 1       .ERRNB   <present>            ; this does.
fig9_err.ASM(59): error A2095: Forced error - string not blank
                             demo1                                 ; blank parameter error
                                 1       .ERRB    <>               ; This generates an error
fig9_err.ASM(60): error A2094: Forced error - string blank

                             demo2     MACRO    param1,param2
                                 IFNB <param2>                     ; Limit to 'good' compares.
                                     %OUT     looking for equal parameters here
                                     .ERRIDN  <param1>,<param2>    ; Error if identical
                                     .ERRIDNI <param1>,<param2>    ; Case insensitive check.
                                     %OUT     Looking for unequals now --
                                     .ERRDIF  <param1>,<param2>    ; Error if different
                                     .ERRDIFI <param1>,<param2>    ; Case insensitive check.
                                 ELSE
                                     %OUT     Looking for equal to xXx now --
                                     .ERRIDN  <param1>,<xXx>       ; Error if identical
                                     .ERRIDNI <param1>,<xXx>       ; Case insensitive check.
                                     %OUT     Looking for unequals now --
                                     .ERRDIF  <param1>,<xXx>       ; Error if different
                                     .ERRDIFI <param1>,<xXx>       ; Case insensitive check.
                                 ENDIF
                                     ENDM
```

Fig. 9-5. (continued)

```
                                    demo2   aaa,aaa              ; identical parameters
                            1               .ERRIDN <aaa>,<aaa>  ; Error if identical
fig9_err.ASM(80): error A2096: Forced error - strings identical
                            1               .ERRIDNI <aaa>,<aaa> ; Case insensitive check.
fig9_err.ASM(80): error A2096: Forced error - strings identical

                                    demo2   aaa,AAA              ; same letters - diff case
                            1               .ERRIDNI <aaa>,<AAA> ; Case insensitive check.
fig9_err.ASM(82): error A2096: Forced error - strings identical
                            1               .ERRDIF <aaa>,<AAA>  ; Error if different
fig9_err.ASM(82): error A2097: Forced error - strings different

                                    demo2   aaa,bbb              ; No match at all
                            1               .ERRDIF <aaa>,<bbb>  ; Error if different
fig9_err.ASM(84): error A2097: Forced error - strings different
                            1               .ERRDIFI <aaa>,<bbb> ; Case insensitive check.
fig9_err.ASM(84): error A2097: Forced error - strings different

                                    demo2   xXx                  ; parameter matches con
                            1               .ERRIDN <xXx>,<xXx>   ; Error if identical
fig9_err.ASM(86): error A2096: Forced error - strings identical
                            1               .ERRIDNI <xXx>,<xXx>  ; Case insensitive check.
fig9_err.ASM(86): error A2096: Forced error - strings identical

                                    demo2   xxx                  ; same letters - diff case
                            1               .ERRIDNI <xxx>,<xXx>  ; Case insensitive check.
fig9_err.ASM(88): error A2096: Forced error - strings identical
                            1               .ERRDIF <xxx>,<xXx>   ; Error if different
fig9_err.ASM(88): error A2097: Forced error - strings different

                                    demo2   yyy                  ; again - no match at all
                            1               .ERRDIF <yyy>,<xXx>   ; Error if different
fig9_err.ASM(90): error A2097: Forced error - strings different
                            1               .ERRDIFI <yyy>,<xXx>  ; Case insensitive check.
fig9_err.ASM(90): error A2097: Forced error - strings different

     0000                   Fig9_err   ENDP
     0000                   code       ENDS
                                       END

        1                              PAGE    55,132
        2                              .386
        3 0000                code     SEGMENT para 'CODE' USE16 PUBLIC
        4                              ASSUME  CS:code, DS:code, SS:code
        5                      ;
        6                      ; Name;    FIG9_ERR
        7                      ;
        8                      ; Purpose: The following procedure provides a vehicle for
        9                      ;          demonstrating the error directives.
       10                      ;
       11                      ; Inputs:  None.
       12                      ;
       13                      ; Process: None.
       14                      ;
       15                      ; Output:  This listing.
       16                      ;
       17 0000                Fig9_err   PROC
       18
       19 = 0005              num1     EQU     5
       20 = 0006              num2     EQU     6
       21 = 0005              num3     EQU     5
       22
       23                              IF2
       24                              %OUT    Pass 2 messages:
       25                              .ERR1                      ; Unconditional error pass 1
       26                              .ERR2                      ; Unconditional error pass 2
fig9_err.ASM(31): error A2088: Forced error - pass2
       27                              ENDIF
       28                              .ERR                       ; Unconditional error
```

Fig. 9-5. (continued)

```
fig9_err.ASM(33): error A2089: Forced error
        29                              .ERRE    num1 EQ num2        ; Force error if 5=6
fig9_err.ASM(34): error A2090: Forced error - expression equals 0
        30                              .ERRE    num1 EQ num3        ; Force error if 5=5
        31                              .ERRNZ   num1 NE num2        ; Force error if 5=6
fig9_err.ASM(36): error A2091: Forced error - expression not equal 0
        32                              .ERRNZ   num1 NE num3        ; Force error if 5=5
        33
        34                              .ERRNDEF Fig9_err            ; No error - fig9_err is def.
        35                              .ERRNDEF FIG9_xxx            ; Error - fig9_xxx is not.
fig9_err.ASM(40): error A2092: Forced error - symbol not defined
        36                              .ERRDEF  Fig9_err            ; Error - fig9_err is defined
fig9_err.ASM(41): error A2093: Forced error - symbol defined
        37                              .ERRDEF  FIG9_xxx            ; No error - fig9_xxx is not.
        38                      ;
        39                      ; The remaining two error directives are valid only within macros.
        40                      ; Thus we make a macro to demo them.
        41                      ;
        42              demo1   MACRO    param1
        43                  IFB <param1>                             ; ensure param1 is omitted
        44                      %OUT     Parameter param1 is omitted
        45                      .ERRB    <param1>                    ; This generates an error
        46                      .ERRNB   <param1>                    ; This doesn't
        47                  ELSE
        48                      %OUT     Parameter param1 is present
        49                      .ERRB    <param1>                    ; This doesn't generate but
        50                      .ERRNB   <param1>                    ; this does.
        51                  ENDIF
        52                      ENDM
        53
        54                      demo1    present            ; non-blank error message
        55          1                    .ERRNB <present>          ; this does.
fig9_err.ASM(59): error A2095: Forced error - string not blank
        56                      demo1                      ; blank parameter error
        57          1                    .ERRB    <>               ; This generates an error
fig9_err.ASM(60): error A2094: Forced error - string blank
        58
        59                      demo2   MACRO    param1,param2
        60                  IFNB <param2>                            ; Limit to 'good' compares.
        61                      %OUT     looking for equal parameters here
        62                      .ERRIDN  <param1>,<param2>  ; Error if identical
        63                      .ERRIDNI <param1>,<param2> ; Case insensitive check.
        64                      %OUT     Looking for unequals now --
        65                      .ERRDIF  <param1>,<param2>  ; Error if different
        66                      .ERRDIFI <param1>,<param2> ; Case insensitive check.
        67                  ELSE
        68                      %OUT     Looking for equal to xXx now --
        69                      .ERRIDN  <param1>,<xXx>     ; Error if identical
        70                      .ERRIDNI <param1>,<xXx>    ; Case insensitive check.
        71                      %OUT     Looking for unequals now --
        72                      .ERRDIF  <param1>,<xXx>     ; Error if different
        73                      .ERRDIFI <param1>,<xXx>    ; Case insensitive check.
        74                  ENDIF
        75                      ENDM
        76
        77                      demo2    aaa,aaa           ; identical parameters
        78          1                    .ERRIDN <aaa>,<aaa>  ; Error if identical
fig9_err.ASM(80): error A2096: Forced error - strings identical
        79          1                    .ERRIDNI <aaa>,<aaa> ; Case insensitive check.
fig9_err.ASM(80): error A2096: Forced error - strings identical
        80
        81                      demo2    aaa,AAA           ; same letters - diff case
        82          1                    .ERRIDNI <aaa>,<AAA> ; Case insensitive check.
fig9_err.ASM(82): error A2096: Forced error - strings identical
        83          1                    .ERRDIF <aaa>,<AAA>  ; Error if different
fig9_err.ASM(82): error A2097: Forced error - strings different
        84
        85                      demo2    aaa,bbb           ; No match at all
        86          1                    .ERRDIF <aaa>,<bbb>  ; Error if different
```

Fig. 9-5. (continued)

```
fig9_err.ASM(84): error A2097: Forced error - strings different
      87                              1                 .ERRDIFI <aaa>,<bbb>   ; Case insensitive check.
fig9_err.ASM(84): error A2097: Forced error - strings different
      88
      89                              demo2    xXx                ; parameter matches con
      90                              1                 .ERRIDN <xXx>,<xXx>    ; Error if identical
fig9_err.ASM(86): error A2096: Forced error - strings identical
      91                              1                 .ERRIDNI <xXx>,<xXx>     ; Case insensitive check.
      92
      93                              demo2    xxx                ; same letters - diff case
      94                              1                 .ERRIDNI <xxx>,<xXx>     ; Case insensitive check.
fig9_err.ASM(88): error A2096: Forced error - strings identical
      95                              1                 .ERRDIF <xxx>,<xXx>     ; Error if different
fig9_err.ASM(88): error A2097: Forced error - strings different
      96
      97                              demo2    yyy                ; again - no match at all
      98                              1                 .ERRDIF <yyy>,<xXx>     ; Error if different
fig9_err.ASM(90): error A2097: Forced error - strings different
      99                              1                 .ERRDIFI <yyy>,<xXx>     ; Case insensitive check.
fig9_err.ASM(90): error A2097: Forced error - strings different
     100
     101 0000                         Fig9_err    ENDP
     102 0000                         code        ENDS
     103                                          END
```

```
                  Macros:

                                N a m e          Lines

                  DEMO1 . . . . . . . . . . . .          9
                  DEMO2 . . . . . . . . . . . .         15

                  Segments and Groups:

                                N a m e          Size    Length   Align  Combine Class

                  CODE . . . . . . . . . . . .   16 Bit  0000     PARA   PUBLIC 'CODE'

                  Symbols:

                                N a m e          Type    Value   Attr

                  FIG9_ERR . . . . . . . . . . .  N PROC  0000    CODE    Length = 0000

                  NUM1 . . . . . . . . . . . . .  NUMBER  0005
                  NUM2 . . . . . . . . . . . . .  NUMBER  0006
                  NUM3 . . . . . . . . . . . . .  NUMBER  0005

                  @CPU . . . . . . . . . . . .    TEXT    3343
                  @FILENAME  . . . . . . . . . .  TEXT    fig9_err
                  @VERSION . . . . . . . . . . .  TEXT    510

                       94 Source  Lines
                      202 Total   Lines
                       12 Symbols

                   47366 + 189030 Bytes symbol space free

                        0 Warning Errors
                       20 Severe  Errors
```

Fig. 9-5. (continued)

Figure 9-6 shows the error messages as they would display on the screen during a MASM run of the program shown in Fig. 9-5.

.ERR, .ERR1, and .ERR2 Directives.

Syntax: .ERR
               .ERR1
               .ERR2

Examples:
```
IFDEF DOS
   :
   :
   ELSE
       IFDEF XENIX
          :
          :
       ELSE
              .ERR
              ENDIF
   ENDIF
```

.ERR, .ERR1, and .ERR2 force errors at the points they occur in a source file. Although the error directives force errors, you can place them inside conditional assembly blocks to limit the directives to certain situations. .ERR forces an error regardless of the pass, while .ERR1 forces an error only during the first MASM pass, and .ERR2 only during the second pass. .ERR1 only appears on the monitor screen or in the listing file if you use the /D option to request a pass one listing. Unlike other conditional error directives, .ERR1 is not a fatal error. For a quick way to see which macros or conditional-assembly blocks are being expanded, place one of these directives in the macro or block.

.ERRB and .ERRNB Directives.

Syntax: .ERRB <*argument*>
               .ERRNB <*argument*>

Examples: See the listing in Fig. 9-5.

.ERRB and .ERRNB test the given *argument* to see if one was passed to a macro. The directives conditionally generate an error based on the result of that test. .ERRB generates an error if *argument* is blank, and .ERRNB generates an error if *argument* is NOT blank. The *argument* can be any name, number, or expression; the angle brackets (< >) are required. These directives are always used within macros to test for the existence of real parameters passed as dummy arguments.

```
Microsoft (R) Macro Assembler Version 5.10
Copyright (C) Microsoft Corp 1981, 1988.  All rights reserved.

Pass 1 messages:
fig9_3.ASM(25): error A2087: Forced error - pass1
fig9_3.ASM(33): error A2089: Forced error
fig9_3.ASM(34): error A2090: Forced error - expression equals 0
fig9_3.ASM(36): error A2091: Forced error - expression not equal 0
fig9_3.ASM(40): error A2092: Forced error - symbol not defined
fig9_3.ASM(41): error A2093: Forced error - symbol defined
Parameter present is present
fig9_3.ASM(59): error A2095: Forced error - string not blank
Parameter  is omitted
fig9_3.ASM(60): error A2094: Forced error - string blank
looking for equal parameters here
fig9_3.ASM(80): error A2096: Forced error - strings identical
fig9_3.ASM(80): error A2096: Forced error - strings identical
Looking for unequals now --
looking for equal parameters here
fig9_3.ASM(82): error A2096: Forced error - strings identical
Looking for unequals now --
fig9_3.ASM(82): error A2097: Forced error - strings different
looking for equal parameters here
Looking for unequals now --
fig9_3.ASM(84): error A2097: Forced error - strings different
fig9_3.ASM(84): error A2097: Forced error - strings different
Looking for equal to xXx now --
fig9_3.ASM(86): error A2096: Forced error - strings identical
fig9_3.ASM(86): error A2096: Forced error - strings identical
Looking for unequals now --
Looking for equal to xXx now --
fig9_3.ASM(88): error A2096: Forced error - strings identical
Looking for unequals now --
fig9_3.ASM(88): error A2097: Forced error - strings different
Looking for equal to xXx now --
Looking for unequals now --
fig9_3.ASM(90): error A2097: Forced error - strings different
fig9_3.ASM(90): error A2097: Forced error - strings different
Pass 2 messages:
fig9_3.ASM(31): error A2088: Forced error - pass2
fig9_3.ASM(33): error A2089: Forced error
fig9_3.ASM(34): error A2090: Forced error - expression equals 0
fig9_3.ASM(36): error A2091: Forced error - expression not equal 0
fig9_3.ASM(40): error A2092: Forced error - symbol not defined
fig9_3.ASM(41): error A2093: Forced error - symbol defined
Parameter present is present
fig9_3.ASM(59): error A2095: Forced error - string not blank
Parameter  is omitted
fig9_3.ASM(60): error A2094: Forced error - string blank
looking for equal parameters here
fig9_3.ASM(80): error A2096: Forced error - strings identical
fig9_3.ASM(80): error A2096: Forced error - strings identical
Looking for unequals now --
looking for equal parameters here
fig9_3.ASM(82): error A2096: Forced error - strings identical
Looking for unequals now --
fig9_3.ASM(82): error A2097: Forced error - strings different
looking for equal parameters here
Looking for unequals now --
fig9_3.ASM(84): error A2097: Forced error - strings different
fig9_3.ASM(84): error A2097: Forced error - strings different
Looking for equal to xXx now --
fig9_3.ASM(86): error A2096: Forced error - strings identical
fig9_3.ASM(86): error A2096: Forced error - strings identical
Looking for unequals now --
Looking for equal to xXx now --
fig9_3.ASM(88): error A2096: Forced error - strings identical
Looking for unequals now --
```

Fig. 9-6. MASM Screen Display of Conditional Error-Directive Error Messages. (continued)

```
fig9_3.ASM(88): error A2097: Forced error - strings different
Looking for equal to xXx now --
Looking for unequals now --
fig9_3.ASM(90): error A2097: Forced error - strings different
fig9_3.ASM(90): error A2097: Forced error - strings different

   47384 + 156436 Bytes symbol space free

       0 Warning Errors
      20 Severe  Errors
```

Fig. 9-6. (continued)

.ERRDEF and .ERRNDEF Directives.

Syntax: .ERRDEF *name*
             .ERRNDEF *name*

Examples: See the listing in Fig. 9-5.

    .ERRDEF and .ERRNDEF test whether or not *name* has been defined. .ERRDEF produces an error if *name* is defined as a label, variable, or symbol. .ERRNDEF produces an error if *name* has not yet been defined. If *name* is a forward reference, MASM considers it undefined on pass one and defined on pass two.

.ERRE and .ERRNZ Directives.

Syntax: .ERRE *expression*
             .ERRNZ *expression*

Examples: See the listing in Fig. 9-5.

    .ERRE and .ERRNZ test the value of an *expression* and generate errors based on the result of the test. .ERRE generates an error if the *expression* is false (0) and .ERRNZ generates an error if the *expression* is true (nonzero). *Expression* must resolve to a constant and must not contain forward references.

.ERRIDN and .ERRDIF Directives.

Syntax: .ERRIDN[I] <*argument1*>,<*argument2*>
             .ERRDIF[I] <*argument1*>,<*argument2*>

Examples: See the listing in Fig. 9-5.

    .ERRIDN and .ERRDIF test whether two arguments are identical. .ERRIDN generates an error if the two arguments are identical and .ERRDIF generates an error if the arguments are different. *Argument1* and *argument2* can be names, numbers, or expressions. To be considered identical, each character in *argument1* must match the corresponding character in *argument2*. The arguments are case sensitive, and the angle brackets (< >) are required. The two arguments must be separated by a comma.

The optional I at the end of the directive name specifies that the directive is case insensitive. Arguments that are spelled the same will be evaluated the same regardless of case. If the I is not given, the directive is case sensitive.

MACRO DIRECTIVES

Macro directives allow the writing of a named block of source statements. You can then use that name in a source file to represent the statements. Define a macro any place in the source file, as long as the definition precedes the first source line that calls the macro. Keep macros in a separate directory or subdirectory and make them available to programs through an INCLUDE directive. In fact, we suggest you set up an MS-DOS subdirectory, generally called a macro library or MACLIB. Group logically similar macros into a single source. For instance, if a series of macros do graphics work (locate cursor, draw lines, and so on), package them into one large source called GRAPHIC.MAC. Then simply INCLUDE GRAPHIC.MAC when you write new graphics source programs.

Macro expansion is a text-producing function that occurs at assembly time. MASM automatically replaces each occurrence of the macro name with the statements in the macro definition. Insert the statements anywhere in the source by simply using the name as many times as the macro is needed. You can also pass parameters to the macros. During assembly, MASM replaces the text of parameter names with the text of the corresponding actual arguments. Because most macros only need to be expanded once, increase efficiency by processing them only during a single pass of the assembler. Do this by enclosing the macros (or an INCLUDE statement that calls them) in a conditional block using the IF1 directive.

Often a task can be completed by using either a macro or a procedure. Macros are expanded on every occurrence of the macro name, so they can increase the length of the executable file if they are called repeatedly. Procedures, on the other hand, are coded only once in the executable file, but the increased overhead of saving and restoring addresses and parameters can make them slower. Ultimately, the choice of whether to code the task as a macro or a procedure comes down to an intuitive feel that you develop after a few programming experiences with macros and procedures.

Figure 9-7 shows an overview of macro directives.

```
        ENDM
        EXITM
        IRP     param,<argument[[,argument,,,]]>
        IRPC    param,string
        LOCAL   name1[[,name,,,]]
name    MACRO   [[parameters,,,]]
        PURGE   macroname[[,macroname,,,]]
        REPT    expression
```

Fig. 9-7. Overview of Macro Directives.

MACRO and ENDM designate the beginning and end of a macro block. LOCAL allows the definitions of labels used only within a macro, and PURGE deletes previously defined macros. EXITM allows you to exit from a macro before all the statements in the block are expanded. REPT, IRP, and IRPC creates contiguous blocks of repeated statements. These repeat blocks are often placed within macros but can also be used independently. You can control the number of repetitions in three separate ways: (1) by specifying a number, (2) by allowing the block to be repeated once for each parameter in a list, or (3) by having the block repeated once for each character in a string.

A macro is called any time its name appears in a source file; however, macro names in comments are ignored. MASM copies the statements in the macro definition to the point of the call, replacing any dummy parameters in these statements with actual parameters passed in the call. All addresses in the assembled code will be relative to the macro call, not the macro definition. The macro definition itself is never assembled.

Macro definitions can be *recursive*; that is, they can call themselves. Using recursive macros is one way of doing repeated operations. The macro does a task, and then calls itself to do the task again. The recursion is repeated until a specific condition is met.

Macro definitions can be nested to any depth; this nesting is limited only by the amount of memory available when a source file is assembled. Nesting means that one macro can be defined within another one. MASM does not process nested definitions until the outer macro has been called. Therefore, you cannot call nested macros until the outer macro has been called at least once.

Macros can be redefined, and you do not need to purge the first macro before redefining it. The new definition replaces the old one. If redefining a macro from within the macro itself, make sure there are no lines between the ENDM directive of the nested redefinition and the ENDM directive of the original macro.

MACRO and ENDM Directives

Syntax: *name* MACRO [*dummyparameter,,,*]
                       statements
                       ENDM

Examples: See the listing in Fig. 9-5.

MACRO and ENDM create a macro having *name* and containing the given *statements*. *Name* must be a valid name and unique; use the *name* in the source file to invoke the macro. The *dummyparameter* is a name that acts as a placeholder for values to be passed to the macro when it is called. Specify any number of *dummyparameter*, but they must all fit on one line. That is, there can be no embedded carriage return. If more than one parameter is entered, they must be separated by commas (,), spaces, or tabs (commas can always be used, but spaces or tabs might cause ambiguity if the arguments are expressions). The *dummyparameter* can be used any number of times in the *statements*. The *statements* are any valid MASM statements, including other macro directives. You can code any number of statements.

Be careful when using the word MACRO after the TITLE, SUBTTL, or NAME directives. Because MACRO overrides these directives, placing the word MACRO immediately after these directives causes MASM to begin to create a macro named TITLE, SUBTTL, or NAME. For instance, take the code line:

TITLE MACRO File

You might intend to give an include file the title *Macro File*, but the effect of the line of code is to create a macro called TITLE that accepts the dummy parameter File. There is no corresponding ENDM directive, so MASM prints an error. To avoid this, alter the word MACRO in some way when using it in a title or name, such as MACRO1 or __MACRO.

MASM replaces all occurrences of a dummy parameter name, even if it was not intended for it to do so. For instance, you might have used a register name such as EAX for a dummy parameter. MASM replaces all occurrences of that register name when it expands the macro.

Remember that MASM assembles the statements in a macro only if the macro is called and only at the point in the source file from which it is called. The macro definition itself is never assembled. A macro definition can include the LOCAL directive (see below), which lets you define labels used only within a macro, or the EXITM directive, (see below) which allows you to exit from a macro before all the statements in the block are expanded.

Macro Calls

Syntax: *name [actualparameter,,,]*

Examples: See the listing in Fig. 9-5.

A macro call directs MASM to copy the statements of the macro *name* to the point of call in the source and to replace any dummy parameters in these statements with the corresponding *actualparameter*. The *name* must be the name of a macro defined earlier in the source file (or INCLUDEd earlier). The *actualparameter* can be any name, number, or other value. It is possible to pass any number of parameters, but they must all fit on one line and be separated by commas (,), spaces, or tabs (commas are the recommended separator).

The *actualparameter* is position sensitive. MASM replaces the first dummy parameter with the first actual parameter, the second with the second, and so on. If the macro call has more actual parameters than dummy parameters, MASM ignores the extra actual parameters. If it finds fewer actual parameters than dummy parameters, MASM replaces any remaining dummy parameters with a null (empty) string. Use the IFB, IFNB, .ERR, and .ERRNB directives to have macros check for null strings and take appropriate action. If passing a list of values as a single *actualparameter*, place angle brackets (< >) around the list. The items in the list must be separated by commas (,).

Macro Operators

Macros use the set of operators shown in Fig. 9-8. When used in a macro definition, these operators carry out special control operations, such as text substitution.

Operator	Definition
&	Substitute Operator
<>	Literal-text enclosure
!	Character escape
%	Espression Operator
;;	Macro Comment

Fig. 9-8. Macro Operators.

Substitute Operator

Syntax: *&dummyparameter*

Examples:

```
THSERROR   MACRO   a,b
           PUBLIC  ERR&a
err&a      DB      'Error &a: &b'
           ENDM
```

The substitute operator comes to microprocessor programming with a long history of usefulness from the mainframe world. For instance, programmers use it in Job Control Language (JCL) to instruct the mainframe operating systems to use various input devices. With MASM, the substitute operator (&) forces the assembler to replace *dummyparameter* with its corresponding actual parameter value. The operator is used anywhere a dummy parameter immediately precedes or follows other characters, or whenever the parameter appears in a quoted string.

With nested macros, use the ampersand (&) to delay the actual replacement of a dummy parameter. In general, supply as many ampersands as there are levels of nesting. For instance, in the following example, the substitute operator is used twice with *z* to make sure its replacement occurs while the IRP directive is being processed:

```
alloc   MACRO X
        IRP     z,<1,2,3>
        x&&z    DB      z
        ENDM
        ENDM
```

In the example, the dummy parameter x is replaced immediately when the macro is called. The dummy parameter z is not replaced until the IRP directive is processed. This means that the parameter is replaced once for each number in the IRP parameter list.

Literal-Text Operator

Syntax: *<text>*

Examples: thiswork 1,2,3,   ; Passes three parameters
                                  ; to thiswork
            thiswork <1,2,3,>   ; Passes a three-element
                                  ; parameter to thiswork

When using the literal-text operator, you direct MASM to treat *text* as a single literal element, regardless of whether it contains spaces, commas, or other separators. This operator is most often used with macro calls and the IRP directive to ensure that values in a parameter list are treated as a single parameter. It is possible also to use the literal-text operator to force MASM to treat special characters (such as the semicolon [;] or the ampersand [&]) literally. For example, the semicolon inside angle brackets <;> becomes a semicolon and not a comment indicator. MASM removes one set of angle brackets each time the parameter is used in a macro. When nesting macros, supply as many sets of angle brackets as there are levels of nesting.

Literal-Character Operator

Syntax: *!character*

Examples: See the listing in appendix G—listing page numbers 1-10 and 1-11.

The literal-character operator forces MASM to treat the *character* as a literal character. It is possible to use this directive to force MASM to treat special characters literally. Therefore, !; is equivalent to <;>.

Expression Operator

Syntax: *%text*

Examples: See the listing in appendix G—listing page numbers 1-10 and 1-11.

The expression operator (%) causes MASM to treat *text* as an expression. MASM computes the expression value, using numbers of the current radix, and replaces *text* with this new value. The *text* must represent a valid expression. Typically, use the expression operator in macro calls where you need to pass the result of an expression to the macro instead of the actual expression.

Macro Comment

Syntax: *;;text*

Examples: See the listing in appendix G.

A macro comment is text in a macro definition that does not need to be copied in the macro expansion. MASM ignores all *text* following the double semicolon (;;). That *text* only appears in the macro definition when the source listing is created.

You can also use the regular comment operator (the single semicolon [;]) in macros. However, regular comments might appear in listings when the macro is expanded. Whether or not regular comments are listed in macro expansions depends on the use of the .LALL, .XALL, and .SALL directives (see chapter 8 for a description of these directives).

EXITM Directive.

Syntax: EXITM

Examples: See the listing in appendix G—listing page number 1-1.

EXITM tells MASM to terminate macro or repeat-block expansion and to continue assembly with the next statement after the macro call or repeat block. Typically, use EXITM with IF directives to allow conditional expansion of the last statements in a macro or repeat block.

When MASM encounters the EXITM, MASM exits the macro or repeat block immediately. Any remaining statements in the macro or repeat block are not processed. If MASM finds an EXITM in a macro or repeat block nested in another macro or repeat block, MASM returns to expanding the outer level block.

Repeat Blocks

Repeat blocks are a special form of macro that creates block of repeated statements. They differ from macros in that they are not named. Thus, they cannot be called. Like macros, however, they can have parameters that are replaced by actual arguments during assembly. Again like macros, repeat blocks always terminate with an ENDM directive.

Repeat blocks are used in macros to repeat some of the macro statements. They can also be used independently, usually for declaring arrays with repeated data elements. MASM processes repeat blocks during assembly. These blocks should not be confused with the 80386 REP prefix instruction, which causes string instructions to be repeated at run time (see appendix B).

Three different kinds of repeat blocks can be defined by using the REPT, IRP, and IRPC directives. The major difference between them is in how the number of repetitions is specified.

REPT Directive.

Syntax: REPT *expression*
                 statements
             ENDM

Examples: See the listing in appendix G—listing page number 1-7.

REPT creates repeat blocks in which you specify the number of repetitions with a numeric argument. REPT and ENDM enclose a block of *statements* to be repeated *expression* number of times. The *expression* must evaluate to a 16-bit unsigned number, and it must not contain external or undefined symbols. The *statements* can be any valid assembler statements.

IRP Directive.

Syntax: IRP *dummyname,* <*parameter,,,* >
                   statements
               ENDM

Examples: See the listing in appendix G—listing page numbers 1-6.

IRP creates repeat blocks in which the number of repetitions are specified (as well as the parameters for each repetition) in a list of arguments. IRP and ENDM designate a block of *statements* to be repeated once for each *parameter* in the list enclosed by angle brackets (< >). *Dummyname* is a name for a placeholder to be replaced by the current *parameter.* This *parameter* can be any legal symbol, numerical, string, or character constant. It is possible to give any number of parameters but separate them with commas (,). You must code angle brackets (< >) around the parameter list. The *statements* can be any valid assembler statements. The *dummyname* can be used any number of times within the macro.

Each time MASM finds an IRP, it makes one copy of the *statements* for each parameter in the enclosed list. When it copies the *statements*, it substitutes the current parameter for all occurrences of *dummyname* in these statements. If MASM finds a null parameter (< >) in the list, the *dummyname* is replaced with a null value. If the parameter list is empty, MASM ignores IRP and does not copy any statements.

IRPC Directive.

Syntax: IRPC *dummyname,string*
                   statements
               ENDM

Examples: See the listing in appendix G—listing page numbers 1-6 and 1-7.

IRPC creates repeat blocks in which the number of repetitions are specified, as well as arguments for each repetition, in a string. IRPC and ENDM enclose a block of *statements* that is repeated once for each character in *string*. *Dummyname* is a name for a placeholder that is replaced by the current character in the *string*. The *string* can be any combination of digits, letters, and other characters. Enclose the *string* with angle brackets (< >) if the string contains spaces, commas, or other separating characters. The *statements* can be any valid assembler statements and *dummyname* can be used any number of times in these statements.

Each time MASM finds an IRPC, it makes one copy of the *statements* for each character in the *string*. When it copies the *statements*, MASM substitutes the current character for all occurrences of *dummyname* in these *statements*.

LOCAL Directive.

Syntax: LOCAL *localname,,,*

Examples: LOCAL This__Num,CALL__HERE

Typically, use LOCAL to create a unique label that will only be used in a macro. If MASM finds a macro that contains a label used more than once, the assembler displays an error message that indicates the file contains a label or symbol with multiple definitions, because the same label appears in both expansions. To avoid this, declare all labels as local names with the LOCAL directive.

Only use LOCAL in a macro definition, LOCAL must precede all other statements in the definitions. If a comment line or an instruction appears before the LOCAL directive, MASM issues a warning message.

LOCAL creates unique symbol names for use in macros. *Localname* is a name for a placeholder that is replaced by a unique name when the macro is called (expanded). MASM creates a new actual name for the *localname* each time the macro is expanded. That actual name has the form: *??number*. The *number* is a hexadecimal number in the range 0000 to 0FFFF. Do not use other symbol names in this format, because doing so might produce a label or symbol with multiple definitions. In listings, the *localname* is shown in the macro definition, but the actual names are shown for each expansion of the macro.

At least one *localname* is required for each LOCAL, although if you give more they must be separated by commas (,). It is possible to use the *localname* in any statement within the macro.

PURGE Directive.

Syntax: PURGE *macroname,,,*

Examples: PURGE THISMAC
            PURGE mac1,mac2

At assembly time, PURGE deletes from memory the current definition of the macro called *macroname*. Any subsequent call to that macro causes MASM to generate an error. Use PURGE to clear memory space no longer needed by a macro. If *macroname* is a reserved name, the reserved name is restored to its previous meaning. Macros need not be purged before being redefined since any redefinition automatically purges the previous definition. Also, any macro can purge itself as long as the PURGE directive is on the last line of the macro.

PURGE works by redefining the macro to a null string. Therefore, calling a purged macro does not cause an error; the macro name is simply ignored.

PURGE is often used with a macro library to choose which macros from the library are needed in the source file. A macro library, by the way, is simply a file that contains macro definitions. Add this library to the source program by using the INCLUDE directive; then remove unwanted definitions using PURGE.

TEXT MACROS

Syntax: *name* EQU [<]*string*[>]

Examples: pi   EQU<3.14>   ; string constant "3.14"
             PROMPT EQU <'Enter number: '>

A string equate (or text macro) is used to assign a string constant to a symbol. It is possible to use text macros in a variety of contexts, including defining aliases and string constants. An alias is a special kind of string equate. It is a symbol that is equated to another symbol or keyword. The EQU directive creates constant symbols by assigning *string* to *name*. MASM replaces each subsequent occurrence of *name* with *string*. Symbols defined to represent strings with the EQU directive can be redefined to new strings. Do not define symbols to represent strings with the equals-sign (=) directive.

The use of angle brackets to force string evaluation is a new feature of MASM version 5.0. Previous versions tried to evaluate equates as expressions. If the string did not evaluate to a valid expression, MASM evaluated it as a string, which sometimes caused unexpected consequences. For example:

RNTME   EQU RUN-TIME

would evaluate as a subtraction of TIME from RUN, even though you might intend to define the string RUN-TIME. If RUN and TIME did not already appear as numerical equates, the statement generates an error. Using angle brackets solves this problem, to evaluate RUN-TIME as a string:

RNTME   EQU <RUN-TIME>

When evaluating existing source, you can leave string equates alone that evaluate correctly, but for new source code that will not be used with previous MASM versions, it is a good idea to enclose all string equates in angle brackets.

Warning: If you originally had MASM 5.0 and ordered the update to 5.1, your reference manual indicates that the following information *was* valid for text macros. We installed the update, used them, and found significant bugs. However, if you simply ordered 5.1 straight (as we did for our second system) and did not pay for the update (which we did for our first system), these text macro directives disappeared without a word—not even in the README.DOC released with the code. As best we can determine, the text macro string directives do not work as released. The full 5.1 release does not document them. So, do not use them until this is resolved. EQU is documented in both and appears to work.

In the update version 5.1, text macros follow the same evaluation rules as regular macros. This change means that text is substituted for the text-macro name when it appears in the operation field. It is now possible to use text macros as short, one-line macros. MASM displays the values of text macros in the program listing when you assign the text macro a value. Text macro values appear in the left column preceded by an equals sign (=).

MASM 5.1 includes four text-macro string directives that allow manipulation of literal strings or text-macro values. Use the four directives in much the same way you use the equals-sign (=) directive (see chapter 6 for the equals-sign directive).

CATSTR Directive.

Syntax: *textlabel* CATSTR *string*[*,string*],,,

The CATSTR directive concatenates a variable number of strings (text macros or literal strings) to form a single string. The CATSTR directive requires a text-macro label. *textlabel* is the text label the result is assigned to, and *string* is the string or strings concatenated and assigned to *textlabel*.

INSTR Directive.

Syntax: *numericlabel* INSTR [*start,*]*string1,string2*

The INSTR directive returns an index indicating the starting position of a substring within another string. INSTR requires a numerical label. The *start* is the starting position for the search. When the *start* is omitted, INSTR starts searching at the first character. The first character in the string has a position of one, not zero. The *numericlabel* is a numerical label the substring position is assigned to. *string1* is the string being searched and *string2* is the string to look for.

SIZESTR Directive.

Syntax: *numericlabel* SIZESTR *string*

SIZESTR returns the length, in characters, of its argument *string*. SIZESTR requires a numerical label. A null string has a length of zero.

SUBSTR Directive.

Syntax: *textlabel* SUBSTR *string,start*[*,length*]

SUBSTR returns a substring of its text macro or literal string argument. SUBSTR requires a text-macro label. *textlabel* is the text label the result is assigned to; *string* is the string the substring is extracted from. *start* is the starting position of the substring, where the first character in the string has a position of one (not zero). *length* is the number of characters to extract. If the *length* is omitted, SUBSTR returns all characters to the right of position *start*, including the character at position *start*.

MASM 5.1 includes three new predefined text macros: @WordSize, @Cpu, and @Version.

@WordSize. @WordSize returns the word size of the segment word size in bytes. It returns 4 when the word size is 32 bits and 2 when the word size is 16 bits. By default, the segment word size is 16 bits with the 80286 and 32 bits with the 80386.

@Cpu. @Cpu returns a 16-bit value containing information about the selected processor (see chapter 8 for instruction-set directives). Select a processor by using one of the processor directives such as the .386 directive. You can use the @Cpu text macro to control assembly of processor-specific code. Individual bits in the value returned by @Cpu are shown in Fig. 9-9.

Bit	If Bit = 1
0	8086 processor
1	80186 processor
2	80286 processor
3	80386 processor
4	Reserved
5	Reserved
6	Reserved
7	Privileged instruction enabled (80286 and 80386)
8	8087 coprocessor instructions enabled
9	Reserved
10	80287 coprocessor instructions enabled
11	80387 coprocessor instructions enabled
12	Reserved
13	Reserved
14	Reserved
15	Reserved

Fig. 9-9. Bits Returned by @Cpu.

Do not use bits that are shown as reserved. They can be changed without notice in future releases. Also, remember that the Intel processors are upwardly compatible; the 80386 instruction set includes all the previous instruction sets (8088 through 80386). Therefore, selecting a higher-numbered processor automatically sets the bits indicating lower-numbered processors. The @Cpu text macro tells information only about the processor used during assembly; it does not provide information about the processor used during run time.

@Version. @Version returns a string containing the MASM version in use. With @Version, it is possible to write macros for future versions of MASM that take appropriate actions when used with inappropriate MASM versions. This macro returns 510 as a string of three characters, for version 5.1.

FINAL NOTE

MASM 5.1 requires the use of a special convention when assembling using the /ML switch; each word in a name must begin with an upper case letter. If, in MASM 5.0, you used @thisfile when assembling with the /ML switch, now it must appear as @ThisFile. This convention does not apply to the predefined equates used with segment directives, such as the equate @curseg.

10

Interfacing Assembly Language with High-Level Languages

MICROSOFT HAS BUILT THEIR LANGUAGES SO THAT A PROGRAM WRITTEN IN ONE LANGUAGE can call modules written in another language. This characteristic is especially handy if you are on a programming team where each programmer is writing code in a different language. It also enables you to pass routines among friends, and the routines are in different Microsoft languages. This chapter gives an overview of mixed-language programming and the conventions Microsoft has set up for its languages. If you need more than an overview, be sure to get Microsoft's *Mixed-Language Programming Guide*, which is a full manual dedicated to the subject with separate sections that detail each language. In this chapter, the focus is on assembly language.

Mixed-language programming is creating programs using two or more source languages. Mixed-language programming is not really difficult, but it requires an understanding of some basic issues. Once you understand those underlying facts, mix and match languages and routines to use the unique strengths of each language.

When writing mixed-language calls, you invoke functions, procedures, or subroutines. For example, the main BASIC program might need to use some of the MS-DOS function calls (see appendix D for BIOS interrupts and calls, and appendix E for MS-DOS interrupts and calls). So, write the function calls in assembly language and then issue a call from the BASIC program for that function. Instead of compiling the code in one large program, code various pieces and assemble each one individually (debugging as you go). Once you are finished, simply link them together. Figure 10-1 shows this process graphically.

CONVENTIONS

A *convention* is a standard and accepted procedure in programs and systems analysis. It includes the abbreviations, symbols, and their meanings as developed for particular systems and programs. The availability of conventions within any software system

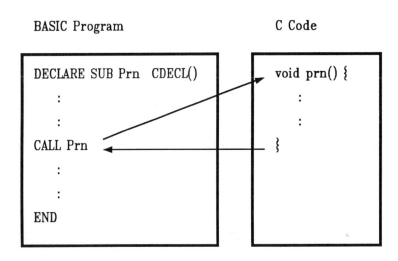

BASIC Program

C Code

```
DECLARE SUB Prn  CDECL()

    :

    :

CALL Prn

    :

    :

END
```

```
void prn() {

    :

    :

}
```

Fig. 10-1. Using Mixed-Language Calls.

provides a basis for writing efficient programs. Microsoft has set certain conventions for naming, calling, and parameter passing for their mixed-language programming.

Naming Conventions

Microsoft compilers and assemblers place machine code into object files. The names (in ASCII format) of all variables and routines which need to be accessed publicly are also stored in the object files. Then the linker (see appendix F for a LINK overview) compares the name called in one module to the name defined in another module, and either finds a match or does not. If the compiler or assembler stores the name of the called routine differently in each object file, then the linker will not be able to find a match and will report an unresolved external reference.

Microsoft's compilers (BASIC, FORTRAN, and Pascal) use almost the same naming convention in that they translate each letter to upper case. At the same time, BASIC type declaration characters (%, &, !, #, and $) are dropped. However, each language recognizes a different number of characters for names. BASIC recognizes the first 40 characters, FORTRAN the first six, and Pascal the first eight. If a name is longer than the language maximum, the additional characters are not placed in the object file.

Unlike the other three languages, C does not translate any letters to upper case. Like Pascal, C recognizes the first 8 characters of a name, but C inserts a leading underscore (_) in front of the name.

Figure 10-2 shows an overview of naming conventions. In the figure, note that the BASIC compiler inserts a leading underscore in front of Prn as it places the name into the object file, because the CDECL keyword directs the BASIC compiler to use the C

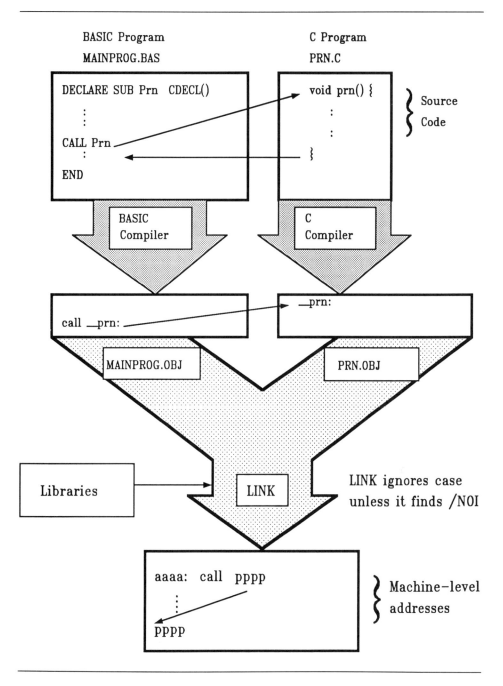

Fig. 10-2. Overview of Naming Conventions.

naming convention. BASIC also converts all letters to lower case when this keyword is used. You will have few problems with naming conventions by following two single rules:

- If using any FORTRAN, keep all names six characters or less.
- When linking, do not use the /NOIGNORE (see appendix F for a LINK overview) option, which causes LINK to distinguish between upper and lower case.

Calling Conventions

A calling convention defines how a language implements a call. The importance in this is how the convention affects the actual machine instructions that the compiler/assembler generates in order to execute and return from a function, procedure, or subroutine call. The calling convention is a low-level protocol, which is essentially a set of conventions, or rules, between processes on the format and content of messages to be exchanged. It is critical that the routine that issues a call and the routine being called recognize the same protocol. Otherwise, the processor might receive confusing instructions, which can cause it to crash. A calling convention affects you two ways:

- The calling routine uses a convention to determine in what order and form to pass parameters to another routine.
- The called routine uses a convention to determine in what order and form it is to receive the parameters that were passed to it.

The calling and the receiving conventions must be compatible. Microsoft's BASIC, FORTRAN, and Pascal use the same standard calling convention; C is different. BASIC, FORTRAN, and Pascal each push parameters onto the stack in the order in which they appear in the source code. (A stack is a reserved area of memory where the CPU saves the contents of various registers and other values; it works on a last-in/first-out basis.) For instance, the statement CALL Calc1 (X,Y) pushes the argument X onto the stack before it pushes Y. Also, these languages specify that the stack be restored (by removing parameters) by the called routine, just before returning control to the caller, see Fig. 10-3. These conventions produce slightly less object code than does the C convention.

C pushes parameters onto the stack in the reverse order in which they appear in the source code. For example, CALL Calc1 (X,Y) pushes Y onto the stack before it pushes X. Also different from the others, C specifies that a calling routine restore the stack immediately after the called routine returns control. The C conventions make calling with a variable number of parameters possible because the first parameter is always the last one pushed. That last parameter is always on the top of the stack so it has the same address relative to the pointer, regardless of how many parameters were actually passed.

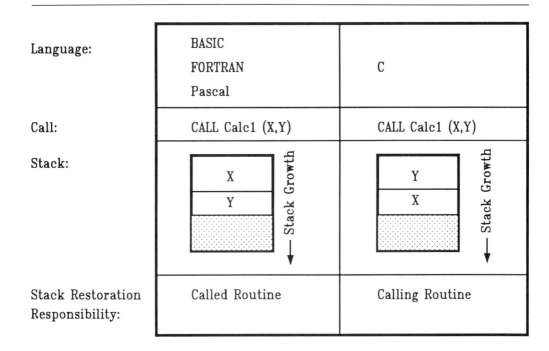

Language:	BASIC FORTRAN Pascal	C
Call:	CALL Calc1 (X,Y)	CALL Calc1 (X,Y)
Stack:		
Stack Restoration Responsibility:	Called Routine	Calling Routine

Fig. 10-3. Calling Convention-Stack Handling.

Parameter-Passing Conventions

If you write procedures that do not mutually agree upon how to pass parameters, a called routine will misinterpret passed data. It is also possible that a program will cause the system to end abnormally (*abend*). Microsoft languages support three ways to pass parameters.

- Value—This method passes only the variable value, not its address. Here, the called routine knows the value of the parameter but has no access to the original variable. Once the called routine terminates, any changes to the parameter value have no effect in the calling routine.

- NEAR Reference—This passes a variable near (offset) address. If you use this method, the called routine gets direct access to the variable itself. Any change that the called routine makes to the parameter is reflected in the calling routine. This also presumes that the two routines share the same data segment.

- FAR Reference—This method passes a FAR (segmented) address of a value. Thus a longer address is passed than with a NEAR reference. This method is necessary if passing data outside the default segment, although it is slower than passing by NEAR reference.

Size	Return location
1	AL
2	AX
4	DX:AX DX high order (or segment) AX low order (or offset)
Long	Spec.FORTRAN & Pascal

Fig. 10-4. Parameter-Passing Defaults.

Figure 10-4 summarizes the parameter-passing defaults for four of Microsoft's languages. Each of the languages has ways to override the defaults, and the details are listed in Microsoft's manual, *Mixed-Language Programming Guide*.

MICROSOFT MEMORY MODEL

All EXTRN, PUBLIC, and PROC items, as well as uses of the .MODEL directive, support a language type. The language type of EXTRN and PUBLIC variables determine whether or not an underscore is prefixed to the name (an underscore is prefixed only for variables with a C language type). The language type of a procedure determines its calling and naming conventions.

The language type consists of the word C or *Pascal* and uses the following syntax. Note that lower-case items are placeholders and bracketed items are optional.

```
EXTRN [<langtype>] <varname>:<type>
PUBLIC [<langtype>] <varname>
procName PROC [NEAR|FAR] [<langtype>] [USES <regs>,] <args>
```

For example, the C and Pascal keywords are used correctly in the following:

```
.MODEL        SMALL,C
EXTRN         Pascal DosOpen:FAR
PUBLIC        C myVar
myOpen PROC   Pascal fName:PTR,mode:WORD
        :
myOpen ENDP
```

Figure 10-5 shows the default segment names created by each directive. Using these segments will ensure compatibility with Microsoft languages and will help access public symbols. The .MODEL directive must be used, or full segment definitions must be used. Memory models are explained further in chapter 11.

MODEL SMALL

Directive	.CODE	.DATA	.CONST	.DATA?	.STACK
Name	—TEXT	—DATA	CONST	—BSS	STACK
Align	WORD	WORD	WORD	WORD	PARA
Combine	PUBLIC	PUBLIC	PUBLIC	PUBLIC	STACK
Class	'CODE'	'DATA'	'CONST'	'BSS'	'STACK'
Group	--	DGROUP	DGROUP	DGROUP	DGROUP

MODEL MEDIUM

Directive	.CODE	.DATA	.CONST	.DATA?	.STACK
Name	name—TEXT	—DATA	CONST	—BSS	STACK
Align	WORD	WORD	WORD	WORD	PARA
Combine	PUBLIC	PUBLIC	PUBLIC	PUBLIC	STACK
Class	'CODE'	'DATA'	'CONST'	'BSS'	'STACK'
Group	--	DGROUP	DGROUP	DGROUP	DGROUP

MODEL COMPACT

Directive	.CODE	.FARDATA	.FARDATA?	.DATA	.CONST	.DATA?	.STACK
Name	—TEXT	FAR—DATA	FAR—BSS	—DATA	CONST	—BSS	STACK
Align	WORD	PARA	PARA	WORD	WORD	WORD	PARA
Combine	PUBLIC	private	private	PUBLIC	PUBLIC	PUBLIC	STACK
Class	'CODE'	'FAR—DATA'	'FAR—BSS'	'DATA'	'CONST'	'BSS'	'STACK'
Group	--	--	--	DGROUP	DGROUP	DGROUP	DGROUP

MODEL LARGE or HUGE

Directive	.CODE	.FARDATA	.FARDATA?	.DATA	.CONST	.DATA?	.STACK
Name	name—TEXT	FAR—DATA	FAR—BSS	—DATA	CONST	—BSS	STACK
Align	WORD	PARA	PARA	WORD	WORD	WORD	PARA
Combine	PUBLIC	private	private	PUBLIC	PUBLIC	PUBLIC	STACK
Class	'CODE'	'FAR—DATA'	'FAR—BSS'	'DATA'	'CONST'	'BSS'	'STACK'
Group	--	--	--	DGROUP	DGROUP	DGROUP	DGROUP

Fig. 10-5. Default Segments and Types.

The directives in Fig. 10-5 refer to the following kinds of segments.

- .CODE   The segment containing all of the code for the module.
- .CONST   Constant data. Microsoft compilers use this segment for items such as string and floating point constants.
- .DATA   Initialized data.
- .DATA?   Uninitialized data. Microsoft compilers store the uninitialized data separately because it can be more efficiently stored than initialized data.
- .FARDATA   Data here will not be combined with the corresponding segments in other modules. The segment of data here can always be determined with the assembler SEG operator (see chapter 7 for a description of SEG).
- .FARDATA?   Same as .FARDATA, except for uninitialized data.
- .STACK   Stack. Normally, this segment is declared in the main module and should not be redeclared.

To create directives, use the information in Fig. 10-5 in the following steps:

- Decide which memory model to use. Then go to Fig. 10-5 to look up the segment name, align type, combine type, and class for the code and data segments for the program. Use all these attributes to define segment. For instance, if using a code segment with a large model:

```
name_TEXT  SEGMENT  WORD PUBLIC 'CODE'
```

If the combine type is private, do not use any combine type.

- If you have segments in the DGROUP group, put them into the DGROUP by using the GROUP directive. For instance:

```
GROUP    DGROUP    _DATA _BSS
```

- Use the two directives ASSUME and ENDS as you would normally use them (see chapter 8 for descriptions of ASSUME and ENDS). On entry, DS and SS will both point to DGROUP. Therefore, a small model procedure that makes use of DGROUP should include the following ASSUME directive:

```
ASSUME    CS:TEXT,DS:DGROUP,SS:DGROUP
```

A large model procedure assumes a different code segment, and could assume a FAR data segment for ES.

ASSEMBLING, COMPILING, AND LINKING

Following is a review of some basic concepts.

Compiling is the preparation of a machine language program from a source program written in another programming language. The process of compiling often generates more than one machine instruction for each symbolic statement (or both) as well as performing the function of an assembler. Among other things, compilers eliminate the need to write detailed code to handle I/O, to handle control loops, to access complex data structures, or to program formulas and functions. One of the main driving forces behind compilers is to lessen detail programming.

A compiler breaks out statements using format identifiers and delimiters, and builds up executable binary code sequences. Compilers are further from machine language than assemblers. Compilers often generate several machine instructions for every compiler language statement, while assembly language generally has a one-for-one comparison between line of code and line of generated machine language. Compilers take care of much of the programmer's decision-making, such as choosing register assignments, assigning memory areas to programs and subroutines, and linking labels in one program with addresses in another program.

An assembler program, on the other hand, is composed of simple but brief expressions that provide a rapid translation from symbolic to machine-language relocatable object coding for the computer. Assembly language includes a wide and sophisticated variety of operators that allows the fabrication of desired fields based on information generated at assembly time. The instruction-operation codes are assigned mnemonics that describe the hardware function of each instruction. Assembler directive commands provide the ability to generate data words and values based on specific conditions at assembly time. A major function of an assembler is to ease the problem of assigning actual storage locations to instructions and data when a program is coded. It also allows the use of mnemonic operational codes rather than numerical operation codes.

Most microcomputer language compilers support modular software development, which is something assembly language did almost from the beginning. Each module is written and compiled separately. The final program consists of several modules linked together by a special utility program. (This program is called a linker, linking loader, or link editor; in OS/2, it is called a binder.) Although this procedure is intended to divide the functions of a final product into smaller more easily manageable projects, it also provides a key performance tool. With the typical linker, any number of programs can be combined with one command, relocatable modules can be ordered in user-specified ways, and external references between modules are automatically resolved. The linker performs library searches for system subroutines and generates a load map of memory that shows locations of main program and subroutines. A cross-reference facility prints out an alphabetic listing of all program variable names along with line numbers and where they are referenced and defined.

With Microsoft's BASIC, FORTRAN, and Pascal, you are not required to give special options to compile source files that are part of a mixed-language program. However, with Microsoft's C, be aware that not all memory models are compatible with other languages. BASIC, FORTRAN, and Pascal use only far (segmented) code addresses. Compiling in small or compact models can cause the mixed-language program to crash as soon as a call is made to or from C. It is possible to avoid this problem if you apply the far keyword to a C-function definition to specify that the function uses a far call and return.

Differences in data addresses can be resolved through compile options or in the source code. Your choice of a memory model affects the default data pointer size in C and FORTRAN, although it is possible to override this default with FAR and NEAR. Your choice of memory model, with C and FORTRAN, also affects whether data objects are located in the default data segment. If a data object is not located in the default data segment, it cannot be passed directly by a near reference.

ASSEMBLY LANGUAGE TO HIGH-LEVEL INTERFACE

Microsoft high-level language routines assume that certain initialization codes have been executed. You need to follow four guidelines when executing an assembly call to a high-level language.

- First, PUSH each parameter onto the stack. Be sure to observe the calling conventions of the high-level language. Also be sure to load constants, such as offset addresses, into a register before PUSHing them.
- Next, with long parameters, always PUSH the segment or high-order portion of the parameter first regardless of the calling convention.
- Execute a call. This call must be FAR unless the high-level language routine is a small model.
- If using the C convention, immediately after the call, clear the stack of parameters with the instruction:

ADD   SP,*size*

where *size* is the total size in bytes of all parameters that were PUSHed.

Before you execute a call to a BASIC, Pascal, or FORTRAN routine, remember to declare an additional parameter if the return value is noninteger. This additional parameter must contain the offset address of the return value, for which you must allocate room within the stack segment (normally DGROUP, the same as the default data segment).

HIGH-LEVEL LANGUAGE TO ASSEMBLY INTERFACE

The standard assembly language interface consists of seven steps. Each step is explained in the sections that follow.

1. Set up the procedure.
2. Enter the procedure.

3. Allocate local data, which is an optional step.
4. Preserve register values.
5. Access parameters.
6. Return a value, which is an optional step.
7. Exit the procedure.

Procedure Setup

LINK cannot combine the assembly language procedure correctly with a calling program unless you use compatible segments and declare the procedure correctly (see appendix F for an overview of Microsoft's LINK). There are four general rules to follow to set up the segments and procedures. Remember that the rules apply to MASM version 5.0 and higher.

First, use the .MODEL directive at the beginning of the source file. This directive automatically causes MASM to generate the correct kind of returns—NEAR for small or compact model, and FAR for the rest. If calling from Pascal, declare the modules as .MODEL LARGE. From BASIC, they should be .MODEL MEDIUM.

Second, use the simplified segment directives .CODE to declare the code segment, and .DATA to declare the data segment.

Third, declare the procedure label public with the PUBLIC directive (see chapter 9 for a description of PUBLIC). This declaration makes the procedure available to other modules. Also, remember to declare all data PUBLIC that must be used in other modules.

Finally, declare as EXTRN any global data or procedures accessed in other routines (see chapter 9 for a description of EXTRN). The best way to use EXTRN is to place the directive outside of any segment definition.

Enter the Procedure

A frame pointer is a mechanism used to access parameters and local data which are located on the stack. So begin the procedure or macro with the ENTER instruction; it does the equivalent of the two instructions:

```
PUSH  BP
MOV   BP,SP
```

This instruction establishes and optionally allocates work space on the stack with BP as the frame pointer. SP cannot be used for this purpose because it is not an index or base register. Also, the value of SP might change as more data are pushed onto the stack. The value of the base register BP remains constant throughout the procedure so that each parameter can be addressed as a fixed displacement from BP. The ENTER instruction saves the value of BP because BP is needed by the calling procedure as soon as the current procedure terminates. Next, ENTER loads the value of SP into BP in order to capture the value of the stack pointer at the time of entry to the procedure.

Allocate Local Data

To set up local data space, use the operands of the ENTER instruction (see the examples in appendix G, which show how to allocate a 10-byte work area).

Preserve Register Values

As a standard practice when writing subroutines or procedures, save all the general registers by a PUSHA (push all). To preserve the values of any segment registers you intend to change, PUSH them as a second step, using PUSH. Be sure to POPA all the registers as the last instruction just before returning from the assembly language procedure, to restore their original values. Figure 10-6 shows an example of the first few and last few lines of code in the procedure.

PUSH	BP	; Save framepointer
MOV	BP,SP	; Set up current framepointer
SUB	SP,4	; Set up local data space
PUSH	SI	; Save SI
PUSH	DI	; Save DI
PUSHA		; Save all general registers
:		
:		
POPA		; Restore general registers
POP	DI	; Restore DI
POP	SI	; Restore SI

Fig. 10-6. Preserving Register Values.

Access Parameters

Once you are through the steps of setting up the procedure, allocating data space, and pushing register values, write the main body of the procedure. You might have parameters that you have passed to it. To figure out how to use those parameters, look at the stack (see Fig. 10-7 for an overview). The stack is established by the following sequence:

- First, the calling program PUSHes each of the parameters onto the stack. After this, SP points after the last parameter PUSHed. For the called procedure, after ENTER, the displacement off BP for a parameter X, is equal to:

     2 plus the size of the return address, plus the total size of parameters PUSHed after X.

```
CALLING PROGRAM              OFFSET        STACK
Has Parameter in AX
                              100
    (SP = 114)
                              102
PUSH AX - Parameter 1
                              104
    (SP = 112)
                              106
CALL PROC  (FAR)
                              108
    Stores 4 bytes
        (the RETURN address)  10A
        at the ENTRY to the   10C      BP
        called PROC           10E      RET Displacement
    (SP = 10E)                110      CS
                              112      AX
ENTER
    (SP = 10C)                114
    Old BP stored at 10C      116
    SP stored in BP

MOV AX,[BP + 6]
    This gets Parameter 1
```

Stack Growth →

Note: SP is the Stack Pointer

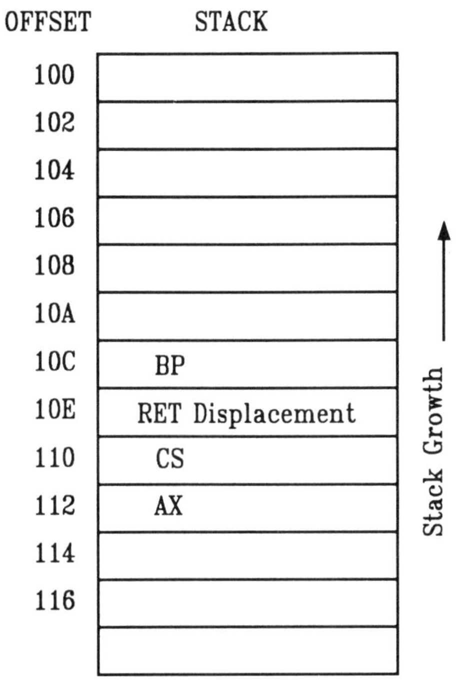

Fig. 10-7. Overview of Stack Changes.

For example, if a FAR procedure has been passed one parameter, a two-byte address. The displacement of that parameter is:

2 + 4 (size of return address) = 6.

The size of the return address is two bytes for NEAR calls and four bytes for FAR calls. The argument can be loaded into BP with the following instruction:

MOV BX,[BP+6]

• The calling program issues a CALL. This causes the return address to be placed on the stack; the return address is the place in the calling program to which control will ultimately return. SP now points to this address.

• ENTER creates a stack frame. This is normally done by most high-level languages at every procedure call. The format for ENTER is:

ENTER   Operand1,Operand2

where Operand1 specifies the number of bytes of local variables for which stack space is automatically allocated. Operand2 specifies the nesting depth of the routine. The nesting depth determines the number of stack frame pointers that are copied from the current stack frame into the new stack frame that is being built by ENTER. In the 80386, EBP is used to copy the frame pointers from the current stack frame into the new stack frame. EBP points to the new stack frame pointer at the end of the instruction.

• LEAVE removes the stack frame that was created by a corresponding EN-TER instruction. The stack space is released by ESP being assigned the value of EBP (the frame pointer). The old frame pointer (seen on the top of the stack following the assignment of ESP to EBP) is POPed into EBP to set up the frame pointer for the calling routine. Normally, a RET instruction is used to complete the control transfer back to the calling procedure. The RET might have an optional size, which is used to remove any parameters that were PUSHed onto the stack for the procedure that is now exiting (not used for C).

• SP can be decreased to provide room on the stack for local data or saved registers. BP remains constant throughout the procedure.

A point to remember: Microsoft high-level languages always PUSH segment addresses before they PUSH offset addresses. In addition, when PUSHing arguments larger than two bytes, high-order words are always PUSHed before low-order words. With USE32, a PUSH of a 32-bit register PUSHes high to low the same as if it were a high word and low word.

Return a Value

The four Microsoft languages (BASIC, C, FORTRAN, and Pascal) have similar conventions for receiving return values. The conventions are the same when the returned data type is simple, not an array or structure, and is no more than four bytes long. This includes all NEAR and FAR address types, all pointers, and all parameters passed by reference. Figure 10-8 shows an overview of where the data is returned.

When the return value is larger than four bytes, a procedure called by BASIC or C allocates space for the return value and then places its address in DX:AX (an easy way to create space for the return value is to declare it in a data segment).

Long return values for FORTRAN and Pascal are more complex. To create an interface for long return values, FORTRAN and Pascal do the following before they call an assembly language procedure:

1. Create space somewhere in the stack segment to hold the actual return value(s).

2. When they call your procedure, they pass an extra parameter that contains the offset address to place the long return value. This parameter is placed immediately above the return address; that is, it is the last one PUSHed. The extra parameters is always located at BP + 6. Its presence automatically increases the displacement of all other parameters by two, as shown in Fig. 10-9.

3. The segment address of the return value is contained in both DS and SS.

Fig. 10-8. Overview of Data Size and Return Location.

Data Size	80386 Register
1 Byte	AL
2 Bytes	AX
4 Bytes	EAX

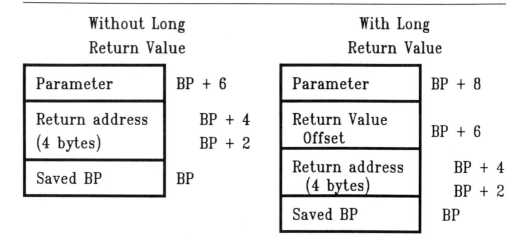

Fig. 10-9. FORTRAN and Pascal Return Values in the Stack. (continued)

```
 1                                        PAGE    55,132
 2
 3                                        .MODEL  Medium          ;
 4                                        .386                    ; After .MODEL sets USE16
 5
 6                              ;
 7                              ; Name:    SAMPLE
 8                              ;
 9                              ; Purpose: The following procedure provides an entry and exit
10                              ;          example.  The example works for BASIC and Pascal.
11                              ;          For FORTRAN the displacement for param1 would be 10
12                              ;          and the number on the return would be 8 (not 4).
13                              ;          For C only the number on the return changes - it is
14                              ;          omitted.
15                              ;
16                              ;
17                              ; Inputs:  Two near reference parameters are assumed.
18                              ;
19                              ; Process: None
20                              ;
21                              ; Output:  One word from the work area
22                              ;
23                              ;
24                              ; Equate parameter and work areas used in the stack frame for
25                              ; this sample procedure.
26                              ;
27 = WORD PTR 8+[BP]    param1       EQU      WORD PTR 8+[BP]
28 = WORD PTR 6+[BP]    param2       EQU      WORD PTR 6+[BP]
29 = WORD PTR [BP]-2    work1        EQU      WORD PTR [BP]-2
30 = WORD PTR [BP]-4    retnv        EQU      WORD PTR [BP]-4
31                              ;
32                              ;
33                                        PUBLIC  Sample          ; Make the name usable
34                                        .CODE                   ; Begin code segment
35 0000                 Sample       PROC
36 0000  C8 0010 00                  enter   16,0                ; Set BP and get work space
37 0004  60                          pusha                       ; Save entry registers
38 0005  1E                          push    DS                  ; Save any affected segment
39 0006  06                          push    ES                  ; registers.
40                              ;
41                              ; Access parameter offset and work area.
42                              ;
43 0007  8B 5E 08                    mov     BX,param1           ; Get first parameter
44 000A  89 5E FE                    mov     work1,BX            ; Save it in my work area
45
46                              ; The body of the procedure
47
48 000D  07                          pop     ES                  ; Restore segment registers
49 000E  1F                          pop     DS                  ; (pop in reverse order from
50                                                               ; the pushs.)
51 000F  61                          popa                        ; Restore the entry registers
52 0010  8B 46 FC                    mov     AX,retnv            ; Set the return value
53 0013  C9                          leave                       ; remove the stack frame
54 0014  CA 0004                     ret     4                   ; and return. (wipe parameters
55                                                               ; off the stack - 4 bytes too)
56 0017                 Sample       ENDP
57                                        END
```

Fig. 10-9. (continued)

```
Segments and Groups:

                N a m e                 Size    Length   Align  Combine Class

DGROUP . . . . . . . . . . . . .        GROUP
     _DATA  . . . . . . . . . . .       16 Bit  0000     WORD   PUBLIC  'DATA'
FIG10_6_TEXT . . . . . . . . .          16 Bit  0017     WORD   PUBLIC  'CODE'

Symbols:

                N a m e                 Type    Value    Attr

PARAM1 . . . . . . . . . . . .          TEXT    WORD PTR 8+[BP]
PARAM2 . . . . . . . . . . . .          TEXT    WORD PTR 6+[BP]

RETNV  . . . . . . . . . . .            TEXT    WORD PTR [BP]-4

SAMPLE . . . . . . . . . . . .          F PROC  0000     FIG10_6_TEXT   Global Length = 0017

WORK1  . . . . . . . . . . . .          TEXT    WORD PTR [BP]-2

aCODE  . . . . . . . . . . .            TEXT    fig10_6_TEXT
aCODESIZE  . . . . . . . . . .          TEXT    1
aCPU . . . . . . . . . . . . .          TEXT    3343
aDATASIZE  . . . . . . . . .            TEXT    0
aFILENAME  . . . . . . . . .            TEXT    fig10_6
aVERSION . . . . . . . . . .            TEXT    510


     57 Source  Lines
     57 Total   Lines
     21 Symbols

  47142 + 184231 Bytes symbol space free

      0 Warning Errors
      0 Severe  Errors
```

Fig. 10-9. (continued)

Exit the Procedure

When exiting a procedure, be sure to POP all registers in the reverse order in which they were PUSHed. If you used local data space and allocated it at the beginning of the procedure, restore SP and BP with the LEAVE instruction. Finally, return to the calling program with the exit of RET.

11

Using MASM

AT THIS POINT IN THE BOOK, YOU HAVE LEARNED HOW PEOPLE LEARN THEIR NATIVE language, how computer languages grew from native languages, and the details of MASM grammar and structure. The next part of the book described the specific details of MASM. This chapter takes the final step. It tells you how to run MASM, explaining the options and environment variables that control its behavior.

You can assemble source files by using one of two different methods: by giving a command line at the MS-DOS prompt or by responding to a series of MASM prompts. Once started, MASM attempts to process the specified source file. If it finds errors, they are output to the screen and MASM terminates. If it finds no errors, MASM automatically outputs an object file; it can also output a listing file and a cross-reference file, if they are specified. You can terminate MASM at any time by pressing control-C or control-break.

Before you get to actually running MASM, take a look at the various options and set-up issues to resolve before turning MASM loose on your source code.

MASM OPTIONS

Options control MASM operation and the format of the output files it generates. Options are not case sensitive; enter them with any combination of upper- and lower-case letters. Figure 11-1 gives an overview of the 22 options. Note that one option, /B, is obsolete as of release 5.1. It is shown here for compatibility with earlier releases, but a detailed description of it is not included.

Previous MASM releases had an /R option that enabled 8087 instructions and real numbers in the IEEE format. MASM 5.1 uses IEEE as default; the /R is no longer needed, just as /B is not needed. MASM still recognizes /R so that older BATCH and MAKE files still work, but it has no effect. The previous default format, Microsoft Binary, can be specified with the .MSFLOAT directive.

MASM OPTION	ACTION
/A	Writes segments in alphabetic order
/B *number*	Sets buffer size (this is an obsolete option)
/C	Specifies a cross-reference file
/D	Creates Pass 1 listing
/D *symbol[=value]*	Defines assembler symbol
/E	Creates code for emulated floating-point instructions
/H	Lists command-line syntax and all assembler options
/I *path*	Sets include-file search path
/L	Specifies an assembly-listing file
/ML	Makes names case sensitive
/MU	Converts names to uppercase letters
/MX	Makes PUBLIC and EXTRN names case sensitive
/N	Suppresses tables in listing file
/P	Checks for impure code
/S	Writes segments in source-code order
/T	Suppresses messages for successful assembly
/V	Displays extra statistics to screen
/W {0|1|2}	Sets error-display level
/X	Includes false conditionals in listings
/Z	Displays error lines on screen
/ZD	Puts line-number information in the object file
/ZI	Puts symbolic and line-number information in the object file

Fig. 11-1. MASM Options.

/A and /S—Specify Segment Order

Syntax: /S   ; Default
           /A

The /A option directs MASM to place the assembled segments in alphabetical order before copying them to the object file. The /S option directs MASM to write segments in the order in which they appear in the source code. Source code order is the default.

If MASM finds neither of these options, it copies the segments in the order found in the source file. /S is provided for compatibility with the XENIX operating system and for overriding a default option in the MASM environment variable.

/C and /L—Specify Cross-Reference and Listing Files

Syntax: /C
           /L

/L directs MASM to create a listing file, even if one was not specified in the command line, or in response to prompts. /C has the same effect for cross-reference files. Files specified with these options always have the base name of the source file plus the extension .LST for listing files or .CRF for cross-reference files. You cannot specify any other file names.

/D—Create a Pass 1 Listing

Syntax: /D

/D tells MASM to add a pass 1 listing to the assembly listing file, making the assembly listing show the results of both assembly passes. You will typically use a pass 1 listing to locate phase errors (phase errors occur when MASM makes assumptions about the program in pass 1 that are not valid in pass 2). /D does not create a pass 1 listing unless you also direct MASM to create an assembly listing. However, it does direct MASM to display errors for both pass 1 and pass 2, even if you forgot or deliberately did not request the assembly listing.

/Dsymbol[=value])—Define Assembler Symbols

When you give the /D option a *symbol* argument, it directs MASM to define a symbol that can be used during the assembly as if it were defined as a text equate in the source file. Multiple symbols can be defined in a single command line. The *value* can be any text string that does not include a space, comma, or semicolon. If MASM does not find a value, it assigns a null string.

/E—Create Code for a Floating-Point Emulator

Syntax: /E

/E directs MASM to generate data and code in the format expected by coprocessor emulator libraries. An emulator library uses the instructions of the 8087, 80287, or 80387 coprocessors, if a coprocessor is present. If there is no coprocessor, the library emulates coprocessor activity. /E cannot be used by stand-alone assembly language programs since emulator libraries are only available with Microsoft's high-level language compilers.

/H—Get Command-Line Help

Syntax: /H

/H displays the command-line syntax and all the MASM options on the screen. Do not give any file names or other options with this option.

/I*path*—Set a Search Path for INCLUDE Files

Syntax: /I

/I is used to set search paths for INCLUDE files. It is possible to set as many as 10 search paths by using the option for each path. The order of searching is the order in which the paths are listed in the command line.

Do not specify a pathname with the INCLUDE directive if you plan to specify search paths from the command line. If you do, MASM will search only the specified path and ignore any search paths specified in the command line if the source file contained any of the following statements:

```
INCLUDE   A:\MACRO\DOS.INC
INCLUDE   ..\dos.inc
INCLUDE   .\DOS.INC
```

/MU, /ML, and /MX—Specify Case Sensitivity

Syntax: /MU
          /ML
          /MX

By default, MASM converts all names to upper case. There are instances where you might not wish this to happen, so you have three options to control how MASM treats case sensitivity.

/ML directs MASM to make all names case sensitive. /MX directs it to make PUBLIC and EXTRN names case sensitive. /MU directs it to convert all names to upper case. /MU is provided for compatibility with XENIX (which uses -ML by default) and to override options given in the environment variable.

If case sensitivity is turned on, all names that have the same spelling but use letters of different cases are considered different. For example, with /ML, DATA and data are different. They would also be different with the /MX option if they were declared EXTRN or PUBLIC. Public and external names include any label, variable, or symbol names defined by using any of the three directives: EXTRN, PUBLIC, or COMM.

Typically, use /ML and /MX when object modules created with MASM are to be linked with object modules created by a case-sensitive compiler (such as the Microsoft C compiler). If case sensitivity is important, use LINK's /NOI option (described in appendix F). If you use the /ZI and /ZD options (see below), the /MX, /ML, and /MU options affect the case of the symbolic data that will be available to a symbolic debugger.

/N—Suppress Tables in the Listing File

Syntax: /N

/N tells MASM to omit all tables from the end of the listing file. If it does not find /N, MASM includes tables of macros, structures, records, segments and groups, and symbols. The code portion of the listing file is not changed by /N.

/P—Check for Impure Code

Syntax: /P

/P directs MASM to check for impure code in the 80286 or 80386 privileged mode. Code that moves data into memory with a CS: override is acceptable in real mode. Any such code might cause problems in protected mode. With /P in effect, MASM checks for these situations and generates an error if it encounters them. The 80386 real and protected modes are described in appendix H. If you need additional information, see TAB Books *80386 A Design and Programming Handbook*. You can use the /P option for XENIX compatibility and to learn about problem programming practices when using OS/2.

/V and /T—Control Display for Assembly Statistics

Syntax: /V
          /T

/V and /T specify the level of information displayed to the screen at the end of an assembly. If MASM finds neither option, it outputs a line telling the amount of symbol space free and the number of warning and error messages. If MASM finds /V, it also reports the number of lines and symbols processed. If it finds /T, it does not output anything to the screen unless it finds errors. /T is useful in BATCH or MAKE files if you do not want the output cluttered with messages.

IF MASM finds errors during assembly, it will display them whether /V or /T is given or not.

/W{0|1|2}—Set the Warning Level

Syntax: /W {0|1|2}

/W sets the MASM warning level. MASM gives warning messages for assembly statements that are ambiguous or questionable but not necessarily illegal. MASM has three levels of errors, as shown in Fig. 11-2. The default warning level is 1. A higher level includes a lower level; that is, if you use 2, it includes severe error, serious warnings, and advisory warnings. If MASM finds severe errors, it does not produce an object file. The advisory warnings also are listed in Fig. 11-2, along with the serious warnings. All other errors are severe.

/X—List False Conditionals

Syntax: /X

/X controls the contents of the program listing and other optional files that are generated as a result of assembly. /X has no effect if the .SFCOND or the .LFCOND directive is used in the source file. If .TFCOND is used, the effects of /X are reversed. The /X switch includes statements inside false conditional statements in the list file. This allows conditionals that do not generate code to be displayed.

/Z—Display Error Lines on the Screen

Syntax: /Z

/Z affects the standard output display. /Z displays the actual source lines producing assembly errors, rather than displaying just the error type and line number.

/ZD and /ZI—Write Symbolic Information to the Object File

Syntax: /ZD

      /ZI

/ZI directs MASM to write symbolic information to the object file. /ZI writes both line-number data and symbolic data. Line-number data relates each instruction to the source line that created it. Symbolic data specifies a size for each variable or label used in the program.

/ZD writes line-number information to the object file only.

MASM WARNING LEVELS

LEVEL	TYPE	DESCRIPTION
0	Severe errors	Illegal statements
1	Serious warnings	Ambiguous statements or questionable programming practices
2	Advisory warnings	Statements that may produce inefficient code

MASM ADVISORY WARNINGS

NUMBER	MESSAGE
104	Operand size does not match word size
105	Address size does not match word size
106	Jump within short distance

MASM SERIOUS WARNINGS

NUMBER	MESSAGE
1	Extra characters on line
16	Symbol is reserved word
31	Operand types must match
57	Illegal size for item
85	End of file, no END directive
101	Missing data; zero assumed
102	Segment near (or at) 64K limit

Fig. 11-2. MASM Warning Levels and Messages.

DEFINE MASM DEFAULT BEHAVIOR

MASM processes sequentially, so any directives that define its behavior must come before the sections affected by the directive. There are three types of directives that can define this behavior:

- Instruction set directives (see chapter 8) that define the processor and coprocessor, such as .386.

- The .MODEL directives that define the memory model. These are overviewed in chapter 10 and described further in the section below that discusses understanding memory models.

- The .MSFLOAT directive and the coprocessor directives that describe how floating-point variables are encoded. These directives are optional. If you use them, they must appear before any statements that they affect. If MASM does not find them, it makes the following default assumptions:

  ○ 8086/8088 processor instruction set.

  ○ 8087 coprocessor instruction set.

  ○ IEEE format for floating-point variables.

.MODEL and .MSFLOAT affect the entire assembly and can only occur once in the source file. Place them at the beginning of your source. .MSFLOAT disables all coprocessor instructions and specifies that initialized real-number variables be encoded in the Microsoft Binary format. Without this directive, MASM encodes initialized real-number variables in IEEE formats. This is a change from earlier MASM versions, which used Microsoft Binary format by default and required a coprocessor directive or the /R to specify IEEE format.

The coprocessor instruction set directives have the opposite effect of .MSFLOAT. .MSFLOAT turns off the coprocessor instruction set and enables the Microsoft Binary format for floating-point variables. Any coprocessor instruction turns on the specified coprocessor instruction set and enables the IEEE format for floating-point variables.

MEMORY MODELS

A memory model specifies the default size of data and code used in a program. To use simplified segment directives (discussed below), you must declare a memory model for your program. Microsoft high-level languages require that each program have a default size, or memory model. Any assembly language routine called from a high level language program should have the same memory model as the calling program. (See chapter 10 for more information about mixed-language programming.) The most commonly used memory models are described here.

• Tiny—All data and code fits in a single segment. Tiny model programs must be written in the .COM format. Microsoft languages do not support this model. Some compilers from other manufacturers support tiny model either as an option or as a requirement. You cannot use simplified segment directives for tiny-model programs.

• Small—All data fits within a 64K segment. All code also fits within a 64K segment. This means that all code and data can be accessed as NEAR. This is the most common model for stand-alone assembler programs. C is the only Microsoft language that supports this model.

• Medium—All data fits within a single 64K segment, but code may be greater than 64K. This means that data is NEAR but code may be FAR. Most recent versions of Microsoft languages support this model.

• Compact—All code fits within a single 64K segment, but the total amount of data can be greater than 64K, although no array can be larger than 64K. This means that code is NEAR but data may be FAR. C is the only Microsoft language that supports this model.

• Large—Both code and data can be greater than 64K. Also, data arrays can be larger than 64K. Both code and data are FAR. All Microsoft languages support this model.

• Huge—Both code and data can be greater than 64K. Also, data arrays can be larger than 64K. Both code and data are FAR, and pointers to elements within an array must also be FAR. Most recent versions of Microsoft languages support this model. Segments are the same for large and huge models.

Mixed-model programs use the default size for most code and data, but override the default for particular data items. Stand-alone assembler programs can be written as mixed-model programs by making specific procedures or variables NEAR or FAR.

Use the .MODEL directive to initialize the memory model and use it early in the source code before any other segment directive. The syntax is as follows:

Syntax: .MODEL   *memorymodel*

The *memorymodel* can be SMALL, MEDIUM, COMPACT, LARGE, or HUGE. You must use the .MODEL directive before defining any segment. If you use the .386 directive before .MODEL, the segment definitions define 32-bit segments. If you want to enable the 80386 processor with 16-bit segments, use the .386 after .MODEL. If one of the other simplified segment directives (such as .CODE or .DATA) are used before .MODEL, MASM generates an error.

Segments are defined the same for large and huge models, but the predefined equate @datasize (see chapter 8) is different. If you are writing an assembler routine for a high-level language, the *memorymodel* should match the memory model used by the compiler or interpreter.

MS-DOS SIMPLIFIED AND FULL-SEGMENT DEFINITIONS

Segments are a fundamental part of assembly-language programming for the Intel family of processors. A segment is a collection of instructions or data whose addresses are all relative to the same segment register. Segments can be defined by using simplified segment directives or full-segment directives.

In most cases, simplified segment definitions are a better choice. They are easier to use and more consistent. They automatically define the segment structure required when combining assembler modules with modules prepared with Microsoft high-level languages. Full-segment definitions give more complete control over segments. A few complex programs might require full-segment definition in order to get unusual segment orders and types.

Specifying Segment Order

Syntax: DOSSEG

DOSSEG specifies that segments be ordered according to the MS-DOS segment-order convention. Using DOSSEG enables you to maintain a consistent logical segment order without actually defining segments in that order in your source file. Without this directive, the final segment order of the executable file depends on factors such as segment order, class name, and order of linking. Because segment order is generally not critical to the proper functioning of most stand-alone assembler programs, simply use DOSSEG and ignore the whole issue of segment order.

The MS-DOS segment order is as follows:

1. All segment names having the class name 'CODE'.
2. Any segments that do not have class name 'CODE' and are not part of the group DGROUP.
3. Segments that are part of DGROUP, in the following order:
    a. Any segments of class BEGDATA (reserved for Microsoft use).
    b. Any segments not of class BEGDATA, BSS, or STACK.
    c. Segments of class BSS.
    d. Segments of class STACK.

Using DOSSEG (or LINK's /DOSSEG) has two side effects. LINK generates symbols called __end and __edata. Do not use these names in programs that contain the DOSSEG directive. Also, LINK increases the offset of the first byte of the code segment by 16 bytes in small or compact models, to give proper alignment to executable files created with Microsoft compilers.

Simplified-Segment Definitions

Syntax:	.STACK[*size*]	; Stack segment
	.CODE[*name*]	; Code segment
	.DATA	; Initialized near-data
		; segment
	.DATA?	; Uninitialized
		; near-data segment
	.FARDATA[*name*]	; Initialized far-data
		; segment
	.FARDATA?[*name*]	; Uninitialized far-data
		; segment
	.CONST	; Constant-data segment

These directives indicate the start of a segment. They also end any open segment definition used earlier in the source code. For segments that take an optional *name*, MASM uses a default name if none is specified. Each new segment ends the previous segment. The END directive closes the last open segment in the source file.

The *size* argument of .STACK is the number of bytes to be declared in the stack. If MASM finds no *size*, it defines the segment with a default size of one kilobyte. Stand-alone assembler programs in the .EXE format should define a stack for the main (or only) module. The compiler or interpreter defines stacks for modules linked with a main module from a high-level language.

Place code in a segment initialized with the .CODE directive, regardless of the memory model. Normally, only one code segment is defined in a source module. If you use multiple code segments in one source file, specify *name* to distinguish between them. The *name* can only be specified for models allowing multiple code segments (medium and large), and will be ignored if given with small or compact models.

Constant-data is data that must be declared in a data segment but is not subject to change at run time. Use of this segment is optional for stand-alone assembler programs. However, if you write assembler routines to be called from a high-level language, use the .CONST directive to declare strings, real numbers, and other constant data that must be allocated as data.

Data in segments defined with .STACK, .CONST, .DATA, or .DATA? are placed in a group called DGROUP. Data in segments defined with .FARDATA or .FARDATA? are not placed in any group. When you initialize the DS register to access data in a group-associated segment, load the value DGROUP into DS.

There are predefined equates that are associated with the simplified-segment system. They are @curseg, @filename, @codesize, and @datasize. They are described in chapter 8.

Simplified-Segment Defaults. If the .386 directive is used, the default align type for all segments is DWORD. In certain other circumstances, defaults are different when using simplified-segment directives than they would be if you gave full-segment definitions.

Those changes are:

- In full-segment definitions, the default size for the PROC directive is always NEAR. If you use .MODEL, the PROC is associated with the specified memory model of NEAR for small and compact models, and FAR is used for medium, large, and huge models.

- If you use full segment definitions, the segment offset used as the base when calculating an offset with OFFSET is the data segment (the segment associated with the DS register). With simplified segment directives, the base address is the DGROUP segment for segments that are associated with a group. This includes segments declared with .DATA, .DATA?, and .STACK, but not segments declared with .CODE, .FARDATA, or .FARDATA?

Figure 10-5 (in chapter 10) shows an overview of default segment names and types, which were discussed as part of mixed-language programming.

Full-Segment Definitions

If you need complete control over segments, you may want to give complete segment definitions. The directives to use were described in chapter 8. The syntax is repeated here.

Syntax: *name* SEGMENT [*align*][*combine*][*use*]['*class*']

             :

      name ENDS

The *name* defines the segment name. This name can be unique or the same name given to other segments in the program. Segments with identical names are treated as the same segment. The optional *align, combine, use,* and '*class*' give both MASM and LINK instructions on how to set up and combine segments. Specify these types in any order, and it is not necessary to enter any or all types for a given segment.

The order in which MASM writes segments to the object file can either be sequential or alphabetical. If you specify sequential, MASM writes segments in the order they appear in the source code. If you specify alphabetical, MASM writes them in an alphabetical order of their segment names. The default is sequential, and if you do not specify an order, MASM uses the default.

You could set the ordering method by using .ALPHA or .SEQ directives in your source. Another way is to use the /S (sequential) or /A (alphabetical) assembler options, described earlier in this chapter. The directives have precedence over the assembler options. In most cases, simply leave the ordering to MASM.

INITIALIZING REGISTERS

The CS and IP registers are initialized by specifying a starting address with the END directive (see chapter 8 for a description of END). CS is initialized to the segment value of the code segment containing the label specified. IP is initialized with the displacement of the specified label. The label will often have the displacement zero associated with it, if it is at the beginning of the code segment in the source. As with all displacements, its final value depends on whether other (code) segments are combined with this one and where.

The DS register must be initialized to the address of the segment that will be used for data. This is done in two statements because an immediate memory value cannot be loaded directly into a segment register. The segment-startup lines typically appear at the start or very near the start of the code segment. See the program listing in appendix G for an example of this.

SS is automatically initialized to the value of the last segment in the source code having the combine type STACK. SP is automatically initialized to the size of the stack segment. Thus, SS:SP initially points to the end of the stack. You can initialize or reinitialize the stack segment directly by changing the values of SS and SP. Because hardware interrupts use the same stack as your program, turn off hardware interrupts while changing the stack.

ES is not automatically initialized. Initialize it by moving the appropriate segment value into the register if your program uses the register. For example:

```
ASSUME   ES,@FARDATA   ; Tell MASM
MOV      AX,@FARDATA   ; Tell the Processor
MOV      ES,AX
```

ASSEMBLING

The classic assembler takes source code and converts it into binary symbolic form for subsequent processing by a linkage editor. The assembler, itself, is a program for a symbolic coding language. That language is composed of simple but brief expressions that allow a rapid translation from symbolic to machine-language relocatable object code. MASM assembly language includes a wide and sophisticated variety of operators that allow the fabrication of desired fields based on information generated at assembly time.

The conversion of source to object is accomplished in two passes (that is, the source code is scanned twice). The basic strategy is simple. The first pass through the source collects all the symbol definitions into a symbol table. The second pass converts the program to binary symbolic form, using the definitions collected in the first pass.

Command-Line Assembly

If you use this method, assemble your program source file(s) by typing the MASM command name and the names of the files you wish to process. Figure 11-3 shows the command-line format.

Note that all the files created during the assembly process are written to the current drive and directory. You can specify another drive or directory for each or all the files.

MASM [*options*] *sourcefile* [,[*objectfile*] [,[*listingfile*] [,[*crossreferencefile*]]]] [;]

Fig. 11-3. MASM Control-Line Format.

However, you must specify them for each file since there is no general override. You can specify a device name instead of a file name; for example, NUL for no file or PRN for the printer.

The *options* can be any combination of the assembler options shown in Fig. 11-1, and the options described below. Precede the option letter or letters by a forward slash (/) or by a dash (-); you cannot mix the two preceding characters in a single command line. The examples used in this book all use the forward slash. The *options* can appear at any point on the line; that is, it is not position sensitive. The *option* affects all the relevant files on the command line even if the option appears at the end of the line.

The *sourcefile* must be the name of the source file to be assembled. If you do not supply an extension to the *sourcefile* name, MASM defaults to .ASM. The optional *objectfile* is the file which receives the relocatable object code. If you do not supply a name, MASM uses the source file name and adds the extension .OBJ. If you supply a name but not an extension, MASM supplies the extension .OBJ.

The optional *listingfile* receives the assembly listing. The listing shows the assembled code for each source statement and the names and types of symbols defined in the program. If you do not supply a name, MASM uses the source file name and adds the extension .LST. If you supply a name but not an extension, MASM uses .LST. The optional *crossreferencefile* is the name of the file to receive the cross-reference output. If you do not supply a name, MASM uses the source file name and adds the extension .CRF. Once again, if you supply a name but not an extension, MASM uses .CRF

You can use the semicolon (;) anywhere after the *sourcefile* to select defaults for the remaining file names. Be careful, though. A semicolon after the *sourcefile* selects a default *objectfile*, but it suppresses creation of the assembly *listingfile* and *crossreferencefile*. A semicolon after the *listingfile* name suppresses only the cross-reference file.

The easiest way to respond to the MASM command line is to enter MASM,,,;. That is, MASM followed by three commas that tell MASM to use the default names and the default extensions. End the line with the semicolon.

Spaces in the command line are optional. If you make an error entering any of the file names, MASM displays an error message and prompts for new file names. See the next section on how the prompts appear.

Using Prompts for Assembly

You can direct MASM to prompt you for the files it needs by starting MASM with just the command name. MASM displays the following lines, one at a time:

Source filename [.ASM]:
Object filename [*source*.OBJ]:
Source listing [NUL.LST]:
Cross-reference [NUL.CRF]:

The prompts correspond to the field of the MASM command line. MASM waits for you to respond to each prompt (you can press ENTER to allow MASM to choose the defaults). The only answer you must give is the first: the source filename.

File names entered at the prompts must follow the command-line rules described above. You can type options after any of the prompts as long as you separate them from the file names with spaces. At any prompt, you can enter the remaining answers by typing a name and separating it from the next name with a comma. You can choose the defaults for the remaining prompts by entering a semicolon (as long as you have entered the source file name).

ASSEMBLY LISTINGS

MASM creates an assembly listing of your source file whenever you give it the name of an assembly-listing file, either in the command line or with the prompts. The listing contains both the statements in the source file and any INCLUDE source files. The listing also shows the names and values of all labels, variables, and symbols used in your source code.

Although this section does not intend to be an all-inclusive description of an assembly listing, Fig. 11-4 gives you an overview of the various, and sometimes cryptic, abbreviations and symbols that may suddenly appear in your listing.

MASM lists the code generated from the statements. Each line has the following syntax:

[linenumber] offset [code] statement

The *linenumber* is the number of the line, starting from the first statement in the assembly listing. Line numbers are produced only if you request a cross-reference file. Note that listing line numbers do not always correspond to line numbers in the source file. The *offset* is the offset from the beginning of the current segment to the code. If the statement generates code or data, *code* shows the numerical value in hexadecimal if the value is known at assembly time. If the value is calculated at run time, MASM indicates what action is necessary to compute the value. The *statement* is the source statement shown exactly as it appears in the source file, or as expanded by a macro.

Any errors that MASM finds, it lists immediately following the statement where the error occurred. See the listing in appendix G for examples of how errors print. Also, appendix A lists all the MASM error messages.

CHARACTER	MEANING
C	Line comes from an INCLUDE file
E	External address (LINK must resolve)
R	Relocatable address (LINK must resolve)
n	Macro-expansion nesting level (+ if more than 9)
nn:	Segment override in statement
nn/	REP or LOCK prefix instruction
nn[xx]	DUP expression: nn copies of the value xx
|	80386 size or address prefix
=	EQU or equal-sign directive
---	Segment/group address (LINK must resolve)

Fig. 11-4. Abbreviations and Symbols in Listings.

Some errors and questionable practices that were ignored by earlier MASM versions are now flagged as errors. As a result, existing source code might produce errors or warnings. The following are examples:

- The OFFSET operator used with a constant causes an error.
- Labels defined only during pass 1 cause errors if used in expressions.
- Reserved words used as labels produce warnings.
- A CS ASSUME that changes from pass 1 to pass 2 causes an error.
- Constants are now checked for type overflow.

12

Macro Library

THE MACROS LISTED IN THIS CHAPTER ARE USEFUL IF YOU HAVE NEED TO CALL THE
normal BIOS or MS-DOS interrupts. We wrote the majority of the interrupts. We did
not write the MS-DOS interrupt 21h 4xh, but left them to you.

MACTEST

MACTEST. Provides a test bed for the macros and their generation. The listing
runs approximately 25 pages with additional symbol listings. Note that errors are printed
out; the lines of code were programmed this way deliberately to illustrate the editing
and error messages the program provides.

```
                        PAGE    55,132

                        .MODEL  Medium          ;
                        .386                     ; After .MODEL sets USE16

                    ;
                    ; Name:   MACTEST
                    ;
                    ; Purpose: The following procedure provides a test bed for
                    ;          macros and their generation.
                    ;
                    ; Inputs:  None
                    ;
                    ; Process: None
                    ;
                    ; Output:  A listing of generations and errors of the macros.
                    ;
                                INCLUDE  MACROS\@BIOS10.MAC ; Bring into the assembly.
C  @BIOS10           MACRO   CODE
C  ;;
C  ;; Inner macro for BIOS int 10 calls.
C  ;;      A macro per functional group of calls is chosen as opposed
C  ;;      to a writing a single macro with the INT number a parameter
C  ;;      The duplication is deemed acceptable.
C  ;;
C  ;; Input:
C  ;;   CODE is the BIOS code to be loaded in AH.
```

```
C  ;;    If omitted it is assumed that AH has been set prior to
C  ;;    invoking the macro.
C  ;;
C                    @SETBYT CODE,AH
C                    INT     10h
C                    ENDM
C
C              INCLUDE  MACROS\@DOS21.MAC
C  @DOS21         MACRO    CODE
C  ;;
C  ;; Inner macro for DOS int 21 calls.
C  ;;    A macro per functional group of calls is chosen as opposed
C  ;;    to a writing a single macro with the INT number a parameter
C  ;;    The duplication is deemed acceptable.
C  ;;
C  ;; Input:
C  ;;    CODE is the DOS code to be loaded in AH.
C  ;;    If omitted it is assumed that AH has been set prior to
C  ;;    invoking the macro.
C  ;;
C                    @SETBYT CODE,AH
C                    INT     21h
C                    ENDM
C
C              INCLUDE  MACROS\@SETBYT.MAC
C  @SETBYT        MACRO    CODE,INTO
C  ;;
C  ;; Inner - Inner macro for loading a byte into a register
C  ;;
C  ;; Input:
C  ;;    CODE is the value to be loaded into the register.
C  ;;       If omitted, it is assumed that the register has
C  ;;       been set prior to the call.
C  ;;    INTO is the byte register that is to be loaded.
C  ;;
C  ;;    invoking the macro.
C  ;;
C              IFB     <CODE>                  ;; If CODE is omitted - ok but
C                 EXITM                        ;; get out fast.
C              ENDIF
C  ;;
C  ;; Edit the register to load
C  ;;
C              IFB     <INTO>                  ;; If INTO is omitted
C                 IF2
C                 %OUT Parameter 2 (register to load) cannot be omitted.
C                 .ERR Parameter 2 (register to load) cannot be omitted.
C                 ENDIF
C                 EXITM                        ;; get out fast.
C              ENDIF
C  ;;
C  ;; It is present - check it out in detail.
C  ;;
C              IF  ((.TYPE INTO) AND 0010h) EQ 010h   ;; Is INTO a register
C                 IFIDNI  <INTO>,<AH>          ;; Check for 1 byte reg.
C                 ELSEIFIDNI <INTO>,<AL>
C                 ELSEIFIDNI <INTO>,<BL>
C                 ELSEIFIDNI <INTO>,<CL>
C                 ELSEIFIDNI <INTO>,<DL>
C                 ELSEIFIDNI <INTO>,<BH>
C                 ELSEIFIDNI <INTO>,<CH>
C                 ELSEIFIDNI <INTO>,<DH>
C                 ELSE
C                    IF2
C                    %OUT  INTO (parameter 2) must be a byte register.
C                    .ERR  INTO (parameter 2) must be a byte register.
C                    ENDIF
C                    EXITM
C                 ENDIF
C              ELSE
C                 IF2
C                 %OUT INTO (parameter 2) must be a byte register.
C                 .ERR INTO (parameter 2) must be a byte register.
```

```
C               ENDIF
C               EXITM
C           ENDIF
C ;;
C ;; Now edit parameter 1, the item to load into the register.
C ;;
C ;; It could be a byte register
C           IF ((.TYPE CODE) AND 0010h) EQ 010h  ;; Is CODE a register
C               IFIDNI  <CODE>,<AH>              ;; Check for 1 byte reg.
C               ELSEIFIDNI <CODE>,<AL>
C               ELSEIFIDNI <CODE>,<BL>
C               ELSEIFIDNI <CODE>,<CL>
C               ELSEIFIDNI <CODE>,<DL>
C               ELSEIFIDNI <CODE>,<BH>
C               ELSEIFIDNI <CODE>,<CH>
C               ELSEIFIDNI <CODE>,<DH>
C               ELSE
C                   IF2
C                   %OUT  CODE must be a byte register.
C                   .ERR  CODE must be a byte register.
C                   ENDIF
C                   EXITM
C               ENDIF
C               IFIDNI  <CODE>,<INTO>           ;; Are the registers the same?
C                   EXITM                       ;; If so - done.
C               ENDIF
C ;;
C ;; CODE is not a register - it can be a constant or 8 bit data.
C ;;
C
C           ELSE
C               IF  (TYPE CODE) GT 1
C                   IF2
C                   %OUT  CODE is an invalid data type - use byte size.
C                   .ERR  CODE is an invalid data type - use byte size.
C                   ENDIF
C                   EXITM
C               ENDIF
C           ENDIF
C                   MOV     INTO,CODE
C                   ENDM
C
C                   INCLUDE  MACROS\@SETWRD.MAC
C @SETWRD         MACRO   WCODE,INTO
C ;;
C ;; Inner - Inner macro for loading a word into a register
C ;;
C ;; Input:
C ;;  WCODE is the value to be loaded into the register.
C ;;      If omitted, it is assumed that the register has
C ;;      been set prior to the call.
C ;;  INTO is the word register that is to be loaded.
C ;;
C ;;  invoking the macro.
C ;;
C           IFB     <WCODE>                     ;; If WCODE is omitted - ok but
C               EXITM                           ;; get out fast.
C           ENDIF
C ;;
C ;; Edit the register to load
C ;;
C           IFB     <INTO>                      ;; If INTO is omitted
C               IF2
C               %OUT Parameter 2 (register to load) cannot be omitted.
C               .ERR Parameter 2 (register to load) cannot be omitted.
C               ENDIF
C               EXITM                           ;; get out fast.
C           ENDIF
C ;;
C ;; It is present - check it out in detail.
C ;;
C           IF  ((.TYPE INTO) AND 0010h) EQ 010h    ;; Is INTO a register
```

```
C                       IFIDNI   <INTO>,<AX>        ;; Check for 1 word reg.
C                       ELSEIFIDNI <INTO>,<BX>
C                       ELSEIFIDNI <INTO>,<CX>
C                       ELSEIFIDNI <INTO>,<DX>
C                       ELSEIFIDNI <INTO>,<SP>
C                       ELSEIFIDNI <INTO>,<BP>
C                       ELSEIFIDNI <INTO>,<SI>
C                       ELSEIFIDNI <INTO>,<DI>
C                       ELSE
C                          IF2
C                          %OUT  INTO (parameter 2) must be a word register.
C                          .ERR  INTO (parameter 2) must be a word register.
C                          ENDIF
C                          EXITM
C                       ENDIF
C              ELSE
C                 IF2
C                 %OUT INTO (parameter 2) must be a word register.
C                 .ERR INTO (parameter 2) must be a word register.
C                 ENDIF
C                 EXITM
C              ENDIF
C  ;;
C  ;; Now edit parameter 1, the item to load into the register.
C  ;;
C  ;; It could be a word register
C              IF ((.TYPE WCODE) AND 0010h) EQ 010h  ;; Is WCODE a register
C                       IFIDNI   <WCODE>,<AX>        ;; Check for 1 word reg.
C                       ELSEIFIDNI <WCODE>,<BX>
C                       ELSEIFIDNI <WCODE>,<CX>
C                       ELSEIFIDNI <WCODE>,<DX>
C                       ELSEIFIDNI <WCODE>,<SP>
C                       ELSEIFIDNI <WCODE>,<BP>
C                       ELSEIFIDNI <WCODE>,<SI>
C                       ELSEIFIDNI <WCODE>,<DI>
C                       ELSE
C                          IF2
C                          %OUT  WCODE must be a word register.
C                          .ERR  WCODE must be a word register.
C                          ENDIF
C                          EXITM
C                       ENDIF
C              IFIDNI <WCODE>,<INTO>        ;; Are the registers the same?
C                 EXITM                      ;; If so - done.
C              ENDIF
C  ;;
C  ;; WCODE is not a register - it can be a constant or 16 bit data.
C  ;;      (TYPE 0 or TYPE 2 are both OK 0 and x is zero as is 2 and D
C  ;;      all other values should be non-zero)
C
C              ELSE
C                 IF  ((TYPE WCODE) AND 0FFFDh) NE 0
C                    IF2
C                    %OUT  WCODE is an invalid data type - use word size.
C                    .ERR  WCODE is an invalid data type - use word size.
C                    ENDIF
C                    EXITM
C                 ENDIF
C              ENDIF
C                       MOV     INTO,WCODE
C                       ENDM
C
C                 INCLUDE MACROS\@OFFSET.MAC
C @OFFSET          MACRO   DISPL,INTO
C  ;;
C  ;; Inner - Inner macro for loading a displacement into a register
C  ;;
C  ;; Input:
C  ;;  DISPL is the value to be loaded into the register.
C  ;;       If omitted, it is assumed that the register has
C  ;;       been set prior to the call.
C  ;;       If a register, it is assumed that the offset is loaded.
```

```
C  ;;          In any case, it is assumed that the segment is properly
C  ;;          accessed for addressability.  i.e. as an over-ride
C  ;; INTO is the word register that is to be loaded.
C  ;;
C  ;; invoking the macro.
C  ;;
C          IFB    <DISPL>                    ;; If DISPL is omitted - ok but
C                 EXITM                      ;; get out fast.
C          ENDIF
C  ;;
C  ;; Edit the register to load
C  ;;
C          IFB    <INTO>                     ;; If INTO is omitted
C              IF2
C              %OUT Parameter 2 (register to load) cannot be omitted.
C              .ERR Parameter 2 (register to load) cannot be omitted.
C              ENDIF
C                 EXITM                      ;; get out fast.
C          ENDIF
C  ;;
C  ;; It is present - check it out in detail.
C  ;;
C          IF  ((.TYPE INTO) AND 0010h) EQ 010h   ;; Is INTO a register
C              IFIDNI    <INTO>,<AX>          ;; Check for 1 word reg.
C              ELSEIFIDNI <INTO>,<BX>
C              ELSEIFIDNI <INTO>,<CX>
C              ELSEIFIDNI <INTO>,<DX>
C              ELSEIFIDNI <INTO>,<SP>
C              ELSEIFIDNI <INTO>,<BP>
C              ELSEIFIDNI <INTO>,<SI>
C              ELSEIFIDNI <INTO>,<DI>
C              ELSE
C                  IF2
C                  %OUT  INTO (parameter 2) must be a word register.
C                  .ERR  INTO (parameter 2) must be a word register.
C                  ENDIF
C                  EXITM
C              ENDIF
C          ELSE
C              IF2
C              %OUT INTO (parameter 2) must be a word register.
C              .ERR INTO (parameter 2) must be a word register.
C              ENDIF
C              EXITM
C          ENDIF
C  ;;
C  ;; Now edit parameter 1, the item to load into the register.
C  ;;
C  ;; It could be a word register
C          IF ((.TYPE DISPL) AND 0010h) EQ 010h  ;; Is DISPL a register
C              IFIDNI    <DISPL>,<AX>         ;; Check for 1 word reg.
C              ELSEIFIDNI <DISPL>,<BX>
C              ELSEIFIDNI <DISPL>,<CX>
C              ELSEIFIDNI <DISPL>,<DX>
C              ELSEIFIDNI <DISPL>,<SP>
C              ELSEIFIDNI <DISPL>,<BP>
C              ELSEIFIDNI <DISPL>,<SI>
C              ELSEIFIDNI <DISPL>,<DI>
C              ELSE
C                  IF2
C                      %OUT  DISPL must be a word register.
C                      .ERR  DISPL must be a word register.
C                  ENDIF
C                      EXITM
C              ENDIF
C              IFIDNI <DISPL>,<INTO>          ;; Are the registers the same?
C                  EXITM                      ;; If so - done.
C              ENDIF
C                  MOV    INTO,DISPL
C          EXITM
C  ;;
C  ;; DISPL is not a register - it must be a data area.
```

```
C  ;;          TYPE 0 or TYPEs 0FFFFh and 0FFFEh are bad.
C  ;;          All other values should be ok.
C
C          ELSE
C              IF   ((TYPE DISPL) GT 0FFFDh) OR ((TYPE DISPL) EQ 0)
C                  IF2
C                  %OUT  DISPL is a constant or code - must be data.
C                  .ERR  DISPL is a constant or code - must be data.
C                  ENDIF
C                  EXITM
C              ENDIF
C          ENDIF
C                  LEA     INTO,DISPL
C                  ENDM
C
C
C
C

              INCLUDE  MACROS\@SETBYT.MAC
C  @SETBYT        MACRO   CODE,INTO
C  ;;
C  ;; Inner - Inner macro for loading a byte into a register
C  ;;
C  ;; Input:
C  ;;  CODE is the value to be loaded into the register.
C  ;;       If omitted, it is assumed that the register has
C  ;;       been set prior to the call.
C  ;;  INTO is the byte register that is to be loaded.
C  ;;
C  ;;  invoking the macro.
C  ;;
C              IFB     <CODE>               ;; If CODE is omitted - ok but
C                  EXITM                    ;; get out fast.
C              ENDIF
C  ;;
C  ;; Edit the register to load
C  ;;
C              IFB     <INTO>               ;; If INTO is omitted
C                  IF2
C                  %OUT Parameter 2 (register to load) cannot be omitted.
C                  .ERR Parameter 2 (register to load) cannot be omitted.
C                  ENDIF
C                  EXITM                    ;; get out fast.
C              ENDIF
C  ;;
C  ;; It is present - check it out in detail.
C  ;;
C              IF  ((.TYPE INTO) AND 0010h) EQ 010h   ;; Is INTO a register
C                  IFIDNI  <INTO>,<AH>           ;; Check for 1 byte reg.
C                  ELSEIFIDNI <INTO>,<AL>
C                  ELSEIFIDNI <INTO>,<BL>
C                  ELSEIFIDNI <INTO>,<CL>
C                  ELSEIFIDNI <INTO>,<DL>
C                  ELSEIFIDNI <INTO>,<BH>
C                  ELSEIFIDNI <INTO>,<CH>
C                  ELSEIFIDNI <INTO>,<DH>
C                  ELSE
C                      IF2
C                      %OUT INTO (parameter 2) must be a byte register.
C                      .ERR INTO (parameter 2) must be a byte register.
C                      ENDIF
C                      EXITM
C                  ENDIF
C              ELSE
C                  IF2
C                  %OUT INTO (parameter 2) must be a byte register.
C                  .ERR INTO (parameter 2) must be a byte register.
C                  ENDIF
C                  EXITM
C              ENDIF
C  ;;
C  ;; Now edit parameter 1, the item to load into the register.
```

```
C   ;;
C   ;; It could be a byte register
C           IF ((.TYPE CODE) AND 0010h) EQ 010h  ;; Is CODE a register
C               IFIDNI   <CODE>,<AH>          ;; Check for 1 byte reg.
C               ELSEIFIDNI <CODE>,<AL>
C               ELSEIFIDNI <CODE>,<BL>
C               ELSEIFIDNI <CODE>,<CL>
C               ELSEIFIDNI <CODE>,<DL>
C               ELSEIFIDNI <CODE>,<BH>
C               ELSEIFIDNI <CODE>,<CH>
C               ELSEIFIDNI <CODE>,<DH>
C               ELSE
C                   IF2
C                   %OUT  CODE must be a byte register.
C                   .ERR  CODE must be a byte register.
C                   ENDIF
C                   EXITM
C               ENDIF
C               IFIDNI <CODE>,<INTO>          ;; Are the registers the same?
C                   EXITM                     ;; If so - done.
C               ENDIF
C   ;;
C   ;; CODE is not a register - it can be a constant or 8 bit data.
C   ;;
C
C           ELSE
C               IF (TYPE CODE) GT 1
C                   IF2
C                   %OUT  CODE is an invalid data type - use byte size.
C                   .ERR  CODE is an invalid data type - use byte size.
C                   ENDIF
C                   EXITM
C               ENDIF
C           ENDIF
C               MOV     INTO,CODE
C               ENDM
C
C               INCLUDE  MACROS\@SETWRD.MAC
C @SETWRD       MACRO   WCODE,INTO
C   ;;
C   ;; Inner - Inner macro for loading a word into a register
C   ;;
C   ;; Input:
C   ;;  WCODE is the value to be loaded into the register.
C   ;;        If omitted, it is assumed that the register has
C   ;;        been set prior to the call.
C   ;;  INTO is the word register that is to be loaded.
C   ;;
C   ;;  invoking the macro.
C   ;;
C           IFB     <WCODE>                   ;; If WCODE is omitted - ok but
C               EXITM                         ;; get out fast.
C           ENDIF
C   ;;
C   ;; Edit the register to load
C   ;;
C           IFB     <INTO>              ;; If INTO is omitted
C               IF2
C               %OUT Parameter 2 (register to load) cannot be omitted.
C               .ERR Parameter 2 (register to load) cannot be omitted.
C               ENDIF
C               EXITM                   ;; get out fast.
C           ENDIF
C   ;;
C   ;; It is present - check it out in detail.
C   ;;
C           IF ((.TYPE INTO) AND 0010h) EQ 010h   ;; Is INTO a register
C               IFIDNI   <INTO>,<AX>          ;; Check for 1 word reg.
C               ELSEIFIDNI <INTO>,<BX>
C               ELSEIFIDNI <INTO>,<CX>
C               ELSEIFIDNI <INTO>,<DX>
```

```
c                   ELSEIFIDNI <INTO>,<SP>
c                   ELSEIFIDNI <INTO>,<BP>
c                   ELSEIFIDNI <INTO>,<SI>
c                   ELSEIFIDNI <INTO>,<DI>
c                   ELSE
c                       IF2
c                       %OUT  INTO (parameter 2) must be a word register.
c                       .ERR  INTO (parameter 2) must be a word register.
c                       ENDIF
c                       EXITM
c                   ENDIF
c               ELSE
c                   IF2
c                   %OUT INTO (parameter 2) must be a word register.
c                   .ERR INTO (parameter 2) must be a word register.
c                   ENDIF
c                   EXITM
c               ENDIF
c ;;
c ;; Now edit parameter 1, the item to load into the register.
c ;;
c ;; It could be a word register
c               IF ((.TYPE WCODE) AND 0010h) EQ 010h  ;; Is WCODE a register
c                   IFIDNI   <WCODE>,<AX>          ;; Check for 1 word reg.
c                   ELSEIFIDNI <WCODE>,<BX>
c                   ELSEIFIDNI <WCODE>,<CX>
c                   ELSEIFIDNI <WCODE>,<DX>
c                   ELSEIFIDNI <WCODE>,<SP>
c                   ELSEIFIDNI <WCODE>,<BP>
c                   ELSEIFIDNI <WCODE>,<SI>
c                   ELSEIFIDNI <WCODE>,<DI>
c                   ELSE
c                       IF2
c                       %OUT  WCODE must be a word register.
c                       .ERR  WCODE must be a word register.
c                       ENDIF
c                       EXITM
c                   ENDIF
c                   IFIDNI <WCODE>,<INTO>         ;; Are the registers the same?
c                       EXITM                     ;; If so - done.
c                   ENDIF
c ;;
c ;; WCODE is not a register - it can be a constant or 16 bit data.
c ;;       (TYPE 0 or TYPE 2 are both OK 0 and x is zero as is 2 and D
c ;;       all other values should be non-zero)
c
c               ELSE
c                   IF  ((TYPE WCODE) AND 0FFFDh) NE 0
c                       IF2
c                       %OUT  WCODE is an invalid data type - use word size.
c                       .ERR  WCODE is an invalid data type - use word size.
c                       ENDIF
c                       EXITM
c                   ENDIF
c               ENDIF
c                       MOV     INTO,WCODE
c                       ENDM
c
c                   INCLUDE  MACROS\@OFFSET.MAC
c @OFFSET         MACRO   DISPL,INTO
c ;;
c ;; Inner - Inner macro for loading a displacement into a register
c ;;
c ;; Input:
c ;; DISPL is the value to be loaded into the register.
c ;;       If omitted, it is assumed that the register has
c ;;       been set prior to the call.
c ;;       If a register, it is assumed that the offset is loaded.
c ;;       In any case, it is assumed that the segment is properly
c ;;       accessed for addressability.  i.e. as an over-ride
c ;; INTO is the word register that is to be loaded.
c ;;
```

```
C  ;;   invoking the macro.
C  ;;
C           IFB      <DISPL>                ;; If DISPL is omitted - ok but
C                    EXITM                  ;; get out fast.
C           ENDIF
C  ;;
C  ;; Edit the register to load
C  ;;
C           IFB      <INTO>                 ;; If INTO is omitted
C              IF2
C              %OUT Parameter 2 (register to load) cannot be omitted.
C              .ERR Parameter 2 (register to load) cannot be omitted.
C              ENDIF
C                    EXITM                  ;; get out fast.
C           ENDIF
C  ;;
C  ;; It is present - check it out in detail.
C  ;;
C           IF  ((.TYPE INTO) AND 0010h) EQ 010h   ;; Is INTO a register
C              IFIDNI   <INTO>,<AX>         ;; Check for 1 word reg.
C              ELSEIFIDNI <INTO>,<BX>
C              ELSEIFIDNI <INTO>,<CX>
C              ELSEIFIDNI <INTO>,<DX>
C              ELSEIFIDNI <INTO>,<SP>
C              ELSEIFIDNI <INTO>,<BP>
C              ELSEIFIDNI <INTO>,<SI>
C              ELSEIFIDNI <INTO>,<DI>
C              ELSE
C                 IF2
C                 %OUT  INTO (parameter 2) must be a word register.
C                 .ERR  INTO (parameter 2) must be a word register.
C                 ENDIF
C                 EXITM
C              ENDIF
C           ELSE
C              IF2
C              %OUT INTO (parameter 2) must be a word register.
C              .ERR INTO (parameter 2) must be a word register.
C              ENDIF
C              EXITM
C           ENDIF
C  ;;
C  ;; Now edit parameter 1, the item to load into the register.
C  ;;
C  ;; It could be a word register
C           IF  ((.TYPE DISPL) AND 0010h) EQ 010h  ;; Is DISPL a register
C              IFIDNI   <DISPL>,<AX>        ;; Check for 1 word reg.
C              ELSEIFIDNI <DISPL>,<BX>
C              ELSEIFIDNI <DISPL>,<CX>
C              ELSEIFIDNI <DISPL>,<DX>
C              ELSEIFIDNI <DISPL>,<SP>
C              ELSEIFIDNI <DISPL>,<BP>
C              ELSEIFIDNI <DISPL>,<SI>
C              ELSEIFIDNI <DISPL>,<DI>
C              ELSE
C                 IF2
C                 %OUT  DISPL must be a word register.
C                 .ERR  DISPL must be a word register.
C                 ENDIF
C                 EXITM
C              ENDIF
C              IFIDNI <DISPL>,<INTO>        ;; Are the registers the same?
C                 EXITM                     ;; If so - done.
C              ENDIF
C              MOV      INTO,DISPL
C              EXITM
C  ;;
C  ;; DISPL is not a register - it must be a data area.
C  ;;    TYPE 0 or TYPEs 0FFFFh and 0FFFEh are bad.
C  ;;    All other values should be ok.
C
C           ELSE
C              IF  ((TYPE DISPL) GT 0FFFDh) OR ((TYPE DISPL) EQ 0)
```

```
                            C               IF2
                            C               %OUT  DISPL is a constant or code - must be data.
                            C               .ERR  DISPL is a constant or code - must be data.
                            C               ENDIF
                            C               EXITM
                            C           ENDIF
                            C         ENDIF
                            C               LEA     INTO,DISPL
                            C               ENDM
                            C
                            C
                            C
                            C
                                    ;
                                    ;
                                    ;
                                            .DATA
                                    ;
                                    ; To provide data type definitions for the test.
                                    ;
0000  00                    dtabyte   DB      0              ; A byte sized field
0001  0000                  dtaword   DW      0              ; A word sized field
0003  00000000              dtadbl    DD      0              ; A double word field
0007  61 62 63 64 65        dtastr    DB      'abcde'        ; A string
000C  0001 ---- R           dtaptr    DD      dtaword        ; A far pointer (USE16)
0010  00000007 ---- R       fdtaptr   DF      dtastr         ; A far pointer (USE32)

                                            .CODE                 ; Begin code segment
0000                        MACTEST   PROC
                                    ;       enter                 ; Set BP and get work space
0000                        BIOS10:
0000  60                              pusha                       ; Save entry registers
                                    ;
                                    ; Check out valid generations of @SETBYT directly.
                                    ;
                                            @SETBYT 33h,DL         ; Constant is OK
0001  B2 33             1               MOV     DL,33h
                                            @SETBYT dtabyte,BL     ; as is a byte field,
0003  8A 1E 0000 R      1               MOV     BL,dtabyte
                                            @SETBYT dtastr,CH      ; a string field,
0007  8A 2E 0007 R      1               MOV     CH,dtastr
                                            @SETBYT AL,AH          ; a byte register,
000B  8A E0             1               MOV     AH,AL
                                            @SETBYT AL,AL          ; and the same byte register.
                                    ;
                                    ; Check out valid generations of @SETWRD directly.
                                    ;
                                            @SETWRD 333h,DX        ; Constant is OK
000D  BA 0333           1               MOV     DX,333h
                                            @SETWRD dtaword,BP     ; as is a word field,
0010  8B 2E 0001 R      1               MOV     BP,dtaword
                                            @SETWRD dtaword,CX     ; another word field,
0014  8B 0E 0001 R      1               MOV     CX,dtaword
                                            @SETWRD SI,DI          ; a word register,
0018  8B FE             1               MOV     DI,SI
                                            @SETWRD ,DI            ; an omitted source,
                                            @SETWRD SP,SP          ; and the same byte register.
                                    ;
                                    ; Check invalid generations of @SETWRD directly.
                                    ;
                                            @SETWRD 330h,dtaword   ; Constant is OK register isn't
                            1               .ERR dtaword (parameter 2) must be a word register.
mactest.ASM(66): error A2089: Forced error
                                            @SETWRD dtabyte,BX     ; nor is a byte field,
                            1               .ERR  dtabyte is an invalid data type - use word size.
mactest.ASM(67): error A2089: Forced error
                                            @SETWRD dtastr,AX      ; a string field,
                            1               .ERR  dtastr is an invalid data type - use word size.
mactest.ASM(68): error A2089: Forced error
                                            @SETWRD AX,AH          ; a byte register target,
                            1               .ERR  AH (parameter 2) must be a word register.
mactest.ASM(69): error A2089: Forced error
                                            @SETWRD AL,AX          ; or a byte register source.
                            1               .ERR  AL must be a word register.
```

```
            mactest.ASM(70): error A2089: Forced error
                                          ;
                                          ; Check out valid generations of @OFFSET directly.
                                          ;
                                          @OFFSET                      ; Both omitted is OK
                                          @OFFSET dtaword,BP           ; as is a word field,
     001A  8D 2E 0001 R         1              LEA     BP,dtaword
                                          @OFFSET dtaword,CX           ; another word field,
     001E  8D 0E 0001 R         1              LEA     CX,dtaword
                                          @OFFSET dtabyte,BX           ; a byte field,
     0022  8D 1E 0000 R         1              LEA     BX,dtabyte
                                          @OFFSET dtastr,AX            ; a string field,
     0026  8D 06 0007 R         1              LEA     AX,dtastr
                                          @OFFSET SI,DI                ; a word register,
     002A  8B FE               1              MOV     DI,SI
                                          @OFFSET ,DI                  ; an omitted source,
                                          @OFFSET SP,SP                ; and the same word register.
                                          ;
                                          ; Check invalid generations of @OFFSET directly.
                                          ;
                                          @OFFSET 333h,DX              ; Constant is BAD
                            1                 .ERR 333h is a constant or code - must be data.
            mactest.ASM(85): error A2089: Forced error
                                          @OFFSET dtabyte,dtaword      ; so is invalid register,
                            1                 .ERR dtaword (parameter 2) must be a word register.
            mactest.ASM(86): error A2089: Forced error
                                          @OFFSET BIOS10,BP            ; a code label,
                            1                 .ERR  BIOS10 is a constant or code - must be data.
            mactest.ASM(87): error A2089: Forced error
                                          @OFFSET AX,AH                ; a byte register target,
                            1                 .ERR  AH (parameter 2) must be a word register.
            mactest.ASM(88): error A2089: Forced error
                                          @OFFSET AL,AX                ; or a byte register source.
                            1                 .ERR  AL must be a word register.
            mactest.ASM(89): error A2089: Forced error
                                          ;
                                          ; Check out valid generations of @BIOS10
                                          ;
     002C  CD 10               1          @BIOS10                      ; Omitted is OK
                                              INT     10h
                                          @BIOS10 35                   ; Decimal con is OK
     002E  B4 23               2              MOV     AH,35
     0030  CD 10               1              INT     10h
                                          @BIOS10 dtabyte              ; A byte field is OK
     0032  8A 26 0000 R        2              MOV     AH,dtabyte
     0036  CD 10               1              INT     10h
                                          @BIOS10 dtastr               ; As is a string field.
     0038  8A 26 0007 R        2              MOV     AH,dtastr
     003C  CD 10               1              INT     10h
                                          ;
                                          ; Check out error generations (and early exits)
                                          ;
                                          @BIOS10 dtaword              ; Can't fit word in byte
                            2                 .ERR  dtaword is an invalid data type - use byte size.
            mactest.ASM(100): error A2089: Forced error
     003E  CD 10               1              INT     10h
                                          @BIOS10 Bios10               ; nor can a data label be used
                            2                 .ERR  Bios10 is an invalid data type - use byte size.
            mactest.ASM(101): error A2089: Forced error
     0040  CD 10               1              INT     10h
                                          @BIOS10 355                  ; MASM will catch this.
     0042  B4 63               2              MOV     AH,355
            mactest.ASM(102): error A2050: Value out of range
     0044  CD 10               1              INT     10h
                                          ;
                                          ; Check out valid generations of @DOS21
                                          ;
     0046  CD 21               1          @DOS21                       ; Omitted is OK
                                              INT     21h
                                          @DOS21 35                    ; Decimal con is OK
     0048  B4 23               2              MOV     AH,35
     004A  CD 21               1              INT     21h
                                          @DOS21 dtabyte               ; A byte field is OK
```

```
     004C  8A 26 0000 R          2                    MOV      AH,dtabyte
     0050  CD 21                 1                    INT      21h
                                                      @DOS21   dtastr          ; As is a string field.
     0052  8A 26 0007 R          2                    MOV      AH,dtastr
     0056  CD 21                 1                    INT      21h
                                                   ;
                                                   ; Check out error generations (and early exits)
                                                   ;
                                                      @DOS21   dtaword              ; Can't fit word in byte
                                   2                   .ERR  dtaword is an invalid data type - use byte size.
mactest.ASM(113): error A2089: Forced error
     0058  CD 21                 1                    INT      21h
                                                      @DOS21   Bios10              ; nor can a data label be used
                                   2                   .ERR  Bios10 is an invalid data type - use byte size.
mactest.ASM(114): error A2089: Forced error
     005A  CD 21                 1                    INT      21h
                                                      @DOS21   355              ; MASM will catch this.
     005C  B4 63                 2                    MOV      AH,355
mactest.ASM(115): error A2050: Value out of range
     005E  CD 21                 1                    INT      21h
                                                   ;
                                                   ; Check generation of 'non-standard' macros.  i.e. those with other
                                                   ; than default editing checked above.
                                                   ;
                                                      INCLUDE  MACROS\BIOS1006.MAC
                                 C  BIOS1006       MACRO    LINENO,DISPLY,LEFTROW,LEFTCOL,RIGHTROW,RIGHTCOL
                                 C  ;;
                                 C  ;; BIOS Interrupt 10h Function 06h - Scroll Active Page Up
                                 C  ;; Input:
                                 C  ;;     AH = 06h
                                 C  ;;     AL = Number of lines blanked at bottom of the screen
                                 C  ;;          (00=blanks entire screen)
                                 C  ;;     BH = Display attribute used on blank lines
                                 C  ;;     CH = Upper left row of area to scroll
                                 C  ;;     CL = Upper left column of area to scroll
                                 C  ;;     DH = Lower right row of area to scroll
                                 C  ;;     DL = Lower right column of area to scroll
                                 C  ;;
                                 C         IFB   <LINENO>                  ; If omitted
                                 C                  XOR      AL,AL         ; clear whole screen.
                                 C         ELSE
                                 C                  @SETBYT LINENO,AL      ; Lines to blank at bottom
                                 C         ENDIF
                                 C                  @SETBYT DISPLY,BH      ; Display attribute on blanks
                                 C                  @SETBYT LEFTROW,CH     ; Upper left row to scroll
                                 C                  @SETBYT LEFTCOL,CL     ; Upper left column to scroll
                                 C                  @SETBYT RIGHTROW,DH    ; Lower right row to scroll
                                 C                  @SETBYT RIGHTCOL,DL    ; Lower right column to scroll
                                 C                  @BIOS10 06h            ; Scroll active page up.
                                 C                  ENDM
                                 C
                                 C
                                                   ;
                                                   ; Check generation when first operand omitted.
                                                   ;
                                                      BIOS1006 dtabyte,BL,CL,DL,CH  ; Present as data byte
     0060  A0 0000 R             2                    MOV      AL,dtabyte
     0063  8A FB                 2                    MOV      BH,BL
     0065  8A E9                 2                    MOV      CH,CL
     0067  8A CA                 2                    MOV      CL,DL
     0069  8A F5                 2                    MOV      DH,CH
     006B  B4 06                 3                    MOV      AH,06h
     006D  CD 10                 2                    INT      10h
                                                      BIOS1006 DL,DH,CL,CH,BL      ; Present as byte reg
     006F  8A C2                 2                    MOV      AL,DL
     0071  8A FE                 2                    MOV      BH,DH
     0073  8A E9                 2                    MOV      CH,CL
     0075  8A CD                 2                    MOV      CL,CH
     0077  8A F3                 2                    MOV      DH,BL
     0079  B4 06                 3                    MOV      AH,06h
     007B  CD 10                 2                    INT      10h
                                                      BIOS1006 ,DH,CL,CH,BL        ; Omitted
```

```
007D  32 C0          1              XOR     AL,AL           ; clear whole screen.
007F  8A FE          2              MOV     BH,DH
0081  8A E9          2              MOV     CH,CL
0083  8A CD          2              MOV     CL,CH
0085  8A F3          2              MOV     DH,BL
0087  B4 06          3              MOV     AH,06h
0089  CD 10          2              INT     10h
                                    PURGE   BIOS1006        ; Get rid of it.
                                    INCLUDE MACROS\DOS2106.MAC
               C DOS2106            MACRO   CHOUT
               C ;;
               C ;; MS-DOS Interrupt 21h Function 06h - Console Input/Output
               C ;;
               C ;; This function allows all possible characters and control codes
               C ;; with values between 00h and 0FEh to be read and written with
               C ;; standard I/O with no filtering by MS-DOS.  Note that the
               C ;; RUBOUT character (0FFh, 255 decimal) can NOT be output with
               C ;; this function.
               C ;;
               C ;; Function 06h does NOT wait for input.  Also, the input character
               C ;; is NOT automatically displayed.  CTRL-BREAK does not terminate
               C ;; operation.
               C ;;
               C ;; Input:
               C ;;      AH = 06h
               C ;;
               C ;;      If DL = FF    AL holds the character, if one is ready
               C ;;         DL < FF    Type ASCII code in DL out
               C ;;
               C              IFB <CHOUT>                    ; If omitted
               C                     @SETBYT 0FFh,DL         ; default to read.
               C              ELSE
               C                     @SETBYT CHOUT,DL        ; write byte otherwise.
               C              ENDIF
               C                     @DOS21  06h             ; Do read or write
               C                     ENDM
               C
                             ;
                             ; Check generation when first operand omitted.
                             ;
                                     DOS2106 dtabyte        ; Present as data byte
008B  8A 16 0000 R   2              MOV     DL,dtabyte
008F  B4 06          3              MOV     AH,06h
0091  CD 21          2              INT     21h
                                    DOS2106 AL             ; Present as byte reg
0093  8A D0          2              MOV     DL,AL
0095  B4 06          3              MOV     AH,06h
0097  CD 21          2              INT     21h
                                    DOS2106                ; Omitted
0099  B2 FF          2              MOV     DL,0FFh
009B  B4 06          3              MOV     AH,06h
009D  CD 21          2              INT     21h
                                    PURGE   DOS2106         ; Get rid of it.

                                    INCLUDE MACROS\DOS210C.MAC
               C DOS210C            MACRO   KBDFUN,BUFFAD
               C ;;
               C ;; MS-DOS Interrupt 21h Function 0Ch - Clear Buffer and Invoke Service
               C ;;
               C ;; This function clears the keyboard buffer before it invokes a
               C ;; keyboard function (01h, 06h, 07h, 08h, or 0Ah).  This function
               C ;; also checks for CTRL-BREAK.
               C ;;
               C ;; Input:
               C ;;      AH = 0Ch
               C ;;      AL = Keyboard function number
               C ;;
               C ;;           If AL = 06h, then DL=FFh
               C ;;           IF AL = 0Ah, DS:DX=the address of the buffer to receive
               C ;;                        the data
               C ;;
               C ;; Output:
```

```
        C  ;;        If AL was 01h, 06h, 07h, or 08h on the call:
        C  ;;            AL = 8-bit ASCII character from standard input
        C  ;;        If AL was 0A on the call:
        C  ;;            Nothing is returned
        C  ;;
        C      IF (TYPE KBDFUN) EQ 0              ; Is function a constant?
        C          IF (KBDFUN - 6) EQ 0          ; Is it a 6?
        C              @SETBYT 0FFh,DL           ; Default to read.
        C              IFNB <BUFFAD>             ; But can't have buffer too
        C                  IF2
        C                      %OUT Function 6 cannot also have a buffer address.
        C                      .ERR Function 6 cannot also have a buffer address.
        C                  ENDIF
        C              ENDIF
        C          ;;
        C          ;; No reasonable default is available for other than 6.
        C          ;; We assume a buffer address otherwise.
        C          ;;
        C          ELSE
        C              @OFFSET BUFFAD,DX         ; point to buffer
        C          ENDIF
        C      ELSE
        C              @OFFSET BUFFAD,DX         ; point to buffer
        C      ENDIF
        C              @SETBYT KBDFUN,AL         ; Set desired function
        C              @DOS21 0Ch                ; and go do it.
        C              ENDM
        C
        C
                ;
                ; Check generation when first operand is or isnt a con of 6.
                ;
                             DOS210C 06h                    ; Con of 6,
009F  B2 FF          2       MOV     DL,0FFh
00A1  B0 06          2       MOV     AL,06h
00A3  B4 0C          3       MOV     AH,0Ch
00A5  CD 21          2       INT     21h
                             DOS210C 6,dtabyte              ; Con of 6 with buffer
00A7  B2 FF          2       MOV     DL,0FFh
                     1       .ERR Function 6 cannot also have a buffer address.
mactest.ASM(144): error A2089: Forced error
00A9  B0 06          2       MOV     AL,6
00AB  B4 0C          3       MOV     AH,0Ch
00AD  CD 21          2       INT     21h
                             DOS210C 5,dtabyte              ; Other con with buffer
00AF  8D 16 0000 R   2       LEA     DX,dtabyte
00B3  B0 05          2       MOV     AL,5
00B5  B4 0C          3       MOV     AH,0Ch
00B7  CD 21          2       INT     21h
                             DOS210C dtabyte,dtabyte        ; Non-con with buffer
00B9  8D 16 0000 R   2       LEA     DX,dtabyte
00BD  A0 0000 R      2       MOV     AL,dtabyte
00C0  B4 0C          3       MOV     AH,0Ch
00C2  CD 21          2       INT     21h
                             DOS210C dtabyte                ; and without
00C4  A0 0000 R      2       MOV     AL,dtabyte
00C7  B4 0C          3       MOV     AH,0Ch
00C9  CD 21          2       INT     21h
                             PURGE   DOS210C                ; Get rid of it.

                             INCLUDE MACROS\DOS2125.MAC
        C  DOS2125        MACRO   INTNUM,HANDLER
        C  ;;
        C  ;; MS-DOS Interrupt 21h Function 25h - Set Interrupt Vector
        C  ;;
        C  ;; Function 25 sets an address in the Interrupt Vector Table to point
        C  ;; to a specified interrupt handler.
        C  ;;
        C  ;; When this function is called, the 4-byte address IN DS:DX is
        C  ;; placed in the correct position in the IVT.  Before using Function 25,
        C  ;; read the address of the current interrupt handler with Function 35
        C  ;; and save the current address for restoration before your program
```

```
            C  ;; terminates.
            C  ;;
            C  ;; Input:
            C  ;;    AH = 25h
            C  ;;    AL = Interrupt number to modify
            C  ;;    DS:DX = Address of new interrupt handler
            C  ;;
            C  ;;    Note: DS:DX IS the address to set.  It is NOT the
            C  ;;          segment value (DS) and offset (DX) of the area
            C  ;;          where the address is located.
            C  ;;
            C               @SETBYT INTNUM,AL          ; Set interrupt number
            C     IFNB <HANDLER>                       ; If HANDLER is present
            C       IF ((.TYPE HANDLER) AND 01h) EQ 01h ; If program related
            C               MOV     DX,CS              ; Set CS as segment.
            C               MOV     DS,DX              ; In DS
            C               LEA     DX,HANDLER         ; Get offset in DX
            C       ELSEIF ((.TYPE HANDLER) AND 02h) EQ 02h ; If data related
            C               LDS     DX,HANDLER         ; Load full pointer
            C       ENDIF
            C     ENDIF
            C               @DOS21  25h                ; and request function.
            C               ENDM
            C
            C
               ;
               ; Check generation for special second operand (seg:offset pair)
               ;
                            DOS2125 06h,dtaptr          ; Coded as pointer,
  00CB  B0 06          2            MOV     AL,06h
  00CD  C5 16 000C R   1            LDS     DX,dtaptr    ; Load full pointer
  00D1  B4 25          3            MOV     AH,25h
  00D3  CD 21          2            INT     21h
                            DOS2125 6,BIOS10            ; as code label, and
  00D5  B0 06          2            MOV     AL,6
  00D7  8C CA          1            MOV     DX,CS        ; Set CS as segment.
  00D9  8E DA          1            MOV     DS,DX        ; In DS
  00DB  8D 16 0000 R   1            LEA     DX,BIOS10    ; Get offset in DX
  00DF  B4 25          3            MOV     AH,25h
  00E1  CD 21          2            INT     21h
                            DOS2125 5,dtabyte           ; od sized data area.
  00E3  B0 05          2            MOV     AL,5
  00E5  C5 16 0000 R   1            LDS     DX,dtabyte   ; Load full pointer
mactest.ASM(156): warning A4057: Illegal size for operand
  00E9  B4 25          3            MOV     AH,25h
  00EB  CD 21          2            INT     21h
                            DOS2125 dtabyte,dtabyte     ; Non-con number and odd size,
  00ED  A0 0000 R      2            MOV     AL,dtabyte
  00F0  C5 16 0000 R   1            LDS     DX,dtabyte   ; Load full pointer
mactest.ASM(157): warning A4057: Illegal size for operand
  00F4  B4 25          3            MOV     AH,25h
  00F6  CD 21          2            INT     21h
                            DOS2125 dtabyte             ; and without.
  00F8  A0 0000 R      2            MOV     AL,dtabyte
  00FB  B4 25          3            MOV     AH,25h
  00FD  CD 21          2            INT     21h
                            PURGE   DOS2125             ; Get rid of it.

                        INCLUDE  MACROS\DOS2129.MAC
            C  DOS2129          MACRO   STRADD,FCBADD
            C  ;;
            C  ;; MS-DOS Interrupt 21h Function 29h - Parse Filename
            C  ;;
            C  ;; This function is useful in parsing file names from the command
            C  ;; line.  Give it the address of the command line.  If it finds a
            C  ;; file name, Function 29h places an unopened FCB for the file at
            C  ;; address ES:DI.  If the command line does not contain a valid
            C  ;; file name, ES:[DI+1] will contain blanks.
            C  ;;
            C  ;; Note this function cannot parse pathnames.
            C  ;;
            C  ;; Input:
```

```
C ;;          AH = 29h
C ;;          AL = Bit 0=0  Stop parsing if file separator is found
C ;;                     1  Leading separators are scanned off the command
C ;;                        line
C ;;                   1=0  Set drive number field in FCB to 0 (current
C ;;                        drive) if string does not include a drive
C ;;                        identifier
C ;;                     1  Drive ID in final FCB will be change ONLY if a
C ;;                        drive was specified
C ;;                   2=0  Set filename field in the FCB to blanks if
C ;;                        string does not include a filename
C ;;                     1  Filename in FCB changed ONLY if command line
C ;;                        includes a filename
C ;;                   3=0  Set extension field in FCB to blanks if string
C ;;                        does not include a filename extension
C ;;                     1  Filename extension in FCB will be changed ONLY
C ;;                        if command line contains a filename extension
C ;;          DS:SI = Command line string to parse
C ;;          ES:DI = Address to put unopened FCB
C ;;
C ;; Output:
C ;;          AL = 00 if string does not contain wildcard character
C ;;               01 if string contains wildcard character
C ;;               FF if drive specifier invalid
C ;;          DS:SI = first byte after parsed string
C ;;          ES:DI = valid unopened FCB
C ;;
C                     @OFFSET STRADD,SI          ; Point to string
C          IF ((.TYPE FCBADD) AND 3) NE 0        ; If a label or variable,
C                     MOV     DI, SEG FCBADD      ; Get segment
C                     MOV     ES,DI               ; into ES.
C          ENDIF
C                     @OFFSET FCBADD,DI           ; and offset to DI.
C                     @DOS21 29h                  ; Parse filename.
C                     ENDM
C
C
;
; Check generation when second operand is in code and data areas.
;
                      DOS2129 dtabyte,BIOS10     ; Code buffer,
00FF 8D 36 0000 R  2            LEA     SI,dtabyte
0103 BF ---- R     1            MOV     DI, SEG BIOS10  ; Get segment
0106 8E C7         1            MOV     ES,DI           ; into ES.
                   2            .ERR BIOS10 is a constant or code - must be data.
mactest.ASM(165): error A2089: Forced error
0108 B4 29         3            MOV     AH,29h
010A CD 21         2            INT     21h
                      DOS2129 dtabyte,dtabyte    ; data buffer,
010C 8D 36 0000 R  2            LEA     SI,dtabyte
0110 BF ---- R     1            MOV     DI, SEG dtabyte  ; Get segment
0113 8E C7         1            MOV     ES,DI            ; into ES.
0115 8D 3E 0000 R  2            LEA     DI,dtabyte
0119 B4 29         3            MOV     AH,29h
011B CD 21         2            INT     21h
                      DOS2129 dtabyte            ; and without
011D 8D 36 0000 R  2            LEA     SI,dtabyte
0121 B4 29         3            MOV     AH,29h
0123 CD 21         2            INT     21h
                      PURGE   DOS2129            ; Get rid of it.


                      INCLUDE  MACROS\DOS212D.MAC
C DOS212D          MACRO  HOUR,MINUTE,SECOND,HUND
C ;;
C ;; MS-DOS Interrupt 21 Function 2D - Set Time
C ;;
C ;; Function 2C sets the current system time in binary form (with
C ;; the hours based on the 24-hour clock), minutes, seconds, and
C ;; hundredths of a second.
C ;;
C ;; Input:
```

```
C  ;;         AH = 2Dh
C  ;;         CH = Hours (0 .. 23)
C  ;;         CL = Minutes (0 .. 59)
C  ;;         DH = Seconds (0 .. 59)
C  ;;         DL = Hundredths of seconds (0 .. 99)
C  ;;
C  ;; Output:
C  ;;         AL = 00 if successful
C  ;;              FF if time is invalid
C  ;;
C      IFB    <HUND>
C              XOR     DL,DL            ; Default hundredths to zero
C      ELSE
C              @SETBYT HUND,DL          ; Load hundredths,
C      ENDIF
C              @SETBYT SECOND,DH        ; seconds,
C              @SETBYT MINUTE,CL        ; minutes, and
C              @SETBYT HOUR,CH          ; hours.
C              @DOS21  2Dh              ; Go set them.
C              ENDM
C
C
       ;
       ; Check generation when fourth operand is omitted
       ;
                        DOS212D dtabyte,AL,AL      ; omit hundredths.
0125  32 D2         1            XOR     DL,DL     ; Default hundredths to zero
0127  8A F0         2            MOV     DH,AL
0129  8A C8         2            MOV     CL,AL
012B  8A 2E 0000 R  2            MOV     CH,dtabyte
012F  B4 2D         3            MOV     AH,2Dh
0131  CD 21         2            INT     21h
                        DOS212D dtabyte,BH,BL,CL   ; refer to hundredths
0133  8A D1         2            MOV     DL,CL
0135  8A F3         2            MOV     DH,BL
0137  8A CF         2            MOV     CL,BH
0139  8A 2E 0000 R  2            MOV     CH,dtabyte
013D  B4 2D         3            MOV     AH,2Dh
013F  CD 21         2            INT     21h
                        DOS212D dtabyte            ; and without
0141  32 D2         1            XOR     DL,DL     ; Default hundredths to zero
0143  8A 2E 0000 R  2            MOV     CH,dtabyte
0147  B4 2D         3            MOV     AH,2Dh
0149  CD 21         2            INT     21h
                        PURGE   DOS212D            ; Get rid of it.


                        INCLUDE  MACROS\DOS212E.MAC
C  DOS212E       MACRO   SWITCH
C  ;;
C  ;; MS-DOS Interrupt 21h Function 2Eh - Set or Reset Verify Switch
C  ;;
C  ;; Function 2Eh turns on and off the verification for disk writing.
C  ;;
C  ;; Input:
C  ;;         AH = 2Eh
C  ;;         AL = 00  Turn verify OFF
C  ;;              01  Turn verify ON
C  ;;         DL = 00  Obsolete DOS requirement.
C  ;;
C          IFIDNI <SWITCH>,<OFF>
C                  XOR     AL,AL            ; Verify OFF
C          ELSEIFIDNI <SWITCH>,<ON>
C                  MOV     AL,1             ; Verify ON
C          ELSE
C                  @SETBYT SWITCH,AL        ; Who knows.
C          ENDIF
C                  @DOS21  2Eh              ; Set the option.
C                  ENDM
C
C
```

```
                      ;
                      ; Check generation of off/on.
                      ;
                                DOS212E oN                      ; mixed case ON
014B  B0 01         1             MOV     AL,1                  ; Verify ON
014D  B4 2E         3             MOV     AH,2Eh
014F  CD 21         2             INT     21h
                                DOS212E OFf                     ; and OFF
0151  32 C0         1             XOR     AL,AL                 ; Verify OFF

0153  B4 2E         3             MOV     AH,2Eh
0155  CD 21         2             INT     21h
                                DOS212E dtabyte                 ; user specified.
0157  A0 0000 R     2             MOV     AL,dtabyte
015A  B4 2E         3             MOV     AH,2Eh
015C  CD 21         2             INT     21h
                                PURGE   DOS212E                 ; Get rid of it.

                                INCLUDE MACROS\DOS2133.MAC
            C  DOS2133           MACRO   GETQ,SETTING
            C  ;;
            C  ;; MS-DOS Interrupt 21h Function 33h - Control Break Check
            C  ;;
            C  ;; MS-DOS uses this function to check if a BREAK is pending each
            C  ;; time a MS-DOS function is called.  Otherwise, the user can wait
            C  ;; a long time for a BREAK to be noticed and processed.  If the
            C  ;; Control-C check flag is off, MS-DOS checks for a Control-C entered
            C  ;; at the keyboard only during servicing of the character I/O functions
            C  ;; (01 through 0C).
            C  ;;
            C  ;; If the Control-C check flag is on, MS-DOS also checks for user entry
            C  ;; of a Control-C during servicing of other functions, such as file and
            C  ;; record operations.
            C  ;;
            C  ;; The state of the Control-C check flag affects all programs.  If a
            C  ;; program needs to change the state of Control-C checking, it should
            C  ;; save the original flag and restore it before terminating.
            C  ;;
            C  ;; Input:
            C  ;;      AH = 33h
            C  ;;      AL = 00 to get the state of Control-C check flag
            C  ;;           01 to set the state of Control-C check flag
            C  ;;      DL = 00 to set the flag to off
            C  ;;           01 to set the flag to on
            C  ;;
            C  ;; Output:
            C  ;;      AL = 00 if flag is set successfully
            C  ;;           FF code in AL on call was not 00 or 01
            C  ;;
            C  ;;      If AL was 00 on the call:
            C  ;;      DL = 00 Control-C check flag is Off
            C  ;;           01 Control-C check flag is On
            C  ;;
            C      IFIDNI <GETQ>,<GET>                     ; If getting the current
            C             XOR     AL,AL                    ; Indicate get request
            C      ELSEIFIDNI <GETQ>,<SET>                 ; If setting
            C             MOV     AL,1                      ; Indicate set
            C         IFIDNI <SETTING>,<OFF>               ; Is it off?
            C             XOR     DL,DL                    ; Indicate off.
            C         ELSEIFIDNI <SETTING>,<ON>            ; how about on?
            C             MOV     DL,1                      ; if so - request on.
            C         ELSE
            C             @SETBYT SETTING,DL               ; Not on or off - but --
            C         ENDIF
            C      ELSE                                    ; Not get or set - so
            C             @SETBYT GETQ,AL                  ; use whatever was coded
            C             @SETBYT SETTING,DL               ; with no defaults.
            C      ENDIF
            C             @DOS21  33h                      ; Issue request
            C             ENDM
            C
            C
```

```
                              ;
                              ; Check generation of get/set and on/off.
                              ;
                                      DOS2133 GET                 ; try GET
015E  32 C0            1              XOR     AL,AL              ; Indicate get request
0160  B4 33            3              MOV     AH,33h
0162  CD 21            2              INT     21h
                                      DOS2133 dtabyte              ; User trys a get.
0164  A0 0000 R        2              MOV     AL,dtabyte
0167  B4 33            3              MOV     AH,33h
0169  CD 21            2              INT     21h
                                      DOS2133 SET,OFf              ; SET it OFF
016B  B0 01            1              MOV     AL,1               ; Indicate set
016D  32 D2            1              XOR     DL,DL              ; Indicate off.
016F  B4 33            3              MOV     AH,33h
0171  CD 21            2              INT     21h
                                      DOS2133 dtabyte,CH           ; user specified both.
0173  A0 0000 R        2              MOV     AL,dtabyte
0176  8A D5            2              MOV     DL,CH
0178  B4 33            3              MOV     AH,33h
017A  CD 21            2              INT     21h
                                      DOS2133 SET,ON               ; try SET ON
017C  B0 01            1              MOV     AL,1               ; Indicate set
017E  B2 01            1              MOV     DL,1               ; if so - request on.
0180  B4 33            3              MOV     AH,33h
0182  CD 21            2              INT     21h
                                      DOS2133 SET,dtabyte          ; SET it to user's desire.
0184  B0 01            1              MOV     AL,1               ; Indicate set
0186  8A 16 0000 R     2              MOV     DL,dtabyte
018A  B4 33            3              MOV     AH,33h
018C  CD 21            2              INT     21h
                                      DOS2133 GET,dtabyte          ; user error specified.
018E  32 C0            1              XOR     AL,AL              ; Indicate get request
0190  B4 33            3              MOV     AH,33h
0192  CD 21            2              INT     21h
                                      PURGE   DOS2133              ; Get rid of it.


                              INCLUDE  MACROS\DOS2138.MAC
C  DOS2138        MACRO   GETQ,CNTRY,BUFF
C  ;;
C  ;; MS-DOS Interrupt 21h Function 38h - Get/Set Country Dependent
C  ;;                                 Information
C  ;; See the Brumm book which contains the complete information for
C  ;; this function, with illustrations as to the specific formats of
C  ;; the various fields.
C  ;;
C  ;; The get/set field must be either get or set for generation of
C  ;; the macro.  The input is edited and passed depending on this
C  ;; value.
C  ;;
C  ;; Input:
C  ;;      AH = 38h
C  ;;      AL = 00   Current country
C  ;;           01-FE Country code between 1 and 254
C  ;;           FF   Country code of 255 or greater, specifiedin BX
C  ;;      BX = Country code, if AL=FF
C  ;;      DX = FFFF - if set country information
C  ;;      DS:DX = 34-byte buffer - if get country information
C  ;;
C  ;; Output:
C  ;;      CF = 0 if successful
C  ;;           Filled in 32-byte block
C  ;;           BX = country code (MS-DOS version 3.x only)
C  ;;           DS:DX = buffer containing country information
C  ;;      CF = 1 if unsuccessful
C  ;;           AX = error code
C  ;;                02 invalid country code
C  ;;
C  ;;
C
C      IFNB <CNTRY>
C  ;;
```

```
C   ;; Edit country - if register, handle it
C   ;;
C   ;; It could be a byte register
C           IF ((.TYPE CNTRY) AND 0010h) EQ 010h  ;; Is CNTRY a register
C               IFIDNI  <CNTRY>,<AH>              ;; Check for 1 byte reg.
C                   @SETBYT CNTRY,AL              ; yes assume < 255
C               ELSEIFIDNI <CNTRY>,<AL>
C                   @SETBYT CNTRY,AL              ; yes assume < 255
C               ELSEIFIDNI <CNTRY>,<BL>
C                   @SETBYT CNTRY,AL              ; yes assume < 255
C               ELSEIFIDNI <CNTRY>,<CL>
C                   @SETBYT CNTRY,AL              ; yes assume < 255
C               ELSEIFIDNI <CNTRY>,<DL>
C                   @SETBYT CNTRY,AL              ; yes assume < 255
C               ELSEIFIDNI <CNTRY>,<BH>
C                   @SETBYT CNTRY,AL              ; yes assume < 255
C               ELSEIFIDNI <CNTRY>,<CH>
C                   @SETBYT CNTRY,AL              ; yes assume < 255
C               ELSEIFIDNI <CNTRY>,<DH>
C                   @SETBYT CNTRY,AL              ; yes assume < 255
C               ELSE
C                   @SETWRD CNTRY,BX
C                   MOV     AL,0FFh
C               ENDIF
C   ;; It wasn't a register - constant?
C           ELSEIF (TYPE CNTRY) EQ 0              ; Country is a constant
C               IF CNTRY LT 255                   ; Will it fit in AL?
C                   MOV     AL,CNTRY              ; Set country < 255
C               ELSE
C                   MOV     BX,CNTRY              ; Set country > 254
C                   MOV     AL,0FFh
C               ENDIF
C           ELSEIF (TYPE CNTRY) EQ 1              ; is country a byte?
C               @SETBYT CNTRY,AL                  ; yes assume < 255
C           ELSE
C               @SETWRD CNTRY,BX
C               MOV     AL,0FFh                   ; Set country > 254
C           ENDIF
C       ENDIF
C       IFIDNI <GETQ>,<GET>                       ; Is this a get request?
C               MOV     DX,-1                     ; Indicate get.
C           IFNB <BUFF>
C               .ERR BUFF is invalid for GET.
C           ENDIF
C       ELSEIFIDNI <GETQ>,<SET>                   ; Is it a set?
C               @OFFSET BUFF,DX                   ; Point to the buffer.
C       ELSE
C           IF2
C               %OUT  The first operand (GETQ) must be get or set.
C           ENDIF
C               .ERR  The first operand (GETQ) must be get or set.
C               EXITM
C       ENDIF
C               @DOS21  38h                       ; Request get/set
C               ENDM
C
C
    ;
    ; Check generation of off/on.
    ;
                DOS2138 GET,35                    ; try GET con
0194  B0 23     1       MOV     AL,35             ; Set country < 255
0196  BA FFFF   1       MOV     DX,-1             ; Indicate get.
0199  B4 38     3       MOV     AH,38h
019B  CD 21     2       INT     21h
                DOS2138 GET,350                   ; try GET con
019D  BB 015E   1       MOV     BX,350            ; Set country > 254
01A0  B0 FF     1       MOV     AL,0FFh
01A2  BA FFFF   1       MOV     DX,-1             ; Indicate get.
01A5  B4 38     3       MOV     AH,38h
01A7  CD 21     2       INT     21h
                DOS2138 GET,dtabyte               ; try GET var
```

```
01A9  A0 0000 R       2        MOV     AL,dtabyte
01AC  BA FFFF         1        MOV     DX,-1           ; Indicate get.
01AF  B4 38           3        MOV     AH,38h
01B1  CD 21           2        INT     21h
                               DOS2138 SET,35,dtabyte       ; try SET con and buffer
01B3  B0 23           1        MOV     AL,35           ; Set country < 255
01B5  8D 16 0000 R    2        LEA     DX,dtabyte
01B9  B4 38           3        MOV     AH,38h
01BB  CD 21           2        INT     21h
                               DOS2138 SET,350,dtabyte      ; try SET con and buffer
01BD  BB 015E         1        MOV     BX,350          ; Set country > 254
01C0  B0 FF           1        MOV     AL,0FFh
01C2  8D 16 0000 R    2        LEA     DX,dtabyte
01C6  B4 38           3        MOV     AH,38h
01C8  CD 21           2        INT     21h
                               DOS2138 SET,dtabyte,dtabyte  ; try SET var and buffer
01CA  A0 0000 R       2        MOV     AL,dtabyte
01CD  8D 16 0000 R    2        LEA     DX,dtabyte
01D1  B4 38           3        MOV     AH,38h
01D3  CD 21           2        INT     21h
                               DOS2138 SET,dtaword,dtabyte  ; try SET var and buffer
01D5  8B 1E 0001 R    2        MOV     BX,dtaword
01D9  B0 FF           1        MOV     AL,0FFh         ; Set country > 254
01DB  8D 16 0000 R    2        LEA     DX,dtabyte
01DF  B4 38           3        MOV     AH,38h
01E1  CD 21           2        INT     21h
                               DOS2138 SET,35,dtaword       ; try SET con and buffer
01E3  B0 23           1        MOV     AL,35           ; Set country < 255
01E5  8D 16 0001 R    2        LEA     DX,dtaword
01E9  B4 38           3        MOV     AH,38h
01EB  CD 21           2        INT     21h
                               DOS2138 SET,350,BP           ; try SET con and buffer
01ED  BB 015E         1        MOV     BX,350          ; Set country > 254
01F0  B0 FF           1        MOV     AL,0FFh
01F2  8B D5           2        MOV     DX,BP
01F4  B4 38           3        MOV     AH,38h
01F6  CD 21           2        INT     21h
                               DOS2138 SET,dtabyte,AH       ; try SET var and buffer err
01F8  A0 0000 R       2        MOV     AL,dtabyte
                      2        .ERR  AH must be a word register.
mactest.ASM(217): error A2089: Forced error
01FB  B4 38           3        MOV     AH,38h
01FD  CD 21           2        INT     21h
                               DOS2138 dtabyte,AX,BP        ; User trys a -what?
01FF  8B D8           2        MOV     BX,AX
0201  B0 FF           1        MOV     AL,0FFh
                      1        .ERR  The first operand (dtabyte) must be get or set.
mactest.ASM(218): error A2089: Forced error
                               DOS2138 SET,dtaword,BIOS10   ; SET it wrong
0203  8B 1E 0001 R    2        MOV     BX,dtaword
0207  B0 FF           1        MOV     AL,0FFh         ; Set country > 254
                      2        .ERR  BIOS10 is a constant or code - must be data.
mactest.ASM(219): error A2089: Forced error
0209  B4 38           3        MOV     AH,38h
020B  CD 21           2        INT     21h
                               DOS2138 GET,CH               ; try GET with byte register.
020D  8A C5           2        MOV     AL,CH
020F  BA FFFF         1        MOV     DX,-1           ; Indicate get.
0212  B4 38           3        MOV     AH,38h
0214  CD 21           2        INT     21h
                               DOS2138 SET,dtabyte          ; SET it to user's desire.
0216  A0 0000 R       2        MOV     AL,dtabyte
0219  B4 38           3        MOV     AH,38h
021B  CD 21           2        INT     21h
                               PURGE   DOS2138              ; Get rid of it.

                               INCLUDE MACROS\DOS213C.MAC
              C  DOS213C       MACRO   STRING,ATTRIB
              C  ;;
              C  ;; MS-DOS Interrupt 21h Function 3Ch - Create a File
              C  ;;
              C  ;; This function creates a file, assigns it the attributes specified,
```

```
C  ;; and returns a 16-bit handle for the file. Function 3Ch needs a string
C  ;; that gives drive, directories (and any subdirectories), and file name
C  ;; (with any extension).  Point DS:DX at the ASCIIZ character string,
C  ;; which is a string that ends in a null (a hex 00).  You might have a
C  ;; string definition in a program such as:
C  ;;
C  ;;            MY_FILE DB        'C:\ASM\MACRO\SQRT.ASM',0
C  ;;
C  ;; If that file already exists in that subdirectory, it is set to a 0
C  ;; length.  However, if that file exists and is marked "read only", error
C  ;; 05 returns in AL.  If this function works correctly, a 16-bit file handle
C  ;; returns in AX.  Use this word to refer the file from then on; it's the file
C  ;; handle.
C  ;;
C  ;; Input:
C  ;;     AH = 3Ch
C  ;;     CX = File attribute, bits 0 through 2 of the 2-byte
C  ;;            attribute:
C  ;;                      00 = normal file
C  ;;                      01 = read-only file
C  ;;                      02 = hidden file
C  ;;                      04 = system file
C  ;;            Bits 3 through 5 are associated with volume
C  ;;            labels, subdirectories, and archive files.  These
C  ;;            bits are invalid for this function and must be set
C  ;;            to zero.  Also, set bits 6 though 15 to zero to
C  ;;            assure future compatibility.
C  ;;     DS:DX points to ASCIIZ string with directory name
C  ;;
C  ;; Output:
C  ;;     Carry Flag = 0 if successful
C  ;;                      AH = File Handle
C  ;;     Carry Flag = 1 if unsuccessful
C  ;;                      AL holds error value
C  ;;                          = 3 Path not found
C  ;;                          = 4 Too many files open
C  ;;                          = 5 Directory full, or previous
C  ;;                                  read-only file exists
C  ;;
C              @OFFSET STRING,DX          ; Point to dir name
C      IFNB <ATTRIB>
C          IF (TYPE ATTRIB) EQ 0          ; If constant
C                  MOV     CX,ATTRIB      ; Load as a word
C          ELSEIF (TYPE ATTRIB) EQ 1      ; If byte data
C                  MOV     CL,ATTRIB      ; Load low half of CX
C                  XOR     CH,CH          ; and clear high byte
C          ELSE
C                  @SETWRD ATTRIB,CX      ; load as word.
C          ENDIF
C      ENDIF
C              @DOS21  3Ch                ; Request create.
C              ENDM
C
;
; Check generation of attribute.
;
                     DOS213C dtabyte              ; omitted
021D  8D 16 0000 R        2        LEA     DX,dtabyte
0221  B4 3C               3        MOV     AH,3Ch
0223  CD 21               2        INT     21h
                     DOS213C dtabyte,dtabyte      ; byte field
0225  8D 16 0000 R        2        LEA     DX,dtabyte
0229  8A 0E 0000 R        1        MOV     CL,dtabyte      ; Load low half of CX
022D  32 ED               1        XOR     CH,CH           ; and clear high byte
022F  B4 3C               3        MOV     AH,3Ch
0231  CD 21               2        INT     21h
                     DOS213C dtabyte,dtaword      ; word field
0233  8D 16 0000 R        2        LEA     DX,dtabyte
0237  8B 0E 0001 R        2        MOV     CX,dtaword
023B  B4 3C               3        MOV     AH,3Ch
023D  CD 21               2        INT     21h
                     DOS213C dtabyte,33           ; byte constant
023F  8D 16 0000 R        2        LEA     DX,dtabyte
```

```
0243  B9 0021          1              MOV     CX,33        ; Load as a word
0246  B4 3C            3              MOV     AH,3Ch
0248  CD 21            2              INT     21h
                                      DOS213C dtabyte,333       ; word constant
024A  8D 16 0000 R     2              LEA     DX,dtabyte
024E  B9 014D          1              MOV     CX,333       ; Load as a word
0251  B4 3C            3              MOV     AH,3Ch
0253  CD 21            2              INT     21h
                                      DOS213C dtabyte,BH        ; byte register
0255  8D 16 0000 R     2              LEA     DX,dtabyte
0259  8B CF            1              MOV     CX,BH        ; Load as a word
mactest.ASM(233): warning A4031: Operand types must match
025B  B4 3C            3              MOV     AH,3Ch
025D  CD 21            2              INT     21h
                                      DOS213C dtabyte,CX        ; word register
025F  8D 16 0000 R     2              LEA     DX,dtabyte
0263  8B C9            1              MOV     CX,CX        ; Load as a word
0265  B4 3C            3              MOV     AH,3Ch
0267  CD 21            2              INT     21h
                                      DOS213C dtabyte           ; and without
0269  8D 16 0000 R     2              LEA     DX,dtabyte
026D  B4 3C            3              MOV     AH,3Ch
026F  CD 21            2              INT     21h
                                      PURGE   DOS213C           ; Get rid of it.

                                      INCLUDE MACROS\DOS213E.MAC
                     C DOS213E        MACRO   HANDLE
                     C ;;
                     C ;; MS-DOS Interrupt 21h Function 3Eh - Close a File Handle
                     C ;;
                     C ;; Function 3Eh needs the file handle loaded into BX.  If the file
                     C ;; has been modified, truncated or extended, Function 3Eh updates the
                     C ;; current date, time, and file size in the directory entry.  With
                     C ;; MS-DOS versions 3.1 and later, a program must remove all file locks
                     C ;; in effect before it closes a file.  The result of closing a file
                     C ;; with active locks is unpredictable.  If there was an error during
                     C ;; the close, the Carry Flag is set.
                     C ;;
                     C ;; Input:
                     C ;;     AH = 3Eh
                     C ;;     BX = Valid file handle
                     C ;;
                     C ;; Output:
                     C ;;     Carry Flag is 0 if successful
                     C ;;     Carry Flag is 1 if unsuccessful
                     C ;;         AL = 6 Invalid file handle
                     C ;;
                     C        IF ((.TYPE HANDLE) AND 4) EQ 4      ; if constant and
                     C          IF HANDLE GT 2                    ; if not < 3 (in, out, err)
                     C              .ERR     HANDLE Is constant over 2 - (last standard)
                     C              EXITM
                     C          ENDIF
                     C        ENDIF
                     C              @SETWRD HANDLE,BX     ; Load handle
                     C              @DOS21  3Eh           ; close the file.
                     C              ENDM
                     C
                       ;
                       ; Check generation of handle edits.
                       ;
                                      DOS213E dtabyte           ; byte field.
                     2                 .ERR  dtabyte is an invalid data type - use word size.
mactest.ASM(242): error A2089: Forced error
0271  B4 3E            3              MOV     AH,3Eh
0273  CD 21            2              INT     21h
                                      DOS213E dtaword           ; word field.
0275  8B 1E 0001 R     2              MOV     BX,dtaword
0279  B4 3E            3              MOV     AH,3Eh
027B  CD 21            2              INT     21h
                                      DOS213E CH                ; byte register.
                     2                 .ERR  CH must be a word register.
```

```
mactest.ASM(244): error A2089: Forced error
027D  B4 3E            3              MOV      AH,3Eh
027F  CD 21            2              INT      21h
                                      DOS213E DX              ; word register.
0281  8B DA            2              MOV      BX,DX
0283  B4 3E            3              MOV      AH,3Eh
0285  CD 21            2              INT      21h
                                      DOS213E 2               ; ok constant.
0287  BB 0002          2              MOV      BX,2
028A  B4 3E            3              MOV      AH,3Eh
028C  CD 21            2              INT      21h
                                      DOS213E 3               ; bad constant.
                       1              .ERR     3 Is constant over 2 - (last standard)
mactest.ASM(247): error A2089: Forced error
                                      PURGE    DOS213E        ; Get rid of it.


028E  61                             popa                     ; Restore the entry registers
                       ;             leave                    ; remove the stack frame
028F  CB                             ret                      ; and return.
0290                   MACTEST       ENDP
                                     END
```

```
                 N a m e           Lines

aBIOS10 . . . . . . . . . . . .      13
aDOS21 . . . . . . . . . . . . .     13
aOFFSET . . . . . . . . . . . .      92
aSETBYT . . . . . . . . . . . .      86
aSETWRD . . . . . . . . . . . .      87
BIOS1006 . . . . . . . . . . .       0
DOS2106 . . . . . . . . . . . .      0
DOS210C . . . . . . . . . . . .      0
DOS2125 . . . . . . . . . . . .      0
DOS2129 . . . . . . . . . . . .      0
DOS212D . . . . . . . . . . . .      0
DOS212E . . . . . . . . . . . .      0
DOS2133 . . . . . . . . . . . .      0
DOS2138 . . . . . . . . . . . .      0
DOS213C . . . . . . . . . . . .      0
DOS213E . . . . . . . . . . . .      0
```

Segments and Groups:

```
                 N a m e          Size    Length  Align  Combine Class

DGROUP . . . . . . . . . . . .    GROUP
   _DATA . . . . . . . . . . .    16 Bit  0016    WORD   PUBLIC  'DATA'
MACTEST_TEXT . . . . . . . . .    16 Bit  0290    WORD   PUBLIC  'CODE'
```

Symbols:

```
                 N a m e          Type    Value   Attr

BIOS10 . . . . . . . . . . . .    L NEAR  0000    MACTEST_TEXT

DTABYTE . . . . . . . . . . . .   L BYTE  0000    _DATA
DTADBL . . . . . . . . . . . . .  L DWORD 0003    _DATA
DTAPTR . . . . . . . . . . . . .  L DWORD 000C    _DATA
DTASTR . . . . . . . . . . . . .  L BYTE  0007    _DATA
DTAWORD . . . . . . . . . . . .   L WORD  0001    _DATA

FDTAPTR . . . . . . . . . . . .   L FWORD 0010    _DATA

MACTEST . . . . . . . . . . . .   F PROC  0000    MACTEST_TEXT   Length = 0290

aCODE . . . . . . . . . . . . .   TEXT    mactest_TEXT
aCODESIZE . . . . . . . . . . .   TEXT    1
aCPU . . . . . . . . . . . . . .  TEXT    3343
aDATASIZE . . . . . . . . . . .   TEXT    0
aFILENAME . . . . . . . . . . .   TEXT    mactest
```

```
@VERSION . . . . . . . . . . .        TEXT  510


   1321 Source  Lines
  20313 Total    Lines
     40 Symbols

  46184 + 363498 Bytes symbol space free

      3 Warning Errors
     24 Severe  Errors




Microsoft (R) Macro Assembler Version 5.10
Copyright (C) Microsoft Corp 1981, 1988.  All rights reserved.

dtaword (parameter 2) must be a word register.
mactest.ASM(66): error A2089: Forced error
dtabyte is an invalid data type - use word size.
mactest.ASM(67): error A2089: Forced error
dtastr is an invalid data type - use word size.
mactest.ASM(68): error A2089: Forced error
AH (parameter 2) must be a word register.
mactest.ASM(69): error A2089: Forced error
AL must be a word register.
mactest.ASM(70): error A2089: Forced error
333h is a constant or code - must be data.
mactest.ASM(85): error A2089: Forced error
dtaword (parameter 2) must be a word register.
mactest.ASM(86): error A2089: Forced error
BIOS10 is a constant or code - must be data.
mactest.ASM(87): error A2089: Forced error
AH (parameter 2) must be a word register.
mactest.ASM(88): error A2089: Forced error
AL must be a word register.
mactest.ASM(89): error A2089: Forced error
dtaword is an invalid data type - use byte size.
mactest.ASM(100): error A2089: Forced error
Bios10 is an invalid data type - use byte size.
mactest.ASM(101): error A2089: Forced error
mactest.ASM(102): error A2050: Value out of range
dtaword is an invalid data type - use byte size.
mactest.ASM(113): error A2089: Forced error
Bios10 is an invalid data type - use byte size.
mactest.ASM(114): error A2089: Forced error
mactest.ASM(115): error A2050: Value out of range
Function 6 cannot also have a buffer address.
mactest.ASM(144): error A2089: Forced error
mactest.ASM(156): warning A4057: Illegal size for operand
mactest.ASM(157): warning A4057: Illegal size for operand
BIOS10 is a constant or code - must be data.
mactest.ASM(165): error A2089: Forced error
AH must be a word register.
mactest.ASM(217): error A2089: Forced error
The first operand (dtabyte) must be get or set.
mactest.ASM(218): error A2089: Forced error
BIOS10 is a constant or code - must be data.
mactest.ASM(219): error A2089: Forced error
mactest.ASM(233): warning A4031: Operand types must match
dtabyte is an invalid data type - use word size.
mactest.ASM(242): error A2089: Forced error
CH must be a word register.
mactest.ASM(244): error A2089: Forced error
mactest.ASM(247): error A2089: Forced error

  46184 + 363498 Bytes symbol space free

      3 Warning Errors
     24 Severe  Errors
```

INNER MACROS

There are five inner macros that were coded to give added facility. They are: @BIOS10, @DOS21, @OFFSET, @SETBYT, and @SETWRD. Most of the editing done within the BIOS and MS-DOS macros is done by these inner macros. Where this standard editing was insufficient, additional edits were added in the macros. Part of the function of MACTEST is to exercise these additional edits.

@BIOS10

The @BIOS10 macro loads the function code and issues an INT 10h. It uses the @SETBYT as an inner macro within itself to load the function code.

```
@BIOS10        MACRO   CODE
;;
;; Inner macro for BIOS int 10 calls.
;;        A macro per functional group of calls is chosen as opposed
;;        to a writing a single macro with the INT number a parameter
;;        The duplication is deemed acceptable.
;;
;; Input:
;;  CODE is the BIOS code to be loaded in AH.
;;  If omitted it is assumed that AH has been set prior to
;;  invoking the macro.
;;
               @SETBYT CODE,AH
               INT     10h
               ENDM
```

@DOS21

The @DOS21 macro loads the function code for the MS-DOS interrupt INT 21h. It also uses @SETBYT as an inner macro within itself to load the function code.

```
@DOS21         MACRO   CODE
;;
;; Inner macro for DOS int 21 calls.
;;        A macro per functional group of calls is chosen as opposed
;;        to a writing a single macro with the INT number a parameter
;;        The duplication is deemed acceptable.
;;
;; Input:
;;  CODE is the DOS code to be loaded in AH.
;;  If omitted it is assumed that AH has been set prior to
;;  invoking the macro.
;;
               @SETBYT CODE,AH
               INT     21h
               ENDM
```

@OFFSET

The @OFFSET macro is an inner macro that is written to provide more complete editing and error messages for the loading of offsets.

```
@OFFSET        MACRO   DISPL,INTO
;;
;; Inner - Inner macro for loading a displacement into a register
;;
;; Input:
;;  DISPL is the value to be loaded into the register.
```

```
;;      If omitted, it is assumed that the register has
;;      been set prior to the call.
;;      If a register, it is assumed that the offset is loaded.
;;      In any case, it is assumed that the segment is properly
;;      accessed for addressability.  i.e. as an over-ride
;;  INTO is the word register that is to be loaded.
;;
;;  invoking the macro.
;;
        IFB    <DISPL>                  ;; If DISPL is omitted - ok but
               EXITM                    ;; get out fast.
        ENDIF
;;
;; Edit the register to load
;;
        IFB    <INTO>                   ;; If INTO is omitted
           IF2
           %OUT Parameter 2 (register to load) cannot be omitted.
           .ERR Parameter 2 (register to load) cannot be omitted.
           ENDIF
               EXITM                    ;; get out fast.
        ENDIF
;;
;; It is present - check it out in detail.
;;
        IF  ((.TYPE INTO) AND 0010h) EQ 010h    ;; Is INTO a register
           IFIDNI  <INTO>,<AX>          ;; Check for 1 word reg.
           ELSEIFIDNI <INTO>,<BX>
           ELSEIFIDNI <INTO>,<CX>
           ELSEIFIDNI <INTO>,<DX>
           ELSEIFIDNI <INTO>,<SP>
           ELSEIFIDNI <INTO>,<BP>
           ELSEIFIDNI <INTO>,<SI>
           ELSEIFIDNI <INTO>,<DI>
           ELSE
               IF2
               %OUT  INTO (parameter 2) must be a word register.
               .ERR  INTO (parameter 2) must be a word register.
               ENDIF
               EXITM
           ENDIF
        ELSE
           IF2
           %OUT INTO (parameter 2) must be a word register.
           .ERR INTO (parameter 2) must be a word register.
           ENDIF
           EXITM
        ENDIF
;;
;; Now edit parameter 1, the item to load into the register.
;;
;; It could be a word register
        IF ((.TYPE DISPL) AND 0010h) EQ 010h  ;
                                        ; Is DISPL a register
           IFIDNI  <DISPL>,<AX>         ;; Check for 1 word reg.
           ELSEIFIDNI <DISPL>,<BX>
           ELSEIFIDNI <DISPL>,<CX>
           ELSEIFIDNI <DISPL>,<DX>
           ELSEIFIDNI <DISPL>,<SP>
           ELSEIFIDNI <DISPL>,<BP>
           ELSEIFIDNI <DISPL>,<SI>
           ELSEIFIDNI <DISPL>,<DI>
           ELSE
               IF2
                  %OUT  DISPL must be a word register.
                  .ERR  DISPL must be a word register.
               ENDIF
               EXITM
           ENDIF
           IFIDNI <DISPL>,<INTO>        ;; Are the registers the same?
               EXITM                    ;; If so - done.
           ENDIF
               MOV     INTO,DISPL
```

```
                EXITM
;;
;; DISPL is not a register - it must be a data area.
;;      TYPE 0 or TYPEs OFFFFh and OFFFEh are bad.
;;      All other values should be ok.

        ELSE
          IF  ((TYPE DISPL) GT OFFFDh) OR ((TYPE DISPL) EQ 0)
              IF2
              %OUT  DISPL is a constant or code - must be data.
              .ERR  DISPL is a constant or code - must be data.
              ENDIF
              EXITM
          ENDIF
        ENDIF
                LEA     INTO,DISPL
                ENDM
```

@SETBYT

The @SETBYT macro loads a byte value, providing editing that ensures that the proper size register is used and that the proper size value (byte) is loaded into that register.

```
@SETBYT         MACRO   CODE,INTO
;;
;; Inner - Inner macro for loading a byte into a register
;;
;; Input:
;; CODE is the value to be loaded into the register.
;;      If omitted, it is assumed that the register has
;;      been set prior to the call.
;; INTO is the byte register that is to be loaded.
;;
;;  invoking the macro.
;;
        IFB   <CODE>                    ;; If CODE is omitted - ok but
              EXITM                     ;; get out fast.
        ENDIF
;;
;; Edit the register to load
;;
        IFB   <INTO>                    ;; If INTO is omitted
            IF2
            %OUT Parameter 2 (register to load) cannot be omitted.
            .ERR Parameter 2 (register to load) cannot be omitted.
            ENDIF
              EXITM                     ;; get out fast.
        ENDIF
;;
;; It is present - check it out in detail.
;;
        IF  ((.TYPE INTO) AND 0010h) EQ 010h   ;; Is INTO a register
            IFIDNI  <INTO>,<AH>          ;; Check for 1 byte reg.
            ELSEIFIDNI <INTO>,<AL>
            ELSEIFIDNI <INTO>,<BL>
            ELSEIFIDNI <INTO>,<CL>
            ELSEIFIDNI <INTO>,<DL>
            ELSEIFIDNI <INTO>,<BH>
            ELSEIFIDNI <INTO>,<CH>
            ELSEIFIDNI <INTO>,<DH>
            ELSE
                IF2
                %OUT  INTO (parameter 2) must be a byte register.
                .ERR  INTO (parameter 2) must be a byte register.
                ENDIF
                EXITM
            ENDIF
        ELSE
            IF2
```

```
            %OUT INTO (parameter 2) must be a byte register.
            .ERR INTO (parameter 2) must be a byte register.
         ENDIF
         EXITM
      ENDIF
;;
;; Now edit parameter 1, the item to load into the register.
;;
;; It could be a byte register
      IF ((.TYPE CODE) AND 0010h) EQ 010h  ;; Is CODE a register
            IFIDNI  <CODE>,<AH>          ;; Check for 1 byte reg.
            ELSEIFIDNI <CODE>,<AL>
            ELSEIFIDNI <CODE>,<BL>
            ELSEIFIDNI <CODE>,<CL>
            ELSEIFIDNI <CODE>,<DL>
            ELSEIFIDNI <CODE>,<BH>
            ELSEIFIDNI <CODE>,<CH>
            ELSEIFIDNI <CODE>,<DH>
            ELSE
               IF2
               %OUT  CODE must be a byte register.
               .ERR  CODE must be a byte register.
               ENDIF
               EXITM
            ENDIF
            IFIDNI <CODE>,<INTO>          ;; Are the registers the same?
               EXITM                      ;; If so - done.
            ENDIF
;;
;; CODE is not a register - it can be a constant or 8 bit data.
;;
      ELSE
         IF  (TYPE CODE) GT 1
            IF2
            %OUT  CODE is an invalid data type - use byte size.
            .ERR  CODE is an invalid data type - use byte size.
            ENDIF
            EXITM
         ENDIF
      ENDIF
            MOV     INTO,CODE
            ENDM
```

@SETWRD

The @SETWRD macro loads a word value, also provides editing that ensures that the proper size register is used and that the proper size value (word) is loaded into that register.

```
@SETWRD       MACRO   WCODE,INTO
;;
;; Inner - Inner macro for loading a word into a register
;;
;; Input:
;;   WCODE is the value to be loaded into the register.
;;        If omitted, it is assumed that the register has
;;        been set prior to the call.
;;   INTO is the word register that is to be loaded.
;;
;;   invoking the macro.
;;
      IFB    <WCODE>                  ;; If WCODE is omitted - ok but
            EXITM                     ;; get out fast.
      ENDIF
;;
;; Edit the register to load
;;
      IFB    <INTO>                   ;; If INTO is omitted
         IF2
```

```
                %OUT Parameter 2 (register to load) cannot be omitted.
                .ERR Parameter 2 (register to load) cannot be omitted.
            ENDIF
                EXITM                       ;; get out fast.
        ENDIF
;;
;; It is present - check it out in detail.
;;
        .IF  ((.TYPE INTO) AND 0010h) EQ 010h   ;; Is INTO a register
                IFIDNI   <INTO>,<AX>        ;; Check for 1 word reg.
            ELSEIFIDNI <INTO>,<BX>
            ELSEIFIDNI <INTO>,<CX>
            ELSEIFIDNI <INTO>,<DX>
            ELSEIFIDNI <INTO>,<SP>
            ELSEIFIDNI <INTO>,<BP>
            ELSEIFIDNI <INTO>,<SI>
            ELSEIFIDNI <INTO>,<DI>
            ELSE
                IF2
                %OUT  INTO (parameter 2) must be a word register.
                .ERR  INTO (parameter 2) must be a word register.
                ENDIF
                EXITM
            ENDIF
        ELSE
            IF2
            %OUT INTO (parameter 2) must be a word register.
            .ERR INTO (parameter 2) must be a word register.
            ENDIF
            EXITM
        ENDIF
;;
;; Now edit parameter 1, the item to load into the register.
;;
;; It could be a word register
        IF ((.TYPE WCODE) AND 0010h) EQ 010h  ;; Is WCODE a register
                IFIDNI   <WCODE>,<AX>       ;; Check for 1 word reg.
            ELSEIFIDNI <WCODE>,<BX>
            ELSEIFIDNI <WCODE>,<CX>
            ELSEIFIDNI <WCODE>,<DX>
            ELSEIFIDNI <WCODE>,<SP>
            ELSEIFIDNI <WCODE>,<BP>
            ELSEIFIDNI <WCODE>,<SI>
            ELSEIFIDNI <WCODE>,<DI>
            ELSE
                IF2
                %OUT  WCODE must be a word register.
                .ERR  WCODE must be a word register.
                ENDIF
                EXITM
            ENDIF
            IFIDNI <WCODE>,<INTO>           ;; Are the registers the same?
                EXITM                       ;; If so - done.
            ENDIF
;;
;; WCODE is not a register - it can be a constant or 16 bit data.
;;      (TYPE 0 or TYPE 2 are both OK 0 and x is zero as is 2 and D
;;       all other values should be non-zero)
;;
        ELSE
            IF ((TYPE WCODE) AND 0FFFDh) NE 0
                IF2
                %OUT  WCODE is an invalid data type - use word size.
                .ERR  WCODE is an invalid data type - use word size.
                ENDIF
                EXITM
            ENDIF
        ENDIF
                MOV     INTO,WCODE
                ENDM
```

The remaining macros are listed without additional documentation other than what appears within the macros.

BIOS1000

```
BIOS1000      MACRO   SCRMODE
;;
;; BIOS INT 10h Function 00h - Set Screen Mode
;;
;; Requires @BIOS10 inner macro.
;;
;; Input:
;;    AH = 00h
;;    AL = mode (in hex):
;;            00      16-shade gray text        40 x 25
;;                    EGA: 64-color
;;            01      16/8-color text           40 x 25
;;                    EGA: 64-color
;;            02      16-shade gray text        80 x 25
;;                    EGA: 64-color
;;            03      16/8-color text           80 x 25
;;                    EGA: 64-color
;;            04      4-color graphics          320 x 200
;;            05      4-shade gray graphics     320 x 200
;;            06      2-shade gray graphics     640 x 200
;;            07      monochrome text            80 x 25
;;            08      16-color graphics         160 x 200
;;            09      16-color graphics         320 x 200
;;            0A      4-color graphics          640 x 200
;;            0B      Reserved
;;            0C      Reserved
;;            0D      16-color graphics         320 x 200
;;
              @SETBYT SCRMODE,AL      ; Screen Mode
              @BIOS10 0               ; Bios 10 call with code 0
              ENDM
```

BIOS1001

```
BIOS1001      MACRO   SCANSTRT,SCANEND
;;
;; BIOS Interrupt 10h Function 01h - Set Cursor Type
;;
;; The cursor on a monochrome screen is 14 pixel lines
;; tall (0 to 13) and on a graphics screen is 8 (0 to 7)
;; pixel lines tall.
;;
;; Input:
;;    AH = 01h
;;    CH = Starting scan line
;;    CL = Ending scan line
;;
;; Note: CH < CL gives normal one-part cursor.
;;       CH > CL gives two-part cursor.
;;       CH = 20h gives no cursor
;;
              @SETBYT SCANSTRT,CH     ; Start Scan Line
              @SETBYT SCANEND,CL      ; End Scan Line
              @BIOS10 01h             ; Set cursor type
              ENDM
```

BIOS1002

```
BIOS1002      MACRO    PAGENO,ROWNO,COLNO
;;
;; BIOS Interrupt 10h Function 02h - Set Cursor Position
;;
;; Input:
;;    AH = 02h - request code
;;    BH = Display Page Number
;;    DH = Row Number
;;    DL = Column Number
;;                                     def 0
    IFB  <PAGENO>                      ; If omitted,
              XOR     BH,BH            ; default to zero.
    ELSE
              @SETBYT PAGENO,BH        ; Screen Page Number
    ENDIF
              @SETBYT ROWNO,DH         ; Screen Row
              @SETBYT COLNO,DL         ; Screen Column
              @BIOS10 02h              ; Set cursor position
              ENDM
```

BIOS1003

```
BIOS1003      MACRO    PAGENO
;;
;; BIOS Interrupt 10h Function 03h - Find Cursor Position
;;
;; This function finds where the cursor is.  0,0 is the upper
;; left of the screen.  If using a graphics screen with 4 pages,
;; put the page number into BH.  If using a monochrome, store a
;; 0 in BH.
;;
;; Input:
;;    AH = 03h
;;    BH = Display Page Number
;;
;; Output:
;;    CH = Matrix Ending Line
;;    CL = Matrix Starting Line
;;    DH = Row Number
;;    DL = Column Number
;;
    IFB  <PAGENO>                      ; If omitted,
              XOR     BH,BH            ; default to zero.
    ELSE
              @SETBYT PAGENO,BH        ; Display Page Number
    ENDIF
              @BIOS10 03h
              ENDM
```

BIOS1004

```
BIOS1004      MACRO
;;
;; BIOS Interrupt 10h Function 04h - Read Light Pen Position
;;
;; Input:
;;    AH = 04h
;;
;; Output:
;;    AH = 00h  Light pen switch not set
;;    AL = 01h  Then:
;;    DH = Row of Light Pen Position
;;    DL = Column of Light Pen position
;;    CH = Pixel line (vertical row) 0-199
;;    CX = Pixel line number (for some EGA modes)
;;    BX = Pixel column (horizontal column) 0-319,639
;;
              @BIOS10 04h              ; Read light pen position.
              ENDM
```

BIOS1005

```
BIOS1005      MACRO   PAGENO
;;
;; BIOS Interrupt 10h Function 05h - Set Active Display Page
;;
;; Move between the various pages in text mode on graphics
;; monitors.  Note that if doing graphics on the graphics
;; monitor, only one page (page 0) is available for use.  Also,
;; monochrome monitors only have page 0.
;;
;; Input:
;;    AH = 05h
;;    AL = Page number:
;;         0-7  Screen modes 0 and 1 = 40-column text modes
;;         0-3  Screen modes 2 and 3 = 80-column text modes
;;         varies                    = EGA graphics modes
;;
;;       Note: Each page = 2Kb in 40-column text mode, 4Kb in
;;         80-column text mode.
;;
              @SETBYT PAGENO,AL      ; Screen page number.
              @BIOS10 05h            ; Set display page number.
              ENDM
```

BIOS1006

```
BIOS1006      MACRO   LINENO,DISPLY,LEFTROW,LEFTCOL,RIGHTROW,RIGHTCOL
;;
;; BIOS Interrupt 10h Function 06h - Scroll Active Page Up
;; Input:
;;    AH = 06h
;;    AL = Number of lines blanked at bottom of the screen
;;         (00=blanks entire screen)
;;    BH = Display attribute used on blank lines
;;    CH = Upper left row of area to scroll
;;    CL = Upper left column of area to scroll
;;    DH = Lower right row of area to scroll
;;    DL = Lower right column of area to scroll
;;
       IFB  <LINENO>                 ; If omitted
              XOR     AL,AL          ; clear whole screen.
       ELSE
              @SETBYT LINENO,AL      ; Lines to blank at bottom
       ENDIF
              @SETBYT DISPLY,BH      ; Display attribute on blanks
              @SETBYT LEFTROW,CH     ; Upper left row to scroll
              @SETBYT LEFTCOL,CL     ; Upper left column to scroll
              @SETBYT RIGHTROW,DH    ; Lower right row to scroll
              @SETBYT RIGHTCOL,DL    ; Lower right column to scroll
              @BIOS10 06h            ; Scroll active page up.
              ENDM
```

BIOS1007

```
BIOS1007      MACRO   LINENO,DISPLY,LEFTROW,LEFTCOL,RIGHTROW,RIGHTCOL
;;
;; BIOS Interrupt 10h Function 07h - Scroll Active Page Down
;;
;;Input:
;;    AH = 07h
;;    AL = Number of lines blanked at top of screen
;;         (00=blank entire screen)
;;    BH = Display attribute used on blank lines
;;    CH = Upper left row of area to scroll
;;    CL = Upper left column of area to scroll
;;    DH = Lower right row of area to scroll
;;    DL = Lower right column of area to scroll
;;
```

```
            @SETBYT LINENO,AL        ; Lines to blank at top
            @SETBYT DISPLY,BH        ; Display attribute on blanks
            @SETBYT LEFTROW,CH       ; Upper left row to scroll
            @SETBYT LEFTCOL,CL       ; Upper left column to scroll
            @SETBYT RIGHTROW,DH      ; Lower right row to scroll
            @SETBYT RIGHTCOL,DL      ; Lower right column to scroll
            @BIOS10 07h              ; Scroll Active Page Down
            ENDM
```

BIOS1008

```
BIOS1008    MACRO   PAGENO
;;
;; BIOS Interrupt 10h Function 08h - Read Attribute and Character
;;                                   at Cursor Position
;;
;;
;; Input:
;;    AH = 08h
;;    BH = Display page number (for text mode only)
;;
;; Output:
;;    If text mode:
;;       AH = Attribute of Character (alphanumerics only)
;;       AL = Character read (in ASCII)
;;    If graphics mode:
;;       AL = ASCII character (00 if unmatched)
;;
            @SETBYT PAGENO,BH        ; Display Page Number
            @BIOS10 08h              ; BIOS Read Attr & Char
            ENDM
```

BIOS1009

```
BIOS1009    MACRO   ASCIICHR,PAGENO,TXTATTR,WRITEIT
;;
;; BIOS Interrupt 10h Function 09h - Write Attribute and Character
;;                                   at Cursor Position
;;
;;
;; Input:
;;    AH = 09h
;;    AL = ASCII Character to write
;;    BH = Display page Number (Graphics 1-4, Monochrome=0)
;;    BL = Text attribute (Alpha Mode)
;;       = Color of foreground (Graphics Mode)
;;    CX = Number of times to write characters (must be > 0)
;;
;;    Note: Function 09 modifies AL, even though this is
;;          undocumented.  AL returns with the last character
;;          in the character string, hex 24, a "$".
;;
            @SETBYT ASCIICHR,AL      ; ASCII Character
            @SETBYT PAGENO,BH        ; Display Page Number
            @SETBYT TXTATTR,BL       ; Text attrib/Foregrnd Color
            @SETWRD WRITEIT,CX       ; Number of times to write it
            @BIOS10 09h              ; Write Attrib & Char
            ENDM
```

BIOS100A

```
BIOS100A    MACRO   ASCIICHR,PAGENO,FOREGRND,WRITEIT
;;
;; BIOS Interrupt 10h Function 0Ah - Write Character Only at
;;                                   Cursor Position
;;
;; Input:
;;    AH = 0Ah
;;    AL = ASCII Character to write
;;    BH = Display page Number (Graphics 1-4, Monochrome=0)
;;    BL = Graphics foreground color (unused in text modes)
```

```
;;      CX = Number of times to write character (must be > 0)
;;
                @SETBYT ASCIICHR,AL     ; ASCII Character to write
                @SETBYT PAGENO,BH       ; Display Page Number
                @SETBYT FOREGRND,BL     ; Graphics Foreground Color
                @SETWRD WRITEIT,CX      ; Number of times to write char
                @BIOS10 0AH             ; BIOS Write Char at Cursor Pos
                ENDM
```

BIOS100B

```
BIOS100B        MACRO   PALLETTE,COLOR
;;
;; BIOS Interrupt 10h Function 0Bh - Select Color Palette
;;
;; Input:
;;      AH = 0Bh
;;      BH = Palette Color ID
;;      BL = Background Color (if BH = 00h)
;;         = Palette Number (if BH = 01h)
;;           0 - Green/Read/Yellow
;;           1 - Cyan/Magenta/White
;;
                @SETBYT PALLETTE,BH     ; Palette Color ID
                @SETBYT COLOR,BL        ; Background or Palette Color
                @BIOS10 0Bh             ; Select Color Palette
                ENDM
```

BIOS100C

```
BIOS100C        MACRO   COLORATR,PIXELCOL,PIXELLIN
;;
;; BIOS Interrupt 10h Function 0Ch = Write Dot
;;
;; Input:
;;      AH = 0Ch
;;      AL = Color attribute of pixel (0-3)
;;      CX = Pixel column number (0-319,639)
;;      DX = Pixel raster line number (0-199)
;;
                @SETBYT COLORATR,AL     ; Color Attribute
                @SETWRD PIXELCOL,CX     ; Pixel Column
                @SETWRD PIXELLIN,DX     ; Raster Line Number
                @BIOS10 0Ch             ; BIOS Write Dot
                ENDM
```

BIOS100D

```
BIOS100D        MACRO   PIXELROW,PIXELCOL
;;
;; BIOS Interrupt 10h Function 0Dh - Write Pixel Dot
;;
;; Input:
;;      AH = 0Dh
;;      DX = Pixel row number (0-199)
;;      CX = Pixel column number (0-319,639)
;;
;; Output:
;;      AL = Pixel color attribute
;;
                @SETWRD PIXELROW,DX     ; Pixel row number
                @SETWRD PIXELCOL,CX     ; Pixel column number
                @BIOS10 0Dh             ; Write Pixel Dot
                ENDM
```

BIOS100E

```
BIOS100E      MACRO    ASCIICHR,PAGENO,COLOR
;;
;; BIOS Interrupt 10h Function 0Eh - Teletype Write to Active Page
;;
;; Input:
;;      AH = 0Eh
;;      AL = ASCII character
;;      BH = Display page number
;;      BL = Foreground Color (Graphics Mode) (unused in text mode)
;;
;;      Note: Cursor position advanced; beep, backspace, linefeed
;;            linefeed, and carriage return active.  All other
;;            characters displayed.
;;
              @SETBYT ASCIICHR,AL    ; ASCII Character
              @SETBYT PAGENO,BH      ; Display Page Number
              @SETBYT COLOR,BL       ; Foreground Color
              @BIOS10 0Eh            ; Teletype Write/Active Pge
              ENDM
```

BIOS100F

```
BIOS100F      MACRO    PAGENO
;;
;; BIOS Interrupt 10h Function 0Fh - Return Video State
;;
;; Input:
;;      AH = 0Fh
;;      BH = Active display page
;;
;; Output:
;;      AH = Characters per line (20, 40,80)
;;      AL = Current video mode
;;           00  16-shade gray text        40 x 25
;;               EGA: 64-color
;;           01  16/8-color text           40 x 25
;;               EGA: 64-color
;;           02  16-shade gray text        80 x 25
;;               EGA: 64-color
;;           03  16/8-color text           80 x 25
;;               EGA: 64-color
;;           04  4-color graphics          320 x 200
;;           05  4-shade gray graphics     320 x 200
;;           06  2-shade gray graphics     640 x 200
;;           07  monochrome text           80 x 25
;;           08  16-color graphics         160 x 200
;;           09  16-color graphics         320 x 200
;;           0A  4-color graphics          640 x 200
;;           0B  Reserved
;;           0C  Reserved
;;           0D  16-color graphics         320 x 200
;;           0E  16-color graphics         640 x 200
;;           0F  monochrome graphics       640 x 350
;;           10  16/64-color graphics      640 x 350
;;
              @SETBYT PAGENO,BH      ; Active Display Page
              @BIOS10 0Fh           ; Return Video State
              ENDM
```

BIOS1013

```
BIOS1013      MACRO   SUBFN,PAGENO,STRATTR,STRLENG,STARTROW,STARTCOL,STRADDR
;;
;; BIOS Interrupt 10h Function 13h - Write Character String
;;
;; Input:
;;      AH = 13h
;;      AL = Subfunction Number
;;            00 String shares attribute in BL, cursor unchanged
;;            01 String shares attribute in BL, cursor advanced
;;            02 Each character has attribute. Cursor unchanged
;;            03 Each character has attribute. Cursor advanced
;;      BH = Active display page
;;      BL = String attribute (for AL = 00 or 01 only)
;;      CX = Length of character string
;;      DH = Starting row number
;;      DL = Starting column number
;;      ES:BP = Address of string to be displayed
;;
;;      Note: For AL = 00 or 01, string=(char,char, ...)
;;            For AL = 02 or 03, string=(char,attr,char,attr . . .)
;;            For AL = 01 or 03, cursor position set to location
;;                                  following last caracter output.
;;
              @SETBYT SUBFN,AL       ; Subfunction Number
              @SETBYT PAGENO,BH      ; Active Display Page Number
              @SETBYT STRATTR,BL     ; String Attribute
              @SETWRD STRLENG,CX     ; String Length
              @SETBYT STARTROW,DH    ; Starting row number
              @SETBYT STARTCOL,DL    ; Starting column number
       IFNB  <STRADDR>               ; If present -
              MOV     BP,SEG STRADDR ; Prepare to set seg in ES
              MOV     ES,BP
              LEA     BP,STRADDR     ; Address of string to display
       ENDIF
              @BIOS10 13h            ; Write Character String
              ENDM
```

BIOS1100

```
BIOS1100      MACRO
;;
;; BIOS Interrupt 11 - Equipment Determination
;;
;; Output:
;;      AX Bits =
;;            0 = 1 if IPL diskette installed
;;            1 = 1 if numerics coprocessor here
;;            2,3 = Unused
;;            4,5 = Video Mode
;;                  00 = Reserved
;;                  01 = 40 x 25 Color Card
;;                  10 = 80 x 25 Color Card
;;                  11 = 80 x 25 Monochrome
;;            6,7 = Number of Diskette Drives
;;                  00 = 1
;;                  01 = 2
;;                  10 = 3
;;                  11 = 4
;;            8 = Unused
;;            9,10,11 = Number of RS-232 Cards
;;            12 = Unused
;;            13 = If internal modem installed
;;            14,15 = Number of Printers Attached
;;
              INT     11h            ; BIOS Equipment Determination
              ENDM
```

DOS2101

```
DOS2101        MACRO
;;
;; MS-DOS Interrupt 21h Function 01h - Keyboard Input
;;
;; With this function is issued, processing stops until a key
;; is pressed.  If the corresponding character is an ASCII
;; printable character, it is printed on the screen.  The TAB
;; character automatically expands to the end of the next
;; eight-column field by adding spaces.  Holding the CTRL key
;; and pressing BREAK terminates operation.  If the pressed key
;; corresponds to an extended code, the AL register contains a
;; value of zero.  Then execute this function again to get the
;; code.  If the second value is less than 84, it represents
;; the scan code of the pressed key.
;;
;; Input:
;;     AH = 01h
;; Output:
;;     AL = ASCII code of struck key
;;
                @DOS21  01H             ; Keyboard input (1 char)
                ENDM
```

DOS2102

```
DOS2102        MACRO   CHOUT
;;
;; MS-DOS Interrupt 21h Function 02h - Character Output on Screen
;;
;; This function displays the character contained in the DL
;; register onto the screen.  It's useful for writing a single
;; character (use Function 09h for a string).  Function 02h
;; is useful for displaying a dollar sign ($), since Function 09h
;; uses the $ as the end of string characters.
;;
;; The BACKSPACE key moves the cursor to the left, but does not
;; erase the character printed there.
;;
;; The output can be sent to another device or disk file by
;; redirecting the standard output.
;;
;; Input:
;;     AH = 02h
;;     DL = ASCII character
;;
                @SETBYT CHOUT,DL        ; Load the character then
                @DOS21  02h             ; Output the char
                ENDM
```

DOS2103

```
DOS2103        MACRO
;;
;; MS-DOS Interrupt 21h Function 03h - Standard Auxiliary Device Input
;;
;; This function is not interrupt driven and does not buffer
;; characters received from the standard auxiliary device.
;;
;; Input:
;;     AH = 03h
;;
;; Output:
;;     The character in AL
;;
                @DOS21  03h             ; Read a byte
                ENDM
```

DOS2104

```
DOS2104      MACRO   CHOUT
;;
;; MS-DOS Interrupt 21h Function 04h - Standard Auxiliary Device
;;                                               Output
;;
;; This function sends the byte in register DL to the auxiliary port
;; AUX or COM1.  Note that Function 04h does NOT ensure that the
;; auxiliary output is connected and working, nor does it perform
;; any error checking or set up the status of auxiliary output
;; device.  Note that it does NOT return an error code if the
;; auxiliary output device is not ready for data.
;;
;; Input:
;;     AH = 04h
;;     DL = The character to output
;;
             @SETBYT CHOUT,DL      ; Load the byte and
             @DOS21  04h           ; have it put out.
             ENDM
```

DOS2105

```
DOS2105      MACRO   CHOUT
;;
;; MS-DOS Interrupt 21h Function 05h - Printer Output
;;
;; This function sends the character in register DL to the standard
;; printer port: PRN or LPT1.  Function 05h does NOT return the status
;; of the standard printer, nor does it return an error code if the
;; standard printer is not ready for characters.  If the printer is
;; busy of off-line, Function 05h waits until it is available.
;;
;; Input:
;;     AH = 05h
;;     DL = The character to output
;;
             @SETBYT CHOUT,DL      ; Load char to print
             @DOS21  05h           ; and print it.
             ENDM
```

DOS2106

```
DOS2106      MACRO   CHOUT
;;
;; MS-DOS Interrupt 21h Function 06h - Console Input/Output
;;
;; This function allows all possible characters and control codes
;; with values between 00h and 0FEh to be read and written with
;; standard I/O with no filtering by MS-DOS.  Note that the
;; RUBOUT character (0FFh, 255 decimal) can NOT be output with
;; this function.
;;
;; Function 06h does NOT wait for input.  Also, the input character
;; is NOT automatically displayed.  CTRL-BREAK does not terminate
;; operation.
;;
;; Input:
;;     AH = 06h
;;
;;     If DL = FF    AL holds the character, if one is ready
;;        DL < FF    Type ASCII code in DL out
;;
      IFB <CHOUT>                  ; If omitted
             @SETBYT 0FFh,DL       ; default to read.
      ELSE
             @SETBYT CHOUT,DL      ; write byte otherwise.
      ENDIF
             @DOS21  06h           ; Do read or write
             ENDM
```

DOS2107

```
DOS2107        MACRO
;;
;; MS-DOS Interrupt 21h Function 07h - Console Input Without Echo
;;
;; Function 07h waits for keyboard entry.  If an ASCII character is
;; entered, the ASCII value is returned in the AL register.  This
;; function does NOT display the input character.  CTRL-BREAK does
;; not terminate the process.
;;
;; Input:
;;     AH = 07h
;;
;; Output:
;;     AL = ASCII code of struck key
;;
               @DOS21  07h            ; Quiet read.
               ENDM
```

DOS2108

```
DOS2108        MACRO
;;
;; MS-DOS Interrupt 21h Function 08h - Console Input without Echo,
;;                                     with BREAK Check
;;
;; Function 08h waits for a character and terminates when CTRL-BREAK
;; is pressed.  The input character is NOT displayed and TAB characters
;; are NOT expanded.
;;
;; Input:
;;     AH = 08h
;;
;; Output:
;;     AL = ASCII code of struck key
;;
               @DOS21  08h            ; Quiet read w/break.
               ENDM
```

DOS2109

```
DOS2109        MACRO   STRNG
;;
;; MS-DOS Interrupt 21h Function 09h - String Print
;;
;; Function 09h is useful for printing a string of characters on
;; the screen.  Note that AL returns with a 24h ($) in it, so
;; don't depend on AL staying the same.
;;
;; Display begins at the current cursor position on the standard
;; output.  After the string is displayed, MS-DOS updates the cursor
;; position to the location immediately following the string.
;;
;; Input:
;;     AH = 09h
;;     DS:DX = The address of the string (that ends in '$')
;;
               @OFFSET STRNG,DX       ; Set offset in DX
               @DOS21  09h            ; Display string.
               ENDM
```

DOS210A

```
DOS210A        MACRO   BUFADR
;;
;; MS-DOS Interrupt 21h Function 0Ah - String Input
;;
;; All characters typed by the user are entered into the keyboard
;; buffer.  When RETURN is pressed, the line is stored into the
;; input buffer.  Be sure to set up a buffer in memory before
;; calling this function.
;;
;; Input:
;;      AH = 0Ah
;;      DS:DX = Address of buffer
;;
;; Output:
;;      Buffer at DS:DX filled
;;      Echo the typed keys
;;
              @OFFSET BUFADR,DX        ; Load displacement in DX
              @DOS21  0Ah              ; and read string
              ENDM
```

DOS210B

```
DOS210B        MACRO
;;
;; MS-DOS Interrupt 21h Function 0Bh - Check Input Status
;;
;; Function 0Bh is useful to check to see if there is any keyboard
;; input waiting.  On return, AL contains a zero if no key has been
;; pressed.  Any other AL value indicates a character is waiting to
;; be read--although this function does NOT read the character.
;;
;; This function does not indicate how many characters are available.
;;
;; Input:
;;      AH = 0Bh
;;
;; Output:
;;      AL = FF, if a character is ready
;;      AL = 00, if nothing is there to be read
;;
              @DOS21  0Bh              ; Get status of kbd.
              ENDM
```

DOS210C

```
DOS210C        MACRO   KBDFUN,BUFFAD
;;
;; MS-DOS Interrupt 21h Function 0Ch - Clear Buffer and Invoke Service
;;
;; This function clears the keyboard buffer before it invokes a
;; keyboard function (01h, 06h, 07h, 08h, or 0Ah).  This function
;; also checks for CTRL-BREAK.
;;
;; Input:
;;      AH = 0Ch
;;      AL = Keyboard function number
;;
;;           If AL = 06h, then DL=FFh
;;           IF AL = 0Ah, DS:DX=the address of the buffer to receive
;;                        the data
;;
;; Output:
;;      If AL was 01h, 06h, 07h, or 08h on the call:
;;           AL = 8-bit ASCII character from standard input
;;      If AL was 0A on the call:
```

```
;;            Nothing is returned
;;
   IF (TYPE KBDFUN) EQ 0              ; Is function a constant?
      IF (KBDFUN - 6) EQ 0           ; Is it a 6?
            @SETBYT 0FFh,DL          ; Default to read.
         IFNB <BUFFAD>               ; But can't have buffer too
            IF2
               %OUT Function 6 cannot also have a buffer address.
               .ERR Function 6 cannot also have a buffer address.
            ENDIF
         ENDIF
      ;;
      ;; No reasonable default is available for other than 6.
      ;; We assume a buffer address otherwise.
      ;;
      ELSE
            @OFFSET BUFFAD,DX        ; point to buffer
      ENDIF
   ELSE
            @OFFSET BUFFAD,DX        ; point to buffer
   ENDIF
            @SETBYT KBDFUN,AL        ; Set desired function
            @DOS21  0Ch              ; and go do it.
            ENDM
```

DOS210D

```
DOS210D        MACRO
;;
;; MS-DOS Interrupt 21h Function 0Dh - Disk Reset
;;
;; This function writes to disk all internal MS-DOS file buffers in
;; memory that have been modified since the last write.  Note that
;; this function does NOT update the disk directory.
;;
;; Input:
;;     AH = 0Dh
;;
            @DOS21  0Dh              ; Request flush
            ENDM
```

DOS210E

```
DOS210E        MACRO   DDRIVE
;;
;; MS-DOS Interrupt 21h Function 0Eh - Set the default drive.
;;
;; Function 21h is how MS-DOS selects a default disk.
;;
;; Input:
;;     AH = 0Eh
;;     DL = Drive number
;;              00 - Drive A
;;              01 - Drive B
;;              02 - Drive C, and so on
;;
;; Output:
;;     AL = The number of logical drives in the system
;;
            @SETBYT DDRIVE,DL        ; Set drive code number.
            @DOS21  0Eh              ; Select the drive.
            ENDM
```

DOS210F

```
DOS210F        MACRO    FCBADR
;;
;; MS-DOS Interrupt 21h Function OF - Open Pre-existing File
;;
;; This function opens a file created some time in the past, which
;; can be just before you used this function.  Function OFh does NOT
;; create the file.
;;
;; Function OFh uses File Control Blocks (FCBs).
;;
;; Interrupt 21 Function 3D is recommended rather than this function.
;;
;; Input:
;;      AH = OFh
;;      DS:DX = Address of an FCB
;;
;; Output:
;;      AL = 00h if successful
;;      AL = FFh if unsuccessful
;;
               @OFFSET FCBADR,DX      ; Set offset
               @DOS21  OFh            ; and open file in FCB.
               ENDM
```

DOS2110

```
DOS2110         MACRO    FCBADR
;;
;; MS-DOS Interrupt 21h Function 10h - Close File
;;
;; Function 10h reads what is in the FCB and writes it to the
;; directory.  Its major use is to give the file a non-zero
;; size.
;;
;; Input:
;;      AH = 10h
;;      DS:DX = Address of previously opened FCB
;;
;; Output:
;;      AL = 00, if successful
;;      AL = FF, if unsuccessful
;;
               @OFFSET FCBADR,DX      ; Set the FCB offset
               @DOS21  010h           ; and close the file.
               ENDM
```

DOS2111

```
DOS2111        MACRO    FCBADR
;;
;; MS-DOS Interrupt 21h Function 11h - Search for First Matching File
;;
;; This function searches a disk for files.  Point DS:DX at an
;; unopened File Control Block (FCB).  The FCB can use the "?"
;; wildcard, but not the "*".  If you want to find all the file
;; names with an ".ASM" extension, fill the FCB file name with
;; ???????? and the extension with .ASM.  The eight question marks
;; will find any length file name, from a single character to eight.
;;
;; If the search finds a match, an unopened FCB for the matching
;; file will be stored in the DTA.
;;
;; Input:
;;      AH = 11h
;;      DS:DX = Address of an unopened FCB
;;
;; Output:
```

```
;;      AL = 00, if successful.  The DTA contains unopened FCB of
;;             the same type (normal or extended) as the search FCB.
;;      AL = FF, if unsuccessful
;;
            @OFFSET FCBADR,DX        ; Set the offset of the FCB
            @DOS21  011h             ; and search for file.
            ENDM
```

DOS2112

```
DOS2112     MACRO   FCBADD
;;
;; MS-DOS Interrupt 21h Function 12h - Search for Next Matching File
;;
;; After finding the first matching file (using INT 21h, Function 11h),
;; MS-DOS fills part of the reserved areas in the FCB.  This function
;; uses that information to find the next match in the directory.
;;
;; Input:
;;      AH = 12h
;;      DS:DX = Address to search FCB
;;
;; Output:
;;      AL = 00, if successful.  DTA contains unopened FCB of the
;;             same type (normal or extended) as the search FCB.
;;      AL = FF, if unsuccessful
;;
            @OFFSET FCBADD,DX        ; Load FCB offset.
            @DOS21  12h              ; Go search for next.
            ENDM
```

DOS2113

```
DOS2113     MACRO   FCBADD
;;
;; MS-DOS Interrupt 21h Function 13h - Delete Files
;;
;; This function simply deletes files.  Point DS:DX at an unopened
;; FCB and issue this interrupt and function.  Note that this does
;; NOT physically erase data.  All files which match the name (with
;; wildcards) are deleted.
;;
;; Input:
;;      AH = 13h
;;      DS:DX = Address of an unopened FCB
;; Output:
;;      AL = 00 if successful
;;         = FF if unsuccessful
;;
            @OFFSET FCBADD,DX        ; Point to FCB
            @DOS21  13h              ; Delete the file.
            ENDM
```

DOS2114

```
DOS2114     MACRO   FCBADD
;;
;; MS-DOS Interrupt 21 Function 14 - Sequential Read
;;
;; This function reads sequential records from an opened file.
;; Set the current block field (bytes 0C-0D in the FCB) and the
;; current record field 0 to 127 in byte 1F.  The data read is
;; dumped in the DTA.
;;
;; If you change the record length from the default 128 bytes,
;; you'd get whatever the change was in the DTA.  The record
;; address increments with each read, which means that if the
;; current record is 127, the next record will be 0.
;;
```

```
;; Input:
;;      AH = 14h
;;      DS:DX = Address of an opened FCB
;;      Current block and record set in FCB
;;
;; Output:
;;      AL = 00 if successful
;;              Requested record put in DTA
;;           01 End of file, no data in record
;;           02 DTA segment too small for record
;;           03 End of file, record padded with 0's, but requested
;;                record put in DTA
;;

            @OFFSET FCBADD,DX      ; Point to the FCB.
            @DOS21  14h            ; Read record.
            ENDM
```

DOS2115

```
DOS2115       MACRO   FCBADD
;;
;; MS-DOS Interrupt 21h Function 15h - Sequential Write
;;
;; Function 15 writes a record from the Disk Transfer Area--DTA
;; (always used in FCB operations) to an open file.  The record
;; address is incremented.  Note that if the record size is
;; significantly smaller than a sector (512 bytes), MS-DOS buffers
;; the data and only writes it when there is enough to write,
;; or when the program ends.  Note: this is one of the tasks that
;; INT 20 or INT 27 takes care of for you.
;;
;; Input:
;;      AH = 15h
;;      DS:DX = Address of an opened FCB
;;      Current block and record set in FCB
;;
;; Output:
;;      AL = 00 if successful, one record read from DTA and written
;;           01 if disk is full, write canceled
;;           02 DTA segment too small for record, write canceled
;;

            @OFFSET FCBADD,DX      ; Point to fcb.
            @DOS21  15h            ; Write record.
            ENDM
```

DOS2116

```
DOS2116       MACRO   FCBADD
;;
;; MS-DOS Interrupt 21h Function 16h - Create File
;;
;; This function creates a file.  If a file already exists with the
;; same name, that file will be opened and set to zero length, which
;; may destroy valid data stored there earlier.  If there is not
;; identical file, a directory entry is opened for this new one.  If
;; there is no space left on the diskette or hard disk, this function
;; returns an FF and you must free some space.
;;
;; Note that pathnames and wildcard characters (* and ?) are NOT
;; supported by Function 16h.
;;
;; Input:
;;      AH = 16h
;;      DS:DX = Address of an unopened FCB
;;
;; Output:
;;      AL = 00 if successful
;;           FF Directory is full
;;

            @OFFSET FCBADD,DX      ; Point to FCB.
            @DOS21  16h            ; Create file.
            ENDM
```

DOS2117

```
DOS2117        MACRO   FCBADD
;;
;; MS-DOS Interrupt 21h Function 17h - Rename File
;;
;; If you need to rename files, use this interrupt and function.
;; Note that the FCB can use the ? wildcard but not the * wildcard.
;;
;; Input:
;;     AH = 17h
;;     DS:DX = Address of a modified FCB
;;             For a modified FCB, the second file name starts six
;;             bytes after the end of the first file name at DS:DX+11.
;;
;; Output:
;;     AL = 00 if successful
;;          FF Directory full
;;
               @OFFSET FCBADD,DX        ; Point to FCB.
               @DOS21  17h              ; Rename the file.
               ENDM
```

DOS2119

```
DOS2119        MACRO
;;
;; MS-DOS Interrupt 21h Function 19h - Find Current Disk
;;
;; This function can find the default disk, or the one on which you're
;; currently working.
;;
;; Input:
;;     AH = 19h
;;
;; Output:
;;     AL = Current Disk
;;          00 Drive A
;;          01 Drive B
;;          02 Drive C, and so on
;;
               @DOS21  19h              ; Reuest drive no.
               ENDM
```

DOS211A

```
DOS211A        MACRO   DTAADD
;;
;; MS-DOS Interrupt 21h Function 1Ah - Set the Disk Transfer Area
;;                                     (DTA) Location
;;
;; The MS-DOS default DTA is located at 80h within the Program
;; Segment Prefix.  If a size larger than 128 bytes is to be
;; transfered at a time or if a different area is desired this
;; function is used to set it.
;; Note that all FCB I/O uses the same DTA.  Reads, writes, and
;; directory I/O uses this area.
;;
;; Input:
;;     AH = 1Ah
;;     DS:DX = Address to new DTA area
;;
               @OFFSET DTAADD,DX        ; Point to DTA.
               @DOS21  1Ah              ; Request the change.
               ENDM
```

DOS211B

```
DOS211B         MACRO
;;
;; MS-DOS Interrupt 21h Function 1Bh - File Allocation Table (FAT)
;;                                     Information for Default Drive
;;
;; This function gets the default drive data.
;;
;; Input:
;;      AH = 1Bh
;;
;; Output:
;;      If successful:
;;          AL = Number of sectors per cluster
;;          DS:DX = Points to the FAT Id byte
;;          DX = Number of clusters
;;          CS = Size of a sector (e.g., 512)
;;      If unsuccessful:
;;          AL = FF
;;
                @DOS21  1Bh             ; Get disk info.
                ENDM
```

DOS211C

```
DOS211C         MACRO   DCODE
;;
;; MS-DOS Interrupt 21h Function 1C - File Allocation Table (FAT)
;;                                    Information for Specified Drive
;;
;; Input:
;;      AH = 1Ch
;;      DL = Drive Code:
;;              00 Default drive
;;              01 Drive A
;;              02 Drive B
;;              03 Drive C, and so on
;;
;; Output:
;;      If successful:
;;          AL = Number of sectors per cluster
;;          CX = Size of a sector (e.g., 512)
;;          DS:DX = Address of the FAT byte
;;          DX = Number of clusters
;;      If unsuccessful:
;;          AL = FF
;;
                @SETBYT DCODE,DL        ; Set desired drive code.
                @DOS21  1Ch             ; Issue the request
                ENDM
```

DOS2121

```
DOS2121         MACRO   FCBADD
;;
;; MS-DOS Interrupt 21h Function 21h - Random Read
;;
;; To write into the Disk Transfer Area (DTA) from a random read,
;; set the random record field in an opened FCB.  When a read is
;; requested, MS-DOS sets the current block and current record
;; fields.
;;
;; Input:
;;      AH = 21h
;;      DS:DX = Address of an opened FCB
;;      Set FCB's Random Record field at DS:DX+21 and DS:DX+23
;;
```

```
;; Output:
;;       AL = 00 if successful, DTA contains data read from file
;;            01 End of file, no more data; no record read
;;            02 Not enough space in DTA segment; read canceled
;;            03 End of File, partial record padded with 0's     ,
;;               DTA contains data read from file
;;
              @OFFSET FCBADD,DX      ; Point to FCB.
              @DOS21  21h            ; Request random read.
              ENDM
```

DOS2122

```
DOS2122       MACRO   FCBADD
;;
;; MS-DOS Interrupt 21h Function 22 - Random Write
;;
;; Fill the Disk Transfer Area (DTA) with the record to write.  Set
;; the Random Record field in the FCB.  Be sure to double-check the
;; record field and record number.  MS-DOS will overwrite whatever
;; you've got set.  Also note that, if the record number is far
;; in excess of what is currently in the file, MS-DOS simply
;; extends the file the requested length, to stack that record at
;; the end of the file and fill in the intervening space (if
;; there's garbage in storage, that's what appears in the
;; intervening space.
;;
;; Input:
;;       AH = 22h
;;       DS:DX = Address of an opened FCB
;;       Set FCB's Random Record field at DS:DX+21 and DS:DX+23
;;
;; Output:
;;       AL = 00 if successful
;;            01 Disk is full
;;            02 Not enough space in DTA segment; write canceled
;;
              @OFFSET FCBADD,DX      ; Point to FCB.
              @DOS21  22h            ; Request random write.
              ENDM
```

DOS2123

```
DOS2123       MACRO   FCBADD
;;
;; MS-DOS Interrupt 21h Function 23h - File Size
;;
;; Use this function to find out the size of a file without having
;; to open it.  The function uses an unopened FCB.  The FCB's record
;; size is used to compute the file size in number of records.  (A
;; size of 1 will return the size in bytes.)
;;
;; Input:
;;       AH = 23h
;;       DS:DX = Address of unopened FCB
;;
;; Output:
;;       AL = 00 if successful, FCB Relative Record field set to file
;;               length in records, rounded up
;;
;;            FF if no file found that matched FCB
;;
              @OFFSET FCBADD,DX      ; Point to FCB.
              @DOS21  23h            ; Request file size
              ENDM
```

DOS2124

```
DOS2124        MACRO   FCBADD
;;
;; MS-DOS Interrupt 21h Function 24h - Set Relative Record Field
;;
;; This function sets the relative-record field of a File Control
;; Block (FCB) to match the file position indicated by the
;; current-block and current-record fields of the same FCB.
;;
;; Note that the AL register is set to 00 by this function.  Before
;; using this function, your program must open the FCB.
;;
;; Input:
;;     AH = 24h
;;     DS:DX = Address of an opened FCB
;;
;; Output:
;;     AL = 00
;;     Random Record Field is set to match Current Record and Current
;;      Block
;;
               @OFFSET FCBADD,DX      ; Point to FCB.
               @DOS21  24h            ; Request Set.
               ENDM
```

DOS2125

```
DOS2125        MACRO   INTNUM,HANDLER
;;
;; MS-DOS Interrupt 21h Function 25h - Set Interrupt Vector
;;
;; Function 25 sets an address in the Interrupt Vector Table to point
;; to a specified interrupt handler.
;;
;; When this function is called, the 4-byte address IN DS:DX is
;; placed in the correct position in the IVT.  Before using Function 25,
;; read the address of the current interrupt handler with Function 35
;; and save the current address for restoration before your program
;; terminates.
;;
;; Input:
;;     AH = 25h
;;     AL = Interrupt number to modify
;;     DS:DX = Address of new interrupt handler
;;
;;     Note: DS:DX IS the address to set.  It is NOT the
;;           segment value (DS) and offset (DX) of the area
;;           where the address is located.
;;
               @SETBYT INTNUM,AL      ; Set interrupt number
       IFNB <HANDLER>                 ; If HANDLER is present
         IF ((.TYPE HANDLER) AND 01h) EQ 01h ; If program related
               MOV     DX,CS          ; Set CS as segment.
               MOV     DS,DX          ; In DS
               LEA     DX,HANDLER     ; Get offset in DX
         ELSEIF ((.TYPE HANDLER) AND 02h) EQ 02h ; If data related
               LDS     DX,HANDLER     ; Load full pointer
         ENDIF
       ENDIF
               @DOS21  25h            ; and request function.
               ENDM
```

DOS2127

```
DOS2127        MACRO   NRECS,FCBADD
;;
;; MS-DOS Interrupt 21h Function 27h - Random Block Read
;;
;; When reading in a random record, INT 21 Function 27 updates the
;; random record field.  When the function is finished, the random
;; record field is set to the number of the next, unread record.
;;
;; Input:
;;     AH = 27h
;;     CX = Number of records to read
;;     DS:DX = Address of an opened FCB
;;     Set FCB's Random Record field at DS:DX+21 and DS:DX+23
;;
;; Output:
;;     AL = 00 if successful
;;          01 End of file, no more data
;;          02 Not enough space in DTA segment
;;          03 End of file, partial record padded with 0's
;;     CX = Number of records read
;;     Random Record fields set to access next record
;;
             @SETWRD NUMREC,CX       ; Set number of records
             @OFFSET FCBADD,DX       ; and FCB offset
             @DOS21  27h             ; Request the read.
             ENDM
```

DOS2128

```
DOS2128        MACRO   NRECS,FCBADD
;;
;; MS-DOS Interrupt 21h Function 28h - Random Block Write
;;
;; Function 28h writes one or more records from the current disk
;; transfer (DTA) to a file.  Data to be written must be placed in
;; the DTA before calling this function.
;;
;; Unless the DTA address has been set with Function 1A (Set DTA
;; Address), MS-DOS uses a default 128-byte DTA at offset 80 in
;; the program segment prefix (PSP).
;;
;; If you set CX to 00 before calling this function, the file will
;; be set to the length given by the random record field.  This may
;; force the file to be truncated or enlarged.  If enlarged, it
;; includes whatever garbage is in the free sectors on the disk.
;;
;; Input:
;;     AH = 28h
;;     CX = Number of records to write
;;          00 The file is set to the size indicated in the Random
;;             Record field
;;     DS:DX = Address of an opened FCB
;;     Set FCB's Random Record field at DS:DX+21 and DS:DX+23
;;
;; Output:
;;     AL = 00 if successful
;;          01 Disk is full
;;          02 Not enough space in DTA segment; write canceled
;;     CX = Number of records written
;;     Random Record field set to access next record
;;
             @SETWRD NUMREC,CX       ; Set number of records
             @OFFSET FCBADD,DX       ; and FCB offset
             @DOS21  28h             ; Request the write.
             ENDM
```

DOS2129

```
DOS2129        MACRO    STRADD,FCBADD
;;
;; MS-DOS Interrupt 21h Function 29h - Parse Filename
;;
;; This function is useful in parsing file names from the command
;; line.  Give it the address of the command line.  If it finds a
;; file name, Function 29h places an unopened FCB for the file at
;; address ES:DI.  If the command line does not contain a valid
;; file name, ES:[DI+1] will contain blanks.
;;
;; Note this function cannot parse pathnames.
;;
;; Input:
;;      AH = 29h
;;      AL = Bit 0=0  Stop parsing if file separator is found
;;               1  Leading separators are scanned off the command
;;                  line
;;           1=0  Set drive number field in FCB to 0 (current
;;                  drive) if string does not include a drive
;;                  identifier
;;               1  Drive ID in final FCB will be change ONLY if a
;;                  drive was specified
;;           2=0  Set filename field in the FCB to blanks if
;;                  string does not include a filename
;;               1  Filename in FCB changed ONLY if command line
;;                  includes a filename
;;           3=0  Set extension field in FCB to blanks if string
;;                  does not include a filename extension
;;               1  Filename extension in FCB will be changed ONLY
;;                  if command line contains a filename extension
;;      DS:SI = Command line string to parse
;;      ES:DI = Address to put unopened FCB
;;
;; Output:
;;      AL = 00 if string does not contain wildcard character
;;           01 if string contains wildcard character
;;           FF if drive specifier invalid
;;      DS:SI = first byte after parsed string
;;      ES:DI = valid unopened FCB
;;
                @OFFSET STRADD,SI        ; Point to string
        IF ((.TYPE FCBADD) AND 3) NE 0   ; If a label or variable,
                MOV     DI, SEG FCBADD   ; Get segment
                MOV     ES,DI            ; into ES.
        ENDIF
                @OFFSET FCBADD,DI        ; and offset to DI.
                @DOS21 29h               ; Parse filename.
                ENDM
```

DOS212A

```
DOS212A        MACRO
;;
;; MS-DOS Interrupt 21h Function 2A - Get Date
;;
;; Function 2A returns the current system date in binary form:
;; year, month, day, and day of week.
;;
;; Note that years outside the range of 1980 through 2099 cannot
;; be returned by this function.
;;
;; Input:
;;      AH = 2Ah
;;
;; Output:
;;      AL = Day of week (0=Sunday .. 7=Saturday)
;;      CX = Year (1980 .. 2099)
;;      DH = Month number (1=January .. 12=December)
;;      DL = Day of the month (1 .. 31)
;;
                @DOS21  2Ah              ; Get the date.
                ENDM
```

DOS212B

```
DOS212B        MACRO    YEAR,MONTH.DAY
;;
;; MS-DOS  Interrupt 21h Function 2B - Set Date
;;
;; Function 2B takes binary values for the year, month, and day of
;; month.  It stores them in the system's date counter as the number
;; of days since January 1, 1980.  The year must be a 16-bit value
;; in the range 1980 .. 2099.  Values outside that range are not
;; accepted.  Also, supplying only the last two digits of the year
;; causes an error.
;;
;; Input:
;;     AH = 2Bh
;;     CX = Year (1980 .. 2099)
;;     DH = Month number (1=January .. 12=December)
;;     DL = Day of month (1 .. 31)
;;
;; Output:
;;     AL = 00 if successful
;;          FF if date not valid
;;
               @SETWRD YEAR,CX       ; Set year
               @SETBYT MONTH,DH      ; month
               @SETBYT DAY,DL        ; and day.
               @DOS21  2Bh           ; Into DOS.
               ENDM
```

DOS212C

```
DOS212C        MACRO
;;
;; MS-DOS Interrupt 21h Function 2C - Get Time
;;
;; Function 2C reports the current system time in binary form (with
;; the hours based on the 24-hour clock), minutes, seconds, and
;; hundredths of a second.
;;
;; Input:
;;     AH = 2Ch
;;
;; Output:
;;     CH = Hours (0 .. 23)
;;     CL = Minutes (0 .. 59)
;;     DH = Seconds (0 .. 59)
;;     DL = Hundredths of seconds (0 .. 99)
;;
               @DOS21  2Ch           ; Get time.
               ENDM
```

DOS212D

```
DOS212D        MACRO    HOUR,MINUTE,SECOND,HUND
;;
;; MS-DOS Interrupt 21 Function 2D - Set Time
;;
;; Function 2C sets the current system time in binary form (with
;; the hours based on the 24-hour clock), minutes, seconds, and
;; hundredths of a second.
;;
;; Input:
;;     AH = 2Dh
;;     CH = Hours (0 .. 23)
;;     CL = Minutes (0 .. 59)
;;     DH = Seconds (0 .. 59)
;;     DL = Hundredths of seconds (0 .. 99)
;;
;; Output:
```

```
;;      AL = 00 if successful
;;           FF if time is invalid
;;
    IFB     <HUND>
            XOR     DL,DL           ; Default hundredths to zero
    ELSE
            @SETBYT HUND,DL         ; Load hundredths,
    ENDIF
            @SETBYT SECOND,DH       ; seconds,
            @SETBYT MINUTE,CL       ; minutes, and
            @SETBYT HOUR,CH         ; hours.
            @DOS21  2Dh             ; Go set them.
            ENDM
```

DOS212E

```
DOS212E         MACRO   SWITCH
;;
;; MS-DOS Interrupt 21h Function 2Eh - Set or Reset Verify Switch
;;
;; Function 2Eh turns on and off the verification for disk writing.
;;
;; Input:
;;      AH = 2Eh
;;      AL = 00  Turn verify OFF
;;           01  Turn verify ON
;;      DL = 00  Obsolete DOS requirement.
;;
    IFIDNI <SWITCH>,<OFF>
            XOR     AL,AL           ; Verify OFF
    ELSEIFIDNI <SWITCH>,<ON>
            MOV     AL,1            ; Verify ON
    ELSE
            @SETBYT SWITCH,AL       ; Who knows.
    ENDIF
            @DOS21  2Eh             ; Set the option.
            ENDM
```

DOS212F

```
DOS212F         MACRO
;;
;; MS-DOS Interrupt 21h Function 2F - Get Current DTA
;;
;; This function returns the base address of the current DTA.
;; MS-DOS has no way of knowing the size of the buffer at that
;; address.  Your program must ensure that the buffer pointed to
;; by the DTA address is large enough to hold any records
;; transferred to it.
;;
;; If the DTA address has not been set by INT 21h Function 1Ah
;; (Set DTA Address), MS-DOS uses a default buffer of 128 bytes
;; located at offset 80 in the program segment prefix (PSP).
;;
;; Input:
;;      AH = 2Fh
;;
;; Output:
;;      ES:BX = Current DTA Address
;;
            @DOS21  2Fh             ; Get DTA
            ENDM
```

DOS2130

```
DOS2130      MACRO
;;
;; MS-DOS Interrupt 21h Function 30h - Get MS-DOS Version Number
;;
;; This function lets you know what version of MS-DOS is running on
;; a system.  AL holds the major version, the "3" in MS-DOS 3.10.
;; AH holds the minor version, the "10" of 3.10.  If AL returns a 0,
;; it's an early MS-DOS, before 2.0.
;;
;; Input:
;;     AH = 30h
;;     AL = 00
;;
;; Output:
;;     AL = Major version number
;;     AH = Minor version number
;;     BH = Original Equipment Manufacturer's serial number,
;;             but usually 00 for PC-DOS and 0FF or other values
;;             for MS-DOS
;;     BL:CX = 24-bit user serial number (this is optional and
;;             OEM dependent)
;;
               XOR    AL,AL           ; Clear for older DOSs
               @DOS21 30h             ; Get version.
               ENDM
```

DOS2131

```
DOS2131      MACRO   MSIZE,RETCD
;;
;; MS-DOS Interrupt 21h Function 31h - Terminate Process and Keep
;;                                 Resident
;;
;; Function 31h terminates a program and returns control to the
;; parent process (usually COMMAND.COM) but keeps the terminated program
;; resident in memory.  The terminating process should return a completion
;; code in the AL register.  If the program terminates normally, the return
;; code should be 00.  A return code of 01 or greater usually indicates
;; that termination was caused by an error encountered by the process.
;;
;; Input
;;     AH = 31h
;;     AL = Return Code
;;     DX = Size of memory request in paragraphs.
;;
               @SETWRD MSIZE,DX       ; Get size required
               @SETBYT RETCD,AL       ; Set return code.
               @DOS21 31h             ; Terminate.
               ENDM
```

DOS2133

```
DOS2133      MACRO   GETQ,SETTING
;;
;; MS-DOS Interrupt 21h Function 33h - Control Break Check
;;
;; MS-DOS uses this function to check if a BREAK is pending each
;; time a MS-DOS function is called.  Otherwise, the user can wait
;; a long time for a BREAK to be noticed and processed.  If the
;; Control-C check flag is off, MS-DOS checks for a Control-C entered
;; at the keyboard only during servicing of the character I/O functions
;; (01 through 0C).
;;
;; If the Control-C check flag is on, MS-DOS also checks for user entry
;; of a Control-C during servicing of other functions, such as file and
;; record operations.
;;
```

```
;; The state of the Control-C check flag affects all programs.  If a
;; program needs to change the state of Control-C checking, it should
;; save the original flag and restore it before terminating.
;;
;; Input:
;;     AH = 33h
;;     AL = 00 to get the state of Control-C check flag
;;          01 to set the state of Control-C check flag
;;     DL = 00 to set the flag to off
;;          01 to set the flag to on
;;
;; Output:
;;     AL = 00 if flag is set successfully
;;          FF code in AL on call was not 00 or 01
;;
;;     If AL was 00 on the call:
;;     DL = 00 Control-C check flag is Off
;;          01 Control-C check flag is On
;;
    IFIDNI <GETQ>,<GET>                  ; If getting the current
              XOR    AL,AL               ; Indicate get request
    ELSEIFIDNI <GETQ>,<SET>              ; If setting
              MOV    AL,1                ; Indicate set
       IFIDNI <SETTING>,<OFF>            ; Is it off?
              XOR    DL,DL               ; Indicate off.
       ELSEIFIDNI <SETTING>,<ON>         ; how about on?
              MOV    DL,1                ; if so - request on.
       ELSE
              @SETBYT SETTING,DL         ; Not on or off - but --
       ENDIF
    ELSE
              @SETBYT GETQ,AL            ; Not get or set - so
              @SETBYT SETTING,DL         ; use whatever was coded
    ENDIF                                ; with no defaults.
              @DOS21 33h                 ; Issue request
              ENDM
```

DOS2135

```
DOS2135        MACRO    INTNO
;;
;; MS-DOS Interrupt 21h Function 35h - Get Interrupt Vector
;;
;; This function works with Function 25h, which sets vectors.
;;
;; Input:
;;     AH = 35h
;;     AL = Interrupt number
;;
;; Output:
;;     ES:BX = Interrupt vector for interrupt specified in AL
;;
              @SETBYT INTNO,AL           ; Set int vector desired
              @DOS21 35h                 ; Request current value
              ENDM
```

DOS2136

```
DOS2136        MACRO    NDISK
;;
;; MS-DOS Interrupt 21h Function 36h - Get Free Disk Space
;;
;; MS-DOS uses this function when it tells how many free bytes are
;; available on a disk.  A cluster is the smallest piece of a disk
;; that MS-DOS keeps track of, so the number of bytes in a cluster
;; multiplied by number of clusters gives the total number of bytes
;; available.
;;
;; Input:
```

```
;;        AH = 36h
;;        DL = Drive Number
;;             00 - Default drive
;;             01 - drive A
;;             02 - drive B, and so on
;;
;; Output:
;;        If successful:
;;        AX = Number of sectors per clusters
;;        BX = Number of available clusters.
;;        CX = Size of a sector in bytes
;;        DX = Number of clusters on the drive
;;        If unsuccessful:
;;        AX = 0FFFF - Drive number is invalid
;;        DL = Invalid drive number
;;
               @SETBYT NDISK,DL        ; Set drive number
               @DOS21  36h             ; and request space.
               ENDM
```

DOS2138

```
DOS2138        MACRO   GETQ,CNTRY,BUFF
;;
;; MS-DOS Interrupt 21h Function 38h - Get/Set Country Dependent
;;                                     Information
;; See the Brumm book which contains the complete information for
;; this function, with illustrations as to the specific formats of
;; the various fields.
;;
;; The get/set field must be either get or set for generation of
;; the macro.  The input is edited and passed depending on this
;; value.
;;
;; Input:
;;        AH = 38h
;;        AL = 00  Current country
;;             01-FE Country code between 1 and 254
;;             FF   Country code of 255 or greater, specifiedin BX
;;        BX = Country code, if AL=FF
;;        DX = FFFF - if set country information
;;        DS:DX = 34-byte buffer - if get country information
;;
;; Output:
;;        CF = 0 if successful
;;             Filled in 32-byte block
;;             BX = country code (MS-DOS version 3.x only)
;;             DS:DX = buffer containing country information
;;        CF = 1 if unsuccessful
;;             AX = error code
;;                  02 invalid country code
;;
;;

    IFNB <CNTRY>
;;
;; Edit country - if register, handle it
;;
;; It could be a byte register
        IF ((.TYPE CNTRY) AND 0010h) EQ 010h  ;; Is CNTRY a register
           IFIDNI <CNTRY>,<AH>          ;; Check for 1 byte reg.
             @SETBYT CNTRY,AL           ; yes assume < 255
           ELSEIFIDNI <CNTRY>,<AL>
             @SETBYT CNTRY,AL           ; yes assume < 255
           ELSEIFIDNI <CNTRY>,<BL>
             @SETBYT CNTRY,AL           ; yes assume < 255
           ELSEIFIDNI <CNTRY>,<CL>
             @SETBYT CNTRY,AL           ; yes assume < 255
           ELSEIFIDNI <CNTRY>,<DL>
             @SETBYT CNTRY,AL           ; yes assume < 255
           ELSEIFIDNI <CNTRY>,<BH>
```

```
                @SETBYT CNTRY,AL          ; yes assume < 255
             ELSEIFIDNI <CNTRY>,<CH>
                @SETBYT CNTRY,AL          ; yes assume < 255
             ELSEIFIDNI <CNTRY>,<DH>
                @SETBYT CNTRY,AL          ; yes assume < 255
             ELSE
                @SETWRD CNTRY,BX
                MOV    AL,0FFh
             ENDIF
;; It wasn't a register - constant?
       ELSEIF (TYPE CNTRY) EQ 0           ; Country is a constant
          IF CNTRY LT 255                 ; Will it fit in AL?
             MOV     AL,CNTRY             ; Set country < 255
          ELSE
             MOV     BX,CNTRY             ; Set country > 254
             MOV     AL,0FFh
          ENDIF
       ELSEIF (TYPE CNTRY) EQ 1           ; is country a byte?
             @SETBYT CNTRY,AL             ; yes assume < 255
       ELSE
             @SETWRD CNTRY,BX
             MOV     AL,0FFh              ; Set country > 254
       ENDIF
    ENDIF
    IFIDNI <GETQ>,<GET>                   ; Is this a get request?
             MOV     DX,-1                ; Indicate get.
       IFNB <BUFF>
          .ERR BUFF is invalid for GET.
       ENDIF
    ELSEIFIDNI <GETQ>,<SET>               ; Is it a set?
             @OFFSET BUFF,DX              ; Point to the buffer.
    ELSE
       IF2
                %OUT  The first operand (GETQ) must be get or set.
       ENDIF
                .ERR  The first operand (GETQ) must be get or set.
             EXITM
    ENDIF
             @DOS21  38h                  ; Request get/set
             ENDM
```

DOS2139

```
DOS2139        MACRO   STRING
;;
;; MS-DOS Interrupt 21h Function 39h - Create a Subdirectory
;;
;; The MS-DOS command MKDIR uses this function to create a subdirectory
;; using a specified path.  Create a subdirectory that points DS:DX
;; to an ASCIIZ string that has the disk, path, and subdirectory
;; information.  An ASCIIZ character string is one that ends in a null
;; (hex 00). For example, use a line in your program like:
;;
;;             MK_SUB  DB       'C:\ASM',0
;;
;; A subdirectory ASM will be created.  If there's one already there, or
;; some other problem is encountered, an error returns in AH.
;;
;; Input:
;;     AH = 39h
;;     DS:DX points to ASCIIZ string with directory name
;;
;; Output:
;;     Carry Flag = 0 if successful
;;     Carry Flag = 1 if unsuccessful
;;                     AH holds the error value
;;                        = 3 Path not found
;;                        = 5 Access denied
;;
             @OFFSET STRING,DX    ; Set name
             @DOS21  39h          ; and call dos.
             ENDM
```

DOS213A

```
DOS213A        MACRO   STRING
;;
;; MS-DOS Interrupt 21 Function 3Ah - Delete a Subdirectory
;;
;; This function is the companion of INT 21 Function 39h.  The MS-DOS
;; RMDIR uses this function to removed directories.  Point DS:DX to an
;; ASCIIZ string with the disk and path in it.  Use a line in your
;; program such as;
;;
;;      RM_DIR  DB       'C:\ASM',0
;;
;; The subdirectory must be empty before it can be removed.  Use INT 21
;; Function 41h to delete the files.  If you try to delete a subdirectory
;; with files, AH returns with an 05h.
;;
;; Input:
;;      AH = 3Ah
;;      DS:DX points to ASCIIZ string with directory name
;;
;; Output:
;;      Carry Flag = 0 if successful
;;      Carry Flag = 1 if unsuccessful
;;                      AH holds error value
;;                      = 3 Path not found
;;                      = 5 Access denied
;;
                @OFFSET STRING,DX      ; Set name
                @DOS21  3Ah            ; and call dos.
                ENDM
```

DOS213B

```
DOS213B        MACRO   STRING
;;
;; MS-DOS Interrupt 21h Function 3Bh - Change a Current Directory
;;
;; Function 3Bh allows a change in the default directory.  It's useful
;; to search for files and you're not certain in which subdirectory
;; the file exists.  MS-DOS uses this function for the CD command.
;; The pathname pointed to by DS:DX must be an ASCIIZ string, one that
;; terminates in a null (hex 00).  The path string is limited to a total
;; of 64 characters, including all separators.
;;
;; Input:
;;      AH = 3Bh
;;      DS:DX points to ASCIIZ string with directory name
;;
;; Output:
;;      Carry Flag = 0 if successful
;;      Carry Flag = 1 if unsuccessful
;;                      AH holds error value
;;                      = 3 Path not found
;;
                @OFFSET STRING,DX      ; Set name
                @DOS21  3Bh            ; and call dos.
                ENDM
```

DOS213C

```
DOS213C        MACRO    STRING,ATTRIB
;;
;; MS-DOS Interrupt 21h Function 3Ch - Create a File
;;
;; This function creates a file, assigns it the attributes specified,
;; and returns a 16-bit handle for the file. Function 3Ch needs a string
;; that gives drive, directories (and any subdirectories), and file name
;; (with any extension).  Point DS:DX at the ASCIIZ character string,
;; which is a string that ends in a null (a hex 00).  You might have a
;; string definition in a program such as:
;;
;;             MY_FILE DB      'C:\ASM\MACRO\SQRT.ASM',O
;;
;; If that file already exists in that subdirectory, it is set to a 0
;; length.  However, if that file exists and is marked "read only", error
;; 05 returns in AL.  If this function works correctly, a 16-bit file handle
;; returns in AX.  Use this word to refer the file from then on; it's the fil
;; handle.
;;
;; Input:
;;      AH = 3Ch
;;      CX = File attribute, bits 0 through 2 of the 2-byte
;;                  attribute:
;;                          00 = normal file
;;                          01 = read-only file
;;                          02 = hidden file
;;                          04 = system file
;;                  Bits 3 through 5 are associated with volume
;;                  labels, subdirectories, and archive files.  These
;;                  bits are invalid for this function and must be set
;;                  to zero.  Also, set bits 6 though 15 to zero to
;;                  assure future compatibility.
;;      DS:DX points to ASCIIZ string with directory name
;;
;; Output:
;;      Carry Flag = 0 if successful
;;                          AH = File Handle
;;      Carry Flag = 1 if unsuccessful
;;                          AL holds error value
;;                              = 3 Path not found
;;                              = 4 Too many files open
;;                              = 5 Directory full, or previous
;;                                          read-only file exists
;;
                @OFFSET STRING,DX        ; Point to dir name
        IFNB <ATTRIB>
            IF (TYPE ATTRIB) EQ 0        ; If constant
                    MOV     CX,ATTRIB    ; Load as a word
            ELSEIF (TYPE ATTRIB) EQ 1    ; If byte data
                    MOV     CL,ATTRIB    ; Load low half of CX
                    XOR     CH,CH        ; and clear high byte
            ELSE
                @SETWRD ATTRIB,CX        ; load as word.
            ENDIF
        ENDIF
                @DOS21  3Ch              ; Request create.
                ENDM
```

DOS213D

```
DOS213D        MACRO    STRING,FACCESS
;;
;; MS-DOS Interrupt 21h Function 3Dh - Open a File with Handle
;;
;; Give this function a ASCIIZ string with the drive, path name,
;; and a file name.  Enter the access code in AL which specifies
;; how to work with the file. If the Carry Flag (CF--bit 0 of
;; the EFLAGS register) is set, there was an error, which returns
```

```
;; in AL.
;; When the file is opened, the position of the file pointer is set
;; to zero.  Interrupt 21 Function 42h (Move File Pointer) can be used
;; to change its position.
;;
;; Input:
;;      AH = 3Dh
;;      AL = File access, file sharing, and inheritance codes
;;              Bits 0-2 Access code, file usage
;;                      000 read-only
;;                      001 write-only
;;                      010 read/write
;;              Bit 3 reserved, set to 0
;;              Bits 4-6 sharing mode; file access granted
;;                      000 compatibility mode
;;                      001 deny read/write access
;;                      010 deny write access
;;                      100 read/write access
;;              Bit 7 inherit bit
;;                      0 child process inherits the file
;;                      1 child process does not inherit the file
;;      DS:DX points to ASCIIZ string with directory name
;;
;; Output:
;;      Carry Flag = 0 if successful
;;              AH = File Handle
;;      Carry Flag = 1 if unsuccessful
;;              AL holds error value
;;                 = 2 File not found
;;                 = 3 Path not found
;;                 = 4 Too many files open
;;                 = 5 Access denied
;;
            @SETBYT FACCESS,AL        ; Set access byte
            @OFFSET STRING,DX         ; and path name
            @DOS21  3Dh               ; then open it.
            ENDM
```

DOS213E

```
DOS213E         MACRO   HANDLE
;;
;; MS-DOS Interrupt 21h Function 3Eh - Close a File Handle
;;
;; Function 3Eh needs the file handle loaded into BX.  If the file
;; has been modified, truncated or extended, Function 3Eh updates the
;; current date, time, and file size in the directory entry.  With
;; MS-DOS versions 3.1 and later, a program must remove all file locks
;; in effect before it closes a file.  The result of closing a file
;; with active locks is unpredictable.  If there was an error during
;; the close, the Carry Flag is set.
;;
;; Input:
;;      AH = 3Eh
;;      BX = Valid file handle
;;
;; Output:
;;      Carry Flag is 0 if successful
;;      Carry Flag is 1 if unsuccessful
;;              AL = 6 Invalid file handle
;;
    IF ((.TYPE HANDLE) AND 4) EQ 4      ; if constant and
        IF HANDLE GT 2                  ; if not < 3 (in, out, err)
                .ERR    HANDLE Is constant over 2 - (last standard)
                EXITM
        ENDIF
    ENDIF
            @SETWRD HANDLE,BX         ; Load handle
            @DOS21  3Eh               ; close the file.
            ENDM
```

DOS213F

```
DOS213F        MACRO   HANDLE,BYTECT,BUFF
;;
;; MS-DOS Interrupt 21h Function 3Fh - Read a File or Device
;;
;; Function 3Fh reads bytes from a file, not records.  Store the
;; number of bytes to read in CX.  This function returns them to
;; the location specified in DS:DX (but not in the disk transfer area,
;; DTA).  AX returns the number of bytes read.  Since MS-DOS won't
;; read past the end of the file, check AX to see that you actually
;; got the full number of bytes expected.
;;
;; Input:
;;      AH = 3Fh
;;      BX = File handle
;;      CX = Number of bytes to read
;;      DS:DX = Data buffer address
;;
;; Output:
;;      Carry Flag = 0 if successful
;;                      AX = Number of bytes read
;;      Carry Flag = 1 if unsuccessful
;;                      AL = 5 Access denied
;;                           6 Invalid handle
;;
    IF (TYPE HANDLE) EQ 0            ; A constant is wrong
            .ERR    HANDLE Is not a valid type.
            EXITM
    ENDIF
            @SETWRD HANDLE,BX        ; Load handle
            @SETWRD BYTECT,CX        ; count and
            @OFFSET BUFF,DX          ; buffer area.
            @DOS21  3Fh              ; request read
            ENDM
```

Appendices

Appendix A

MASM Error Messages

THIS APPENDIX LISTS AND EXPLAINS THE MESSAGES MASM DISPLAYS WHEN IT ENCOUNTERS an error during processing. MASM will give you warnings when it finds an instance of questionable statement syntax. You can ignore the warnings if you are certain that what you have coded will work as you wish it to. Otherwise, go back and correct all instructions which give either errors or warnings.

MASM EXIT CODES

MASM returns one of the codes shown in Fig. A-1. These codes can be tested by a MAKE file or a BATCH file.

NUMBERED MESSAGES

MASM displays messages on the screen whenever it finds an error while processing your source file(s). It displays warning messages when it encounters questionable syntax. General errors related to the entire assembly rather than a particular line are unnumbered (see the unnumbered messages section of this appendix). MASM displays the numbered messages in the following format:

$$sourcefile(line):code:message$$

The *sourcefile* is the name of the source file where the error occurred. If the error occurred in a macro from an INCLUDE file, the *sourcefile* is the file where the macro was called and expanded, not the file where it was defined. The *line* shows the point in the source file where MASM was no longer able to assemble. The *code* starts with

CODE	MEANING
0	No error
1	Argument error
2	Unable to open input file
3	Unable to open listing file
4	Unable to open object file
5	Unable to open cross–reference file
6	Unable to open INCLUDE file
7 *	Assembly error
8	Memory–allocation error
9	Not used
10	Error defining symbol from command line (/D)
11	User interrupted

* If MASM exits with a code 7, it automatically deletes the invalid object file.

Fig. A-1. MASM Exit Codes.

the word *error* or *warning* followed by a five-character code. The first character of the code indicates the program or language (for example, A = assembler). The first digit indicates the warning level (for example, 2 for severe errors, 4 for serious warnings, and 5 for advisory messages). The next three digits are the error number. The *message* is a line that describes the error.

In the messages below, you will see that some numbers are not assigned in MASM 5.1. Some of the numbers were generated by earlier releases and are no longer applicable.

Code   **Message**

0   **Block nesting error**
Nested procedures, segments, structures, macros, and repeat blocks (IRC, IRP, or REPT) are not properly terminated. An example of this error occurs when you close an outer level of nesting with inner level(s) still open.

1   **Extra characters on line**

You get this error when MASM has read sufficient information to define the instruction directive and it finds additional characters on the line. You might have provided too many arguments.

2   **Internal error - register already defined:** *symbol*

Error 2 indicates a MASM internal error. You should document how you got this error and notify Microsoft Product Assistance.

3   **Unknown type specifier**

MASM did not recognize the size type specified in a label or external declaration. You might have misspelled the specifier.

4   **Redefinition of symbol**

If you define a symbol in two places, you get this error printed during pass 1 when MASM finds the second declaration of the symbol.

5   **Symbol is multidefined**

If you have defined the symbol in two places, MASM prints this message in pass 2 on each declaration of the symbol.

6   **Phase error between passes**

Your program has an ambiguous instruction or directive, such that the location of a label in your program changed in value between MASM pass 1 and pass 2. For example, you may have coded a forward reference without a segment override where one is required. An additional byte (the code segment override) is generated in pass 2 which causes the label to change. You can use the /D option to produce a pass 1 listing to help you resolve phase errors between the passes.

7   **Already had ELSE clause**

You attempted to define more than one ELSE clause within a conditional assembly block. You cannot nest an ELSE without nesting its own IF...ENDIF.

8   **Must be in conditional block**

You specified an ENDIF or ELSE without a previous conditional-assembly directive (IF).

9   **Symbol not defined**

You used a symbol without defining it. MASM prints this error for forward references on the first pass and ignores it if the reference is resolved on the second pass.

10 **Syntax error**
You coded a statement that does not match any of those recognized by MASM.

11 **Type illegal in context**
The type specifier is of an unacceptable size.

12 **Group name must be unique**
A name assigned as a group name was already defined as another type of symbol.

13 **Must be declared during pass 1:** *symbol*
You referenced an item before it was defined in pass 1.

14 **Illegal public declaration**
MASM found an illegal use of a PUBLIC symbol. For example, you might have tried to declare a text equate as PUBLIC.

15 **Symbol already different kind:** *symbol*
You attempted to define a symbol differently from a previous definition.

16 **Reserved word used as symbol:** *symbol*
Your program attempted to use an assembler reserved word as a symbol. For example, perhaps you tried to define JMP or LOOP as variables. This is a warning message, which you can choose to ignore. If you do, remember that the keyword is no longer usable for its original purposes.

17 **Forward reference is illegal**
You attempted to reference something before you defined it in pass 1. For example, if you code:

```
                DB      amount    DUP (?)

        amount    EQU    10
```

you will get an error message. If you reverse the lines, it is legal code.

18 **Operand must be register:** *operand*
MASM expected a register as an operand, but it found a symbol or constant.

19 **Wrong type of register**
The specified register (in the operand field) is incompatible with the directive

or instruction in the operation field. For example, the following instruction causes this error because you cannot increment the code segment register:

INC CS

20   **Operand must be segment or group**
MASM expected a segment or group, but it found something else.

21   **Not used in MASM 5.1**

22   **Operand must be type specifier**
MASM expected a type specifier such as NEAR, but it found something else.

23   **Symbol already defined locally**
You tried to define a symbol as EXTRN when the symbol had already been defined within the current module.

24   **Segment parameters are changed**
The list of arguments to SEGMENT was not identical to the list the first time this segment was declared.

25   **Improper align/combine type**
The SEGMENT parameters are incorrect. Check the align and combine types to be sure you have entered valid types.

26   **Reference to multidefined symbol**
An instruction referenced a symbol that has been defined in more than one place.

27   **Operand expected**
MASM expected an operand, but it found an operator.

28   **Operator expected**
MASM expected an operator, but it found an operand.

29   **Division by 0 or overflow**
You coded an expression that results in a division by zero or a number larger than the variable or system can represent.

30   **Negative shift count**
You coded a shift expression (SHL or SHR) that results in a negative shift count.

31   **Operand types must match**
MASM found different kinds (or sizes) of arguments in a case where they must match. For instance, you may have erroneously coded a move from a byte register to a word register: MOV BX,CH. If you coded MOV BX,CX, you would have a legal statement.

32   **Illegal use of external**
You coded an external variable in an illegal manner. For instance, if you code INDEX__IT as external, you cannot code: DB INDEX__IT DUP(?).

33   **Not used in MASM 5.1**

34   **Operand must be record or field name**
MASM expected a record name or field name, and it found something else.

35   **Operand must have size**
MASM expected an operand to have a size, but you did not code it. You can often correct this by using the PTR operator to specify a size type.

36   **Extra NOP inserted**
During pass 1, MASM did not have enough information to correctly infer the length of the encoding for the instruction. During pass 2, the encoding was found to be shorter than the space allocated from pass 1, so MASM inserted one or more NOP instructions as padding. It might be possible to generate a smaller amount of code by eliminating a forward reference to a symbol.

37   **Not used in MASM 5.1**

38   **Left operand must have segment**
The left operand of a segment-override expression must be a segment name, a segment register, or a group name. For instance, if you define a variable in another segment and do not define it in the segment in which the code executes, you will get this error.

39   **One operand must be constant**
If you illegally use the addition operator, you will get this error. For example, two memory operands cannot be added in an expression.

40   **Operands must be in same segment or one must be constant**
Here, you illegally used the subtraction operator. For example, a memory operand in a data segment cannot be subtracted from a memory operand in a code segment.

41 **Not used in MASM 5.1**

42 **Constant expected**
MASM expected a constant operand, and you coded an item that does not evaluate to a constant, such as a variable name or an external.

43 **Operand must have segment**
You incorrectly used the SEG directive.

44 **Must be associated with data**
You used a code-related item where MASM expected a data-related item.

45 **Must be associated with code**
This error is a reverse of error 44. Here, you used a data-related item where MASM requires a code-related item. For instance, you might declare the item TEST_IT in the data segment and then try to JMP TEST_IT.

46 **Multiple base registers**
You tried to use more than one base register in an operand. For example: MOV AX,[BX + BP].

47 **Multiple index registers**
You tried to use more than one index register in an operand. For example: MOV BX,[DI + SI].

48 **Must be index or base register**
The instruction you used requires a base or index register and some other register was specified in square brackets ([ ]). An indirect-memory operand requires a base or index register. Only BP, BX, DI, or SI can be used in indirect operands, except with 32-bit registers on the 80386.

49 **Illegal use of register**
You used a register with an instruction where no valid register is possible.

50 **Value out of range**
The value is too large for the use. For example: MOV BH,7500. In this case, you used a value too big for a byte register. You could code: MOV BX,7500.

51 **Operand not in current CS ASSUME segment**
You used an operand to represent a code address outside the code segment assigned with the current ASSUME statement. This often happens with a call or jump to a label outside the current code segment.

52   **Improper operand type:** *symbol*
You used an operand in some way that prevents MASM from generating an opcode.

53   **Jump out of range by** *number* **bytes**
For all Intel processors except the 80386, conditional jumps must be within the range of −128 to +127 bytes of the current instruction. For the 80386, the default is −32768 to +32767. The jump you coded goes too far. Generally, you correct the condition by reversing the condition of the jump and using an unconditional jump (JMP) to the label.

54   **Not used in MASM 5.1**

55   **Illegal register value**
The register value was specified with illegal syntax.

56   **Immediate mode illegal**
You supplied immediate data as an operand for an instruction that cannot use immediate data. For instance, you cannot move the segment address into a data segment register, such as MOV DS,SEG__ADDR. You have to move SEG__ADDR into a general register and then into DS.

57   **Illegal size for operand**
The size of the operand item is illegal with the specified instruction. This message is a warning. MASM still tries to assemble the instruction. This error often occurs when you try to assemble source code written for assemblers that have less strict type checking than does MASM. You can generally correct this error by changing the size of the item with the PTR operator.

58   **Byte register illegal**
You used one of the byte registers in a context where it is illegal. For instance, you will get this message if you try to PUSH CH. Instead, PUSH CX.

59   **Illegal use of CS register**
You will get this error if you use the code segment register (CS) illegally. For instance, you cannot exchange data in CS with a general register when you code something like: XCHG CS,BX.

60   **Must be accumulator register**
There are instructions which only use the AL, AX or EAX registers. If you use that instruction (such as the IN instruction), you have to use either AL, AX or EAX as the left operand (the destination).

61 **Improper use of segment register**
You specified a segment register in an illegal situation. For instance, you cannot make an immediate move to a segment register.

62 **Missing or unreachable code segment**
You attempted to jump to a label that is unreachable as your program now stands or that MASM does not recognize as a code segment. This occurs, for instance, when there is no ASSUME statement that associates the CS register with a segment.

63 **Operand combination illegal**
You coded a two-operand instruction where the combination specified is illegal.

64 **Near JMP/CALL to different code segment**
You attempted to do a NEAR jump or call to a location in a code segment defined with a different ASSUME:CS. To correct this error, you can use a FAR call or jump, or you can use an ASSUME statement to change the code segment.

65 **Label can't have segment override**
You illegally used a segment override.

66 **Must have instruction after prefix**
You used a repeat instruction (such as REP, REPE, or REPNE) without specifying an opcode after it.

67 **Cannot override ES for destination**
You tried to override the ES segment in a string instruction where this override is not legal. The default source (DS:SI) can have a segment override, but not the destination (ES:DI).

68 **Cannot address with segment register**
There is not an ASSUME directive that would make the variable reachable.

69 **Must be in segment block**
A directive (for example, EVEN) that MASM expects within a segment is used outside a segment.

70 **Cannot use EVEN or ALIGN with byte alignment**
You used the EVEN or ALIGN directive, even though the segment was declared to be byte aligned.

71   **Forward reference needs override or FAR**
A call or jump attempted to access a FAR label that was not declared FAR earlier in the source code.

72   **Illegal value for DUP count**
The DUP count must be a constant that evaluates to a positive integer greater than zero.

73   **Symbol is already external**
You declared a symbol already as external that MASM later found defined locally.

74   **DUP nesting too deep**
You nested a DUP operator more than 17 levels.

75   **Illegal use of undefined operator (?)**
This signals an improper use of the undefined operand (?).

76   **Too many values for structure or record initialization**
You entered too many initial values when you defined a variable using a REC or STRUC type. The number in the definition must match the number of values in the declaration.

77   **Angle brackets required around initialized list**
You attempted to define STRUC variable without the required angle brackets (< >).

78   **Directive illegal in structure**
The only allowable statements within a STRUC block is one of the define directives (that is, DB), a comment preceded by a semicolon (;), or a conditional-assembly directive.

79   **Override with DUP illegal**
In a STRUC initialization statement, you used a DUP.

80   **Field cannot be overridden**
In a STRUC initialization, you tried to give a value to a field that cannot be overridden.

81   **Not used in MASM 5.1**

82   **Not used in MASM 5.1**

83   **Circular chain of EQU aliases**
Check your EQU statements, because they form a circle. That is, an alias declared with the EQU directive points to itself.

84   **Cannot emulate coprocessor opcode**
Either the coprocessor opcode, or the operands you used with it, produce an instruction that the coprocessor emulator cannot support.

85   **End of file, no END directive**
Check to see that you end your source code with an END. There could also be a nesting error.

86   **Data emitted with no segment**
Some code that is not located within a segment attempted to generate data. Any statement that generates code or allocates data must be within a segment, although directives that specify assembler behavior—without generating code—can be outside segments.

87   **Forced error - pass1**
You forced an error with the .ERR1 directive.

88   **Forced error - pass2**
You forced an error with the .ERR2 directive.

89   **Forced error**
You forced an error with the .ERR directive.

90   **Forced error - expression true (0)**
You forced an error with the .ERRE directive.

91   **Forced error - expression false (not 0)**
You forced an error with the .ERRNZ directive.

92   **Forced error - symbol not defined**
You forced an error with the .ERRNDEF directive.

93   **Forced error - symbol defined**
You forced an error with the .ERRDEF directive.

94   **Forced error - string blank**
You forced an error with the .ERRB directive.

95   **Forced error - string not blank**
You forced an error with the .ERRNB directive.

96 **Forced error - strings identical**
You forced an error with the .ERRIDN directive.

97 **Forced error - strings different**
You forced an error with the .ERRDIF directive.

98 **Wrong length for override value**
If you try to override a value for a structure field with too large a value to fit the field, you will get this error. For instance, you declared a string value as one byte and then you try to store two characters.

99 **Line too long expanding symbol:** *symbol*
You get this error if a symbol defined by an EQU or equals-sign (=) directive is so long that expanding it overflows internal MASM buffers. The message might also indicate a recursive text macro.

100 **Impure memory reference**
The code attempts to store data into the code segment when the .286p directive (for privileged instructions) and the /P option are in effect.

101 **Missing data; zero assumed**
This is a warning message and occurs if you code a statement which requires two operands. For instance, if you code:

MOV EAX,

the code is assembled as if you coded:

MOV EAX,0

102 **Segment near (or at) 64K limit**
There is a bug in the 80286 which causes jump errors when a code segment approaches within a few bytes of the 64K limit in privileged mode. This error warns you about code that might fail because of the bug; the error can only be generated when the .286 directive is given.

103 **Align must be power of 2**
You used a number that is not a power of two with the ALIGN directive.

104 **Jump within short distance**
You used a JMP instruction to jump to a short label (128 or fewer bytes beyond the instruction). By default, MASM assumes that all jumps are NEAR (greater than short, but still in one segment). If it finds a short jump, MASM uses a

short form of the JMP instruction (two bytes) instead of the long form (three bytes with 16-bit segments, or five bytes with 32-bit segments). You can make your code more efficient by using the SHORT operator to specify that a jump is short rather than near.

105 Expected *element*

You omitted an element such as an operator or punctuation, such as comma between source and destination operands.

106 Line too long

You coded a source line longer than 128 characters.

107 Illegal digit in number

A constant number contains a digit that is not allowed in the current radix.

108 Empty string not allowed

A statement used an empty string. In many languages, an empty string represents ASCII character 0. In assembly, you have to give the value of 0.

109 Missing operand

The directive or instruction requires more operands than you provided.

110 Open parenthesis or bracket

In a statement, MASM found only one parenthesis or bracket.

111 Directive must be in macro

A directive that is expected only in macro definitions was used outside a macro.

112 Unexpected end of line

A statement line ended before the complete statement was formed. MASM expects more information, but cannot identify what is missing.

113 Cannot change processor in segment

MASM encountered a processor directive within a segment. Processor directives must be given before the first segment directive, or between segments.

114 Operand size does not match segment word size

You used a 32-bit operand in a 16-bit segment, or vice versa. MASM only gives this warning when you use an 80386. The message is a warning that you can choose to ignore.

115   **Address size does not match segment word size**
You used a 32-bit address in a 16-bit segment, or vice versa. This is a warning message which you can choose to ignore. It only appears when you use an 80386.

UNNUMBERED MESSAGES

MASM uses unnumbered messages when an error occurs that cannot be associated with a particular line of code. These errors often indicate problems with file access, the command line, or memory allocation.

File-Access Errors

These eleven errors can occur when MASM tries to access a file for processing. They usually indicate insufficient disk space or a corrupted file.

MESSAGE

End of file encountered on input file

Include file *filename* not found

Read error on standard input

Unable to access input file: *filename*

Unable to open cref file: *filename*

Unable to open input file: *filename*

Unable to open listing file: *filename*

Unable to open object file: *filename*

Write error on cross-reference file

Write error on listing file

Write error on object file

Command-Line Errors

Any of the seven following errors can occur if you type an invalid command line when you start MASM.

MESSAGE

Buffer size expected after B option

Error defining symbol "*name*" from command line

Extra filename ignored

Line invalid, start again

Path expected after I option

Unknown case option: *option*

Unknown option: *option*

Miscellaneous Errors

These seven errors are not related to a specific source line. They often indicate a problem with memory allocation or other assembler problems.

MESSAGE

Out of Memory
All available memory has been used. This occurs either because there are too many symbols defined in the symbol table or the source file is too large. You can try assembling with no listing or cross-reference file. If this works, you can reassemble by specifying a null object file to get a listing or cross-reference file.

Internal Error
This is a severe error within MASM. Document as much about it as you can and contact Microsoft Product Assurance.

Internal error - Problem with expression analyzer
This problem could indicate an expression that MASM does not understand. This is another problem to document and for which you should contact Microsoft Product Assurance.

Internal unknown error
The internal error table might have become corrupted, and MASM cannot figure out what the problem is. This is another problem to document and contact Microsoft Product Assurance.

Number of open conditionals: <*number*>
Conditional-assembly directives (those that start with IF) were given without a corresponding ENDIF directives. This also might indicate a problem with memory allocation or some other assembler problem not related to a specific source line.

Open procedures
A PROC directive was given without a corresponding ENDP directive. This also might indicate a problem with memory allocation or some other assembler problem not related to a specific source line.

Open segments
You defined a segment, but never terminated it with an ENDS directive. This error does not occur with simplified segment directives. This also might indicate a problem with memory allocation or some other assembler problem not related to a specific source line.

Appendix B

80386 Instruction Set

THE 80386 INSTRUCTION SET IS A SUPERSET OF INSTRUCTIONS FROM PREVIOUS GENERA-
tions with additional instructions for specific 80386 uses. The instruction set is listed
in this appendix in alphabetical order by mnemonic opcode. Along with each instruction,
the forms are given for each operand combination, including the object code that is
produced, the operands required, and a description of the instruction.

There are 14 new instructions on the 80386. They are: BSF, BSR, BT, BTC, BTR,
BTS, MOVSX, MOVZX, SETcc, SHLD, SHRD, LSS, LFS, and LGS. These instructions
are described in detail in this appendix, along with the remaining instructions. See appendix
C for an overview of the 80386/80387 coprocessor floating-point instructions.

INSTRUCTION FORMAT

The 80386 instructions are made up of various elements and have various formats.
Of the elements described below, only one (the opcode) is always present in each individual
instruction. The other items are optional; that is, they might not be present, depending
on the operation involved and on the location and type of the operands.

Instructions are made up of:

- Optional instruction prefixes.
- One or two primary opcode bytes.
- Possibly an address specifier, which consists of the Mod R/M byte and the
scale index base byte.
- A displacement—if required.
- An immediate data field—if required.

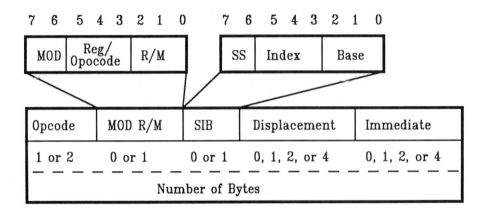

Fig. B-1. General Instruction Format.

All the instruction encodings are subsets of the general instruction format shown in Fig. B-1.

The elements of an instruction, in their order of occurrence are as follows:

• Prefixes—One or more bytes preceding an instruction that modify the operation of that instruction. There are four types of prefixes:

    ○ Repeat—Used with a string instruction to cause the instruction to act on each element of the string.
    ○ Operand size—Switches between 32-bit and 16-bit operands.
    ○ Address size—Switches between 32-bit and 16-bit address generation.
    ○ Segment override—Explicitly specifies which segment register an instruction should use. This overrides the default segment-register selection normally used by the 80386 for that instruction.

• Opcode—This specifies the operation performed by the instruction. Some operations have several different opcodes. Each specifies a different variant of the operation.

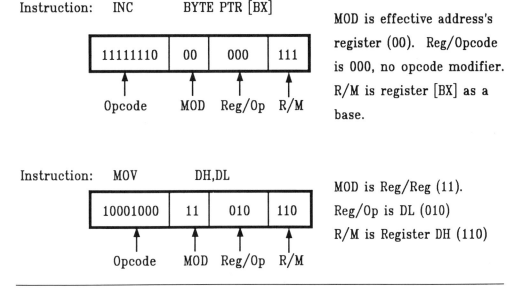

Fig. B-2. MOD R/M Examples.

• Register specifier—The instruction can specify one or two register operands. Register specifiers can occur in either the same byte as the opcode or in the same byte as the addressing-mode specifier.

• Addressing-mode specifier—When present, this element specifies whether an operand is a register or a memory location. If it is in memory, this specifies whether a displacement, an index register, a base register, and scaling is to be used.

• MOD R/M (register/memory) and SIB (scale index base) bytes—If present, a MOD R/M operand specifier follows the opcode byte(s). The opcode determines if this specifier is present. It also determines whether this field specifies two operands or one operand plus extra opcode bits. See Fig. B-2 for MOD R/M examples. The bits that indicate registers are shown in the encoding below.

Most instructions that can refer to an operand in memory have an addressing form byte following the primary opcode byte(s). This byte specifies the address form to be used. Some encodings of the MOD R/M byte indicate a second addressing byte, the scale index base (SIB) byte.

The MOD R/M and SIB bytes contain the following information:

  ○ The indexing type or register number to be used in the instructions.

○ The register to be used, or more information to select the instruction.
○ The base, index, and scale information.

The MOD R/M byte contains these three fields:

○ MOD (bits 7 and 6) occupies the two most significant bits of the byte. They combine with the R/M field to form 32 possible values: eight registers and 24 indexing modes.
○ REG (bits 5, 4, and 3) specifies either a register number or three more bits of opcode information. The meaning of REG is specified by the first (opcode) byte of the instruction.
○ R/M (bits 2, 1, and 0) can specify a register as the location of an operand, or it can form part of the addressing-mode encoding in combination with the MOD field as described above.

The SIB byte includes the three fields:

○ SS (bits 7 and 6) specifies the scale factor.
○ INDEX (bits 5, 4, and 3) specifies the register number of the index register.
○ BASE (bits 2, 1, and 0) specifies the register number of the base register.

Encoding of 32-bit address mode:

Register modifiers for address computation are all 32-bit registers (EAX for example). Address computations without scale index base (SIB) byte include:

○ A MOD of 00, which specifies address computation of DS:[R/M], which specifies a register as follows:

000 DS:[EAX]
001 DS:[ECX]
010 DS:[EDX]
011 DS:[EBX]
100 SIB Present
101 DS:32 bit displacement
110 DS:[ESI]
111 DS:[EDI]

Thus, the effective address is DS:32 bit modifier from register or memory.

○ A MOD of 01 adds an 8-bit displacement to the above so that R/M:

> 000 DS:[EAX + 8 bit displacement]
> 100 SIB Present
> 101 SS:[EBP + 8 bit displacement]

○ A MOD of 10 adds a 32-bit displacement. An R/M of 000 is DS:[EAX + a displacement]:

> 000 DS:[EAX + 32-bit displacement]
> 100 SIB Present
> 101 SS:[EBP + 32-bit displacement]

○ A MOD of 11 specifies a register in the R/M so that an R/M of:

> 000 AL or EAX
> 001 CL or ECX
> 010 DL or EDX
> 011 BL or EBX
> 100 AH or ESP
> 101 CH or EBP
> 110 DH or ESI
> 111 BH or EDI

The register selected depends on whether an 8-bit operation or a 32-bit operation is specified in the W bit.

The MOD value indicates the length of the displacement field to address:

> 00—no displacement, except for base 101
> 01—8-bit displacement
> 10—32-bit displacement

Therefore, the SIB modifies the computed address (DS:[base + scaled index + displacement]), except for the base where the base is ESP or EBP. Then, the logical substitution of SS: is made for the segment, instead of DS:.

Where an SIB is present, R/M = 100 for MOD = 00, 01, or 10. The address computation is done using a combination of the following.

A 32-bit scaled index value is computed as index $* 2^{scale}$ where scale is the first two bits of the SIB byte and specified by its binary value. The index register is specified as an index of the following.

000	EAX
001	ECX
010	EDX
011	EBX
100	no index value; scale must be 0
101	EBP
110	ESI
110	EDI

If the byte is laid out, the bits appear as SSIIIBBB, where SS is the scale, III is the index and BBB is the base. The base is selected as follows:

000	EAX
001	ECX
010	EDX
011	EBX
100	ESP
101	Special (a 32-bit displacement if MOD is 00, and the EBP register is otherwise)
110	ESI
111	EDI

• Displacement—An address displacement, if present, follows the MOD R/M field. The mod subfield of the MOD R/M field indicates if the displacement is present and its length. When the addressing-mode specifier indicates that a displacement will be used to compute the address of an operand, the displacement is encoded in the instruction. A displacement is a signed integer of 8, 16, or 32 bits. The 8-bit form is used when the displacement is sufficiently small.

• Immediate operand—This is the simplest type of operand specifier, where the value of the operand is given directly in the instruction. The number of bits in the immediate operand depends on the operand size of the instruction and on the opcode. If present, an immediate operand is always the last field in an instruction, coming after any opcode fields or address mode fields.

When present, this element provides the value of an operand of the instruction. Immediate operands may be 8, 6, or 32 bits wide. In cases where an 8-bit immediate operand is combined in some way with a 16- or 32-bit operand, the processor automatically extends the size of the 8-bit operand, taking into account the sign.

DESCRIPTION NOTATIONS

The following explains the notational conventions used and abbreviations used for illustrating the instruction set.

- **+rb, +rw, +rd** A register code, 0 through 7, which is added to the hexadecimal byte given at the left of the plus sign, in order to form a single opcode byte. The codes are:

rb	rw	rd
AL = 0	AX = 0	EAX = 0
CL = 1	CX = 1	ECX = 1
DL = 2	DX = 2	EDX = 2
BL = 3	BX = 3	EBX = 3
AH = 4	SP = 4	ESP = 4
CH = 5	BP = 5	EBP = 5
DH = 6	SI = 6	ESI = 6
BH = 7	DI = 7	EDI = 7

- **/digit** The digit is generally between 0 and 7. It indicates that the MOD R/M byte of the instruction uses only the register or memory (r/m) operand. The reg field contains the digit that provides an extension to the instruction opcode.

- **/r** This shows that the instruction MOD R/M byte contains both a register operand and an r/m operand.

- **cb, cw, cd, cp** A one-byte (cb), two-byte (cw), four-byte (cd), or a six-byte (cp) value that follows the opcode is used to specify a code offset and possibly a new value for the code segment register.

- **ib, iw, id** A one-byte (ib), two-byte (iw), or four-byte (id) immediate operand to the instruction that follows the opcode, MOD R/M bytes or scale-indexing bytes. The opcode determines if the operand is a signed value. Note that all words and doublewords are given with the low-order byte first.

- **imm8** An immediate byte value. imm8 is a signed number between −128 and +127, inclusive. For those instructions where imm8 combines with a word or doubleword operand, the immediate value is sign-extended to form a word or doubleword. The upper byte of the word/doubleword is filled with the topmost bit of the immediate value.

- **imm16** An immediate word value. It is used for instructions whose operand-size attribute is 16 bits. Inclusive, this number runs from −32768 to +32767.

- **imm32**   An immediate doubleword. imm32 is used for instructions whose operand-size attribute is 32 bits. The range of numbers is from -2147483648 to $+2147483647$ inclusive.

- **m8**   A memory byte. It is addressed by DS:SI or ES:DI.

- **m16**   A memory word. It is addressed by DS:SI or ES:DI.

- **m32**   A memory doubleword. It is addressed by DS:SI or ES:DI.

- **moffs8, moffs16, moffs32**   A memory offset. A simple memory variable of type BYTE, WORD, or DWORD, used by some variants of the MOV instruction. The actual address is given by a simple offset relative to the segment base. The number shown with the *moffs* indicates its size, which is determined by the address-size attribute of the instruction. No MOD R/M byte is used in the instruction.

- **ptr16:16, ptr16:32**   FAR pointer. Typically it is in a code segment different from that of the instruction. The notation 16:16 shows that the pointer value has two parts. The value to the left of the colon is the offset within the destination segment. The value to the right of the colon is a 16-bit selector or value destined for the code segment register. When the instruction operand has a size attribute of 16, use 16:16. For the 32-bit attribute, use 16:32.

- **r8**   One of the byte registers: AL, CL, DL, BL, AH, CH, DH, or BH.

- **r16**   One of the word registers: AX, CS, DX, BX, SP, BP, SI or DI.

- **r32**   One of the doubleword registers: EAX, ECX, EDX, EBX, ESP, EBP, ESI, or EDI.

- **rel8**   A relative address in the range from 128 bytes before the end of the instruction to 127 bytes after the end of the instruction.

- **rel16, rel32**   A relative address within the same code segment as the instruction assembled. rel16 is applied to instructions whose operand-size attribute is 16 bits. rel32 is applied to the instructions with a 32-bit operand-size attribute.

- **r/m8**   A one-byte operand. It is either the contents of a byte from memory or from a byte register—AL, BL, CL, DL, AH, BH, CH, or DH.

- **r/m16**   A word register or memory operand. It is used for instructions whose operand-size attribute is 16 bits. The contents of memory are found at the address provided by the effective address computation. The word registers are: AX, BX, CX, DX, SP, BP, SI and DI.

- **r/m32**   A doubleword register or memory operand. It is used for instructions whose operand-size attribute is 32 bits. The contents of memory are found at the address provided by the effective address computation. The doubleword registers are: EAX, EBX, ECX, EDX, ESP, EBP, ESI and EDI.

- **rrr**   When rrr appears in the binary equivalent column, it appears as the last three digits of the binary figure and indicates a particular register is referenced. The rrr translates to the following:

000	= AX/EAX	100	= SP/ESP
001	= CX/ECX	101	= BP/EBP
010	= DX/EDX	110	= SI/ESI
011	= BX/EBX	111	= DI/EDI

- **Sreg**   A segment register. The segment register bit assignments are ES = 0, CS = 1, SS = 2, DS = 3, FS = 4, and GS = 5.

DESCRIPTION OF MODIFIERS AND SPECIFICATIONS

In the descriptions that illustrate each instruction, there are some extensions that show modifiers, register specifications and register/memory specifications. The notation mm 00 r/m specifies memory and mm 11 r/m specifies rrr. A further explanation of how those interact with the opcode follows where:

> disp8 is an 8-byte displacement
> disp16 is a 16-byte displacement
> disp32 is a 32-byte displacement

8 Bit

rrr	8-bit registers	16- or 32-bit
000	AL	AX, EAX
001	CL	CX, ECX
010	DL	DX, EDX
011	BL	BX, EBX
100	AH	SP, ESP
101	CH	BC, EBP
110	DH	SI, ESI
111	BH	DI, EDI

16 Bit

r/m or mm	00	01	10	11
000	[BX + SI]	+ disp8	+ disp16	rrr
001	[BX + DI]			
010	[BP + SI]			
011	[BP + DI]			
100	[SI]			
101	[DI			
110	disp16	[BP] + disp8	[BP] + disp16	[BP] + disp16
111	[BX]	+ disp8	+ disp16	

32 Bit

r/m & mm	00	01	10	11
000	[EAX]	+ disp8	+ disp32	rrr
001	[ECX]	+ disp8		
010	[EDX]	+ disp8		
011	[EBX]	+ disp8		
100	SIB Follows			
101	disp32	[EBC + disp8	[EBP] + disp32	
110	[ESI]	[EBC] + disp8		
111	[EDI]			

Scaled-Index Byte (SIB)

Where SS = the scale factor:

SS		
	00	Times 1
	01	Times 2
	10	Times 4
	11	Times 8

Index	Base
000 EAX	000 EAX
001 ECX	001 ECX
010 EDX	010 EDX
011 EBX	011 EBX
100 None	100 ESP
101 EBP	101 Special
110 ESI	110 ESI
111 EDI	111 EDI

Addition notes: the instruction demonstrations show the various flags. If a flag changes after an instruction executes, that flag is shown in bold-face print.

AAA   ASCII Adjust After Addition

Instruction	Opcode	Binary
AAA	37	00110111

Purpose: AAA changes the contents of register AL to a valid unpacked decimal number and zeros the top four bits. AAA follows the addition of two unpacked decimal operands in AL, but it can be used for other BCD conversions also. If a decimal carry results from the addition, or the contents of the lower nibble of AL are greater than nine, then AL is incremented by six, AH is incremented by one, and the carry flag (CF) and auxiliary carry flag (AF) are set to one. If no decimal carry occurred, AH is unchanged, CF and AF are set to zero, and the lower four bits of AL are unchanged. Whether or not a decimal carry occurred, the upper four bits of AL are cleared.

Instruction Demonstration: This demonstration of the AAA instruction shows the adjustments made after addition to keep unpacked BCD as BCD even though the addition is binary.

The instruction sequence:

```
4C25:0000 B80800   MOV   AX,0008
4C25:0003 80C004   ADD   AL,04
4C25:0006 37       AAA
4C25:0007 80C004   ADD   AL,04
4C25:000A 37       AAA
```

The registers (which change) and flags at the start:

EAX = 00000000   IP = 0000   NV UP EI PL NZ NA PO NC

Note that an asterisk appears under each flag that has changed in that step.

```
4C25:0000 B80800         MOV      AX,0008
```

EAX = 00000008   IP = 0003   NV UP EI PL NZ NA PO NC

A pair of BCD digits (0,8) are loaded into AH,AL by the move into AX. The move does not affect the flags.

```
4C25:0003 80C004         ADD      AL,04
```

    EAX = 0000000C IP = 0006 NV UP EI PL NZ NA **PE** NC

The add of 4 only changes the value to 12 (hex C) and the parity flag.

    4C25:0006 37   AAA

    EAX = 00000102 IP = 0007 NV UP EI PL NZ **AC** PE **CY**

    The AAA instruction inspects AL for a value greater than nine. If it is, (in this case C, which is greater) 10 (hex A) is subtracted from AL, and 1 is added to AH. The adjust flag is set as is the carry flag indicating a BCD carry has occurred.

    4C25:0007 80C004   ADD   AL,04

    EAX = 00000106 IP = 000A NV UP EI PL NZ **NA** PE **NC**

    This add results in neither a carry nor an adjustment. Both flags are reset. The result of the addition is 06 a valid BCD digit.

    4C25:000A 37   AAA

    EAX = 00000106 IP = 000B NV UP EI PL NZ NA PE NC

    The result of the AAA is no change which is what would be expected since the value does not need any.

AAD   ASCII Adjust Register AX Before Division

Instruction	Opcode	Binary
AAD	D5 0A	11010101 00001010

    Purpose: AAD modifies the numerator in AH and AL, to prepare for the division of two valid unpacked decimal operands. The result of the modification is that the quotient produced by the division is a valid unpacked decimal number. AH should contain the high-order digit, and AL should contain the low-order digit. AAD adjusts the value and places the result in AL. AH will contain zero.

    Instruction Demonstration: AAD and AAM are demonstrated together because they reverse the action of the other. The effect of each is shown below.

    The instruction sequence:

```
4C25:0000 B80508          MOV       AX,0805
4C25:0003 D50A            AAD
4C25:0005 D40A            AAM
```

The registers and the flags at the start:

EAX = 00000000   IP = 0000   NV UP EI PL NZ NA PO NC

4C25:0000 B80508   MOV   AX,0805

EAX = 00000805   IP = 0003   NV UP EI PL NZ NA PO NC

The MOV has loaded two BCD digits into AX. The setting of the flags is unaffected by MOV.

4C25:0003 D50A   AAD

EAX = 00000055   IP = 0005   NV UP EI PL **NZ** NA **PE** NC

The result of the AAD is to combine the BCD digits and convert them to their binary equivalent (55 Hex = 85 decimal). The zero flag is set according to the result in AL (non zero in this case) as is the parity flag (to even in this case). If the sign flag were set to negative it would be set to positive for all valid conversions.

4C25:0005 D40A   AAM

EAX = 00000805   IP = 0007   NV UP EI PL NZ NA PE NC

The result of the AAM is to convert the value in the AL register into two BCD digits in AH and AL.

AAM   ASCII Adjust AX Register After Multiplication

Instruction	Opcode	Binary
AAM	D4 0A	11010100 00001010

Purpose: Two BCD digits multiplied together *may* produce an invalid BCD result. AAM corrects the result of a multiplication of two valid unpacked decimal numbers back into a pair of digits in AH and AL. AAM follows the multiplication of two decimal numbers to produce a valid result. The high-order digit is left in AH, the low-order in AL.

Instruction Demonstration: Demonstrated with AAD.

AAS   ASCII Adjust AL Register After Subtraction

Instruction	Opcode	Binary
AAS	3F	00111111

Purpose: AAS changes the contents of register AL to a valid unpacked decimal number and zeros the top four bits. AAS follows the subtraction of one unpacked decimal operand from another in AL. If a decimal borrow results from the subtraction, then AL is decremented by six, AH is decremented by one, and the carry flag (CF) and auxiliary carry flag (AF) flags are set. If no decimal carry occurred, AH is unchanged, CF and AF are set to zero, and the lower four bits of AL are unchanged. Whether a decimal carry occurred or not, the upper four bits of AL are cleared.

Instruction Demonstration: This demonstration of the AAS instruction shows its effect in BCD subtraction.

The instruction sequence:

```
4C25:0000 B80500          MOV      AX,0005
4C25:0003 80E804          SUB      AL,04
4C25:0006 3F              AAS
4C25:0007 80E804          SUB      AL,04
4C25:000A 3F              AAS
```

The registers (which change) and flags at the start:

EAX = 00000000 IP = 0000 NV UP EI PL NZ NA PO NC

```
4C25:0000 B80500          MOV      AX,0005
```

EAX = 00000005 IP = 0003 NV UP EI PL NZ NA PO NC

The move changes the register contents without changing the flags.

```
4C25:0003 80E804          SUB      AL,04
```

EAX = 00000001 IP = 0006 NV UP EI PL NZ NA PO NC

The result of the subtraction is still a positive value.

```
4C25:0006 3F              AAS
```

EAX = 00000001 IP = 0007 NV UP EI PL NZ NA PO NC

The AAS does not change the result or the flags because no adjustment is made.

  4C25:0007 80E804   SUB   AL,04

  EAX=000000FD IP=000A NV UP EI **NG** NZ **AC** PO **CY**

This subtract results in a negative value. The sign flag is set, the carry flag is set because of the borrow required to set the sign flag. The adjust flag is set because of the borrow from the high nibble of AL.

  4C25:000A 3F   AAS

  EAX=0000FF07 IP=000B NV UP EI NG NZ AC PO CY

The result of the AAS is to set the proper decimal value in AL and to subtract one from AH. The carry and auxiliary carry flags are set according to the result (since these flags were set prior to the AAS no change is indicated).

ADC   Add Integers with Carry

Instruction	Opcode	Binary
ADC AL,imm8	14 ib	00010100
ADC AX,imm16	15 iw	00010100
ADC EAX,imm32	15 id	00010101
ADC r/m8,imm8	90 /2 ib	10010000 mm 010 r/m
ADC r/m16,imm16	90 /2 /w	10010000 mm 010 r/m
ADC r/m32,imm32	91 /2 id	10010001 mm 010 r/m
ADC r/m16,imm8	93 /2 ib	10010011 mm rrr r/m
ADC r/m32,imm8	93 /2 ib	10010011 mm rrr r/m
ADC r/m8,r8	10 /r	00010000 mm rrr r/m
ADC r/m16,r16	11 /r	00010001 mm rrr r/m
ADC r/m32,r32	11 /r	00010001 mm rrr r/m
ADC r8,r/m8	12 /r	00010010 mm rrr r/m
ADC r16,r/m16	13 /r	00010011 mm rrr r/m
ADC r32,r/m32	13 /r	00010011 mm rrr r/m

Purpose: ADC sums the operands, adds one if the carry flag (CF) is set and replaces the destination operand with the result. If CF is cleared, ADC does the same operation as the ADD instruction. An ADD followed by multiple ADC instructions can be used to add numbers longer than 32 bits.

Instruction Demonstration: This demonstration of the ADC instruction shows the effect of the carry flag being set on when the instruction is executed. Note that the carry flag being set adds one to the sum.

The instruction sequence:

```
4C25:0000 29C0              SUB      AX,AX
4C25:0002 80C040            ADD      AL,40
4C25:0005 80D040            ADC      AL,40
4C25:0008 80D080            ADC      AL,80
4C25:000B 80D080            ADC      AL,80
```

The registers (which change) and flags at the start:

EAX = 00000000 IP = 0000 NV UP EI PL NZ NA PO NC

First ensure a clear register.

```
4C25:0000 29C0              SUB      AX,AX
```

EAX = 00000000 IP = 0002 NV UP EI PL **ZR** NA **PE** NC

The sequence of ADCs begins with an ADD which ignores the state of the carry flag. This would normally be the add of the lowest order numbers in the extended summation. The carry flag could have been forced off with the CLC (clear carry) instruction also.

```
4C25:0002 80C040            ADD      AL,40
```

EAX = 00000040 IP = 0005 NV UP EI PL **NZ** NA **PO** NC

ADD changes the value of the register and the flags change to reflect the result.

```
4C25:0005 80D040            ADC      AL,40
```

EAX = 00000080 IP = 0008 **OV** UP EI **NG** NZ NA PO NC

Note that because the sign bit (the high-order bit of the register) is now set, the minus flag is also set. Also note that the overflow flag has been set because the result cannot be contained in the target register as a signed quantity.

```
4C25:0008 80D080            ADC      AL,80
```

EAX = 00000000 IP = 000B OV UP EI **PL ZR** NA **PE CY**

This addition caused a carry out of the register (AL). The carry flag is now set. (Note the effect on the next ADC instruction.) It also left a sum of zero as its result.

This caused the zero flag and even parity to be set. Because zero has a sign bit of zero, the sign flag is set to positive.

        4C25:000B 80D080   ADC   AL,80

        EAX=00000081   IP=000E   **NV** UP EI **NG NZ** NA PE **NC**

Because the carry flag was on, an additional 1 was added in the operation. This result did not cause a carry so the carry flag is reset. Because the result is not zero, the zero flag is also reset.

ADD   Add Integers

Instruction	Opcode	Binary
ADD AL,imm8	04 ib	00000100
ADD AX,imm16	05 /w	00000101
ADD EAX,imm32	05 id	00000101
ADD r/m8,imm8	80 /0 ib	10000000 mm 000 r/m
ADD r/m16,imm16	81 /0 iw	10000001 mm 000 r/m
ADD r/m32,imm32	81 /0 id	10000001 mm 000 r/m
ADD r/m16,imm8	83 /0 ib	10000011 mm 000 r/m
ADD r/m32,imm8	83 /0 ib	10000011 mm 000 r/m
ADD r/m8,r8	00 /r	00000000 mm rrr r/m
ADD r/m16,r16	01 /r	00000001 mm rrr r/m
ADD r/m32,r32	01 /r	00000001 mm rrr r/m
ADD r8,r/m8	02 /r	00000010 mm rrr r/m
ADD r16,r/m16	03 /r	00000011 mm rrr r/m
ADD r32,r/m32	03 /r	00000011 mm rrr r/m

Purpose: ADD replaces the destination operation with the sum of the source and destination operands. It sets the carry flag (CF) it there is an overflow. CF is bit zero of the EFLAGS register (see appendix H).

Instruction Demonstration: This demonstration of the ADD instruction shows that it executes its addition without interrogating the carry flag.

The instruction sequence:

        4C13:0000 6629C0   SUB   EAX,EAX
        4C13:0003 80C040   ADD   AL,40
        4C13:0006 80C040   ADD   AL,40
        4C13:0009 80C080   ADD   AL,80
        4C13:000C 80C040   ADD   AL,40

The registers and flags at the start:

EAX = 00000000   IP = 0000   NV UP EI PL NZ NA PO NC

4C13:0000 6629C0   SUB   EAX,EAX

EAX = 00000000   IP = 0003   NV UP EI PL **ZR** NA **PE** NC

The subtract ensures the register contents are zero. It also sets the zero and parity flags.

4C13:0003 80C040   ADD   AL,40

EAX = 00000040   IP = 0006   NV UP EI PL **NZ** NA **PO** NC

The ADD sets the parity flag to odd because the number of bits in the low eight bits is odd. The zero flag is reset because the result of the addition is not zero.

4C13:0006 80C040   ADD   AL,40

EAX = 00000080   IP = 0009   **OV** UP EI **NG** NZ NA PO NC

The result of the addition cannot be contained as a signed 8-bit number so the overflow flag is set. The sign bit (of AL) is also set, which causes the sign flag to be set to negative.

4C13:0009 80C080   ADD   AL,80

EAX = 00000000   IP = 000C   OV UP EI **PL ZR** NA **PE CY**

This ADD causes a carry out of the target register. The carry flag is set. Because the result has a zero sign bit, the sign flag changes to positive. The result is a zero register so the zero flag is set.

4C13:000C 80C040   ADD   AL,40

EAX = 00000040   IP = 000F   **NV** UP EI PL **NZ** NA **PO NC**

This ADD changes the zero flag to non zero, resets the carry flag, and changes the parity flag to odd. Note that the state of the carry flag does not affect the result of the instruction.

AND   Logical AND

Instruction	Opcode	Binary
AND AL,imm8	24 ib	00100100
AND AX,imm6	25 iw	00100101
AND EAX,imm32	25 id	00100101
AND r/m8,imm8	A0 /4 ib	10100000 mm 100 r/m
AND r/m16,imm16	A1 /4 iw	10100001 mm 100 r/m
AND r/m32,imm32	A1 /4 ib	10100001 mm 100 r/m
AND r/m16,imm8	A3 /4 ib	10100011 mm 100 r/m
AND r/m32,imm8	A3 /4 ib	10100011 mm 100 r/m
AND r/m8,r8	20 /r	00100000 mm rrr r/m
AND r/m16,r16	21 /r	00100001 mm rrr r/m
AND r/m32,r32	21 /r	00100001 mm rrr r/m
AND r8,r/m8	22 /r	00100010 mm rrr r/m
AND r16,r/m16	23 /r	00100011 mm rrr r/m
AND r32,r/m32	23 /r	00100011 mm rrr r/m

Purpose: AND is used to ensure that user-specified bits are off, for example, the parity bit in an ASCII input stream from a terminal. When AND is used in conjunction with a compare, AND makes certain that the specified bits are on. In use, AND is executed prior to the compare. Both AND and the compare use known masks.

Instruction Demonstration: This demonstration of the AND instruction shows its effect as it is used to mask bits of its destination off.

The instruction sequence:

```
4C20:0000 66B8EE11F0F0         MOV      EAX,F0F011EE
4C20:0006 81E0FFFF             AND      AX,FFFF
4C20:000A 81E0F5F5             AND      AX,F5F5
4C20:000E 81E0123E             AND      AX,3E12
4C20:0012 676681E0EE11F000 AND          EAX,00F011EE
```

The registers and flags at the start:

EAX = 00000000   IP = 0000 NV UP EI PL NZ NA PO NC

```
4C20:0000 66B8EE11F0F0         MOV      EAX,F0F011EE
```

EAX = F0F011EE   IP = 0006   NV UP EI PL NZ NA PO NC

MOV sets the register value with no changes to the flags.

    4C20:0006 81E0FFFF   AND   AX,FFFF

    EAX=F0F011EE IP=000A NV UP EI PL NZ NA **PE** NC

Note that ANDing with a mask which has all bits set does not affect the target. It does set the carry flag off, sets the parity flag, and the zero flag according to the result. It also sets overflow off and the sign flag according to the result. Note also that the extended register bits are not affected.

    4C20:000A 81E0F5F5   AND   AX,F5F5

    EAX=F0F011E4 IP=000E NV UP EI PL NZ NA PE NC

This AND has masked out bits 0 and 2 of the low nibble. The result is nonzero with even parity so no flags change.

    4C20:000E 81E0123E   AND   AX,3E12

    EAX=F0F01000 IP=0012 NV UP EI PL NZ NA PE NC

This AND has masked the value in AL to zero, leaving AX with only one bit in AH. Note the parity, which is calculated on the low eight bits of the result is even. The zero flag is nonzero because it is set based on the total result.

    4C20:0012 676681E0EE11F000 AND   EAX,00F011EE

    EAX=00F01000 IP=001A NV UP EI PL NZ NA PE NC

This AND affects the high bits of EAX. Note the address and the width prefixes necessary because of the 16-bit width default which must be overridden.

ARPL Adjust Requester Privilege Level of Selector

Instruction	Opcode	Binary
ARPL r/m16,r16	63 /r	01100011 mm rrr r/m

Purpose: ARPL is used by systems software to guarantee that selector parameters to a subroutine do not request more privilege than allowed to the caller. (Appendix H gives an overview of the 80386, and also discusses selectors and descriptors.) ARPL has two operands. The first is a 16-bit word register or memory variable that contains the value of the selector. The second operand is generally a register that contains the caller CS (code segment) selector value.

ARPL checks that the requested privilege level (RPL) of the first operand against the RPL of the second. The RPL is specified in the least significant bits of each operand. If RPL of the first operand is less than that of the second, the zero flag (ZF) is set to one.

Instruction Demonstration: The ARPL instruction is used by system software to validate selectors passed as parameter pointers. It checks a selector against a model which contains the maximum privilege allowed (usually the caller CS selector is used) and adjusts the tested value to the lesser of the privilege levels (highest number). If no change is necessary, the zero flag is reset. If a change was needed, the zero flag is set (a possible attempt to breach security).

The instruction sequence:

```
0070:0100 8CCB          MOV     BX,CS
0070:0102 B87300        MOV     AX,0073
0070:0105 63C3          ARPL    BX,AX
```

The registers and flags at the start:

EAX=00000000 EBX=00000000 CS=0070 IP=0100   NV UP EI PL NZ NA PO NC

For the purpose of the demonstration, the normal was reversed, and CS was the tested value (the demonstration was done at level 0).

```
0070:0100 8CCB          MOV     BX,CS
```

EAX=00000000 EBX=00000070 CS=0070 IP=0102   NV UP EI PL NZ NA PO NC

Set a comparand with a lower privilege (3).

```
0070:0102 B87300        MOV     AX,0073
```

EAX=00000073 EBX=00000070 CS=0070 IP=0105   NV UP EI PL NZ NA PO NC

Issue the ARPL, which adjusts the tested descriptor to the least privilege and sets the zero flag because the adjustment was needed.

```
0070:0105 63C3          ARPL    BX,AX
```

EAX=00000073 EBX=00000073 CS=0070 IP=0107   NV UP EI PL **ZR** NA PO NC

BOUND   Check Array Index Against Bounds

Instruction	Opcode	Binary
BOUND r16,m16&16	62 /r	01100010 mm rrr r/m
BOUND r32,m32&32	62 /r	01100010 mm rrr r/m

Purpose: BOUND verifies that the signed value contained in the specified register lies within specified limits. Interrupt 5 occurs if the value in the register is less than the lower bound or greater than the upper bound. The upper- and lower-limit values can each be a word or a doubleword.

The block of memory that specifies the lower and upper limits of an array may typically reside just before the array itself. This makes the array bounds accessible at a constant offset from the beginning of the array. Because the address of the array is already present in a register, extra calculations to obtain the effective address of the array bounds are avoided.

BOUND includes two operands. The first specifies the register being tested. The second contains the effective address of the two signed BOUND limit values. BOUND assumes that the upper limit and the lower limit are in adjacent memory locations. These limit values cannot be register operands. If they are, an invalid opcode exception occurs.

BSF   Bit Scan Forward

Instruction	Opcode	Binary
BSF r16,r/m16	0F BC	00001111 10111100 mm rrr r/m
BSF r32,r/m32	0F BC	00001111 10111100 mm rrr r/m

Purpose: This instruction scans a word or doubleword (from the least significant bit to the most significant bit) for a one-bit and stores the number of the first set bit into a register. The bit string being scanned can be either in a register or in memory. The zero flag (ZF) is set if the entire word is zero; that is, no set bits are found. ZF is cleared if a one bit is found. ZF is bit six of the EFLAGS register (see appendix H).

Note: If no set bit is found, the value of the destination register is undefined.

This instruction is new with the 80386. It is useful for scanning allocation bitmaps for an allocatable or free bit. Returning the number of the bit provides the relative number of the item within the word being examined.

BSR   Bit Scan Reverse

Instruction	Opcode	Binary
BSR r16,r/m16	0F BD	00001111 10111101 mm rrr r/m
BSR r32,r/m32	0F BD	00001111 10111101 mm rrr r/m

Purpose: This instruction scans a word or doubleword (from the most significant bit to the least significant bit) for a one bit and stores the index of the first set bit into a register. The bit string being scanned can be either in a register or in memory. The zero flag (ZF) is set if the entire word is zero; that is, no set bits are found. ZF is cleared if a one bit is found. ZF is bit six of the EFLAGS register (see appendix H). BSR is a new instruction with the 80386.

Note: If no set bit is found, the value of the destination register is undefined.

BT   Bit Test

Instruction	Opcode	Binary
BT r/m16,r16	0F A3	00001111 10100011 mm rrr r/m
BT r/m32,r32	0F A3	00001111 10100011 mm rrr r/m
BT r/m16,imm8	0F BA /r ib	00001111 10111010 mm 100 r/m
BT r/m32,imm8	0F BA /r ib	00001111 10111010 mm 100 r/m

Purpose: BT is a means of determining if a bit in a bitmap is set or not. BT sets the carry flag (CF) to the same value as the bit being tested. This instruction is new with the 80386. Do not use BT to reference memory-mapped I/O registers directly. Use MOV to load from or store to the memory-mapped device registers and then use the register form of BT.

BTC   Bit Test and Complement

Instruction	Opcode	Binary
BTC r/m16,r16	0F BB	00001111 10111011 mm rrr r/m
BTC r/m32,r32	0F BB	00001111 10111011 mm rrr r/m
BTC r/m16,imm8	0F BA /7 ib	00001111 10111010 mm 111 r/m
BTC r/m32,imm8	0F BA /7 ib	00001111 10111010 mm 111 r/m

Purpose: BTC tests a specific bit, copies that bit to the carry flag (CF—bit zero of the EFLAGS register), and inverts the original bit (for example, if the bit was a one, it is changed to a zero, and CF set to one). This instruction is new with the 80386. Do not use BTC to reference memory-mapped I/O registers directly. Use MOV to load from or store to the memory-mapped device registers and then use the register form of BTC.

BTS   Bit Test and Set

Instruction	Opcode	Binary
BTS r/m16,r16	0F AB	00001111 10101011 mm rrr r/m

```
BTS r/m32,r32     0F AB        00001111 10101011 mm rrr r/m
BTS r/m16,imm8    0F BA /5 ib  00001111 10111010 mm 101 r/m
BTS r/m32,imm8    0F BA /5 ib  00001111 10111010 mm 101 r/m
```

Purpose: BTS tests a specific bit, copies that bit to the carry flag (CF—bit zero of the EFLAGS register), and sets the original bit to one. This instruction is new with the 80386. Do not use BTC to reference memory-mapped I/O registers directly. Use MOV to load from or store to the memory-mapped device registers, and then use the register form of BTS.

CALL   Call a Procedure

Instruction	Opcode	Binary
CALL rel16	E8 cw	11101000
CALL r/m16	FF /2	11111111 mm 010 r/m
CALL ptr16:16	9A cd	10011010
CALL m16:16	FF /3	11111111 mm 011 r/m
CALL rel32	E8 cd	11101000
CALL r/m32	FF /2	11111111 mm 010 r/m
CALL ptr16:32	9A cp	10011010
CALL ptr32:32	9A cp	10011010
CALL m16:32	FF /3	11111111 mm 011 r/m

Purpose: CALL transfers control from one code segment location to another. These locations can be within the same code segment (near) or in different ones (far). Prior to actual transfer, CALL saves the address of the instruction following the CALL, and the current value of extended instruction pointer (EIP) on the stack.

CALL instructions have relative, direct, and indirect versions. Indirect instructions specify an absolute address in one of two ways: (1) the 80386 can obtain the destination address from a memory operand specified in the instruction, or (2) the program CALLs a location specified by a general register (EAX, EDX, ECX, EBX, EBP, ESI, or EDI).

CBW   Convert Byte to Word

CWDE   Convert Word to Doubleword

Instruction	Opcode	Binary
CBW	98	10011000
CWDE	99	10011001

Purpose: These instructions extend the sign bit into the top portion of the larger register so that arithmetic operations can occur with correct results. The value of bit seven of AX or bit 15 of EAX is placed in every bit of AH or the upper 16 bits of EAX.

CLC   Clear Carry Flag (CF)

Instruction	Opcode	Binary
CLC	F8	11111000

Purpose: This instruction sets the carry flag (CF—bit zero of the EFLAGS register) to zero. No other flags are affected.

CLD   Clear Direction Flag (DF)

Instruction	Opcode	Binary
CLD	FC	11111100

Purpose: CLD sets the direction flag (DF—bit 10 of the EFLAGS register) to zero. No other flags are affected. By setting DF to zero, DF now signals the automatic indexing feature to increment the index registers ESI and EDI. Automatic indexing is used by string instructions.

CLI   Clear Interrupt Flag (IF)

Instruction	Opcode	Binary
CLI	FA	11111010

Purpose: If the current privilege level is at least as privileged as the input/output privilege level (IOPL—bits 12 and 13 of the EFLAGS register), CLI sets the interrupt flag (IF—bit 9 of EFLAGS) to zero. No other flags are affected. An exception is raised if the program does not have the correct I/O privilege.

Note: External interrupts are ignored at the end of CLI until the interrupt flag is set.

CLTS   Clear Task-Switched Flag in Control Register Zero (CR0)

Instruction	Opcode	Binary
CLTS	0F 06	00001111 00000110

Purpose: CLTS sets the task-switched bit (TS bit in CR0) to zero. TS is set to one by the 80386 at each occurrence of a task switch. If a task switch has occurred and the new task attempts to use the 80387 coprocessor, a fault occurs. The fault handler must save the content of the 80387 and execute a CLTS instruction. The new task can then use the 80387 without destroying any data of the previous task. This way, only tasks which use the 80387 incur the overhead of saving the prior state of the 80387.

Note: CLTS is used in systems programming. It is a privileged instruction, running at privilege level zero only.

CMC   Complement Carry Flag (CF)

Instruction	Opcode	Binary
CMC	F5	11110101

Purpose: CMC reverses the value of the carry flag (CF—bit zero of the EFLAGS register), for example, CF becomes a zero if it was a one. No other flags are affected. EFLAGS is described in appendix H.

CMP   Compare

Instruction	Opcode	Binary
CMP AL, imm8	3C ib	00111100
CMP AX,imm16	3D iw	00111101
CMP EAX,imm32	3D id	00111101
CMP r/m8,imm8	80 /7 ib	10000000 mm 111 r/m
CMP r/m16,imm16	81 /7 iw	10000001 mm 111 r/m
CMP r/m32,imm32	81 /7 id	10000001 mm 111 r/m
CMP r/m16,imm8	83 /7 ib	10000011 mm 111 r/m
CMP r/m32,imm8	83 /7 ib	10000011 mm 111 r/m
CMP r/m8,r8	38 /r	00111000 mm rrr r/m
CMP r/m16,r16	39 /r	00111001 mm rrr r/m
CMP r/m32,r32	39 /r	00111001 mm rrr r/m
CMP r8,m8	3A /r	00111010 mm rrr r/m
CMP r16,r/m16	3B /r	00111011 mm rrr r/m
CMP r32,r/m32	3B /r	00111011 mm rrr r/m

Purpose: CMP subtracts the source operand from the destination operand but does not store the result. Only the flags are changed. That is, CMP updates the overflow flag (OF—bit 11 of EFLAGS), the sign flag (SF—bit 7 of EFLAGS), the zero flag (ZF—bit 6 of EFLAGS), the auxiliary carry flag (AF—bit 4 of EFLAGS), the parity flag (PF—bit 2 of EFLAGS), and the carry flag (CF—bit 0 of EFLAGS), but does not alter the source and destination operands. EFLAGS is described in appendix H.

CMPS   Compare String Operands

CMPSB   Compare String - Byte

CMPSW   Compare String - Word

CMPSD   Compare String - Doubleword

Instruction	Opcode	Binary
CMPS m8,m8	A6	10100110
CMPS m16,m16	A7	10100111
CMPS m32,m32	A7	10100111

Note:

CMPSB is a common assembler mnemonic for CMPS m8,m8
CMPSW is a common assembler mnemonic for CMPS m16,m16
CMPSD is a common assembler mnemonic for CMPS m32,m32

Purpose: These instructions operate on strings rather than on logical or numerical values. They operate on one element of a string, which may be a byte, a word, or a doubleword. The string elements are addressed by the registers ESI and EDI. After each string operation, ESI and/or EDI are automatically updated to point to the next element of the string. If DF is zero, the index registers are incremented. If DF is one, they are decremented. The amount incremented or decremented is one, two, or four, depending on the size of the string element.

CMPS subtracts the destination string element (at ES:EDI) from the source string element (at DS:ESI). It then updates the flags auxiliary carry flag (AF—bit 4 of the EFLAGS register), the sign flag (SF—bit 7 of EFLAGS), parity flag (PF—bit 2 of EFLAGS), the carry flag (CF—bit 0 of EFLAGS), and the overflow flag (OF—bit 11 of EFLAGS). (See appendix H for a description of EGLAGS.) If the string elements are equal, ZF is set to 1; otherwise, ZF is set to 0. If DF is 0, the 80386 increments the memory pointers ESI and EDI for two strings. The segment register used for the source address can be changed with a segment register override prefix. The destination segment register cannot be overridden.

The assembler always translates CMPS into one of the oher types. CMPSB compares bytes. CMPSW compares words. CMPSD compares doublewords.

If the REPE or REPNE prefix modifies this instruction, the 80386 compares the value of the destination string element to the value of the source string element. It then steps SI and DI in the direction indicated by DF by the indicated size, until either the REPE/REPNE condition is false or ECX counts to 0.

CWD   Convert Word to Doubleword

CDQ   Convert Doubleword to Quad-Word

CWDE   Convert Word to Doubleword Extended

Instruction	Opcode	Binary
CWD	99	10011001
CDQ	99	10011001

Note: CDQ is for the 32-bit mode.

Purpose: CWD doubles the size of the source operand. CWD extends the sign of the word in register AX throughout register DX. CWD can be used to produce a doubleword dividend from a word before a word division.

CWDE extends the sign of the word in register AX throughout EAX.

CDQ extends the sign of the doubleword in EAX throughout EDX. CDQ can be used to produce a quad-word dividend from a doubleword before doubleword division.

DAA   Decimal Adjust AL Register After Addition

Instruction	Opcode	Binary
DAA	27	00100111

Purpose: DAA adjusts the result of adding two valid packed decimal operands in AL. DAA must always follow the addition of two pairs of packed decimal numbers (one digit in each half byte) to obtain a pair of valid packed decimal digits as results.

If the low nibble of AL is greater than nine, AF is set and six added to AL. Otherwise AF is reset. If the high nibble is greater than 9h or the carry flag (CF) is set, then add 60h to AL and set CF. Otherwise, CF is reset.

DAS   Decimal Adjust AL Register After Subtraction

Instruction	Opcode	Binary
DAS	2F	00101111

Purpose: DAS adjusts the result of subtracting two valid packed decimal operands in AL. DAS follows subtraction of one pair of packed decimal numbers (one digit in each half byte) from another to obtain a pair of valid packed decimal digits as results. If the low nibble of AL is greater than nine or if auxiliary carry flag (AF—bit 4 of the EFLAGS register) is set, then AL has six subtracted from it and AF is set. Otherwise, AF is reset. If the high nibble of AL is greater than 9h or the carry flag (CF—bit 0 of EFLAGS) bit is set, then AL has 60h subtracted from it, and CF is set. Otherwise, CF is reset.

DEC   Decrement by One

Instruction	Opcode	Binary
DEC r/m8	FE /1	11111110 mm 001 r/m
DEC r/m16	FF /1	11111111 mm 001 r/m
DEC r/m32	FF /1	11111111 mm 001 r/m
DEC r16	48 + rw	01001rrr
DEC r32	48 + rw	01001rrr

Purpose: DEC subtracts one from the destination operand and replaces the result into the destination operand. DEC does not update the carry flag (CF—bit 0 of the EFLAGS register). Use SUB with an operand of one if a carry flag update is desired.

DIV   Unsigned Integer Divide

Instruction	Opcode	Binary
DIV AL,r/m8	F6 /6	11110110 mm 110 r/m
DIV AX,r/m16	F7 /6	11110111 mm 110 r/m
DIV EAX,r/m32	F7 /6	11110111 mm 110 r/m

Purpose: DIV divides an unsigned number in the accumulator by the source operand. The dividend (which is the accumulator) is twice the size of the divisor (which is the source operand); the dividend is AX, DC:AX, or EDX:EAX, for divisors of 8, 16, or 32 bits. The quotient and the remainder have the same size as the divisor. The quotient is placed in AL, AX, or EAX for 8-, 16-, or 32-bit operands, respectively. The remainder is in AH, DX, or EDX.

A divisor of zero or a quotient too large for the designated register causes an 80386 interrupt zero (0). Figure B-3 summarizes the registers and operands for DIV.

Note: Non-integer quotients are truncated to integers. The remainder is always less than the divisor. For unsigned byte division, the largest quotient is 255. For unsigned word division, the largest quotient is 65,535. For unsigned doubleword division, the largest quotient is $2^{32} - 1$.

ENTER   Make Stack Frame for Procedure Parameter

Instruction	Opcode	Binary
ENTER imm16,0	C8 iw 00	11001000
ENTER imm16,1	C8 /2 01	11001000
ENTER imm16,imm8	C8 iw ib	11001000

Length of Operand 1	Dividend	Divisor	Quotient	Remainder
8	AX	Operand 1	AL	AH
16	DS:AX	Operand 1	AX	DX
32	EDX:EAX	Operand 1	EAX	EDX

Fig. B-3. Summary of Registers and Operands for DIV.

Purpose: ENTER creates a stack frame that can be used to implement the rules of block-structured, high-level languages. A LEAVE instruction at the end of the procedure complements the ENTER.

ENTER has two parameters. The first specifies the number of bytes of dynamic storage to be allocated on the stack for the routine being entered. The second parameter corresponds to the lexical nesting level of the routine: 0 to 31. This level determines how many sets of stack frame pointers the CPU copies into the new stack frame from the proceeding frame. This list of stack frames is often called the display. Lexical level has no relationship to either the protection levels or to the I/O privilege level.

ENTER creates the new display for a procedure. Then it allocates the dynamic storage space for that procedure by decrementing ESP by the number of bytes specified in the first parameter. This new value of ESP serves as the starting point for all PUSH and POP operations within that procedure.

ENTER can be used either nested or non-nested. If the lexical level is zero, the non-nested form is used. The main procedure operates at the highest logical level, level 1. The first procedure it calls operates at the next deeper level, level 2. And so on. A level 2 procedure can access the variables in the main program because a program operating at a higher logical level (calling a program at a lower level) requires that the called procedure have access to the variables of the calling program.

A procedure calling another procedure at the same level implies that they are parallel procedures and should not have access to the variables of the calling program. The new stack frame does not include the pointer for addressing the calling procedure stack frame. ENTER treats a re-entrant procedure as a procedure calling another procedure at the same level.

HLT   Halt

Instruction	Opcode	Binary
HLT	F4	11110100

Purpose: HALT stops the execution of all instructions and places the 80386 in a HALT state. AN NMI, reset, or an enabled interrupt will resume execution. An HLT would normally be the last instruction in a sequence which shuts down the system (that is, for a checkpoint after a power failure is detected).

IDIV   Signed Divide

Instruction	Opcode	Binary
IDIV r/m8	F6 /7	11110110 mm 111 r/m
IDIV AX,r/m16	F7 /7	11110111 mm 111 r/m
IDIV EAX,r/m32	F7 /7	11110111 mm 111 r/m

Purpose: IDIV does signed division. The dividend, quotient, and remainder are implicitly allocated to fixed registers (see below), while only the divisor is given as an explicit r/m (register or memory) operand. The divisor determines which registers are used. Figure B-4 shows which registers to use for IDIV. Nonintegral quotients are truncated toward zero. Remainders are always the same sign as the dividend and always have less magnitude than the divisor.

Size	Divisor	Quotient	Remainder	Dividend
Byte	r/m 8	AL	AH	AX
Word	r/m 16	AX	DX	DX:AX
Dword	r/m 32	EAX	EDX	EDX:EAX

Fig. B-4. Registers to Use for IDIV.

An 80386 interrupt zero (0) is taken if a zero divisor or a quotient too large for the destination register is generated. If a divide by zero occurs, the quotient and remainder are undefined.

IMUL   Signed Integer Multiply

Instruction	Opcode	Binary
IMUL r/m8	F6 /5	11110110 mm 101 r/m
IMUL r/m16	F7 /5	11110111 mm 101 r/m
IMUL r/m32	F7 /5	11110111 mm 101 r/m
IMUL r16,r/m16	0F AF /r	00001111 10101111 mm rrr r/m
IMUL r32,r/m32	0F AF /r	00001111 10101111 mm rrr r/m

IMUL r16,r/m16,imm8	6B /r ib	01101011 mm rrr r/m
IMUL r32,r/m32,imm8	6B /r ib	01101011 mm rrr r/m
IMUL r16,imm8	6B /r ib	01101011 mm rrr r/m
IMUL r32,imm8	6B /r ib	01101011 mm rrr r/m
IMUL r16,r/m16,imm16	69 /r iw	01101001 mm rrr r/m
IMUL r32,r/m32,imm32	69 /r id	01101001 mm rrr r/m
IMUL r16,imm16	69 /r iw	01101001 mm rrr r/m
IMUL r32,imm32	69 /r id	01101001 mm rrr r/m

Purpose: IMUL performs a signed multiplication operation. This instruction has three variations:

- A one-operand form. The operand can be a byte, word, or doubleword located in memory or in a general register. IMUL uses EAX and EDX as implicit operands in the same way that MUL does.

- A two-operand form. One of the source operands can be in any general register while the other can be either in memory or in a general register. The product replaces the general-register operand. If the result is within the range of the first operand, CF and OF are zero. Otherwise, CF and OF are set to 1.

- A three-operand form. The second and third operands are source, and the first operand is the destination. One of the source operands is an immediate value stored in the instruction. The second can be in memory or in any general register. The product can be stored in any general register. The immediate operand is treated as signed. If the immediate operand is a byte, the processor automatically sign-extends it to the size of the second operand before doing the multiplication. If the result is within the range of the first operand, CF and OF are 0. Otherwise, CF and OF are set to 1.

IN   Input from Port

Instruction	Opcode	Binary
IN AL,imm8	E4 ib	11100100
IN AX,imm8	E5 ib	11100101
IN EAX,imm8	E5 ib	11100101
IN AL,DX	EC	11101100
IN AX,DX	ED	11101101
IN EAX,DX	ED	11101101

Purpose: IN brings a byte, word, or dword from a specified port and stores it in a register AL, AX, or EAX, respectively. The port is specified by the second operand and is in the range of 0 to 64K – 1. The port is accessed by using an immediate operand or by placing its number into the DX register and using an IN instruction with DX as the second parameter. The immediate byte allows ports 0 to 255 to be accessed, in which case the upper bits of the port are always zero. The register form (DX) allows for the full range to be used. An exception occurs if the current task has insufficient privilege for the I/O.

INC   Increment by 1

Instruction	Opcode	Binary
INC r/m8	FE /0	11111110 mm 000 r/m
INC r/m16	FF /0	11111111 mm 000 r/m
INC r/m32	FF /0	11111111 mm 000 r/m
INC r16	40 + rw	01000rrr
INC r32	40 + rd	01000rrr

Purpose: INC adds one to the destination operand, but (unlike ADD) INC does not affect CF. Other flags are set according to the result. Use ADD with an operand of 1 if the carry flag update is desired.

INS   Input String from Port

INSB   Input Byte

INSW   Input Word

INSD   Input Doubleword

Instruction	Opcode	Binary
INS r/m8,DX	6C	01101100
INS r/m16,DX	6D	01101101
INS r/m32,DX	6D	01101101

Note:

INSB is a common assembler mnemonic for INS r/m8,DX
INSW is a common assembler mnemonic for INS r/m16,DX
INSD is a common assembler mnemonic for INS r/m32,DX

Purpose: These instructions allow a read from a specified device into memory (ES:EDI), the input device being specified in the DX register. After the transfer is made, EDI is updated to point to the next string location, depending on how DF (the direction flag) is set. If DF = 0, EDI increments by 1, 2, or 4. If DF = 1, EDI is decremented by −1, −2, or −4. The data is read into the segment specified by ES and no segment override is possible. INS does not allow port number specification as an immediate value. The port must be addressed through DX.

These instructions normally use a REP prefix to indicate the reading of the number of bytes as specified in CX.

An exception is raised if the current task has insufficient privilege to perform I/O.

INT   Call to Interrupt Procedure

INTO   Interrupt on Overflow

Instruction	Opcode	Binary
INT 3	CC	11001100
INT imm8	CD ib	11001101
INTO	CE	11001110

Purpose: INT transfers control from one code segment location to another. These locations can be within the same code segment (*near*) or in different code segments (*far*). INT is a software-generated interrupt that allows a programmer to transfer control to an interrupt service routine from within a program.

When any of the INTs are used, the flags register, the code segment register, and the instruction pointer are pushed onto the stack. When CS is PUSHed onto the stack, a full 32-bit word is PUSHed. This keeps the stack aligned which improves the 80386 performance.

INT *n* activates the interrupt service that corresponds to the number coded in the instruction. INT can specify any interrupt type. Note that interrupts 0–31 are reserved by Intel. INT *n* returns control at the end of the service routine with an IRET.

INTO invokes interrupt 4 if the overflow flag (OF) is set, and interrupt 4 is reserved for this purpose. OF is set by several arithmetic, logical, and string instructions. See appendix H for a discussion of where the various flags are stored.

INT 3 is a single-byte form (the breakpoint instruction) that is useful for debugging.

IRET   Return from Interrupt

IRETD   Return from Interrupt—32-bit mode

Instruction	Opcode	Binary
IRET	CF	11001111
IRETD	CF	11001111

Purpose: IRET returns control to an interrupted procedure. IRET differs from RET in that it also POPs the flags register, the code segment register, and the instruction pointer from the stack. The registers are PUSHed onto the stack by the interrupt mechanism. When CS is POPed, the full 32-bit word is POPed for stack alignment, and the upper 16 bits are discarded. Stack alignment improves 80386 performance.

Note: In the case of IRET, the flags register is flags. If IRETD is used, then it is the EFLAGS register.

JMP   Jump

Jcc   **Jump on some Condition Code**

Instruction	Opcode	Binary
JA rel8	77 cb	01110111
JAE rel8	73 cb	01110011
JB rel8	72 cb	01110010
JBE rel8	76 cb	01110110
JC rel8	72 cb	01110010
JCXZ rel8	E3 cb	11100011
JECXZ rel8	E3 cb	11100011
JE rel8	74 cb	01110100
JZ rel8	74 cb	01110100
JG rel8	7F cb	01111111
JGE rel8	7D cb	01111101
JL rel8	7C cb	01111100
JLE rel8	7E cb	01111110
JNA rel8	76 cb	01110110
JNAE rel8	72 cb	01110010
JNB rel8	73 cb	01110011
JNBE rel8	77 cb	01110111
JNC rel8	73 cb	01110011
JNE rel8	75 cb	01110101
JNG rel8	7E cb	01111110
JNGE rel8	7C cb	01111100
JNL rel8	7D cb	01111101
JNLE rel8	7F cb	01111111
JNO rel8	71 cb	01110001
JNP rel8	7B cb	01111011
JNS rel8	79 cb	01111001
JNZ rel8	75 cb	01110101
JO rel8	70 cb	01110000
JP rel8	7A cb	01111010
JPE rel8	7A cb	01111010
JPO rel8	7B cb	01111011
JS rel8	78 cb	01111000

JZ rel8	74 cb	01110100
JA rel16/32	0F 87 cw/cd	00001111 10000111
JAE rel16/32	0F 83 cw/cd	00001111 10000011
JB rel16/32	0F 82 cw/cd	00001111 10000010
JBE rel16/32	0F 86 cw/cd	00001111 10000110
JC rel16/32	0F 82 cw/cd	00001111 10000010
JE rel16/32	0F 84 cw/cd	00001111 10000100
JZ rel16/32	0F 84 cw/cd	00001111 10000100
JG rel16/32	0F 8F cw/cd	00001111 10001111
JGE rel16/32	0F 8D cw/cd	00001111 10001101
JL rel16/32	0F 8C cw/cd	00001111 10001100
JLE rel16/32	0F 8E cw/cd	00001111 10001110
JNA rel16/32	0F 86 cw/cd	00001111 10000110
JNAE rel16/32	0F 82 cw/cd	00001111 10000010
JNB rel16/32	0F 83 cw/cd	00001111 10000011
JNBE rel16/32	0F 87 cw/cd	00001111 10000111
JNC rel16/32	0F 83 cw/cd	00001111 10000011
JNE rel16/32	0F 85 cw/cd	00001111 10000101
JNG rel16/32	0F 8E cw/cd	00001111 10001110
JNGE rel16/32	0F 8C cw/cd	00001111 10001100
JNL rel16/32	0F 8D cw/cd	00001111 10001101
JNLE rel16/32	0F 8F cw/cd	00001111 10001111
JNO rel16/32	0F 81 cw/cd	00001111 10000001
JNP rel16/32	0F 8B cw/cd	00001111 10001011
JNS rel16/32	0F 89 cw/cd	00001111 10001001
JNZ rel16/32	0F 85 cw/cd	00001111 10000101
JO rel16/32	0F 80 cw/cd	00001111 10000000
JP rel16/32	0F 8A cw/cd	00001111 10001010
JPE rel16/32	0F 8A cw/cd	00001111 10001010
JPO rel16/32	0F 8B cw/cd	00001111 10001011
JS rel16/32	0F 88 cw/cd	00001111 10001000
JZ rel16/32	0F 84 cw/cd	00001111 10000100

Purpose: JMP transfers control from one code segment location to another. The Jcc jumps depend on the flags, as shown below. These locations can be within the same code segment (near) in different code segments (far). JMP unconditionally transfers control to the target location and is a one-way transfer. JMP does not save a return address on the stack as CALL does.

JMP implementation varies depending on whether the address is directly specified within the instruction or indirectly through a register or memory. A direct JMP includes the destination address as part of the instruction. An indirect JMP gets the destination address through a register or a pointer variable. An indirect JMP specifies an absolute address in one of the following ways: (1) a register modifies the address of the memory pointer to select a destination address; (2) the program can JMP to a location specified by a general register (EAX, EDX, ECX, EBX, EBP, ESI, or EDI)—the 80386 moves this 32-bit value into EIP and resumes execution; or (3) the 80386 obtains the destination address from a memory operand specified in the instruction.

The following Jcc conditional transfer instructions might or might not transfer control, depending on the state of the flags when the instruction executes. The flags are assumed to have been set in some meaningful way by proceeding instruction(s).

JA/JNBE	Above, not below nor equal	CF = 0, ZF = 0
JAE/JNB	Above or equal, not below	CF = 0
JB/JNAE	Below, not above nor equal	CF = 1
JBE/JNA	Below or equal, not above	CF = 1, ZF = 1
JC	Carry	CF = 1
JE/JZ	Equal, zero	ZF = 1
JNC	Not carry	CF = 0
JNE/JNZ	Not equal, not zero	ZF = 0
JNP/JPO	Not parity, parity odd	PF = 0
JP/JPE	Parity, parity even	PF = 1

The following Jcc instructions are signed control transfers:

JG/JNLE	Greater, not less nor equal	ZF = 0, SF = OF
JGE/JNL	Greater or equal, not less	SF = OF
JL/JNGE	Less, not greater nor equal	SF = OF
JLE/JNG	Less or equal, not greater	SF = OF, ZF = 1
JNO	Not overflow	OF = 0
JNS	Not sign	SF = 0
JO	Overflow	OF = 1
JS	Sign (negative)	SF = 1

JCXZ (jump if ECX is zero) branches to the label specified in the instruction if it finds a value of zero in the ECX register. JCXZ is useful when it is desirable to design a loop that executes zero times if the count variable in ECX is initialized to zero. When used with repeated string scan and compare instructions, JCXZ determines whether the repetitions ended due to a zero in ECX or to satisfaction of the scan or compare conditions.

LAHF   Load Flags into AH Register

Instruction	Opcode	Binary
LAHF	9F	10011111

Purpose: Though specific instructions exist to alter CF and DF, there is no direct way of altering the other applications-oriented flags. The flag-transfer instructions (LAHF and SAHF) allow a program to alter the other flag bits with the bit manipulation instructions after transferring these flags to the stack or the AH register.

LAHF copies SF, ZF, AF, PF, and CF to AH bits 7, 6, 4, 2, and 0, respectively. The contents of the remaining bits (5, 3, and 1) are undefined. The flags remain unaffected. See Fig. B-5 for the layout of the flags in the flags register, the low 16 bits of EFLAGS.

See appendix H for a discussion of the various flags and where they are stored.

7	6	5	4	3	2	1	0
SF	ZF	0	AF	0	PF	1	CF

Fig. B-5. Low Byte of the Flags Register.

SF – Sign Flag

ZF – Zero Flag

AF – Auxiliary Carry Flag

PF – Parity Flag

CF – Carry Flag

LAR   Load Access Rights Byte

Instruction	Opcode	Binary
LAR r16,r/m16	0F 02 /r	00001111 00000010 mm rrr r/m
LAR r32,r/m32	0F 02 /r	00001111 00000010 mm rrr r/m

Purpose: LAR reads a segment descriptor and puts the granularity (bit 23), programmer available (bit 20), present (bit 15), DPL (bit 14), type (bit 9-11), and accessed (bit 8) into a 32-bit register, the first operand. If you specify a 16-bit register as the first operand, the granularity, and programmer available bits are not moved.

The segment attribute field is simply the high-order four bytes of the descriptor ANDed with 00FxFF00h, where x indicates that bits 16 through 19 are undefined in the value loaded by LAR.

Note: Only the following are valid special segment and gate descriptor types as shown in Fig. B-6. See appendix H for a discussion of gates.

Type	Name
0	Undefined, invalid
1	Available 80286 TSS
2	Local Descriptor Table
3	Busy 80286 TSS
4	80286 Call Gate
5	80286/80386 Task Gate
6	80286 Interrupt Gate
7	80286 Trap Gate
8	Undefined, invalid
9	Available 80386 TSS
A	Undefined, invalid
B	Busy 80386 TSS
C	80386 Call Gate
D	Undefined, invalid
E	80386 Interrupt Gate
F	80386 Trap Gate

Fig. B-6. Valid Special-Segment and Gate-Descriptor Types for LAR.

The descriptor specified by the selector in the first operand must be within the descriptor table limits, have a valid type field, and be accessible at both CPL (current privilege level) and RPL (requestor's privilege level) of the selector in the second operand compared to DPL (descriptor privilege level). If so, ZF is set to 1 and the segment attributes are loaded to operand 1. If not, ZF is set to 0, and the first operand is unmodified.

LEA   Load Effective Address

Instruction	Opcode	Binary
LEA r16,m	8D /r	10001101 mm rrr r/m
LEA r32,m	8D /r	10001101 mm rrr r/m

Purpose: LEA transfers the offset of the source operand, rather than its value, to the destination operand. The source operand must be a memory operand. The destination operand must be a general register. LEA is particularly useful for initializing registers before the execution of the string primitives or the XLAT.

LEAVE   High Level Procedure Exit

Instruction	Opcode	Binary
LEAVE	C9	11001001

Purpose: LEAVE reverses the action of a previous ENTER. LEAVE does not use any operands. LEAVE copies EBP to ESP to release all stack space allocated to the procedure by the most recent ENTER. Then LEAVE POPs the old value of EBP from the stack. A subsequent RET can then remove any arguments that were pushed on the stack by the calling program for use by the called procedure.

LGDT   Load Global Descriptor Table Register

LIDT   Load Interrupt Descriptor Table Register

Instruction	Opcode	Binary
LGDT m16&32	0F 01 /2	00001111 00000001 mm 010 r/m
LIDT m16&32	0F 01 /3	00001111 00000001 mm 011 r/m

Purpose: LGDT loads the global descriptor table (GDT) register. LGDT loads the global descriptor table register (GDTR) from the 48-bit pseudodescriptor given in the instruction. This 48-bit descriptor has two components: the limit and base. The 16-bit limit is stored at the low word, and the 32-bit base is stored at the high doubleword.

LIDT tells the hardware where to go in case of interrupts. LIDT loads the interrupt descriptor table register (IDTR) from the 48-bit pseudodescriptor given in the instruction. This 48-bits has two components: the limit and base. The 16-bit limit is stored at the low word, and the 32-bit base is stored at the high doubleword.

Both global descriptor table (GDT) and the interrupt descriptor table (IDT) are loaded at system reset (initialization of the operating system). This generally happens at the beginning of the work session.

LGS   Load Full Pointer

LSS   Load Pointer Using SS

LDS   Load Pointer Using DS

LES   Load Pointer Using ES

LFS   Load Pointer Using FS

Instruction	Opcode	Binary
LDS r16,m16:16	C5 /r	11000101 mm rrr r/m
LDS r32,m16:32	C5 /r	11000101 mm rrr r/m
LSS r16,m16:16	0F B2 /r	00001111 10110010 mm rrr r/m
LSS r32,m16:32	0F B2 /r	00001111 10110010 mm rrr r/m
LES r16,m16:16	C4 /r	11000100 mm rrr r/m
LES r32,m16:32	C4 /r	11000100 mm rrr r/m
LFS r16,m16:16	0F B4 /r	00001111 10110100 mm rrr r/m
LFS r32,m16:32	0F B4 /r	00001111 10110100 mm rrr r/m
LGS r16,m16:16	0F B5 /r	00001111 10110101 mm rrr r/m
LGS r32,m16:32	0F B5 /r	00001111 10110101 mm rrr r/m

Purpose: The data pointer instructions load a pointer which consists of a segment selector and an offset into a segment register and a general register.

LDS transfers a pointer variable from the source operand to DS and the destination register. The source operand must be a memory operand. The destination operand must be a general register. DS receives the segment-selector of the pointer. The destination register receives the offset part of the pointer, which points to a specific location within the segment.

The other instructions use the various registers, as noted in the instruction mnemonic.

LSS is particularly important because it allows the two registers that identify the stack (SS:ESP) to be changed in one uninterruptible operation. See appendix H for an overview of the 80386, which includes a discussion of the various system registers and their contents.

LLDT   Load Local Descriptor Table Register

Instruction	Opcode	Binary
LLDT r/m16	0F 00 /2	00001111 00000000 mm 010 r/m

Purpose: The local descriptor table (LDT) is loaded whenever a task or major subsystem gains or regains control of the system. LLDT loads the local descriptor table register (LDTR). The operand (memory or register) should hold a selector to the global descriptor table (GDT). The descriptor registers are not affected, and the LDT field in the task state segment does not change. The first operand can be a null selector, which causes the LDT to be marked invalid. Loading a selector naming an LDT segment raises a segment load exception if LDTR contains a null selector. See appendix H, which gives an overview of the 80386; there is also a discussion of registers, selectors, and descriptors.

LMSW   Load Machine Status Word

Instruction	Opcode	Binary
LMSW r/m16	0F 01 /6	00001111 00000001 mm 110 r/m

Purpose: LMSW loads the machine status word (MSW) into CR0 from the source as specified in the first operand. The MSW is the low-order 16 bits of control register zero (CR0), see Fig. B-7. LMSW can be used to switch to protected mode, by setting the PE (protection enable) bit to 1. If so, the instruction queue must be flushed and LMSW followed by an intrasegment jump instruction. LMSW will not switch back to real address mode; that is, you cannot alter the PE bit to zero with an LMSW.

For compatibility with the 80286, the ET (extension type) bit of MSW is not altered by the LMSW instruction.

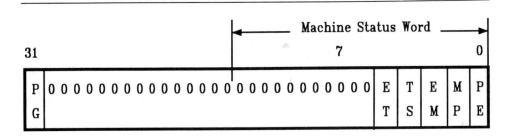

Control Register Zero (CR0)

PG – Paging Enable   EM – Emulate Coprocessor

ET – Processor Extension Type   MP – Monitor Coprocessor

TS – Task Switched   PE – Protection Enable

Note: Zero bits indicate Intel reserved. Do not define.

Fig. B-7. Machine-Status Word.

LOCK   Assert LOCK# Signal Prefix

Instruction	Opcode	Binary
LOCK	F0	11110000

Purpose: LOCK asserts a hold on shared memory so that the 80386 has exclusive use of it during the instruction which immediately follows the LOCK. LOCK integrity is not affected by memory field alignment. LOCK will only work with:

BT, BTS, BTR, BTC	memory, reg/imm
ADD, OR, ADC, SBB, AND, SUB, XOR	memory, reg/imm
NOT, NEG, INC, DEC	memory
XCHG	reg, memory or memory, reg

An undefined opcode trap is generated if LOCK is used with any instruction not listed here. Note that XCHG always asserts LOCK# whether or not it has the LOCK prefix.

Note: LOCK is not assured if another 80386 is concurrently executing an instruction that has any of the following characteristics:

- If it is not one of the instructions in the list above.
- If it is not preceded by a LOCK prefix.
- If it specifies a memory operand that does not exactly overlap the destination operand. LOCK is not guaranteed for partial overlap, even if one memory is contained wholly within the other.

LODS   Load String Operand

LODSB   Load Byte

LODSW   Load Word

LODSD   Load Doubleword

Instruction	Opcode	Binary
LODS m8	AC	10101100
LODS m16	AD	10101101
LODS m32	AD	10101101

Purpose: These instructions operate on strings rather than on logical or numerical values. They operate on one element of a string, which can be a byte, a word, or a doubleword. The string elements are addressed by the DS (default) and ESI registers. After each string operation, ESI is automatically updated to point to the next element of the string. If DF = 0, the index register is incremented. If DF = 1, it is decremented. The amount incremented or decremented is 1, 2, or 4, depending on the size of the string element.

LODS places the source string element at ESI into AL for byte strings, AX for word strings, and in EAX for doubleword strings. LODS increments or decrements ESI according to DF.

The operand specifies the length of the operand; for example, AH specifies eight bits, AX 16, and EAX 32. The actual transfer is always done with the address specified in ESI. A segment override prefix can be specified in the operand, which is applied to [ESI].

LOOP   Loop Control While ECX Counter Not Zero

LOOP*cond*

LOOPE   Loop while Equal

LOOPZ   Loop while Zero

LOOPNE   Loop while Not Equal

LOOPNZ   Loop while Not Zero

Instruction	Opcode	Binary
LOOP rel8	E2 cb	11100010
LOOPE rel8	E1 cb	11100001
LOOPNE rel8	E1 cb	11100001

Note:

LOOPZ is an alternate mnemonic for LOOPE rel8
LOOPNZ is an alternate mnemonic for LOOPNE rel8

Purpose: The LOOP instructions are conditional jumps that use a value stored in ECX to specify the number of times a section of software loops to a label. All LOOPs automatically decrement ECX and terminate when ECX = 0. LOOP is placed at the bottom of the loop and the label at the top. See appendix H for a discussion of the 80386 registers and their contents (flags and bits).

LOOP first decrements ECX before testing ECX for the branch condition. If ECX is not zero, the program branches to the target label specified in the instruction. If

ECX = 0, control transfers to the instruction immediately following the LOOP. ECX is decremented without affecting any of the flags.

LOOPE and LOOPZ are synonymous. These instructions decrement ECX before testing ECX and ZF (zero flag) for branch condition. If ECX is nonzero and ZF = 1, the program branches to the target label as specified in the instruction. If LOOPE or LOOPZ finds ECX = 0 or ZF = 0, control transfers to the instruction immediately following the LOOPE or LOOPZ.

LOOPNE and LOOPNZ are synonymous. These instructions decrement ECX before testing ECX or ZF for branch conditions. If ECX is nonzero and ZF = 0, the program branches to the target label specified by the instruction. If ECX = 0 or ZF = 1, control transfers to the instruction immediately following LOOPNE or LOOPNZ.

LSL   Load Segment Limit

Instruction	Opcode	Binary
LSL r16,r/m16	0F 03 /r	00001111 00000011 mm rrr r/m
LSL r32,r/m32	0F 03 /r	00001111 00000011 mm rrr r/m

Purpose: LSL loads a user-specified register with a segment limit. The limit comes from the descriptor for the segment specified by the selector in the second operand. If the source selector is visible at the CPL and the descriptor is a type accepted by LSL (see Fig. B-8), LSL sets ZF to 1. Otherwise, LSL sets ZF to 0 and keeps the destination register unchanged.

The 32-bit forms of LSL store the 32-bit granular limit in the 16-bit destination register.

Note that this segment limit is a byte-granular value. If the descriptor uses a page granular (the G bit = 1) segment limit, LSL translates that value to a byte limit (shifts it left 12 bits and fills the low 12 bits with 1s) and then loads it into the destination register.

LTR   Load Task Register

Instruction	Opcode	Binary
LTR r/m16	0F 00 /3	00001111 00000000 mm 011 r/m

Purpose: The first operand of LTR specifies the source register or memory location, which contains information for the task register. LTR loads data from that location into the task register. The loaded TSS is marked busy; however, a task switch does not occur. The given selector must point to a global descriptor table (GDT) entry that is of the descriptor type TSS (task state segment). If this is the case, the task register (TR) is loaded. See appendix H for an overview of the 80386, which includes a discussion of the various registers.

Type	Name
0	Undefined, invalid
1	Available 80286 TSS
2	Local Descriptor Table
3	Busy 80286 TSS
4	80286 Call Gate
5	80286/80386 Task Gate
6	80286 Interrupt Gate
7	80286 Trap Gate
8	Undefined, invalid
9	Available 80386 TSS
A	Undefined, invalid
B	Busy 80386 TSS
C	80386 Call Gate
D	Undefined, invalid
E	80386 Interrupt Gate
F	80386 Trap Gate

Fig. B-8. Valid System Segments and Gates for LSL.

MOV   Move Data

Instruction	Opcode	Binary
MOV r/m8,r8	88 /r	10001000 mm rrr r/m
MOV r/m16,r16	89 /r	10001001 mm rrr r/m
MOV r/m32,r32	89 /r	10001001 mm rrr r/m
MOV r8,r/m8	8A /r	10001010 mm rrr r/m
MOV r16,r/m16	8B /r	10001011 mm rrr r/m
MOV r32,r/m32	8B /r	10001011 mm rrr r/m
MOV r/m16,sreg	8C /r	10001100 mm rrr r/m
MOV Sreg,r/m16	8D /r	10001101 mm rrr r/m
MOV AL,moffs8	A0	10100000
MOV AX,moffs16	A1	10100001
MOV EAX,moffs32	A1	10100001

MOV moffs8,AL	A2	10100010
MOV moffs16,AX	A3	10100011
MOV moffs32,EAX	A3	10100011
MOV reg8,imm8	B0 + rb	10110rrr
MOV reg16,imm16	B8 + rw	10111rrr
MOV reg32,imm32	B8 + rd	10111rrr
MOV r/m8,imm8	C6	11000110 mm rrr r/m
MOV r/m16,imm16	C7	11000111 mm rrr r/m
MOV r/m32,imm32	C7	11000111 mm rrr r/m

Purpose: MOV transfers a byte, word, or doubleword from the source operand to the destination operand. MOV is useful for transferring data along these paths:

- Immediate data to a memory.
- Immediate data to a register.
- Between general registers.
- To a register from memory.
- To memory from a register.

There are some variations of MOV that operate on segment registers, which is how the segment registers are initialized in programs in this book.

Note: MOV cannot move from memory to memory or from segment register to segment register. Memory to memory can be done with the string move MOVS.

MOV   Move To/From Special Registers

Instruction	Opcode	Binary
MOV r32,CR0/CR2/CR3	0F 20 /r	00001111 00100000 mm ccc r/m
MOV CR0/CR2/CR3,r32	0F 22 /r	00001111 00100010 mm ccc r/m
MOV r32,TR6/TR7	0F 24 /r	00001111 00100100 mm + + + r/m
MOV TR6/TR7,r32	0F 26 /r	00001111 00100110 mm + + + r/m
MOV r32,DR0-3/6/7	0F 21 /r	00001111 00100001 mm ddd r/m
MOV DR0-3/6/7,r32	0F 23 /r	00001111 00100011

Purpose: These forms of MOV load or store special registers or from a general register. They are particularly designed for the control registers (CR0, CR2, CR3), test registers (TR6 and TR7), and the debug registers (DR0, DR1, DR2, DR3, DR6, and DR7). See appendix H which gives an overview of the 80386, which includes a discussion on the various registers.

MOVS   Move Data from String to String

MOVSB   Move String Byte

MOVSW   Move String Word

MOVSD   Move String Doubleword

Instruction	Opcode	Binary
MOVS m8,m8	A4	10100100
MOVS m16,m16	A5	10100101
MOVS m32,m32	A5	10100101

Note:

> MOVSB is a common assembler mnemonic for MOVS m8,m8
> MOVSW is a common assembler mnemonic for MOVS m16,m16
> MOVSD is a common assembler mnemonic for MOVS m32,m32

Purpose: These instructions operate on strings rather than on logical or numerical values. They operate on one element of a string (addressed by [ESI]), which may be a byte, a word, or a doubleword and move it to the area addressed by ES:[EDI]. After each string operation, ESI and/or EDI are automatically updated to point to the next element of the string. If the direction (DF) is 0, the index registers are incremented. If DF = 1, they are decremented. The amount incremented or decremented is one, two, or four, depending on the size of the string element.

When prefixed by REP, MOVS operates as a memory-to-memory block transfer and repeats for the number of times specified by the value stored in ECX. To set this up, be sure your program initializes ECX and the register pairs ESI and EDI. ECX specifies the number of bytes, words, or doublewords in the block. If the direction flag (DF) is 0, the program must point ESI to the first element of the source string and point EDI to the destination address for the first element. IF DF = 1, the program points these two registers to the last element of the source string and to the destination address for the last element, respectively.

MOVSX   Move with Sign Extension

Instruction	Opcode	Binary
MOVSX r16,r/m8	0F BE /r	00001111 10111110 mm rrr r/m
MOVSX r32,r/m8	0F BE /r	00001111 10111110 mm rrr r/m
MOVSX r32,r/m16	0F BF /r	00001111 10111111 mm rrr r/m

Purpose: MOVSX extends the sign of an 8-bit value to a 16-bit value and an 8-bit or a 16-bit value to a 32-bit value. If both operands are words, a normal move occurs. This instruction is new to the 80386.

MOVZX   Move with Zero Extension

Instruction	Opcode	Binary
MOVZX r16,r/m8	0F B6 /r	00001111 10110110 mm rrr r/m
MOVZX r32,r/m8	0F B6 /r	00001111 10110110 mm rrr r/m
MOVZX r32,r/m16	0F B7 /r	00001111 10110111 mm rrr r/m

Purpose: MOVZX extends an 8-bit value to a 16-bit value and an 8- or 16-bit value to a 32-bit value by padding with high-order zeros. If both operands are words, a normal move occurs. This instruction is new to the 80386.

MUL   Unsigned Integer Multiply of AL, AX, or EAX

Instruction	Opcode	Binary
MUL AL,r/m8	F6 /4	11110110 mm 100 r/m
MUL AX,r/m16	F7 /4	11110111 mm 100 r/m
MUL EAX,r/m32	F7 /4	11110111 mm 100 r/m

Purpose: MUL multiplies the numbers in the source operand and the accumulator (AL, AX, or EAX). If the source is a byte, the 80386 multiplies it by the contents of AL and returns the double-length result in AH and AL. If the source operand is a word, the 80386 multiplies it by the contents of AX and returns the double-length result to DX and AX. If the source is a doubleword, the processor multiplies it by the contents of EAX and returns the 64-bit result in EDX and EAX. MUL sets CF (carry flag) and OF (overflow flag) to zero, if AH, DX, or EDX is all zeros for 8-, 16-, or 32-bit operations. Otherwise CF and OF are set to 1. See appendix H for an overview of the 80386, which discusses the various registers and their contents (flags and bits).

NEG   Negate (Two's Complement)

Instruction	Opcode	Binary
NEG r/m8	F6 /3	11110110 mm 011 r/m
NEG r/m16	F7 /3	11110111 mm 011 r/m
NEG r/m32	F7 /3	11110111 mm 011 r/m

Purpose: NEG subtracts a signed integer operand from zero. Its effect is to make a positive into a negative or vice versa. That is, NEG forms a two's complement of a given operand, which is subtracted from zero. The result is placed in the operand. The carry flag (CF) is set to 1, except when the operand prior to the NEG was 0.

NOP   No Operation

Instruction	Opcode	Binary
NOP	90	10010000

Purpose: NOP occupies a byte of storage. It affects nothing but the instruction pointer, EIP. NOP is useful for providing space in fixing up branch addresses, that is, the address might require an 8- or 16-bit displacement—if 16 bits are reserved, an 8-bit displacement and a NOP can be used to fill the 16 bits.

NOT   Negate (One's Complement)

Instruction	Opcode	Binary
NOT r/m8	F6 /2	11110110 mm 010 r/m
NOT r/m16	F7 /2	11110111 mm 010 r/m
NOT r/m32	F7 /2	11110111 mm 010 r/m

Purpose: NOT inverts the bits in the specified operand to form a one's complement of the operand. NOT is a unary operation (refers to an arithmetic operator having only one term) that uses a single operand in a register or memory. The result is stored in the operand. NOT has no effect on flags.

OR   Logical Inclusive OR

Instruction	Opcode	Binary
OR AL,imm8	0C ib	00001100
OR AX,imm16	0D iw	00001101
OR EAX,imm32	0D id	00001101
OR r/m8,imm8	80 /1 ib	10000000 mm 001 r/m
OR r/m16,imm16	81 /1 iw	10000001 mm 001 r/m
OR r/m32,imm32	81 /1 id	10000001 mm 001 r/m
OR r/m16,imm8	83 /1 ib	10000011 mm 001 r/m
OR r/m32,imm8	83 /1 ib	10000011 mm 001 r/m
OR r/m8,r8	08 /r	00001000 mm 001 r/m
OR r/m16,r16	09 /r	00001001 mm 001 r/m
OR r/m32,r32	09 /r	00001001 mm 001 r/m
OR r8,r/m8	0A /r	00001010 mm rrr r/m
OR r16,r/m16	0B /r	00001011 mm rrr r/m
OR r32,r/m32	0B /r	00001011 mm rrr r/m

Purpose: OR compares its two operands and computes the following: if each corresponding bit in the operands is zero, the result is a zero; otherwise, the result is a 1.

$$
\begin{array}{llll}
\text{Operand 1} & 0\ 0\ 1\ 1 \\
\text{Operand 2} & 0\ 1\ 1\ 0 \\
\text{Result} & 0\ 1\ 1\ 1
\end{array}
$$

The result is stored in the operand.

OUT   Output to Port

Instruction	Opcode	Binary
OUT imm8,AL	E6 ib	11100110
OUT imm8,AX	E7 ib	11100111
OUT imm8,EAX	E7 ib	11100111
OUT DX,AL	EE	11101110
OUT DX,AX	EF	11101111
OUT DX,EAX	EF	11101111

Purpose: OUT transfers data from a register to an output port. The source is a register (AL, AX, or EAX) and is given as the second operand. The output port is specified in the first operand. To output data to any port from 0 to 65536, the port number is placed in the DX register. OUT is then used with DX as the first operand. If the instruction contains an 8-bit port ID, the value is zero-extended to 16 bits in DX. If the immediate 8 is used, only ports from 0 to 255 are valid. In this case, the upper bits of the port address are zero.

Note: I/O ports 00F8 through 00FF are reserved by Intel.

OUTS   Output String to Port

OUTSB   Output Byte

OUTSW   Output Word

OUTSD   Output Doubleword

Instruction	Opcode	Binary
OUTS DX,r/m8	6E	01101110
OUTS DX,r/m16	6F	01101111
OUTS DX,r/m32	6F	01101111

Note:

> OUTSB is a common assembler mnemonic for OUTS DX,r/m8
> OUTSW is a common assembler mnemonic for OUTS DX,r/m16
> OUTSD is a common assembler mnemonic for OUTS DX,r/m32

Purpose: OUTS operates much like OUT, in that it transfers data (memory byte, word, or doubleword) at the source-index register to the output port addressed by the DX register. After the data transfer, the source-index register (SI or ESI, see below) is advanced; that is, it is either incremented or decremented. If the DF is 0 (CLD was executed), the index is incremented. If DF is 1 (STD was executed), it is decremented. The amount it is changed depends on the size of the output: a 1 if it is a byte, a 2 if a word, or 4 if a doubleword.

The source data address is determined by the contents of a source-index register. The correct index value must be loaded into either SI or ESI prior to executing these instructions. SI is used for the source-index register if the address size attribute for these instructions is 16 bits. Otherwise, ESI is used, and the address size attribute is 32 bits.

The port must be addressed through the DX register value. OUTS does not allow specification of the port number as an immediate value.

OUTS can be preceded by the REP prefix. In this case, ECX bytes, words, or dwords are transferred.

POP Pop a Word from the Stack

Instruction	Opcode	Binary	
POP m16	8F /0	10001111 mm	000 r/m
POP m32	8F /0	10111111 mm	000 r/m
POP r16	58 + rw	01011rrr	
POP r32	58 + rd	01011rrr	
POP DS	1F	00011111	
POP ES	07	00000111	
POP SS	17	00010111	
POP FS	0F A1	00001111 10100001	
POP GS	0F A9	00001111 10101001	

Purpose: POP transfers the word or doubleword at the current top of stack (indicated by SS:ESP) to the destination operand. It then increments SS:ESP to point to the new top of stack. When POPping 16-bit operands, avoid misaligning the stack, which causes performance degradation. See Fig. B-9 for an overview of how stacks PUSH and POP.

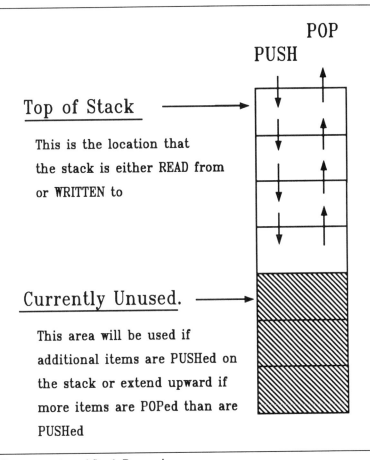

POP

PUSH

Top of Stack ———————→

This is the location that
the stack is either READ from
or WRITTEN to

Currently Unused. ———————→

This area will be used if
additional items are PUSHed on
the stack or extend upward if
more items are POPed than are
PUSHed

Fig. B-9. Representation of Stack Processing.

POPA   POP All Registers

POPAD   POP All Registers—32-bit Mode

Instruction	Opcode	Binary
POPA	61	01100001
POPAD	61	01100001

Purpose: POPA restores the eight general-purpose registers saved on the stack by PUSHA. It discards the saved value of ESP. The order the registers are POPed is: DI, SI, BP, SP, BX, DX, CX, and AX for POPA, or EDI, ESI, EBP, ESP, EBX, EDX, ECX, and EAX for POPAD. See appendix H for an overview of the 80386, which includes a description of the various registers.

POPF   POP Stack into FLAGS or EFLAGS Register

POPFD   POP Stack—32-bit Mode

Instruction	Opcode	Binary
POPF	9D	10011101
POPFD	9D	10011101

Purpose: POPF transfers specific bits from the word at the top of stack into the low-order byte of EFLAGS. Then POPF increments ESP by two. POPFD transfers the 16 or 32 bits and increments ESP by four. The RF and VM flags are not changed by either POPF or POPFD.

PUSHF and POPF are useful for storing the flags in memory where they can be examined and modified. They are also useful for preserving the state of the flags register while executing a procedure.

The IOPL (I/O privilege level) flag will only be altered if the current privilege level (CPL) is 0. If not 0, IOPL is not altered and no exception results. If CPL is as privileged or more privileged than the current IOPL, the interrupt enable flag (IF) is altered. If not, IF is unchanged and no exception results.

PUSH   Push Operand onto the Stack

Instruction	Opcode	Binary
PUSH m16	FF /6	11111111 mm 110 r/m
PUSH m32	FF /6	11111111 mm 110 r/m
PUSH r16	50 + /r	01010rrr
PUSH r32	50 + /r	01010rrr
PUSH imm8	6A	01101010
PUSH imm16	68	01101000
PUSH imm32	68	01101000
PUSH CS	0E	00001110
PUSH SS	16	00010110
PUSH DS	1E	00011110
PUSH ES	06	00000110
PUSH FS	0F A0	00001111 10100000
PUSH GS	0F A8	00001111 10101000

Purpose: PUSH decrements the stack pointer (ESP) then transfers the source operand to the top of stack (TOS) indicated by ESP. PUSH is often used to place parameters on the stack before calling a procedure. It is also the means of storing temporary variables on the stack. PUSH operates on memory operands, register operands (including segment registers), and immediate operands. Immediate data is always considered to be 32 bits in size, although it can be encoded in the instruction as an 8-bit immediate.

Be careful when PUSHing 16-bit operands. Avoid misaligning the stack, which causes performance degradation.

PUSHA   Push All General Registers

PUSHAD

Instruction	Opcode	Binary
PUSHA	60	01100000
PUSHAD	60	01100000

Purpose: PUSHA saves the contents of the eight general-purpose registers on the stack. PUSHA eliminates the need for eight consecutive PUSH instructions. The order of the registers PUSHed is: AX, CX, DX, BX, SP, BP, SI and DI for word, or EAX, ECX, EDX, EBX, ESP, EBP, ESI and EDI for dword. Note that the value PUSHed for SP or ESP is the original value. The order of the registers PUSHed is correct for a subsequent POPA.

PUSHF   Push Flags Register EFLAGS onto the Stack

PUSHFD

Instruction	Opcode	Binary
PUSHF	9C	10011100
PUSHFD	9C	10011100

Purpose: PUSHF decrements ESP (stack pointer) by two and then transfers the low-order word of EFLAGS to the word at the top of stack pointed to by ESP. PUSHFD decrements ESP by four then transfers both words of the EFLAGS to the top of stack pointed to by ESP. Note that the VM and RF flags are not moved.

PUSHF and POPF are useful for storing the flags in memory where they can be examined and modified. They are useful also for preserving the state of the flags register while executing a procedure.

RCL   Rotate Left through Carry—Uses CF for Extension

RCR   Rotate Right through Carry—Uses CF for Extension

ROL   Rotate Left—Wrap bits around

ROR   Rotate Right—Wrap bits around

Instruction	Opcode	Binary
RCL r/m8,1	D0 /2	11010000 mm 010 r/m
RCL r/m8,CL	D2 /2	11010010 mm 010 r/m
RCL r/m8,imm8	C0 /2 ib	11000000 mm 010 r/m
RCL r/m16,1	D1 /2	11010001 mm 010 r/m
RCL r/m16,CL	D3 /2	11010011 mm 010 r/m
RCL r/m16,imm8	C1 /2 ib	11000001 mm 010 r/m
RCL r/m32,1	D1 /2	11010001 mm 010 r/m
RCL r/m32,CL	D3 /2	11010011 mm 010 r/m
RCL r/m32,imm8	C1 /2 ib	11000001 mm 010 r/m
RCR r/m8,1	D0 /3	11010000 mm 011 r/m
RCR r/m8,CL	D2 /3	11010010 mm 011 r/m
RCR r/m8,imm8	C0 /3 ib	11000000 mm 011 r/m
RCR r/m16,1	D1 /3	11010001 mm 011 r/m
RCR r/m16,CL	D3 /3	11010011 mm 011 r/m
RCR r/m16,imm8	C1 /3 ib	11000001 mm 011 r/m
RCR r/m32,1	D1 /3	11010001 mm 011 r/m
RCR r/m32,CL	D3 /3	11010011 mm 011 r/m
RCR r/m32,imm8	C1 /3 ib	11000001 mm 011 r/m
ROL r/m8,1	D0 /0	11010000 mm 000 r/m
ROL r/m8,CL	D2 /0	11010010 mm 000 r/m
ROL r/m8,imm8	C0 /0 ib	11000000 mm 000 r/m
ROL r/m16,1	D1 /0	11010001 mm 000 r/m
ROL r/m16,CL	D3 /0	11010011 mm 000 r/m
ROL r/m16,imm8	C1 /0 ib	11000001 mm 000 r/m
ROL r/m32,1	D1 /0	11010001 mm 000 r/m
ROL r/m32,CL	D3 /0	11010011 mm 000 r/m
ROL r/m32,imm8	C1 /0 ib	11000001 mm 000 r/m
ROR r/m8,1	C0 /1	11000000 mm 001 r/m
ROR r/m8,CL	D2 /1	11010010 mm 001 r/m
ROR r/m8,imm8	C0 /1 ib	11000000 mm 001 r/m
ROR r/m16,1	D1 /1	11010001 mm 001 r/m
ROR r/m16,CL	D3 /1	11010011 mm 001 r/m
ROR r/m16,imm8	C1 /1 ib	11000001 mm 001 r/m
ROR r/m32,1	D1 /1	11010001 mm 001 r/m
ROR r/m32,CL	D3 /1	11010011 mm 001 r/m
ROR r/m32,imm8	C1 /1 ib	11000001 mm 001 r/m

Purpose: Rotate refers to a process of moving in a circular manner each bit in a register, either to the right or left. Bits rotated out of an operand are not lost as in a shift but are circled back into the other end of the operand. Rotate instructions affect only the carry and overflow flags. CF can act as an extension of the operand in two of the rotate instructions. This allows a bit to be isolated and then tested by a conditional jump instruction (JC or JNC). CF always contains the value of the last bit rotated out, even if the instruction does not use this bit as an extension of the rotated operand.

In single-bit rotates, OF is set if the operation changes the high-order (sign) bit of the destination operand. If the sign bit retains its original value, OF is cleared. On multibit rotates, the value of OF is always undefined.

RCL rotates bits in the byte, word, or doubleword destination operand left by one or by the number of bits specified in the count operand. RCL differs from ROL in that it treats CF as a high-order, one-bit extension of the destination operand. Each high-order bit that exits from the left side of the operand moves to CF before it returns to the operand as the low-order bit on the next rotation cycle.

RCR rotates bits in the byte, word, or doubleword destination right by one or by the number of bits specified in the count operand. RCR differs from ROR in that it treats CF as a low-order, one-bit extension of the destination operand. Each low-order bit that exits from the right side of the operand moves to CF before it returns to the operand as the high-order bit on the next rotation cycle.

ROL rotates the byte, word, or doubleword destination operand left by one or by the number of bits specified in the count operand, ECX. For each rotation specified, the high-order bit that exits from the left of the operand returns at the right to become the new low-order bit of the operand. If the ROL count is 1, the overflow flag (OF) is set to 0 if the carry flag (after the ROL) equals the high bit of the resultant operand. Otherwise, OF is set to 1. If ROL is not 1, OF is undefined. ROL with a 0 count does not affect OF or CF.

ROR rotates the byte, word, or doubleword destination operand right by one or by the number of bits specified in the count operand. For each rotation, the low-order bit that exits from the right of the operand returns at the left to become the new high-order bit of the operand. If the ROR count is 1, the overflow flag (OF) is set to 0 if the top two bits of the resultant operand are equal. Otherwise, OF = 1. If the ROR count is not 1, OF is undefined. Rotates with a zero count do not alter OF or CF.

Note: A rotate instruction with a count equal to 0 does not alter the carry flag. Also, RCL or RCR of 32 or 33 bits (for dwords) cannot be done because only a count of 0 to 31 are valid.

REP   **Repeat Following String Operation**

REPE   **Repeat while Equal**

REPZ   **Repeat while Zero**

REPNE   Repeat while Not Equal

REPNZ   Repeat while Not Zero

Instruction	Opcode	Binary
REP INS r/m8,DX	F3 6C	11110011 01101100
REP INS r/m16,DX	F3 6D	11110011 01101101
REP INS r/m32,DX	F3 6D	11110011 01101101
REP MOVS m8,m8	F3 A4	11110011 10100100
REP MOVS m16,m16	F3 A5	11110011 10100101
REP MOVS m32,m32	F3 A5	11110011 10100101
REP OUTS DX,r/m8	F3 6E	11110011 01101110
REP OUTS DX,r/m16	F3 6F	11110011 01101111
REP OUTS DX,r/m32	F3 6F	11110011 01101111
REP STOS m8	F3 AA	11110011 10101010
REP STOS m16	F3 AB	11110011 10101011
REP STOS m32	F3 AB	11110011 10101011
REPE CMPS m8,m8	F3 A6	11110011 10100110
REPE CMPS m16,m16	F3 A7	11110011 10100111
REPE CMPS m32,m32	F3 A7	11110011 10100111
REPE SCAS m8	F3 AE	11110011 10101110
REPE SCAS m16	F3 AF	11110011 10101111
REPE SCAS m32	F3 AF	11110011 10101111
REPNE CMPS m8,m8	F2 A6	11110010 10100110
REPNE CMPS m16,m16	F2 A7	11110010 10100111
REPNE CMPS m32,m32	F2 A7	11110010 10100111
REPNE SCAS m8	F2 AE	11110010 10101110
REPNE SCAS m16	F2 AF	11110010 10101111
REPNE SCAS m32	F2 AF	11110010 10101111

Purpose: The REP prefixes specify repeated operation of a string, which enables the 80386 to process strings much faster than with a regular software loop. When a string operation has one of these repeat prefixes, the operation is executed repeatedly for ECX times. Each time, the operation uses a different element of the string. The repetition ends when one of the conditions specified by the prefix is satisfied.

At the repetition of the instruction, the string operation can be suspended temporarily to handle an external interrupt or exception. After that interrupt has been handled, the string operation begins where it left off.

REPE repeats ECX times or until zero flag (ZF) becomes zero. REPZ is synonymous with REPE. REPNE repeats ECX times, or until ZF becomes one. REPNZ is synonymous with REPNE.

RET   Return from Procedure

Instruction	Opcode	Binary
RET	C3	11000011
RET imm16	CA /w	11001010

Purpose: RET ends the execution of a CALLed procedure and transfers control through the back-link on the top of the stack, which is the extended instruction pointer (EIP) value. The back-link points to the program that originally invoked the procedure. RET restores the value of EIP (instruction pointer) that was saved on the stack by the previous CALL instruction.

RET can optionally specify an immediate operand. By adding this constant to the new top-of-stack pointer, RET removes any arguments that the CALLing program pushed onto the stack before the CALL executed.

SAHF   Store AH into Flags Register

Instruction	Opcode	Binary
SAHF	9E	10011110

Purpose: Though specific instructions exist to alter CF and DF, there is no direct way of altering the other applications-oriented flags. The flag transfer instructions (LAHF and SAHF) allow a program to alter the other flag bits with the bit manipulation instructions after transferring these flags to the stack or the AH register. Then SAHF stores the contents of AH to the low byte of EFLAGS. See appendix H, which gives an overview of the 80386 and includes a discussion of the various registers and their contents (bits and flags).

SAL   Shift Instructions

SAR

SHL

SHR

Instruction	Opcode	Binary
SAL r/m8,1	D0 /4	11010000 mm 100 r/m
SAL r/m8,CL	D2 /4	11010010 mm 100 r/m
SAL r/m8,imm8	C0 /4 ib	11000000 mm 100 r/m
SAL r/m16,1	D1 /4	11010001 mm 100 r/m

SAL r/m16,CL	D3 /4	11010011 mm 100 r/m
SAL r/m16,imm8	C1 /4 ib	11000001 mm 100 r/m
SAL r/m32,1	D1 /4	11000001 mm 100 r/m
SAL r/m32,CL	D3 /4	11010011 mm 100 r/m
SAL r/m32,imm8	C1 /4 ib	11000001 mm 100 r/m
SAR r/m8,1	D0 /7	11010000 mm 111 r/m
SAR r/m8,CL	D2 /7	11000010 mm 111 r/m
SAR r/m8,imm8	C0 /7 ib	11000000 mm 111 r/m
SAR r/m16,1	C1 /7	11000001 mm 111 r/m
SAR r/m16,CL	D3 /7	11010011 mm 111 r/m
SAR r/m16,imm8	C1 /7 ib	11000001 mm 111 r/m
SAR r/m32,1	D1 /7	11010001 mm 111 r/m
SAR r/m32,CL	D3 /7	11010011 mm 111 r/m
SAR r/m32,imm8	C1 /7 ib	11000001 mm 111 r/m
SHR r/m8,1	D0 /5	11010000 mm 101 r/m
SHR r/m8,CL	C2 /5	11000010 mm 101 r/m
SHR r/m8,imm8	C0 /5 ib	11000000 mm 101 r/m
SHR r/m16,1	D1 /5	11010001 mm 101 r/m
SHR r/m16,CL	D3 /5	11010011 mm 101 r/m
SHR r/m16,imm8	C1 /5 ib	11000001 mm 101 r/m
SHR r/m32,1	D1 /5	11010001 mm 101 r/m
SHR r/m32,CL	D3 /5	11010011 mm 101 r/m
SHR r/m32,imm8	C1 /5 ib	11000001 mm 101 r/m

Note: SHL is an alternate assembler opcode for SAL.

Purpose: The bits in bytes, words, and doublewords can be shifted logically or arithmetically. Bits can be shifted up to 31 places, depending on a specified count in ECX. Shift instructions specify the count in one of three ways: (1) implicitly by specifying the count as a single shift; (2) specifying the count as an immediate value; or (3) specifying the count as the value contained in ECX. The result is stored back into the first operand.

The shift instructions provide a convenient way to multiply or divide by binary. The division of signed numbers by shifting right is not the same kind of division performed by IDIV.

CF always contains the value of the last bit shifted out of the destination operand. In a single-bit shift, OF is set if the value of the high-order (sign) bit was changed by the operation. If the sign bit was not changed, OF is cleared. After a multibit shift, the contents of OF is always undefined.

SAL shifts the destination byte, word or doubleword operand left by one or by the number of bits specified in the count register. The processor shifts zeros in from the right (low-order) side of the operand as bits exit from the left (high-order) side. If the shift count is one, the overflow flag (OF) is set to zero if the carry flag (CF) after the shift equals the high bit of the first operand. Otherwise, OF is set to one. If the shift count is not one, OF is undefined.

SAR shifts the destination byte, word, or doubleword operand to the right by one or by the number of bits specified in the count operand. The processor preserves the sign of the operand by shifting in zeros on the left (high-order) side if the value is positive or by shifting in ones if the value is negative. If the shift count is one, OF is set to zero; otherwise it is unchanged. Another way to think of SAR is that operand 1 is being divided by two shift-count times. The divide rounds to negative infinity (which is different than IDIV) for negative numbers. Shifts of zero do not alter any flags.

SHL is a synonym for SAL.

SHR shifts the destination byte, word, or doubleword operand right by one or by the number of bits specified in the count operand. The processor shifts zeros in from the left (high-order) side of the operand as bits exit from the right (low-order) side.

SBB Subtract Integers with Borrow

Instruction	Opcode	Binary
SBB AL,imm8	1C ib	00011100
SBB AX,imm16	1D iw	00011101
SBB EAX,imm32	1D id	00011101
SBB r/m8,imm8	80 /3 ib	10000000 mm 011 r/m
SBB r/m16,imm16	81 /3 iw	10000001 mm 011 r/m
SBB r/m32,imm32	81 /3 id	10000001 mm 011 r/m
SBB r/m16,imm8	83 /3 ib	10000011 mm 011 r/m
SBB r/m32,imm8	83 /3 ib	10000011 mm 011 r/m
SBB r/m8,r8	18 /r	00011000 mm rrr r/m
SBB r/m16,r16	19 /r	00011001 mm rrr r/m
SBB r/m32,r32	19 /r	00011001 mm rrr r/m
SBB r8,r/m8	1A /r	00011010 mm rrr r/m
SBB r16,r/m16	1B /r	00011011 mm rrr r/m
SBB r32,r/m32	1B /r	00011011 mm rrr r/m

Purpose: SBB subtracts the source operand from the destination operand and then returns the results to the destination operand. It subtracts one if CF is set. If CF is cleared, SBB performs the same operation as SUB. SUB followed by multiple SBB instructions can be used to subtract numbers longer than 32 bits.

SCAS Compare String Data

SCASB Compare Byte

SCASW Compare Word

SCASD   Compare Doubleword

Instruction	Opcode	Binary
SCAS m8	AE	10101110
SCAS m16	AF	10101111
SCAS m32	AF	10101111

Note:

> SCASB is a common assembler mnemonic for SCAS m8
> SCASW is a common assembler mnemonic for SCAS m16
> SCASD is a common assembler mnemonic for SCAS m32

Purpose: These instructions operate on strings rather than on logical or numerical values. They operate on one element of a string, which might be a byte, a word, or a doubleword. SCAS subtracts ES:[EDI] from AL, AX, or EAX (for byte, word, or dword) operations. The result of the subtraction is not stored; only the flags are changed. After each string operation, EDI is updated to point to the next element of the string. If the direction flag (DF) is zero, the index register is incremented. If DF = one, it is decremented. The amount incremented or decremented is one, two, or four, depending on the size of the string element.

If the values are equal, the zero flag (ZF) is set to one; otherwise, ZF = zero. If DF = zero, the 80386 increments the memory pointer (EDI) for the string. The destination segment register (ES) cannot be overridden.

SCAS can be preceded by REPE (REPZ) or REPNE (REPNZ). If preceded by REPE, SCAS is repeated while ECX is not zero, and the string elements are equal to AL, AX, or EAX (ZF = one). If preceded by REPNE, SCAS is repeated while ECX is not zero, and the string element is not equal to AL, AX, or EAX (ZF = zero). In this way, SCAS is useful to find the first mismatch (REPE) or match (REPNE) to AL, AX, or EAX in the string if they exist.

The specification of mem is used by the assembler to determine the length of the operation only. The string is always taken from ES:[EDI]. No segment override is possible for SCAS.

SETcc   Set Byte on Condition Code

Instruction	Opcode	Binary
SETA r/m8	0F 97	00001111 10010111 mm rrr r/m
SETAE r/m8	0F 93	00001111 10010011 mm rrr r/m
SETB r/m8	0F 92	00001111 10010010 mm rrr r/m
SETBE r/m8	0F 96	00001111 10010110 mm rrr r/m
SETC r/m8	0F 92	00001111 10010010 mm rrr r/m

SETE r/m8	0F 94	00001111 10010100 mm rrr r/m
SETG r/m8	0F 9F	00001111 10011111 mm rrr r/m
SETGE r/m8	0F 9D	00001111 10011101 mm rrr r/m
SETL r/m8	0F 9C	00001111 10011100 mm rrr r/m
SETLE r/m8	0F 9E	00001111 10011110 mm rrr r/m
SETNA r/m8	0F 96	00001111 10010110 mm rrr r/m
SETNAE r/m8	0F 92	00001111 10010010 mm rrr r/m
SETNB r/m8	0F 93	00001111 10010011 mm rrr r/m
SETNBE r/m8	0F 97	00001111 10010111 mm rrr r/m
SETNC r/m8	0F 93	00001111 10010011 mm rrr r/m
SETNE r/m8	0F 95	00001111 10010101 mm rrr r/m
SETNG r/m8	0F 9E	00001111 10011110 mm rrr r/m
SETNGE r/m8	0F 9C	00001111 10011100 mm rrr r/m
SETNL r/m8	0F 9D	00001111 10011101 mm rrr r/m
SETNLE r/m8	0F 9F	00001111 10011111 mm rrr r/m
SETNO r/m8	0F 91	00001111 10010001 mm rrr r/m
SETNP r/m8	0F 9B	00001111 10011011 mm rrr r/m
SETNS r/m8	0F 99	00001111 10011001 mm rrr r/m
SETNZ r/m8	0F 95	00001111 10010101 mm rrr r/m
SETO r/m8	0F 90	00001111 10010000 mm rrr r/m
SETP r/m8	0F 9A	00001111 10011010 mm rrr r/m
SETPE r/m8	0F 9A	00001111 10011010 mm rrr r/m
SETPO r/m8	0F 9B	00001111 10011011 mm rrr r/m
SETS r/m8	0F 98	00001111 10011000 mm rrr r/m
SETZ r/m8	0F 94	00001111 10010100 mm rrr r/m

Purpose: New to the 80386, SETcc sets a byte to zero or one depending on any of the conditions defined by the status flags, and shown below. They byte can be in memory or can be a one-byte general register. SETcc sets the byte to one if the condition cc is true; otherwise, it sets the byte to zero.

The condition codes are:

SETB/SETNAE/SETC	CF = 1
SETBE/SETNA	CF = 1, ZF = 1
SETE/SETZ	ZF = 1
SETL/SETNGE	SF = OF
SETLE/SETNG	SF = OF, ZF = 1
SETNB/SETAE/SETNC	CF = 0
SETNBE/SETA	CF = 0, ZF = 1
SETNE/SETNZ	ZF = 0
SETNL/SETGE	SF = OF
SETNLE/SETG	ZF = 0, SF = OF
SETNO	OF = 0
SETNP/SETPO	PF = 0

SETNS	SF = 0
SETO	OF = 1
SETP/SETPE	PF = 1
SETS	SF = 1

SGDT   Store Global Descriptor Table

SIDT   Store Interrupt Descriptor Table

Instruction	Opcode	Binary
SGDT m	0F 01 /0	00001111 00000001 mm 000 r/m
SIDT m	0F 01 /1	00001111 00000001 mm 001 r/m

Purpose: These instructions copy the contents of the global descriptor table register (GDTR) or the interrupt descriptor table register (IDTR) the six bytes (48 bits) indicated by the operand. The 16-bit forms of the SGDT/SIDT instructions are compatible with the 80286, but only if the value in the upper eight bits is not referenced. The 80286 stores 1s in these bits while the 80386 stores 0s.

The 16-bit limit is stored in the low word, and the 32-bit base is stored in the high doubleword. See appendix H for an overview of the 80386, which also contains a description of the various registers and their contents (bits and flags).

SHLD   Double Precision Shift Left

SHRD   Double Precision Shift Right

Instruction	Opcode	Binary
SHLD r/m16,r16,imm8	0F A4	00001111 10100100 mm rrr r/m
SHLD r/m32,r32,imm8	0F A4	00001111 10100100 mm rrr r/m
SHLD r/m16,r16,CL	0F A5	00001111 10100101 mm rrr r/m
SHLD r/m32,r32,CL	0F A5	00001111 10100101 mm rrr r/m
SHRD r/m16,r16,imm8	0F AC	00001111 10101100 mm rrr r/m
SHRD r/m32,r32,imm8	0F AC	00001111 10101100 mm rrr r/m
SHRD r/m16,r16,CL	0F AD	00001111 10101101 mm rrr r/m
SHRD r/m32,r32,CL	0F AD	00001111 10101101 mm rrr r/m

Purpose: New to the 80386, SHLD and SHRD provide the basic operations needed to implement operations on long unaligned bit strings. The double shifts either (1) take two-word operands as input and produce a one-word output, or (2) take two doubleword operands as input and produce a doubleword output. The result is stored back in the first operand.

One of the two input operands can either be in a general register or in memory; the other can only be in a general register. The results replace the memory or register operand. The number of bits to be shifted is specified either in the CL register or in an immediate byte of the instruction. This count is masked to five bits; thus, shifts of zero to 31 bits are performed. CF is set to the value of the last bit shifted out of the destination operand. SF, ZF, and PF are set according to the value of the result. OF and AF are left undefined. (See appendix H, which contains a description of the various 80386 registers and their bits and flags.)

If the count in CL is zero, the instructions are equivalent to a NOP and do not alter the flags. If the shift count is greater than the operand length, the flags and the result in the first operand are undefined.

SLDT   Store Local Descriptor Table Register (LDTR)

Instruction	Opcode	Binary
SLDT r/m16	0F 00 /0	00001111 00000000 mm 000 r/m

Purpose: The local descriptor table is pointed to by a selector that resides in the LDTR. SLDT stores the LDTR in the register or memory location indicated by the effective address operand.

Note: The operand-size attribute has no effect on the operation of SLDT.

SMSW   Store Machine Status Word

Instruction	Opcode	Binary
SMSW r/m16	0F 01 /4	00001111 00000001 mm 100 r/m

Purpose: The machine status word is part of control register zero (CR0), as shown in Fig. B-7. SMSW stores this word in the two-byte register or memory location indicated by the effective address operand. SMSW provides compatibility with the 80286. 80386 programs should use MOV CR0.

STC   Set Carry Flag (CF)

Instruction	Opcode	Binary
STC	F9	11111001

Purpose: STC sets the carry flag (CF) to one. CF is bit zero of the EFLAGS register.

STD   Set Direction Flag (DF)

Instruction	Opcode	Binary
STD	FD	11111101

Purpose: STD sets the direction flag (DF) to one; DF is bit 10 of EFLAGS. This causes all subsequent string operations to decrement the index register(s) SI (or ESI), DI (or EDI).

STI   Set Interrupt Flag (IF)

Instruction	Opcode	Binary
STI	FB	11111011

Purpose: STI sets the interrupt flag (IF) to one; IF is bit 9 of the EFLAGS register. After executing the next operation, the 80386 responds to external interrupts, but only if the next instruction allows the interrupt flag to remain enabled. However, if external interrupts are disabled, code STI, RET (such as at the end of a subroutine), and RET is allowed to execute before external interrupts are recognized. Also, if external interrupts are disabled, and STI, CLI are coded, the interrupts are not recognized because CLI clears the interrupt flag during its execution.

If the current task has insufficient privilege to alter IF, an undefined opcode fault is generated.

STOS   Store String Data

STOSB   Store Byte

STOSW   Store Word

STOSD   Store Doubleword

Instruction	Opcode	Binary
STOS m8	AA	10101010
STOS m16	AB	10101011
STOS m32	AB	10101011

Purpose: These instructions operate on strings rather than on logical or numerical values. They operate on one element of a string, which can be a byte, a word, or a doubleword. The string elements are transferred from AL, AX, or EAX into ES:EDI. After each string operation, EDI is automatically updated to point to the next element of the string. If DF = zero, the index registers are incremented. If DF = one, they are decremented. The amount incremented or decremented is one, two, or four, depending on the size of the string element.

STOS can be preceded by a REP prefix. This allows a string to be filled with the contents of the accumulator register (AL, AX, or EAX).

STR   Store Task Register

Instruction	Opcode	Binary
STR r/m16	0F 00 /1	00001111 00000000 mm 001 r/m

Purpose: STR copies the contents of the task register to the two-byte register or memory location specified in the first operand. The operand-size attribute has no effect on STR.

SUB   Subtract Integers

Instruction	Opcode	Binary
SUB AL, imm8	2C ib	00101100
SUB AX,imm16	2D iw	00101101
SUB EAX,imm32	2D id	00101101
SUB r/m8,imm8	80 /5 ib	10000000 mm 101 r/m
SUB r/m16,imm16	81 /5 iw	10000001 mm 101 r/m
SUB r/m32,imm32	81 /5 id	10000001 mm 101 r/m
SUB r/m16,imm8	83 /5 ib	10000011 mm 101 r/m
SUB r/m32,imm8	83 /5 ib	10000011 mm 101 r/m
SUB r/m8,r8	28 /r	00101000 mm rrr r/m
SUB r/m16,r16	29 /r	00101001 mm rrr r/m
SUB r/m32,r32	29 /r	00101001 mm rrr r/m
SUB r8,r/m8	2A /r	00101010 mm rrr r/m
SUB r16,r/m16	2B /r	00101011 mm rrr r/m
SUB r32,r/m32	2B /r	00101011 mm rrr r/m

Purpose: SUB subtracts the source operand from the destination operand and then replaces the destination operand with the result. If a borrow is required, the carry flag (CF) is set; CF is bit 0 of EFLAGS (see appendix H for a discussion of the 80386 registers and their contents). The operands can be signed or unsigned bytes, words, or doublewords.

TEST   Logical Compare

Instruction	Opcode	Binary
TEST AL,imm8	A8 ib	10101000
TEST AX,imm16	A9 iw	10101001
TEST EAX,imm32	A9 id	10101001
TEST r/m8,imm8	F6 /0 ib	11110110 mm 000 r/m
TEST r/m16,imm16	F7 /0 iw	11110111 mm 000 r/m
TEST r/m32,imm32	F7 /0 id	11110111 mm 000 r/m
TEST r/m8,r8	84 /r	10000100 mm rrr r/m
TEST r/m16,r16	85 /r	10000101 mm rrr r/m
TEST r/m32,r32	85 /r	10000101 mm rrr r/m

Purpose: TEST "ANDs" two operands. It then clears the overflow flag (OF) and carry flag (CF), leaves auxiliary carry (AF) undefined and updates the sign flag (SF), zero flag (ZF), and parity flag (PF). These flags are all contained in the EFLAGS register (see appendix H). The flags can be tested by conditional control transfer instructions or by the byte-set-on condition instructions.

The difference between TEST and AND is that TEST does not store the result in the first operand. TEST differs from BT (bit test) in that TEST tests the value of multiple bits in one operation, while BT tests a single bit.

VERR   Verify a Segment for Reading

VERW   Verify a Segment for Writing

Instruction	Opcode	Binary
VERR r/m16	0F 00 /4	00001111 00000000 mm 100 r/m
VERW r/m16	0F 00 /5	00001111 00000000 mm 101 r/m

Purpose: These instructions verify whether a segment noted by the selector can be reached with the current privilege level (CPL) and if the segment is readable. If the segment is accessible, the zero flag (ZF) is set to one. If not, ZF is set to zero. The validation done is the same as if the segment were loaded into DS, ES, FS or GS and the indicated read was performed.

Because ZF receives the result of the validation, the selector value does not result in a protection exception. This allows software to anticipate possible segment access problems.

XCHG   Exchange Register/Memory with Register

Instruction	Opcode	Binary
XCHG AX,r16	90 + r	10010rrr
XCHG r16,AX	90 + r	10010rrr
XCHG EAX,r32	90 + r	10010rrr
XCHG r32,EAX	90 + r	10010rrr
XCHG r/m8,r8	86 /r	10000110 mm rrr r/m
XCHG r8,r/m8	86 /r	10000110 mm rrr r/m
XCHG r/m16,r16	87 /r	10000111 mm rrr r/m
XCHG r16,r/m16	87 /r	10000111 mm rrr r/m
XCHG r/m32,r32	87 /r	10000111 mm rrr r/m
XCHG r32,r/m32	87 /r	10000111 mm rrr r/m

Note that XCHG, AX,AX is an NOP.

Purpose: XCHG swaps the contents of two operands and takes the place of three MOV instructions. It does not require a temporary location to save the contents of one operand while loading the other. XCHG is useful for implementing semaphores or similar data structures for process synchronization.

If one of the operands is memory, the bus transfer is always performed as if a LOCK prefix is given, even if LOCK was not specified.

XLAT   Table Lookup-Translation

XLATB

Instruction	Opcode	Binary
XLAT m8	D7	11010111

Purpose: XLAT is useful for translating from one coding system to another, such as from EBCDIC to ASCII. The translate table can be up to 256 bytes long. The value placed in AL serves as an index to the location of the corresponding translation value.

XLAT replaces a byte in AL with a byte from a user-coded translation table at [EBX + AL]. AL is always an unsigned value. When XLAT is executed, AL should have the unsigned index to the table addressed by EBX. XLAT changes the contents of AL from the table index to the table entry. EBX is unchanged.

The table is always based at [EBX], regardless of the m8. m8, however, does allow a segment override to be specified rather than the default DS:[EBX].

XOR Logical, Exclusive OR

Instruction	Opcode	Binary
XOR AL,imm8	34 ib	00110100
XOR AX,imm16	35 iw	00110101
XOR EAX,imm32	35 id	00110101
XOR r/m8,imm8	80 /6 ib	10000000 mm 110 r/m
XOR r/m16,imm16	81 /6 iw	10000001 mm 110 r/m
XOR r/m32,imm32	81 /6 id	10000001 mm 110 r/m
XOR r/m16,imm8	83 /6 ib	10000011 mm 110 r/m
XOR r/m32,imm8	83 /6 ib	10000011 mm 110 r/m
XOR r/m8,r8	30 /r	00110000 mm rrr r/m
XOR r/m16,r16	31 /r	00110001 mm rrr r/m
XOR r/m32,r32	31 /r	00110001 mm rrr r/m
XOR r8,r/m8	32 /r	00110010 mm rrr r/m
XOR r16,r/m16	33 /r	00110011 mm rrr r/m
XOR r32,r/m32	33 /r	00110011 mm rrr r/m

Purpose: XOR compares the bits in its two operands and stores the result into the first operand. Each bit of the result is one if the corresponding bits in the operands are different. Each bit is zero if the corresponding bits are the same. The result replaces the first operand.

Operand 1	110001
Operand 2	001101
Result	111100

Appendix C

80387 Coprocessor Instruction Set

THIS APPENDIX GIVES THE COMPLETE SET OF FLOATING-POINT INSTRUCTIONS AVAILABLE in an 80386/80387 system, along with the two instructions that access the 80387: ESC and WAIT. Some of the syntax for the floating-point instructions is different from that used for the 80386. That is discussed, and the examples of operands are kept simpler (for instance, there is no binary form of the instructions shown). There is a control word register, a tag-word register, and a status-word register that control the operation of the floating-point instructions and provide status information.

80387 DATA FORMATS

The 80387 supports seven data types, summarized in Fig. C-1. The largest integer number supported is 2^{32}, or $4.29 * 10^9$ in decimal.

Integer Data Types

The integer data types represented by the two's complement notation used by integer data types on the 80386. All these integers are common to the two chips, except that the 80386 supports an 8-bit integer, and the 80387 supports a 64-bit integer. The 80387 word integer can represent numbers from -32768 to 32767. The short integer supports $-2.147 * 10^9$ to $2.147 * 10^9$, and the long integer supports $-9.233 * 10^{18}$ to $9.233 * 10^{18}$.

Binary-Coded Decimal (BCD)

BCD supported by the 80387 is a packed-decimal type that is 80 bits long, which holds 18 decimal digits and one sign bit. The 80387 packed BCD leaves seven unused bits in the representation because, at 18 digits, it meets the COBOL standard. COBOL

Data Type	Bits	Significant Digits (in decimal)	Approximate Range (in decimal)		
Word Integer	16	4	−32768	≪ X ≫	+32767
Short Integer	32	9	$-2*10^9$	≪ X ≫	$+2*10^9$
Long Integer	64	18	$-9*10^{18}$	≪ X ≫	$+9*10^{18}$
Packed Decimal (BCD)	80	18	−99..99	≪ X ≫	+99..99 (18 digits)
Short Real	32	6 – 7	$-3.39*10^{-38}$	≪ X ≫	$+3.39*10^{38}$
Long Real	64	15 – 16	$-1.80*10^{-308}$	≪ X ≫	$+1.80*10^{308}$
Temporary Real	80	19	$-1.19*10^{-4932}$	≪ X ≫	$+1.19*10^{4932}$

Fig. C-1. Data Types Supported by the 80387.

is one of the prime languages that uses BCD, and there is no reason to complicate the design past 18 digits.

Real Formats

The format of a real floating-point number is composed of three parts: significand, exponent, and sign. Figure C-2 shows the bits that are used for each part of the format and the detailed bit locations of the data types.

The *sign* is simply that—a sign bit. If this bit is 1, the number is negative. If 0, the number is positive. The *significand* gives the significant bits of the number; the significand is often referred to as a mantissa. To make computations always yield the maximum precision, the results are *normalized*. That is, numbers always have their exponent adjusted such that the most significant (leftmost) bit of the binary significand is 1, with the binary point just to the right of this 1 bit.

The *exponent* field contains the power of two needed to scale the significand to achieve the final result. The exponent is stored in a biased form (biased numbers are discussed in chapter 6). Biased forms ease numerical comparisons. The biases are 127, 1023, and 16383 for short, long, and temporary real formats. Thus, an exponent of 10000000b (short real) is really 2^1.

Temporary Real Formats

The temporary real format is the internal form used by the 80387. No matter what data type you give (short integer, BCD, short real, and so on) the 80387 immediately converts it into temporary real. Temporary real maximizes the precision and range of computations.

Data Type	Total	Sign	Exponent	Significand
Short Real	32	1	8	23
Long Real	64	1	11	52
Temporary Real	80	1	15	64

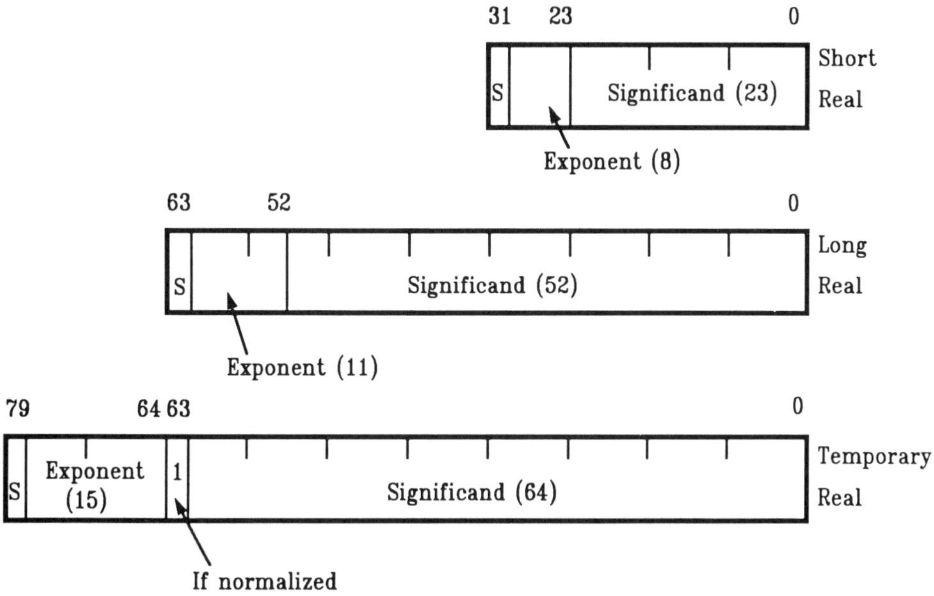

S = Sign

$$\text{VALUE} = (-1)^{\text{Sign}} * \text{Significand} * 2^{\text{Exponent}}$$

Fig. C-2. Real Formats.

Special Cases

There are five special cases: zero, infinity, denormal, pseudodenormal, and NaN (signaling and quiet). *Zero* is simply a biased exponent of 00...00b and a significand of 00...00b in all three formats. The biased exponent of zero cannot be used to represent a normal real number because it is reserved. Both positive and negative zero can be represented. The 80387 distinguishes between the two forms of zero only when it is dividing by zero.

Infinities have a biased exponent value of 11...11b, which is reserved. If the significand is also zero, you have infinity. Both positive and negative infinity can be represented. *Denormals* are a special case in representing very small numbers. Denormals allow a representation of gradual underflow or a gradual loss of precision. Most processors do not gradually underflow as does the 80387, but abruptly underflow. This means that when they get to the least normalized number, the next smaller representation used is zero. As a contrast, gradual underflow uses representations that are not normalized (denormal). This action results in a loss of precision, but it significantly extends the range of very small numbers.

The 80387 supports *pseudodenormals*, but can never produce them. Denormals normally have 0 as the most significant bit of the significand. Pseudodenormals have 1 for this bit. Pseudodenormals are unusual because they can be represented in a normalized form but have not been. This is true since the special-case biased exponent of 00...00 has the same exponential value as the normal biased exponent of 00...01. Also, the significand of a pseudodenormal is normalized; that is, the most significant bit is a 1.

NaN stands for *not a number* and has two forms, signaling and quiet. A signaling NaN causes an invalid operation exception to be raised when used in an operation. A quiet NaN does not. The signaling NaN has a 0 as the most significant significand bit, except for temporary real where the second most significant bit is a 0, and the most significant significand bit is a 1. You can use the signaling NaN to be sure that the program initializes all variables before use. You could initialize each variable in your program to a signaling NaN so that an exception is raised if an uninitialized value is used.

A NaN can have anything in the remainder of its fraction portion, which you can use to store information about where or why the NaN was produced. The 80387 never produces a signaling NaN.

A quiet NaN has 1 in the most significant significand bit except for the temporary real number, where the second most significant significand bit is 1, and the most significant bit is also 1. A quiet NaN is produced when an invalid operation exception occurs. Under all circumstances (except for FCOM, FIST, and FBSTP), quiet and signaling NaNs are preserved through operations.

80387 REGISTERS

The 80387 is used with the 80386 for high-performance operations on data. When used with the 80386, the numerical coprocessor adds three sets of registers to support floating-point calculations. Those registers are:

- Four 32-bit error pointer registers to identify the instruction and memory operand causing an exception—FOS, FOO, FCS, and FIP

- Three 16-bit status and control registers—one for a status word, one for a control word, and one for a tag word.

- A stack of eight 80-bit accumulators to hold up to eight floating-point operands.

Floating-Point Accumulator Registers

The accumulator stack is an array of eight physical registers, with a separate three-bit field that identifies the current stack top, as shown in Fig. C-3. A three-bit field (named TOP) in the status word contains the absolute register number of the current top of the accumulator stack, ST. After a PUSH, the previous ST becomes ST(1), and all the stacked accumulators have their ST-relative names incremented by 1.

Tag-Word Register

The 16-bit tag-word register, as shown in Fig. C-4, contains eight two-bit fields, one for each of the eight floating-point registers. Each TAG field indicates whether the corresponding floating-point register holds a valid, zero, special floating-point number,

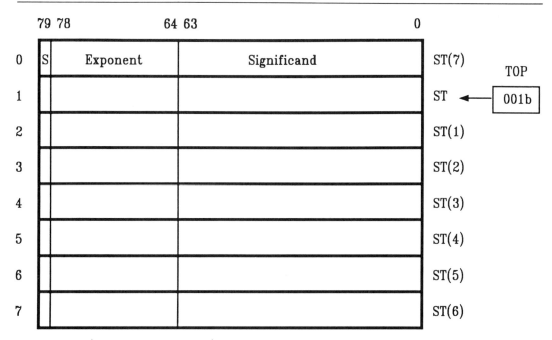

If TOP (in the Status Word) = 001b, then ST is at the second register, or register 1. After a PUSH, TOP increments by 1 and all the registers have their values incremented also. The increments and decrements ignore wrap-around. If TOP = 000b, a PUSH decrements TOP to 111b and stores the new value in register 7.

Fig. C-3. 80387 Accumulator Registers.

	15 14	13 12	11 10	9 8	7 6	5 4	3 2	1 0
TW	TAG7	TAG6	TAG5	TAG4	TAG3	TAG2	TAG1	TAG0

(Tag Word)

Tag Field Encoding

TAG	Meaning
00	Valid
01	Zero
10	Special – Infinity, NaN, Denormal
11	Empty

Fig. C-4. Tag-Word Register.

or is empty. To avoid the need to rotate the tag word as the accumulator stack is PUSHed and POPped, the fields in the TAG word correspond to the physical registers, rather than being relative to the stack top.

Control-Word Register

The control-word register contains three fields, all under program control:

• Bits 0 to 5—Contain the exception masks for the conditions that occur in the 80387.

• Bits 8 to 9—Precision control (PC). The results of floating-point arithmetic are rounded to one of the precisions as shown in Fig. C-5, before they are stored in the destination.

• Bits 10 to 11—Rounding control (RC). There are four rounding modes, as shown in Fig. C-5.

Status-Word Register

The 80387 sets certain bits in the status-word register, and these bits can be tested under program control. Figure C-6 shows the format of the status-word register. The fields are:

• Bits 0 to 5—These bits are set if an exception is detected and are sticky bits. That is, the 80387 sets them, and they must be explicitly reset under program control.

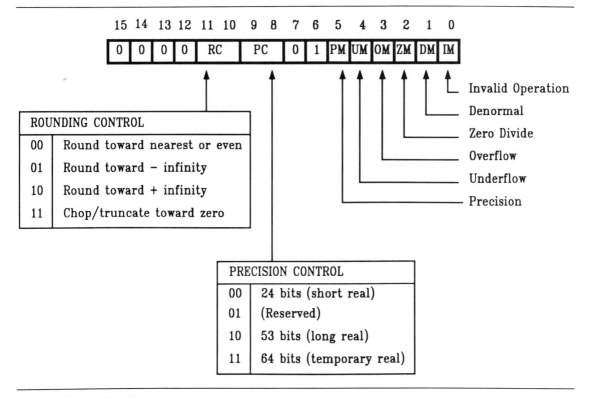

Fig. C-5. Control-Word Register.

- Bit 6—Stack fault (SF). This flag is set if an invalid operation exception is due to overflow, or underflow of the accumulator stack. Otherwise, it is reset.
- Bit 7 and Bit 15—These bits are set to 1 if any unmasked exception is indicated by the exception bits in the lower six bits of the status word. The status-word low-order six bits are masked by the exception mask in the lower six bits of the control word. Otherwise, bit 7 and 15 are set to 0.
- Bits 8 (C0), 9 (C1), 10 (C2), and 14 (C3)—Condition-code flags. These flags are set depending on the floating-point operations. They can be moved to the lower eight bits of the 80386 EFLAGS register.
- Bit 11 to 13—TOP. This field indicates which of the seven accumulator registers is the top of the stack.

Error-Pointer Registers

There are four 32-bit registers that hold pointers to the last 80387 instruction executed and that instruction data, as shown in Fig. C-7. These four registers are useful

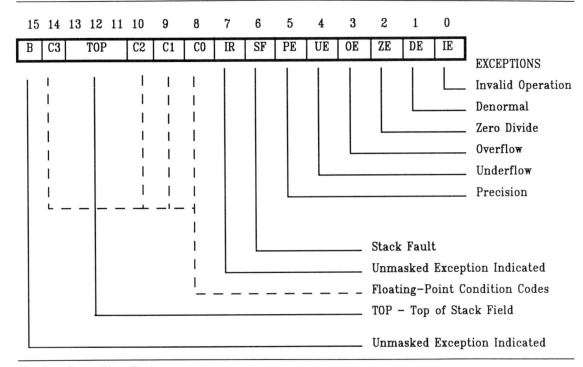

Fig. C-6. Status-Word Register.

in analyzing and reporting exceptions that occur during floating-point instruction execution. You need these registers, since the 80386 and 80387 can operate in parallel, and you could lose the error if the registers were not present.

FIP and FCS point to the 80387 instruction, along with the first two opcode bytes of that instruction, ignoring prefixes. FCS holds the selector and opcode, and FIP holds the offset. The opcode field is formed by combining the low-order three bits of the first instruction byte with the second instruction byte. The two bytes selected come after any prefixes, which means they contain the opcode field and the first byte of the MODRM field.

FOO and FOS, the second pair of registers, point to the memory operand of the last instruction executed. FOS holds the selector, and FOO holds the offset. Note that if the last instruction did not have a memory operand, FOO and FOS are undefined.

80387 INSTRUCTIONS

The assembler mnemonics follow a standard notation. That is:

• F—All floating-point instructions begin with F. No other 80386 instruction does.

- FB—The instructions that operate on BCD data types begin with FB.
- FI—The instructions that operate upon integer data begin with FI.
- FNxx—All instructions except for those that begin with FN check for unmasked numerical exceptions prior to execution.
- FxxP—Instructions that cause the stack to be POPped once end with P.
- FxxPP—Instructions that cause the stack to be POPped twice end in PP.

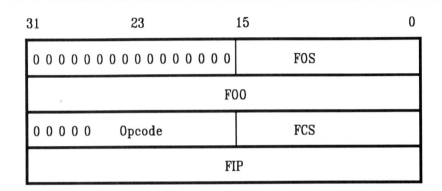

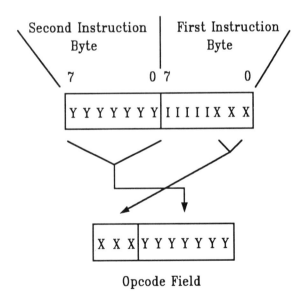

Opcode Field

Fig. C-7. Error-Pointer Registers.

The 80387 uses an accumulator stack, and almost all operations must have the stack top (referred to as ST) as one operand. The other accumulators are referenced in relation to ST, using the notation ST(n), which indicates the nth stack element beneath the current top of stack.

ESC Escape

Instruction	Opcode	Binary
ESC	D8 + TTT	11011TTT mod LLL r/m TTT and LLL are opcode information for the coprocessor.

Purpose: A numerical coprocessor provides an extension to the instruction set of the 80386. The coprocessor supports high-precision integer and floating-point calculations, in addition to containing a set of useful constants to enhance the speed of numerical calculations. The coprocessor operates in parallel with the CPU to provide maximum instruction throughput.

A program contains coprocessor instructions in the same instruction stream as the 80386 instructions. The system executes the coprocessor set in the same order as they appear in the stream.

ESC is a five-bit sequence that begins with the opcode that identifies floating-point numerical instructions. This sequence is 11011B. This pattern tells the 80386 to send the opcode and addresses of operands to the numerics coprocessor.

F2XM1 $2^x - 1$

Instruction	Operands
F2XM1	

Purpose: The item at the top of the stack is ST in the computation of $2^{ST} - 1$. The result of this computation replaces the initial ST. The input operand range is bounded by -0.5 and 0.5. If the operand is out of this range, the results are undefined.

FABS Absolute Value

Instruction	Operands
FABS	

Purpose: The top stack element is changed to its absolute value. The top stack element is always positive, following the FABS instruction execution.

FADD   **Real Addition**

FIADD   **Integer Addition**

FADDP   **Real Addition and POP**

Instruction	Operands
FADD	
	Operand1
	ST(n)
	m32
	m64
	Operand1,Operand2
	ST,ST(n)
	ST(n),ST
FIADD	Operand1
	m16
	m32
FADDP	Operand1,Operand2
	ST,ST(n)
	ST(n),ST

Purpose: The explicitly defined or implicitly specified floating-point operands are added, and the result is stored in the first operand. The destination (or first) operand in all cases is the stack top, except the two-operand form where the destination can be ST(n) where *n* is the accumulator in the stack with reference to the top of stack.

If the first operand is a memory operand, it is automatically converted to temporary real (which is the 80387 internal format) before any operations are performed on it.

Note: An FADDP or FADD without operands causes the stack to be POPped. Thus FADD with no operands is synonymous with FADDP ST(1),ST.

FBLD   **BCD Load**

Instruction	Operands
FBLD	m80

Purpose: The ten-byte packed BCD memory operand pointed to by m80 is converted to a temporary real value and PUSHed onto the top of the stack. The conversion is always exact. The BCD digits must be in the range 0h to 9h. An attempt to load invalid BCD digits puts an undefined temporary real value into ST.

FBSTP   BCD Store and POP

Instruction	Operands
FBSTP	m80

Purpose: The stack top is converted to an 18-digit BCD number, which is then stored into the ten-byte location pointed to by m80, and then the stack is POPped. ST is rounded to an integer. This instruction is very slow and may cause an interrupt latency problem.

ST for FBSTP can be a denormal (it could not be for an 80287). If ST is a quiet NaN, an invalid operation will be generated. Operations with quiet NaNs do not usually generate exceptions.

FCHS   Change Sign

Instruction	Operands
FCHS	

Purpose: The sign of the top of stack element is complemented. If the stack top was $+0.9$, it is changed to -0.09 by FCHS.

FCLEX   Clear Exceptions

FNCLEX

Instruction	Operands
FCLEX	
FNCLEX	

Purpose: These instructions cause the 80387 to clear all exceptions and the busy bit of the status-word register. FCLEX checks for unmasked numerical exceptions, while FNCLEX does not.

FCOM   Compare

FCOMP   Compare and POP

FCOMPP   Compare and POP Two

Instruction	Operands
FCOM	Operand1
	m32

                              m64
                              ST(i)

            FCOMP   Operand1
                              m32
                              m64
                              ST(i)

            FCOMPP

Purpose: The given operand is numerically compared with the top of stack. The condition codes are set according to the table shown in Fig. C-8.

Operation	C3	C2	C0
ST > Operand 1	0	0	0
ST < Operand 1	0	0	1
ST = Operand 1	1	0	0
Unordered	1	1	1

Note: See the section on the Status Word Register

for locations of C0, C2, and C3

Fig. C-8. Compare Condition Codes.

If the opcode was FCOMPP, the operand compared against the top of stack is ST(1)—the first below the top of stack. If the operand was FCOMP, the stack is POPped once after comparison. Unordered comparison occurs if either of the two operands are NaNs. The sign of zero is ignored in comparisons.

FCOM generates an invalid operation exception if either operand is a quiet NaN. Usually, operations with quiet NaNs do not cause operation exceptions.

FCOS   Cosine

                    Instruction   Operands

                    FCOS

Purpose: New to the 80387, the cosine of ST (top of stack) is computed. After the computation, the stack top is set to the cosine of ST and 1.0 is PUSHed onto the stack. The input operand to FCOS must be in the range of 0 to PI $* 2^{62}$. If the source operand is within this range, C2 is set to 0 (see the section on the status word for location of C2). Otherwise, C2 is set to 1, ST is left intact, and the stack-top pointer is unchanged.

FDECSTP   Decrement Stack Pointer

Instruction	Operands
FDECSTP	

Purpose: One is subtracted from the stack-top pointer TOP in the status word. See the section on the status word register for the location of TOP. This instruction allows direct control of the stack pointer, which can be useful if a virtual accumulator stack is needed that is larger than the eight hardware accumulators provided on the 80387. The virtual-stack registers would reside in memory, and software would manage this stack when stack invalid operation exceptions are detected.

Using FDECSTP, the tag word and the stack top itself are not updated. If an FDECSTP is executed when TOP is 0, ST becomes 7. PUSHing a new element onto the stack causes the stack pointer to be decremented, as does FDECSTP.

FDIV   Real Division

FIDIV   Integer Divide

FDIVP   Real Divide and POP

Instruction	Operands
FDIV	
	Operand1
	ST(n)
	m32
	m64
	Operand1,Operand2
	ST,ST(n)
	ST(n),ST
FIDIV	Operand1
	m16
	m32

FDIVP   Operand1,Operand2
              ST,ST(n)
              ST(n),ST

Purpose: The explicitly or implicitly specified floating-point operands are divided, with the result placed back into the first operand, the destination. The destination is the stack top in all cases except the two-operand form, where the destination can be ST(n). If operand1 is a memory operand, it is automatically converted to temporary real (the internal 80387 format) before any operations are performed with it.

An FDIV without operands causes the stack to be POPped. FDIV with no operands is synonymous with FDIVP ST(1),ST.

FDIVR   Division Reverse

FIDIVR   Integer Divide Reverse

FDIVRP   Real Divide Reverse and POP

Instruction	Operands
FDIVR	Operand1
	ST(n)
	m32
	m64
	Operand1,Operand2
	ST,ST(n)
	ST(n),ST
FDIVR	Operand1
	m16
	m32
FDIVRP	Operand1,Operand2
	ST,ST(n)
	ST(n),ST

Purpose: The explicitly or implicitly specified operands are divided with the result stored into the first operand, the destination. The destination is the stack top in all cases except the two-operand form where the destination can be ST(n). These operations are equivalent to FDIV/FIDIV/FDIVP, except numerator and divisor are reversed.

If operand1 is a memory operand, it is automatically converted to temporary (the 80387 internal format) before any operations are performed on it. An FDIVR without operands causes the stack to be POPped, which makes it synonymous with FDIVRP ST(1),ST.

FFREE   Free Register

Instruction	Operands
FFREE	ST(n)

Purpose: The tag-word bits associated with the specified register are set to 11b, which indicates that the specified stack element is changed to empty. Neither the floating-point stack nor the floating-point stack pointer is modified. The tag word describes the physical stack registers, and FFREE gives an accumulator stack reference that is relative to the stack top.

FICOM   Integer Compare

FICOMP   Integer Compare and POP

Instruction	Operands
FICOM	Operand1 m16 m32
FICOMP	Operand1 m16 m32

Purpose: The given operand is converted from word or short integer into temporary real, and numerically compared against the top of stack. The condition codes are set according to the table shown in Fig. C-9.

Unordered comparison occurs if the stack top is a NaN. The sign of zero is ignored in comparisons. If the operand is FICOMP, the stack is POPped.

FILD   Integer Load

Instruction	Operands
FILD	Operand1 m16 m32 m64

Operation	C3	C2	C0
ST > Operand 1	0	0	0
ST < Operand 1	0	0	1
ST = Operand 1	1	0	0
Unordered	1	1	1

Note: See the section on the Status Word Register

for locations of C0, C2, and C3

Fig. C-9. Integer Compare Condition Codes.

Purpose: The memory word, short integer, or long integer specified by the first operand is read from memory and converted into temporary real (the 80387 internal format). The stack is PUSHed, and the temporary real is placed in the new top of stack.

FINCSTP   Increment Stack Pointer

Instruction   Operands

FINCSTP

Purpose: This instruction allows direct control of the stack pointer. One is added to the stack pointer in the status word (see the section on the status-word register for the location of the pointer). The tag word (TW) and the contents of the floating-point stack are not updated. If FINCSTP is executed when the stack-top pointer (TOP) is 7, ST becomes 0. POPping an element off the stack causes the stack pointer to be incremented.

FINIT   Initialize Processor

FNINIT

Instruction   Operands

FINIT
FNINIT

Purpose: These two instructions set all the control-word, status-word, and tag-word registers to their default values. After execution, the machine rounding control is set to round to nearest, all exceptions are masked, precision is set to 64 bits, the status word (SW) is cleared except for the four condition code bits (which are undefined), and all floating-point stack registers (TW) are set to empty. FINIT checks for unmasked numerical exceptions, while FNINIT does not.

FIST   Integer Store

Instruction	Operands
FIST	Operand1
	m16
	m32

Purpose: The stack top is rounded to an integer whose length matches that of the first operand. The rounding is as specified by the round control (RC) bits of the control word (CW) register. The integer is then stored into the first operand. Negative zero is converted to two's complement to a positive zero before storing. FIST cannot store a long integer. If ST is a quiet NaN, an invalid operation exception is generated.

FISTP   Integer Store and POP

Instruction	Operands
FISTP	Operand1
	m16
	m32
	m64

Purpose: The stack top is rounded to an integer, whose length matches that of the first operand. The rounding is as specified by RC in the control-word register. The integer is then stored into the first operand. FISTP can store a long integer, where FIST cannot. Negative zero is converted to two's complement positive zero. The stack is POPped.

FLD   Real Load

Instruction	Operands
FLD	Operand1
	m32
	m64

m80
ST(i)

The i is any position on the stack.

Purpose: The operand specified in operand1 is PUSHed onto the top of the stack. If the operand is a short or long real, it is converted to a temporary real (the 80387 internal format) prior to being PUSHed onto the stack.

FLDcon   Load Constant

Instruction	Operands
FLD1	
FLDL2E	
FLDL2T	
FLDLG2	
FLDLN2	
FLDPI	
FLDZ	

Purpose: The constant value that is specified by the instruction itself is PUSHed onto the stack and becomes the new top of stack. FLD is 1.0. FLDL2E is $\log_2 e$. FLDL2T is $\log_2 10$. FLDLG2 is $\log_{10} 2$. FLDLN2 is $\log_e 2$. FLDPI is the value of PI. FLDZ is 0.0.

FLDCW   Load Control Word

Instruction	Operands
FLDCW	m16

Purpose: This instruction loads the control word (CW) register with the value found in m16. An exception is flagged if any of the exception flags in SW (the status word) register are unmasked by the new control word.

FLDENV   Load Environment

Instruction	Operands
FLDENV	m

Purpose: This instruction loads the machine environment from the given memory area. This environment consists of the tag-word register, the status-word register, and the control-word register, along with the error-pointer registers of the most recent floating-point instruction executed. Note that the error-pointer registers contain information on the most recent opcode and the data referenced.

FMUL   Real Multiply

FIMUL   Integer Multiply

FMULP   Real Multiply and POP

Instruction	Operands
FMUL	
	Operand1
	ST(n)
	m32
	m64
	Operand1,Operand2
	ST,ST(n)
	ST(n),ST
FIMUL	Operand1
	m16
	m32
FMULP	Operand1,Operand2
	ST,ST(n)
	ST(n),ST

Purpose: The specified operands are multiplied, with the result being stored in the first operand, the destination. The destination is the top of stack in all cases except the two-operand form where the destination can be ST(n).

If the first operand is a memory operand, it is automatically converted to temporary real (the 80387 internal format) before any operations are performed on it. An FMUL without operands causes the stack to be POPped, which makes it synonymous with FMULP ST(1),ST.

FNOP   No Operation

Instruction   Operands

FNOP

Purpose: FNOP stores the stack to the stack top, which is effectively a NOP.

FPATAN   Partial Arctangent

Instruction   Operands

FPATAN

Purpose: The arctangent of ST(1)/ST is computed. After the computation, the stack is POPped once, and the result placed in the new top of stack.

FPREM   Partial Remainder

Instruction   Operands

FPREM

Purpose: FPREM computes the partial remainder of ST/ST(1). The remainder is computed by a series of successive scaled subtractions, so that the remainder produced is exact with no precision error possible. If the operands differ greatly in magnitude, this series of subtractions can take a very long time. To prevent severe performance degradation, the instruction only partially computes the remainder and a software loop is required to complete the reduction.

FPREM reduces a magnitude difference up to 2^{64} in one execution. If the reduction is complete, condition code 2 is set to 0 and condition code 0, 3, and 1 (in that order) reflect the least significant 3 bits of the quotient. If the reduction was incomplete, condition code 2 is set to 1. See the section on the control word to find the location of the condition codes.

The result follows the relation:

$$REM = ST - ST(1) * \text{Quotient}$$

where the remainder always has the sign of the original ST.

FPREM1 Partial Remainder - IEEE

Instruction   Operands

FPREM1

Purpose: New with the 80387, this instruction computes the partial remainder of ST/ST(1). It is for the purpose of IEEE compatibility.

The remainder is computed by a series of successive scaled subtractions, so the remainder is exact with no precision error. When the operands differ greatly in magnitude, these subtractions can take a very long time. To prevent severe degradation of interrupt latency, the instruction only partially computes the remainder. A software loop is required to complete the reduction.

FPREM1 reduces a magnitude difference up to 2^{64} in one execution. If the reduction is complete, condition code 2 is set to 0, and condition codes 0, 3, and 1 (in that order) reflect the three least significant bits of the quotient. If the reduction is incomplete, condition code 2 is set to 1. See the section on the control word for the location of the condition codes.

The result obeys the relation:

$$REM = ST - ST(1) * Quotient$$

where the quotient is the integer nearest to the exact value of ST/ST(1). Rounding mode and precision control do not affect the results except when ST(1) exactly divides into ST. In this case, the result is plus zero for rounding control of nearest, up, or chop; it is minus zero for down. If ST(1) was initially infinity, ST is unchanged and the quotient (condition codes) is set to zero.

FPTAN Partial Tangent

Instruction   Operands

FPTAN

Purpose: The tangent of ST is computed. After the computation, the stack top is set to the tangent of ST and 1.0 PUSHed onto the stack. Thus:

$$ST(1)/ST = tan(ST')$$

where ST' is the stack top prior to the tangent instruction. ST is always 1.0, and ST(1) is the tangent of ST'.

FRNDINT   Round to Integer

Instruction   Operands

FRNDINT

Purpose: FRNDINT rounds the top of stack element to an integer. The rounding obeys the RC (rounding control) setting found in the control word (see the section on the control word for the location of RC). The four rounding modes are: 00 = nearest, 01 = minus infinity, 10 = plus infinity, and 11 = chop.

FRSTOR   Restore State

Instruction   Operands

FRSTOR   m

Purpose: This instruction reloads the complete state of the 80387 from a 108-byte location given by m. The format of the load memory is identical to that of the FSAVE instruction. Included in the restore are the 80387 environment and the eight 80-bit floating-point stack registers. Any exception is possible, if the combination of the status word and the control word are in an exception condition.

FSAVE   Save State

FNSAVE

Instruction   Operands

FSAVE   m
FNSAVE   m

Purpose: These instructions store the complete state of the 80387 into the memory location m. This environment consists of the control-word register, the status-word register, and the tag-word registers, the error-pointer registers, and the complete floating-point stack (eight 80-bit registers). See the beginning of this appendix for the formats of these registers.

After storing the 80387 state, FSAVE initializes the 80387 in the same way the FINIT instruction does. FSAVE checks for unmasked numerical exceptions, while FNSAVE does not.

FSCALE   Power of Two Scaling

Instruction   Operands

FSCALE

Purpose: FSCALE scales the top or stack by the power of two given in ST(1). This ST(1) value is treated as an integer (chopped) and is added to the exponent of ST, which is useful as a quick way of multiplying by powers of two. Operands that cause overflow or underflow signal exceptions.

FSIN   Sine

Instruction   Operands

FSIN

Purpose: New with the 80387, FSIN computes the sine of ST. After the computation, the stack top is set to the sine of ST, and 1.0 is PUSHed onto the stack. Thus:

$$ST(1)/ST = \sin (ST')$$

where ST′ is the stack top prior to the sine operation. ST is always 1.0, and ST(1) is the sine of ST′. The input operand to FSIN must be in the range of 0 to PI $* 2^{62}$. If the source operand is in this range, C2 is set to 0; otherwise, C2 is set to 1, and ST and TOP are unchanged. See the beginning of this appendix for the locations of C2 and TOP.

FSINCOS   Sine and Cosine

Instruction   Operands

FSINCOS

Purpose: New with the 80387, this instruction computes both the sine and cosine of ST. After the computation is complete, the stack top is set to the sine of ST; then the cosine is PUSHed onto the stack. Thus, at the end of the execution:

$$ST(1) = \sin (ST')$$

and

$$ST = \cos (ST')$$

where ST′ is the stack top prior to FSINCOS. The input operand to this instruction must be in the range of 0 to PI $* 2^{62}$. If it is, C2 is set to 0. Otherwise, C2 is set to 1, and ST and TOP are unchanged. See the beginning of this appendix for the locations of the condition codes and TOP.

FSQRT   Square Root

Instruction   Operands

FSQRT

Purpose: The top of the stack is replaced with the square root of the top of the stack.

$$\text{FSQRT}(-0) \qquad = -0$$
$$\text{FSQRT}(+ \text{ infinity}) \qquad = \text{ plus infinity}$$
$$\text{FSQRT}(- \text{ infinity}) \qquad \text{ is invalid}$$

FST   Real Store

Instruction   Operands

FST   Operand1
              m32
              m64
              ST(i)

The i is any position in the stack.

Purpose: The top of stack is stored in operand1. If it is a short or long real, the top of stack is first converted to the type according to RC (round control) in the control word—see the beginning of this appendix for the location and meaning of the round control. If the top of stack is a NaN or an infinity, the stack-top exponent and significant are chopped rather than rounded to fit the destination sizes.

FST cannot store a temporary real operand to memory, whereas FSTP can.

FSTCW   Store Control Word

FNSTCW

Instruction   Operands

FSTCW   m16
FNSTCW   m16

Purpose: These instructions store the control word into m16. FSTCW checks for unmasked numerical exceptions, while FNSTCW does not.

FSTENV   Store Environment

FNSTENV

Instruction	Operands
FSTENV	m
FNSTENV	m

Purpose: These instructions store the machine environment to the given memory location. This environment consists of the control-word register, the status-word register, and the tag-word register, and the error pointers of the most recent floating-point instruction executed. See the beginning of this appendix for the formats of the registers. FSTENV checks for unmasked numerical exceptions, and FNSTENV does not.

FSTP   Real Store and POP

Instruction	Operands
FSTP	Operand1
	m32
	m64
	m80
	ST(i)

The i is any position on the stack.

Purpose: The top of stack is stored into the first operand. If it is a short or long real, the top of stack is first converted as specified by RC (rounding control)—see the beginning of this appendix for the location and meaning of RC. If the top of stack is a NaN or infinity, the stack-top exponent and the significand are chopped rather than rounded to fit the destination sizes. FSTP can store a temporary real number to memory, where FST cannot.

FSTSW   Store Status Word

FNSTSW

Instruction	Operands
FSTSW	m16
FNSTSW	m16

Purpose: These instructions store the current status word into m16. FSTSW checks for unmasked numerical exceptions, while FNSTSW does not.

FSTSW AX   Store Status Word into AX

FNSTSW AX

Instruction	Operands
FSTSW	AX
FNSTSW	AX

Purpose: These instructions store the current status word into the 80386 AX register. FSTSW checks for unmasked numerical exceptions, while FNSTSW does not. These instructions are useful for control-flow changes based on the condition flag settings of the 80387.

FSUB   Real Subtraction

FISUB   Integer Subtraction

FSUBP   Real Subtraction and POP

Instruction	Operands
FSUB	Operand1
	ST(n)
	m32
	m64
	Operand1,Operand2
	ST,ST(n)
	ST(n),ST
FISUB	Operand1
	m16
	m32
FSUBP	Operand1,Operand2
	ST,ST(n)
	ST(n),ST

Purpose: The operands are subtracted with the result being stored in the first operand, the destination. The destination is the stack top in all cases, except the two-operand form where the destination can be ST(n). If the first operand is a memory operand, it is automatically converted to temporary real (the 80387 internal format) before any operations are performed with it. An FSUB without operands causes the stack to be POPped, which makes it synonymous with FSUBP ST(1),ST.

FSUBR   Real Subtraction Reverse

FISUBR   Integer Subtraction Reverse

FSUBRP   Real Subtraction Reverse with POP

Instruction	Operands
FSUBR	Operand1 ST(n) m32 m64
	Operand1,Operand2 ST,ST(n) ST(n),ST
FISUBR	Operand1 m16 m32
FSUBRP	Operand1,Operand2 ST,ST(n) ST(n),ST

Purpose: The operands are subtracted, with the result being placed in the first operand, the destination. The destination is the stack top in all cases except the two-operand form where the destination can be ST(n). If the first operand is a memory operand, it is automatically converted to temporary real (the 80387 internal format) before any operations are performed with it. An FSUBR without operands causes the stack to be POPped, which makes it synonymous with FSUBRP ST(1),ST.

FTST   Test

Instruction   Operands

FTST

Purpose: The stack top is numerically compared against 0. The condition code bits in the status word are set according to the table shown in Fig. C-10.

Operation	C3	C2	C0
ST > 0.0	0	0	0
ST < 0.0	0	0	1
ST = 0.0	1	0	0
Unordered	1	1	1

Note: See the section on the Status Word Register

for locations of C0, C2, and C3

Fig. C-10. Test Condition Codes.

See the beginning of this appendix for the location of the condition codes. Unordered comparison occurs if ST is a NaN. The sign of zero is ignored in comparisons.

FUCOM   Unordered Compare

FUCOMP   Unordered Compare with POP

FUCOMPP   Unordered Compare with POP Two

Instruction   Operands

FUCOM   Operand1
             m32
             m64
             ST(i)

FUCOMP   Operand1
            m32
            m64
            ST(i)

FUCOMPP

The i is any position on the stack.

Purpose: The operand is numerically compared with the top of the stack. The condition codes are set according to the table shown in Fig. C-11.

Operation	C3	C2	C0
ST > Operand 1	0	0	0
ST < Operand 1	0	0	1
ST = Operand 1	1	0	0
Unordered	1	1	1

Note: See the section on the Status Word Register

for locations of C0, C2, and C3

Fig. C-11. Unordered Compare Condition Codes.

See the beginning of this appendix for the location of the condition codes. If the opcode was FUCOMPP, the operand compared against the top of stack is ST(1), and the stack POPped twice. If the operand was FUCOMP, the stack is POPped once. Unordered comparison occurs if either the operands is a NaN. The sign of zero is ignored in the comparisons.

FXAM Examine

Instruction   Operands

FXAM

Purpose: The stack top is examined. The condition codes of the status word are modified according to the table in Fig. C-12.

See the beginning of this appendix for the location of the condition codes in the status word. The unsupported entry in the table refers to pseudo-NaN, pseudoinfinity, unnormal, or pseudozero.

ST Value	C3	C2	C1	C0
+ Unsupported	0	0	0	0
+ NaN	0	0	0	1
− Unsupported	0	0	1	0
− NaN	0	0	1	1
+ Normal	0	1	0	0
+ Infinity	0	1	0	1
− Normal	0	1	1	0
− Infinity	0	1	1	1
+ 0	1	0	0	0
+ Empty	1	0	0	1
− 0	1	0	1	0
− Empty	1	0	1	1
+ Denormal	1	1	0	0
+ Empty	1	1	0	1
− Denormal	1	1	1	0
− Empty	1	1	1	1

Note: See the section on the Status Word Register
for locations of C0, C1, C2 and C3

Fig. C-12. Examine Condition Codes.

FXCH Exchange Registers

Instruction	Operands
FXCH	Operand1
	ST(n)

Purpose: The contents of the first operand are exchanged with the contents of the top of stack. This provides a convenient way to use the various 80387 instructions that operate only on the top of stack, such as FSQRT and FSIN.

FXTRACT Extract Exponent and Significant

Instruction	Operands
FXTRACT	

Purpose: The unbiased exponent of the original stack top is placed on the stack top as a real number. The significand and sign are pushed onto the stack, as the new top of stack. Thus, the original stack top is decomposed into a true exponent, ST(1), and a significant, ST, portion. The significand has an exponent of zero.

If the operand is zero, ST(1)—the exponent—is set to negative infinity, and ST—the significand—is set to 0 with the same sign as the original stack top. This differs from the 80287. If the operand was infinity, the ST(1) exponent is positive infinity, and the ST significand is infinity with the sign of the original stack top.

FYL2X Y * $\log_2$X

Instruction	Operands
FYL2X	

Purpose: The top two stack elements are used in the comparison of the function:

$$ST(1) * \log_2 ST$$

The stack is POPped, and the new stack top is replaced with the result of the computation. ST must be in the range of 0 to positive infinity. The ST(1) operand can be minus infinity to plus infinity. If the operands are not in this range, the instruction produces an undefined result, and no exception will be detected.

FYL2XP1 Y * log₂(X+1)

$$\text{FYL2XP1 Y} * \log_2(X+1)$$

Instruction   Operands

FYL2XP1

Purpose: The top two stack elements are used in the computation:

$$ST(1) * \log_2(ST + 1.0)$$

The stack is POPped, and the new stack top is replaced with the result of the computation. ST must be in the range of that shown in Fig. C-13.

$$-(1 - \sqrt{2}/2) \quad \text{to} \quad +(1 - \sqrt{2}/2)$$

Fig. C-13. ST Range.

ST(1) can be in the range of minus infinity to plus infinity. If the operands are not in this range, the instruction will produce an undefined result, and no exception will be detected.

WAIT   Wait until BUSY# Pin is Inactive (High)

Instruction	Opcode	Binary
WAIT	9B	10011011

Purpose: A numerical coprocessor provides an extension to the instruction set of the 80386. The coprocessor supports high-precision integer and floating-point calculations, in addition to containing a set of useful constants to enhance the speed of numerical calculations. The coprocessor operates in parallel with the CPU to provide maximum instruction throughput.

A program contains coprocessor instructions in the same instruction stream with the 80386 instructions. The system executes the coprocessor set in the same order as they appear in the stream.

WAIT suspends 80386 program execution until the 80386 CPU detects that the BUSY pin is inactive. This indicates that the coprocessor has completed its processing task and that the CPU can now obtain the results.

Appendix D

Overview of BIOS Interrupts/Calls

BIOS MEANS BASIC INPUT/OUTPUT SYSTEM. IT DOES JUST WHAT THE NAME IMPLIES; IT HANdles system I/O while keeping track of equipment connected to the system. BIOS updates appear as often (or perhaps more so) than DOS updates. This means that some of the information in this appendix will change at some point in time. However, MS-DOS and BIOS designers seem to be keeping the basic user interfaces the same, which is good news, even if the underlying code changes.

Note that the interrupt numbers below are hexadecimal; for example, interrupt 1 is really INT 1h, and interrupt 10 function 3 is INT 10 function 03h.

Interrupt 0 - Divided by Zero

If the processor executes a divide by zero, INT 0 is called. Generally, this stops program execution.

Interrupt 1 - Single Step

INT 1 single steps through code, a necessity for program debugging. There is a call to INT 1 in between each line of program code.

Interrupt 2 - Non-Maskable Interrupt (NMI)

INT 2 is a hardware interrupt that cannot be blocked off by using either STI or CLI. INT 2 executes when called.

Interrupt 3 - Breakpoint

INT 3 is another important debug interrupt. In fact, the programs DEBUG uses INT 3 with the GO command. For instance, if you want to execute code to a particular address and then stop, DEBUG inserts INT 3 into the code at that point and gives control to the program. When the INT 3 is reached, DEBUG takes control again.

Interrupt 4 - Overflow

If there is an overflow condition, INT 4 is called. Generally, no action is called for, and BIOS returns.

Interrupt 5 - Print Screen

The PrtSc key uses INT 5 to print the screen. Your program can do the same by simply calling this interrupt.

Interrupt 6 & 7 - Reserved for Future Development

As with undefined bits in registers, you can use these interrupts for your own uses, but it is highly recommended that you do not because future development will cause you to go back and reprogram.

Interrupt 8 - Time of Day

INT 8 updates the internal time of day in the computer. It does this however many times a second your internal clock runs. This interrupt calls INT 1C (timer tick interrupt). We recommend that you actually use INT 1C if you need to write a handler that interacts with the clock.

Interrupt 9 - Keyboard Input

Each time you press a keyboard key, INT 9 is generated. The waiting keystroke is read from the keyboard port, processed, and stored in the keyboard buffer (if required). INT 9 does a lot of work, so we recommend that you allow INT 9 to do its job and read from the keyboard buffer (if anything is stored there).

Interrupt 0A - Reserved for Future Development

The same caveat mentioned above is stressed here. You can use this if you are willing to invest the future time to go back and rewrite when BIOS finally uses this interrupt.

Interrupt 0B - 0F

These interrupts point to the BIOS routine end-of-interrupt (D__EOI) routine. D__EOI simply resets the interrupt handler at port 20h and return.

Interrupt 10 - Screen/Character Handling

The INT 10 includes a whole collection of routines that use AH as input with various quantities as output. Each of the functions have input and output notations. Input values are always in AH. In the notation below, B&W means black and white on a graphics screen and does not refer to a monochrome screen.

INT 10 Function 00 - Set Screen Mode

Input: AH = 00
            AL = mode:
            00   16-shade gray text   40 × 25
                  EGA: 64-color
            01   16/8-color text   40 × 25
                  EGA: 64-color
            02   16-shade gray text   80 × 25
                  EGA: 64-color
            03   16/8-color text   80 × 25
                  EGA: 64-color
            04   4-color graphics   320 × 200
            05   4-shade gray graphics   320 × 200
            06   2-shade gray graphics   640 × 200
            07   Monochrome text   80 × 25
            08   16-color graphics   160 × 200
            09   16-color graphics   320 × 200
            0A   4-color graphics   640 × 200
            0B   Reserved
            0C   Reserved
            0D   16-color graphics   320 × 200
            0E   16-color graphics   640 × 200
            0F   Monochrome graphics   640 × 350
            10   16/64-color graphics   640 × 350

INT 10 Function 01 - Set Cursor Type

INT 10 Function 1 allows you to change how your cursor looks. The cursor on a monochrome screen is 14 pixel lines tall (0 to 13) and on a graphics screen is 8 (0-7) pixel lines tall. You put the starting of the cursor matrix in CH and the end in CL. For instance, if you want the cursor to be only one line tall, store 0C in CH and 0D in CL before you issue INT 10. If you wanted the cursor to be at both the top and bottom, use the wrap-around feature: store 0D in CH and 00 in CL. You cannot stop the cursor from blinking—that is set in hardware—but you can redesign or eliminate it.

```
Input:      AH  =  01
            CH  =  Starting scan line
            CL  =  Ending scan line

   Note:              CH  <  CL gives normal one-part cursor.
                      CH  >  CL gives two-part cursor.
                      CH  =  20 gives no cursor.
```

INT 10 Function 02 - Set Cursor Position

This function changes the position of the cursor. Store the row number in DH and the column in DL, remembering that 0,0 is the upper left of your screen. If you are using a graphics screen with a possibility of four pages, put the page number in BH. If you are using a monochrome display, store a 0 in BH.

```
Input:      AH  =  02
            BH  =  Display page number (0 in graphics)
            DH  =  Row number
            DL  =  Column number
```

INT 10 Function 03 - Find Cursor Position

This function allows you to find where your cursor is, remembering that 0,0 is the upper left of the screen. If you are using a graphics screen with four pages, put the page number into BH. If you are using monochrome, store a 0 in BH. Function 3 of INT 10 returns the row number in DH, the column number in DL, the cursor mode in CH,CL (where the matrix starting line is in CL and the ending line is in CH).

```
Input:      AH  =  03
            BH  =  Display page number

Output:     CH  =  Matrix ending line
            CL  =  Matrix starting line
            DH  =  Row number
            DL  =  Column number
```

INT 10 Function 04 - Read Light Pen Position

Input: AH = 04

Output: AH = 00 Light pen switch not set
                    AL = 01   Then:
                              DH = Row of light pen position
                              DL = column of light pen
                                       position
                              CH = Pixel line (vertical row)
                                       0-199
                              CX = Pixel line number (for some
                                       EGA modes)
                              BX = Pixel column (horizontal
                                       column) 0-319,639

INT 10 Function 05 - Set Active Display Page

By using INT 10 Function 05, you can move between the various pages in text mode on graphics monitors. Note that if you are doing graphics on the graphics monitor, only one page (page 0) is available for your use. Also, on monochrome monitors, you only have page 0.

Input: AH = 05
         AL = Page number:
         0-7   Screen modes 0 and 1 = 40-column text modes
         0-3   Screen modes 2 and 3 = 80-column text modes
         varies   = EGA graphics modes

Note: Each page = 2kb in 40-column text mode, 4kb in 80-column text mode.

INT 10 Function 06 - Scroll Active Page Up

INT 10 Function 06 is useful when you have ''fill in the blank'' types of applications and you selectively clear parts of the screen; see Fig. D-1 for an example. It is also useful for scrolling windows.

Input: AH   =   06
         AL   =   Number of lines blanked at bottom of the screen
                    (00 = blanks entire screen)
         BH   =   Display attribute used on blank lines
         CH   =   Upper left row of area to scroll

Fig. D-1. Example of Selectively Scrolling.

CL = Upper left column of area to scroll
DH = Lower right row of area to scroll
DL = Lower right column of area to scroll

INT 10 Function 07 - Scroll Active Page Down

Input: AH = 07
        AL = Number of lines blanked at top of screen
             (00 = blank entire screen)
        BH = Display attribute used on blank lines
        CH = Upper left row of area to scroll
        CL = Upper left column of area to scroll
        DH = Lower right row of area to scroll
        DL = Lower right column of area to scroll

INT 10 Function 08 - Read Attribute and Character at Cursor Position

Input: AH = 08
        BH = Display page number (for text mode only)

Output: If text mode:
                AL = Character read (in ASCII)
                AH = Attribute of character
                        (alphanumerics only)
            If graphics mode:
                AL = ASCII character (00 if unmatched)

INT 10 Function 09 - Write Attribute and Character at Cursor Position

Input: AH = 09
           AL = ASCII character to write
           BH = Display page number (graphics 1–4, monochrome = 0)
           BL = Text attribute (alpha mode)
               = Color of foreground (graphics mode)
           CX = Number of times to write characters (must be > 0)

Note: Function 09 modifies AL, even though this is undocumented. AL returns with the last character in the character string, hex 24, a $.

INT 10 Function 0A - Write Character ONLY at Cursor Position

Input: AH = 0A
           AL = ASCII character to write
           BH = Display page number (graphics 1–4, Monochrome = 0)
           BL = Graphics foreground color (unused in text modes)
           CX = Number of times to write character (must be > 0)

INT 10 Function 0B - Select Color Palette

Input: AH = 0B
           BH = Palette color ID
           BL = Background color (if BH = 0)
               = Palette number (if BH = 1)
               0 - Green/red/yellow
               1 - Cyan/magenta/white

INT 10 Function 0C - Write Dot

Note that in this function, the column number is in CX, instead of using DX for row/column.

Input: AH = 0C
           AL = Color attribute of pixel (0–3)
           CX = Pixel column number (0–319,639)
           DX = Pixel raster line number (0–199)

INT 10 Function 0D - Read Pixel Dot

In this function, if bit 7 of AL = 1, then the color value is XORed with the current value of the dot. Position 0,0 is the upper left of the screen.

Input: AH = 0D
         DX = Pixel row number (0–199)
         CX = Pixel column number (0–319,639)

Output: AL = Pixel color attribute

INT 10 Function 0E - Teletype Write to Active Page

Input: AH = 0E
         AL = ASCII character
         BH = Display page number
         BL = Foreground Color (graphics mode) (unused in text mode)

Note: Cursor position advanced; beep, backspace, linefeed, and carriage return active. All other characters displayed.

INT 10 Function 0F - Return Video State

Input: AH = 0F
         BH = Active display page

Output: AH = Characters per line (20, 40,80)
         AL = Current video mode

00	16-shade gray text EGA: 64-color	40 × 25
01	16/8-color text EGA: 64-color	40 × 25
02	16-shade gray text EGA: 64-color	80 × 25
03	16/8-color text EGA: 64-color	80 × 25
04	4-color graphics	320 × 200
05	4-shade gray graphics	320 × 200
06	2-shade gray graphics	640 × 200
07	Monochrome text	80 × 25
08	16-color graphics	160 × 200
09	16-color graphics	320 × 200
0A	4-color graphics	640 × 200
0B	Reserved	

0C	Reserved	
0D	16-color graphics	320 × 200
0E	16-color graphics	640 × 200
0F	Monochrome graphics	640 × 350
10	16/64-color graphics	640 × 350

INT 10 Function 13 - Write Character String

Input: AH   = 13
        AL   = Subfunction Number
               00 String shares attribute in BL, cursor unchanged
               01 String shares attribute in BL, cursor advanced
               02 Each character has attribute, cursor unchanged
               03 Each character has attribute, cursor advanced
        BH   = Active display page
        BL   = String attribute (for AL = 00 or 01 only)
        CX   = Length of character string
        DH   = Starting row number
        DL   = Starting column number
        ES:BP = Address of string to be displayed

Note:

For AL = 00 or 01, string = (*char,char*, ...)
For AL = 02 or 03, string = (*char,attr,char,*
                        attr, ...)
For AL = 01 or 03, cursor position set to location
        following last character output

Interrupt 11 - Equipment Determination

This interrupt returns you the current configuration of your computer.

Output: AX Bits =
                0 = 1 if IPL diskette installed
                1 = 1 if numerics coprocessor here
                2,3 = Unused
                4,5 = Video mode
                      00 = Reserved
                      01 = 40 × 25 Color Card
                      10 = 80 × 25 Color Card
                      11 = 80 × 25 Monochrome
                6,7 = Number of Diskette Drives
                      00 = 1

```
01 = 2
10 = 3
11 = 4
8 = Unused
9,10,11 = Number of RS-232 cards
12 = Unused
13 = If internal modem installed
14,15, = Number of printers attached
```

Interrupt 12 - Determine Memory Size

INT 12 checks the size of installed memory, as shown by the internal DIP switches.

Output: AX = Number of contiguous 1K memory blocks

Interrupt 13 - Disk I/O

INT 13 is used as the fundamental channel to most disk activities in most IBM PCs and clones (compatibles). INT 13 works for both hard disk drives and floppy disk drives. Different drive numbers are used to distinguish between the two. For floppy drives, use the numbers 0 to 3. For hard disks, use 80 to 87 (remember all numbers are hex, unless it is stated specifically that they are not). Note that floppy disks only support functions 00 through 05 of INT 13. Hard drives support all INT 13 functions.

INT 13 Function 00 - Reset Disk

INT 13, Function 00, is a hard reset to the disk controller to restore things to the boot status. If there is an error using this function, CF (the carry flag) is set and AH will contain the error code. The disk error codes are shown in Fig. D-2.

```
Input:    AH = 00
          AL = Drive number
               00–07 Floppy disk
               80–FF Fixed disk

Output:   Carry flag = 0 (AL = 0) success
          Carry flag = 1 (AL = error code)
```

INT 13 Function 01 - Read Status of Last Operation

If this function does not go to correct completion, an error code is stored into AL. See Fig. D-2 for a list of error codes and their meanings.

```
Input:    AH = 01

Output:   AH = Disk status (00 if successful)
```

Input

AH = Function Number of INT 13

Output

AL = Disk Error Code

00	No error
01	Bad command passed to controller
02	Address mark not found
03	Diskette is write-protected
04	Sector not found
05	Reset failed
06	Floppy Disk Removed
07	Drive parameters wrong
08	DMA Overflow
09	DMA across segment end
0A	Bad sector flag
0B	Bad track flag seen
10	Data error
11	Data is error-corrected
20	Controller failure
40	Seek operation failed
80	No response from disk , Time out
AA	Drive not ready
BB	Undefined error
E0	Status Error
0FF	Sense operation failed

Note: All error codes are in hexadecimal.

Fig. D-2. Disk Error Codes.

INT 13 Function 02 - Read Sectors into Memory

As with function 00 and 01, if this function is not successful, AL contains an error code. See Fig. D-2 for a list of the error codes and their meanings. For hard disks, the drive number (in DL) can range from 80 to 87.

Input: AH   = 02
AL   = Number of sectors to read
           Floppies 1–8
           Hard disk 1–80
           Hard disk read/write long 1–79
CH   = Cylinder or track (floppy disk) number
CL   = Sector number
DH   = Head number
DL   = Drive number
ES:BX = Buffer address

Output: Carry flag = 0 (AL = 0) successful
Carry flag = 1 (AL contains error code)

INT 13 Function 03 - Write Sectors to Disk

As with functions 00 through 02, if this function is not successful, AL contains an error code. See Fig. D-2 for a list of the error codes and their meanings. For hard disks, the drive number (in DL) can range from 80 to 87.

Input: AH   = 03
AL   = Number of sectors to write
           Floppy diskettes = 1–8
           Hard disks = 1–80
           Hard disks read write long = 1–79
CH   = Cylinder or track (floppy) number
CL   = Sector number
DH   = Head number
DL   = Drive number
ES:BX = Address of buffer for reads/writes

Output: Carry flag = 0 (AL = 00) successful
Carry flag = 1 (AL has error code)

INT 13 Function 04 - Verify Sectors

As with functions 00 through 03, if this function is not successful, AL contains an error code. See Fig. D-2 for a list of the error codes and their meanings. For hard disks, the drive number (in DL) can range from 80 to 87.

Input:	AH	= 04
	AL	= Number of sectors to verify
		Floppy diskettes = 1–8
		Hard disks = 1–80
		Hard disks read/write long = 1–79
	CH	= Cylinder (hard drive) or track (floppy) number
	CL	= Sector number
	DH	= Head number
	DL	= Drive number
Output:	Carry flag = 0 (AL = 0) successful	
	Carry flag = 1 (AL has error code)	

INT 13 Functions 05, 06, and 07 - Formatting

Function 05 is supported only by floppy diskettes. Functions 06 and 07 work only on hard disks. As with functions 00 through 04, if this function is not successful, AL contains an error code. See Fig. D-2 for a list of the error codes and their meanings. For hard disks, the drive number (in DL) can range from 80 to 87.

Input:	AH	= 05 Format desired track
		= 06 Format desired track and set bad sector flags
		= 07 Format the desired disk starting at the
		= indicated track
		Cylinder (hard drive) or track (floppy) number
	CH	= Head number
	DH	= Drive number (80–87 only allowed for hard
	DL	= disks)
	ES:BX	= 4-byte address field entries, 1 per sector
		byte 0 - Cylinder number
		byte 1 - Head number
		byte 2 - Sector number
		byte 3 - Sector-size code
		00 - 128 bytes/sector
		01 - 256 bytes/sector
		02 - 512 bytes/sector
		03 - 1024 bytes/sector
Output:	Carry flag = 0 (AL = 0) successful	
	Carry flag = 1 (AL has error code)	

INT 13 Function 08 - Return Drive Parameters

Function 08 of INT 13 only works on hard disks.

Input:	AH	= 08
	DL	= Drive number

Output:	AH	= 00
	BH	= 00
	BL	= Drive type
	CH	= Low-order 8 bits of 10-bit maximum of cylinders
	CL	= Bits 7 and 6 - High-order 2 bits of 10-bit maximum number of cylinders
		Bits 5–0 - Maximum number of sectors/track
	DH	= Maximum value for head number
	DL	= Number of drives attached to the controller
	ES:DI	= Address of floppy-disk drive parameter table

INT 13 Function 09 - Initialize Drive

Function 09 is used by BIOS to initialize the drive and to point INT 41 to the drive parameter block.

Input: AH = 09

INT 13 Functions 0A and 0B - Read/Write Long Sectors

As with most INT 13 functions, if function 0A/0B is not successful, AL will contain an error code. See Fig. D-2 for a list of the error codes and their meanings. For hard disks, the drive number (in DL) can range from 80 to 87. Function 0A is for read, and 0B is for write. This function is only for hard disks.

Input:	AH	= 0A,0B
	AL	= Number of sectors to read
		Floppies 1–8
		Hard disk 1–80
		Hard disk read/write long 1–79
	CH	= Cylinder or track (floppy disk) number
	CL	= Sector number
	DH	= Head number
	DL	= Drive number
	ES:BX	= Buffer address

Output: Carry flag = 0 (AL = 0) successful
          Carry flag = 1 (AL has error code)

INT 13 Function 0C - Seek

As with most INT 13 functions, if function 0C is not successful, AL will contain an error code. See Fig. D-2 for a list of the error codes and their meanings. This function is only for hard disks, and the drive number (in DL) can range from 80 to 87.

Input: AH   = 0C
          AL   = Number of sectors to read
                  Floppies 1–8
                  Hard disk 1–80
                  Hard disk read/write long 1–79
          CH   = Cylinder or track (floppy disk) number
          CL   = Sector number
          DH   = Head number
          DL   = Drive number
          ES:BX = Buffer address

Output: Carry flag = 0 (AL = 0) successful
          Carry flag = 1 (AL has error code)

INT 13 Function 0D - Alternate Disk Reset

This alternate disk reset is used only for hard disk drives. Function 0 also works to reset diskettes as well.

Input: AH = 0D
          DL = Drive number

INT 13 Function 0E and 0F - Read/Write Sector Buffer

As with most INT 13 functions, if function 0D is not successful, AL contains an error code. See Fig. D-2 for a list of the error codes and their meanings. For hard disks, the drive number (in DL) can range from 80 to 87. Function 0E is for read and 0F is for write. This function is only for hard disks.

Input: AH   = 0E,0F
          DH   = Head number
          DL   = Drive number (80–87 allowed)
          CH   = Cylinder number
          CL   = Sector number
          ES:BX = Address of buffer address for reads/writes

Output: Carry flag = 0 (AL = 0) successful
           Carry flag = 1 (AL has error code)

INT 13 Function 10 - Test Drive Ready

Function 10 of INT 13 tests whether or not a hard disk is ready for a read or write.

INT 13 Function 11 - Recalibrate Hard Drive

As with most INT 13 functions, if function 11 is not successful, AH contains an error code. See Fig. D-2 for a list of the error codes and their meanings. For hard disks, the drive number (in DL) can range from 80 to 87. This function is only for hard disks.

Input: AH = 11
           DL = Drive number (80–87 allowed)

Output: Carry flag = 0 (AL = 0) successful
           Carry flag = 1 (AL has error code)

INT 13 Function 12 & 13 - Diagnostic Services

As with most INT 13 functions, if function 13 is not successful, AH contains an error code. See Fig. D-2 for a list of the error codes and their meanings. For hard disks, the drive number (in DL) can range from 80 to 87. This function is only for hard disks.

Input: AH =
                   12 = RAM diagnostics
                   13 = Drive diagnostics
                   14 = Controller diagnostics
           DL = Drive number (80–87 allowed)

Output: Carry flag = 0 (AL = 0) successful
           Carry flag = 1 (AL has error code

INT 13 Function 14 - Controller Diagnostic

As with other INT 13 functions, if function 14 is not successful, AH contains an error code. See Fig. D-2 for a list of status codes and their meanings.

Input: AH = 14

Output: AH = Status

INT 13 Function 15 - Get Disk Type

As with other INT 13 functions, if function 15 is not successful, AH contains an error code. See Fig. D-2 for a list of status codes and their meanings.

Input: AH = 15
          DL = Drive number

Output: AH = Disk drive code:
                 00 - No drive present
                 01 - Cannot sense when floppy is changed
                 02 - Can sense when floppy is changed
                 03 - Fixed disk, also
          CX:DX - Number of sectors

INT 13 Function 16 - Check for Change of Floppy Disk Status

As with other INT 13 functions, if function 16 is not successful, AH contains an error code. See Fig. D-2 for a list of status codes and their meanings.

Input: AH = 16
          DL = Number of drive to check

Output: AH = 00 - No change
                 06 - Floppy disk change

INT 13 Function 17 - Set Disk Type

As with other INT 13 functions, if function 17 is not successful, AH contains an error code. See Fig. D-2 for a list of status codes and their meanings.

Input: AH = 17
          AL = Floppy-disk type code
          DL = Drive number

Interrupt 14 - Port Usage

The various functions of INT 14 initialize RS-232 ports, send characters to them, receive characters from them, or return the status of the port.

INT 14 Function 00 - Initialize RS-232 Port

This function configures the RS-232 port for one of 8 baud rates and sets up the other parameters necessary for correct transmission of data. There must be an RS-232 card installed in your system before this function works.

Input: AH = 00
          AL =
                 Bits 0,1 = Character length

$$00 = \text{Unused}$$
$$01 = \text{Unused}$$
$$10 = 7 \text{ bits}$$
$$11 = 8 \text{ bits}$$

```
2      = Stop bits
         0 = 1 stop bit
         1 = 2 stop bits
3,4    = Parity
         00 = None
         01 = Odd
         10 = None
         11 = Even
5,6,7  = Baud rate
         000 = 110 baud
         001 = 150 baud
         010 = 300 baud
         011 = 600 baud
         100 = 1200 baud
         101 = 2400 baud
         110 = 4800 baud
         111 = 9600 baud
```

DX = Serial port number (0 = first port)

INT 14 Function 01 - Send One Character

INT 14 Function 01 allows you to send data over your system serial port. You load the character to send in AL, store 1 in AH, and call INT 14. AH holds the status on return. See Fig. D-3 for a list of the status and error codes and their meanings.

```
Input:    AH = 01
          AL = Character to send
          DX = Serial port number (0 = first port)

Output:   AX = Status (See Fig. D-3)
```

INT 14 Function 02 - Receive Character

Function 02 allows you to read a character from the RS-232 port. AH holds the status on return. See Fig. D-3 for a list of the status and error codes and their meanings.

```
Input:    AH = 02
          DX = Serial port number (0 = first)

Output:   AH = Status (See Fig. D-3)
              If successful, AL holds the character
```

Return Value	Meaning
8000	Time out
4000	Transfer shift register empty
2000	Transfer holding register empty
1000	Break detect
0800	Framing error
0400	Parity error
0200	Overrun error
0100	Data ready
0080	Received line signal detect
0040	Ring indicator
0020	Data set ready
0010	Clear to send
0008	Delta receive line signal detect
0004	Trailing edge ring detector
0002	Delta data set ready
0001	Delta clear to send

Fig. D-3. RS-232 Status and Error Codes.

INT 14 Function 03 - Return Status

Function 03 gives you the status of an RS-232 port. The status is returned in AH. For a list of the status and error codes, see Fig. D-3.

Input: AH = 03
          DX = Serial port number (0 = first)

Output: AH = Status

Interrupt 15 - Cassette I/O

INT 15 is the only BIOS support for cassettes because they are rarely used. They can supply a large amount of storage and accurate, rapid backups are coming into the market.

Input: AH = 00, 01, 02, 03
           AH = 00 Turn cassette motor on
              = 01 Turn cassette motor off
              = 02 Read one or more 256 byte blocks. Store data
                   at ES:BX.
                   CX = Count of bytes to read
                   On return, DX holds number of bytes read
                              ES:BX points to one byte past the
                              last read.
              = 03 Write one or more 256 byte blocks from ES:BX.
                   CX = Count of bytes to write
                   On return, CX = 00
                              ES:BX points to location
                              following last byte written.

Output: DX = Number of bytes actually read
           Carry flag = 1, if an error is found. Than AH is set.
           AH = 01 CRC error
              = 02 Data transitions lost
              = 03 No data found

Interrupt 16 - Keyboard Services

INT 16 handles keyboard input. AL will contain the ASCII code on return. However, if the key pressed was in the extended code, AH will contain the scan code.

INT 16 Function 00 - Read Key from Keyboard

Input: AH = 00

Output: If standard ASCII:
                   AH = Standard keyboard scan code
                   AL = ASCII Code

           If extended ASCII:
                   AH = Extended ASCII code
                   AL = 00

Note: Does not return until a character is read; this interrupt removes the character from the keyboard buffer.

INT 16 Function 01 - Check if Key Ready to be Read

This function returns immediately and does not remove the character from the keyboard buffer.

Input: AH = 01

Output: Zero flag (ZF) = 0
          Zero flag (ZF) = 1 Buffer is empty

          If standard ASCII:
              AH = Standard keyboard scan code
              AL = ASCII code

          If extended ASCII:
              AH = Extended ASCII code
              AL = 00

INT 16 Function 02 - Get Shift Status

This function returns the status of the various shift keys. There can be multiple shifts active at the same time.

Input: AH = 02

Output: AL = Shift status
               01 - Right shift active
               02 - Left shift active
               04 - CTRL active
               08 - ALT active
               10 - Scroll lock active
               20 - Num lock active
               40 - Caps lock active
               80 - Insert state active

Interrupt 17 - Printer Services

INT 17 Function 00 - Send Byte to Printer

INT 17 Function 00 is how BIOS talks to your printer. Set DX to the printer number you will print on (numbers range from 0 to 2 and correspond to printer cards). Generally, you will choose 0. To print a character, store it in AL, set AH to 0, and issue INT 17.

Return Value	Meaning
80	Printer not busy
40	Printer Acknowledgement
20	Out of paper
10	Printer selected
08	I/O Error
04	Unused
02	Unused
01	Time out

Fig. D-4. Printer Status Codes.

Note: Multiple states can be active simultaneously

Input: AH = 00
           AL = Character to be printed
           DX = Printer number (0, 1, 2)

Output: AH = Printer status (see Fig. D-4)

INT 17 Function 01 - Initialize Printer Port

INT 17 Function 01 resets the printer and prepares it for output. On return AH holds the printer status as shown in Fig. D-4. If you select a printer you do not have, you get a time-out for status.

Input: AH = 01
           DX = Printer number (0, 1, 2)

Output: AH = Printer status

INT 17 Function 02 - Read Printer Status into AH

If your program seems to be having problems getting information out to the printer, you can check on its status. See Fig. D-4 for a list of the status codes that will return in AH.

Input: AH = 02
         DX = Printer number (0, 1, 2)

Output: AH = Status

Interrupt 18 - Resident BASIC

INT 18 starts ROM-resident BASIC.

Interrupt 19 - Bootstrap (Warm Start)

INT 19 loads the BOOT record from disk, if there is one. If not, ROM-resident BASIC is executed.

Interrupt 1A - Time of Day

Your system clock increments at a rapid rate, depending on the megahertz tempo of its clock. The functions of INT 1A work with that timer.

INT 1A Function 00 - Read Time of Day

Input: AH = 00

Output: AL = 0 if timer has not passed 24 hours
                since last read
         CX = High word of timer count
         DX = Low word of timer count

INT 1A Function 01 - Set Time of Day

Input: AH = 01
         CX = High word of timer count
         DX = Low word of timer count

INT 1A Function 02 - Read Real-Time Clock

Input: AH = 02

Output: CF = 0 Clock running
            = 1 Clock stopped
         CH = Hours in BCD
         CL = Minutes in BCD
         DH = Seconds in BCD

INT 1A Function 03 - Set Real-Time Clock

Input: AH = 03
            CH = Hours in BCD
            CL = Minutes in BCD
            DH = Seconds in BCD
            DL = 00 Standard time
                      01 Daylight saving time

INT 1A Function 04 - Read Date from Real-Time Clock

Input: AH = 04

Output: CF = 0 Clock running
                     1 Clock stopped
            CH = Century in BCD
            CL = Year in BCD
            DH = Month in BCD
            DL = Day in BCD

INT 1A Function 05 - Set Date in Real-Time Clock

Input: AH = 05
            CH = Century in BCD
            CL = Year in BCD
            DH = Month in BCD
            DL = Day in BCD

INT 1A Function 06 - Set Alarm

If the set is unsuccessful, the carry flag (CF) is set.

Input: AH = 06
            CH = Hours in BCD
            CL = Minutes in BCD
            DH = Seconds in BCD

Output: CF = 0 Operation successful
               = 1 Alarm already set or clock stopped

INT 1A Function 07 - Reset Alarm (Turn Alarm Off)

Input: AH = 07

Interrupt 1B - Keyboard Break Address

INT 1B holds the address that control will be transferred to if your program is interrupted with a BREAK. You can write your own BREAK handler by intercepting and redirecting this interrupt. This is useful if you do not want your user to be able to interrupt the running of your program.

Interrupt 1C - Timer Tick Interrupt

INT 1C is called by INT 8. Originally, INT 1C points only to an IRET instruction. You can redirect it where you wish.

Interrupt 1D - Video Parameter Tables

INT 1D points to the address of the video controller parameter tables.

DOS Memory 0000:0078

Byte 0,1	Contain step rate time and head load/unload times
2	The time it takes diskette motors to turn off after an operation
3	Number of bytes per sector
4	Number of sectors per track
5,6,7	These bytes are concerned with the layout of the disk sectors
8	Fill byte – The byte used to fill newly formatted disk sectors
9	Head settle time – the time given for the diskette head to come to rest after it has shot into position over the track
10	Diskette motor start and warm–up time.

Note: it is recommended that you do NOT change these values.

Fig. D-5. Diskette Base Table.

Interrupt 1E - Diskette Parameters

INT 1E is like INT 1D in that is points to a parameter table, the diskette base table, which is 11 bytes long. Since it is in ROM, you cannot change it. However, MS-DOS also stores it in low memory, at 0000:0078, which you can change. See Fig. D-5 for the table format. It is recommended, however, that you leave the values as they are.

Interrupt 1F - Graphics Character Definitions

INT 1F points to a table in memory that allows you to define the top 128 ASCII characters in high-resolution graphics mode—for graphics screens only. The table is a list of 128 characters, with eight bytes each, for a total of 1,024 bytes.

Appendix E

Overview of MS-DOS Interrupts/Calls

MANY OPERATING SYSTEMS ARE DISK-BASED AND OFFER INTERACTIVE OPERATION TO USERS. MS-DOS offers many special features in tightly-coded system interrupts. These interrupts allow multitasking and pipeline processing, both of which keep a processor busy instead of waiting for work. This feature allows more processes to flow through a computer, which means that more tasks are accomplished in a shorter time.

The MS-DOS interrupts, 20-F0, are usable by systems programmers. Note that the numbers used in this appendix are in hexadecimal unless specifically stated otherwise; that is, interrupt 21, function 15 is really INT 21h function 15h.

You will see several functions listed as internal to MS-DOS. These functions are not unassembled or described in great detail. This is deliberate. One of the reasons most software people do not use undocumented functions is that the manufacturer can change them without notice. This means that you have to retrofit old code, in an unending loop of updating software you thought was finished. In addition, this kind of update seems to appear only during the tightest deadlines on new code.

Several functions (such as INT 21 function 4B and INT 21 function 62) refer to a program segment prefix. The PSP is a special 256-byte (16 paragraph) page of memory, built by MS-DOS in front of all .EXE and .COM programs when they are loaded into memory. The PSP does contain several fields of use to newer programs; it exists, however, primarily as a remnant of CP/M. Microsoft adopted the PSP for ease in porting the vast number of programs available under CP/M to the MS-DOS environment. The PSP contains items that are of interest when using the FCB file and record operations. See Fig. E-1 for an overview of a PSP structure.

Offset (in hex)	Size (in bytes)	CONTENTS
00	2	INT 21 instruction
02	2	Address of last segment allocated to program
04	1	Reserved: Normally 0
05	5	Long call to MS-DOS Function Dispatcher
0A	4	Terminate program interrupt vector (INT 22)
0E	4	Control-C handler interrupt vector (INT 23)
12	4	Critical error handler interrupt vector (INT 24)
16	22	Reserved
2C	2	Segment address of environment
2E	34	Reserved
50	9	INT 21, RETF instructions
53	9	Reserved
5C	16	Default file control block 1
6C	108	Default file control block 2 (overlaid if FCB 1 opened)
80	127	Command tail and default DTA
FF		

Fig. E-1. Program Segment Prefix (PSP) Structure.

Interrupt 20 - Terminate

At the end of user programs, INT 20 terminates the program and gives control back to MS-DOS. In response to this interrupt, MS-DOS does the following:

- Restores the termination handler vector (INT 22) from PSP:000A.
- Restores the control-C vector (INT 23) from PSP:000A.
- Restores the critical error handler vector (INT 24) from PSP:0012.
- Flushes the file buffers.
- Transfers to the termination handler address.

The termination handler releases all memory blocks allocated to the program, including its environment block and many dynamically allocated blocks that were not previously explicitly released. It closes any files opened with handles that were not previously closed and, finally, returns control to the parent process—usually COMMAND.COM.

Note: Any files that have been written by a program (using FCBs) should be closed before using INT 21; otherwise, data might be lost.

The recommended way to terminate programs is to use INT 21 function 4C (terminate process with return code) instead of using INT 20.

Interrupt 21 - Service Interrupts

INT 21 is a power-packed interrupt, with a great number of subfunctions. To call one of its functions, load the function number into AH (and any other register values as shown in each of the functions), and issue INT 21.

INT 21 Function 00 - Program Terminate

Function 00 of INT 21 is exactly the same as INT 20. It ends a program and returns control to MS-DOS. MS-DOS restores the following interrupt vectors from the PSP of the terminated program: 0A (INT 22), 0E (INT 23), and 12 (INT 24). MS-DOS writes all file buffers to disk and closes all handles and, finally, transfers control to INT 22 (terminate routine address).

Any file that was opened with an FCB and which changed in length should be closed before calling this function. If you do not, the file length, date, and time are not recorded correctly in the directory.

This function is really obsolete with MS-DOS versions 2.0 and later. INT 21 function 4C is recommended to end programs.

Input: AH = 0

INT 21 Function 01 - Keyboard Input

With function 01, any key pressed (that has a graphic) is echoed to the display screen. When function 1 is issued, processing stops until a key is pressed; that is, the operating system waits for input. If the corresponding character is an ASCII printable character, it is printed on the screen. The tab character is automatically expanded to the end of the next eight-column field by adding spaces. Holding the CTRL key and pressing BREAK terminates operation.

If the pressed key corresponds to an extended code, the AL register contains a value of zero. Then execute this function again to get the code. If the second value is less than 84, it represents the scan code of the pressed key. For example, a value of 30 says that the ALT key and the letter A were pressed. Input can be read from another device or disk file by redirection of the standard input.

Remember that the carriage-return character (0D) does not echo a line feed; likewise, the line-feed character (0A) does not echo a carriage return.

Input: AH = 01

Output: AL = ASCII code of struck key

INT 21 Function 02 - Character Output on Screen

Function 02 displays the character contained in the DL register onto the screen. It is useful for writing a single character (use function 09 for a string). Function 02 is useful for displaying the dollar sign ($), because function 09 uses the $ as the end of string characters. The BACKSPACE key moves the cursor to the left but does not erase the character printed there. The output can be sent to another device or disk file by redirecting the standard output.

With MS-DOS versions 2.0 and later, INT 21 function 40 (write file or device) is recommended in preference to function 02.

Input: AH = 02
           DL = ASCII character

INT 21 Function 03 - Standard Auxiliary Device Input

Function 03 reads a character from the standard auxiliary device, generally the serial port, defined as AUX or COM1. However, you can change the standard auxiliary port to COM2. Function 03 waits until a byte is available.

Function 03 is not interrupt driven and does not buffer characters received from the standard auxiliary device. As a result, it might not be fast enough for some telecommunications applications, and data might be lost. Also, this function does not ensure that auxiliary input is connected and working. Also, it does not perform any error checking, nor does it set up the auxiliary input device. With MS-DOS versions 2.0 and later, INT 21 function 3F (read file or device) is recommended instead of function 03.

Input: AH = 03

Output: Character in AL

INT 21 Function 04 - Standard Auxiliary Device Output

Function 04 sends the byte in register DL to the auxiliary port AUX or COM1. Function 04 does not ensure that auxiliary output is connected and working, nor does it perform any error checking or set up the auxiliary output device. Also, it does not return the status of auxiliary output, nor does it return an error code if the auxiliary output device is not ready for data. If the device is busy, function 04 waits until it is availablc. With MS-DOS vcrsions 2.0 and later, INT 21 function 40 (write file or device) is recommended instead of function 04.

Input: AH = 04
          DL = The character to output

INT 21 Function 05 - Printer Output

Function 05 sends the character in register DL to the standard printer port, PRN or LPT1. As with function 04, the byte to be written to the printer is passed in DL. You could also use INT 17 for this purpose.

Function 05 does not return the status of the standard printer, nor does it return an error code if the standard printer is not ready for characters. If the printer is busy or off line, function 05 waits until it is available. With MS-DOS versions 2.0 and later, INT 21 function 40 (write file or device) is recommended instead of function 05.

Input: AH = 05
          DL = The character to output

INT 21 Function 06 - Console Input/Output

Function 06 can do both input and output; it can also determine the input status. It does not wait for input. Also, the input character is not automatically displayed, and CTRL-BREAK does not terminate the operation.

Function 06 allows all possible characters and control codes with values between 00 and 0FE to be read and written with standard input and output with no filtering by MS-DOS. The rubout character (0FF, 255 decimal), however, cannot be output with this function. Use function 02 (character output) instead.

```
Input:   AH = 06

         If   DL = FF     AL holds the character if one is ready
              DL < FF     Type ASCII code in DL out
```

INT 21 Function 07 - Console Input Without Echo

INT 21 function 07, like function 01, waits for keyboard entry. If an ASCII character is entered, the ASCII value is returned in the AL register. The IBM graphics characters can be entered by holding the ALT key and typing the decimal value with the keypad numbers. If an extended character (such as a function key) is entered, a 00 is stored in AL. This function must then be called a second time to determine the character. Unlike function 01, function 07 does not display the input character. Also, CTRL-BREAK does not terminate the process.

```
Input:   AH  = 07

Output: AL   = ASCII code of struck key
```

INT 21 Function 08 - Console Input Without Echo, with BREAK Check

Function 08 waits for a character and terminates when CTRL-BREAK is pressed. A wait can be avoided by calling function 0B (check keyboard status), which checks whether a character is available, and then calling function 08 if a character is ready. The input character is not displayed and tab characters are not expanded.

On IBM PCs and compatibles, extended characters (such as those produced by the ALT-O and F8 keys) are returned as two bytes. The first byte, 00, signals an extended character; the second byte completes the key code. To read these characters, function 08 must be called twice.

With MS-DOS versions 2.0 and later, function 03F (read file or device) is recommended.

```
Input:   AH = 08

Output:  AL = ASCII code of struck key
```

INT 21 Function 09 - String Print

INT 21 function 09 is useful for printing a string of characters on the screen. Function 09 is easy to use. To use it, place the string somewhere in memory and terminate it with a dollar sign ($), which means that you cannot include a dollar sign as part of the string (use function 02 to print a $). Place the address of the string in the DS:DX register.

Although it is undocumented, AL returns with a hex 24 ($) in it, so do not depend on AL staying the same.

Display begins at the current cursor position on the standard output. After the string is completely displayed, MS-DOS updates the cursor position to the location immediately following the string. On IBM PCs and compatibles, if the end of a line is reached before the string is completely displayed, a carriage return and line feed are issued, and the next character is displayed in the first position of the following line. If the cursor reaches the bottom right corner of the display before the character string has been sent, the display is scrolled up one line.

Input: AH = 09
             DS:DX = The address of the string that ends in '$'

INT 21 Function 0A - String Input

All characters typed by the user are entered into the keyboard buffer. When the RETURN key is pressed, the line is stored into the input buffer.

Before using this function, set up a buffer in memory. Remember that there are two auxiliary bytes located at the beginning of the buffer, as shown in Fig. E-2. The first byte defines the maximum length of text that can be stored in the buffer. The second byte gives the number of characters that were entered by the user. You set the value of the first byte. MS-DOS fills in the second byte after the buffer has been read. MS-DOS also adds a carriage return to the end of the input string. However, this carriage return is not included in the count that MS-DOS enters in the second byte. So, set the maximum size of the buffer to be one byte larger than needed.

Input: AH = 0A
             DS:DX = Address of buffer

Output: Buffer at DS:DX filled
            Echo the typed keys

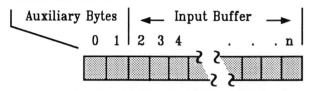

Aux byte 0 = The maximum length of the input (set by user)

1 = The number of bytes actually entered (set by DOS)

This count does NOT include the carriage return

that DOS adds to the end of the string.

Fig. E-2. Input Buffer Format.

INT 21 Function 0B - Check Input Status

Function 0B is useful for checking to see if there is any keyboard input waiting, which avoids having a program wait for something if there is no need to. On return from this function, AL contains a zero if no key has been pressed. Any other AL value indicates a character is waiting to be read—although this function does not read the character.

Function 0B does not indicate how many characters are available; it merely indicates whether at least one character is available. If the available character is control-C, MS-DOS calls INT 24 (control-C handler address). Function 0B does not remove characters from standard input. Thus, if a character is present, repeated calls return 0FF in AL until all characters in the buffer are read, either with one of the character-input functions (01, 06, 07, 08, or 0A) or with function 3F (read file or device) using the handle for standard input.

Input: AH = 0B

Output: AL = FF if a character is ready
           AL = 00 if nothing is there to be read in

INT 21 Function 0C - Clear Buffer and Invoke Service

INT 21 function 0C clears the keyboard buffer before it invokes a keyboard function (01, 06, 07, 08, or 0A). This is important when a user might be typing ahead. Because of familiarity with a software package, the user knows what question comes next and will type an answer before the question appears on the screen. If a program finds an error (such as an abort, retry, or ignore?), the program must have a correct answer to that prompt before it can go on. So flush the keyboard buffer and wait for that answer to be entered.

INT 21 function 0C also checks for BREAK.

Input: AH = 0C
           AL = Keyboard function number

           If AL = 06, then DL = FF
           If AL = 0A, DS:DX = the segment:offset of the buffer to receive the data.

Output: If AL was 01, 06, 07, or 08 on the call:
                   AL = 8-bit ASCII character from standard input
           If AL was 0A on the call:
                   Nothing is returned.

Note 1: A function number other than 01, 06, 07, 08, or 0A in AL simply flushes the standard-input buffer and returns control to the calling program.

Note 2: If AL contains 0A, DS:DX must point to the buffer in which MS-DOS is to place the string read from the keyboard.

Note 3: Because the buffer is flushed before the input function is carried out, any control-C characters pending in the buffer are discarded. If subsequent input is a control-C, however, INT 23 (control-C handler address) is called.

INT 21 Function 0D - Disk Reset

Function 0D writes to disk all internal MS-DOS file buffers in memory that have been modified since the last write. This function ensures that the information stored on disk matches changes made by write requests to file buffers in memory. This function does not update the disk directory. A program must issue function 10 (close file with FCB) or function 3E (close file) to update directory information correctly.

Input: AH = 0D

INT 21 Function 0E - Select Disk

INT 21 function 0E is how MS-DOS selects a default disk. Whenever you type C: at a prompt, INT 21 function 0E is called. This was one of the early MS-DOS interrupts. INT 21 function 3B is more comprehensive—it allows the change of the current directory, including the default drives.

A logical drive is defined as any block-oriented device. This category includes floppy-disk drives, RAM disks, tape devices, fixed disks, and network drives. Drive letters should be limited to A through P (00 through 0F) to ensure than an application runs on all versions on MS-DOS.

Input: AH = 0E
          DL = Drive number
               00 = Drive A
               01 = Drive B
               02 = Drive C, and so on

Output: AL = The number of logical drives in the system

INT 21 Function 0F - Open Pre-Existing File

Function 0F opens a file created some time in the past, which can be just before you used this function. INT 21 function 0F does not create the file. It uses file control blocks (FCBs). FCBs are supported under all MS-DOS versions, although it is now recommended that you use file handles, because FCBs do not allow the specification of subdirectories. See Fig. E-3 for the format of an opened FCB.

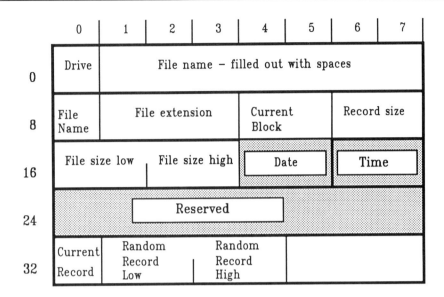

Note: Shaded areas are reserved by MS-DOS

Fig. E-3. File Control Block Format (Opened File).

There is no space in the "normal" FCB for either the file creation time or its attribute. It is possible to add the attribute by using an extended FCB. An extended FCB looks the same as an FCB, with an added seven bytes at the beginning: a byte of FF, five bytes of zeros, and the attribute byte. See Fig. E-4 for a list of file attributes and their meanings.

Using the FCBs (instead of file handles) is somewhat awkward, so instead of continuing, study the MS-DOS manual carefully. There are two ways to read files: sequentially and randomly. Sequential files need a marker between records (because MS-DOS knows that the records may be of differing lengths). When it uses sequential reading and writing functions, MS-DOS takes care of worrying about the markers. Random files, on the other hand, need records of the same size. MS-DOS defaults to a size of 128 bytes. If the record size is different, modify the record size in the FCB after a successful open.

With MS-DOS versions 2.0 and later, INT 21 function 3D (open file with handle) is recommended.

Input: AH = 0F
           DS:DX points to an FCB

Output: AL = 00 if successful
           AL = FF if unsuccessful

Attribute Bit	Meaning
0	Read-only
1	Hidden. Directory searches will not find.
2	System file, same attribute as IBMDOS.COM
3	Volume file, the eleven letters of the file name actually are the disk's label
4	Directory
5	Archive, this bit is checked by BACKUP to see if the file has been rewritten since last BACKUP run
6	Reserved
7	Reserved

Fig. E-4. File Attribute (Extended FCB).

INT 21 Function 10 - Close File

To keep data intact, be sure to close all files before exiting a program. INT 21 function 10 reads what is in the FCB and writes it to the directory. Its major use is to give the file a nonzero size. MS-DOS usually keeps track of file size, but you can use this function to do so.

A successful call to function 10 flushes to disk all MS-DOS internal buffers associated with the file, and it updates the directory entry and file allocation table (FAT). Function 10 thus ensures that correct information is contained in the copy of the file on the disk. With MS-DOS versions 2.0 and later, INT 21 function 3E (close file) is recommended.

Input: AH = 10
         DS:DX points to a previously opened FCB

Output: AL = 00 if successful
         AL = FF if unsuccessful

INT 21 Function 11 - Search for First Matching File

MS-DOS itself uses INT 21 function 11 to search the disk for files. Point DS:DX at an unopened FCB and call this function. The FCB can use a ? wildcard (but not the

*, which file-handle functions can use). For example, if you want to find all the file names with a .ASM extension, fill the FCB file name with ???????? and the extension with .ASM. The eight question marks will find any length file name, from a single character to eight.

If the search finds a match, an unopened FCB (for the matching file) will be stored in the DTA.

If necessary, use function 1A (set DTA address) before function 11, to set the location of the DTA in which the results of the search will be placed.

With MS-DOS versions 2.0 and later, INT 21 function 4E (Find First File) and INT 21 function 4F (find next file) are recommended.

Input: AH = 11
         DS:DX points to an unopened FCB

Output: AL = 00 if successful
              The DTA contains unopened FCB of the same type
              (Normal or extended) as search FCB.
         AL = FF if unsuccessful

INT 21 Function 12 - Search for Next Matching File

After finding the first matching file (using INT 21 function 11), MS-DOS fills part of the reserved areas in the FCB. This function uses that information to find the next match in the directory.

Input: AH = 12
         DS:DX points to search FCB

Output: AL = 00 if successful
              DTA contains unopened FCB of the same type (normal or
              extended) as the search FCB.
         AL = FF if unsuccessful

INT 21 Function 13 - Deletes Files

INT 21 function 13 simply deletes files. All you have to do is to point DS:DX at an unopened FCB and issue this interrupt and function. Note that this function does not physically erase data. INT 21 function 41 is recommended instead of function 13.

Input: AH = 13
         DS:DX points to an unopened FCB

Output: AL = 00 if successful
         AL = FF if unsuccessful

INT 21 Function 14 - Sequential Read

INT 21 function 14 reads sequential records from an opened file. Set the current block field (bytes 0C-0D in the FCB) and the current record field from 0 to 127 in byte 1F. The data read is dumped in the DTA. If you change the record length from the default 128 bytes, you would get whatever the change was in the DTA. The record address increments with each read, which means that if the current record is 127 the next record will be 0.

If necessary, use function 1A (set DTA address) before function 14. This sets the base address of the DTA. With MS-DOS versions 2.0 and later, INT 21 function 3F (read file or device) is recommended instead of function 14.

Input: AH = 14
           Current block and record set in FCB
           DS:DX points to an opened FCB

Output: AL = 00 if successful
                    requested record put in DTA
                 01 end of file, no data in record
                 02 DTA segment too small for record
                 03 end of file, record padded with 0s
                    requested record put in DTA

INT 21 Function 15 - Sequential Write

INT 21 function 15 writes a record from the disk transfer area—DTA (always used in FCB operations)—to an open file. The record address is incremented. Note that if the record size is significantly smaller than a sector (512 bytes), MS-DOS buffers the data and only writes it when there is enough to write, or when the program ends. Note: this is one of the tasks that INT 20 or INT 27 takes care of for you.

With MS-DOS versions 2.0 and later, INT 21 function 40 is recommended instead of function 15.

Input: AH = 15
           Current block and record set in FCB
           DS:DX points to an opened FCB

Output: AL = 00 if successful
                    One record read from DTA and written
                 01 disk full; write canceled
                 02 DTA segment too small for record; write canceled

INT 21 Function 16 - Create File

INT 21 function 16 creates a file. If a file already exists with the same name (the one put into the FCB), that file will be opened and set to zero length (which might destroy valid data stored there earlier if your overwrite it by accident). If there is no identical file, a directory entry is opened for this new one. If there is no space left on the diskette or hard disk, this function returns an FF and you must free some space.

Note that pathnames and wildcard characters (* and ?) are not supported by function 16. With MS-DOS versions 2.0 and later, function 16 has been superseded by functions 3C (create file with handle), 5A (create temporary file), and 5B (create new file).

Input: AH = 16
           DS:DX points to an unopened FCB

Output: AL = 00 if successful
                FF directory full

INT 21 Function 17 - Rename File

If you need to rename files, use this interrupt and function (it is the way MS-DOS does it). The FCB can use a ? wildcard (but not the *, which file handle functions can). For example, if your want to find all the file names with a .ASM extension, fill the FCB file name with ???????? and the extension with ASM. The eight question marks will find any length file name, from a single character to eight.

To use INT 21 function 17, set up an unopened FCB for the file(s) to rename.

With MS-DOS versions 2.0 and later, INT 21 function 56 (rename file) is recommended instead of function 17.

Input: AH = 17
           DS:DX points to a modified FCB
                For a modified FCB, the second file name starts six bytes after
                the end of the first file name at DS:DX+11

Output: AL = 00 if successful
                FF directory full

INT 21 Function 18 - Internal to MS-DOS

Function 18 is used only by MS-DOS. It is listed here so you can see that it is used and unavailable for use.

INT 21 Function 19 - Find Current Disk

INT 21 function 19 is handy to find which disk is the default or on which you are currently working. The drive code returned by this function is zero-based; that is, drive

A = 0, drive B = 1, and so on. This value is unlike the drive code used in FCBs and some other MS-DOS functions where a 0 indicates the default rather than the current drive.

Input: AH = 19

Output: AL = Current disk
                00 = A
                01 = B
                02 = C
                03 = D (and so on)

INT 21 Function 1A - Set the Disk Transfer Area (DTA) Location

The MS-DOS default DTA (disk transfer area) and record size in the FCB are only 128 bytes, but a larger size might be needed. One area to use for more bytes is the end of your program in memory. Be careful not to overwrite the stack that MS-DOS supplies at the top of every .COM file segment. If no DTA is specified, MS-DOS uses a default buffer at offset 80 in the program segment prefix (PSP).

Input: AH = 1A
          DS:DX points to new DTA address

INT 21 Function 1B - File Allocation Table (FAT) Information for Default Drive

Function 1B gets the default drive data. For MS-DOS versions 3.2 and later, obtain additional drive information by checking the media descriptor byte (at offset 0A) in the BIOS parameter block with INT 21 function 44 (IOCTL), subfunction 0D (generic I/O control for block devices). With MS-DOS versions 2.0 and later, function 1C (get drive data) provides the same types of information as function 1B, but for a disk in a drive rather than just the default drive.

Input: AH = 1B

Output: If successful—
                AL = Number of sectors/cluster
                CX = Size of a sector (for example, 512)
                DS:DX points to the FAT byte
                DX = Number of clusters
          If unsuccessful—
                AL = FF
                In this case, the most common errors are:
                      Drive door was open

Disk was unformatted
Medium was bad
Disk was not ready

INT 21 Function 1C - File Allocation Table (FAT) Information for Specified Drive

After issuing this interrupt, DX holds the number of usable clusters. AL holds the number of sectors per cluster, and CX holds the size of a physical sector on the drive selected. With MS-DOS versions 3.2 and later, obtain additional drive information by checking the media descriptor byte at offset 0A in the BIOS parameter block with function 44 (IOCTL) subfunction 0D (generic I/O control for block devices).

Input: AH   =   1C
           DL   =   Drive Code
                    00 = Default drive
                    01 = Drive A
                    02 = Drive B
                    03 = Drive C, and so on

Output: If successful—
                    AL = Number of sectors/cluster
                    CX = Size of a sector (for example, 512)
                    DS:DX points to the FAT byte
                    DX = Number of clusters

          If unsuccessful—
                    AL = FF
                    In this case, the most common errors are:
                    Disk was unformatted
                    Disk was not ready
                    Drive door was open
                    Medium was bad

INT 21 Function 1D to 20 - Internal to MS-DOS

Functions 1D to 20 are used only by MS-DOS. They are shown here so you can see that they are used and unavailable for use.

INT 21 Function 21 - Random Read

To write into the disk transfer area (DTA) from a random read, set the random record field in an opened file control block (FCB). DS:DX+21 holds the low word of the random record number and DS:DX+23 holds the high word. When a read is requested, MS-DOS sets the current block and current record fields.

With MS-DOS versions 2.0 and later, INT 21 function 3F (read file or device) is recommended instead of function 21.

Input: AH = 21
          DS:DX points to an opened FCB
          Set the FCBs random record filed at DS:DX + 21 and DS:DX + 23

Output: AL = 00 Successful
                    DTA contains data read from file
             01 end of file, no more data; no record read
             02 not enough space in DTA segment; read canceled
             03 end of file, partial record padded with 0s
                    DTA contains data read from file

INT 21 Function 22 - Random Write

To use INT 21 function 22, fill the disk transfer area (DTA) with the record to write. Set the random record field in the file control block (FCB). It is recommended that you doublecheck the record field and record number. If you use an incorrect record field, MS-DOS might overwrite something you do not want destroyed. Also, if the record number is far in excess of what is currently in the file, MS-DOS will simply extend the file the required length to stick that record at the end and fill in the intervening space (if there was garbage in storage, that is what appears in the intervening space). MS-DOS sets the current block and current record fields.

With MS-DOS versions 2.0 and later, INT 21 function 40 (write file or device) is recommended instead of function 22.

Input: AH = 22
          DS:DX points to an opened FCB
          Set the FCBs random record field at DS:DX + 21 and DS:DX + 23

Output: AL = 00 successful
             01 disk is full
             02 not enough space in DTA segment; write
                    canceled

INT 21 Function 23 - File Size

If you want to know the size of a file (without having to open it), use this function. Point DS:DX at the unopened FCB, and MS-DOS searches the current directory for a match to the file name. If it finds a match, the random record fields of the FCB will be set to the total length of the file in records—rounded up. If you set the record length to a value, the total bytes are divided by that number, and the result is rounded up.

If you want the total size in bytes, set the record length to one byte. If MS-DOS does not find a match in the directory, AL returns FF.

With MS-DOS versions 2.0 and later, INT 21 function 42 (move file pointer) is recommended instead of function 23.

```
Input:     AH = 22
           DS:DX points to an unopened FCB

Output:    AL = 00  if successful
                    Random record field set to file length in records, rounded
                    up
              = FF no file found that matched FCB
```

INT 21 Function 24 - Set Random Record Field

Function 24 sets the relative-record field of a file control block (FCB) to match the file position indicated by the current-block and current-record fields of the same FCB. The AL register is always set to 00 by this function. This overwrites any preexisting information in the AL register. Before function 24 is called, your program must open the FCB with function 0F (open file with FCB) or function 16 (create file with FCB). With MS-DOS versions 2.0 and later, INT 21 function 42 (move file pointer) is recommended instead of function 24.

```
Input:     AH = 24
           DS:DX points to an opened FCB

Output:    AL = 00
```

The random record field is set to match current record and current block.

INT 21 Function 25 - Set Interrupt Vector

Function 25 sets an address in the interrupt vector table to point to a specified interrupt handler. When this function is called, the four-byte address in DS:DX is placed in the correct position in the interrupt vector table. Before using function 25, read the address of the current interrupt handler with function 35 (get interrupt vector) and save the current address for restoration before your program terminates.

```
Input:     AH = 25
           AL = Interrupt number
           DS:DX = New address of interrupt handler
```

Note: DS:DX is the address. It is not a segment value (DS) and an offset (DX).

INT 21 Function 26 - Create a New Program Segment

This is an old implementation of this need for creating new segments. Instead, use function 4B (load and execute program), which can be used to load .COM files, .EXE files, and overlays.

INT 21 Function 27 - Random Block Read

When reading in a random record, INT 21 function 27 updates the random record field. When the function is finished, the random record field is set to the number of the next unread record.

With MS-DOS versions 2.0 and later, INT 21 function 3F (read file or device) is recommended instead of function 27.

```
Input:    AH = 27
          CX = Number of records to read
          DS:DX points to an opened FCB
          Set the FCB random-record field at DS:DX + 21 and DS:DX + 23

Output:   AL = 00 Successful
          CX = Number of records read
          Random record fields set to access next
          record
                  01 end of file, no more data
                  02 not enough space in DTA segment
                  03 end of file, partial record padded with 0s
          CX = Number of records read
          Random record fields set to access next
          record
```

INT 21 Function 28 - Random Block Write

This function writes one or more records from the current disk transfer area (DTA) to a file. Data to be written must be placed in the DTA before this function is called. Unless the DTA address has been set with function 1A (set DTA address), MS-DOS uses a default 128-byte DTA at offset 80 in the program segment prefix (PSP).

If you set CX to 00 when calling this function, the file will be set to the length given by the random record field. This might force the file to be truncated or enlarged. If it enlarges, it includes whatever garbage is in the free sectors on the disk.

With MS-DOS versions 2.0 and later, INT 21 function 40 (write file or device) is recommended instead of function 28.

```
Input:    AH = 28
          CX = Number of records to write.
```

    00 - The file is set to the size indicated in the random record field.

  DS:DX points to an opened FCB

  Set FCB random record file at DS:DX+21 and DS:DX+23

Output: AL = 00 Successful

    CX = number of records written

    Random-record fields set to access next record

   01 disk is full

    CX = number of records written

   02 Not enough space in DTA segment; write canceled

INT 21 Function 29 - Parse Filename

INT 21 function 29 is useful in parsing file names from the command line. Give it the address of the command line. If it finds a file name, the function places an unopened FCB for the file at address ES:DI. If the command line does not contain a valid file name, ES:[DI+1] will contain blanks.

This function cannot parse pathnames. With MS-DOS versions 2.0 and later, the following characters are filename separators:

    : . ; , space tab / " " [ ]

The following characters are filename terminators:

    / " [ ] < > | : . ; , space tab / " [ ]

Input: AH = 29

  AL = Bit 0 = 0 Stop parsing if file separator is found

      = 1 leading separators are scanned off the command line

     1 = 0 set drive number field in FCB to 0 (current drive) if string does not include a drive identifier

      = 1 drive ID in final FCB will be changed ONLY if a drive was specified

     2 = 0 set filename field in the FCB to blanks if string does not include a filename

      = 1 filename in FCB changed ONLY if command line includes filename

     3 = 0 set extension field in FCB to blanks if string does not include a filename extension

      = 1 filename extension in FCB will be changed ONLY if command line contains a filename extension

  DS:SI = Command line string to parse

  ES:DI = Address to put unopened FCB

Output: AL   = 00 if string does not contain wildcard characters
                  01 if string contains wildcard characters
                  FF if drive specifier invalid
          DS:SI = First byte after parsed string
          ES:DI = Valid unopened FCB

INT 21 Function 2A - Get Date

Function 2A returns the current system date in binary form: year, month, day, and day of the week. Note that years outside the range 1980 through 2099 cannot be returned by function 2A.

Input: AH = 2A

Output: AL = Day of the week (0 = Sunday, 1 = Monday, and so on)
          CX = Year (1980 through 2099)
          DH = Month number (1 = January, 2 = February, and so on)
          DL = Day of the month (1 through 31)

INT 21 Function 2B - Set Date

Function 2B accepts binary values for the year, month, and day of the month. It stores them in the systems date counter as the number of days since January 1, 1980. The year must be a 16-bit value in the range 1980 through 2099. Values outside this range are not accepted. Also, supplying only the last two digits of the year causes an error.

Input: AH = 2B
          CX = Year (1980 through 2099)
          DH = Month number (1 = January, 2 = February, and so on)
          DL = Day of the month (1 through 31)

Output: AL = 00 if successful
          AL = FF if date not valid

INT 21 Function 2C - Get Time

Function 2C reports the current system time in binary form, (hours based on the 24-hour clock), minutes, seconds, and hundredths of a second. The accuracy of the time returned depends on the accuracy of the system's timekeeping hardware. On systems unable to resolve time to the hundredth of a second, DI might contain either 00 or an approximate value calculated by an MS-DOS algorithm.

Input: AH = 2C

Output: CH = Hours (0–23)
           CL = Minutes (0–59)
           DH = Seconds (0–59)
           DL = Hundredths of seconds (0–99)

INT 21 Function 2D - Set Time

Function 2D accepts binary values for the hour (based on a 24-hour clock), minute, second, and hundredths of a second and stores them in the operating system's time counter. On systems unable to resolve the time to the hundredth of a second, set DL to 00 before calling function 2D.

Input: AH = 2D
           CH = Hours (0–23)
           CL = Minutes (0–59)
           DH = Seconds (0–59)
           DL = Hundredths of seconds (0–99)

Output: AL = 00 if successful
           AL = FF if time is invalid

INT 21 Function 2E - Set or Reset Verify Switch

INT 21 function 2E turns verification for disk writing on or off. This helps protect against disk errors.

Input: AH = 2E
           AL = 00 Turn verify off
                 01 Turn verify on
           DL = 00

INT 21 Function 2F - Get Current DTA

Function 2F is useful if the DTA location is moved often. Function 2F returns the base address of the current DTA. MS-DOS has no way of knowing the size of the buffer at that address. Your program must ensure that the buffer pointed to by the DTA address is large enough to hold any records transferred to it. If the DTA address has not been set (by INT 21 function 1A—set DTA address), MS-DOS uses a default buffer of 128 bytes located at offset 80 in the program segment prefix (PSP).

Input: AH = 2F

Output: ES:BX = Current DTA address

INT 21 Function 30 - Get MS-DOS Version Number

Function 30 lets you know what version of MS-DOS is running on a system. AL holds the major version, the 3 in MS-DOS 3.10. AH holds the minor version, the 10 of 3.10. If AL returns a 0, it is an early MS-DOS, before 2.0.

Input: AH   = 30
         AL   = 00

Output: AL   = Major version number
         AH   = Minor version number
         BX   = Original equipment manufacturer's (OEM) serial number, but usually 00 for PC-DOS and 0FF or other values for MS-DOS
         BL:CX = 24-bit user serial number (this is optional and OEM dependent)

INT 21 Function 31 - Terminate Process and Keep Resident

Function 31 terminates a program and returns control to the parent process (usually COMMAND.COM) but keeps the terminated program resident in memory. The terminating process should return a completion code in the AL register. If the program terminates normally, the return code should be 00. A return code of 01 or greater usually indicates that termination was caused by an error encountered by the process.

Input: AH = 31
         AL = Return Code
         DX = Size of memory request in paragraphs.

Note 1: The minimum amount of memory a process can reserve is 6 paragraphs (60 bytes), which makes up the initial portion of the process PSP (including the reserved area).

Note 2: The amount of memory required by the program is not necessarily the same as the size of the file that holds the program on disk. The program must allow for its PSP and stack in the amount of memory reserved. On the other hand, the memory occupied by code and data used only during program initialization frequently can be discarded as a side effect of the INT 21 function 31 call.

INT 21 Function 32 - Internal to MS-DOS

Function 32 is used only by MS-DOS. It is shown here so you can see that it is used and unavailable.

INT 21 Function 33 - Control Break Check

MS-DOS uses function 33 to check if a BREAK is pending each time a MS-DOS function is called. Otherwise, the user can wait a long time for a BREAK to be noticed and processed. If the control-C check flag is off, MS-DOS checks for a control-C entered at the keyboard only during servicing of the character I/O functions (01 through 0C). If the control-C check flag is on, MS-DOS also checks for user entry of a control-C during servicing of other functions, such as file and record operations.

The state of the control-C check flag affects all programs. If a program needs to change the state of control-C checking, it should save the original flag and restore it before terminating.

```
Input:     AH  = 33
           AL  = 00 to get the state of control-C check flag
                 01 to set the state of control-C check flag
              DL = 00 control-C flag is off
                   01 control-C check flag is on


Output:   AL  =  00 if flag is set successfully
                 FF code in AL on call was not
                 00 or 01

           If AL was 00 on the call:
           DL =   00 control-C flag is off
                  01 control-C check flag is on
```

INT 21 Function 34 - Internal to MS-DOS

Function 34 is used only by MS-DOS. It is shown here so you can see that it is used and unavailable. This function returns the address of the InDOS flag, which reflects the current state of INT 21 function processing. The InDOS flag is a byte within the MS-DOS kernel. The InDOS value is incremented when MS-DOS begins execution of an INT 21 function and decremented when MS-DOS's processing of that function is completed.

INT 21 Function 35 - Get Interrupt Vector

Function 35 works with function 25 which sets vectors.

```
Input:     AH = 35
           AL = Interrupt number

Output:   ES:BX = Interrupt vector for the interrupt specified in AL
```

INT 21 Function 36 - Get Free Disk Space

MS-DOS uses function 36 when it tells how many free bytes are available on a disk. A cluster is the smallest piece of a disk that MS-DOS keeps track of, so the number of bytes in a cluster multiplied by cluster number gives the total number of bytes available. INT 21 function 36 returns about the same information as INT 21 function 1C, except that instead of pointing at the file allocation table (FAT) byte, BX holds the number of free clusters.

Check AX for a value of FFFF (error) before information returned by this function is used. With MS-DOS versions 2.0 and later, this INT 21 function 36 is recommended instead of using the older FCB functions 1B (get default drive data) and 1C (get drive data).

```
Input:    AH  =  36
          DL  =  Drive number
                 00 - Default drive
                 01 - Drive A
                 02 - Drive B, and so on

Output:   If successful—
                 AX  =  Number of sectors per clusters
                 BX  =  Number of available clusters
                 CX  =  Size of a sector in bytes
                 DX  =  Number of clusters on the drive
          If unsuccessful—
                 AX  =  0FFFF - Drive number is invalid
                 DL  =  Invalid drive number
```

INT 21 Function 37 - Internal to MS-DOS

Function 37 is used only by MS-DOS. It is shown here so you can see that it is used and unavailable.

INT 21 Function 38 - Get/Set Country Dependent Information

Function 38 is valuable if you are writing or modifying international software. See Fig. E-5 for the formats of the various fields. With MS-DOS versions 2.0 and later, if DX contains any value other than FFFF, the get current country subfunction is invoked. Information on date, currency, and other country-specific formats is then returned in a buffer specified by the calling program. The country code is usually the same as the international telephone prefix for the country.

```
Input:    AH  =  38
          AL  =  00     Current country
                 01-FE Country code between 1 and 254
                 FF Country code of 255 or greater, specified in BX
```

BX = Country code, if AL = FF
DX = FFFF - if set country information
DS:DX = 34-byte buffer - if get country information

Output: CF = 00 if successful
Filled in 32-byte block (see Fig. E-5)
BX   = Country code (MS-DOS version 3.x only)
DS: DX = Buffer containing country information

CF = 1 if unsuccessful
AX
=   Error code
02 invalid country code

The 32-byte block format:

0,1	Date/Time Format 0 = USA (H:M:S M/D/Y) 1 = Europe (H:M:S D/M/Y) 2 = Japan (H:M:S D:M:Y)
2	Currency symbol ASCII
3	Set to 0
4	Thousands separator ASCII
5	Set to 0
6	Decimal separator ASCII
7	Set to 0
8–31	Used internally, do not use

Fig. E-5. Country-Dependent Information.

INT 21 Function 39 - Create a Subdirectory

The MS-DOS command MKDIR uses this function to create a subdirectory using a specified path. Create a subdirectory that points DS:DX to an ASCIIZ string that has the disk, path, and subdirectory information. An ASCIIZ character string is one that ends in a null (hex 00). For example, use a line in your program like:

```
MK_SUB     DB     'C:\ASM',0
```

A subdirectory ASM will be created. If there is one already there, or if some problem is encountered, an error returns in AH.

Input: AH = 39
          DS:DX points to ASCIIZ string with directory name

Output: Carry flag = 0 if successful
          Carry flag = 1 if unsuccessful
                          AH   holds the error value
                             = 3 path not found
                             = 5 access denied

Note: If AH has a return code of 05, the following are the most common reasons:

- File or directory with the same name already exists in the specified path.
- Print directory is the root directory, and this root directory is full.
- Path specifies a device.
- The program is running on a network under MS-DOS version 4.1 or later, and the user does not have create access to the parent directory.

INT 21 Function 3A - Delete a Subdirectory

INT 21 function 3A is the companion of INT 21 function 39. The MS-DOS command RMDIR uses this function to remove directories. Point DS:DX to an ASCIIZ string with the disk, and path in it. An ASCIIZ string is one that ends in a null (hex 00). Use a line in your program such as:

```
RM_DIR     DB     'C:\ASM',0
```

As with the MS-DOS command, the subdirectory must be empty before it can be removed. Use INT 21 function 41 to delete all the files in it. If you try and delete a subdirectory that still has files, AH returns with an 05.

Input: AH = 3A
          DS:DX points to ASCIIZ string with directory name

Output: Carry flag = 0 if successful
          Carry flag = 1 if unsuccessful

AH   holds error value
           = 3 path not found
           = 5 access denied

Note: if AH returns with an 05, the most common reasons are as follows:

- Path did not specify a valid directory.
- User has insufficient access rights on a network running under MS-DOS version 3.1 or later.
- Directory is not empty.
- Root directory was specified.
- Current directory was specified.
- Directory is malformed (. and .. not the first two entries).

INT 21 Function 3B - Change a Current Directory

INT 21 function 3B allows a change in the default directory. It is useful if you need to search for a file and you are not certain in which subdirectory the file exists. MS-DOS uses this function for the CD command. The pathname pointed to by DS:DX must be an ASCIIZ string, one that terminates in a null (hex 00). The path string is limited to a total of 64 characters, including all separators.

Input: AH = 3B
           DS:DX points to ASCIIZ string with directory name

Output: Carry flag = 0 if successful
           Carry flag = 1 if unsuccessful
                         AH   holds error value
                             = 3 Path not found

INT 21 Function 3C - Create a File

Function 3C creates a file, assigns it the attributes specified, and returns a 16-bit handle for the file. INT 21 function 3C needs a string that gives drive, directories (and any subdirectories), and file name (with any extension). Point DS:DX at the ASCIIZ character string, which is a string that ends in a null (hex 00). You might have a string definition in a program such as:

```
MY_FILE    DB    'C:\ASM\MACRO\SQRT.ASM' ,0
```

If that file already exists in that subdirectory, it is set to a 0 length. However, if that file exists and is marked read only, error 5 returns in AL. If this function works correctly, a 16-bit handle returns in AX. Use this word to refer to the file from then on; it is the file handle.

Input: AH = 3C
          CX = File attribute, bits 0 through 2 of the two-byte attribute:
                    00 = Normal file
                    01 = Read-only file
                    02 = Hidden file
                    04 = System file
          Bits 3 through 5 are associated with volume labels, subdirectories, and archive files. These bits are invalid for this function and must be set to zero. Also, set bits 6 through 15 to zero to assure future compatibility.
          DS:DX points to ASCIIZ string with directory name

Output: Carry flag = 0   if successful
                    AH = File handle
          Carry flag = 1   if unsuccessful
                    AL holds error value
                        = 3 path not found
                        = 4 too many files open
                        = 5 directory full, or previous read-
                              only file exists

   Note 1: Because this function truncates an existing file to zero length, use INT 21 function 3D (open file with handle) or function 4E (find first file), which can be used to check for the previous existence of the file before function 3C is called. Also there is function 5A (create temporary file) that creates a file in the specified subdirectory and gives it a unique name assigned by MS-DOS
   Note 2: On networks running under MS-DOS version 3.1 or later, the user must have create access to the directory that contains the specified file.

INT 21 Function 3D - Open a File

   This function uses the file handle (see INT 21 function 3C how the handle can be created). You do not need to specify if the file is being opened for sequential or random access, or specify a record size. Just give this function an ASCIIZ string with the drive, path name, and a file name. An ASCIIZ character string is a string which ends in a null (hex 00). Enter the access code in AL, which specifies how to work with the file. The access codes are shown below. If the carry flag (CF—bit 0 of the EFLAGS register) is set, there was an error, which returns in AL.
   When the file is opened, the position of the file pointer is set to zero. INT 21 function 42 (move file pointer) can be used to change its position.

Input: AH = 3D
           AL = File access, file sharing, and inheritance codes
                    Bits   0-2 access code, file usage
                                000 read-only
                                001 write-only
                                010 read/write
                    Bit 3   reserved, set to 0
                    Bits   4-6 sharing mode; file access granted
                                000 compatibility mode
                                001 deny read/write access
                                010 deny write access
                                100 read/write access
                    Bit 7   inherit bit
                                    0 child process inherits the file
                                    1 child process does not inherit the file
           DS:DX points to ASCIIZ string with directory name

Output: Carry flag = 0 if successful
                                AH   = File handle
           Carry flag = 1 if unsuccessful
                                AL   holds error value
                                    = 2 file not found
                                    = 3 path not found
                                    = 4 too many files open
                                    = 5 access denied

INT 21 Function 3E - Close a File Handle

INT 21 function 3E needs the file handle loaded into BX. If the file has been modified, truncated or extended, function 3E updates the current date, time, and file size in the directory entry. With MS-DOS versions 3.1 and later, a program must remove all file locks in effect before it closes a file. The result of closing a file with active locks is unpredictable. If there was an error during the close, the carry flag is set.

Input: AH = 3E
           BX = Valid file handle

Output: Carry flag is 0 if successful
           Carry flag is 1 if unsuccessful
                                AL = 6 invalid file handle

INT 21 Function 3F - Read from a File or Device

Function 3F reads bytes from a file, not records. Store the number of bytes to read in CX. This function returns them to the location specified in DS:DX (but not in the disk transfer area, DTA). AX returns the number of bytes read. Since MS-DOS will not read past the end of the file, check AX to see that you actually got the full number of bytes expected.

```
Input:     AH = 3F
           BX = File handle
           CX = Number of bytes to read
           DS:DX = Data buffer address

Output:    Carry flag = 0 if successful
                        AX   = Number of bytes read

           Carry flag = 1 if unsuccessful
                        AL   = 5 access denied
                             = 6 invalid handle
```

INT 21 Function 40 - Write to a File or Device

To use function 40, load the number of bytes to write into DX. AX returns the number of bytes actually written. If the numbers do not match, an error occurs—most likely the disk is full. Note that INT 21 function 40 does not consider a full disk an error, and the carry flag is not set.

Redirecting output is easy, using file handles. To change output from the screen to the printer, change the handle number from 1 to 4. One caution, if the keyboard is used as an input file, the input buffer is limited to 80 bytes, no matter what limit is set.

Data is written to the file or device beginning at the current location of the file pointer. After writing the specified data, function 40 updates the position of the file pointer and returns the actual number of bytes written in AX. The handle number in BX must be one of the predefined device handles (0 through 4) or a handle obtained through a previous call to open or create a file (such as function 3C, 3D, 5A, or 5B). If CX is zero, the file is truncated or extended to the current file pointer location. Clusters are allocated or released in the file allocation table (FAT) as required to fulfill the request.

```
Input:     AH = 40
           BX = File handle
           CX = Number of bytes to write
           DS:DX = Data buffer address

Output:    Carry flag = 0 if successful
                        AX = Number of bytes written
```

Carry flag = 1 if unsuccessful
>>AL = 05 access denied
>>= 06 invalid handle

INT 21 Function 41 - Delete a File

Function 41 deletes the directory entry of the specified file. Because function 41 supports the use of full pathnames, it is preferable to function 13. In this function, wildcards cannot be used in the file names. Also, strings that identify drive, pathname and file name are limited to 63 characters. The string stored in DS:DX is an ASCIIZ string, one that ends in a null (hex 00). The string can look like:

```
DEL__FILE     DB      'C:\ASM\FILE.OBJ' ,0
```

Input: AH = 41
>>DS:DX = ASCIIZ pathname

Output: Carry flag = 0 if successful
>>Carry flag = 1 if unsuccessful
>>>>AL = 02 file not found
>>>>= 05 access denied

INT 21 Function 42 - Move Read/Write Pointer

The read/write pointer points to the current position in a file. You can skip around in the file by moving the pointer. The value in CX:DX is an offset that specifies how far the file pointer is to be moved.

Set AL with a method code. With method 00, MS-DOS always interprets the value in CX:DX as a positive 32-bit integer, meaning the file pointer is always set relative to the beginning of the file. Method 00, with an offset of 0, positions the file pointer at the beginning of the file.

With methods 01 and 02, the value in CX:DX can be either a positive or negative 32-bit integer. Thus, method 01 can move the file pointer either forward or backward from its current position. Method 02 can move the file pointer either forward or backward from the end of the file. Method 02, with an offset of 0, positions the file pointer at the end of the file. Also, method 02 offset 0 can find the size of the file by examining the pointer position returned by the function.

Input: AH = 42
>>AL = Method value
>>>>00 byte offset from beginning of the file
>>>>01 byte offset from the current location of the
>>>>>>file pointer
>>>>02 byte offset from the end of the file

BX = File handle
CX:DX = Offset
        CX Most significant half of a doubleword value
        DX Least significant half of a doubleword value

Output: Carry flag = 0 if successful
                  DS:AX = new pointer location at an
                        absolute byte offset from the
                        beginning of the file
      Carry flag = 1 if unsuccessful
                  AL = 01 illegal function number
                     = 06 invalid handle

INT 21 Function 43 - Change a File's Attribute

Function 43 gets or sets the attributes of the specified file. The pathname must be an ASCIIZ character string, one that ends in a null (hex 00). This function cannot be used to set or change either a volume-label or directory attribute. Figure E-4 lists the possible file attributes. To summarize: 0 is normal, 1 is read only, 2 is hidden, 4 is a system file, 8 is a volume file, 10 is a subdirectory, and 20 is an archive. Use INT 21 function 43 to change the attributes needed.

Input: AH = 43
            AL = 00 file current attribute returned in CX
                    01 file attribute changed, CX holds new attribute
            DS:DX = ASCIIZ pathname

Output: Carry flag = 0 if successful
           Carry flag = 1 if unsuccessful

                        AL = 00, CX returns attribute
                     = 02 file not found
                     = 03 path not found
                     = 05 access denied

INT 21 Function 44 - Input/Output Control

INT 21 function 44 is used for I/O control (IOCTL) when you set up and define your own devices. It has many, many options and cautions in its use. Because of its complexity, study the the MS-DOS manual.

This function is called with 44 in AH and the subfunction number in AL. If the subfunction has minor functions, those values are specified in CL. Otherwise, the BX,

Subfunction (in hex)	Name
00	Get Device Data
01	Set Device Data
02	Receive Control Data from Character Device
03	Send Control Data to Character Device
04	Receive Control Data from Block Device
05	Send Control Data to Block Device
06	Check Input Status
07	Check Output Status
08	Check if Block Device is Removable
09	Check if Block Device is Remote
0A	Check if Handle is Remote
0B	Change Sharing Retry Count
0C	Generic I/O Control for Handles
	Minor code 45: Set Iteration Count
	65: Get Iteration Count
0D	Generic I/O Control for Block Devices
	Minor code 40: Set Device Parameters
	60: Get Device Parameters
	41: Write Track on Logical Drive
	61: Read Track on Logical Drive
	42: Format/Verify Track on Logical Drive
	62: Verify Track on Logical Drive
0E	Get Logical Drive Map
0F	Set Logical Drive Map

Fig. E-6. INT 21 Function 44 Subfunctions.

CX, and DX registers are used for such information as handles, drive identifiers, buffer addresses, and so on. Figure E-6 shows a list of the subfunctions.

INT 21 Function 45 - Duplicate a File Handle

Use function 45 to refer to a file with more than one handle. This service duplicates the handle. When you move around in the file using one handle, the duplicate one moves, too.

```
Input:    AH = 45
          BX = File handle to duplicate

Output:   Carry flag = 0 if successful
                          AX = New, duplicated handle
          Carry flag = 1 if unsuccessful
                          AL = 04 too many files open
                             = 06 invalid file handle
```

Note 1: The file pointer for the new handle is set to the same position as the original handle. That means that any further changes to the file are reflected in both handles.

Note 2: A use for this function is to keep a file open while its directory entry is being updated to reflect a change in length.

INT 21 Function 46 - Force Duplication of a File Handle

If you are locked into a particular file handle, function 46 can help. Note that handle 2 (standard error output) cannot be redirected and the program will crash if you try it. The function does not return an error in that case. If the handle in CX refers to an open file, the file is closed. The file pointer for the duplicate handle is set to the same position as the pointer for the original handle. Changing the position of either file pointer moves the other pointer as well.

```
Input:    AH = 46
          BX = File handle to duplicate
          CX = Second file handle

Output:   Carry flag = 0 if successful
                          Handles refer to same stream
          Carry flag = 1 if unsuccessful
                          AL = 04 too many open files
                             = 06 invalid handle
```

INT 21 Function 47 - Get Current Directory on Specified Drive

Function 47 returns the path, excluding the drive and leading backslash, of the current directory for the specified drive. The string representing the pathname is returned as an ASCIIZ string, one that ends in a null (hex 00). Function 47 returns the name of the current default directory at a location pointed to by DS:SI. To call INT 21 function 47, point DS:SI at a 64-byte free region and store the drive number in DL.

Input: AH = 47
            DL = Drive number
                  0 = default
                  1 = drive A
                  2 = drive B, and so on
            DS:SI Points to 64-byte buffer

Output: Carry flag = 0 if successful
                            ASCIIZ string at DS:SI
            Carry flag = 1 if unsuccessful
                            AH = 0F invalid drive specified

INT 21 Function 48 - Allocate Memory

When loading a .COM file, MS-DOS gives all memory to it. When loading an .EXE file, this is not always the case. Your program can request more memory by using this function. If too much is asked for, the maximum number allowed returns in BX, so the trick is to request a huge number and then use whatever returns in BX as your real request. However, if you actively use this function, the transient program area (TPA) can become fragmented; that is, small blocks of memory can be orphaned because the memory-management strategy seeks contiguous blocks of memory.

Input: AH = 48
            BX = Number of paragraphs requested

Output: Carry flag = 0 if successful
                            AX: 0000 Memory block address
            Carry flag = 1 if unsuccessful
                            AL = 07 memory control blocks destroyed
                               = 08 insufficient memory
                                  BX contains max. allowed

Note: If a process writes to memory outside the limits of the allocated block, it can destroy control structures for other memory blocks. This could result in failure of subsequent memory-management functions. Also, it could cause MS-DOS to print an error message and halt when the process terminates.

INT 21 Function 49 - Free Allocated Memory

Function 49 frees memory that was allocated by function 48. A program that loads and runs another program must first free the memory in which it is to load the second program. As a normal practice, it is not good for memory-resident programs to use these memory-allocation functions, because you might just free memory that belongs to another program. MS-DOS would then crash.

Input: AH = 49
         ES = Segment address of block being freed

Output: Carry flag = 0 if successful
         Carry flag = 1 if unsuccessful
                         AL = 07 memory control blocks destroyed
                            = 09 incorrect memory block address

INT 21 Function 4A - SETBLOCK

INT 21 function 4A allows expansion or shrinkage of memory blocks. If you are expanding, ask for a huge amount, let it come back with an error and the actual maximum allowable in BX. Then issue this again, using BX as the real request. Because the MS-DOS loader allocates all available memory to .COM programs, such a program should use function 4A immediately (with the segment address of its program segment prefix—PSP) to load a child process or overlay. Also, if using this function to adjust the amount of memory allocated to a .COM program, the stack pointer must be adjusted so that it is within the limits of the revised memory allocation of the program.

Input: AH = 4A
         BX = Requested size in paragraphs
         ES = Segment address of block to modify

Output: Carry flag = 0 if successful
         Carry flag = 1 if unsuccessful
                         AL = 07 memory blocks destroyed
                            = 08 insufficient memory
                                 BX holds maximum allowed
                            = 09 invalid memory block address

INT 21 Function 4B - Load or Execute a Program (EXEC)

INT 21 function 4B allows you to load another program and run it. The environment mentioned in the segment address, below, is a set of strings that indicate something about the PCs operating environment. For example, if VERIFY is set on, the environment holds the string VERIFY + ON. Before loading another program into memory, free memory for it (with function 4A). If you load another program and run it, control returns to the instruction after the INT 21 when the second program finishes. The pathname must be an ASCIIZ, an ASCII string that ends in a null (hex 00).

The handles for any files opened by the parent process before the call to this function are inherited by the child process, unless the parent specified otherwise in calling. All standard devices remain open and available to the child process. In this way, the parent process can control the files used by the child process and control redirection for the child process.

Input: AH = 4B

If AL = 00 Load and execute the program

Parameter block:

Segment address of environment (word)

Address of command to put a PSP + 80 (dword)

Address of default FCB to put at PSP + 5C (dword)

Address of second default FCB to put at PSP + 6C (doubleword)

Note 1: If AH = 00, MS-DOS creates a PSP for the new process and sets the terminate and control-C addresses to the instruction in the parent process that follows the call to this function.

Note 2: Before AL = 00 is used, the system must contain enough free memory to accommodate the new process. Use function 4A (resize memory block), if necessary, to reduce the amount of memory allocated to the parent process. If the parent is a .COM program, allocated memory must be reduced because a .COM program is given ownership of all available memory when it is executed.

Note 3: The EXEC function with AL = 00 is commonly used to load a new copy of COMMAND.COM and then execute an MS-DOS command from within another program.

If AL = 03 Load but create no PSP. Do not run (overlay).

Parameter block:

Segment address to load file at (word)

Relocation factor for image (word)

Note 1: This function with AL = 03 is useful for loading program overlays or for loading data to be used by the parent process, if that data requires location.

Note 2: If you use AL = 03, free memory is not a factor because MS-DOS assumes the new process is being loaded into the address space of the calling process.

Note 3: if you use AL = 03, no PSP is created.

DS:DX = ASCIIZ string with drive, pathname, file name
ES:BX = Parameter block address for AL

Output: Carry flag = 0   if successful
          Carry flag = 1   if unsuccessful
                                AL = 01 invalid function number
                                    = 02 file not found
                                    = 03 path not found
                                    = 05 access denied
                                    = 08 insufficient memory
                                    = 0A invalid environment
                                    = 0B invalid format

INT 21 Function 4C - Exit

Use INT 21 function 4C to end a program if you want to communicate with a calling program. A program that was loaded and run can send a return code to the parent program if the parent program uses INT 21 function 4D. So these two functions can work together. This is the recommended program exit.

When the process is terminated with this function, MS-DOS restores the termination handler (INT 22), control-C handler (INT 23), and critical error handler (INT 24) addresses from the program segment prefix (PSP—offsets 0A, 0E, and 12). MS-DOS also flushes the file buffers to disk, updates the disk directory, closes all files with open handles belonging to the terminated process, and then transfers control to the termination-handler address. On termination, all memory owned by the process is freed.

If the terminated process was invoked by a command line or batch file, control returns to COMMAND.COM, and the transient portion of the command interpreter is reloaded, if necessary. If a batch file was in process, execution continues with the next line of the file, and the return code can be tested with an IF ERRORLEVEL statement. Otherwise, the command prompt is issued.

If working in a networking environment, remove all file locks before calling function 4C.

Input: AH = 4C
          AL = Binary return code

INT 21 Function 4D - Get Return Code of Child Process

The binary return code loaded into AL (before issuing INT 21 function 4C) can be retrieved with this call in the child program. Also, AH tells how the child process ended—normally, with a control-C error, or with function 31. This function can be used only once to retrieve the return code of a terminated process. Subsequent calls do not yield meaningful results. Also, function 4D does not set the carry flag (CF—bit 0 of EFLAGS) to indicate an error. If no previous child process exists, the information returned in AH and AL is undefined.

Input: AH = 4D

Output: AH = Termination method:
                  00 if subprocess ended normally
                       by INT 20, INT 21 function 00, or INT 21 function 4C
                = 01 if subprocess ended with control-C
                = 02 if subprocess ended with a critical
                      device error
                = 03 if terminated and stayed resident
                      INT 27, or INT 21 function 31
          AL = Binary return code from child process
                  00 if terminated with INT 21, INT 21 function 00, or INT 27

INT 21 Function 4E - Find First Matching File

Point DS:DX at an ASCIIZ string that has the drive letter, path name, and wildcards. An ASCIIZ string is one that ends with a null (hex 00). The file name and extension portions of the pathname can contain the MS-DOS wildcards (? or *). If MS-DOS finds the file(s), the disk transfer area (DTA) is filled with 43 bytes of information as shown in Fig. E-7.

Disk Transfer Area – First 43 bytes

0-20	Reserved
21	Found Attribute
22-23	File's Time
24-25	File's Date
26-27	Size – Low word
28-29	Size – High word
30-42	Name and extension of found file in ASCIIZ form

Note: there is NO path name or drive returned

Fig. E-7. DTA Information from INT 21 Function 4E.

Because the file name is returned without drive or pathname, construct the pathname if you want to do anything with the file.

Input: AH = 4E
         CX = Attribute to match

00 only normal files are included in search

any combination of bits 1, 2, and 4, the search
    includes normal files as well as hidden, system, or subdirectory
    files

Bit 3 set (volume-label), only a matching volume
    is returned

Bits 0 and 5 (read-only and archive), these bits
    are ignored by function 4E

DS:DX = ASCIIZ file string

Output: Carry flag = 0 if successful
            DTA filled with:
                21 reserved bytes
                1 byte found attribute
                2 bytes files time
                2 bytes files date
                2 bytes low word - size
                2 bytes high word - size
                13 bytes name and extension of found
                    file in ASCIIZ form—no pathname

Carry flag = 1 if unsuccessful
            AL = 02 no match found
               = 03 path not found
               = 12 no more files; no match found

INT 21 Function 4F - Find Next Matching File

Use INT 21 function 4D before function 4F. This function finds all subsequent matches to a file name, but only after the first one has been found. The 21 reserved bytes (as shown in Fig. E-7) in the DTA that MS-DOS used contain information that this function requires.

Input: AH = 4F

Output: Carry flag = 0 if successful
            DTA filled with information, see Fig. E-7.
          Carry flag = 1 if unsuccessful
            AL = 12 no more files; no match found,
                or no previous function 4E call

INT 21 Function 50-53 - Internal to MS-DOS

These functions are used only by MS-DOS. They are shown here so you can see that they are used and unavailable.

INT 21 Function 54 - Get/Verify State

INT 21 function 54 checks to see if disk writes are being verified or not (the default is 00). If so, AL returns 01. If not, AL returns 00. Verify can be turned on and off with function 2E.

Input: AH = 54

Output: AL = 00 verify is off, no read after write
                = 01 verify is on; read after write operation

INT 21 Function 55 - Internal to MS-DOS

Function 55 is used only by MS-DOS. It is shown here so you can see that it is used and unavailable.

INT 21 Function 56 - Rename a File

Function 56 renames a file and/or moves it to a new location in the hierarchical directory structure. The directory paths specified in DS:DX and ES:DI need not be identical. Thus, specifying different directory paths effectively moves a file from one directory to another. However, when using this function, remember that a file cannot be sent to another drive. The pathname must be an ASCIIZ string, one that terminates in a null (hex 00).

Function 55 should not be used to rename open files. Close open files with function 10 or 3E before calling function 56 to rename it.

Input: AH = 56
               DS:DX = ASCIIZ file string to be renamed
               ES:DI = ASCIIZ file string that holds the new name

Output: Carry flag = 0 if successful
               Carry flag = 1 if unsuccessful
                               AL = 02 file not found
                                    = 03 path not found
                                    = 05 access denied
                                    = 11 not the same device

INT 21 Function 57 - Get/Set a File's Date and Time

To use function 57, the file must already be open. Store the file handle in BX and load AL with a 01 or 00, depending on what is wanted. To set the date and time, store the values in CX and DX first. Before the date and time in a directory of a file can be retrieved or changed with function 57, a handle must be obtained by opening or creating the file using function 3C (create file with handle), 3D (open file with handle), 5A (create temporary file), or 5B (create new file).

Input: AH = 57
        AL = 00 get date and time
        AL = 01 store time as located in CX
                store date as located in DX

Output: Carry flag = 0 if successful
                CX returns Time
                DX returns Date
        Carry flag = 1 if unsuccessful
                AL = 01 invalid function number
                   = 06 invalid handle

      Time: $(2{,}045 \times hours) + (32 \times minutes) + (seconds/2)$
      Date: $512 \times (Year\text{-}1980) + (32 \times Month\ number) + Day$

INT 21 Function 58 - Internal to MS-DOS

Function 58 is used only by MS-DOS. It is shown here so you can see that it is used and unavailable. This function retrieves or sets the method MS-DOS uses to allocate memory blocks for a process that issues a memory-allocation request. Allocation strategies determine how MS-DOS finds and allocates a block of memory to an application that issues a memory-allocation request with either function 48 (allocate memory block) or function 4A (resize memory block). The three strategies are carried out as follows:

- First fit (the default)—MS-DOS works upward from the lowest available block and allocates the first block it encounters that is large enough to satisfy the request for memory. This strategy is followed consistently, even if the block allocated is much larger than requested.

- Best Fit—MS-DOS searches all available memory blocks and then allocates the smallest block that satisfies the request, regardless of its location in the empty-block chain. This strategy maximizes the use of dynamically allocated memory at a slight cost in speed of allocation.

- Last Fit—This is the reverse of first fit. MS-DOS works downward from the highest available block and allocates the first block it encounters that is large enough to satisfy the request for memory. This strategy is followed consistently, even if the block allocated is much larger than required.

INT 21 Function 59 - Get Extended Error

Function 59 only works with MS-DOS releases newer than 3.0. When there was an error, function 59 returns an extended error code and tells where the error was physically located, plus suggests corrective action. Function 59 gives these returns only if it is the next function called after the error. Any intervening calls to other MS-DOS functions, either explicit or implicit, loses the error value for the unsuccessful function. Unlike many of the MS-DOS functions, function 59 alters some registers that are not used to return results: CL, DX, DI, SI, ES, and DS. If the contents of these registers are needed, preserve them before calling function 59. Figure E-8 gives the return codes and suggested actions.

Input: AH = 59
          BX = 00

Output: AH = Extended error code (see Fig. E-8)
          BH = Error class (see Fig. E-8)
          BL = Suggested action (see Fig. E-8)
          CH = Location of error (see Fig. E-8)

Other altered registers: DI, SI, DS, and ES

Function 59 extended error codes correspond to the error values returned in AX by MS-DOS that set the carry flag (CF) on error.

AX = Extended Error Code (in hexadecimal)	Meaning
00	No error encountered
01	Invalid function number
02	File not found
03	Path not found
04	Too many files open; no handles available
05	Access denied
06	Invalid handle
07	Memory control blocks destroyed
08	Insufficient memory
09	Invalid memory–block address
0A	Invalid environment
0B	Invalid environment

Fig. E-8. INT 21 Function 59 Extended-Error Information. (continued)

0C	Invalid access code
0D	Invalid data
0E	Reserved
0F	Invalid disk drive
10	Attempt to remove current directory
11	Device not the same
12	No more files
13	Write-protected disk
14	Unknown unit
15	Drive not ready
16	Invalid command
17	Data error based on cyclic redundancy check (CRC)
18	Length of request structure invalid
19	Seek error
1A	non-MS-DOS disk
1B	Sector not found
1C	Printer out of paper
1D	Write fault
1E	Read fault
1F	General failure
20	Sharing violation
21	Lock violation
22	Invalid disk change
23	FCB unavailable
24	Sharing buffer exceeded
25-31	Reserved
32	Unsupported network request
33	Remote machine not listening
34	Duplicate name on network

Fig. E-8. (continued)

35	Network name not found
36	Network busy
37	Device no longer exists on network
38	Net BIOS command limit exceeded
39	Error in network adapter hardware
3A	Incorrect response from network
3B	Unexpected network error
3C	Remote adapt incompatible
3D	Print queue full
3E	Queue not full
3F	Not enough room for print file
40	Network name deleted
41	Access denied
42	Incorrect network device type
43	Network name not found
44	Network name limit exceeded
45	Net BIOS session limit exceeded
46	Temporary pause
47	Network request not accepted
48	Print or disk redirection paused
49–4F	Reserved
50	File already exists
51	Reserved
52	Cannot make directory
53	Failure on Interrupt 24 (Critical Error)
54	Out of structures
55	Already assigned
56	Invalid password
57	Invalid parameter

Fig. E-8. (continued)

58	Net write fault

BH = Error class

01	Out of resource (such as storage)
02	Temporary situation, expected to end; not an error
03	Authorization problem
04	Internal error in system software
05	Hardware failure
06	System software failure, such as missing or incorrect configuration files; not the fault of the active process
07	Application program error
08	File or item not found
09	File or item of invalid format or type or otherwise unsuitable
0A	File or item interlocked
0B	Drive contains wrong disk, disk has bad spot or other problem with storage medium
0C	Already exists
0D	Unknown

BL = Suggested action

01	Perform a reasonable number of retries before prompting user to choose Abort or Ignore in response to error message
02	Perform a reasonable number of retries, with pauses between, before prompting user to choose Abort or Ignore in response to error message

Fig. E-8. (continued)

03	Prompt user to enter corrected information, such as drive letter or filename
04	Clean up and exit application
05	Exit immediately without cleanup
06	Ignore; information error
07	Prompt user to remove cause of error (for example, change disk) and then retry
CL = Location of error	
01	Unknown
02	Block device
03	Network
04	Serial device
05	Memory related

Fig. E-8. (continued)

INT 21 Function 5A - Create Temporary File

Function 5A only works with MS-DOS releases newer than 3.0. This function uses the systems clock to create a temporary file and returns an ASCIIZ string with the file name. An ASCIIZ string is one that ends in a null (hex 00). Only the drive and path to use should be specified in the buffer pointed to by DS:DX. The function appends an eight-character file name to the specified path and opens the temporary file.

Function 5A is useful in such situations as print spooling on a network, where temporary files are created by many users. In this networking situation, MS-DOS opens the temporary file in compatibility mode.

Note: MS-DOS does not delete the temporary files. Your program must do this.

Input: AH = 5A
           CX = File attribute
                  00 normal file
                  01 read-only file
                  02 hidden file
                  04 system file
           DS:DX = ASCIIZ pathname, ending with a backslash character (\) and followed by 13 bytes of memory to receive the generated filename

Output: Carry flag = 0 if successful
                          AX   = Handle
                          DS:DX = Full pathname for temporary file
          Carry flag = 1 if unsuccessful
                          AX   = Error code
                                  = 03 path not found
                                  = 04 too many open files
                                  = 05 access denied

INT 21 Function 5B - Create a New File

Function 5B creates a new file with the specified pathname. This function works like function 3C (create file with handle) but it fails if the pathname references a file that already exists. The pathname must be an ASCII character string that terminates with a null (hex 00).

Input: AH = 5B
          CS = File attribute
                 00 normal file
                 01 read-only file
                 02 hidden file
                 04 system file
          DS:DX = ASCIIZ pathname

Output: Carry flag = 0 if successful
                          AX = File handle
          Carry flag = 1 if unsuccessful
                          AX = Error code
                             = 03 path not found
                             = 04 too many open files
                             = 05 access denied
                             = 50 file already exists

INT 21 Function 5C - Lock/Unlock Access to a File

Function 5C enables a process running in a networking or multitasking environment to lock or unlock a range of bytes in an open file. This function is useful in ensuring that competing programs or processes do not interfere while a record is being updated. Function 5C can also be used to check the lock status of a file. If an attempt to lock a needed portion of a file fails and error code 21 is returned in AH, the region is already locked by another process.

This function only works with MS-DOS releases newer than 3.0. Locking a portion of a file denies all other processes, both read and write, access to the specified region of the file. This restriction also applies when open file handles are passed to a child process with function 4B (load and execute program). Duplicate file handles created with function 45 (duplicate file handle) and 46 (force duplicate file handle) are allowed to access the locked portions within the current process.

Note that locking a region that goes beyond the end of a file does not cause an error.

Any region locked with a call to function 5C must also be unlocked, and the same four-byte integer values must be used for each operation. Two adjacent regions of a file cannot be locked separately and then unlocked with a single unlock call.

Input: AH = 4C
        AL = 00 lock region
                01 unlock region
        BX = File handle
        CX:DX = 4-byte integer that specifies the beginning of the region to be locked or unlocked (offset in bytes from the beginning of the file)
        SI:DI = 4-byte integer that specifies the length of the region to be blocked (measured in bytes)

Output: Carry flag = 0   if successful
        Carry flag = 1   if unsuccessful
                            AX = Error code
                               = 01 invalid function
                            AL not 00 or 01 or file sharing not loaded
                       = 06 invalid file handle
                       = 21 lock violation
                       = 24 sharing buffer exceeded

INT 21 Function 5E00 - Get Machine Name

Function 5E00 only works with MS-DOS releases newer than 3.0. With this function, load the full word into AX. MS-DOS uses the full word to distinguish between functions, such as between function 5E00 and 5E02. INT 21 5E00 returns an ASCIIZ string filled with the computer name—a 15-character string that is set in PC networks. An ASCIIZ string is one that ends in a null (hex 00).

Input: AH = 5E
        AL = 00
        DS:DX = 16-byte buffer

Output: Carry flag = 0   if successful
                            CH = Validity of machine name
                               00 invalid
                               nonzero valid

CL = NETBIOS number assigned to machine
DS:DX - ASCIIZ machine name

Note: The NETBIOS number in CL and the name at
DS:DX are valid only if the value returned in
CL is nonzero.

Carry flag = 1 if unsuccessful
AX = Error code
01 invalid function, or Microsoft
Network not running

INT 21 Function 5E02 - Set Printer Setup

Function 5E02 sets the setup string that MS-DOS adds to the beginning of a file sent to a network printer. With this function, load the full word into AX. This function only works with MS-DOS releases newer than 3.0. Function 5E02 and 5E03 enable multiple users on a network to configure a shared printer as required. The *assign-list* number is an index to a table that identifies the printer as a device on the network. A process can determine the assign-list number for the printer by using function 5F02 subfunction 02 (get assign-list entry).

Input: AH = 5E
AL = 02 set printer setup string
BX = Assign-list index number (obtained with function 5F subfunction 02)
CX = Length of setup string in bytes (64 bytes max)
DS:SI = ASCII setup string

INT 21 Function 5E03 - Get Printer Setup

With function 5E03, load the full word into AX. This function only works with MS-DOS releases newer than 3.0.

Input: AH = 5E
AL = 03 get printer setup string
BX = Assign-list index number (obtained with function 5F subfunction 02)
ES:DI = 64-byte buffer to receive string

Output: Carry flag = 0 if successful
CX = Length of printer setup string in bytes
ES:DI = ASCII printer setup string
Carry flag = 1 if unsuccessful
AX = Error code
= 01 invalid subfunction

INT 21 Function 5F02 - Get Assign-List Entry

Function 5F subfunction 02 obtains the local and remote (network) names of a device. To find the names of MS-DOS uses the user-assigned index number of the device (set with function 5F subfunction 03) to search a table of redirected devices on the network. Microsoft Networks must be running with file sharing loaded for this subfunction to operate successfully. This function only works with MS-DOS releases newer than 3.0. With this function, load the full word into AX. All strings returned by this subfunction are ASCIIZ strings, ones that terminate with a null (hex 00).

Note that a call to this subfunction destroys the contents of the DX and BP registers.

```
Input:    AH = 5F
          AL = 02
          BX = Assign-list index number
       DS:SI = 16-byte buffer for local device name
       ES:DI = 128-byte buffer to receive remote (network)
               name
Output:   Carry flag = 0 if successful
                          BH = Device status
                               00 valid device
                               01 invalid device
                          BL = Device type
                               03 printer
                               04 drive
                          CX = User data
                       DS:SI = ASCIIZ local device name
                       ES:DI = ASCIIZ network name
          Carry flag = 1 if unsuccessful
                          AX = error code
                             = 01 invalid function or Microsoft
                                  networks not running
                             = 12 no more files
```

INT 21 Function 5F03 - Redirect Device

Function 5F subfunction 03 redirects a local printer or disk drive to a network device and establishes an assign-list index number for the redirected device. Microsoft Networks must be running with file sharing loaded for this subfunction to operate successfully. With this function, load the full word into AX. This function only works with MS-DOS releases newer than 3.0.

The strings used by this subfunction must be ASCIIZ, ones that end in a null (hex 00). The ASCIIZ string pointed to by ES:DI (the destination, or remote, device) cannot be more than 128 bytes including the password (which can be a maximum of eight characters). If the password is omitted, the pathname must be followed by two null bytes.

Input: AH = 5F
           AL = 03
           BL = Device type
                03 printer
                04 drive
           CX = User data
           DS:SI = 16-byte ASCIIZ local device name
           ES:DI = 128-byte ASCIIZ remote network device name and password in the
           form:

           <machinename> <pathname> <null> <password> <null>

Output: Carry flag = 0 if successful
          Carry flag = 1 if unsuccessful
                          AX = Error code
                             = 01 invalid function or Microsoft
                                  Networks not running
                             = 03 path not found
                             = 05 access denied
                             = 08 insufficient memory
                             = 0F redirection paused on server
                             = 12 no more files

Note 1: If BL = 03, the ASCIIZ string pointed to by DS:SI must be one of the following names: PRN, LPT2, or LPT3. If the call is successful, output is redirected to a network print spooler, which must be named in the destination string. When redirection for the printer is canceled, all printing is sent to the first local printer (LPT1).

Note 2: If BL = 04, the ASCIIZ string pointed to by DS:SI can be a drive letter followed by a colon (:) such as C: or it can be a null string. If the string represents a valid drive, a successful call redirects drive requests to the network directory named in the destination string. If DS:SI points to a null string, MS-DOS attempts to provide access to the network directory named in the destination string without redirecting any service.

INT 21 Function 5F04 - Cancel Redirection

Function 5F04 cancels the action of function 5F03. Microsoft Networks must be running with file sharing loaded for this subfunction to operate correctly. With this function, load the full word into AX. This function only works with MS-DOS releases newer than 3.0.

The strings must be ASCIIZ, ones that end in a null (hex 00). The string can be any one of the following:

- The letter, followed by a colon, of a redirected local drive. This function restores the drive letter to its original, physical meaning.
- The name of a redirected printer: PRN, LPT1, LPT2, or LPT3, or its machine-specific equivalent. This function restores the printer name to its original, physical meaning at the local workstation.
- A string, beginning with two backslashes (\ \ ) followed by the name of a network directory. This function terminates the connection between the local workstation and the directory specified in the string.

Input: AH = 5F
            AL = 04
            DS:SI = ASCIIZ device name or path

Output: Carry flag = 0 if successful
          Carry flag = 1 if unsuccessful
                          AX = Error code
                             = 01   invalid function or Microsoft
                                     Networks not running
                             = 03   path not found
                             = 05   access denied
                             = 08   insufficient memory
                             = 0F   redirection paused on server
                             = 12   no more files

INT 21 Function 62 - Get PSP

INT 21 function 62 returns the program segment prefix (PSP) of the currently executing process. This function only works with MS-DOS releases newer than 3.0.

Input: AH = 62

Output: BX = Segment address of PSP for current process

Interrupt 21 Function 63 - Get Lead Byte Table

This function only occurs in MS-DOS version 2.25. Because the concentration is on MS-DOS 5.1 and higher function 63 will not be discussed here.

Interrupt 22 - Terminate Address

The machine interrupt vector for INT 22 (memory locations 0000:008B) contains the address of the routine that receives control when the currently executing program terminates by means of INT 20, INT 27, or INT 21 function 00, INT 21 function 31, or INT 21 function 4C. This interrupt stores the address to which control will be transferred when your program is done. Let MS-DOS functions use this terminate address and do not call it yourself.

MS-DOS copies the address in this vector into offsets 0A through 0D of the program segment prefix (PSP) when a program is loaded, but before it begins executing. The address is restored from the PSP as part of MS-DOS termination handling.

Interrupt 23 - Control-C Break Exit Address

INT 23 stores the address to which control will be transferred when BREAK (control-C) is typed. The machine interrupt vector contains the address of the routine that receives control when a control-C is detected during any character I/O function and, if the break flag is on, during most other MS-DOS calls.

When MS-DOS detects a control-C and a program interrupt 23 handler receives control, MS-DOS sets all registers to the original values they had when the function call that is being interrupted was made. Any MS-DOS function call can be used within the body of an interrupt 23 handler.

MS-DOS copies the address of this vector into offsets 0E through 11 of the program segment prefix (PSP) when a program is loaded but before it begins executing. MS-DOS restores the address from the PSP in case it was modified by an application. It does this as part of its termination handling.

Interrupt 24 - Critical Error Handler

INT 24 holds the address to which control transfers if there is a critical error, such as a seek error. It is possible to intercept the INT 24 handler and install your own handler. If the most significant bit of AH is zero, the error was a disk error; otherwise bit 7 is set to one. Error codes are found in the lower four bits of DI and are shown in Fig. E-9. If MS-DOS detects an IRET, MS-DOS takes an action based on the values in AL.

Interrupt 25 - Absolute Disk Read

Interrupt 25 provides direct linkage to the MS-DOS BIOS module to read data from a logical disk sector into a specified memory location. INT 25 destroys the contents of all registers. Also, flags are PUSHed onto the stack because this INT call is returned in current flags. Error type is returned in AH, as shown in Fig. E-9. After checking the current flags, be sure to POP the flags off the stack. The difference between this interrupt and the BIOS interrupts is that here you use the logical sector number. MS-DOS calculates the head number, cylinder number, and so on (that BIOS needs) and passes the information to BIOS, which does the work.

A logical sector starts from 0 and runs (on a double-sided, nine-sectored diskette) up to:

$$2 \text{ (sides)} \times 40 \text{ (tracks)} \times 9 \text{ (sectors)} - 1 = 719$$

DI – Lower Four Bits:		Meaning
0	0000	Diskette is write protected
1	0001	Unknown unit
2	0010	The requested drive is not ready
3	0011	Unknown Command
4	0100	Cyclic Redundancy Check error in the data
5	0101	Bad request structure length
6	0110	Seek error
7	0111	Media type unknown
8	1000	Sector not found
9	1001	Printer is out of paper
A	1010	Write fault
B	1011	Read fault
C	1100	General failure
D	1101	Not used
E	1110	Not used
F	1111	Invalid disk change

Fig. E-9. Critical Error Handler Error Codes.

BIOS does not start sectoring at 0, but at 1 (this instance appears to be the only time that counting begins at 1). For that reason, logical sector zero is track 0, head 0, sector 1. This continues until all sectors in the current track, and current head (side) are used. For example, logical sector 8 is track 0, head 0, sector 9, which means that logical sector 9 is track 0, head 1, sector 1. The values change from right to left, which says that head changes before track does.

Input: AH = 25
           AL = Drive number
                0 = Drive A
                1 = Drive B, and so on
           CX = Number of sectors to read
           DX = First logical sector
        DS:BX = Buffer address of disk transfer area (DTA)

If Carry Flag (CF) = 1, AH =	Meaning
80 10000000	Disk did not respond
40 01000000	Seek failed
20 00100000	Controller failure
10 00010000	Bad Cyclic Redundancy Check
08 00001000	DMA overrun
04 00000100	Sector not found
03 00000011	Write protect error
02 00000010	Address Mark missing
00 00000000	Bad command

Fig. E-10. Absolute Disk Read Error Flags.

Output: Carry flag = 0 if successful
           Carry flag = 1 if unsuccessful
                    AH = See Fig. E-10

Interrupt 26 - Absolute Disk Write

Interrupt 26 provides direct linkage to the MS-DOS BIOS module to write data from a specified memory buffer to a logical disk sector. INT 26 destroys the contents of all registers. Also, flags are PUSHed onto the stack because this INT call is returned in current flags. Error type is returned in AH, as shown in Fig. E-10. After checking the current flags, be sure to POP the flags off the stack. The difference between this interrupt and the BIOS interrupts is that here you use the logical sector number. MS-DOS calculates the head number, cylinder number, and so on (that BIOS needs) and passes the information to BIOS, which does the work.

A logical sector starts from 0 and runs (on a double-sided, nine-sectored diskette) up to:

$$2 \text{ (sides)} \times 40 \text{ (tracks)} \times 9 \text{ (sectors)} - 1 = 719$$

BIOS does not start sectoring at 0, but at 1 (this instance and INT 25 appear to be the only times that counting begins at 1). For that reason, logical sector zero is track 0, head 0, sector 1. This continues until all sectors in the current track, and current head (side) are used. For example, logical sector 8 is track 0, head 0, sector 9, which means that logical sector 9 is track 0, head 1, sector 1. The values change from right to left, which says that head changes before track does.

Input: AH = 26
             AL = Drive number
                0 = Drive A
                1 = Drive B, and so on
             CX = Number of sectors to write
             DX = First logical sector
      DS:BX = Buffer address of disk transfer area (DTA)

Output: Carry flag = 0 if successful
         Carry flag = 1 if unsuccessful
                   AH = See Fig. E-10

Interrupt 27 - Terminate and Stay Resident

Interrupt 27 terminates execution of the currently executing program but reserves part or all of its memory so that it will not be overlaid by the next transient program to be loaded. INT 27 makes .COM files code memory-resident, but not .EXE files. If additional memory space is needed, use INT 21 .AW function 31. To use INT 27, set DS:DX to the address at which programs may be loaded; that is, set DS:DX to the end of the program you want to keep in memory and ADD one to DX.

This interrupt is typically used to allow user-written drivers or interrupt handlers to be loaded as ordinary .COM or .EXE programs and then remain resident. Subsequent entrance to the code is by means of a hardware or software interrupt.

If a program is returning to COMMAND.COM rather than to another program, control transfers first to COMMAND.COMs resident portion, which reloads COMMAND.COMs transient portion if necessary and passes it control. If a batch file is in progress, the next line of the file is then fetched and interpreted; otherwise, a prompt is issued for the next user command.

Input: AH = 27
        DX = Offset of last byte plus 1 (relative to the PSP of the program to
               be protected)
        CS = Segment address of PSP

Note: The maximum amount of memory that can be reserved with this interrupt is 64kB. Therefore, INT 27 should be used only for applications that must run under MS-DOS versions 1.0 and later.

Interrupt 28–2E - Internal to MS-DOS

Interrupts 28–2E are used only by MS-DOS. They are shown here so you can see that they are used and unavailable.

Interrupt 2F - Multiplex Interrupt

INT 2F sets up communication between two processes. It can also create queues. This is a complex interrupt, so study the MS-DOS manual carefully before you use the function.

This interrupt with AH = 01 submits a file to the print spooler, removes a file from the print spooler queue of pending files, or obtains the status of the printer. Other values for AH are used by various MS-DOS extensions, such as APPEND.

```
Input:   AH  =  01 print spooler call
         AL  =  00 get installed status
                01 submit file to be printed
                      DS:DX = packet address
                02 remove file from print queue
                      DS:DX = ASCIIZ file specification
                03 cancel all files in queue
                04 hold print jobs for status read
                05 end hold for status read
```

Note 1: For subfunction 01, the packet consists of five bytes. The first byte contains the level (must be zero); the next four bytes contain the doubleword address (segment and offset) of an ASCIIZ file specification. The filename cannot contain MS-DOS wildcard characters. If the file exists, it is added to the end of the print queue.

Note 2: For subfunction 02, wildcard characters (* and ?) are allowed in the file specification, which makes it possible to delete multiple files from the print queue with one call.

Note 3: For subfunction 04, the address returned for the print queue points to a series of filename entries. Each entry in the queue is 64 bytes and contains an ASCIIZ file specification. The first file specification in the queue is the one currently being printed. The last file in the queue has a null (hex 00) in the first byte.

```
Output:  Carry flag = 0 if  successful
                        If AL was 00 on call, then
                            AL = Status
                                 00 not installed-OK to install
                                 01 not installed-do not install
                                 FF installed
                        If AL was 04 on call, then
                            DX = Error count
                            DS:SI = Print queue
         Carry flag = 1 if unsuccessful
                            AX = Error code
                               = 01 function invalid
                               = 02 file not found
```

$$= \text{03 path not found}$$
$$= \text{04 too many open files}$$
$$= \text{05 access denied}$$
$$= \text{08 queue full}$$
$$= \text{09 spooler busy}$$
$$= \text{0C name too long}$$
$$= \text{0F drive invalid}$$

Interrupt 30-3F - Internal to MS-DOS

Interrupts 30-3F are used only by MS-DOS. They are shown here so you can see that they are used and unavailable.

Interrupt 40-5F - Reserved

Interrupts 40-5F are reserved for future use only by MS-DOS. They are shown here so you can see that they could be used, but it is better to consider them unavailable.

Interrupt 60-67 - Reserved for User Software

Interrupts 60-67 are specifically set aside for your use. Programs can use them without fear of overlapping current MS-DOS implementation.

Interrupt 68-7F - Not Used

To date, interrupts 68-7F have not been used by MS-DOS software.

Interrupt 80-85 - Reserved by BASIC

BASIC compilers use interrupts 80-85.

Interrupt 86-F0 - Used by BASIC Interpreter

The interpreted BASIC uses interrupts 68-F0. So, consider them usable only if you never use BASIC.

Interrupt F1-FF - Not Used

Appendix F

LINK—The Microsoft Object Linker

ASSEMBLERS AND COMPILERS TRANSLATE SOURCE CODE MODULES INTO OBJECT MODULES. An object module consists of a sequence of object records and machine language code that describes the form and content of an executable program. Object modules can be stored as either object files or object libraries. By Microsoft convention, object files have the file-name extension .OBJ and object libraries have the extension .LIB.

Input to LINK consists of one or more object files and, optionally, one or more libraries containing binary data that can be loaded directly from the file into memory and executed. LINK also can generate a symbolic address map listing. This map is a text file that describes the organization of the .EXE file, and it defines the correspondence of symbols declared in the object modules to addresses in the executable file.

LINK first extracts executable code and data from records in object modules, arranges them in a specified order according to its rules for segment combination and relocation, and copies the result into the .EXE file. Then LINK builds a header for the .EXE file, as shown in Fig. F-1.

That header describes the size of the executable program and contains a table of load-time segment relocations and initial values for certain CPU registers. LINK always uses all the object modules in the object files it processes. In contrast, it extracts specific object modules from libraries; it uses only those object modules needed to resolve references to public symbols. This difference comes from the order in which LINK reads its input files. First, LINK uses object files specified in the command line or in response to the *Object Modules* prompt. Second, it uses libraries specified in the command line or in response to the *Libraries* prompt. Third, it uses libraries specified in COMENT records.

LINK resolves external references in the order in which it encounters the corresponding public declarations (see chapter 9 for PUBLIC and EXTRN). This fact is important to remember because the order determines the order in which LINK extracts

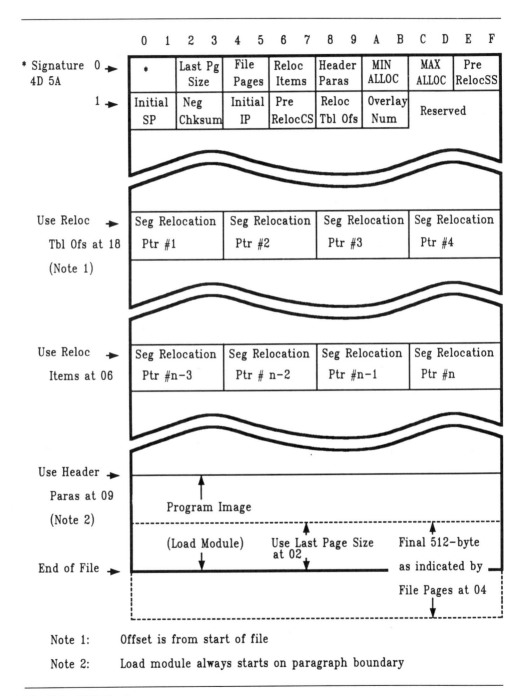

Note 1:   Offset is from start of file

Note 2:   Load module always starts on paragraph boundary

Fig. F-1. .EXE Header.

object modules from libraries. When you declare a public symbol required to resolve an external reference more than once among the object modules in the input libraries, LINK uses the first object module that contains the public symbol. This means that you can vary the actual executable code or data associated with a particular external by changing the order in which LINK processes its internal libraries. See Fig. F-2 for an overview of ordered object module processing by LINK.

TWO-PASS LINKER

LINK is a two-pass linker, which means that it reads all its input object modules twice. On pass 1, it builds an address map of the segments and symbols in the object modules. On pass 2, it extracts the executable code and program data from the object modules and builds a memory image of the executable file.

During pass 1, LINK processes the CRDEF, EXTDEF, GRPDEF, LNAMES, and SEGDEF records in each input object module and uses the information in these object records to construct a symbol table and an address map of segments and segment groups. As each object module is processed, LINK uses the symbol table to resolve external references that are declared in EXTDEF and COMDEF records. If LINK processes all the object files without resolving all the external references in the symbol table, it searches the input libraries for public symbols that match the unresolved external references (which is a good reason to build LINKLIBs). After all the object files have been read and all the external references in the symbol table have been resolved, LINK has a complete map of the addresses of all segments and symbols in the full program. If it finds a request for a .MAP file, LINK creates the file and writes the address map to it. Then LINK goes to pass 2.

During pass 2, LINK extracts executable code and program data from records in the object modules. LINK builds the code and data into a memory image of the executable file. During this pass, LINK also carries out all the address relocations and fixups related to segment relocation, segment grouping, and resolution of external references, as well as any other address fixups specified explicitly in object module FIXUPP records. LINK reads each of the input object modules in the same order as it did in pass 1. This time, however, it copies the information from the records of each object module into the memory image of each segment in the proper sequence. When all the data has been extracted from the object modules, the memory image is complete. LINK now has all the information it needs to build the .EXE header (see Fig. F-1).

LIBRARY MANAGER (LIB)

Although LIB is technically not a part of LINK, it is included here because it is allied in that LIB creates or modifies object module library file. It checks existing library files for consistency and prints listings of the contents of library files. A library file consists of relocatable object modules that are indexed by their names and public symbols. LINK uses these files during the creation of an executable program to resolve external references to routines and variables contained in other object modules. LIB is supplied

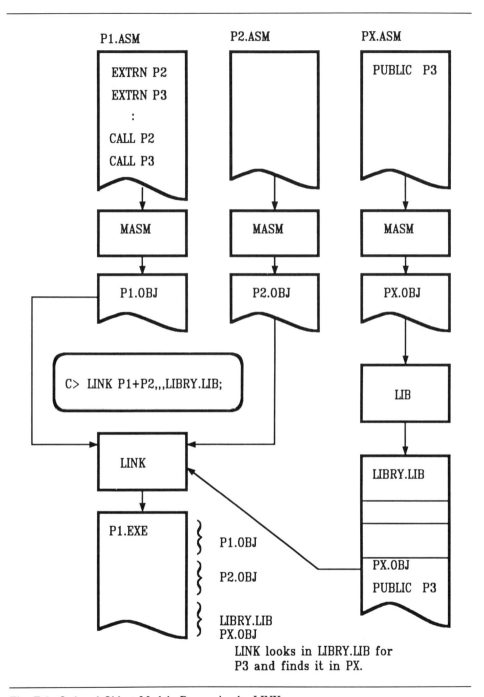

Fig. F-2. Ordered Object Module Processing by LINK.

with the Microsoft Macro Assembler (MASM), C compiler, FORTRAN compiler, and Pascal compiler.

In the delete step, LIB does not actually delete object modules from the specified library file. Instead, it marks the selected object modules for deletion, creates a new library file, and copies only the modules not marked for deletion into the new file. This means that, if LIB is terminated for any reason other than a normal ending, the original file is not lost. Enough space must be available on the disk for both the original library file and the copy, or LIB will abort the run.

Syntax

LIB

or

LIB   *library__file* [/PAGESIZE:*n*] [/NOIGNORECASE] [*operation*] [,[*list__file*] [,[*new__libraryfile*]]][;]

or

LIB   @*response__file*

Where:

•   *library__file* is the name of the object module library file to be created or modified. The default extension is .LIB. This parameter is required. If you forget it, LIB prompts for it.

•   */PAGESIZE:n* is the page size of the library file (in bytes) and must immediately follow *library__file* if used. *n* is a power of 2 between 16 and 32768, inclusive, and the default is 16. This option can be abbreviated /P:*n*. Because the index to a library file is contained in a fixed number of pages, setting a larger page size increases the number of index entries—and thus the number of object modules—that a library file can obtain but results in more wasted disk space, an average of half a library page per object module.

•   */NOIGNORECASE* tells LIB not to ignore case when it compares symbol names. By default, LIB ignores case. Multiple symbols that are the same except for case can be put in the same library. An example of this is "__Open" and "__open". Normally, you could not add both these symbols to the same library. Note that if a library is built with /NOI (the abbreviation), the library is internally marked to indicate /NOI. All libraries built with earlier versions of LIB are not marked. If you combine multiple libraries, and any one of them is marked /NOI, then /NOI is assumed for the output library.

• */IGNORECASE* LIB also supports the option /IGNORECASE, which is completely analogous to /NOIGNORECASE. */I* is the default. The only reason to use it would be if you have an existing library marked */NOI* (see /NOIGNORECASE), you wanted to combine it with other libraries that were not marked, and you wanted the output library to not be marked. If you do not use /IGNORECASE, the output is marked */NOI*.

• *operation* is one or more library manipulations to be performed. Specify each *operation* as a code followed by an object module name; case is not significant.

> + *name* Add object module or another library to the library. This operation also can be used to add the contents of another entire object module library file to the library file being updated, in which case the extension .LIB must be included in the *name*.
> − *name* Delete object module from library.
> − + *name* Replace object module in library.
> * *name* Copy object module from library to object file.
> − * *name* Copy object module to object file and then delete object module from library.

When an object module is copied or moved from the library file, the drive and pathname of the object module are set to the default drive, current directory, and specified module name, and the extension of the object module defaults to .OBJ. When an object module is added or replaced, LIB assumes a default extension of .OBJ.

• *list__file* is the name of the file or character device to receive the cross-reference listing for the library file; the default is NUL device. Any valid drive, pathname, and extension or any valid character device (such as PRN) is permitted. If this parameter is omitted, no listing is generated.

• *new__libraryfile* is the name to be assigned to the modified object module library file. The default name is the same as *library__file*. If the default is used, the original *library__file* is renamed with the extension .BAK. When a new library file is being created, this parameter is not necessary.

• [;] When the command line is used to supply LIB with filenames and switches, typing a semicolon (;) after any parameter (except *library__file*) causes LIB to use the default values for the remaining parameters. When it finds a semicolon after *library__file*, LIB simply checks the file for consistency and usability.

@response_file is the name of a text file containing LIB parameters in the same order in which they are supplied if entered interactively. The name of the response file must be preceded by the at (@) symbol and also can be preceded by a path and/or drive letter. This parameter allows the automation of complex LIB sessions involving many files. A response file contains ASCII text that corresponds line for line to the responses that are entered in a normal interactive LIB session. If *library_file* is a new file, the letter Y must appear by itself on the second line of the response file to approve the creation of a library file. The last line of the response file must end with a semicolon or a carriage return. LIB ignores any lines following the semicolon. If all the parameters required by LIB are not present in the response file or the response file does not end with a semicolon, LIB prompts for the missing information.

If you enter the LIB command without any parameters, LIB prompts for each parameter needed. If there are too many operations to fit on one line, end the line with an ampersand (&), which causes LIB to repeat the *Operations:* prompt. If it finds any response except *library_file* ended with a semicolon, LIB uses the default values for the remaining file names. If the *library_file* parameter is followed by a semicolon or if a semicolon is entered at the *Operations:* prompt, LIB takes no action except to verify that the contents of the specified file are consistent and usable.

Return Codes

0   No error. LIB operation was successful.
1   An error that terminated execution of the LIB utility was encountered.
2   Program error. Something is wrong with the commands or files input to the utility.
4   System error. The utility ran out of memory, was interrupted by the user, or experienced an internal error.

Error Messages

LIB error messages begin with the input file name *filename*, if one exists, or with the name of the utility. If possible, LIB prints a warning and continues operation. For some fatal errors, LIB terminates processing. LIB error messages have one of the following formats:

> {*filename*|LIB} : fatal error U1*xxx*: *messagetext*
> {*filename*|LIB} : warning U4*xxx*: *messagetext*

Number   **LIB Error Message**

U1150   **page size too small**
The page size of an input library was too small, which indicates LIB found an invalid input .LIB file.

U1151 **syntax error : illegal file specification**
A command operator such as a minus sign (–) was given without a following module name.

U1152 **syntax error : option name missing**
LIB found a forward slash (/) without an option after it.

U1153 **syntax error : option value missing**
LIB found a /PAGESIZE option without a value following it.

U1154 **option unknown**
Currently, LIB only recognizes the /PAGESIZE option, and it found some other one.

U1155 **syntax error : illegal input**
The given command did not follow correct LIB syntax.

U1156 **syntax error**
The given command did not follow correct LIB syntax.

U1157 **comma or new line missing**
LIB expected a comma or carriage return in the command line but did not find one. This might indicate an inappropriately placed comma. Check the command line.

U1158 **terminator missing**
Either the response to the *Output Library* prompt or the last line of the response file used to start LIB did not end with a carriage return.

U1159 **Reserved**

U1160 **Reserved**

U1161 **cannot rename old library**
LIB could not rename the old library with a .BAK extension because the .BAK version already exists with read-only protection.

U1162 **cannot reopen library**
LIB could not reopen the old library after it was renamed with a .BAK extension.

U1163 **error writing to cross-reference file**
The disk root directory is full.

U1164–U1169   Reserved

U1170   too many symbols
More than 4609 symbols appear in the library file.

U1171   insufficient memory
LIB did not have enough memory to run. Remove any shells or resident programs and try again, or add more memory.

U1172   no more virtual memory
This is a problem that should be reported to Microsoft Product Assistance.

U1173   internal failure
This is a problem that should be reported to Microsoft Product Assistance.

U1174   mark : not allowed
This is a problem that should be reported to Microsoft Product Assistance.

U1175   free : not allocated
This is a problem that should be reported to Microsoft Product Assistance.

U1176–U1179   Reserved

U1180   write to extract file failed
The disk or root directory is full. Delete files to make space.

U1181   write to library file failed
The disk or root directory is full. Delete files to make space.

U1182   *filename* : cannot create extract file
The disk or root directory is full, or the specified extract file already exists with read-only protection.

U1183   cannot open response file
LIB could not find the response file.

U1184   unexpected end-of-file on command input
An end-of-file character was received prematurely in response to a prompt.

U1185   cannot create new library
The disk or root directory is full, or the library file already exists with read-only protection. Make space on the disk or change the protection of the library file.

U1186   **error writing to new library**
The disk or root directory is full. Delete or move files to make space.

U1187   **cannot open VM.TMP**
The disk or root directory is full. Delete or move files to make space.

U1188   **cannot write to VM.TMP**
This is a problem that should be reported to Microsoft Product Assistance.

U1189   **cannot read from VM.TMP**
This is a problem that should be reported to Microsoft Product Assistance.

U1190   **interrupted by user**
You interrupted LIB during operation with a control-C or control-break.

U1191–U1199   **Reserved**

U1200   **name : invalid library header**
The input library has an invalid format. It is either not a library file or it has been corrupted.

U1201–U1202   **Reserved**

U1203   *name* **: invalid object module near** *location*
The module specified by *name* is not a valid object module.

U1204–U2151   **Reserved**

U2152   *filename* **: cannot create listing**
The directory or disk is full, or the cross-reference listing file already exists with read-only protection. Make space on the disk or change the protection of the cross-reference listing file.

U2153–U2154   **Reserved**

U2155   *modulename* **: module not in library**
LIB did not find the specified module in the input library.

U2156   **Reserved**

U2157   *filename* **: cannot access file**
LIB was unable to open the specified file.

U2158   *libraryname* **: invalid header; file ignored**
The input library had an incorrect format.

U2159   *filename* : **invalid format** *hexnumber*; **file ignored**
The signature byte (see Fig. F-1) or word *hexnumber* of the given file was not one of the following recognized types: Microsoft library, Microsoft object, Xenix archive, or Intel library.

U2160–U4149   Reserved

U4150   *modulename* : **module redefinition ignored**
A module with the same name was already in a library when you specified another one to be added.

U4151   *name* : **symbol defined in module** *modulename*, **redefinition ignored**
The specified symbol was defined in more than one module.

U4152   **Reserved**

U4153   *number* : **page size too small; ignored**
The value specified in the /PAGESIZE option was less than 16.

U4154   **Reserved**

U4155   *modulename* : **module not in library**
A module specified to be replaced does not already exist in the library. LIB adds the module anyway.

U4156   *libraryname* : **output-library specification ignored**
You specified an output library in addition to a new library name.

U4157   **Insufficient memory, extended dictionary not created**
The library is still valid, but LINK is not able to take advantage of the extended dictionary to speed linking.

U4158   **Internal error, extended dictionary not created**
The library is still valid, but LINK is not able to take advantage of the extended dictionary to speed linking.

LINK - CREATE .EXE FILE

LINK combines relocatable object modules into an executable (.EXE) file. Use LINK with object files produced by any of the high-level language compilers or assemblers that support the Microsoft object module format. Microsoft supplies LINK with their Macro Assembler (MASM), FORTRAN compiler, C compiler, and Pascal compiler. LINK supports many options that can be invoked by including a switch in the command line, as part of the response to a LINK prompt, or in a response file. Those switches are described below.

If LINK is unable to hold in RAM all the data it is processing, it creates a temporary disk file named VM.TMP in the current directory of the default disk drive. If a floppy disk is in the default drive, LINK issues a warning message to prevent disk changes until the LINK session is completed. After LINK finishes, it deletes this temporary file. Remember, any file named VM.TMP that is already on the disk will be destroyed if LINK creates the temporary disk file.

Syntax
LINK

or

LINK *@response__file*

or

LINK*obj__file*[+ *obj__file*...][,[*exe__file*]] [,[*map__file*]]
[,[*library*[+ *library*...]]] [*options*] [;]

Where:

- *@response__file* is the name of a text file that contains LINK parameters in the order in which they are supplied during an interactive LINK session. The *response__file* must be the name of an ASCII file that corresponds line for line to the responses that are entered in a normal interactive LINK session. The last line of this file must end with a semicolon (;) or a carriage return. If all parameters required by LINK are not present in the response file or if the response file does not end with a semicolon or carriage return, LINK prompts the user for the missing information.

- *obj__file* is the name of a file that contains a relocatable object module produced by MASM or by a high-level language compiler (default is .OBJ). If multiple object files are linked, their names should be separated by a plus operator (+) or a space. If LINK does not find an extension, LINK supplies the .OBJ extension. If you use one of the high-level language compilers that support partitioning of the executable program into a root segment and one or more overlay segments (and which include a special overlay manager in their libraries), surround the object modules that compose each overlay segment with parentheses in the LINK command line.

- *exe__file* is the name of the executable file to be produced by LINK (default extension is .EXE).

• *map_file* is the name of the file or character device to receive a listing of the names, load addresses, and lengths of the segments in *exe_file* (default is NUL device; default extension is .MAP). The map file also includes the names and load addresses of any groups in the program, the program entry point and (if the /M switch is used) all public symbols and their addresses. If you use the /LI switch and if line numbers were inserted into *obj_file* by the compiler, the starting address of each *obj_file* program is also copied to *map_file*. If neither the /M nor the /LI switch is used and *map_file* is not specified, no listing is created.

• *library* is the name of an object module library to be searched to resolve external references in the object file(s) (default is .LIB). Separate multiple library names by plus operators (+) or spaces. A maximum of 16 search paths can be specified in the LINK command line. If you precede a library name by a drive and/or path, LINK searches only the specified location. If no drive or path precedes a library name, LINK searches for library files in the following order:

1) Current drive and directory.
2) Any other library search paths specified in the command line, in the order they were entered.
3) Directories specified in the LIB = environment variable, if one exists.

If you specify default libraries within the object files through special records inserted by certain high-level language compilers, those libraries will be searched *after* the libraries named in the command line or response file.

• *options* specifies one or more of the following switches. Switches can be either upper case or lower case.

• /CP:*n* (/CPARMAXALLOC:*n*) sets the maximum number of extra memory paragraphs required by *exe_file* (default is 65535).

• /DS (/DSALLOCATE) loads the data in DGROUP at the high end of the data segment.

• /DO (/DOSSEG) arranges segments according to the Microsoft language segment-ordering convention.

• /E (/EXEPACK) compresses repetitive sequences of bytes and optimizes the *exe_file* relocation file. This /E switch does not always save a significant amount of disk space and might even increase the file size when used with small programs that have few load-time relocations or repeated characters. Microsoft's Symbolic Debugger (SYMDEB) cannot be used with packed files.

- /HE (/HELP) lists LINK options on the screen. No other switches or filenames should be used with this switch.

- /HI (/HIGH) causes *exe__file* to be loaded as high as possible in memory when *exe__file* is executed.

- /LI (/LINENUMBERS) copies line-number information (if available) from *obj__file* to *map__file*. If a map file was not specified, this switch creates one.

- /M (/MAP) copies a list of all public symbols declared in *obj__file* to *map__file*. If a map file was not specified, this switch creates one.

- /NOD (/NODEFAULTLIBRARYSEARCH) causes LINK to ignore any library names inserted in the object file by the language compiler. This switch restricts library searches to those libraries specified in the command line.

- /NOG (/NOGROUPASSOCIATION) causes LINK to ignore GROUP associations when assigning addresses.

- /NOI (/NIGNORECASE) causes LINK to be case sensitive when resolving external names. This switch is typically used with object files created by high-level language compilers that differentiate between upper-case and lower-case letters.

- /O:*n* (/OVERLAYINTERRUPT:*n*) overrides the interrupt number used by the overlay manager (0–255, where the default is 63 or 3Fh). This switch should be used only when linking with a run-time module from a language compiler that supports overlays. Interrupt numbers that conflict with the software interrupts used to obtain MS-DOS or ROM BIOS services or with hardware interrupts assigned to peripheral device controllers should not be used in the /O:*n* switch.

- /P (/PAUSE) causes LINK to pause and prompt the user to change disks before writing the *exe__file*. This can allow the insertion of a disk with more available space for the LINK.

- /SE:*n* (/SEGMENT:*n*) sets the maximum number of segments that can be processed (1–1024, where the default is 128). The *n* must be a decimal, octal, or hexadecimal number. Octal numbers must have a leading zero; hexadecimal numbers must begin with 0x.

- /ST:*n* (/STACK:*n*) sets the size of the *exe__file* stack segment to *n* bytes (1–65535).

If LINK is used without parameters, LINK prompts for each filename needed. In square brackets, LINK displays the default response for each prompt, except the *obj__file* prompt. Select the defaults by simply pressing the ENTER key. If there are too many *obj__file* or *library* names to fit on one line, terminate the line by entering a plus operator (+) and pressing the ENTER key. LINK then repeats the prompt. If any response is ended with a semicolon (;), LINK uses the default values for any remaining fields.

If the command line contains switches and filenames, separate the parameters with commas. If you do not supply a filename, use a comma to mark its place. If LINK finds a semicolon after any parameter in the command line, it terminates the command line at the semicolon and uses the default values for any remaining parameters.

Return Codes

0   LINK encountered no errors or unresolved references during the creation of *exe__file*.

1   A miscellaneous LINK error occurred that was not covered by the other return codes.

16   A data record was too large to process.

32   No object files were specified in the command line or response file.

33   The map file could not be created.

66   A COMMON area was declared that is larger than 65535 (one segment).

96   Too many libraries specified.

144   LINK detected an invalid object module *obj__file*.

145   LINK found too many TYPDEFs in the specified object modules.

146   LINK found too many group, segment, or class names in one object module.

147   LINK found too many segments in all the object modules combined, or too many segments in one object module.

148   Too many overlays specified.

149   The size of a segment exceeded 65535.

150   LINK found too many groups or GRPDEFs in one object module.

151   LINK found too many external symbols in one object module.

177   The size of a group exceeded 65535.

Error Messages

There are three kinds of LINK error messages: warnings, nonfatal errors that do not stop execution, and fatal errors that stop execution. In all three types of messages, *location* is the input file associated with the error, or LINK if there is no input file. If the input file is an .OBJ or .LIB file and has a module name, the module name is printed enclosed in parentheses. Note that, in the error messages, warnings have a prefix of L4, nonfatal errors have L2, while fatal errors have L1.

Warnings indicate possible problems in the executable file although LINK does produce the executable file. Warnings have the following format:

location : warning L4*xxx*: *messagetext*

Nonfatal errors indicate problems in the executable file, although LINK does produce the executable file. Nonfatal messages have the following format:

location : error L2*xxx*: *messagetext*

Fatal errors cause LINK to stop execution. Fatal error messages have the following format:

location : error L1*xxx*: *messagetext*

Number   **LINK Error Message**

L1001   *option* : **option name ambiguous**
A unique option name did not appear after the option indicator (/).

L1002   *option* : **unrecognized option name**
An unrecognized character followed the option indicator (/).

L1003   **/QUIKLIB, /EXECPACK incompatible**
You cannot link with both the /QU option and the /E option.

L1004   *option* : **invalid numerical value**
An incorrect value appeared for one of the LINK options.

L1004–L1005   **Reserved**

L1006   *option-text* : **stack size exceeds 65535 bytes**
The value given as a parameter to the /STACKSIZE option exceeds the maximum allowed.

L1007   *option* : **interrupt number exceeds 255**
A number greater than 255 was given as a value for the /OVERLAYINTERRUPT option.

L1008   *option* : **segment limit set too high**
The /SEGMENTS option specified a limit greater than 3072 on the number of segments allowed.

L1009 *number* : **CPARMAXALLOC : illegal value**
The /CPARMAXALLOC number specified was not in the range of 1 to 65535.

L1010 *option* : **stack size exceeds 65536 bytes**
The stack size specified in the /STACK option in the LINK command was more than 65536 bytes.

L1011–L1019   Reserved

L1020   no object module specified
LINK did not find any object-file names specified.

L1021   cannot nest response files
LINK found a response file nested within another response file.

L1022   response line too long
A line in the response file is longer than 127 characters.

L1023   terminated by user
You entered a control-C or control-break to end the LINK run.

L1024   nested right parenthesis
The command line contains an incorrectly typed entry.

L1025   nested left parentheses
The command line contains an incorrectly typed entry.

L1026   unmatched right parentheses
A right parenthesis is missing from the contents specification of any overlay on the command line.

L1027   unmatched left parenthesis
A left parenthesis is missing from the contents specification of an overlay on the command line.

L1028–L1042   Reserved

L1043   relocation table overflow
More than 32,768 long calls, long jumps, or other long pointers appear in your program.

L1044   Reserved

L1045   **too many TYPDEF records**
An object module contains more than 255 TYPDEF records (they describe communal variables). This error occurs only with programs produced by the Microsoft FORTRAN compiler or other compilers that support communal variables.

L1046   **too many external symbols in one module**
An object module specifies more than the limit of 1023 external symbols.

L1047   **too many group, segment, and class names in one module**
Your program contains too many group, segment, and class names. Reduce the number and recreate the object file.

L1048   **too many segments in one module**
An object module has more than 255 segments. Split the module or combine segments.

L1049   **too many segments**
Your program has more than the maximum number of segments. The /SEGMENT option specifies the maximum legal number; the default is 128. Relink and use the /SEGMENTS option with the appropriate number of segments.

L1050   **too many groups in one module**
LINK found more than 21 group definitions (GRPDEF) in a single module. Reduce the number of group definitions or split the module.

L1051   **too many groups**
Your program defines more than 20 groups. This does not count DGROUP. Reduce the number and relink.

L1052   **too many libraries**
You tried to link more than 32 libraries. Either use modules that require fewer libraries or combine the libraries.

L1053   **out of memory for symbol table**
Your program has more than 256K of symbolic information (such as public, external, segment, group, class, and file names) than the amount that could fit in the available real memory. Try freeing memory by linking from the DOS command level instead of from a MAKE file or from an editor. Otherwise, combine modules or segments and try to eliminate as many public symbols as possible.

L1054   **requested segment limit too high**
LINK did not have enough memory to allocate the tables that describe the number of segments you requested. The default is 128 or the value specified with the /SEGMENTS option. Either try linking again and use the /SEGMENTS option to select a smaller number of segments or free some memory by eliminating resident programs or shells.

L1055   **Reserved**

L1056   **too many overlays**
Your program defined more than 63 overlays.

L1057   **data record too large**
In an object module, a LEDATA record contained more than 1024 bytes of data. This is a translator error.

L1058–L1062   **Reserved**

L1063   **out of memory for CodeView information**
LINK was given too many object files with debug information, and it ran out of space to store it. Reduce the number of object files that have debug information.

L1064–L1069   **Reserved**

L1070   **segment size exceeds 64k**
A single segment contains more than 64k of code or data. Try compiling and linking using the LARGE model.

L1071   **segment __TEXT larger than 65520 bytes**
This error generally occurs only in small-model C programs, but it can occur when any program with a segment named __TEXT is linked using the /DOSSEG option of the LINK command. Small-model C programs must reserve code addresses 0 and 1; this range is increased to 16 for alignment. See Fig. 10-5 for an overview of the default segments and types.

L1072   **common area longer than 65536 bytes**
Your program has more than 64k of communal variables. This error cannot appear with object files generated by MASM. It occurs only with programs produced by Microsoft's FORTRAN compiler or other compilers that support communal variables.

L1073–L1079   **Reserved**

L1080   **cannot open list file**
The disk or the root directory is full. Delete or move files to make space.

L1081   **out of space for run file**
The disk is full on which the .EXE file is being written. Free more space on the disk and restart the LINK run.

L1082   **Reserved**

L1083   **cannot open run file**
The disk or root directory is full. Delete or move files to make space.

L1084   **cannot create temporary file**
The disk or root directory is full. Delete or move files to make space.

L1085   **cannot open temporary file**
The disk or root directory is full. Delete or move files to make space.

L1086   **scratch file missing**
An internal error has occurred. Note the circumstances and notify Microsoft Product Assistance.

L1087   **unexpected end-of-file on scratch file**
You removed the disk with the temporary linker-output file.

L1088   **out of space for list file**
The disk is full where the listing file is being written. Free more space on the disk and restart the LINK run.

L1089   *filename* **: cannot open response file**
LINK could not find the specified response file. This might be a typing error or an incorrectly specified pathname.

L1090   **cannot reopen list file**
The original disk was not replaced at the prompt. Restart the linker.

L1091   **unexpected end-of-file on library**
In this case, you might have removed the disk with the library. Replace that disk and rerun the LINK run.

L1092   **Reserved**

L1093   **object not found**
LINK could not find one of the object files specified in the input. Restart the LINK run and specify the object file.

L1094–L1100   Reserved

L1101   **invalid object module**
One of the object modules is invalid. If the error persists after recompiling, contact Microsoft Product Assistance.

L1102   **unexpected end-of-file**
LINK encountered an invalid format for a library.

L1103   **attempt to access data outside segment bounds**
A data record in an object module specified data that extended beyond the end of a segment. This is a translator error. Note the conditions and which translator was used and contact Microsoft Product Assistance.

L1104   *filename* **: not valid library**
LINK aborted because the specified file was not a valid library file.

L1105–L1112   Reserved

L1113   **unresolved COMDEF; internal error**
This is an internal error. Note the circumstances and contact Microsoft Product Assistance.

L1114   **file not suitable for /EXEPACK option**
For the linked program, the size of the packed load image (plus packing overhead) is larger than that of the unpacked load image. Relink without the /EXEPACK option.

L1115   **/QUICKLIB, overlays incompatible**
You specified overlays and used the /QUICKLIB option. These cannot be used together.

L1116–L1125   Reserved

L1126   **starting address __aulstart not found**
You tried to create a quick library without linking with the required LIB library.

L1127–L2000   Reserved

L2001   **fixup(s) without data**
LINK found a FIXUPP record without a data record immediately preceding it. This is an internal error that should be reported to Microsoft Product Assistance.

L2002   **fixup overflow near *number* in frame seg *segname* target seg *segname* target offset *number***
The following conditions can cause this error:

• An EXTRN declaration in an assembly language source file appeared inside the body of a segment. Change the source and recreate the object file.
• A group is larger than 64k.
• The name of a data item in the program conflicts with that of a library subroutine included in the link process.
• Your program contains an intersegment short jump or intersegment short call.

L2003   **intersegment self-relative fixup**
An intersegment self-relative fixup is not allowed.

L2004   **LOBYTE-type fixup overflow**
A LOBYTE fixup generated an address overflow. See your MS-DOS manual for the FIXUPP record. The FIXUPP record contains information that allows the linker to resolve (fix up) addresses whose values cannot be determined by the language translator.

L2005   **fixup type unsupported**
A fixup type occurred that is not supported by the Microsoft LINK. This is most likely a compiler error. Note the circumstances and contact Microsoft Product Assistance.

L2006–L2010   Reserved

L2011   ***name* : NEAR/HUGE conflict**
You gave conflicting NEAR and HUGE attributes for a communal variable in a FORTRAN program.

L2012   ***name* : array-element size mismatch**
In a FORTRAN program, a far communal array was declared with two or more different array-element sizes.

L2013   **LIDATA record too large**
An LIDATA record contained more than 512 bytes. This is probably a compiler error, so note the circumstances and contact Microsoft Product Assistance.

L2014–L2023   Reserved

L2024   *name* : special symbol already defined
Your program defined a symbol name that is already used by LINK for one of its own low-level symbols. For example, LINK generates special symbols used in overlay support and other operations. Choose another name for the symbol in order to avoid conflict.

L2025   *name* : segment with > 1 class name not allowed with /INC
Your program defined a segment more than once, giving the segment different class names. Different class names for the same segment are not allowed when you link with the /INCREMENTAL option. Normally, this error should never appear unless you are programming with MASM. For example, if you give the two MASM statements

and

    _BSS segment 'BSS'

    _BSS segment 'DATA'

then the statements have the effect of declaring two distinct segments. LINK does not support this situation, so it is disallowed when the /INCREMENTAL option is used.

L2026–L2028   Reserved

L2029   unresolved externals
One (or more) symbols declared as external in one or more modules was (were) not publicly defined in any of the modules or libraries. A list of the unresolved externals appears after the message. The name that comes before the *in file(s)* is the unresolved external symbol. On the next line is a list of object modules that have made references to this symbol. The message and list are also written to the map file, if one exists. For example, the list could appear as—

    NUM1 in file(s):

    MAINPROC.OBJ
    NEXTPROC.OBJ

L2030–L2040   Reserved

L2041   stack plus data exceeds 64k
The total of NEAR data and requested stack size exceeds 64k. The program will not run correctly so reduce the stack size. LINK only checks for this

condition if /DOSSEG is enabled, which is done automatically in the library startup module.

L2042–L2043   Reserved

L2044   *name* : **symbol multiply defined, use /NOE**
LINK found what it interprets as a public-symbol redefinition, probably because you redefined a symbol that is defined in a library. Relink with the /NOEXTDICTIONARY (/NOE) option. If error L2025 results for the same symbol, then you have a genuine symbol-redefinition error.

L2045–L4002   Reserved

L4003   **intersegment self-relative fixup at** *offset* **in segment** *name*
pos: *offset* Record type: 9C target external *name* LINK found an intersegment self-relative fixup. This error may be caused by compiling a small model program with the /NT option.

L4004–L4011   Reserved

L4012   **load-high disables EXEPACK**
The /HIGH and /EXEPACK options cannot be used at the same time.

L4015   **/CODEVIEW disables /DSALLOCATE**
The /CODEVIEW and /DSALLOCATE options cannot be used at the same time.

L4016   **/CODEVIEW disables /EXEPACK**
The /CODEVIEW and /EXEPACK options cannot be used at the same time.

L4017–L4019   Reserved

L4020   *name* : **code-segment size exceeds 65500**
This is an 80286 possible problem. Code segments of 65501 through 65536 bytes in length may be unreliable on the Intel 80286 processor.

L4021   **no stack segment**
Your program does not contain a stack segment defined with STACK combine type.

L4022–L4030   Reserved

L4031   *name* : **segment declared in more than one group**
Your program contains a segment that is declared to be a member of two different groups. Correct the source and rerun MASM.

L4032–L4033   Reserved

L4034   **more than 239 overlay segments; extra put in root**
Your program designated more than the limit of 239 segments to go in overlays. Starting with the 234th segment, they are assigned to the root (that is, the permanently resident portion of the program).

L4035–L4044   Reserved

L4045   *name* : **is name of output file**
The prompt for the run-file field gave an inaccurate default because /QUICKLIB was not used early enough. The output will be a quick library with the *name* in the error message.

L4046–L4049   Reserved

L4050   **too many public symbols for sorting**
LINK uses the stack and all available memory in the near heap to sort public symbols for the /MAP option. If the number of public symbols exceeds the available space, LINK issues this warning. The symbols are not sorted in the map file but are listed in arbitrary order.

L4051   *filename* : **cannot find library**
LINK could not find the specified file. Enter a new file name, a new path specification, or both.

L4052   **Reserved**

L4053   **VM.TMP : illegal file name; ignored**
VM.TMP appeared as an object-file name. Rename the file and rerun LINK.

L4054   *filename* : **cannot find file**
LINK could not find the specified file. Enter a new file name, a new path specification, or both.

Appendix G

Program Listing of Directives Examples

THE LISTING AND EXAMPLE OF THE SCREEN DISPLAY SHOW THE CORRECT AND, OFTEN MORE important, the incorrect ways to use MASM directives.

LISTING OF USE OF DIRECTIVES

```
                PAGE    55,132
                .386
                .LALL                   ; Turn macro expansion list on
                .LFCOND                 ; list false conditionals too

;
; Name:   EXAMPLES.ASM
;
; Purpose: This program is used to provide examples of legal and
;          illegal syntax and usage.
;
; Inputs:  None.
;
; Process: None.
;
; Outputs: A listing, including error messages, which provides
;          examples of usage.
;
;
; Declare routines near and far which are used in calls and in
; conjuction with the linkage editor to demonstrate how an error
; can slip by.
;
                EXTRN   EXTNPROC:FAR    ; A near proc external
                EXTRN   EXTFPROC:NEAR   ; A far proc external
;
;
; A sample macro skeleton showing the main parts of a macro.
;
; The macro definition statement -  (the beginning)
; name     MACRO directive  dummy parameters

samp01    MACRO             dummy00,dummy01
;; A comment which is internal to a macro - ie it does not print when
;; macro expansion occurs.
```

```
                        ;; The body of the macro includes everything between the MACRO line
                        ;; and the ENDM line
                                mov     AX,dummy00              ; A prototype statement

                                EXITM                           ; A pseudo-op (directive)
                        ENDM                                    ; End of the macro (the end)


                        ;
                        COMMENT + This starts a multi-line comment which can contain any
                        character except the specified delimiter (in this case +


0000                    stack       SEGMENT PARA 'STACK' STACK USE16
0000  0100[                         dq      256 DUP(?)
      ??????????????????
      ?
                    ]

0800                    stack       ENDS

                        ;
                        ; Note: MASM release 5.1 changes the default size applied to data
                        ;       segments.  For .386, .386p mode assemblies R5.1 assumes a
                        ;       USE32.  R5.0 assumes a USE16.  The first data segment is
                        ;       forced to a size of 16 in order to allow compatable sized
                        ;       examples to generate.

0000                    data        SEGMENT PARA USE16
0000  00000000          data32      dd      0                   ; a 32 bit data area
0004  0000              data16      dw      0                   ; a 16 bit data area
0006  00                data8       db      0                   ; an 8 bit data area
                        ;
                        ; Examples of the use of label to allow access to an area using
                        ; different types for the same area.
                        ;
0007                    bytelabel   LABEL   BYTE                ; Refer as byte type,
0007                    wordtype    LABEL   WORD                ; word type,
0007                    dwordtype   LABEL   DWORD               ; and as double word type.
                        ;
                        ; Examples of DUP and initializations.
                        ;
0007  000A[                         dw      10 DUP (1,2,3,4)
      0001
      0002
      0003
      0004
                    ]

0057  0003[                         dw      3  DUP (3)
      0003
                    ]


                        ;
                        ; Example of record definitions which show the sizes which result,
                        ; results of initialization (when used below), and masking.
                        ;
                        ; Because this is a USE16 segment, record size is limited to 16 bits.
                        ; (This apears to be a bug in MASM R5.1 - probably associated with the
                        ;  change in data segment USE defaulting.)  Note that 32 bit records
                        ; are generated if USE32 is specified for the data segment.

                        recd16      record  flda:3, fldb:7, fldc:4=0fh  ; A 16 bit record
                        ;                   14 bits of the record defined (bits 13-11, 10-4, 3-0).
                        ;
                        recd08      record  flda3:6, fldb3:1=1  ; An 8 bit record
                        ;                   7 bits defined (0<bits<=8 allows 8 bit size).
                        ;
                        recd08a     record  flda4:5, fldb4:3=0fh ; A 3 bit field initialized
EXAMPLES.ASM(93): error A2050: Value out of range
```

```
                                      ;                           ; with 4.
                                      ;
                             encode      record hi:4,mid:3,lo:3
                                      ;
                             recdbt      record bit7:1, bits6t1:6, bit00:1 ;
                                      ;
                             recdbt16    record bit15:1, bitsmid:14, bit0a:1 ;
                                      ;
                             ; Bits defined
                                      ;
  005D  80                                    recdbt   <1,0,0>        ; First defined
  005E  01                                    recdbt   <0,0,1>        ; Last defined
                                      ;
  005F  8000                                  recdbt16 <1,0,0>        ; First defined
  0061  0001                                  recdbt16 <0,0,1>        ; Last defined
                                      ;
                             ; Example generation for records
                                      ;
  0063  03C7                                  encode <15,0,7>         ; Initialize hi and lo
                                      
  0065  000F                                  recd16 <>              ; an uninitialized record
  0067  00FF                                  recd16 <0,15,>         ; use fldc's default value
  0069  0000                                  recd16 <,,0>           ; override the default for fldc
                                      ;
                             ; Mask generation examples
                                      ;
  006B  03C0                                  dw      MASK hi         ; A mask to isolate hi
  006D  0038                                  dw      MASK mid        ; A mask to isolate mid
  006F  0007                                  dw      MASK lo         ; A mask to isolate lo
                                      ;
  0071  FFFF                                  dw      NOT MASK mid    ; A mask to clear mid
EXAMPLES.ASM(124): error A2050: Value out of range
  0073  FFFFFFC7                              dd      NOT MASK mid    ; A mask to clear mid
  0077  25 FFC7                               and     AX,NOT MASK mid ; A mask to clear mid
                                      ;
                             ; Structure definition
                                      ;
                             mystruct    STRUC                       ; Provide name & begin def.
  0000  0021                  mywd0       dw      33                  ; Define initialized field
                                                                     ; which can be over-ridden
                                      ;
  0002  0001 0002             mywd1       dw      1,2                 ; non-over-ride-able
  0006                        mystruct    ENDS
                                      ;
                             ; Structure use
                                      ;
  007A  6300                 usestruct  mystruct <99,>
  007C  0001[
        0100
        0200
                      ]

                             ; Example string initialization for word/double word
                                      ;
  0080  0061                                  dw      'a'             ; A small string (1 byte).
  0082  6162                                  dw      'ab'            ; A word size string
  0084  FFFF                                  dw      'abc'           ; An oversize string for word
EXAMPLES.ASM(144): error A2050: Value out of range
  0086  00616263                              dd      'abc'           ; Fits a double word
  008A  61626364                              dd      'abcd'          ; A double word size string
  008E  62636465                              dd      'abcde'         ; Oversize for double word
EXAMPLES.ASM(147): error A2010: Syntax error
                                      ;
  0092  6564636200000000                      dq      'abcdefgh'      ; A string which fits in qw
EXAMPLES.ASM(149): error A2010: Syntax error
                                      ;
                             ; Equated values using the = form of equate.
                                      ;
  = FF00                     equ16       =       256*255             ; 0 ff 00h    (ok  16 bit)
  = 01000000                 equ32       =       256*256*256         ; 1 00 00 00h (ok  32 bit)
  = 0000                     equ64       =       256*256*256*256     ; 1 00 00 00 00h (bad 33 bit)
                                      ;
```

```
                                              ; Note that there is no warning of the overflow beyond 32 bits.

  009A  FF00                          dw      equ16           ; use is ok
  009C  FFFF                          dw      equ32           ; error - value out of range
EXAMPLES.ASM(161): error A2050: Value out of range

  009E  0000FF00                      dd      equ16
  00A2  01000000                      dd      equ32
  00A6  00000000                      dd      equ64           ; Nor is there an error at use.

  00AA  0000000100000000              dq      equ32
  00B2  0000000000000000              dq      equ64

                                      ;
                                      ; Equates to strings -
                                      ;
  = 6162                         equ16s     =    'ab'
  = 00616263                     equ16s1    =    'abc'
  = 61626364                     equ32s     =    'abcd'
  = 62636465                     equ32s1    =    'abcde'        ; syntax error (equates to bcde)
EXAMPLES.ASM(176): error A2010: Syntax error

  00BA  6162                          dw      equ16s
  00BC  FFFF                          dw      equ16s1         ; error - value out of range
EXAMPLES.ASM(179): error A2050: Value out of range

  00BE  61626364                      dd      equ32s
  00C2  62636465                      dd      equ32s1         ; No error at use though.
                                      ;
                                      ; Equates using the EQU directive.
                                      ;
  = FF00                         equ16e     EQU    256*255

  = FF000000                     equ32e     EQU    256*256*256*255
  = 0000                         equ64e     EQU    equ32e*256    ; Overflow is not detected.

  00C6  FF00                          dw      equ16e
  00C8  FFFF                          dw      equ32e
EXAMPLES.ASM(191): error A2050: Value out of range
  00CA  0000FF00                      dd      equ16e
  00CE  FF000000            word32s   dd      equ32e
  00D2  00000000                      dd      equ64e

                                      ;
                                      ; Sample equates for the book
                                      ;
  = 3.141592                     pi         EQU    3.141592
  = XOR EAX,EAX                  clear_reg  EQU    XOR EAX,EAX
  = 'Enter number: '            prompt     EQU    'Enter number: '
  = BYTE PTR                     byte_ptr   EQU    BYTE PTR
                                      ;
                                      ; and their use
  00D6  40490FD8                      dd      pi              ; A real
  00DA  66| 33 C0                     clear_reg               ; An instruction
  00DD  45 6E 74 65 72 20   dprompt   db      prompt          ; A string
        6E 75 6D 62 65 72
        3A 20
  00EB  A0 00CE R                     mov     AL, byte_ptr DS:word32s ; A type modifier
                                      ;
                                      ; Conditionals as they generate into data

  00EE  00                            db      ( 1 EQ 0ffffh)    ; Values do not compare equal
  00EF  FF                            db      ( 1 NE 0ffffh)    ; This is true (they don't =)
  00F0  FF                            db      ( 1 GT -1 )       ; 1 is greater than -1
  00F1  00                            db      ( 1 GT 0ffffh)    ; It is not greater than 64K-1
  00F2  00                            db      ( 1 GT 0ffffffffh) ; nor greater than 4G-1
  00F3  FF                            db      ( 1 GT 0ffffffffh+1) ; Expression = 0 (32 bits)
                                      ;
                                      ; Conditional assembly examples (as used in open code)
                                      ;
                                 IF        equ32s GT equ16s    ; Is a longer string greater?
  00F4  59 45 53                        db      'YES'
                                 ELSE
                                         db      'NO'
```

```
                             ENDIF
                             ;
                             ; An example of a pass 1 only error forced by IF2.
                             ;
                             IF1                                 ; Check for pass 1
                                 IFDEF Begin                     ; This forward reference is not
                                       %OUT    'WHAT?'
                                 ELSE
                                       %OUT    'EXPECTED'        ; 'EXPECTED' is displayed
                                 ENDIF
                             ELSEIF2                             ; Note address assignment below
                                                                 ; and the re-use at the phase
                                                                 ; error.
                                 IFDEF Begin                     ; Should be defined now
                                       db      'DEFINED'
                                 ELSE
                                       db      'WRONG!'
                                 ENDIF
                             ELSE
                                       db      'PASS3?'
                             ENDIF
00F7   00000000                     dd      0                   ; no phase error
                             ;
                             ; It is instructive to examine the phase 1 listing and the phase 2
                             ; listings together here.  The simple dd which follows becomes a
                             ; problem because it has a symbol associated with it.  The generation
                             ; of the 'phase 2 only' db 'DEFINED' changes the offset of the label
                             ; dummydd which was assigned in phase 1.  It doesn't have any effect
                             ; on the unlabled dd above other than changing its location.
                             ;
00FB   00000000             dummydd dd      0                   ; Phase error
                             ;
                             ; IRP used in a macro
                             ;
                             irpmac  MACRO   param1
                                             IRP     zz,<1,2,3,4,5,6,7>
                             param1&&zz db   zz
                                             ENDM
                                     ENDM
                                     irpmac  first               ; Generate data and labels
                           1         IRP     zz,<1,2,3,4,5,6,7>
                           1 first&zz db     zz
                           1         ENDM
00FF   01                  2 first1 db       1
0100   02                  2 first2 db       2
0101   03                  2 first3 db       3
0102   04                  2 first4 db       4
0103   05                  2 first5 db       5
0104   06                  2 first6 db       6
0105   07                  2 first7 db       7
                             ;
                             ; IRPC used in a macro
                             ;
                             irpcmac MACRO   param1
                                             IRPC    zz,param1
                             irpcm&&zz db    '&zz'
                                             ENDM
                                     ENDM
                                     irpcmac abcdef
                           1         IRPC    zz,abcdef
                           1 irpcm&zz db     '&zz'
                           1         ENDM
0106   61                  2 irpcma db       'a'
0107   62                  2 irpcmb db       'b'
0108   63                  2 irpcmc db       'c'
0109   64                  2 irpcmd db       'd'
010A   65                  2 irpcme db       'e'
010B   66                  2 irpcmf db       'f'
                             ;
                             ; Check size of rept expression
                             ;
                                             .SFCOND             ; (Don't list false conditional)
                                             x = 0               ; initiallize inner counter
 = 0000
```

```
= 0000                            y = 0                       ; and check for over 16 bits.
                   REPT    256*512                            ; try for 18 bit repeat ct.
                                  x = x+1                     ;
                          IF x EQ 1                           ; Ensure repeat ct. not 0
                                  dd      x                   ; Won't generate if it is.
                          ENDIF

                          IF y
                                  dd      y                   ; Generate one for y
                                  y = 0                       ; and only one!
                          ELSE
                                  y = (x AND 0ffffh) EQ 0     ; Force zero if not x0000h
                                  y = y AND ((x SHR 16) NE 0) ; then or to high bits
                          ENDIF
                   ENDM
                   ;
                   ;
                   ; Check on validity of check above - If the repeat count wraps at 16
                   ; bits, we should get generation below.
= 0000             ;
= 0000                            x = 0                       ; initiallize inner counter
                                  y = 0                       ; and check for over 16 bits.
                   REPT    256*512+18                         ; A wrap gives a count of 18
                                  x = x+1                     ;
                          IF x EQ 1                           ; Ensure repeat ct. not 0
                                  dd      x                   ; Won't generate if it is.
                          ENDIF

                          IF y
                                  dd      y                   ; Generate one for y
                                  y = 0                       ; and only 1.
                          ELSE
                                  y = (x AND 0fh) EQ 0        ; Force zero if not x0h
                                  y = y AND ((x AND 30h) NE 0) ; then or to high bits
                          ENDIF
                   ENDM
= 0001        1                   x = x+1                     ;
              1           IF x EQ 1                           ; Ensure repeat ct. not 0
010C 00000001 1                   dd      x                   ; Won't generate if it is.
              1           ENDIF
              1
              1           ELSE
= 0000        1                   y = (x AND 0fh) EQ 0        ; Force zero if not x0h
= 0000        1                   y = y AND ((x AND 30h) NE 0) ; then or to high bits
              1           ENDIF
= 0002        1                   x = x+1                     ;
              1           ELSE
= 0000        1                   y = (x AND 0fh) EQ 0        ; Force zero if not x0h
= 0000        1                   y = y AND ((x AND 30h) NE 0) ; then or to high bits
              1           ENDIF
= 0003        1                   x = x+1                     ;
              1           ELSE
= 0000        1                   y = (x AND 0fh) EQ 0        ; Force zero if not x0h
= 0000        1                   y = y AND ((x AND 30h) NE 0) ; then or to high bits
              1           ENDIF
= 0004        1                   x = x+1                     ;
              1           ELSE
= 0000        1                   y = (x AND 0fh) EQ 0        ; Force zero if not x0h
= 0000        1                   y = y AND ((x AND 30h) NE 0) ; then or to high bits
              1           ENDIF
= 0005        1                   x = x+1                     ;
              1           ELSE
= 0000        1                   y = (x AND 0fh) EQ 0        ; Force zero if not x0h
= 0000        1                   y = y AND ((x AND 30h) NE 0) ; then or to high bits
              1           ENDIF
= 0006        1                   x = x+1                     ;
              1           ELSE
= 0000        1                   y = (x AND 0fh) EQ 0        ; Force zero if not x0h
= 0000        1                   y = y AND ((x AND 30h) NE 0) ; then or to high bits
              1           ENDIF
= 0007        1                   x = x+1                     ;
              1           ELSE
= 0000        1                   y = (x AND 0fh) EQ 0        ; Force zero if not x0h
= 0000        1                   y = y AND ((x AND 30h) NE 0) ; then or to high bits
```

```
                                    1        ENDIF
= 0008                              1             x = x+1                          ;
                                    1        ELSE
= 0000                              1             y = (x AND 0fh) EQ 0         ; Force zero if not x0h
= 0000                              1             y = y AND ((x AND 30h) NE 0) ; then or to high bits
                                    1        ENDIF
= 0009                              1             x = x+1                          ;
                                    1        ELSE
= 0000                              1             y = (x AND 0fh) EQ 0         ; Force zero if not x0h
= 0000                              1             y = y AND ((x AND 30h) NE 0) ; then or to high bits
                                    1        ENDIF
= 000A                              1             x = x+1                          ;
                                    1        ELSE
= 0000                              1             y = (x AND 0fh) EQ 0         ; Force zero if not x0h
= 0000                              1             y = y AND ((x AND 30h) NE 0) ; then or to high bits
                                    1        ENDIF
= 000B                              1             x = x+1                          ;
                                    1        ELSE
= 0000                              1             y = (x AND 0fh) EQ 0         ; Force zero if not x0h
= 0000                              1             y = y AND ((x AND 30h) NE 0) ; then or to high bits
                                    1        ENDIF
= 000C                              1             x = x+1                          ;
                                    1        ELSE
= 0000                              1             y = (x AND 0fh) EQ 0         ; Force zero if not x0h
= 0000                              1             y = y AND ((x AND 30h) NE 0) ; then or to high bits
                                    1        ENDIF
= 000D                              1             x = x+1                          ;
                                    1        ELSE
= 0000                              1             y = (x AND 0fh) EQ 0         ; Force zero if not x0h
= 0000                              1             y = y AND ((x AND 30h) NE 0) ; then or to high bits
                                    1        ENDIF
= 000E                              1             x = x+1                          ;
                                    1        ELSE
= 0000                              1             y = (x AND 0fh) EQ 0         ; Force zero if not x0h
= 0000                              1             y = y AND ((x AND 30h) NE 0) ; then or to high bits
                                    1        ENDIF
= 000F                              1             x = x+1                          ;
                                    1        ELSE
= 0000                              1             y = (x AND 0fh) EQ 0         ; Force zero if not x0h
= 0000                              1             y = y AND ((x AND 30h) NE 0) ; then or to high bits
                                    1        ENDIF
= 0010                              1             x = x+1                          ;
                                    1        ELSE
=-0001                             1             y = (x AND 0fh) EQ 0         ; Force zero if not x0h
= FFFFFFFF                          1             y = y AND ((x AND 30h) NE 0) ; then or to high bits
                                    1        ENDIF
= 0011                              1             x = x+1                          ;
                                    1        IF y
0110  FFFFFFFF                      1             dd      y                        ; Generate one for y
= 0000                              1             y = 0                            ; and only 1.
                                    1        ENDIF
= 0012                              1             x = x+1                          ;
                                    1        ELSE
= 0000                              1             y = (x AND 0fh) EQ 0         ; Force zero if not x0h
= 0000                              1             y = y AND ((x AND 30h) NE 0) ; then or to high bits
                                    1        ENDIF
                                             .LALL                           ; Turn macro expansion list on
                                             .LFCOND                         ; list false conditionals too
                                    ;
                                    ; Show use of IFB/IFNB
                                    ;
                                    ifbnb    MACRO   param1,param2,param3
                                       IFB <param1>                         ; If parameter 1 is omitted
                                         IFNB <param3>                      ; and parameter 3 is present
                                                                           ;; The & forces substitution
                                                                           ;; of parameter 2.
                                                  db      '&param2'        ; define param2
                                                                           ;; See the example without
                                                                           ;; the & below.

                                                  db      'param2'         ; different param2
                                         ENDIF
                                       ENDIF
                                             ENDM
```

```
                          ifbnb   this,"won't",generate
            1    IFB <this>                           ; If parameter 1 is omitted
            1      IFNB <generate>                         ; and parameter 3 is present
            1                                              ;
            1             db      '"won't"'               ; define param2
            1                                              ;
            1             db      'param2'                ; different param2
            1      ENDIF
            1    ENDIF
                          ifbnb   ,<this will>,generate
            1    IFB <>                               ; If parameter 1 is omitted
            1      IFNB <generate>                         ; and parameter 3 is present
            1                                              ;
0114  74 68 69 73 20 77  1      db      'this will'        ; define param2
      69 6C 6C            1
            1                                              ;
011D  70 61 72 61 6D 32  1      db      'param2'           ; different param2
            1      ENDIF
            1    ENDIF
                          ifbnb   ,<!!>,generate
            1    IFB <>                               ; If parameter 1 is omitted
            1      IFNB <generate>                         ; and parameter 3 is present
            1                                              ;
0123  21           1      db      '!'                 ; define param2
            1                                              ;
0124  70 61 72 61 6D 32  1      db      'param2'           ; different param2
            1      ENDIF
            1    ENDIF
                          ifbnb   ,%(equ16e mod 227),will_too
            1    IFB <>                               ; If parameter 1 is omitted
            1      IFNB <will_too>                         ; and parameter 3 is present
            1                                              ;
012A  31 33 31     1      db      '131'               ; define param2
            1                                              ;
012D  70 61 72 61 6D 32  1      db      'param2'           ; different param2
            1      ENDIF
            1    ENDIF
                          ifbnb   ,(equ16e mod 227),will_also
            1    IFB <>                               ; If parameter 1 is omitted
            1      IFNB <mod>                              ; and parameter 3 is present
            1                                              ;
0133  28 65 71 75 31 36  1      db      '(equ16e'          ; define param2
      65            1
            1                                              ;
013A  70 61 72 61 6D 32  1      db      'param2'           ; different param2
            1      ENDIF
            1    ENDIF
                     ;
                     ; Show use of IFIDN[I]/IFDIF[I]
                     ;
                     idndif  MACRO   param1,param2
                         IFIDN <param1>,<param2>              ; If p1 and p2 are the same
                             db      '1 and 2 same'
                         ENDIF
                         IFIDNI <param1>,<param2>             ; same ignoring case
                             db      '1 = 2 case'
                         ENDIF
                         IFDIF <param1>,<param2>              ; If p1 and p2 NOT the same
                             db      '1 and 2 diff'
                         ENDIF
                         IFDIFI <param1>,<param2>             ; not same ignoring case
                             db      '1, 2 diff case'
```

```
                                 ENDIF
                                        ENDM

                                        idndif   aaa,aaa
                               1         IFIDN <aaa>,<aaa>              ; If p1 and p2 are the same
0140  31 20 61 6E 64 20        1          db      '1 and 2 same'
      32 20 73 61 6D 65        1
                               1         ENDIF
                               1         IFIDNI <aaa>,<aaa>            ; same ignoring case
014C  31 20 3D 20 32 20        1          db      '1 = 2 case'
      63 61 73 65              1
                               1         ENDIF
                               1         IFDIF <aaa>,<aaa>             ; If p1 and p2 NOT the same
                               1          db      '1 and 2 diff'
                               1         ENDIF
                               1         IFDIFI <aaa>,<aaa>           ; not same ignoring case
                               1          db      '1, 2 diff case'
                               1         ENDIF
                                        idndif   AAA,aaa
                               1         IFIDN <AAA>,<aaa>              ; If p1 and p2 are the same
                               1          db      '1 and 2 same'
                               1         ENDIF
                               1         IFIDNI <AAA>,<aaa>            ; same ignoring case
0156  31 20 3D 20 32 20        1          db      '1 = 2 case'
      63 61 73 65              1
                               1         ENDIF
                               1         IFDIF <AAA>,<aaa>             ; If p1 and p2 NOT the same
0160  31 20 61 6E 64 20        1          db      '1 and 2 diff'
      32 20 64 69 66 66        1
                               1         ENDIF
                               1         IFDIFI <AAA>,<aaa>           ; not same ignoring case
                               1          db      '1, 2 diff case'
                               1         ENDIF
                                        idndif   bbb,aaa
                               1         IFIDN <bbb>,<aaa>              ; If p1 and p2 are the same
                               1          db      '1 and 2 same'
                               1         ENDIF
                               1         IFIDNI <bbb>,<aaa>            ; same ignoring case
                               1          db      '1 = 2 case'
                               1         ENDIF
                               1         IFDIF <bbb>,<aaa>             ; If p1 and p2 NOT the same
016C  31 20 61 6E 64 20        1          db      '1 and 2 diff'
      32 20 64 69 66 66        1
                               1         ENDIF
                               1         IFDIFI <bbb>,<aaa>           ; not same ignoring case
0178  31 2C 20 32 20 64        1          db      '1, 2 diff case'
      69 66 66 20 63 61        1
      73 65                    1
                               1         ENDIF
0186                                 data       ENDS

                               ;
                               ; This, the second data segment, is allowed to default in size.
                               ; If you have MASM R5.0 the default to a USE16 will provide a
                               ; different generation than R5.1 which defaults to USE32 if the
                               ; .386/.386p directive has been coded.
                               ;

0000                               data2      SEGMENT PARA            ; Default allowed
0000  00000000                     d2ta32 dd      0                   ; a 32 bit data area
0004  0000                         d2ta16 dw      0                   ; a 16 bit data area
0006  00                           d2ta8  db      0                   ; an 8 bit data area
                               ;
                               ; Example of record definitions which show the sizes which result,
                               ; results of initialization (when used below), and masking.
                               ;
                                   recd32     record flda1:10, fldb1:6=3fh, fldc1:2  ; A 32 bit record
                               ;                 18 bits defined (16<bits<=32 causes 32 bit size).
                               ;
                                   recd32a    record flda1a:14=3f3ch, fldb1a:2, fldc1a:2, fldd1a:18=3cffh
EXAMPLES.ASM(381): error A2050: Value out of range: FLDD1A
```

```
                              ;                Note that the error message is not precise.
                              ;
                              code_it    record bulk:16,hia:4,mida:3,lo1:3  ; bulk added for 32 bit
                              ;
                              recdbt32   record bit000:1, bitsmida:30, bit31:1 ;
                              ;
                              ; Bits defined and sample generations.
                              ;
 0007  80000000                          recdbt32  <1,0,0>        ; First defined
 000B  00000001                          recdbt32  <0,0,1>        ; Last defined

 000F  000003C7                          code_it <0,15,0,7>       ; Initialize hia and lo1
                              ;
                              ; Equates to strings -
                              ;
 = 61626364                   equ32s    =         'abcd'
 = 62636465                   equ32s1   =         'abcde'         ; syntax error (equates to bcde)
EXAMPLES.ASM(398): error A2010: Syntax error

 0013  61626364                          dd        equ32s
 0017  62636465                          dd        equ32s1        ; No error at use though.
                              ;
                              ; Equates using the EQU directive.
                              ;
 = FF000000                   equ32e    EQU       256*256*256*255
 = 0000                       equ64e    EQU       equ32e*256      ; Overflow is not detected.

 001B  FF00                              dw        equ16e
 001D  FFFF                              dw        equ32e
EXAMPLES.ASM(409): error A2050: Value out of range
 001F  0000FF00                          dd        equ16e
 0023  FF000000             word32s1     dd        equ32e
 0027  00000000                          dd        equ64e

 002B  7A008BFCFA210940                  dq        pi             ; A real
 0033  33 C0                             clear_reg                ; An instruction
 0035  45 6E 74 65 72 20                 db        prompt         ; A string
       6E 75 6D 62 65 72
       3A 20
 0043  A0 000000CE R                     mov    AL, byte_ptr DS:word32s ; A type modifier

 0048                        data2       ENDS



 0000                        code        SEGMENT para 'CODE' PUBLIC USE16
                                         ASSUME  CS:code, DS:data


                              ;
                              ; Set up the environment
                              ;
 0000                        Begin:
 0000  B8 ---- R                         mov    AX,data           ; Get data segment pointer
 0003  8E D8                             mov    DS,AX             ; into DS,
 0005  8E C0                             mov    ES,AX             ; and ES.
 0007  2B F6                             sub    SI,SI             ; Clear indicies
 0009  2B FF                             sub    DI,DI
                              ;
                              ; Calls as generated for locally defined near and far procs.
                              ;
                              ;       Note: the qualifier (FAR PTR) is necessary for the forward
                              ;             reference to the procedure farproc in order to avoid
                              ;             a phase error.

 000B  E8 0000 U                         call   lclproc           ; Call the near proc
EXAMPLES.ASM(444): error A2009: Symbol not defined: LCLPROC
 000E  9A 0000 ---- U                    call   FAR PTR farproc   ; and the far proc.
EXAMPLES.ASM(445): error A2009: Symbol not defined: FARPROC
                              ;
                              ; Similar calls for externally declared procs.
                              ;
```

```
0013  E8 0000 E                          call    extfproc        ; Check FAR external call
0016  9A 0000 ---- E                     call    extnproc        ; and NEAR external call
                                  ;
                                  ; Use of labels defined as examples of use of the LABEL directive.
                                  ;
001B  8A 26 0007 R                        mov     AH,bytelabel    ; As a byte,
001F  A1 0007 R                           mov     AX,wordtype     ; a word, and
0022  66| A1 0007 R                       mov     EAX,dwordtype   ; a double word.


                                  ;
                                  ; Addressing modes.
                                  ; For 8088, 8086, 80186, and 80286 CPUs the registers usable as
                                  ; either base or index registers were limited.  This limitation
                                  ; is enforced on the 80386 when 16 bit registers are used.
                                  ;
                                  ;
                                  ; Registers as operands
                                  ;       and displacement only addressing.
                                  ;
0026  B1 20                               mov     CL,32           ; 8 bit register as destination
0028  88 0E 0006 R                        mov     data8,CL        ; and as source operand.
002C  8A E1                               mov     AH,CL           ; 8 bit registers as both
                                  ;
002E  8B 36 0004 R                        mov     SI,data16       ; 16 bit register destination
0032  89 26 0004 R                        mov     data16,SP       ; and source operands.
0036  8B F8                               mov     DI,AX           ; 16 bit registers as both.
                                  ;
0038  66| 8B 2E 0000 R                    mov     EBP,data32      ; 32 bit register destination
003D  66| 89 16 0000 R                    mov     data32,EDX      ; and source operands.
0042  66| 8B F1                           mov     ESI,ECX         ; 32 bit registers as both.


                                  ; Base register addressing.  In 32 bit mode there is no distinction
                                  ;     between this and index register addressing.  In 16 bit mode,
                                  ;     base registers are BP and BX, index registers are SI and DI
                                  ;     (other than the registers used, no real distinction exists).
                                  ;
                                  ; The location of the operand within the segment is the sum of the
                                  ;     displacement and the value in the base or index register.
                                  ;     The use of BP or EBP is a special case in that SS is assumed
                                  ;     instead of DS.
                                  ;     In the 80386 any 32 bit general register can be a base, and
                                  ;     any 32 bit general register except ESP can be used as an index.
                                  ;
0045  8B 46 04                            mov     AX,data16-data [BP] ; Assumes SS as a segment reg.
0048  8B 87 0004 R                        mov     AX,data16 [BX]      ; Assumes DS as a segment reg.
004C  26: 8B 87 0004 R                    mov     AX,ES:data16 [BX]   ; Either can be overriden.
0051  67| 8B 01                           mov     AX,WORD PTR [ECX]   ; 32 bit address can use any
                                  ;       indexed
0054  8B 84 0004 R                        mov     AX,data16 [SI]      ; Assumes DS as a segment reg.
0058  26: 8B 85 0004 R                    mov     AX,ES:data16 [DI]   ; Either can be overriden.
                                  ;       alternate forms
005D  67| 66| 8B 42 0A                    mov     EAX, DWORD PTR [EDX+10] ; imbedded
0062  67| 66| 8B 42 0A                    mov     EAX, DWORD PTR [EDX]+10 ; added after
0067  67| 66| 8B 42 0A                    mov     EAX, DWORD PTR [EDX].10 ; as displ into structure


                                  ; Based + indexed mode.
                                  ;
006C  8B 42 04                            mov     AX,data16-data [BP] [SI] ; Assumes SS.
006F  8B 81 0004 R                        mov     AX,data16 [BX] [DI] ; Assumes DS.
0073  26: 8B 80 0004 R                    mov     AX,ES:data16 [BX] [SI] ; Either can be overriden.
0078  67| 8B 0411                         mov     AX,WORD PTR [ECX] [EDX]  ; 32 bit mode can use any
                                  ;       alternate forms
007C  8B 43 0A                            mov     AX,WORD PTR [BP+DI+10] ; imbedded displacement
007F  8B 40 0A                            mov     AX,WORD PTR [BX+SI]+10 ; added after
0082  8B 40 0A                            mov     AX,WORD PTR [BX]+10+[SI] ; added in the center
0085  8B 42 0A                            mov     AX,WORD PTR [BP+SI].10 ; as displ into structure


                                  ; Based + scaled index mode
                                  ;
0088  67| 66| 8B 448A 20                  mov     EAX, DWORD PTR 32+[EDX] [ECX*4]
```

```
008E  67| 66| 8B 848A 0000              mov      EAX, data32+[EDX] [ECX*4]
            0000 R

                            ; Location counter reference

= 0097                      count0    equ     $
0097                        count1:                           ; if used as a transfer label

0097  50                              push     AX
0098  66| 50                          push     EAX

                            ;
                            ; Some examples of expressions using operators as they might be
                            ; used.
                            ;
009A  66| A1 0054 R                   mov      EAX,data32+14*6    ; We add 14*6 to the
                            ;                                         displacement.
009E  8A 26 0026 R                    mov      AH,data16+(word32s-data32) MOD 43 ; the computations
EXAMPLES.ASM(537): warning A4031: Operand types must match
                            ;                                     can be complicated.
                            ;
                            ;
00A2  66| B8 00CE R                   mov      EAX, OFFSET word32s ; This loads the offset
00A8  66| 8D 06 00CE R                lea      EAX,word32s         ; as does the lea instruction
00AD  67| 66| 8D 84D3 0000            lea      EAX,word32s[EBX] [EDX*8] ; lea, however, can be
            00CE R
                            ;                                     used with complex addressing.
00B6  03 06 00CE R                    add      AX, WORD PTR [word32s] ; use the low word of dbl
00BA  C6 06 00CE R 61                 mov      BYTE PTR word32s,'a' ; and change the low byte

                                      ASSUME   DS:data2           ; Change segment addressed
                            ; Addressing modes using default sized data segment.
                            ;
                            ; The above examples are duplicated where they would show the
                            ; different generation due to the USE32 default of MASM R5.1
                            ;
                            ;
                            ; Registers as operands
                            ;         and displacement only addressing.
                            ;
00BF  67| 88 0D 00000006 R            mov      d2ta8,CL           ; and as source operand.
                            ;
00C6  67| 8B 35 00000004 R            mov      SI,d2ta16          ; 16 bit register destination
00CD  67| 89 25 00000004 R            mov      d2ta16,SP          ; and source operands.
                            ;
00D4  67| 66| 8B 2D 0000              mov      EBP,d2ta32         ; 32 bit register destination
            0000 R
00DC  67| 66| 89 15 0000              mov      d2ta32,EDX         ; and source operands.
            0000 R

                            ; Base register addressing.  In 32 bit mode there is no distinction
                            ;     between this and index register addressing.  In 16 bit mode,
                            ;     base registers are BP and BX, index registers are SI and DI
                            ;     (other than the registers used, no real distinction exists).
                            ;
                            ; The location of the operand within the segment is the sum of the
                            ;     displacement and the value in the base or index register.
                            ;     The use of BP or EBP is a special case in that SS is assumed
                            ;     instead of DS.
                            ;     In the 80386 any 32 bit general register can be a base, and
                            ;     any 32 bit general register except ESP can be used as an index.
                            ;
00E4  8B 87 0004 R                    mov      AX,d2ta16 [BX]     ; Assumes DS as a segment reg.
00E8  26: 8B 87 0004 R                mov      AX,ES:d2ta16 [BX]  ; Either can be overriden.
                            ;   indexed
00ED  8B 84 0004 R                    mov      AX,d2ta16 [SI]     ; Assumes DS as a segment reg.
00F1  26: 8B 85 0004 R                mov      AX,ES:d2ta16 [DI]  ; Either can be overriden.
```

```
                                      ; Based + indexed mode.

00F6  8B 81 0004 R                    mov     AX,d2ta16 [BX] [DI] ; Assumes DS.
00FA  26: 8B 80 0004 R                mov     AX,ES:d2ta16 [BX] [SI] ; Either can be overriden.

00FF  67| 66| 8B 848A 0000            mov     EAX, d2ta32+[EDX] [ECX*4]
      0000 R


0108                          Exit:
0108  B0 00                           mov     AL,0            ; Set return code
010A  B4 4C                           mov     AH,04ch         ; Set goodby
010C  CD 21                           int     21h             ; Return to the system
                              ;
                              ; Define local and far procedures
                              ; Near first, this is the default
                              ;
010E                          lclproc PROC                    ; Could have added NEAR type
010E  C3                              ret                     ; and return.
010F                          lclproc ENDP
                              ;
010F                          farproc PROC    FAR             ; Must use FAR to get type
010F  CB                              ret
0110                          farproc ENDP

0110                          code    ENDS
                                      END     Begin
   1                                  PAGE    55,132
   2                                  .386
   3                                  .LALL                   ; Turn macro expansion list on
   4                                  .LFCOND                 ; list false conditionals too
   5
   6                          ;
   7                          ; Name:   EXAMPLES.ASM
   8                          ;
   9                          ; Purpose: This program is used to provide examples of legal and
  10                          ;          illegal syntax and usage.
  11                          ;
  12                          ; Inputs:  None.
  13                          ;
  14                          ; Process: None.
  15                          ;
  16                          ; Outputs: A listing, including error messages, which provides
  17                          ;          examples of usage.
  18
  19                          ;
  20                          ; Declare routines near and far which are used in calls and in
  21                          ; conjuction with the linkage editor to demonstrate how an error
  22                          ; can slip by.
  23                          ;
  24                                  EXTRN   EXTNPROC:FAR    ; A near proc external
  25                                  EXTRN   EXTFPROC:NEAR   ; A far proc external
  26                          ;
  27                          ;
  28                          ; A sample macro skeleton showing the main parts of a macro.
  29                          ;
  30                          ; The macro definition statement - (the beginning)
  31                          ; name    MACRO directive  dummy parameters
  32
  33                          samp01  MACRO           dummy00,dummy01
  34                          ;; A comment which is internal to a macro - ie it does not print when
  35                          ;; macro expansion occurs.
  36                          ;; The body of the macro includes everything between the MACRO line
  37                          ;; and the ENDM line
  38                                  mov     AX,dummy00      ; A prototype statement
  39
  40                                  EXITM                   ; A pseudo-op (directive)
  41                          ENDM                            ; End of the macro (the end)
  42
  43
  44                          ;
  45                          COMMENT + This starts a multi-line comment which can contain any
  46                          character except the specified delimiter (in this case +
```

```
47
48
49
50
51 0000                              stack     SEGMENT PARA 'STACK' STACK USE16
52 0000   0100[                                dq        256 DUP(?)
53        ??????????????????
54        ?
55                          ]
56
57 0800                              stack     ENDS
58
59                          ;
60                          ; Note: MASM release 5.1 changes the default size applied to data
61                          ;       segments.  For .386, .386p mode assemblies R5.1 assumes a
62                          ;       USE32.  R5.0 assumes a USE16.  The first data segment is
63                          ;       forced to a size of 16 in order to allow compatable sized
64                          ;       examples to generate.
65
66 0000                              data      SEGMENT PARA USE16
67 0000   00000000          data32    dd        0                      ; a 32 bit data area
68 0004   0000              data16    dw        0                      ; a 16 bit data area
69 0006   00                data8     db        0                      ; an 8 bit data area
70                          ;
71                          ; Examples of the use of label to allow access to an area using
72                          ; different types for the same area.
73                          ;
74 0007                     bytelabel LABEL     BYTE                   ; Refer as byte type,
75 0007                     wordtype  LABEL     WORD                   ; word type,
76 0007                     dwordtype LABEL     DWORD                  ; and as double word type.
77                          ;
78                          ; Examples of DUP and initializations.
79                          ;
80 0007   000A[                                dw        10 DUP (1,2,3,4)
81             0001
82             0002
83             0003
84             0004
85                      ]
86
87 0057   0003[                                dw        3  DUP (3)
88             0003
89                      ]
90
91                          ;
92                          ; Example of record definitions which show the sizes which result,
93                          ; results of initialization (when used below), and masking.
94                          ;
95                          ; Because this is a USE16 segment, record size is limited to 16 bits.
96                          ; (This apears to be a bug in MASM R5.1 - probably associated with the
97                          ;  change in data segment USE defaulting.)  Note that 32 bit records
98                          ; are generated if USE32 is specified for the data segment.
99                          ;
100                         recd16    record    flda:3, fldb:7, fldc:4=0fh  ; A 16 bit record
101                         ;                   14 bits of the record defined (bits 13-11, 10-4, 3-0).
102                         ;
103                         recd08    record    flda3:6, fldb3:1=1   ; An 8 bit record
104                         ;                   7 bits defined (0<bits<=8 allows 8 bit size).
105                         ;
106                         recd08a   record    flda4:5, fldb4:3=0fh ; A 3 bit field initialized
EXAMPLES.ASM(93): error A2050: Value out of range
107                         ;                                        ; with 4.
108                         ;
109                         encode    record    hi:4,mid:3,lo:3
110                         ;
111                         recdbt    record    bit7:1, bits6t1:6, bit00:1 ;
112                         ;
113                         recdbt16  record    bit15:1, bitsmid:14, bit0a:1 ;
114                         ;
115                         ; Bits defined
116                         ;
117 005D   80                                  recdbt    <1,0,0>              ; First defined
```

```
118 005E  01                              recdbt   <0,0,1>          ; Last defined
119                           ;
120 005F  8000                            recdbt16 <1,0,0>          ; First defined
121 0061  0001                            recdbt16 <0,0,1>          ; Last defined
122                           ;
123                           ; Example generation for records
124                           ;
125 0063  03C7                            encode   <15,0,7>         ; Initialize hi and lo
126
127 0065  000F                            recd16   <>               ; an unintialized record
128 0067  00FF                            recd16   <0,15,>          ; use fldc's default value
129 0069  0000                            recd16   <,,0>            ; override the default for fldc
130                           ;
131                           ; Mask generation examples
132                           ;
133 006B  03C0                            dw       MASK hi          ; A mask to isolate hi
134 006D  0038                            dw       MASK mid         ; A mask to isolate mid
135 006F  0007                            dw       MASK lo          ; A mask to isolate lo
136                           ;
137 0071  FFFF                            dw       NOT MASK mid     ; A mask to clear mid
EXAMPLES.ASM(124): error A2050: Value out of range
138 0073  FFFFFFC7                        dd       NOT MASK mid     ; A mask to clear mid
139 0077  25 FFC7                         and      AX,NOT MASK mid  ; A mask to clear mid
140                           ;
141                           ; Structure definition
142                           ;
143                           mystruct STRUC                        ; Provide name & begin def.
144 0000  0021               mywd0    dw       33                   ; Define initialized field
145                           ;                                         which can be over-ridden
146 0002  0001 0002          mywd1    dw       1,2                  ; non-over-ride-able
147 0006                     mystruct ENDS
148                           ;
149                           ; Structure use
150                           ;
151 007A  6300               usestruct mystruct <99,>
152 007C  0001[
153         0100
154         0200
155                                  ]
156
157                           ;
158                           ; Example string initialization for word/double word
159                           ;
160 0080  0061                            dw       'a'              ; A small string (1 byte).
161 0082  6162                            dw       'ab'             ; A word size string
162 0084  FFFF                            dw       'abc'            ; An oversize string for word
EXAMPLES.ASM(144): error A2050: Value out of range
163 0086  00616263                        dd       'abc'            ; Fits a double word
164 008A  61626364                        dd       'abcd'           ; A double word size string
165 008E  62636465                        dd       'abcde'          ; Oversize for double word
EXAMPLES.ASM(147): error A2010: Syntax error
166                           ;
167 0092  6564636200000000                dq       'abcdefgh'       ; A string which fits in qw
EXAMPLES.ASM(149): error A2010: Syntax error
168                           ;
169                           ;
170                           ; Equated values using the = form of equate.
171                           ;
172 = FF00                    equ16    =        256*255             ; 0 ff 00h    (ok  16 bit)
173 = 01000000                equ32    =        256*256*256         ; 1 00 00 00h (ok  32 bit)
174 = 0000                    equ64    =        256*256*256*256     ; 1 00 00 00 00h (bad 33 bit)
175
176                           ; Note that there is no warning of the overflow beyond 32 bits.
177
178 009A  FF00                            dw       equ16            ; use is ok
179 009C  FFFF                            dw       equ32            ; error - value out of range
EXAMPLES.ASM(161): error A2050: Value out of range
180
181 009E  0000FF00                        dd       equ16
182 00A2  01000000                        dd       equ32
183 00A6  00000000                        dd       equ64            ; Nor is there an error at use.
184
185 00AA  0000000100000000                dq       equ32
```

```
186 00B2  0000000000000000                    dq      equ64
187
188                                    ;
189                                    ; Equates to strings -
190                                    ;
191 = 6162                             equ16s   =      'ab'
192 = 00616263                         equ16s1  =      'abc'
193 = 61626364                         equ32s   =      'abcd'
194 = 62636465                         equ32s1  =      'abcde'                 ; syntax error (equates to bcde)
EXAMPLES.ASM(176): error A2010: Syntax error
195
196 00BA  6162                         dw      equ16s
197 00BC  FFFF                         dw      equ16s1                         ; error - value out of range
EXAMPLES.ASM(179): error A2050: Value out of range
198
199 00BE  61626364                     dd      equ32s
200 00C2  62636465                     dd      equ32s1                         ; No error at use though.
201
202                                    ; Equates using the EQU directive.
203                                    ;
204 = FF00                             equ16e   EQU    256*255
205 = FF000000                         equ32e   EQU    256*256*256*255
206 = 0000                             equ64e   EQU    equ32e*256              ; Overflow is not detected.
207
208 00C6  FF00                         dw      equ16e
209 00C8  FFFF                         dw      equ32e
EXAMPLES.ASM(191): error A2050: Value out of range
210 00CA  0000FF00                     dd      equ16e
211 00CE  FF000000      word32s        dd      equ32e
212 00D2  00000000                     dd      equ64e
213
214
215                                    ; Sample equates for the book
216                                    ;
217 = 3.141592                         pi          EQU    3.141592
218 = XOR EAX,EAX                       clear_reg   EQU    XOR EAX,EAX
219 = 'Enter number: '                 prompt      EQU    'Enter number: '
220 = BYTE PTR                          byte_ptr    EQU    BYTE PTR
221                                    ;
222                                    ; and their use
223 00D6  40490FD8                     dd      pi                    ; A real
224 00DA  66| 33 C0                    clear_reg                     ; An instruction
225 00DD  45 6E 74 65 72 20  dprompt   db      prompt                ; A string
226       6E 75 6D 62 65 72
227       3A 20
228 00EB  A0 00CE R                    mov     AL, byte_ptr DS:word32s ; A type modifier
229                                    ;
230                                    ; Conditionals as they generate into data
231
232 00EE  00                           db      ( 1 EQ 0ffffh)        ; Values do not compare equal
233 00EF  FF                           db      ( 1 NE 0ffffh)        ; This is true (they don't =)
234 00F0  FF                           db      ( 1 GT -1 )           ; 1 is greater than -1
235 00F1  00                           db      ( 1 GT 0ffffh)        ; It is not greater than 64K-1
236 00F2  00                           db      ( 1 GT 0ffffffffh)    ; nor greater than 4G-1
237 00F3  FF                           db      ( 1 GT 0ffffffffh+1)  ; Expression = 0 (32 bits)
238                                    ;
239                                    ; Conditional assembly examples (as used in open code)
240                                    ;
241                          IF       equ32s GT equ16s               ; Is a longer string greater?
242 00F4  59 45 53                     db      'YES'
243                          ELSE
244                                     db      'NO'
245                          ENDIF
246                                    ;
247                                    ; An example of a pass 1 only error forced by IF2.
248                                    ;
249                          IF1                                      ; Check for pass 1
250                              IFDEF Begin                          ; This forward reference is not
251                                    %OUT    'WHAT?'
252                              ELSE
253                                    %OUT    'EXPECTED'             ; 'EXPECTED' is displayed
254                              ENDIF
255                          ELSEIF2                                  ; Note address assignment below
```

```
256                                                        ; and the re-use at the phase
257                                                        ; error.
258                              IFDEF Begin               ; Should be defined now
259 00F7  44 45 46 49 4E 45            db      'DEFINED'
260       44
261                              ELSE
262                                     db      'WRONG!'
263                              ENDIF
264                       ELSE
265                              db      'PASS3?'
266                       ENDIF
267 00FE  00000000               dd      0                 ; no phase error
268                       ;
269                       ; It is instructive to examine the phase 1 listing and the phase 2
270                       ; listings together here.  The simple dd which follows becomes a
271                       ; problem because it has a symbol associated with it.  The generation
272                       ; of the 'phase 2 only' db 'DEFINED' changes the offset of the label
273                       ; dummydd which was assigned in phase 1.  It doesn't have any effect
274                       ; on the unlabled dd above other than changing its location.
275                       ;
276 00FB  00000000       dummydd dd      0                 ; Phase error
EXAMPLES.ASM(255): error A2006: Phase error between passes
277                       ;
278                       ; IRP used in a macro
279                       ;
280                       irpmac   MACRO   param1
281                                IRP     zz,<1,2,3,4,5,6,7>
282                       param1&&zz db   zz
283                                ENDM
284                              ENDM
285                              irpmac   first             ; Generate data and labels
286                     1        IRP     zz,<1,2,3,4,5,6,7>
287                     1 first&zz db    zz
288                     1        ENDM
289 00FF  01            2 first1 db      1
290 0100  02            2 first2 db      2
291 0101  03            2 first3 db      3
292 0102  04            2 first4 db      4
293 0103  05            2 first5 db      5
294 0104  06            2 first6 db      6
295 0105  07            2 first7 db      7
296                       ;
297                       ; IRPC used in a macro
298                       ;
299                       irpcmac  MACRO   param1
300                                IRPC    zz,param1
301                       irpcm&&zz db    '&zz'
302                                ENDM
303                              ENDM
304                              irpcmac abcdef
305                     1        IRPC    zz,abcdef
306                     1 irpcm&zz db    '&zz'
307                     1        ENDM
308 0106  61            2 irpcma db      'a'
309 0107  62            2 irpcmb db      'b'
310 0108  63            2 irpcmc db      'c'
311 0109  64            2 irpcmd db      'd'
312 010A  65            2 irpcme db      'e'
313 010B  66            2 irpcmf db      'f'
314                       ;
315                       ; Check size of rept expression
316                       ;
317                              .SFCOND                    ; (Don't list false conditional)
318 = 0000                       x = 0                      ; initiallize inner counter
319 = 0000                       y = 0                      ; and check for over 16 bits.
320                       REPT    256*512                    ; try for 18 bit repeat ct.
321                              x = x+1                    ;
322                       IF x EQ 1                          ; Ensure repeat ct. not 0
323                              dd      x                  ; Won't generate if it is.
324                       ENDIF
325
326                       IF y
327                              dd      y                  ; Generate one for y
```

```
328                                              y = 0                              ; and only one!
329                                  ELSE
330                                              y = (x AND 0ffffh) EQ 0     ; Force zero if not x0000h
331                                              y = y AND ((x SHR 16) NE 0) ; then or to high bits
332                                  ENDIF
333                          ENDM
334                          ;
335                          ;
336                          ; Check on validity of check above - If the repeat count wraps at 16
337                          ; bits, we should get generation below.
338                          ;
339 = 0000                               x = 0                              ; initiallize inner counter
340 = 0000                               y = 0                              ; and check for over 16 bits.
341                          REPT    256*512+18                             ; A wrap gives a count of 18
342                                  x = x+1                                ;
343                                  IF x EQ 1                              ; Ensure repeat ct. not 0
344                                  dd        x                           ; Won't generate if it is.
345                                  ENDIF
346
347                                  IF y
348                                  dd        y                           ; Generate one for y
349                                              y = 0                      ; and only 1.
350                                  ELSE
351                                              y = (x AND 0fh) EQ 0       ; Force zero if not x0h
352                                              y = y AND ((x AND 30h) NE 0) ; then or to high bits
353                                  ENDIF
354                          ENDM
355 = 0001                  1                   x = x+1                     ;
356                         1          IF x EQ 1                            ; Ensure repeat ct. not 0
357 010C  00000001          1          dd        x                         ; Won't generate if it is.
358                         1          ENDIF
359                         1          ELSE
360 = 0000                  1                   y = (x AND 0fh) EQ 0        ; Force zero if not x0h
361 = 0000                  1                   y = y AND ((x AND 30h) NE 0) ; then or to high bits
362                         1          ENDIF
363 = 0002                  1                   x = x+1                     ;
364                         1          ELSE
365 = 0000                  1                   y = (x AND 0fh) EQ 0        ; Force zero if not x0h
366 = 0000                  1                   y = y AND ((x AND 30h) NE 0) ; then or to high bits
367                         1          ENDIF
368 = 0003                  1                   x = x+1                     ;
369                         1          ELSE
370 = 0000                  1                   y = (x AND 0fh) EQ 0        ; Force zero if not x0h
371 = 0000                  1                   y = y AND ((x AND 30h) NE 0) ; then or to high bits
372                         1          ENDIF
373 = 0004                  1                   x = x+1                     ;
374                         1          ELSE
375 = 0000                  1                   y = (x AND 0fh) EQ 0        ; Force zero if not x0h
376 = 0000                  1                   y = y AND ((x AND 30h) NE 0) ; then or to high bits
377                         1          ENDIF
378 = 0005                  1                   x = x+1                     ;
379                         1          ELSE
380 = 0000                  1                   y = (x AND 0fh) EQ 0        ; Force zero if not x0h
381 = 0000                  1                   y = y AND ((x AND 30h) NE 0) ; then or to high bits
382                         1          ENDIF
383 = 0006                  1                   x = x+1                     ;
384                         1          ELSE
385 = 0000                  1                   y = (x AND 0fh) EQ 0        ; Force zero if not x0h
386 = 0000                  1                   y = y AND ((x AND 30h) NE 0) ; then or to high bits
387                         1          ENDIF
388 = 0007                  1                   x = x+1                     ;
389                         1          ELSE
390 = 0000                  1                   y = (x AND 0fh) EQ 0        ; Force zero if not x0h
391 = 0000                  1                   y = y AND ((x AND 30h) NE 0) ; then or to high bits
392                         1          ENDIF
393 = 0008                  1                   x = x+1                     ;
394                         1          ELSE
395 = 0000                  1                   y = (x AND 0fh) EQ 0        ; Force zero if not x0h
396 = 0000                  1                   y = y AND ((x AND 30h) NE 0) ; then or to high bits
397                         1          ENDIF
398 = 0009                  1                   x = x+1                     ;
399                         1          ELSE
400 = 0000                  1                   y = (x AND 0fh) EQ 0        ; Force zero if not x0h
```

```
401 = 0000              1          y = y AND ((x AND 30h) NE 0) ; then or to high bits
402                     1      ENDIF
403 = 000A              1          x = x+1                    ;
404                     1      ELSE
405 = 0000              1          y = (x AND 0fh) EQ 0        ; Force zero if not x0h
406 = 0000              1          y = y AND ((x AND 30h) NE 0) ; then or to high bits
407                     1      ENDIF
408 = 000B              1          x = x+1                    ;
409                     1      ELSE
410 = 0000              1          y = (x AND 0fh) EQ 0        ; Force zero if not x0h
411 = 0000              1          y = y AND ((x AND 30h) NE 0) ; then or to high bits
412                     1      ENDIF
413 = 000C              1          x = x+1                    ;
414                     1      ELSE
415 = 0000              1          y = (x AND 0fh) EQ 0        ; Force zero if not x0h
416 = 0000              1          y = y AND ((x AND 30h) NE 0) ; then or to high bits
417                     1      ENDIF
418 = 000D              1          x = x+1                    ;
419                     1      ELSE
420 = 0000              1          y = (x AND 0fh) EQ 0        ; Force zero if not x0h
421 = 0000              1          y = y AND ((x AND 30h) NE 0) ; then or to high bits
422                     1      ENDIF
423 = 000E              1          x = x+1                    ;
424                     1      ELSE
425 = 0000              1          y = (x AND 0fh) EQ 0        ; Force zero if not x0h
426 = 0000              1          y = y AND ((x AND 30h) NE 0) ; then or to high bits
427                     1      ENDIF
428 = 000F              1          x = x+1                    ;
429                     1      ELSE
430 = 0000              1          y = (x AND 0fh) EQ 0        ; Force zero if not x0h
431 = 0000              1          y = y AND ((x AND 30h) NE 0) ; then or to high bits
432                     1      ENDIF
433 = 0010              1          x = x+1                    ;
434                     1      ELSE
435 =-0001              1          y = (x AND 0fh) EQ 0        ; Force zero if not x0h
436 = FFFFFFFF          1          y = y AND ((x AND 30h) NE 0) ; then or to high bits
437                     1      ENDIF
438 = 0011              1          x = x+1                    ;
439                     1      IF y
440 0110  FFFFFFFF      1          dd      y                  ; Generate one for y
441 = 0000              1          y = 0                      ; and only 1.
442                     1      ENDIF
443 = 0012              1          x = x+1                    ;
444                     1      ELSE
445 = 0000              1          y = (x AND 0fh) EQ 0        ; Force zero if not x0h
446 = 0000              1          y = y AND ((x AND 30h) NE 0) ; then or to high bits
447                     1      ENDIF
448                              .LALL                        ; Turn macro expansion list on
449                              .LFCOND                      ; list false conditionals too
450                      ;
451                      ; Show use of IFB/IFNB
452                      ;
453                      ifbnb     MACRO   param1,param2,param3
454                        IFB <param1>                       ; If parameter 1 is omitted
455                          IFNB <param3>                    ; and parameter 3 is present
456                                                           ;; The & forces substitution
457                                                           ;; of parameter 2.
458                              db      '&param2'            ; define param2
459                                                           ;; See the example without
460                                                           ;; the & below.
461                              db      'param2'             ; different param2
462                          ENDIF
463                        ENDIF
464                              ENDM
465
466                              ifbnb   this,"won't",generate
467 IFB <this>          1      IFB <this>                     ; If parameter 1 is omitted
468                     1        IFNB <generate>              ; and parameter 3 is present
469                     1                                     ;
470                     1                                     ;
471                     1              db      '"won't"'      ; define param2
472                     1                                     ;
```

```
473                          1                              ;
474                          1              db      'param2'           ; different param2
475                          1          ENDIF
476                          1      ENDIF
477                                     ifbnb   ,<this will>,generate
478                          1      IFB <>                             ; If parameter 1 is omitted
479                          1        IFNB <generate>                        ; and parameter 3 is present
480                          1                                         ;
481                          1                                         ;
482 0114  74 68 69 73 20 77  1          db      'this will'          ; define param2
483       69 6C 6C           1
484                          1                                         ;
485                          1                                         ;
486 011D  70 61 72 61 6D 32  1          db      'param2'           ; different param2
487                          1          ENDIF
488                          1      ENDIF
489                                     ifbnb   ,<!!>,generate
490                          1      IFB <>                             ; If parameter 1 is omitted
491                          1        IFNB <generate>                        ; and parameter 3 is present
492                          1                                         ;
493                          1                                         ;
494 0123  21                 1          db      '!'              ; define param2
495                          1                                         ;
496                          1                                         ;
497 0124  70 61 72 61 6D 32  1          db      'param2'           ; different param2
498                          1          ENDIF
499                          1      ENDIF
500                                     ifbnb   ,%(equ16e mod 227),will_too
501                          1      IFB <>                             ; If parameter 1 is omitted
502                          1        IFNB <will_too>                        ; and parameter 3 is present
503                          1                                         ;
504                          1                                         ;
505 012A  31 33 31           1          db      '131'            ; define param2
506                          1                                         ;
507                          1                                         ;
508 012D  70 61 72 61 6D 32  1          db      'param2'           ; different param2
509                          1          ENDIF
510                          1      ENDIF
511                                     ifbnb   ,(equ16e mod 227),will_also
512                          1      IFB <>                             ; If parameter 1 is omitted
513                          1        IFNB <mod>                             ; and parameter 3 is present
514                          1                                         ;
515                          1                                         ;
516 0133  28 65 71 75 31 36  1          db      '(equ16e'            ; define param2
517       65                 1
518                          1                                         ;
519                          1                                         ;
520 013A  70 61 72 61 6D 32  1          db      'param2'           ; different param2
521                          1          ENDIF
522                          1      ENDIF
523                              ;
524                              ; Show use of IFIDN[I]/IFDIF[I]
525                              ;
526                              idndif  MACRO   param1,param2
527                                  IFIDN <param1>,<param2>              ; If p1 and p2 are the same
528                                      db      '1 and 2 same'
529                                  ENDIF
530                                  IFIDNI <param1>,<param2>             ; same ignoring case
531                                      db      '1 = 2 case'
532                                  ENDIF
533                                  IFDIF <param1>,<param2>              ; If p1 and p2 NOT the same
534                                      db      '1 and 2 diff'
535                                  ENDIF
536                                  IFDIFI <param1>,<param2>             ; not same ignoring case
537                                      db      '1, 2 diff case'
538                                  ENDIF
539                                      ENDM
540
541                                      idndif aaa,aaa
542                          1      IFIDN <aaa>,<aaa>              ; If p1 and p2 are the same
543 0140  31 20 61 6E 64 20  1          db      '1 and 2 same'
544       32 20 73 61 6D 65  1
545                          1      ENDIF
```

```
546                             1       IFIDNI <aaa>,<aaa>              ; same ignoring case
547 014C  31 20 3D 20 32 20     1               db      '1 = 2 case'
548       63 61 73 65           1
549                             1       ENDIF
550                             1       IFDIF <aaa>,<aaa>              ; If p1 and p2 NOT the same
551                             1               db      '1 and 2 diff'
552                             1       ENDIF
553                             1       IFDIFI <aaa>,<aaa>             ; not same ignoring case
554                             1               db      '1, 2 diff case'
555                             1       ENDIF
556                                             idndif  AAA,aaa
557                             1       IFIDN <AAA>,<aaa>              ; If p1 and p2 are the same
558                             1               db      '1 and 2 same'
559                             1       ENDIF
560                             1       IFIDNI <AAA>,<aaa>             ; same ignoring case
561 0156  31 20 3D 20 32 20     1               db      '1 = 2 case'

562       63 61 73 65           1
563                             1       ENDIF
564                             1       IFDIF <AAA>,<aaa>              ; If p1 and p2 NOT the same
565 0160  31 20 61 6E 64 20     1               db      '1 and 2 diff'
566       32 20 64 69 66 66     1
567                             1       ENDIF
568                             1       IFDIFI <AAA>,<aaa>            ; not same ignoring case
569                             1               db      '1, 2 diff case'
570                             1       ENDIF
571                                             idndif  bbb,aaa
572                             1       IFIDN <bbb>,<aaa>              ; If p1 and p2 are the same
573                             1               db      '1 and 2 same'
574                             1       ENDIF
575                             1       IFIDNI <bbb>,<aaa>             ; same ignoring case
576                             1               db      '1 = 2 case'
577                             1       ENDIF
578                             1       IFDIF <bbb>,<aaa>              ; If p1 and p2 NOT the same
579 016C  31 20 61 6E 64 20     1               db      '1 and 2 diff'
580       32 20 64 69 66 66     1
581                             1       ENDIF
582                             1       IFDIFI <bbb>,<aaa>            ; not same ignoring case
583 0178  31 2C 20 32 20 64     1               db      '1, 2 diff case'
584       69 66 66 20 63 61     1
585       73 65                 1
586                             1       ENDIF
587 0186                        data    ENDS
588
589                             ;
590                             ; This, the second data segment, is allowed to default in size.
591                             ; If you have MASM R5.0 the default to a USE16 will provide a
592                             ; different generation than R5.1 which defaults to USE32 if the
593                             ; .386/.386p directive has been coded.
594                             ;
595
596 0000                        data2   SEGMENT PARA                  ; Default allowed
597 0000  00000000              d2ta32  dd      0                     ; a 32 bit data area
598 0004  0000                  d2ta16  dw      0                     ; a 16 bit data area
599 0006  00                    d2ta8   db      0                     ; an 8 bit data area
600                             ;
601                             ;
602                             ; Example of record definitions which show the sizes which result,
603                             ; results of initialization (when used below), and masking.
604                             ;
605                             ;
606                             recd32      record  flda1:10, fldb1:6=3fh, fldc1:2   ; A 32 bit record
607                             ;              18 bits defined (16<bits<=32 causes 32 bit size).
608                             ;
609                             recd32a     record  flda1a:14=3f3ch, fldb1a:2, fldc1a:2, fldd1a:18=3cffh
EXAMPLES.ASM(381): error A2050: Value out of range: FLDD1A
610                             ;              Note that the error message is not precise.
611                             ;
612                             code_it     record  bulk:16,hia:4,mida:3,lo1:3  ; bulk added for 32 bit
613                             ;
614                             recdbt32    record  bit000:1, bitsmida:30, bit31:1 ;
615                             ;
616                             ; Bits defined and sample generations.
617                             ;
```

```
618 0007  80000000                     recdbt32  <1,0,0>            ; First defined
619 000B  00000001                     recdbt32  <0,0,1>            ; Last defined
620
621 000F  000003C7                     code_it <0,15,0,7>           ; Initialize hia and lo1
622                          ;
623                          ; Equates to strings -
624                          ;
625 = 61626364              equ32s   =        'abcd'
626 = 62636465              equ32s1  =        'abcde'               ; syntax error (equates to bcde)
EXAMPLES.ASM(398): error A2010: Syntax error
627
628 0013  61626364                     dd       equ32s
629 0017  62636465                     dd       equ32s1             ; No error at use though.
630                          ;
631                          ; Equates using the EQU directive.
632                          ;
633 = FF000000              equ32e   EQU      256*256*256*255
634 = 0000                  equ64e   EQU      equ32e*256            ; Overflow is not detected.
635
636 001B  FF00                         dw       equ16e
637 001D  FFFF                         dw       equ32e
EXAMPLES.ASM(409): error A2050: Value out of range
638 001F  0000FF00                     dd       equ16e
639 0023  FF000000          word32s1 dd       equ32e
640 0027  00000000                     dd       equ64e
641
642 002B  7A008BFCFA210940             dq       pi                  ; A real
643 0033  33 C0                        clear_reg                    ; An instruction
644 0035  45 6E 74 65 72 20            db       prompt              ; A string
645        6E 75 6D 62 65 72
646        3A 20
647 0043  A0 000000CE R                mov      AL, byte_ptr DS:word32s ; A type modifier
648
649 0048                    data2    ENDS
650
651
652
653
654 0000                    code     SEGMENT para 'CODE' PUBLIC USE16
655                                   ASSUME  CS:code, DS:data
656
657
658                          ;
659                          ; Set up the environment
660                          ;
661 0000                    Begin:
662 0000  B8 ---- R                    mov      AX,data             ; Get data segment pointer
663 0003  8E D8                        mov      DS,AX               ; into DS,
664 0005  8E C0                        mov      ES,AX               ; and ES.
665 0007  2B F6                        sub      SI,SI               ; Clear indicies
666 0009  2B FF                        sub      DI,DI
667                          ;
668                          ; Calls as generated for locally defined near and far procs.
669                          ;
670                          ;    Note: the qualifier (FAR PTR) is necessary for the forward
671                          ;          reference to the procedure farproc in order to avoid
672                          ;          a phase error.
673
674 000B  E8 010E R                    call     lclproc             ; Call the near proc
675 000E  9A 010F ---- R               call     FAR PTR farproc     ; and the far proc.
676                          ;
677                          ; Similar calls for externally declared procs.
678                          ;
679 0013  E8 0000 E                    call     extfproc            ; Check FAR external call
680 0016  9A 0000 ---- E               call     extnproc            ; and NEAR external call
681                          ;
682                          ; Use of labels defined as examples of use of the LABEL directive.
683                          ;
684 001B  8A 26 0007 R                 mov      AH,bytelabel        ; As a byte,
685 001F  A1 0007 R                    mov      AX,wordtype         ; a word, and
686 0022  66| A1 0007 R                mov      EAX,dwordtype       ; a double word.
687
```

```
688                                   ; Addressing modes.
689                                   ; For 8088, 8086, 80186, and 80286 CPUs the registers usable as
690                                   ; either base or index registers were limited.  This limitation
691                                   ; is enforced on the 80386 when 16 bit registers are used.
692                                   ;
693                                   ;
694                                   ;
695                                   ; Registers as operands
696                                   ;       and displacement only addressing.
697                                   ;
698 0026  B1 20                             mov     CL,32               ; 8 bit register as destination
699 0028  88 0E 0006 R                      mov     data8,CL            ; and as source operand.
700 002C  8A E1                             mov     AH,CL               ; 8 bit registers as both
701                                   ;
702 002E  8B 36 0004 R                      mov     SI,data16           ; 16 bit register destination
703 0032  89 26 0004 R                      mov     data16,SP           ; and source operands.
704 0036  8B F8                             mov     DI,AX               ; 16 bit registers as both.
705                                   ;
706 0038  66| 8B 2E 0000 R                  mov     EBP,data32          ; 32 bit register destination
707 003D  66| 89 16 0000 R                  mov     data32,EDX          ; and source operands.
708 0042  66| 8B F1                         mov     ESI,ECX             ; 32 bit registers as both.
709
710
711                                   ; Base register addressing.  In 32 bit mode there is no distinction
712                                   ;       between this and index register addressing.  In 16 bit mode,
713                                   ;       base registers are BP and BX, index registers are SI and DI
714                                   ;       (other than the registers used, no real distinction exists).
715                                   ;
716                                   ; The location of the operand within the segment is the sum of the
717                                   ;       displacement and the value in the base or index register.
718                                   ;       The use of BP or EBP is a special case in that SS is assumed
719                                   ;       instead of DS.
720                                   ;       In the 80386 any 32 bit general register can be a base, and
721                                   ;       any 32 bit general register except ESP can be used as an index.
722                                   ;
723
724 0045  8B 46 04                          mov     AX,data16-data [BP] ; Assumes SS as a segment reg.
725 0048  8B 87 0004 R                      mov     AX,data16 [BX]      ; Assumes DS as a segment reg.
726 004C  26: 8B 87 0004 R                  mov     AX,ES:data16 [BX]   ; Either can be overriden.
727 0051  67| 8B 01                         mov     AX,WORD PTR [ECX]   ; 32 bit address can use any
728                                   ;   indexed
729 0054  8B 84 0004 R                      mov     AX,data16 [SI]      ; Assumes DS as a segment reg.
730 0058  26: 8B 85 0004 R                  mov     AX,ES:data16 [DI]   ; Either can be overriden.
731                                   ;   alternate forms
732 005D  67| 66| 8B 42 0A                  mov     EAX, DWORD PTR [EDX+10] ; imbedded
733 0062  67| 66| 8B 42 0A                  mov     EAX, DWORD PTR [EDX]+10 ; added after
734 0067  67| 66| 8B 42 0A                  mov     EAX, DWORD PTR [EDX].10 ; as displ into structure
735
736                                   ; Based + indexed mode.
737
738 006C  8B 42 04                          mov     AX,data16-data [BP] [SI] ; Assumes SS.
739 006F  8B 81 0004 R                      mov     AX,data16 [BX] [DI]      ; Assumes DS.
740 0073  26: 8B 80 0004 R                  mov     AX,ES:data16 [BX] [SI]   ; Either can be overriden.
741 0078  67| 8B 0411                       mov     AX,WORD PTR [ECX] [EDX]  ; 32 bit mode can use any
742                                   ;   alternate forms
743 007C  8B 43 0A                          mov     AX,WORD PTR [BP+DI+10]    ; imbedded displacement
744 007F  8B 40 0A                          mov     AX,WORD PTR [BX+SI]+10    ; added after
745 0082  8B 40 0A                          mov     AX,WORD PTR [BX]+10+[SI]  ; added in the center
746 0085  8B 42 0A                          mov     AX,WORD PTR [BP+SI].10    ; as displ into structure
747
748                                   ; Based + scaled index mode
749
750 0088  67| 66| 8B 448A 20                mov     EAX, DWORD PTR 32+[EDX] [ECX*4]
751 008E  67| 66| 8B 848A 0000              mov     EAX, data32+[EDX] [ECX*4]
752         0000 R
753
754                                   ; Location counter reference
755
756 = 0097                            count0    equ     $
757 0097                              count1:                             ; if used as a transfer label
758
759 0097  50                                 push    AX
760 0098  66| 50                             push    EAX
```

```
761
762
763                                          ; Some examples of expressions using operators as they might be
764                                          ; used.
765                                          ;
766 009A  66| A1 0054 R                      mov     EAX,data32+14*6    ; We add 14*6 to the
767                                          ;                                            displacement.
768 009E  8A 26 0026 R                       mov     AH,data16+(word32s-data32) MOD 43 ; the computations
EXAMPLES.ASM(537): warning A4031: Operand types must match
769                                          ;                                          can be complicated.
770                                          ;
771                                          ;
772 00A2  66| B8 00CE R                      mov     EAX, OFFSET word32s ; This loads the offset
773 00A8  66| 8D 06 00CE R                   lea     EAX,word32s        ; as does the lea instruction
774 00AD  67| 66| 8D 84D3 0000               lea     EAX,word32s[EBX] [EDX*8] ; lea, however, can be
775       00CE R
776                                          ;                                          used with complex addressing.
777                                          ;
778 00B6  03 06 00CE R                       add     AX, WORD PTR [word32s] ; use the low word of dbl
779 00BA  C6 06 00CE R 61                    mov     BYTE PTR word32s,'a' ; and change the low byte
780
781
782                                                  ASSUME  DS:data2           ; Change segment addressed
783                                          ;
784                                          ; Addressing modes using default sized data segment.
785                                          ;
786                                          ; The above examples are duplicated where they would show the
787                                          ; different generation due to the USE32 default of MASM R5.1
788                                          ;
789                                          ;
790                                          ; Registers as operands
791                                          ;         and displacement only addressing.
792                                          ;
793 00BF  67| 88 0D 00000006 R               mov     d2ta8,CL           ; and as source operand.
794                                          ;
795 00C6  67| 8B 35 00000004 R               mov     SI,d2ta16          ; 16 bit register destination
796 00CD  67| 89 25 00000004 R               mov     d2ta16,SP          ; and source operands.
797                                          ;
798 00D4  67| 66| 8B 2D 0000                 mov     EBP,d2ta32         ; 32 bit register destination
799       0000 R
800 00DC  67| 66| 89 15 0000                 mov     d2ta32,EDX         ; and source operands.
801       0000 R
802
803
804                                          ; Base register addressing.  In 32 bit mode there is no distinction
805                                          ;         between this and index register addressing.  In 16 bit mode,
806                                          ;         base registers are BP and BX, index registers are SI and DI
807                                          ;         (other than the registers used, no real distinction exists).
808                                          ;
809                                          ; The location of the operand within the segment is the sum of the
810                                          ;         displacement and the value in the base or index register.
811                                          ;         The use of BP or EBP is a special case in that SS is assumed
812                                          ;         instead of DS.
813                                          ;         In the 80386 any 32 bit general register can be a base, and
814                                          ;         any 32 bit general register except ESP can be used as an index.
815                                          ;
816
817 00E4  8B 87 0004 R                       mov     AX,d2ta16 [BX]     ; Assumes DS as a segment reg.
EXAMPLES.ASM(583): error A2057: Illegal size for operand
818 00E8  26: 8B 87 0004 R                   mov     AX,ES:d2ta16 [BX]  ; Either can be overriden.
EXAMPLES.ASM(584): error A2057: Illegal size for operand
819                                          ;         indexed
820 00ED  8B 84 0004 R                       mov     AX,d2ta16 [SI]     ; Assumes DS as a segment reg.
EXAMPLES.ASM(586): error A2057: Illegal size for operand
821 00F1  26: 8B 85 0004 R                   mov     AX,ES:d2ta16 [DI]  ; Either can be overriden.
EXAMPLES.ASM(587): error A2057: Illegal size for operand
822
823                                          ; Based + indexed mode.
824
825 00F6  8B 81 0004 R                       mov     AX,d2ta16 [BX] [DI] ; Assumes DS.
EXAMPLES.ASM(591): error A2057: Illegal size for operand
826 00FA  26: 8B 80 0004 R                   mov     AX,ES:d2ta16 [BX] [SI] ; Either can be overriden.
```

```
EXAMPLES.ASM(592): error A2057: Illegal size for operand
    827
    828 00FF  67| 66| 8B 848A 0000              mov     EAX, d2ta32+[EDX] [ECX*4]
    829        0000 R
    830
    831
    832 0108                          Exit:
    833 0108  B0 00                           mov     AL,0          ; Set return code
    834 010A  B4 4C                           mov     AH,04ch       ; Set goodby
    835 010C  CD 21                           int     21h           ; Return to the system
    836                              ;
    837                              ; Define local and far procedures
    838                              ; Near first, this is the default
    839                              ;
    840 010E                          lclproc  PROC                  ; Could have added NEAR type
    841 010E  C3                              ret                   ; and return.
    842 010F                          lclproc  ENDP
    843                              ;
    844 010F                          farproc  PROC    FAR           ; Must use FAR to get type
    845 010F  CB                              ret
    846 0110                          farproc  ENDP
    847
    848 0110                          code     ENDS
    849                                       END     Begin
```

Macros:

Name	Lines
IDNDIF	12
IFBNB	10
IRPCMAC	3
IRPMAC	3
SAMP01	6

Structures and Records:

Name	Width Shift	# fields Width	Mask	Initial
CODE_IT	001A	0004		
BULK	000A	0010	03FFFC00	00000000
HIA	0006	0004	000003C0	00000000
MIDA	0003	0003	00000038	00000000
LO1	0000	0003	00000007	00000000
ENCODE	000A	0003		
HI	0006	0004	03C0	0000
MID	0003	0003	0038	0000
LO	0000	0003	0007	0000
MYSTRUCT	0006	0002		
MYWD0	0000			
MYWD1	0002			
RECD08	0007	0002		
FLDA3	0001	0006	007E	0000
FLDB3	0000	0001	0001	0001
RECD08A	0008	0002		
FLDA4	0003	0005	00F8	0000
FLDB4	0000	0003	0007	0007
RECD16	000E	0003		
FLDA	000B	0003	3800	0000
FLDB	0004	0007	07F0	0000
FLDC	0000	0004	000F	000F
RECD32	0012	0003		
FLDA1	0008	000A	0003FF00	00000000
FLDB1	0002	0006	000000FC	000000FC
FLDC1	0000	0002	00000003	00000000
RECD32A	0012	0004		
FLDA1A	0004	000E	0003FFF0	0003F3C0
FLDB1A	0002	0002	0000000C	00000000
FLDC1A	0000	0002	00000003	00000000

```
     FLDD1A . . . . . . . . . . . .    0000    0000    00000000      00000000
     RECDBT . . . . . . . . . . . .    0008    0003
        BIT7 . . . . . . . . . . . .   0007    0001    0080    0000
        BITS6T1 . . . . . . . . . .    0001    0006    007E    0000
        BIT00 . . . . . . . . . . .    0000    0001    0001    0000
     RECDBT16 . . . . . . . . . . .    0010    0003
        BIT15 . . . . . . . . . . .    000F    0001    8000    0000
        BITSMID . . . . . . . . . .    0001    000E    7FFE    0000
        BIT0A . . . . . . . . . . .    0000    0001    0001    0000
     RECDBT32 . . . . . . . . . . .    0020    0003
        BIT000 . . . . . . . . . . .   001F    0001    80000000 00000000
        BITSMIDA . . . . . . . . . .   0001    001E    7FFFFFFE 00000000
        BIT31 . . . . . . . . . . .    0000    0001    00000001      00000000
```

Segments and Groups:

	N a m e	Size	Length	Align	Combine	Class
CODE		16 Bit	0110	PARA	PUBLIC	'CODE'
DATA		16 Bit	0186	PARA	NONE	
DATA2		32 Bit	0048	PARA	NONE	
STACK		16 Bit	0800	PARA	STACK	'STACK'

Symbols:

	N a m e	Type	Value	Attr	
BEGIN		L NEAR	0000	CODE	
BIT00			0000		
BIT000			001F		
BIT0A			0000		
BIT15			000F		
BIT31			0000		
BIT7			0007		
BITS6T1			0001		
BITSMID			0001		
BITSMIDA			0001		
BULK			000A		
BYTELABEL		L BYTE	0007	DATA	
BYTE_PTR		TEXT	BYTE PTR		
CLEAR_REG		TEXT	XOR EAX,EAX		
COUNT0		NEAR	0097	CODE	
COUNT1		L NEAR	0097	CODE	
D2TA16		L WORD	0004	DATA2	
D2TA32		L DWORD	0000	DATA2	
D2TA8		L BYTE	0006	DATA2	
DATA16		L WORD	0004	DATA	
DATA32		L DWORD	0000	DATA	
DATA8		L BYTE	0006	DATA	
DPROMPT		L BYTE	00DD	DATA	
DUMMYDD		L DWORD	00FB	DATA	
DWORDTYPE		L DWORD	0007	DATA	
EQU16		NUMBER	FF00		
EQU16E		NUMBER	FF00		
EQU16S		NUMBER	6162		
EQU16S1		NUMBER	00616263		
EQU32		NUMBER	01000000		
EQU32E		NUMBER	FF000000		
EQU32S		NUMBER	61626364		
EQU32S1		NUMBER	62636465		
EQU64		NUMBER	0000		
EQU64E		NUMBER	0000		
EXIT		L NEAR	0108	CODE	
EXTFPROC		L NEAR	0000	External	
EXTNPROC		L FAR	0000	External	
FARPROC		F PROC	010F	CODE	Length = 0001
FIRST1		L BYTE	00FF	DATA	
FIRST2		L BYTE	0100	DATA	
FIRST3		L BYTE	0101	DATA	

```
FIRST4 . . . . . . . . . . . . .    L BYTE 0102    DATA
FIRST5 . . . . . . . . . . . . .    L BYTE 0103    DATA
FIRST6 . . . . . . . . . . . . .    L BYTE 0104    DATA
FIRST7 . . . . . . . . . . . . .    L BYTE 0105    DATA
FLDA . . . . . . . . . . . . . .           000B
FLDA1 . . . . . . . . . . . . .            0008
FLDA1A . . . . . . . . . . . . .           0004
FLDA3 . . . . . . . . . . . . .            0001
FLDA4 . . . . . . . . . . . . .            0003
FLDB . . . . . . . . . . . . . .           0004
FLDB1 . . . . . . . . . . . . .            0002
FLDB1A . . . . . . . . . . . . .           0002
FLDB3 . . . . . . . . . . . . .            0000
FLDB4 . . . . . . . . . . . . .            0000
FLDC . . . . . . . . . . . . . .           0000
FLDC1 . . . . . . . . . . . . .            0000
FLDC1A . . . . . . . . . . . . .           0000
FLDD1A . . . . . . . . . . . . .           0000

HI . . . . . . . . . . . . . . .           0006
HIA . . . . . . . . . . . . . . .          0006

IRPCMA . . . . . . . . . . . . .    L BYTE 0106    DATA
IRPCMB . . . . . . . . . . . . .    L BYTE 0107    DATA
IRPCMC . . . . . . . . . . . . .    L BYTE 0108    DATA
IRPCMD . . . . . . . . . . . . .    L BYTE 0109    DATA
IRPCME . . . . . . . . . . . . .    L BYTE 010A    DATA
IRPCMF . . . . . . . . . . . . .    L BYTE 010B    DATA

LCLPROC . . . . . . . . . . . .     N PROC 010E    CODE    Length = 0001
LO . . . . . . . . . . . . . . .           0000
LO1 . . . . . . . . . . . . . .            0000

MID . . . . . . . . . . . . . .            0003
MIDA . . . . . . . . . . . . . .           0003
PI . . . . . . . . . . . . . . .    TEXT  3.141592
PROMPT . . . . . . . . . . . . .    TEXT  'Enter number: '

USESTRUCT . . . . . . . . . . .     L FWORD 007A   DATA

WORD32S . . . . . . . . . . . . .   L DWORD 00CE   DATA
WORD32S1 . . . . . . . . . . . .    L DWORD 0023   DATA2
WORDTYPE . . . . . . . . . . . .    L WORD  0007    DATA

X . . . . . . . . . . . . . . .     NUMBER 0012

Y . . . . . . . . . . . . . . .     NUMBER 0000

@CPU . . . . . . . . . . . . . .    TEXT  3343
@FILENAME . . . . . . . . . . .     TEXT  EXAMPLES
@VERSION . . . . . . . . . . . .    TEXT  510


     614 Source  Lines
     917 Total   Lines
     108 Symbols

  46940 + 174623 Bytes symbol space free

       1 Warning Errors
      19 Severe  Errors
```

SCREEN OUTPUT OF PROGRAM

```
Microsoft (R) Macro Assembler Version 5.10
Copyright (C) Microsoft Corp 1981, 1988.  All rights reserved.

EXAMPLES.ASM(93): error A2050: Value out of range
EXAMPLES.ASM(124): error A2050: Value out of range
EXAMPLES.ASM(144): error A2050: Value out of range
EXAMPLES.ASM(147): error A2010: Syntax error
EXAMPLES.ASM(149): error A2010: Syntax error
EXAMPLES.ASM(161): error A2050: Value out of range
EXAMPLES.ASM(176): error A2010: Syntax error
EXAMPLES.ASM(179): error A2050: Value out of range
EXAMPLES.ASM(191): error A2050: Value out of range
'EXPECTED'          ; 'EXPECTED' is displayed
EXAMPLES.ASM(381): error A2050: Value out of range: FLDD1A
EXAMPLES.ASM(398): error A2010: Syntax error
EXAMPLES.ASM(409): error A2050: Value out of range
EXAMPLES.ASM(444): error A2009: Symbol not defined: LCLPROC
EXAMPLES.ASM(445): error A2009: Symbol not defined: FARPROC
EXAMPLES.ASM(537): warning A4031: Operand types must match
EXAMPLES.ASM(93): error A2050: Value out of range
EXAMPLES.ASM(124): error A2050: Value out of range
EXAMPLES.ASM(144): error A2050: Value out of range
EXAMPLES.ASM(147): error A2010: Syntax error
EXAMPLES.ASM(149): error A2010: Syntax error
EXAMPLES.ASM(161): error A2050: Value out of range
EXAMPLES.ASM(176): error A2010: Syntax error
EXAMPLES.ASM(179): error A2050: Value out of range
EXAMPLES.ASM(191): error A2050: Value out of range
EXAMPLES.ASM(255): error A2006: Phase error between passes
EXAMPLES.ASM(381): error A2050: Value out of range: FLDD1A
EXAMPLES.ASM(398): error A2010: Syntax error
EXAMPLES.ASM(409): error A2050: Value out of range
EXAMPLES.ASM(537): warning A4031: Operand types must match
EXAMPLES.ASM(583): error A2057: Illegal size for operand
EXAMPLES.ASM(584): error A2057: Illegal size for operand
EXAMPLES.ASM(586): error A2057: Illegal size for operand
EXAMPLES.ASM(587): error A2057: Illegal size for operand
EXAMPLES.ASM(591): error A2057: Illegal size for operand
EXAMPLES.ASM(592): error A2057: Illegal size for operand

  46940 + 174623 Bytes symbol space free

    1 Warning Errors
   19 Severe  Errors
```

Appendix H

80386 Architecture Overview

THE 80386 FEATURES MULTITASKING, ON-CHIP MEMORY MANAGEMENT, VIRTUAL MEMORY with paging, software protection, and large address space. Compatibility with earlier Intel chips (8086 through 80286) is preserved through the instruction set, register handling, and bus sizing. This appendix gives an overview of the 80386 architecture; for more complete information, see *80386: A Programming and Design Handbook*, from TAB BOOKS.

The 80386 is designed for applications needing high performance and is optimized for multitasking. The 32-bit registers support 32-bit addresses and data types. Instruction pipelining and on-chip address translation ensure execution at sustained rates of three to four million instructions per second.

The 80386 consists of six elements: an execution unit, a segment unit, a paging unit, an instruction decode unit, a code prefetch unit, and a bus interface unit (BIU). See Fig. H-1 for a graphic view of the six units of the 80386. The BIU unit provides the interface between the 80386 and its environment, accepting internal requests for code fetches (from the code prefetch unit) and data transfers (from the execution unit). The code prefetch unit implements the program look-ahead function of the 80386. When the BIU is not performing bus cycles to execute instructions, the code prefetch unit uses the BIU to fetch sequentially along the instruction byte stream. These prefetched instructions are stored in the 16-byte code queue to wait processing by the instruction decode unit.

The instruction decode unit takes instruction bytes from the prefetch queue and translates them into microcode. The decoded instructions are then stored in a three-deep instruction queue on a first-in-first-out basis to await processing by the execution unit. Immediate data and opcode offsets are taken from the prefetch queue.

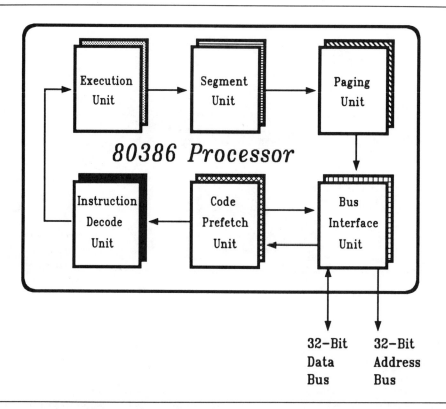

Fig. H-1. Six Basic Units of the 80386.

BASIC DEFINITIONS

• *Segment*—Beginning with the 8086, Intel introduced the concept of segments, which were defined as units of contiguous (adjacent) address space. In the 8086, this space has a maximum of 64k or 65536 bytes. In the 80386, that limitation no longer applies, and programmers can now view segments as one-dimensional subspaces, each with some specified length up to four gigabytes.

• *Gates*—A gate is a logic design that allows only certain processes to pass through it. The 80386 provides protection for control transfers among executable segments at differing privilege levels by use of gate descriptors. There are four gates: call gates, trap gates, interrupt gates, and task gates.

• *Descriptor*—A descriptor is a specific data structure used to define the characteristics of a program element. For example, descriptors describe a data record, a segment, or a task.

- *Table*—A table is a collection or ordering of data laid out in rows and columns for reference or stored as an array. Elements of a table can be obtained by direct calculation from a known selector or base address.

- *Linear Address Space*—An address indicates the location of a register, a particular place in storage, or some other data source or destination. In the 80386, the linear address space of the memory runs from byte 0 to four gigabytes. A linear address points to a particular byte within this space. See Fig. H-2.

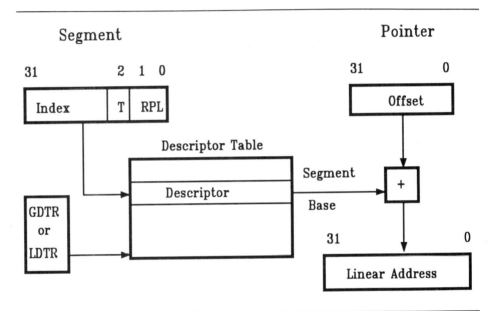

Fig. H-2. Linear Address Translation.

- *Logical Address*—First, there is no conceptual parallel from linear address space to the space used by logical addressing. A logical address consists of a selector and offset. The selector points to some segment descriptor (part of which is the linear base address of that segment). The offset tells how far into the segment the required byte is (see Fig. H-3).

- *Physical Address*—The address that actually selects the memory where a required byte is located. In the 80386, linear and physical addresses differ only when paging is in effect (see Fig. H-12).

- *Task*—A task is a basic, unique function of a program or system. It can be one instance of the execution of a program. Tasks are also referred to as processes.

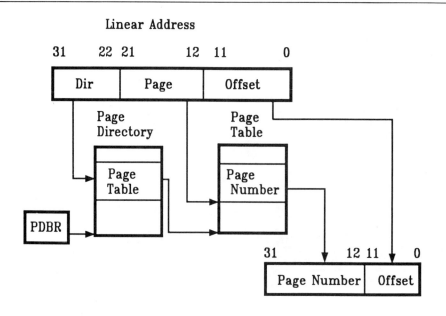

Fig. H-3. Physical Address Translation.

• *Task State Segment (TSS)*—A TSS is a data structure delineated and pointed to by a descriptor, wherein the (interrupted) state of a task is stored. Systems software creates the TSSs and places the initial information, such as correct stack pointers for interrupt handlers, in the TSSs.

• *Microcode*—A list of small program steps; also a set of control functions performed by the instruction decoding and executing logic of a computer system. It is code that is below the level of assembly language.

• *Paging*—Paging refers to a procedure that transmits the consecutive bytes called a page between locations, such as between disk storage and memory. A paging function simplifies the operating system swapping algorithms because it provides a uniform mechanism for managing the physical structure of memory.

• *Flag*—A flag is an indicator whose state is used to inform a later section of a program that a condition has occurred. The condition is identified with the flag and designated by the state of the flag; that is, the flag is either set or not set.

80386 DATA HANDLING

Memory is viewed from the 80386 processor as if it were a sequential array of bytes. Think of it as beginning from your left hand, moving to your right, and continuing to the right for as many bytes as are built into your system. However, the bits within the bytes are counted (or positioned) from right to left, as shown in Fig. H-4. The byte address

Memory is viewed from the processor as if it were a sequential array of bytes.

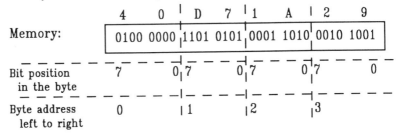

Example 1: Move a memory byte "40" to a byte register, AL, the low order byte of AX. The 80386 moves memory byte 0, the "40".

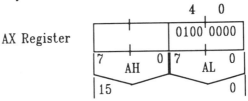

Example 2: Move a word to a word register AX. When memory word "40 D7" is moved to AX, the 80386 moves "40" to AL (low order byte of AX). Then the "D7" is moved to AH (high order byte of AX). Memory byte 0 is moved first ("40"). Memory byte 1 is moved second ("D7").

Note: See how memory shows as "40 D7" and the register shows "D7 40".

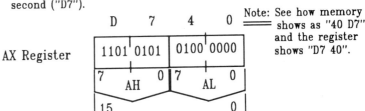

Example 3: Move a double word (dword) to the EAX register. Again, memory moves one byte at a time, going from AL to AH and then to the byte 3 and 4 of EAX.

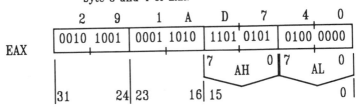

Fig. H-4. Storage Examples of Memory and Registers.

starts at the left with zero and moves to the right. In the example, the byte for 40 is stored in memory storage location zero (0). However, the least significant bit (LSB) is on the right, and the most significant bit (MSB) is on the left.

The 80386 moves data from memory a byte at a time into the specified registers. The registers begin their counting from the right. So, the 80386 stores it from the first byte in the right-hand slot (the AL byte register in the example). The second byte goes in the second slot (the AH register in the example). Therefore, if you look at a dump of a location in memory, it probably will not look like a dump of a register that holds the same data.

REAL- AND PROTECTED-MODE ARCHITECTURE

The 80386 has two modes of operation: real-address mode (called real mode) and protected mode. *Real mode* is required primarily to set up the processor for the protected mode operation and to allow execution of previous chip generation software. *Protected mode* provides access to the advanced paging, memory management, and privilege capabilities of the 80386. These design features allow the object-code compatibility with previous Intel chip generations.

Real Mode

When the processor is reset or powered up, it initializes in real mode. In this mode, the 80386 operates as a very fast 8086, but with 32-bit extensions if the programmer desires. Real mode has the same base architecture as the 8086, but it also allows access to the 32-bit register set of the 80386. The 8086 addressing mechanism, memory size, and interrupt handling (and their consequent limitations) are all identical to the real mode on the 80386.

Like protected mode, real mode uses two components to form the logical address. A 16-bit selector is used to determine the linear base address of a segment. The base address is then used as the 32-bit physical address. The difference between the two modes lies in how the base address is calculated.

Relocatability is a property of programs or data such that they can be located in different places in memory at different times without requiring modification to system or application software. Segment relocation is done in the 80386 real mode as it is in the 8086. The 16-bit value in a segment selector is shifted left by four bits (multiplied by 16) to form the 20-bit base address of a segment. The effective address is extended with four high-order zeros (to give a 20-bit value) and added to the base to form a linear address. This linear address is equivalent to the physical address because paging is not used in the real-address mode.

Interrupts and exceptions are breaks in the normal flow of a system or routine. Interrupts and exceptions in 80386 real-address mode work exactly as they do on the 8086. In real mode, the interrupt descriptor table (IDT) is an 8086 real interrupt vector table, starting at real zero and extending through real 1024 (four bytes per interrupt with 256 possible entries).

The only way to leave the real-address mode is to explicitly switch to protected mode. The 80386 enters the protected mode when a MOV to CR0 (move to control register zero) instruction sets the protection enable (PE) bit in CR0. For compatibility with the 80286, the LMSW (load machine status word) instruction can also be used to set the PE bit.

The processor reenters the real-address mode if software clears the PE bit in CR0 with a MOV to CR0 instruction.

Protected Mode

The complete capabilities of the 80386 are available when it operates in protected mode. Software can perform a task switch to enter tasks designated as virtual 8086 mode tasks. Each such task behaves with 8086 semantics (the relationship between symbols and their intended meanings independent of their interpretation devices). This allows 8086 software—an application program or an entire operating system—to execute on the 80386. At the same time, the virtual 8086 tasks are isolated and protected from one another and from the host 80386 operating system.

In protected mode, the 16-bit selector is used to specify an index into an operating system-defined table that contains the 32-bit base address of a given segment. The physical address is formed by adding the base address obtained from the table to the offset.

In general, programs designed for the 80286 will execute without modification on the 80386. Also, the 80386 supports the descriptors used by the 80286 as long as the Intel-reserved word (the last word) of the 80286 descriptor is zero.

REGISTERS

The 80386 registers are a superset of the previous 8086, 80186, and 80286 registers. All the previous generation 8- and 16-bit registers are contained within the 32-bit architecture. The register set available to programmers consists of eight 32-bit general purpose registers (EAX, EBX, ECX, EDX, ESP, EBP, ESI, and EDI), 32-bit status registers (EIP and EFLAGS), 16-bit segment pointer registers (ES, CS, SS, DS, FS, and GS), 32-bit test registers (TR6 and TR7) and the 32-bit debug registers (DR0, DR1, DR2, DR3, DR6, and DR7; DR4 and DR5 are Intel reserved).

General Registers

The eight general-purpose registers are 32 bits long and hold addresses or data. They support data operands of 1, 8, 16, 32 and 64 bits (which require two registers) and bit fields of 1 to 32 bits, in addition to address operands of 16 and 32 bits. The 32-bit registers are named EAX, EBX, ECX, EDX, ESI, EDI, EBP, and ESP.

The least significant 16 bits of the registers are separately accessible. This is done by using the 16-bit names of the registers: AX, BX, CX, DX, SI, DI, BP, and SP. The 8-bit operations can individually access the low byte (bits 0–7) and the high byte (bits 8–15) of the general registers AX, BX, CX, and DX. The low bytes are named AL, BL, CL, and DL, respectively, and the high bytes are named AH, BH, CH, and DH.

Again, this selection is done by using the register names. If one of the 8-bit registers is accessed, the contents of the remaining 24 bits are undisturbed.

Segment Registers

The 80386 architecture includes six directly accessible segment selector registers, which contain values that point to the segments. These selector values can be loaded as a program executes and are task specific, which means that the segment registers are automatically reloaded upon a task switch operation. Six 16-bit segment registers hold the segment selector values that identify the currently addressable memory segments. The registers are:

- Code Segment (CS)—The CS points to the segment that contains the currently executing sequence of instructions. The 80386 fetches all instructions from this segment, using as an offset the contents of the instruction pointer. CS is changed as the result of inter-segment control-transfer instructions, interrupts, and exceptions. The CS cannot be explicitly loaded. See the programs in this book. Values are loaded into a general register and then the contents of that register can be MOVed to CS.

- Stack Segment (SS)—Subroutine calls, parameters, and procedure-activation records usually require a region of memory that is allocated for a stack. All stack operations use SS to locate that stack. Unlike the CS register, the SS register can be loaded explicitly by program instructions.

- Data Segment Registers (DS, ES, FS, and GS)—The next four registers are data segment registers, each of which is addressable by the currently executing program. Having access to four separate data areas aids program efficiency by allowing them to access different types of data structures. These four registers can be changed under program control.

To use the data segment registers, the 80386 associates a base address with each segment selected. To address a data unit within a segment, a 32-bit offset is added to the segment base address. Once a segment is selected, by loading the segment selector into a segment register, a data manipulation instruction needs only to specify the offset.

Segmented Memory-Management Registers

These registers are also known as system-address registers. Four registers locate the data structures that control segmented memory management. These registers are defined to reference the tables or segments supported by the 80286/80386 protection model.

The addresses of these tables and segments are stored in special system-address and system-segment registers.

- Global Descriptor Table Register (GDTR)—The GDTR holds the 32-bit linear base address and the 16-bit limit of the global descriptor table.

- Local Descriptor Table Register (LDTR)—This register holds the 16-bit selector for the local descriptor table. Because the LDT is a task-specific segment, it is defined by selector values stored in the system segment registers.

- Interrupt Descriptor Table Register (IDTR)—The IDTR points to a table of entry points for interrupt handlers (the IDT). The register holds the 32-bit linear base address and the 16-bit limit of the interrupt descriptor table.

- Task Register (TR)—This register points to the information needed by the processor to define the current task. The register holds the 16-bit selector for the task state segment descriptor. Because the TSS segment is task-specific, it is defined by selector values stored in the system segment registers. Figure H-14 shows how TR assists in linking TSSs.

Processor-Control Registers

Two registers control the operation of the 80386 processor: EFLAGS (the processor status and control flags register) and EIP (the instruction-pointer register).

EFLAGS System Flags Register. The EFLAGS register controls I/O, maskable interrupts, debugging, task switching, and enabling of virtual 8086 execution in a protected, multitasking environment. All this is in addition to providing status flags that represent the result of instruction execution. The low 16 bits (0–15) of EFLAGS contain the 80286 16-bit status or flag register named FLAGS, which is most useful when executing 8086 and 80286 code. See Fig. H-5.

- Virtual 8086 Mode (VM) Bit 17—VM bit provides virtual 8086 mode within the protected mode. If it is set while the processor is in protected mode, the 80386 switches to virtual 8086 operation. The VM flag can be set only two ways: in protected mode by the IRET instruction and only if current privilege level is zero; and by task switches at any privilege level.

- Resume Flag (RF) Bit 16—This flag temporarily disables debug exceptions (breaks to normal program flow) so that an instruction can be restarted after a debug exception without immediately causing another debug exception.

- Nested Task (NT) Bit 14—The 80386 uses this flag to control chaining of interrupted and CALLed tasks. A CALL transfers the program execution sequence on a temporary basis to a subroutine or subprogram. On termination of that subroutine, execution is resumed at the instruction following the CALL. NT influences the operation of the IRET instruction.

- Input/Output Privilege Level (IOPL) Bits 13-12—This two-bit field applies to protected mode. IOPL shows the highest current privilege level (CPL) value permitted to execute I/O instructions without generating an exception-13 fault or consulting the I/O permission bitmap. It also shows the highest CPL value

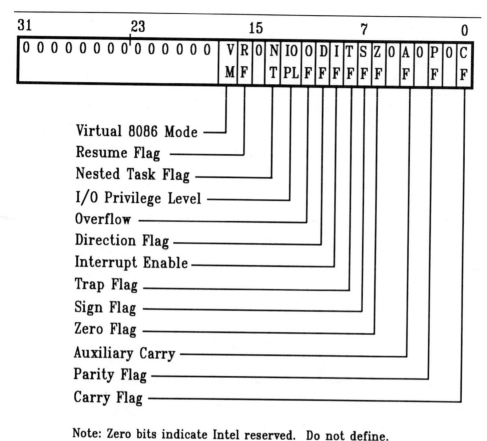

Note: Zero bits indicate Intel reserved. Do not define.

Fig. H-5. EFLAGS Register.

that allows change of the IF (INTR enable flag) bit when new values are POPped into the EFLAGS register.

• Overflow Flag (OF) Bit 11—OF is set if the operation resulted in carry/borrow into the sign bit (high-order bit) of the result but did not result in a carry/borrow out of the high-order bit, or vice versa.

• Direction Flag (DF) Bit 10—DF defines whether the ESI and/or EDI registers are to decrement or increment during string operations. If DF = 0, the registers increment. If DF = 1, they decrement.

• Interrupt-Enable (IF) Bit 9—Setting IF allows the CPU to recognize external (maskable) interrupt requests. Clearing this bit disables these interrupts. IF has no effect on either nonmaskable external interrupts or exceptions.

• Trap Flag (TF) Bit 8—Setting TF puts the processor into single-step mode for debugging. The CPU automatically generates an exception 1 after each instruction, which allows a program to be inspected as it executes each instruction. When TF is reset, exception 1 traps occur only as a function of the breakpoint addresses loaded into debug registers DR0–DR3. Further information is given in discussion of the debug registers.

• Sign Flag (SF) Bit 7—SF is set if the high-order bit of the result is set. It is reset otherwise. For 8-, 16-, and 32-bit operations, SF reflects the state of bit 7, 15, and 31, respectively.

• Zero Flag (ZF) Bit 6—ZF is set if all bits of the result are 0. Otherwise, it is reset.

• Auxiliary Carry Flag (AF) Bit 4—This flag is used to simplify the addition and subtraction of packed BCD quantities. Regardless of the operand length (8, 16, or 32 bits), AF is set if the operation resulted in a borrow into bit 3 (which is a subtraction) or a carry out of bit 3 (which is an addition). Otherwise, AF is reset. Remember that BCD uses bits 0 through 3 to represent decimal digits.

• Parity Flag (PF) Bit 2—PF is set if the low-order eight bits of the operation contains an even number of 1s (even parity). PF is reset if the low-order eight bits have odd parity. PF is a function of only the low-order bits, regardless of operand size.

• Carry Flag (CF) Bit 0—CF is set if the operation resulted in a carry out of the high-order bit (an addition), or a borrow into the high-order bit (a subtraction). Otherwise, CF is reset. For 8-, 16-, or 32-bit operations, CF is set according to the carry/borrow at bit 7, 15, or 31 respectively.

EIP Instruction Pointer Register. The extended instruction pointer (EIP) is a 32-bit register. EIP contains the offset address of the next sequential instruction to be executed. This offset is relative to the start (or base address) of the current code segment. The EIP is not directly visible to programmers, but is controlled explicitly by control-transfer instructions, interrupts, and exceptions.

The low-order 16 bits of EIP are named IP and can be used by the processor as a unit. This feature is useful when executing instructions designed for the 8086 and 80286 processors, which only have an IP.

Control Registers

The 80386 has three 32-bit control registers (CR0, CR2, and CR3; CR1 is reserved by Intel) to hold machine states or global statuses. A global status is one that can be accessed by (or that controls) any of the logical units of the system. Along with the system address registers, these registers hold machine state information that affects all tasks in the system. Load and store instructions have been defined to access the control registers.

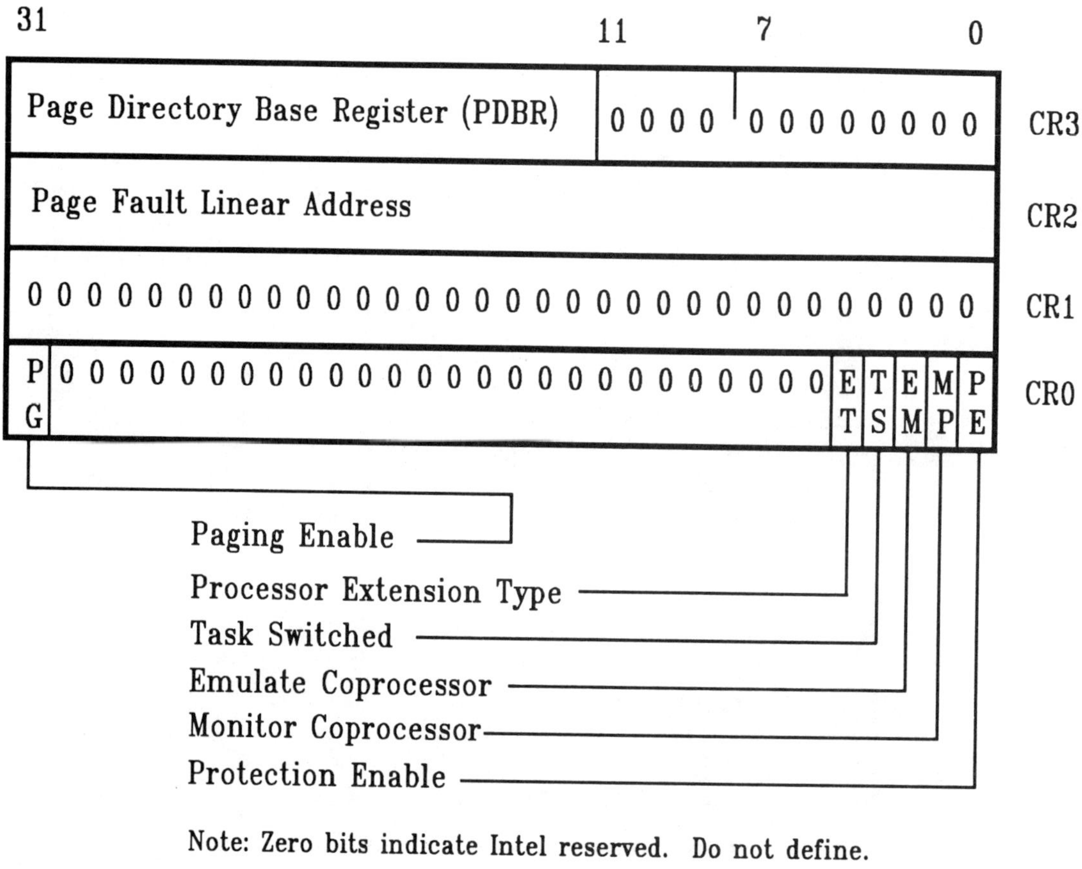

```
 31                                    11      7            0
┌─────────────────────────────────────┬────┬──────────────┐
│ Page Directory Base Register (PDBR)  │0000│0 0 0 0 0 0 0 0│ CR3
├─────────────────────────────────────┴────┴──────────────┤
│ Page Fault Linear Address                                │ CR2
├──────────────────────────────────────────────────────────┤
│0 0 0 0 0 0 0 0 0 0 0 0 0 0 0 0 0 0 0 0 0 0 0 0 0 0 0 0 0 0│ CR1
├─┬──────────────────────────────────────────┬──┬──┬──┬──┬──┤
│P│0 0 0 0 0 0 0 0 0 0 0 0 0 0 0 0 0 0 0 0 0 0│ET│TS│EM│MP│PE│ CR0
│G│                                          │  │  │  │  │  │
└─┴──────────────────────────────────────────┴──┴──┴──┴──┴──┘
```

Paging Enable ──────────┘

Processor Extension Type ───────────────┘

Task Switched ───────────────────────┘

Emulate Coprocessor ──────────────────┘

Monitor Coprocessor ──────────────────┘

Protection Enable ────────────────────┘

Note: Zero bits indicate Intel reserved. Do not define.

Fig. H-6. Control Register Formats.

Control registers are accessible to systems programmers only via variants of the MOV instruction, which allows them to be loaded from or stored in general registers. See Fig. H-6.

CR0. CR0 contains flags that control or indicate conditions that apply to the system as a whole, not to an individual task. The low-order 15 bits of this register is the machine status word (MSW), bits 0–15, for compatibility with 80286 protected mode. CR0 contains bits that enable and disable paging and protection, and bits that control the operation of the floating-point coprocessor. Bits 30 through 5 are reserved and must be loaded with zeros. The PE bit (bit 0) and the PG bit (bit 31) control the operation of the segmentation and paging mechanisms. See Fig. H-7.

- Paging (PG) Bit 31—PG indicates whether the 80386 uses page tables to translate linear addresses into physical addresses. If PG = 1, paging is enabled. If PG = 0, paging is disabled and the linear addresses produced by the segmentation mechanism are passed through as physical addresses.

- Extension Type (ET) Bit 4—ET indicates the type of coprocessor present in the system, either a 80287 or 80387.

- Task Switched (TS) Bit 3—The processor sets TS with every task switch. It also tests TS when it interprets coprocessor instructions because the only time the coprocessor status needs to be saved is when a new task requires the coprocessor. Loading into the CR0 register can reset TS. Also, the CLTS instruction specifically resets the TS.

- Emulation (EM) Bit 2—EM indicates whether coprocessor functions are to be emulated. Emulation is designed to imitate one system or process with another so that the imitating system accepts the same data, executes the same programs, and achieves the same results as the imitated system or function. Setting EM often occurs when there is no coprocessor present.

- Math Present (MP) Bit 1—MP controls the function of the WAIT instruction, which is used to coordinate a coprocessor.

- Protection Enable (PE) Bit 0—If PE = 1, the 80386 operates with segmentation mechanism enabled. When PE = 1, the 80386 is said to be operating in protected mode. If PE = 0, segmentation is turned off, and the processor operates in real mode as an 8086.

PG	PE	Execution Mode
0	0	Real mode
0	1	Protected mode, paging disabled
1	0	Illegal combination, do not use
1	1	Protected mode, paging enabled

Fig. H-7. Processor Modes with PG and PE.

CR1. CR1 is reserved for future Intel processors.

CR2. CR2 is used for handling page faults when the PG bit in CR0 is set. The 80386 stores in CR2 the linear address that triggers the fault. The error code pushed onto the page fault handler stack when it is invoked provides additional status information on this page fault.

CR3. CR3 is used when PG (paging) is set in CR0. CR3 enables the processor to locate the page table directory for the current task. This register contains the physical base address of the page directory table. The 80386 page directory table is always page aligned (four kbyte aligned). The lowest 12 bits of CR3 are ignored when written, and they store as undefined. A task switch through a TSS that changes the value in CR3 (or as an explicit load to CR3) invalidates all cached page table entries in the paging unit cache. Note that if the value in CR3 does not change during the task switch, the cached page table entries are not flushed.

Debug Registers

A breakpoint allows you to set a specific condition at a particular linear address that causes program execution to jump into the exception handler. The 80386 supports four simultaneous breakpoint conditions, which allows you to set up to four locations in a program for which the 80386 will jump to the exception handler. To support the four breakpoints, additional registers are added to the 80386. These registers can only be read or written at privilege level 0; any attempted access at other levels raises an invalid opcode exception.

These six programmer-accessible debug registers (DR0–DR3 and DR6–DR7) bring advanced debugging abilities to the 80386, including data breakpoints and the ability to set instruction breakpoints without modifying code segments. Debug registers DR0–DR3 specify the four linear breakpoints. DR4 and DR5 are reserved by Intel for future development. DR6 displays the current state of the breakpoints. DR7 is used to set the breakpoints. See Fig. H-8.

Debug Register DR6.

- BT Bit 15—The BT bit indicates that the cause for the debug exception was a task switch into a task where the debug trap bit in the TSS is enabled.

- BS Bit 14—The BS bit is set if a single-step exception occurs. The single-step condition is enabled by the TF bit in the EFLAGS register. The BS bit is set only if a single-step trap actually occurs, not if a single-step condition (enabled or not) was detected.

- BD Bit 13—The BD bit is set at an instruction boundary if the next instruction reads or writes to one of the eight debug registers (debug register protection). BD is set whenever a read or write to the debug registers is about to occur. The condition does not need to be enabled by the GD bit of DR7.

- B0, B1, B2, and B3, Bits 3 to 0—Bits B0–B3 indicate that the breakpoint condition specified by the corresponding breakpoint linear address register was detected.

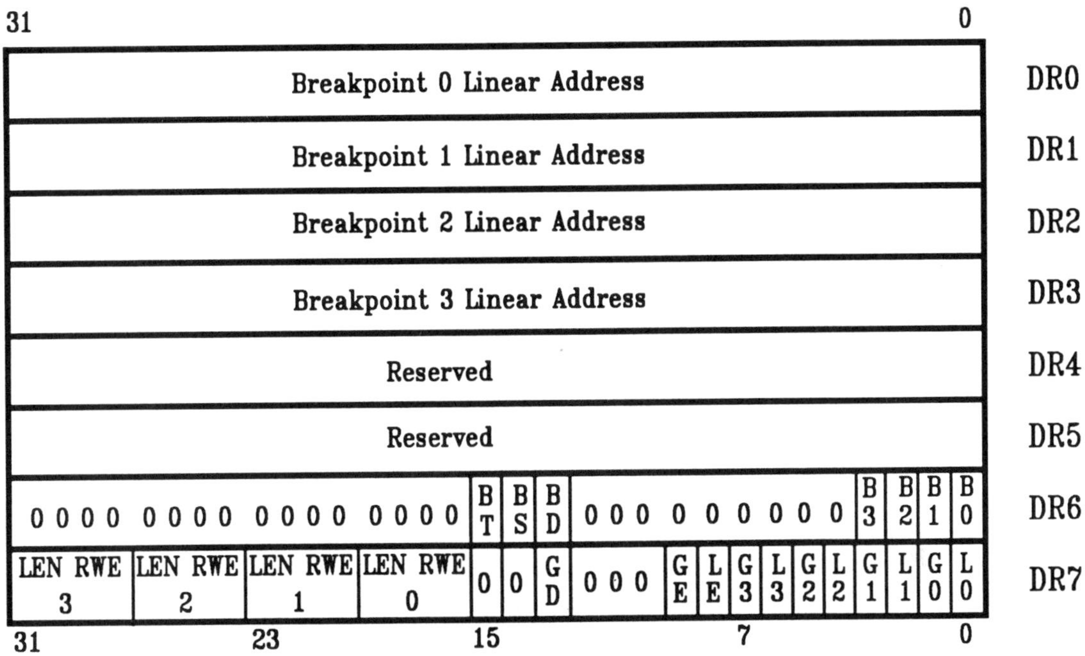

31		0	
Breakpoint 0 Linear Address			DR0
Breakpoint 1 Linear Address			DR1
Breakpoint 2 Linear Address			DR2
Breakpoint 3 Linear Address			DR3
Reserved			DR4
Reserved			DR5

DR6: `0 0 0 0  0 0 0 0  0 0 0 0  0 0 0 0  BT BS BD  0 0 0  0 0 0 0 0  B3 B2 B1 B0`

DR7: `LEN RWE 3 | LEN RWE 2 | LEN RWE 1 | LEN RWE 0 | 0 0 | GD | 0 0 0 | GE LE | G3 L3 | G2 L2 | G1 L1 | G0 L0`

```
31          23          15              7              0
```

Fig. H-8. Debug Register Formats.

Debug Register DR7.

- LEN—The four two-bit LEN fields indicate the length of the breakpoint for each of the four breakpoint registers. The encoding is:

  00 - One-byte length
  01 - Two-byte length
  10 - Reserved
  11 - Four-byte length

- RWE—The four two-bit RWE fields indicate the type of access that causes a breakpoint exception to be raised. The encoding is:

  00 - Instruction execution only
  01 - Data writes only
  10 - Reserved
  11 - Data reads or writes

- GD Bit 13—The GD bit enables the debug register protection condition that is flagged by BD of DR6. GD is cleared at entry to the debug exception handler by the processor which allows the handler free access to the debug registers.

- GE/LE—GE/LE bits indicate the exact data breakpoints (global and local, respectively). If GE or LE is set, the 80386 slows execution such that data breakpoints are reported on exactly the instruction that causes them. If these bits are not set, the 80386 may get slightly ahead of the reporting of the breakpoint conditions on instructions that perform data writes near the end of their execution.

- L0–L3/G0–G3 Bits 7 through 0—The L0 through L3 and G0 through G3 bits are the local and global enable signals for the four debug breakpoint registers. If either the local or global enable is set, the breakpoint specified by the corresponding breakpoint register DRn is enabled.

Test Registers

Two test registers are used to control the testing of the RAM/CAM (content addressable memories) in the translation lookaside buffer (TLB), the cache used for storing information from page tables. TR6 is the command test register, and TR7 is the data register, that contains the data of the TLB test. (TR0 through TR5 do not exist.) These registers are accessed by variants of the MOV instruction, which is defined in both real-address mode and protected mode. In the protected mode, the MOV instruction that accesses them can be executed only at privilege level 0. Any attempt to read from or write to either of the test registers when executing in any other privilege level causes a general protection exception. See Fig. H-9.

- C Bit 0—TR6 contains a command and an address tag. To cause an immediate TLB lookup, move a doubleword into TR6 that contains a 1 in this bit. To cause an immediate write to the TLB, move a doubleword that has a 0 in this bit.

- Linear Address Bits 12–31—On a TLB write, a TLB entry is allocated to this linear address. The rest of the TLB entry is set depending on the value of TR7 and the value just written into TR6. On a TLB lookup, the TLB is interrogated per this value. If one and only one TLB entry matches, the rest of the fields of TR6 and TR7 are set from the matching TLB entry.

- V Bit 11—V bit is the valid bit. The TLB uses it to identify entries that contain valid data. Valid means a successful translation has been made. Entries in the TLB that have not been assigned values have zero in the valid bit. All valid bits can be cleared by writing to control register 3 (CR3).

- D, D# Bits 10 and 9—Bit 10 is the dirty bit (the entry has been changed), and bit 9 is its complement for/from the TLB entry.

- U, U# Bits 8 and 7—Bit 8 is the U/S (user accessible) bit, and bit 7 is its complement for/from the TLB entry.

- W, W# Bits 6 and 5—Bit 6 is the R/W (writeable) bit, and bit 5 is its complement for/from the TLB entry.

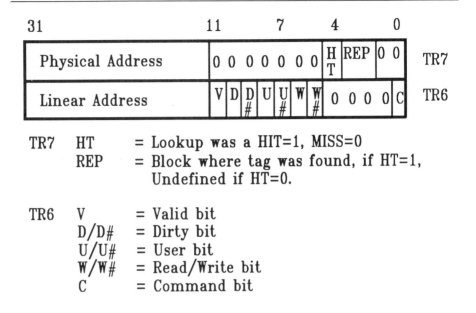

Fig. H-9. Test Registers TR6 and TR7.

• Physical Address Bits 31–12—This is the data field of the TLB. On a write to TLB, the TLB entry allocated to the linear address in TR6 is set to this value. On a TLB lookup, if HT is set, the data field (physical address) from the TLB is read out to this field. If HT bit is not set, this field is undefined.

• HT Bit 4—For a TLB write, HT must be set to 1. For a TLB lookup, the HT bit indicates whether the lookup was a hit (HT = 1) or a miss (HT = 0).

• REP Bit 3 and 2—For a TLB write, one of four associative blocks of the TLB is to be written. These bits indicate which. For a TLB read, if HT is set, REP shows in which of the four associative blocks the tag was found. If HT is not set on a TLB read, REP is undefined.

Translation Lookaside Buffer (TLB)

The translation lookaside buffer (TLB) is a cache used for translating linear addresses to physical addresses.

Warning: the TLB testing mechanism is unique to the 80386 and may be continued in the same way in future processors. Software that uses this mechanism as it currently is may be incompatible with future processors.

The TLB is a four-way, set-associative memory. A set is a collection of elements that have some feature in common or which bear a certain relation to one another. In the TLB, there are:

- Content-Addressable Memory (CAM). CAM holds 32 linear addresses and associated tag bits, which are used for data protection and cache implementation.

- Random Access Memory (RAM). RAM holds the upper 20 bits of the 32 physical addresses that correspond to the linear addresses in the CAM.

- Logic implements the four-way cache and includes a two-bit replacement pointer that decides which of the four sets into which a new entry is directed during a write to the TLB.

Addresses and commands are written to the TLB through the command register, while data is read from or written to the TLB through the data register. Test register six (TR6) is the command register for TLB accesses, and test register seven (TR7) is used as the data register.

SEGMENTATION

Segmentation organizes virtual memory as a collection of variable-sized units, called segments. The 80386 supports a wide range of segmentation strategies; each uses a two-part virtual address: a segment part and an offset part. Segments form the basis of the virtual-to-linear address translation mechanism. Each segment is defined by three parameters, two of which relate virtual addresses given by offsets within the segment to linear addresses. Those three parameters are:

- Base Address—This is the starting address of the segment in the linear address space. The base address is the linear address corresponding to the virtual address at offset 0 within the segment.

- Limit—This is the largest offset that can be used with the segment in a virtual address and defines the size of the segment.

- Attributes—These indicate segment characteristics such as whether the segment can be read from, written to, or executed as a program, the privilege level of the segment, and so on.

Address space comes as one or more segments, any size from one byte to four gigabytes (four billion bytes). Each segment can be protected individually by privilege levels, and selectively shared between tasks.

Segment-Descriptor Tables

The global descriptor table (GDT) and the local descriptor table (LDT) are special segments that contain the segment descriptor tables. The hardware maintains the descriptor tables and references them by memory-management mechanism. These segments should be stored in protected memory accessible only by operating system software, to prevent application software from modifying the address translation information.

The virtual address space divides into two equal halves, one half mapped by the GDT and the other half by the LDT. The total virtual address space consists of 2^{14} segments. A segment descriptor is located by indicating a descriptor table (either the GDT or the LDT) along with a descriptor number within the indicated table. See Fig. H-10 for descriptor formats.

- BASE—BASE defines the location of the segment within the four gigabyte linear address space. The 80386 concatenates the three fragments of the base address to form a single 32-bit value.

- LIMIT—This field defines the size of the segment. The 80386 links the two parts of the LIMIT field, to form a 20-bit result. The processor then interprets the LIMIT field in one of two ways, depending on the setting of the granularity bit.

  ○ In units of one byte, to define a LIMIT of up to one megabyte.
  ○ In units of four kilobytes (one page), to define a LIMIT of up to four gigabytes. The LIMIT is shifted left by 12 bits when loaded, and low-order one-bits are inserted.

- Granularity Bit (G)—This bit specifies the units with which the LIMIT field is interpreted. When G = 0, LIMIT is interpreted as units of one byte. If G = 1, LIMIT is interpreted in units of four kilobytes. The G bit only affects the granularity of the segment LIMIT; the segment BASE is always byte granular.

- Default (D)—The D bit gives a default for segments that are executable or expand down, or that are addressed by the SS register.

  ○ Segments addressed by the SS register use the D bit to determine if they should use the 32-bit ESP register (if D =1) for implicit stack references such as PUSH and POP, or to use the 16-bit SP register (D = 0) for 80286 compatibility.
  ○ Executable segments use the D bit to set the default size for addresses and operands referenced by the instructions in the segment. If D = 1, the default is 32-bit addresses and 32-bit or 8-bit operands, the normal setting for 80386 programs. If D = 0, the default is 16-bit addresses and 16-bit or 8-bit operands, for compatibility with the 80386.
  ○ Expand-down segments use D to determine the upper segment bound. If D = 1, it's a 4G upper limit. If D = 0, it's a 64k upper limit for compatibility with the 80286.

Data Segment Descriptor

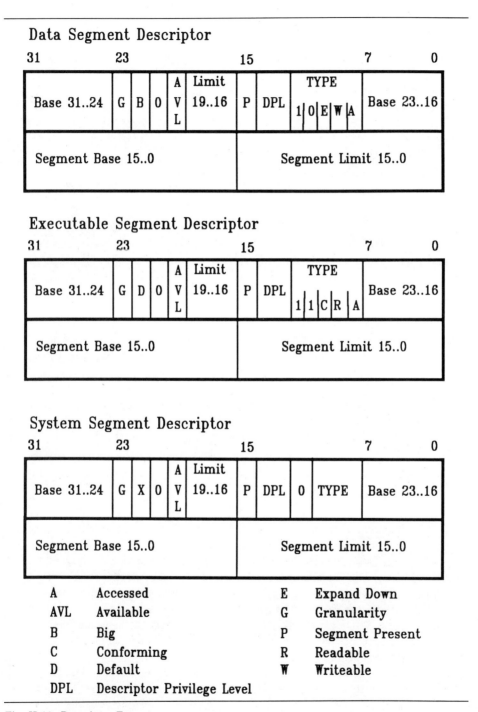

31				23			15			7			0

Executable Segment Descriptor

System Segment Descriptor

A	Accessed	E	Expand Down
AVL	Available	G	Granularity
B	Big	P	Segment Present
C	Conforming	R	Readable
D	Default	W	Writeable
DPL	Descriptor Privilege Level		

Fig. H-10. Descriptor Format.

This bit should always be 1 for 80386 software. 80286 software should have this bit set to 0.

• AVL—AVL is the available-to-software bit. The 80386 does not interpret this bit. Intel states that all future processors compatible with the 80386 also will not define a use for this bit.

• P Bit—The segment present bit determines if the descriptor is valid for address translation, P = 1. If P = 0, the descriptor is not valid and use of it causes an exception.

• DPL (Descriptor Privilege Level)—DPL is used by the protection mechanism.

• Bit 12—This bit distinguishes memory segments (= 1) from the system segments and gates (= 0).

• TYPE—This four-bit field differentiates between various kinds of descriptors. Code and data descriptors split TYPE into a three-bit TYPE and one-bit of accessed flag. System segments use the following set of values in TYPE:

0 = Invalid	8 = Invalid
1 = Available 286 TSS	9 = Available 386 TSS
2 = LDT	A = Intel reserved
3 = Busy 286 TSS	B = Busy 386 TSS
4 = 286 Call gate	C = 386 Call gate
5 = Task gate (286 or 386)	D = Intel reserved
6 = 286 Interrupt gate	E = 386 Interrupt gate
7 = 286 Trap gate	F = 386 Trap gate

• Accessed Bit (A)—The 80386 sets this bit when the segment is accessed in data and code descriptors. Operating systems that implement virtual memory at the segment level may monitor the frequency of segment usage by periodically testing and clearing this bit.

Segment Selectors

Segment selectors identify a segment and can be thought of as the name of the segment. A selector is a 16-bit pointer that, when loaded into a register or used with certain instructions, selects certain descriptors. That is, a selector names a segment by locating the descriptor for the segment. In a logical address, the selector portion identifies an individual descriptor by first specifying the descriptor table and then indexing to the descriptor within that table. See Fig. H-11 for selector format.

In a general selector, the fields are:

• Index—Selects one of up to 8192 descriptors in a descriptor table. The 80386 multiplies this index value by eight (the length of a descriptor) and then adds

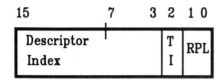

RPL = Requestor Privilege Level

TI = Identifies the Descriptor Table which
       contains the descriptor of the segment
       TI = 0, Descriptor is in the GDT

       TI = 1, Descriptor is in the LDT

Descriptor Index = The index within the GDT or
       LDT where the segment descriptor is

Fig. H-11. Selector Format.

the result to the base address of the descriptor table. This accesses the correct entry in the table.

• Table Indicator (TI)—This bit specifies the descriptor table to which the selector refers: a zero points to the GDT (global descriptor table) and a one indicates the current LDT (local descriptor table).

• Requested Privilege Level (RPL)—Used by the system protection mechanism. See chapter 7 for more on protection and privilege.

Segment Descriptors

Descriptors are those objects to which the segment selector points. They are eight-byte quantities which contain attributes about a given linear address space (that is, about a segment). These attributes include the segment 32-bit base linear address; the segment 30-bit length and granularity; the protection level; read, write, or execute privileges; the default size of the operands (16- or 32-bit); and the type of segment.

All descriptor-attribute information is contained in 12 bits of the segment descriptor. All segments on the 80386 have three attribute fields in common: the P (present) bit, the DPL (descriptor privilege level) bits, and the S (segment descriptor) bit.

Segment descriptors are stored in either a global descriptor table (GDT) or local descriptor table (LDT). These descriptor tables are stored in special segments maintained by the operating system and referenced by memory management hardware. The 80386 locates the GDT and the current LDT in protected memory by means of the GDTR and LDTR registers.

A segment descriptor provides the 80386 with the data it needs to map a logical address into a linear address. These descriptors are not created by programs but by compilers, linkers, loaders, or the operating system.

INTERRUPTS AND EXCEPTIONS

Both hardware and software-generated interrupts alter the programmed execution of the 80386. A hardware-generated interrupt occurs in response to an active input on one of two 80386 interrupt inputs: NMI, which is nonmaskable, or INTR, which is maskable.

The NMI input signals a catastrophic event such as an imminent power loss, a memory error, or a bus parity error. The NMI causes the 80386 to execute the service routine that corresponds to location 2 in the IDT. The processor does not service subsequent NMI requests until the current one has been serviced.

Entry point descriptors to the service routines or the interrupt tasks are stored in memory in the interrupt descriptor table (IDT). The IDT associates each interrupt or except identifies with a descriptor for the instructions that service the associated event. The IDT is an array of eight-byte descriptors and can hold up to 256 identifiers. To locate the correct descriptor, the processor multiplies the identifier by eight.

Exceptions are classified as faults, aborts, or traps, depending on the way they are reported and also whether restart of the instruction that caused the exception is supported. Aborts are used to report severe errors such as illegal, inconsistent values in system tables, or hardware errors. An abort allows neither the restart of the program that caused the exception nor the identification of the precise location of the instruction causing the exception. Faults are exceptions that are either detected before the instruction begins to execute or during execution. A trap is reported at the instruction boundary immediately after the instruction in which the exception was detected.

MEMORY ORGANIZATION

Segmentation is the division of memory into logical blocks for use by a computer. In the 80386, memory is organized into one or more variable-length segments, from one byte up to four gigabytes in size. Every task in the 80386 can have up to 16,381 segments (each up to four gigabytes in length), which provides 64 terabytes of virtual memory. Any given location of the linear address space (a segment of the physical memory) has several attributes associated with it: size, location, type (stack, code, or data), and protection characteristics.

The 80386 physical memory organizes into a sequence of 8-bit bytes. Each byte has a unique address that ranges from zero to $2^{32} - 1$, or four gigabytes. The three distinct address spaces are : physical, logical, and linear.

Physical addresses are the actual addresses used to select the physical memory chips which contain the data. A logical address consists of a segment selector and an offset into that segment. A linear address is the address formed by adding the offset to the base address of the segment.

Paging

Paging is a type of memory management useful in multitasking operating systems. Paging operates underneath segmentation to complete the virtual-to-physical address translation process. Segmentation translates virtual addresses to linear address. Paging translates the linear address put out by segmentation to physical addresses.

In the 80386, paging operates only in protected mode and provides a means of managing the very large segments that the 80386 supports. Paging divides programs into uniformly sized pages—unlike segmentation, which modularizes programs and data into variable length segments. In a real sense, paging operates beneath segmentation; that is, the paging mechanism translates the protected linear address, which comes from the segmentation unit, into a physical address.

The paging mechanism is enabled by the PG bit in CR0. If PG = 1, paging is enabled and linear addresses are translated to physical addresses. If PG = 0, paging is disabled and the linear addresses generated by the segmentation mechanism are used directly as physical addresses (see Fig. H-12).

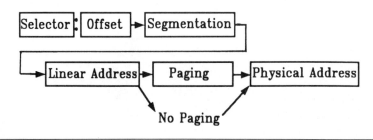

Fig. H-12. Virtual-to-Physical Address Translation.

The paging translation function is described by a memory-resident table called the page table. This page table is stored in the physical address space and can be thought of as a simple array of 2^{30} physical addresses. The linear-to-physical mapping function is simply an array lookup. Each page table entry is 32 bits in size.

80386 Cache Memory

Cache memory is a mechanism interposed in the memory hierarchy between main memory and the processor to improve effective memory transfer rates and to raise processor speeds. The cache anticipates the likely use of the CPU of data in main storage by organizing a copy of it in cache memory. The cache also includes data in adjacent blocks to the actual data needed; it is likely that the adjacent data will be requested next. This principle is called *locality of reference*.

The 80386 prototype cache is 64 kbyte, direct-mapped cache, organized as 16,384 entries. Each entry contains 32 bits of data along with 16 bits of tag information. The line size (the unit of transfer) between the cache and dynamic random access memory

(DRAM) is 32 bits. Together, the tag and index fields uniquely identify a doubleword location in main memory.

PRIVILEGE AND PROTECTION

The concept of privilege is central to the 80386. As applied to procedures, privilege is the degree to which the procedure can be trusted not to make a mistake that might affect other procedures or data. Applied to data, privilege is the degree of protection that a data structure should have from less-trusted procedures. Privilege is implemented by assigning a value (from zero to three) to key objects which are recognized by the processor. This value is called the *privilege level*. The value zero is the greatest privilege, while the value three is the least privilege.

There are two broad classes of protection supported by the 80386. The first is the ability to separate tasks completely by giving each task a different virtual address space; this is accomplished by giving each task a different virtual-to-physical address translation map. The other protection mechanism operates within a task to protect operating system memory segments and special processor registers from access by application program.

The key items the processor recognizes are:

- Descriptor Privilege Level (DPL)—Descriptors contain a field called the DPL. This is the least privilege that a task must have to access the descriptor.

- Requester's Privilege Level (RPL)—The RPL represents the privilege level requested by the procedure that originates a selector.

- Current Privilege Level (CPL)—The CPL is equal to the segment DPL of the code segment which the processor is currently executing. CPL changes when control transfers to segments with differing DPLs.

MULTITASKING

To switch tasks efficiently, the 83086 uses special high-speed hardware. Only a single instruction or interrupt keys the processor to do a switch. Running at 16 megahertz, the 80386 can save the state of one task (all registers), load the state of another task, and resume execution in less than 16 microseconds. The 80386 uses no special instructions to control multitasking. Instead, it interprets ordinary control-transfer instructions when they refer to the special data structures.

Task State Segment (TSS)

A TSS is a data structure (a special segment) that holds the state of a task virtual processor (see Fig. H-13). The TSS for the active task is addressed by the TR register. The 80386 schedules and executes tasks based on a priority set by the operating system. To switch tasks, the operating system issues a jump (JMP) or call (CALL) instruction whose operand is a selector for the TSS or the task gate of the new task.

31	23	16	15	7	0	

I/O Permission Bitmap Base		0 0 0 0 0 0 0 0 0 0 0 0 0 0 0 T	64
0 0 0 0 0 0 0 0 0 0 0 0 0 0 0 0		Local Descriptor Table (LDT)	
0 0 0 0 0 0 0 0 0 0 0 0 0 0 0 0		GS	
0 0 0 0 0 0 0 0 0 0 0 0 0 0 0 0		FS	
0 0 0 0 0 0 0 0 0 0 0 0 0 0 0 0		DS	
0 0 0 0 0 0 0 0 0 0 0 0 0 0 0 0		SS	
0 0 0 0 0 0 0 0 0 0 0 0 0 0 0 0		CS	
0 0 0 0 0 0 0 0 0 0 0 0 0 0 0 0		ES	48
EDI			
ESI			
EBP			
ESP			
EBX			
EDX			
ECX			2C
EAX			
EFLAGS			
EIP			
CR3 (PDBR)			
0 0 0 0 0 0 0 0 0 0 0 0 0 0 0 0		SS2	18
ESP2			
0 0 0 0 0 0 0 0 0 0 0 0 0 0 0 0		SS1	
ESP1			0C
0 0 0 0 0 0 0 0 0 0 0 0 0 0 0 0		SS0	
ESP0			
0 0 0 0 0 0 0 0 0 0 0 0 0 0 0 0		Back Link to Previous TSS	0

Note: Zeros indicate Intel reserved bits.

Fig. H-13. Task State Segment (TSS).

To resume execution of the old task, the operating system issues a JMP instruction to the TSS of the old task. The privilege level at which execution restarts in the incoming task is not restricted by the privilege level of the outgoing task. The tasks are isolated by their separate address spaces and TSSs and privilege access rules are used to prevent improper access to a TSS.

The TSS link field is at offset 0 in the TSS and it is a 32-bit field with a selector in the low-order 16 bits. This link field is used in conjunction with the NT bit in the EFLAGS register to link the TSSs for task suspended by CALL instructions or interrupts. Figure H-14 shows how TSSs are linked.

Also in the TSS is an I/O permission bitmap that defines what addresses in the 64 k-byte I/O space can be accessed by programs executing at any privilege level. A 64k bit string is stored in the current TSS, with each bit corresponding to a single byte-wide I/O address. Bit 0 corresponds to I/O address 0, bit 1 to I/O address 1, and so on. A zero stored in the bitmap indicates that the corresponding I/O address is accessible to programs at any privilege level. A 1 indicates that the I/O address is only accessible to program at IOPL, or an inner level. An exception is raised if a program attempts to access an I/O address corresponding to a 1 in the bitmap while executing at an outer level relative to IOPL.

The T bit in the TSS causes the debug handler to be invoked whenever a task switch through this TSS occurs. This provides a convenient way for the debugger to monitor the activities of certain tasks. The BT bit of DR6 notes that this condition was detected. There is no specific enable bit for this condition in DR7.

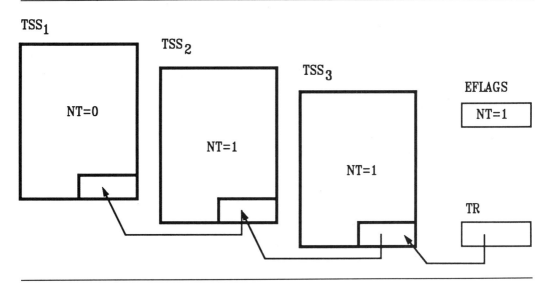

Fig. H-14. Linked TSSs.

BUS INTERFACING

The 80386 features 32-bit wide internal and external data paths and eight general-purpose 32-bit registers. The processor communicates with external memory, I/O, and other devices through a parallel bus interface. This interface consists of a bidirectional data bus, a separate address bus, five bus status pins, and three bus control pins.

The 80386 uses a double-frequency clock (CLK2) that generates the 80386s internal processor clock signal (CLK). This internal clock matches the external clock generator (82384) CLK.

Each bus cycle is made up of at least two states. Each of the states in turn is comprised of two CLK2 cycles. The maximum data transfer rate for a bus operation is determined by the 80386 internal clock, and it is 32 bits for every two CLK cycles. That works out to 32 megabytes per second, when CLK2 = 32 megahertz and the internal CLK = 16 MHz.

The 80386 offers both pipelined and nonpipelined bus cycles. When pipelining is selected, the 80386 overlaps bus cycles, which allows longer access times. Because cache memory can be accessed without wait states, nonpipelined cycles are often preferred. Using nonpipelined cycles minimizes latency between the processor requesting information from the outside world and data becoming available at the 80386 pins.

PROCESSOR CONTROL

Intel designed several instructions to specifically control the processor. Some of the instructions are available on all processors; others are for the protected-mode operations on the 80286 and 80386. System-control instructions have only limited use in applications programming. They are used by systems programmers who write operating systems and other control software. The control instructions are outlined below; they are described in some detail in appendix B (80386 instruction set) and appendix C (80387 coprocessor instruction set).

Controlling Processors

There are four instructions that control aspects of the processors: ESC (escape), HLT (halt), LOCK, and WAIT.

- ESC provides an instruction and possibly a memory operation for use by a coprocessor. MASM automatically inserts ESC instructions, when required, for use with the 8087-family of coprocessors.

- HLT stops the processor until it receives an interrupt.

- LOCK locks out other processors until a specified instruction is finished. LOCK is a prefix that precedes the instruction opcode. It can be used to ensure that a coprocessor does not change data being worked on by the main processor.

• WAIT tells the processor to do nothing until it receives a signal that a coprocessor has finished with a task that the coprocessor is working on.

Protected-Mode Processor Control

The 80286 and 80386 can operate in two modes: real mode and protected mode. When either processor is operating in real mode, it is perceived by MS-DOS as a fast 8086. Programs written for the 8086 run the same on the 80286 and 80386 (real modes)—only faster. These programs cannot, however, take advantage of 80286 or 80386 features unless they can run in protected mode. Note that MS-DOS does not support protected mode.

Instructions that control protected mode are privileged and can only be used in the .286p or .386 directives have been coded. Some privileged-mode instructions use internal registers of the 80286 and 80386 processors. Instructions are provided for loading values from these registers into memory where the values can be modified; other instructions can then store the values back to the special registers. Privileged-mode instructions are:

ARPL	Adjusts requested privilege level
CLTS	Clears task-switched flag
LAR	Loads access rights
LGDT	Loads global descriptor table
LIDT	Load eight-byte interrupt descriptor table
LLDT	Loads local descriptor table
LMSW	Loads machine status word
LSL	Loads segment limit
LTR	Loads task register
SGDT	Stores global descriptor table
SIDT	Stores eight-byte interrupt descriptor table
SLDT	Stores local descriptor table
SMSW	Stores machine status word
STR	Stores task register
VERR	Verifies read access
VERW	Verifies write access

The 80386 can use all the privileged-mode instructions of the 80286, but it also allows you to use MOV to transfer data between general purpose registers and special registers. The following special registers can be accessed with MOV.

Control	CR0, CR2, CR3
Debug	DR0, DR1, DR2, DR3, DR6, DR7
Test	TR6, TR7

Glossary

Glossary

access—To make use of a reference; that is, to execute the statement in which the reference is contained.

access time—The interval between a request for data from the memory unit and its actual availability to the processing unit.

accumulator—A register used to hold sums during arithmetic operations. In 80386 terms, this is another name for the AX register.

address—Information used to identify individual storage locations or words in a memory unit.

address, absolute—The fully defined address by a memory address number.

address, memory—Every word in memory has a unique address. A word can be defined as a set of bits that makes the largest addressable unit of information in a programmable memory.

address space—The total area accessible to a program.

address translation—In 80386 terms, this function is the conversion of a selector and offset into a physical address.

addressability—The characteristic of certain storage devices in which each storage area or location has a unique address. This address is then usable by the programmer to access the information stored at that location.

addressing capacity—The programming addressing range determines how large a program can be written without resorting to special external hardware and internal software techniques.

algorithm—A strategy or plan or series of steps for the solution of a problem.

aliases—Two or more descriptors referring to the same segment.

alternate return—A module linkage convention that allows the subordinate to return to a location other than the normal return location.

American Standard Code for Information Interchange (ASCII)—A binary encoding scheme using seven bits to represent characters, numbers, and special symbols. ASCII was originally designed for information interchange among data processing systems, data communication systems, and associated equipment.

anticipatory loading—An automatic storage management discipline that loads modules into memory before they are invoked, based on knowledge of the hierarchy of modules in the system.

applications software—Programs written to perform particular business functions (such as inventory, payroll, or accounts receivable) as opposed to systems software, which operates a computer system.

architecture—An orderly organization of subsystems to satisfy overall system objectives.

ASCII—See American Standard Code for Information Interchange.

assembler—A software program that translates assembly language into binary machine language.

assembly language—A symbolic notation for writing machine instructions. The language is at a high enough level to free the programmer from working directly in machine code.

auxiliary storage—A place for the long-term storage of data. Storage of this type is usually on magnetic media, such as diskette, and has the capability of storing millions or even billions of characters. Also known as secondary storage.

balanced systems—Systems that are not input driven or output driven. Such systems usually have a deep hierarchy of modules to obtain inputs and to deliver outputs.

base address—In 80386 terms, the physical address of the start of a segment.

base load—A set of modules activated by an unbroken chain of explicit commands.

benchmark testing—The process of actually testing for time, accuracy, ability to perform the job as described, and so on.

binary—A term used to describe the base-two number system.

binary search—A method of searching an index in which the system first goes to the middle of the index to see which half of the index could contain the item wanted. Each succeeding test goes to the midpoint of the remaining part of the index that is being searched. The net effect is that a large index can be searched very quickly.

bit—binary digit, a single binary position that can exist in only one of two states: ON (1) or OFF (0).

bit field—A contiguous sequence of bits. A bit field might begin at any bit location of any byte and might contain up to 32 bits (in the 80386).

bit string—A contiguous sequence of bits. A bit string might begin at any bit position of any byte and (in the 80386) might contain up to $2^{32} - 1$ bits.

bottom-up testing—A testing strategy in which bottom-level modules are tested first and then are integrated into higher-level superordinates. This testing is usually contrasted with top-down testing.

branch—The act of causing control to be shifted to another part of the program.

buffer—Storage elements such as registers or memory locations for the temporary storage of information prior to its use by the intended system, such as a peripheral device.

byte—A collection of eight adjacent bits.

cache—A buffer type of high-speed memory that is filled at medium speed from main memory. Cache memory (especially in the 80386) is the fastest portion of the overall memory that stores only the data that the processor might need in the immediate future.

central processing unit (CPU)—The electronic device that controls all other parts of the computer system.

channel—Circuitry responsible for generating memory references for use in direct memory accessing (DMA).

character—This general term refers to all alphabetic characters, alphabetic punctuation marks, mathematical operators, and the coded representation of such symbols.

clear/reset—This process sets all relevant data to binary zero.

code—A set of unambiguous rules specifying the manner in which data can be represented in a discrete form. Also, a computer program or part of a computer program.

coding—The process of writing the computer instructions.

common-data environment—A means of describing data such that the data can be accessed by any module in a system.

compiler—A software program that translates procedure-oriented or problem-oriented instructions into machine language.

complexity of interface—One of the factors influencing coupling between modules. The complexity of the interface is approximately equal to the number of different items being passed—the more items, the higher the complexity.

computer—A programmable electronic device that can store, retrieve, and process data.

conditioned transfer—A jump out of the current execution sequence with the condition that control eventually will be returned to the execution sequence from which the jump was made (for example, a subroutine call).

conforming—In 80386 terms, a property of a segment that indicates that each procedure in that segment will move outward to the privilege ring of its caller when it is called.

constant—A value that does not change during the execution of a program. Compare with variable.

control register—In the 80386, these registers hold data of machine states of a global nature. They are called CR0, CR1, CR2, and CR3. The low-order 15 bits of CR0 are called the machine status word (MSW) for 80286 compatibility with the 80386.

control structure—The structure of a program defined by references which represent transfers of control.

control transfer—In the 80386, transfer of control is done by use of exceptions, interrupts, and by the instructions CALL, JMP, INT, IRET, and RET. A near transfer goes to a place within the current code segment. Far transfers go to other segments.

control unit—The electronic part of the central processing unit (CPU) that, under program direction, coordinates the action of the system hardware.

conversion—Changing from one method to another, such as converting the data representation of characters from EBCDIC to ASCII.

coprocessor—An auxiliary processor that operates in coordination with the CPU, allowing architectural capabilities which, in view of the limitations of contemporary technology, could not otherwise be provided. Coprocessors furnish the hardware to perform functions that would otherwise be performed in software. In addition, they extend the instruction set of the main processor.

counter—A programming device used to control the number of times a process is executed.

coupling—A measure of the strength of interconnection between one module and another.

data—A representation of facts, concepts, or instructions in a formalized manner suitable for communication, interpretation, or processing by humans or automatic means. Also, any representations such as characters to which meaning is, or might be, assigned.

data conversion—The act of changing data from one form to another.

data coupling—A form of coupling caused by an intermodule connection that provides output from one module and that serves as input to another module.

data field—The column or consecutive columns used to store a particular piece of information.

data file—A collection of data records usually organized on a logical basis.

data item—The smallest accessible element in a database.

data record—A collection of data fields pertaining to a particular subject.

data-structure design—A type of design strategy that derives a structural design from consideration of the structure of data sets associated with the problem.

debugger—A program that helps a programmer locate the source of problems found during run-time testing of a program.

debugging—The act of removing errors or bugs from a computer program.

decoupling—Any systematic method or technique by which modules can be made more independent.

descriptor—In the 80386, a descriptor is an eight-byte quantity specifying an independently protected object. The descriptor for an object specifies the object base address or the address of its entry point, in addition to protection information.

descriptor privilege level (DPL)—In the 80386, the DPL is a field in a descriptor that indicates how protected the descriptor is. The DPL is the least privileged level at which a task can access a particular descriptor and access the segment associated with that descriptor.

design principles—Very broad principles that favor increasing quality for decreased development cost.

device driver—A program that transforms I/O requests made in a standard, device-independent fashion into the operations necessary to make a specific piece of hardware fulfill that request.

device monitor—A mechanism that allows data processes to track and/or modify device data streams.

digital computer—A general-purpose computer that handles data in numerical or digital form.

direct addressing—Specifying a memory location by an address embedded in an instruction.

direct memory addressing (DMA)—This is a technique for transferring data in or out of memory without disturbing the program being executed by the processing unit.

disk storage—A magnetic storage device that closely resembles a phonograph record. However, the tracks of data are in concentric rings instead of a single spiral that a phonograph record has.

displacement—In the 80386, this is a 16-bit value specified in an instruction and used for computing address offsets.

DMA—See direct memory addressing.

documentation—The sum total of the forms, flow charts, program listings, and so on, associated with a computer program.

driver—A program which controls external devices or executes other programs.

dump—Recording the system memory contents on an external medium, such as magnetic tape or printer.

dynamic recursion—A form of recursion that exists wherever a module is shared by two or more tasks that can be among active jobs at the same time. For example, it is used by routines handling different interrupts.

E notation—Also known as scientific notation, E notation is a format for the representation of numbers that are larger than six digits. The notation consists of two parts: a mantissa and an exponent. For example, in the number $.12345E + 10^2$, the $.12345$ is the mantissa and the 10^2 is the exponent.

editing—As used by a programmer, editing instructions allow the programmer to add, replace, and otherwise modify code. As done by a computer, editing allows humans to modify storage.

effective privilege level (EPL)—In the 80386, the EPL is the least privileged of the RPL and DPL.

EIP—See instruction pointer.

emulation—The act of executing a program written for one computer on a different computer.

encapsulation—The principle of hiding the internal implementation of a program, function, or service so that its users can tell what it does, but not how it does it.

ESC (escape) instruction—An instruction having an ESC opcode. Escape instructions are executed by the numeric (or mathematic) coprocessor in concert with the main processor.

exception—A condition that occurs when an instruction violates the rules of normal operation. An exception generally causes an interrupt.

expand down—A property of a segment that causes the processor to check that, in all accesses to that segment, offsets are greater than the segment limits. This property is used for stack segments.

expand up—A property of a segment that causes the processor to check that all accesses to that segment are no greater than the segment limit. Generally, all segments other than stack segments have this property.

exponent—The rightmost part of a number that has been converted into E notation. This position tells the power of 10 to which the mantissa must be raised in order to generate the original number.

far pointer—In the 80386, a 48-bit logical address of two components: a 16-bit segment selector and a 32-bit offset.

field—One or more contiguous bits that represent a piece of a large item of data.

firmware—Memory chips with the software programs already built-in.

fixed-point arithmetic—Operations on numbers without decimal points. It is a type of arithmetic in which the operands and results of all arithmetic operations must be properly scaled so as to have a magnitude between certain fixed values.

flag—A field in the flags register. A flag indicates the status of a previously executed instruction or controls the operation of the processor.

flag bit—A single bit that indicates one of two mutually exclusive conditions or states.

flexibility—A measure of the degree to which a system, as is, can be used in a variety of ways.

flowcharting—A representation of a data processing activity by the use of special graphic symbols.

function—In programming, a function is a prebuilt series of instructions that can be used or called by means of a single word or term. A typical function is SQRT, which finds square root.

function key—A specific key on a keyboard that, when operated, causes a receiving device to perform a certain mechanical function so that a message will be received in proper form. Also, keys on keyboards that are used to query the system or have it perform certain operations.

function key, programmable—By changing the keyboard handling routine, the user can change the function of any key or symbol that will be displayed on the screen.

functional requirements—A precise description of the requirements of a computer system. They include a statement of the inputs to be supplied by the user, the outputs desired by the user, the algorithms involved in any computations desired by the user, and a description of such physical constraints as response time, volumes, and so on.

gate—The simplest logic circuit. In the 80386, there are four types of gates: a call gate, a trap gate, an interrupt gate, and a task gate.

GDT—See global descriptor table.

GDTR—See global descriptor table register.

general register—In the 80386, one of the 32-bit registers: EAX, EBX, ECX or EDX.

generality—A measure of the degree to which a system exhibits the properties of a general-purpose system.

generation—A differentiation of the ages to which computer equipment belongs. The first generation is characterized by the use of vacuum tubes as active elements. The development of a reliable magnetic core memory was a major turning point in moving to the second generation; the use of transistors is the basis of the second generation. Computers that use integrated circuit technology led the way into the third generation, which is considered to have started in 1964. From there on, it is unclear, and there is considerable controversy as to what computer generation is in existence as this book is being written. It is most probably the end of a fourth generation (which is characterized by very large systems integration—VLSI). The fifth generation is just beginning.

giga—A prefix meaning one billion (10^9). Also, the power of 2 closest to one billion, $2^{30} = 1,073,741,824$. This latter description is used when referring to computer memory (gigabyte, gigabit, and so on).

global descriptor table (GDT)—In the 80386, a table in memory that contains descriptors for segments that are shared by all tasks.

global descriptor table register (GDTR)—In the 80386, this register holds the 32-bit linear base address and the 16-bit limit of the global descriptor table.

graphic display—A communications terminal linked to a computer that displays data in shapes and drawings, usually a CRT.

graphics—Symbols produced by a process such as handwriting or printing, synonymous with graphic symbol.

hardware—The physical parts of a computer system, usually a printer, video screen device, circuit chips, and so on.

hashing routine—A mathematical formula that is applied to a key field to determine where the record is stored.

hexadecimal—A base-16 number system, most often called hex. The hex digits are 0, 1, 2, 3, 4, 5, 6, 7, 8, 9, A (= 10), B (= 11), C (= 12), D (= 13), E (= 14), and F (= 15).

high-order position—The leftmost position in a string of characters.

identifier—The name, address, label, or distinguishing index of an object in a program.

IDT—See interrupt descriptor table.

IDTR—See interrupt descriptor table register.

immediate operand—In the 80386, a constant contained in an instruction and used as an operand.

incremental implementation—A testing/implementation strategy for adding a new (potentially error-prone) module to a tested collection of modules and then testing the new combination.

index—A listing of the data records and the disk areas on which they are stored.

index register—In the 80386, one of the 32-bit registers: ESI or EDI. Generally, an index register holds an offset into the current data or extra segment.

indirect addressing—Accessing a memory location by first fetching the desired address from some other memory location or register.

initialize—A programming term that refers to the act of establishing fixed values in certain areas of memory. Generally, the term refers to all the housekeeping that must be completed before the main part of the program can be executed.

input—The general term used to describe the act of entering data into a data processing system or to describe the data being entered.

input/output (I/O)—Pertaining to a device or to a channel that might be involved in an input process, and at a different time, in an output process. Also pertaining to a device whose parts can be performing an input process and an output process at the same time.

instruction pointer (IP)—A register that contains the offset of the instruction currently being executed. A selector for the segment containing this instruction is stored in the CS register. In the 80386, the EIP (an extended instruction pointer) is a 32-bit register that contains the offset address of the next sequential instruction to be executed. The low-order 16 bits of the EIP are the IP.

instruction register—A register that stores the current instruction being executed.

instruction set—The set of all machine-language instructions that can be executed by a processor.

interactive program—A program whose function is to obey commands from a user, such as an editor or a spreadsheet program. Programs such as compilers can literally interact by asking for file names and compilation options, but they are considered noninteractive because their function is to compile a source program, not to provide answers to user-entered commands.

interface—A connecting point between two systems.

intermodular connection—A reference from one module to an identifier in a different module.

interpreter—A computer program that is essentially a closed subroutine that translates a stored code program into machine code, and performs the desired and specified operations. An interpreter translates and executes each source language statement before translating and executing the next one.

interrupt—To suspend execution of the current program in order to service one or more peripheral devices. Also, a forced call, not appearing explicitly in a program, which is triggered by an exception, by a signal from a device external to the processor, or by a special interrupt instruction.

interrupt descriptor table (IDT)—In the 80386, this is a table in memory that is indexed by interrupt number and that contains gates to the corresponding interrupt handlers.

interrupt descriptor table register (IDTR)—In the 80386, this register points to a table of entry points for interrupt handlers. The IDTR holds the 32-bit linear base address and the 16-bit limit of the IDT.

interrupt handler—A procedure or task that is called in response to an interrupt.

interrupt module—A module activated by an interrupt.

I/O permissions bitmap—The mechanism that allows the 80386 to selectively trap references to specific I/O addresses. The permissions bitmap resides in the task state segment (TSS). The map is a bit vector, and its size and location in the TSS are variable. The 80386 locates the map by means of the I/O map base field in the fixed portion of the TSS.

IP—See instruction pointer.

jump—An instruction that causes a transfer of control from one part of the program to another.

k—Kilo, a prefix meaning one thousand (10^3). Also, the power of 2 closest to one thousand, namely $2^{10} = 1024$. This latter definition is used when referring to computer memory (kilobytes).

kB—Kilobyte, a thousand bytes.

label—Identifying statements or numbers used to describe locations. Also, a set of symbols used to identify or describe an item, record, message, or file.

LDT—See local descriptor table.

LDTR—See local descriptor table register.

lexical—Of or pertaining to the program as written, as it appears in a program listing. Also, the order in which items appear.

linear address space—Address space that runs from zero bytes to the maximum physical address that a processor can address. In the 80386, the linear address space runs up to four gigabytes.

local address space—In the 80386, this is the collection of segments accessible through a task LDT.

local descriptor table (LDT)—A table in memory that contains descriptors for segments that are private to a task.

local descriptor table register (LDTR)—In the 80386, this register holds the 16-bit selector for the local descriptor table.

localization—A technique of decoupling done by subdividing the data elements communicated through a common environment into a number of regions common to a smaller number of modules.

lock—In a multiple processor system, this is the signal from one processor that prevents the others from accessing memory. The processor has exclusive use of the memory until it stops sending the local signal.

logic design—The design of the procedural logic within a single module.

logical address—In the 80386, a logical address consists of a selector and offset. The selector points to some segment descriptor, which includes a segment linear-base address. The offset tells how far into the segment the required byte is.

logical device—A symbolic name for a device that the user can cause to be mapped to any physical (actual) device.

logical directory—A symbolic name for a directory that the user can cause to be mapped to any actual drive and directory.

low-order position—The rightmost position in a string of characters.

M—Mega, a prefix meaning one million (10^6). Also, the power of 2 that is closest to one million, $2^{20} = 1,048,576$. This latter definition is used when referring to computer memories (megabytes).

machine language—A programming language that is used directly by a machine. Also, another term for computer instruction code. At this level, instructions are usually in the form of a string of digits that have particular meaning to the internal circuitry of the computer.

machine status word (MSW)—A register that contains a bit for controlling the mode (real versus virtual) and bits which control the processor execution of WAIT and ESC instructions. In the 80386, the low-order 15 bits of the control register zero (CR0) are the MSW, for upward compatibility from the 80286.

macro—A module whose body is effectively copied in line during translation (compilation or assembly) as a result of being invoked by name.

macro instruction—An instruction that is replaced by several other instructions.

maintainability—The extent to which a system can be easily corrected when errors are discovered during the productive lifetime of the system.

mantissa—The leftmost part of a number that has been put into E notation. In the mantissa portion, all numbers are reduced to a single-digit whole number plus a decimal fraction.

mask bit—A bit used to cover up or disable some condition.

masking—A means of examining only certain bits in a word. This is usually done by ANDing the word with a mask containing 1s in the desired bit locations.

memory address—A value that selects one specific memory location.

memory map—The list of memory locations addressed directly by the computer.

memory-mapped input/output—A technique whereby a peripheral device masquerades as a memory location.

microprocessor—A central processing unit implemented on a single chip.

microsecond—One millionth of a second.

millisecond—One thousandth of a second.

mnemonic—Symbol or symbols used instead of terminology more difficult to remember. Usually a mnemonic has two or three letters.

mode—A method of operation, for example, the binary mode.

module—A contiguous sequence of program statements, bounded by boundary elements, having an aggregate identifier.

monitor—A device that observes and verifies the operation of a data processing system and indicates any specific departure from the norm. Also, a television type display such as a monochrome monitor.

MSW—See machine status word.

n—Nano, a prefix meaning one billionth (10^{-9}).

nanosecond—One billionth of a second.

near pointer—In the 80386, this is a 32-bit logical address. A near pointer is an offset within a segment.

NMI—See nonmaskable interrupt.

nonmaskable interrupt (NMI)—A signal to the processor from an external device that indicates that a problem has arisen or is imminent.

not present—In a virtual memory, this describes a segment that is on disk but not in main memory.

null selector—A selector in which all bits are zero (0).

object program—The numeric, machine language output of an assembler.

offset—A quantity specifying the position of a byte within a segment.

opcode—The part of an instruction that specifies the operation to be performed, such as ADD, as opposed to the items upon which the operation is performed.

open system—Hardware or software design that allows third-party additions and upgrades in the field.

operand—The part of an instruction that specifies the data operated on arithmetically or logically by a processor.

operating system (OS)—The collection of programs for operating a computer.

output—Pertaining to a device, process, or channel involved in an output process or pertaining to the data or states involved in an output process.

output-driven system—A system in which the top-level module produces the output of the system in elementary (or raw) form.

overflow—An exception which occurs when a number is too large in absolute value to be represented. Stack overflow is an exception which occurs when too much data is PUSHed onto a stack.

packaging—The assignment of the modules of a total system into sections handled as distinct physical units for execution on a computer.

packed BCD—A packed byte representation of two decimal digits, each in the range of 0 through 9. One digit is stored in each half byte. The digit in the high-order half byte is the most significant.

page—A set of consecutive bytes. In the 80386, pages begin on 4k byte boundaries. Paging divides programs into multiple uniform sized pages which have no direct relationship to the logical structure of the program.

page fault—In the 80386, if the processor finds one of the two following conditions, it issues an interrupt 14: (1) if the current procedure does not have enough privilege to access the indicated page; or (2) if the page-table entry or page-directory that is needed for the address translation has a zero in its P (present) bit. That is, the page is not currently loaded from auxiliary storage.

page frame—A four-kilobyte unit of contiguous addresses of a physical memory. The page frame address specifies the physical starting address of a page. The low-order 12 bits are always zero.

page table—In the 80386, this is an array of 32-bit page specifiers. The table itself is a page, containing pointers to four kilobytes of memory, or up to 1k 32-bit entries.

phased implementation—A form of testing/implementation in which several untested modules are combined together at once, and the collection tested for correctness.

physical address—A number transmitted to the memory hardware in order to specify the location of a memory access. Also, the mechanism which actually selects the memory where a required byte is located. In the 80386, the physical address differs from linear address only when paging is in effect.

pointer—An entity containing or having the value of an identifier. Also, in the 80386, this is an address that is used by software and consists of a selector and offset. In real mode, pointers are real addresses. In virtual mode, they are virtual addresses.

pointer register—In the 80386, one of the BP or BX registers. Generally, a pointer register holds an offset into the current stack segment.

portability—A property of a program representing ease of movement among distinct solution environments.

prefix—A byte preceding the opcode of an instruction. It specifies that the instruction should be repeated, or locked, or that an alternate segment should be used.

priority—A precedence relationship applied to simultaneous occurrences.

privilege level—A number in a predetermined range that indicates the degree of protection or degree of privilege.

processing element—Any part of the task performed by a module—not only the processing accomplished by statements executed within that module, but also that which results from calls on subroutines.

program—As used in this book, a series of ordered code statements designed to achieve a certain result.

program counter—A register in a processor that stores the address of the next instruction to be executed.

program status word (PSW)—A special register used to keep track of the address of the next instruction to be executed; also, often other status flags are stored in the PSW.

programmer—An informal term used to describe the person who designs and writes the programming instructions to implement a module. Often, the programmer is also responsible for the structural design of the system.

protected virtual address mode—A mode of operation in which the processor offers multitasking, advanced protection facilities, and virtual memory.

PSW—See program status word.

real address—In the 80386, this is an address that consists of a selector and offset in real address mode.

real address mode—In the 80386, this is a mode of operation in which the processor closely mimics the behavior of a lower-level chip in the same chip family. For example, the 80386 mimics an 8086.

recursion—The act of invoking a module as a subroutine of itself.

reentrant—A module is reentrant if it can be activated correctly at any time, whether or not it has been suspended by a conditioned transfer or return.

register—Fast, temporary-storage locations, usually in the processor itself.

reliability—A measure of the quality of a program or system, sometimes expressed as mean time between failure (MTBF).

requested privilege level (RPL)—In the 80386, this is a field in a selector that indicates the degree of trust or privilege a program has in the selector. RPL is determined by the least two significant bits of a selector.

RPL—See requested privilege level.

scatter read—Reading a block of data into noncontiguous locations in memory.

scope of control—The scope of control of a module consists of the module itself and all of its subordinates.

security kernel—That part of an operating system devoted to protection and security.

segment—A region of memory, in a range of one byte to the maximum that can be handled by the processor. Also, units of contiguous address space.

segment descriptor table—A memory array of eight-byte entries that contain descriptors. An 80386 descriptor table may contain up to 8192 descriptors.

segment register—In the 80386, one of the registers: CS, DS, ES, FS, GS, or SS.

segmented memory organization—An address space that consists of up to 16,383 linear address spaces up to four gigabytes each. The total space, as viewed by a program in the 80386, can be as large as up to 2^{46} bytes (64 terabytes).

selector—In the 80386, this is a quantity that specifies a segment.

semaphore—A software flag or signal used to coordinate the activities of two or more threads, commonly used to protect a critical section.

shared memory—A memory segment that can be accessed simultaneously by more than one process.

signals—Notification mechanisms implemented in software that operate in a fashion analogous to hardware interrupts.

single stepping—Executing a program one instruction at a time and pausing after each instruction. This is a means by which programmers determine the effect of a line of code.

software—The computer programs, procedures, rules, and possibly associated documentation concerned with the operation of a data processing system.

software reliability—A measure of the quality of a program or system, sometimes expressed as mean time between failure (MTBF).

source program—The original program submitted to the computer for translation or compilation.

stack—This refers to a reserved area of memory where the CPU saves the contents of various registers. The stack is referenced in a last-in/first-out (LIFO) basis. It is coordinated with a stack pointer that keeps track of storage and retrieval of each entry in the stack.

stack pointer—A register that stores the memory address of the top (last-in) element of a stack in memory.

statement—A line, sentence, or other similar well-defined construct of a programming language that defines, describes, or directs one step or part of the problem, or part of the solution of the problem.

string—A contiguous sequence of bytes, words, or double words. In the 80386, a string may contain from zero bytes through $2^{32} - 1$ bytes (or four gigabytes).

structural design—The design of the structure of a system, the specification of the pieces and the interconnection between the pieces.

structured design—A set of guidelines and techniques that assists a systems designer in determining which modules, interconnection in which way, will best solve a well-stated problem.

structured programming—A disciplined programming technique that ensures a single entry point and a single exit point from every processing module.

subroutine—A module activated at execution time by a conditioned transfer.

swapping—Moving a segment from disk to memory (swapping in) or from memory to disk (swapping out).

systems analyst—An informal title of a person whose job it is to analyze the user's needs and to then derive the functional requirements of a system.

task—A defined function that is unique within the computer.

task register (TR)—In the 80386, this register points to the information needed by the processor to define the current task.

task state segment (TSS)—In the 80386, a TSS is a segment which holds the contents of a task registers when the processor is executing another task.

task switch—Switching from one task to another.

terminal failure—A software error that causes a system to completely stop functioning.

test registers—In the 80386, registers TR6 and TR7 are used to control testing of the CAM (content addressable memory) in the translation lookaside buffer (TLB).

testing—A process of demonstrating that a system carries out its functions as specified.

text—In ASCII and data communications, a sequence of characters treated as an entity.

text editing—The general term that covers any additions, changes, or deletions made to electronically stored material.

thread—An OS/2 mechanism that allows more than one path of execution through the same instance of an application program.

TLB—See translation lookaside buffer.

top-down design—A design strategy in which the major functions of a system are identified and their implementation expressed in terms of lower-level primitives. The design process is then repeated on the primitives until the designer has identified primitives of a sufficiently low level that their implementation can be expressed in terms of available program statements.

top-down testing—A testing/implementation strategy in which high-level modules are tested before low-level modules.

TR—See task register.

track—That portion of a moving-type storage, such as a diskette, that is accessible to a given reading station such as a read/write head.

transaction—Any element of data, control, signal, event or change of state which causes, triggers, or initiates some action or sequence of actions.

translation lookaside buffer (TLB)—In the 80386, the TLB is a cache used for translating linear addresses to physical addresses. The TLB testing mechanism is unique to the 80386, and might not be implemented in the same way in future Intel processors.

TSS—See task state segment.

unconditional transfer—A transfer of control from one module to another with no tacit condition of return.

underflow—A numeric underflow is an exception that occurs when a number is too small in absolute value to be represented as a normalized floating-point number. Stack underflow is an exception that occurs when an instruction attempts to POP more data off the stack than is currently on the stack.

unpacked BCD—A representation for integers in which each decimal digit is represented by four bits, and each byte contains only a single decimal digit.

user—A term describing the person, persons, or organizations that expects to benefit from the development of a computer hardware or software system.

variable—As opposed to a constant, a variable is a value that does change during the execution of a program.

vectored interrupt—A technique of interrupt processing in which each interrupt specifies the address of the first instruction of its service routine.

virtual address—An address that consists of selector and offset in protected virtual address mode.

virtual memory—A technique for running programs that are larger than the available physical memory. Pieces of the program are stored on disk and are moved into memory only as necessary. This movement is automatically performed by the operating system and is invisible to the program.

virtual mode—See protected virtual address mode.

virtualization—The general technique of hiding a complicated actual situation behind a simple, standard interface.

wait state—An extra processor cycle added to the bus cycle in order to allow for slower devices on the bus to respond.

word—A machine-dependent unit of storage that is generally the width of the data bus or internal registers. In the 80386, a word is 32 bits.

word processing—A system comprising people, procedures, and automated electronic equipment to produce written communication more effectively.

Bibliography

Bibliography

Barrett, William A. and John D. Couch, *Compiler Construction: Theory and Practice*, Science Research Associates, NY, 1979.

Beck, M. Susan, *Kindspeak*, New American Library, NY, 1982.

Brown, Roger, *A First Language*, Harvard University Press, MA, 1973.

Brumm, Penn and Don Brumm, *80386 A Programming and Design Handbook*, TAB BOOKS, Inc., NY, 1988.

Chomsky, Noam, *Rules and Representations*, Columbia University Press, NY, 1980.

Frank, Werner L., *Critical Issues in Software*, John Wiley and Sons, NY, 1983.

Ghezzi, Carlo Mehdi Jazayeri, *Programming Language Concepts*, John Wiley and Sons, NY, 1982.

Hartman, R.R.K. and F.C. Stork, *Dictionary of Language and Linguistics*, John Wiley and Sons, NY, 1972.

Keller, Helen, *The Story of My Life*, Dell Publishing, NY, 1974.

Leopold, W.F., *Bibliography of Child Language*, Northwestern University Press, IL, 1970.

Marcotty, Michael and Henry Legard, *The World of Programming Languages*, Springer-Verlag, NY, 1987.

Microsoft Corporation, *Mixed-Language Programming Guide For the MS-DOS Operating System*, WA, 1987.

—, *MS-DOS Encyclopedia*, Microsoft Corporation, WA, 1988.

Nash, Walter, *Our Experience of Language*, St. Martin's Press, NY, 1971.

Pei, Mario, *Invitation to Linguistics*, Doubleday & Company, NY, 1965.

Spender, Dale, *Man Made Languages*, Routledge & Kagan Paul, London, 1980.

Tonkin, H., *A Research Bibliography on Esperanto and International Language Problems*, Esperanto Information Center, NY, 1967.

Wexelblat, Richard L., ed., *History of Programming Languages*, Academic Press, NY, 1981.

Index

80386 Macro Assembler and Toolkit

If you are intrigued with the possibilities of the macros included in *80386 Macro Assembler and Toolkit* (TAB Book No. 3247), you definitely should consider having them on disk. This software is guaranteed free from manufacturer's defects. (If you have any problems, simply return the disk within 30 days, and we'll send you a new one.) Not only will you save the time and tedium of typing in the code, the disk eliminates the possibility of errors that can prevent the programs from functioning. Interested?

Available at $34.95 on a double density disk for 80386-based computers (AT-style bus or PS/2 Micro Channel) running MS-DOS 3.1 and Microsoft Macro Assembler 5.1 or later. Please include $1.50 per unit ordered for shipping and handling.

I'm interested. Send me:

_____ double-density disk   (6692S)
_____ TAB BOOKS catalog ($1.00) (with a coupon worth $1.00 on your next TAB purchase)
Check/Money Order enclosed for $34.95 plus $1.50 shipping and handling for each disk ordered.
☐ VISA   ☐ MasterCard   ☐ American Express
Account No. _____ Expires _____

Name _____

Address _____

City _____ State _____ Zip _____

Signature _____

Mail To: **TAB BOOKS Inc.**
           Blue Ridge Summit, PA 17294-0850

OR CALL TOLL-FREE TODAY: **1-800-822-8158**
IN PENNSYLVANIA AND ALASKA CALL: **717-794-2191**

(In PA, NY, and ME add applicable sales tax. Orders subject to credit approval. Orders outside U.S. must be prepaid with international money orders in U.S. dollars.)
*Prices subject to change without notice.

TAB 3247